# THE PRELUDE

OR

## GROWTH OF A POET'S MIND

**WILLIAM WORDSWORTH (1805)**
*From a tinted pencil drawing by* HENRY EDRIDGE, A.R.A.

# WILLIAM WORDSWORTH

# THE PRELUDE

## OR

# GROWTH OF A POET'S MIND

EDITED FROM THE MANUSCRIPTS
WITH INTRODUCTION, TEXTUAL AND
CRITICAL NOTES BY

## ERNEST DE SELINCOURT

SECOND EDITION

REVISED BY

HELEN DARBISHIRE

OXFORD
AT THE CLARENDON PRESS

*Oxford University Press, Ely House, London W.1*

GLASGOW  NEW YORK  TORONTO  MELBOURNE  WELLINGTON
CAPE TOWN  SALISBURY  IBADAN  NAIROBI  LUSAKA  ADDIS ABABA
BOMBAY  CALCUTTA  MADRAS  KARACHI  LAHORE  DACCA
KUALA LUMPUR  HONG KONG  TOKYO

FIRST EDITION 1926
SECOND EDITION 1959
REPRINTED LITHOGRAPHICALLY IN GREAT BRITAIN
AT THE UNIVERSITY PRESS, OXFORD
FROM SHEETS OF THE SECOND EDITION
1965, 1968

TO

GORDON WORDSWORTH

IN GRATITUDE AND FRIENDSHIP

# PREFACE TO THE SECOND EDITION

When in 1956 a new printing of E. de Selincourt's great edition of *The Prelude* was called for, and I was asked to supply the copy for this purpose, it soon became clear that not merely a reprinting but a revised edition was required. After the first publication of de Selincourt's edition in 1926 an important early manuscript, JJ, came to light containing the first drafts of many vital passages which belong to Book I. De Selincourt gave a close account of these in Addenda to Notes printed on a separate sheet. To print the whole text was desirable but not practicable in the lithographic reprinting of the book in 1928 and 1950. I have been able to supply this in the present edition (*v.* p. 633), and also to include matter from other manuscripts in Dove Cottage which de Selincourt had not fully drawn upon, in particular an early version of Book II which I have called RV, apparently not seen by him; and the notebooks *Alfoxden*, *Christabel*, and *18a*.

I have checked the text of 1805 and *apparatus criticus* throughout and made some minor corrections. For instance, I have put right here and there a mistaken reading in the 1805 text: thus *a memorable* for *in memorable* IV. 331; *Dweller* for *Reveller* VII. 61; *the nature's* for *Nature's* VIII. 514; *downy Plain* for *dreary Plain* XII. 339; *strains* for *streams* XIII. 212. And I have restored a few characteristic spellings: *Bethkelet* (Wordsworth himself corrects to *Bethkelert*) for *Bethgelert* XIII. 3 (Wordsworth was with his Welsh friend Robert Jones, and echoes his speech); *vistos*, the 'period' spelling for *vistas* III. 345; *Lu*, the older spelling for *Loo* (card game) I. 543; *incumbences* for *incumbencies* III. 115. In two places a line had inadvertently been left out, and this meant renumbering the lines in Book VIII from 211 onwards, and in Book IX from l. 300. In the *apparatus criticus* also I have occasionally been able to supply a right reading: for example, I read the name of the old Dame who kept her stall in the Hawkshead market-place as *Rowe*, II. 38 *app. crit.* Some interesting additional passages, not used by Wordsworth in the issue—the harvest of a new raking of the manuscripts, will be found in the *apparatus criticus* and the Notes, e.g. I. 663 and II. 1 *app. crit.*; V. 525 and XIII. 1–119 Notes.

Partly through the emergence of early manuscripts new material has come to light since 1926 which illuminates the substance of de Selincourt's Introduction and Notes. The only passages which called for substantial rewriting were the second and fourth sections of the Introduction, dealing with the evolution and the chronology of the composition of the poem. Here and there in other places an alteration of perspective or the discovery of new facts has made necessary some adjustment or addition. This I have tried to supply in the Introduction and the Notes with the least possible interference with his work. His edition of *The Prelude* is a classic.

I have profited throughout by the friendly help of Professor James MacGillivray of Toronto, to whose close knowledge of Wordsworth and careful scholarship I am greatly in debt. I am grateful to Miss Eva Hutchinson for expert help in filling gaps in my knowledge of educational theory in the early nineteenth century (*v.* notes on *The Prelude* V. 226–388). To other scholars and critics who have thrown light and increased knowledge I have recorded my debt in my notes: to Mr. H. M. Margoliouth, to Mrs. Moorman, and to Professor Chester L. Shaver I should like in particular to express my gratitude.

Finally I wish to record my gratitude to my friend Vera Farnell for unstinted expert labour in copying my script, and to my former pupil Beatrix Hogan, a true Wordsworthian, for her close reading of my Introduction and Notes, and welcome corrections; and, with Mr. John P. Hogan, for compiling the Index.

H. D.

*1958*

# ORIGINAL PREFACE, 1926

THE object of this volume is to provide a complete critical text of
*The Prelude*. On the right-hand pages is a reprint of the authorized
text, as it appeared in 1850, a few months after the poet's death ;
on the left, the text of the poem as it was read to Coleridge at
Coleorton, in the winter after his return from Malta (1806–7).
These two versions are accompanied by an *apparatus criticus*,
recording the readings of all manuscript drafts of the poem known
to exist, and tracing the development of the text from 1805 to
1850. All but the most trivial changes have been noted.

In the Introduction, *apparatus criticus*, and notes at the end of
the volume (*v.* especially pp. lvi, 52, 53, 291, 525, 545, 571–8, 581,
612–14, 620–2, 623–8) will be found several passages written for
*The Prelude* but not finally incorporated in it, and hitherto unpublished. These are for the most part rough drafts rapidly written
down and left imperfect, and Wordsworth would not have printed
them before they had been carefully revised. But students of his
poetry will be glad to possess them ; for they are contemporary
with his best work and are eminently characteristic of his thought.
Moreover, some of them contain the raw material of better poetry
than he produced in the more finished but less inspired writings
of his later years.

In the Introduction I have given a description of all the known
manuscripts of *The Prelude*, and some account of its genesis
and growth ; and I have discussed the general significance of the
changes introduced into the text. A full expository commentary
on *The Prelude* is hardly called for, and it would inevitably
traverse ground already covered by many critics, in particular
by Professor Legouis in his exhaustive and illuminating study
of 'La Jeunesse de Wordsworth' ; but in my notes, though I have
paid attention chiefly to the elucidation of the text and to the
significance of the earlier readings, I have added some new matter
on the topography of the poem and on the sources of the poet's
inspiration, and have attempted to throw fresh light on the history
of his mind in that obscure but highly important period of its
development—the years 1793–7.

The publication of this volume has been made possible through
the kindness and generosity of the poet's grandson, Mr. Gordon
Wordsworth, the owner of the manuscripts on which it is based.

Mr. Wordsworth has not only allowed me free access to the manuscripts, but given constant help in deciphering what was almost illegible in them, and he has placed at my disposal his unrivalled knowledge of the details of the poet's life and of the country which will always be associated with him.

The portrait of Wordsworth which appears as the frontispiece to this book is the reproduction of a fine carnation-tinted pencil drawing by the miniature-painter, Henry Edridge (b. 1769, A.R.A. 1820, d. 1821). Edridge was introduced to Wordsworth in 1804 by Sir George Beaumont, and may have executed the portrait early in the following year,[1] i.e. while Wordsworth was at work upon *The Prelude*. Sir George wrote of him to Wordsworth (March 3, 1805): 'I admire him both as a man and an artist, and wish he had drawn all your portraits when he was at Grasmere.' This is the only known portrait of the poet in his prime, and its suitability as an illustration to this volume needs no emphasis. For permission to include it I am greatly indebted to Mrs. Rawnsley, of Allan Bank, Grasmere, its present owner.

After more than thirty years during which Wordsworth has been my constant companion, it is not easy for me to distinguish what I have learnt in direct study of the poems from what has reached me through the medium of his critics and editors; but wherever I have been conscious of an obligation I have acknowledged it. Of Professor Legouis I have already spoken. Professor Harper's admirable *Life of Wordsworth* is a mine of accurate biographical information of which I have frequently availed myself. The late Professor Knight collected a mass of material concerning the poet's life and work: it always needs careful verification, but when so verified often proves of considerable value. To Professor Garrod I am indebted, not only for his brilliant study of Wordsworth, which I have shared with a larger public, but for much private help and encouragement ungrudgingly bestowed. My colleague, Miss J. J. Milne, has given me valuable assistance in writing those notes that deal with Wordsworth's life in France.

---

[1] Mr. Gordon Wordsworth, however, thinks that the date at the foot of the portrait should be read as 1806, *not* 1805. Edridge, he says, was in the Lake country in 1804, but there is no evidence that he went there in 1805, nor that W. W. went to London. But W. W. was in London from April 4 to May 25, 1806, for the greater part of the time staying with the Beaumonts at Grosvenor Square, where Edridge was a constant visitor (*v.* Farington Diary, vol. iii). On the other hand, the letter quoted above, in which Beaumont wishes 'he had drawn all your portraits when he was at Grasmere', suggests to me that he *had* drawn W. W.'s.

To my old pupil, Miss Darbishire, of Somerville College, Oxford, a profound and acute student of Wordsworth, this book owes much. Throughout its preparation I have had the advantage of discussing with her many of the problems raised by the earlier texts, and both my introduction and commentary are the richer for her suggestions; whilst her careful reading of the proofs has directed my attention to several errors that had escaped me.

The printing of a book of this character presents obvious technical difficulties, and I am deeply grateful to the staff of the Clarendon Press, and in particular to Mr. Kenneth Sisam, for the care and skill that they have devoted to it. Finally, I must express my thanks to the Research Committee of the University of Birmingham for their generous contribution to the expenses of its production.

E. DE S.

*November 1925*

# PREFACE TO
# SECOND IMPRESSION

I HAVE taken the opportunity afforded me by the reissue of this book to correct a few misstatements and a number of smaller faults—chiefly errors of letter, numeral, or punctuation—which escaped my notice in reading the proofs of the first edition. Many of these have been pointed out to me by different friends and scholars, and I am especially grateful to Professor Beatty of Wisconsin, Mr. J. C. Smith, and Mr. R. H. Coats, for the care and vigilance with which they read the book and noted its imperfections.

E. DE S.

*January 1928*

# CONTENTS

# LIST OF ILLUSTRATIONS

# TABLE OF SIGLA, ABBREVIATIONS, ETC.

## USED IN THE INTRODUCTION, APPARATUS CRITICUS, AND NOTES

A B C D E *Alf.* JJ Chr. 18*a* RV U V J W M X Y Z = the various MSS. of *The Prelude*, or parts of *The Prelude*, as described on pp. xix to xxxii.

*Chr.* = *Christabel* notebook, *Alf.* = *Alfoxden* notebook.

1850 = the text of the first printed edition of *The Prelude*.

A² or B² = a first correction of A or B (and so with other letters).

𝕬 = a consensus of A and B.

[ ] = A number in square brackets denotes the number of the line in 1850, e.g. [175] = l. 175 in 1850.

[     ] = a blank space in the MS.

[ ? ] = an illegible word or words in the MS.

Letters or words in round brackets have been either added to the MS. or taken from it by the editor, as the obvious sense requires.

A word followed by ? and enclosed in square brackets is an editorial suggestion to fill a vacant or illegible space in the MS.

A word enclosed in square brackets and printed in italics represents a rejected alternative in the MS.

**Unless otherwise stated in the *apparatus criticus*, it may be in general assumed that of the passage in question all MSS. earlier than D have the reading of the A text, and that D and E have the reading of 1850.**

W. W., D. W., and M. W. = William Wordsworth, Dorothy Wordsworth, and Mary Wordsworth.

S. H. = Sarah Hutchinson; S. T. C. = Samuel Taylor Coleridge.

*Oxf. W.* = The one-volume edition of Wordsworth's Poems, ed. by Thomas Hutchinson, Oxford University Press.

*P.W.* = *The Poetical Works of W. W.*, vols. i–v, ed. by E. de Selincourt and Helen Darbishire, 1940–9.

Nowell Smith = *Poems of W. W.*, ed. by Nowell Charles Smith, 3 vols., 1896 (vol. iii contains *The Prelude*).

Moore Smith = *The Prelude*, ed. by G. C. Moore Smith (Temple Classics).

Worsfold = *The Prelude*, ed. by Basil Worsfold, 1907.

Grosart = *The Prose Works of W. W.*, ed. by Alexander B. Grosart, 3 vols., 1876.

Havens = *The Mind of a Poet, A Study of Wordsworth's Thought with particular reference to The Prelude*, by Raymond D. Havens, 1941.

I. F. notes = Notes on the different poems dictated by Wordsworth in later life to Miss Fenwick, and first printed in full in Grosart.

*Letters: E.L.; M.Y.; L.Y.* = *The Early Letters of W. W. and D. W.*, Oxford, 1935; *The Letters of W. W. and D. W. : Middle Years*, 1937; *The Letters of W. W. and D. W. : Later Years*, 1939. Ed. by E. de Selincourt.

*C.R.* = *Correspondence of Crabb Robinson and the Wordsworth Circle*, ed. by Edith J. Morley, 2 vols., 1927.

*Journals* = *The Journals of Dorothy Wordsworth*, ed. by E. de Selincourt, 1941.

*Memoirs* = *Memoirs of W.*, by Christopher Wordsworth, 2 vols., 1851.

Legouis trans. = *The Early Life of W. W., 1770–99*, by Émile Legouis, translated by J. W. Matthews, 1897.

Harper = *W. W., his Life, Works, and Influence*, by George McLean Harper, 2 vols., 1916.

Moorman = *William Wordsworth. The Early Years 1770–1803*, by M. Moorman, 1957.

Garrod = *W. W. : Lectures and Essays*, by H. W. Garrod, 1923.

Griggs = *Collected Letters of Samuel Taylor Coleridge*, edited by Earl Leslie Griggs, 2 vols., 1956.

# INTRODUCTION

## § 1. *The Manuscripts*

*THE PRELUDE* is the essential living document for the interpretation of Wordsworth's life and poetry; any details, therefore, that can be gathered of the manner and circumstances of its composition must be of interest alike to biographer and critic. But of more vital importance than these is a knowledge of its original text. It has long been known that Wordsworth revised *The Prelude* in his later years, and conjectures have been inevitable on the character and extent of that revision. How far does the authorized text, as it was given to the world by the poet's executors, actually represent what he had written nearly half a century before, when he was in the fullness of his powers ? Did he confine himself to purely stylistic correction and embellishment; or did he go further, and in any real sense rehandle his theme, in the spirit of his later thought ? A study of this volume will supply the answer. The original version may now for the first time be compared with the edition published in 1850, and the development from the one to the other traced through its successive stages. If the comparison does not show a change as fundamental as some critics have anticipated, it reveals much that is highly significant in the history of the poet's mind and art.

But first it is necessary to have some knowledge of the MSS., and of their relation with one another.

There are five almost complete extant MSS. of *The Prelude* (A B C D E) covering the years 1805–39, as well as several notebooks and other MSS. (JJ, the *Alfoxden, Christabel,* and 18*a* notebooks, J RV U V W M X Y Z) which contain drafts of parts of the poem, and belong to an earlier period. The main MSS. fall clearly into two groups, according as they are more closely related to the first complete text or to the authorized version. A B C are thus related to the text of 1805–6, D E to the text of 1850. *In the* apparatus criticus, *therefore, unless otherwise stated, it may be assumed that B and C are in agreement with A: D and E with 1850.* A description of all the MSS. follows.

## A and B
### (The MSS. on which the new text of this edition is based)

On November 29, 1805, Dorothy Wordsworth wrote to Lady Beaumont: 'I am now engaged in making a fair and final transcript of the Poem on his own Life.—I mean *final* till it is prepared for the press, which will not be for many years. No doubt before that time he will . . . have some alterations to make, but it appears to us at present to be finished.'

On December 25 she wrote to Mrs. Clarkson: 'I have . . . written 8 books of his Poem.'

During November and December Mrs. Wordsworth was staying at Park House, near Dacre, Cumberland. Sarah Hutchinson was with her, and Wordsworth appears to have divided his time between Dove Cottage and Park House. Dorothy was much alone, looking after the two children with the help of a young servant. On December 29 Mrs. W. returned, accompanied by S. H., who stayed at Grasmere till the following July. On March 2, 1806, Dorothy wrote to Mrs. Clarkson: '[We have] been engaged in making two copies of William's poem, and I also in re-copying my Journal in a fair hand to be bequeathed to my Niece and Namesake. These works are finished, and also Sara's copy for Coleridge.'

It seems certain the MSS. of *The Prelude*, to which Dorothy alludes, are those referred to in this book as A and B. Dorothy speaks of her copy as 'fair and final'; and in her voluminous correspondence, in which she gives much detail of her daily life and occupations, there is no suggestion that she made any subsequent copy of *The Prelude*. My view that B is the copy which S. H. made for Coleridge is corroborated by the fact that a blank page after Book VI is filled with annotations in Coleridge's handwriting. These will be found, marked 'S. T. C.', distributed among the other notes at the end of this volume.

A consists of 342 pages, $7\frac{1}{2} \times 4\frac{5}{8}$ inches in size, stitched together in small sections: B comprises two notebooks (I–VII, VIII–end) of 348 pages, $7\frac{1}{2} \times 4\frac{1}{2}$ inches, bound in blue paper boards. Both MSS. are beautifully written,[1] with hardly a slip of the pen or a writer's correction from one end of the poem to the other. This is all the more remarkable in B, for it would not be possible to

---

[1] B's elaborately decorated title-page, which is reproduced to face the title-page of the 1850 ed., was the work of George Hutchinson, Sarah's brother. He also contributed the heading to each book. A's title-page is missing.

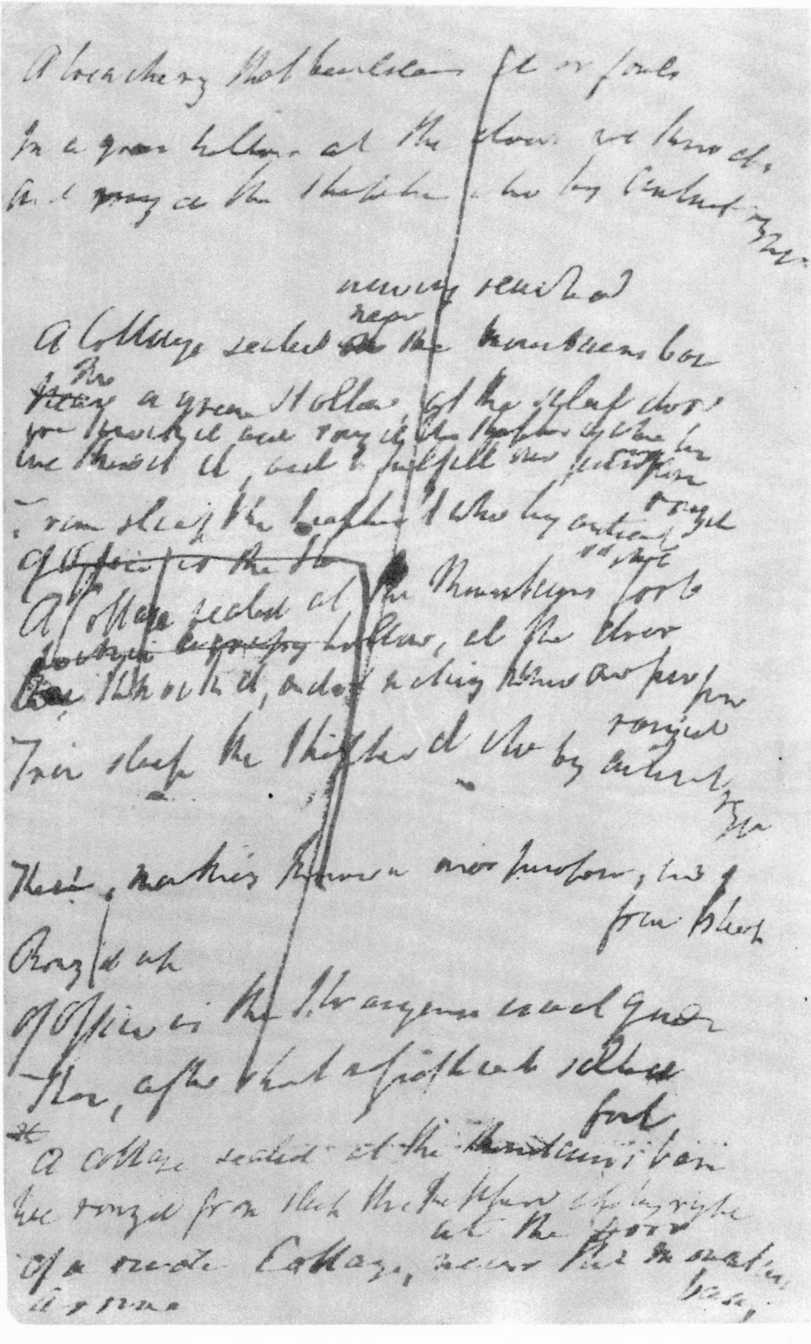

MS. A. Book XIII [XIV]. 1–16 with

_The Most Correct Copy of this Book_

In one of those Excursions (may they ne'er
Fade from my thoughts nor be with less delight
Remember'd) travelling with a youthful Friend
Along the northern tract of Wales, I left
*[heavily struck-through and revised lines]*

Through Stiles, on foot, and with a youthful Friend
I left Bethkelert's huts at couching time,
And westward took my way to see the sun
Rise from the top of Snowdon.                    At the Door
               rude                                 base
Of a low Cottage at the Mountain's
                            the Shepherd, who by ——— night
Of office is the Stranger's usual guide,
And after short refreshment sallied forth. —
       It was a Summer's night, a close warm night,
Wan, dull, and glaring, with a dropping mist
Low hung and thick that cover'd all the sky,
                                        but as we went
                                          ——— hoary faith
In out tired ——— little could we see
Summit round on every side with fog & damp

corrections in Wordsworth's hand. _v._ pp. 478–9.

remove a faulty page from a bound notebook and to substitute another without detection. Both MSS. are easily legible except where the poet himself, in revising, has heavily scored out or written over the original lines. From this A has suffered more seriously than B, for it was written on one side of the paper only, and was therefore used more consistently for the insertion of corrections and additions. But with the help of B, A can generally be read, even where it has been most fiercely defaced. B has many pages left without an alteration upon them, but the number of corrections in it is larger towards the end of the poem than at the beginning. Most of these corrections correspond with those in A, but there are a few not found in A. The blank pages between the books, and at the beginning and end of the two volumes of which B consists, contain drafts in Wordsworth's hand of some of the passages that he wished to alter.

It would be natural to suppose that B would be simply copied from A; for when S. H. began her work Dorothy had already completed eight books, and her 'fair and final copy' must have been far more legible than the MS. from which she took it. But though B's variations from A are few and slight they are enough to give to B some independent authority, and to support the view that both were taken from a common original, in which, for some few passages, either two readings had been preserved, or the text copied was illegible and Wordsworth had to be called in to solve the difficulty. No one who has attempted to decipher the poet's autograph MSS.[1] will believe that two copies so perfect as A and B could have been made from a MS. in his handwriting, unless he was constantly at the writers' elbows to instruct them.

The punctuation of both MSS. errs, perhaps, on the side of lightness; but except for the omission of stops at the end of the line, where the natural pause of the voice makes them less necessary to bring out the meaning of the passage, it is substantially correct. The original punctuation of A cannot always be deter-

[1] Wordsworth's handwriting was always bad, though in early days he could write a good copy-book hand, and he had a constitutional aversion to penmanship. Cf. his letter to De Quincey, March 6, 1804 (*Letters, E.L.* 368): 'I have a kind of derangement . . . which makes writing painful to me, and indeed almost prevents me from holding correspondence with anybody: and this (I mean to say the unpleasant feelings which I have connected with the act of holding a Pen) has been the chief cause of my long silence.' This letter dates from the time when several of the MS. notebooks were written (*v. infra*); as the 'derangement' above referred to was constantly recurrent, the task of deciphering the MSS. has not always been easy. Cf. also *Letters, M.Y.* 487, 704.

mined; sometimes it is very faint, sometimes written over by an alteration in the text, sometimes darkened in at a later period (when it may or may not cover an original stop). But though Wordsworth admitted that he was not 'an adept' at punctuation, and though in writing his rough drafts he almost entirely omitted the stops, there is no doubt that these MSS. represent his own intention in the matter far more accurately than either D or E.

My text (1805–6) is printed from A, with the help of B when A is illegible or defective, or when B seems more clearly to represent the poet's intention at the time the copies were made. In every important case where I have followed B rather than A the fact is recorded in the *apparatus criticus*.

In A and B the poem is divided into thirteen books: Books X and XI of the 1850 edition, as in D and E, form Book X in A and.B.

## C

C is a stout quarto volume of 333 pages, $9\frac{1}{16} \times 7$ inches, written on both sides, in the fine clerkly hand of John Carter. Its exact date is uncertain, but as Carter only entered the service of the Wordsworths, as gardener and handyman, in the year 1813 he is hardly likely to have been entrusted with this task, or indeed to have been equal to it, for some years afterwards. On the other hand, it must have been written before and not after the separate publication of *Vaudracour and Julia* in 1820; for its version of this story, omitted altogether by D and E, has many pencil corrections which were incorporated in the 1820 version. Elsewhere in C there are very few readings that are not found in A and its corrections. Its importance lies in the help it gives us in determining the relative dates of corrections found in A. For the evidence is incontestable that C was copied from the corrected A, and therefore corrections in A not incorporated in C must be regarded as later than C. I should be inclined to attribute it to the years 1817–19, and to regard those alterations of A that imply a change of spirit, or point of view, as introduced after the publication of *The Excursion*. Some, at least, of those changes which are purely stylistic were certainly made earlier, possibly soon after the poem had been read to Coleridge. C stops abruptly at XII. 187 [XIII. 188]. It contains, especially in the later part of the volume, a number of pencil corrections, written, obviously, when Wordsworth was preparing D; these have, therefore, no independent interest, and are not recorded in the *apparatus criticus*.

MS. B. On a page originally blank opposite the opening of Book III. 1–18

& fond with a curious patience &c &c

Laboured the subtile process to detect

By which like thoughts &c

Book Third

From the conflicting powers of flood & fire

Escaped, I stood fixed in permanence serene

Residence at Cambridge

To record                of prime & usual hours

And the           tablets of the earth

It was a dreary morning when the Chaise

Roll'd over the flat plains of Huntingdon

And through the open windows first I saw

The long backed Chapel of Kings College

Its pinnacles above the dusky groves

we espied upon the road

A Student cloathed in gown and tassell'd cap,

He pass'd nor was I master of my eyes

Till he was left a hundred yards behind.

The place as we approach'd seem'd more and more

To have an eddy's force and such'd us in

More eagerly at every step we took

Onward we drove beneath the Castle, down

By Magdalene bridge we went and cross'd the

And at the Hoop we landed, famous Inn!

My spirit was                 my thoughts were full of hope

Some Friends I had, Acquaintance who there

Seem'd Friends, poor simple School boys now hung round

Wordsworth has written a passage related to Book II. 181-3. v. p. 52.

## D

D is written on both sides of the paper on small quarto sheets ($7\frac{1}{2} \times 6$ in.) sewn together in separate books, each book paged separately. It is in the handwriting of M. W. The water-marks on the paper show the dates 1824–8: the work would presumably have been completed in or after 1828. At the beginning of the MS. is a note stating that it was corrected in 1832, and it is clear that Wordsworth devoted the early months of 1832 to a thorough overhauling of the MS. Dora writes to Miss Kinnaird on February 17, 1832: 'Father is particularly well and busier than 1000 bees. Mother and he work like slaves from morning to night—an arduous work—correcting a long Poem written thirty years back and which is not to be published during his life—The Growth of his own Mind—the Ante-Chapel as he calls it to The Recluse . . .'; and on October 15, 1832, Dora reports her father as still correcting the old poem. Christopher Wordsworth senior writes to Christopher Wordsworth junior, April 18, 1832: 'They were very loath to part with him [his son John] at Rydal for he has been of great value to all the family—more especially to your uncle—who having John to talk to in his walks, was very industrious through the whole winter at all other times of the day—and worked very hard, especially in the revising and finishing of his long autobiographic poem' [B.M. Add. MSS. 46137]. These corrections made in 1832 are reinforced by others made in another overhauling of the MS. in 1839. Miss Fenwick writes, March 28, 1839:[1] 'Our journey was postponed for a week, that the beloved old poet might accomplish the work that he had in hand, the revising of his grand autobiographical poem, and leaving it in a state fit for publication. At this he has been labouring for the last month, seldom less than six or seven hours a day, or rather one ought to say the whole day, for it seemed always in his mind—quite a possession, and much, I believe, he has done to it, expanding it in some parts, and perfecting it in all. I could not have imagined the labour that he has bestowed on all his works, had I not been so much with him at this time.'

For the first time in D, Book X is split into two—Books X and XI—so that the poem now extends to fourteen books. The changes introduced into the D text are numerous and important, and a new version is often stuck by means of wafers over the old one. In such places it is reasonable to conjecture that the obliterated

---

[1] *Correspondence of Sir Henry Taylor*, p. 87.

reading is that of C. The punctuation of D is deficient, and much of it was added at a later date. MS. D in its corrected state was used as the copy for MS. E.

## E

E is in the handwriting of the poet's daughter Dora—Books I–VII, and of Elizabeth Cookson—Books VIII–XIV. Dora and Elizabeth Cookson were making copies in May 1839. Wordsworth writes to Dora: 'Now let me thank you and Elizabeth C. for the labours you have gone through in transcribing that long Poem; pray, when it is done, let it be sealed, and deposited with Mr Carter, to provide against any unlucky accident befalling the other.'[1]

E is written on one side of the paper ($7\frac{1}{2} \times 6\frac{1}{4}$ in.) and from marks and instructions upon it is proved to be the copy from which the text of 1850 was printed. E contains a few corrections of D, and was obviously intended to be the final fair copy. On Book XIV is written 'reviewed July 1839'. Wordsworth must have gone through the MS. on his return to Rydal Mount from London and Oxford early that month. E is not quite so carefully copied as the previous MSS., and has a few errors, obviously due either to misreading D or mishearing a dictation of D. Its punctuation is very deficient and sometimes incorrect, and stops have in many places been added later in pencil.

Apart from punctuation and the use of capitals, in which the editor allowed himself a very free discretion, the text of 1850 represents, with few exceptions, the reading of E. Some of its divergences from E are clearly printer's errors: for other changes either Carter, who saw the poem through the press, or the poet's nephew Christopher Wordsworth, or Edward Quillinan, were responsible. Christopher Wordsworth writes from Rydal Mount, June 14, 1850: 'My first duty here is conjointly with Mr Carter and Mr Quillinan to prepare the posthumous Poem for publication, I mean so far as revising the Proof Sheets is concerned, for it was left ready for the Press by the Author' [B.M. Add. MSS. 46137]. E. Quillinan's diary corroborates: June 10, 1850. 'Revised first six sheets of W.'s posthumous Poem, "Growth of a Poet's Mind" at Mrs W.'s request'; July 9: 'Finished the revisal of *The Prelude*, or *Growth of a Poet's Mind* the last proof this day, having as well as Dr C. W. and Mr Carter, revised the whole carefully.' Christopher is more likely than Carter, and even than

[1] *L.Y.* 977.

Quillinan, to have been responsible for deliberate changes in the text. These changes have no authority from the MSS. In correcting proofs for the press the use both of capitals and stops has been strenuously revised. In E the punctuation is deficient: the text of 1850 is throughout over-punctuated.

## Alfoxden Notebook

This is a small leather-bound book ($6\frac{1}{4} \times 4$ in.). At one end is a fragment of D. W.'s *Journal* for January 20, 1798, copied in by W. W., and a few tentative lines of blank verse in W. W.'s hand, followed on the next page by a quotation copied by D. W. from Boswell's *Life of Johnson* on the subject of blank verse. At the other end of the book are drafts of passages (1) for *The Old Cumberland Beggar*; (2) for *The Ruined Cottage*, with passages descriptive of 'The Wanderer', some of them afterwards incorporated in *The Excursion* Book I, others finally to be adapted to *The Prelude* (*v.* notes to VII. 716–29; II. 321–41); (3) portions of an early version of the passage describing his encounter with the discharged soldier (*Prelude*, IV. 450–95); (4) other fragments of blank verse not used by him in the issue;[1] and (5) first drafts of the opening of *The Thorn*, and the whole of 'A Whirl-blast from behind the hill'; and a fragment of *Peter Bell* afterwards made into the poem *Andrew Jones*.

In four places a few pages have been cut out (a common practice with W. W. when he was composing or rewriting, and wanted passages for copying). What is left is mainly drafts of passages in process of composition, not fair copies; but there is one fair copy in D. W.'s hand which seems to have been inserted at a later date —forty-three consecutive lines corresponding (with some omissions) to Addendum IV of MS. D of *The Ruined Cottage*.[2] The other portions of passages in this notebook which belong to *The Ruined Cottage* are trial drafts, or indications on stubs of pages cut out, which suggest in all much less than the 900 lines mentioned in D. W.'s letter to M. H. of March 5, 1798, where she gives a fair copy of a large part of the then completed poem. Some of the verse in this notebook must therefore belong to the period between January 20, 1798, when W. W. copied in a part of D. W.'s *Journal* for that day, and March 5, when he had worked out a complete draft of *The Ruined Cottage*: the rest, except for D. W.'s copy afore-

---

[1] *v. P.W.* v. 340–1.
[2] Perhaps written in 1801–2; *v. P.W.* v. 405.

mentioned of a later addendum to *The Ruined Cottage*, would seem to belong to the later spring months of 1798.

## JJ

JJ is a small notebook used by D. W. in Germany 1798–9, and afterwards for her Grasmere Journal February 14–May 2, 1802. In it Wordsworth has written a succession of passages in blank verse[1] which turn out to be the earliest surviving drafts of a large part of Book I of *The Prelude*, together with two other passages used in later books. It seems quite certain that all the entries apart from the Grasmere Journal date from the German period. After two pages of pencil scribblings and two blank pages there follow an account in W. W.'s hand of his visit to Klopstock, then D. W.'s narrative of the journey from Hamburg to Goslar, and some pages of very elementary German exercises and grammar, and then the aforesaid Journal, which occupies the larger part of the book; after this follow a fragment of a moral essay exposing the weakness of 'systems' such as Godwin's and Paley's; more German exercises, and lastly early drafts of blank verse passages corresponding with passages in *The Prelude*, chiefly occurring in Book I. In writing them W. W. began on the last page of the notebook and apparently worked backwards towards the middle; and, so read, they suggest a different order of composition from that in which the passages were finally arranged. Thus I. 271–350, 428–41, 490–501, 311–32, 577–608, 373–420; V. 389–413; I. 405–27 2nd draft; 351–71; XII. 47–52; I. 659–63 (I. 20–47 fragments).

It is to be noted that the passage corresponding to *The Prelude* I. 372–427 (the stolen boat episode) is in process of composition, one draft following another; whilst the version of it copied by D. W. in her letter to Coleridge December or January 1798–9 (*E.L.* 209–10) is a revision bringing it near to its final form.

This MS. JJ, representing Wordsworth's first coherent attempt to embark upon the poem which afterwards became *The Prelude*, is sufficiently interesting and significant to merit printing as a whole (*v.* Appendix, p. 633 *infra*).

I have tried to place the passages in the order in which they were written: this is partly guess-work, for the writer sometimes turns back to fill in blank spaces.

### Christabel Notebook and MS. 18a

These are two similar pocket-books in red leather measuring $7\frac{3}{4} \times 5$ inches: (1) The *Christabel* notebook, containing at one end

---

[1] *v.* Appendix, p. 633 *infra*.

a fair copy of *Christabel*, Part I, in D. W.'s hand, Part II in Mary Hutchinson's.[1] (2) Pocket-book stamped with initials 'D. W.' Both notebooks have been used by D. W. for fair copies of W. W.'s poems, and also by W. W. for neat copies as well as rough scrawls of his own compositions. When both books contain copies of the same passage or poem the *Christabel* notebook generally gives the earlier version; the 18*a* version is often emended in W. W.'s hand.

Of *The Prelude* Book I, *Christabel* notebook gives ll. 271–304, 310–14; MS. 18*a* gives ll. 452–89 (the skating-scene), 566–70, 653–end; and an abortive beginning of Book II, headed *2nd Part*:

> Friend of my heart and Genius we had reach'd
> A small green island which I was well pleas'd
> To pass not lightly by for though I felt
> Strength unabated yet I seem'd to need
> Thy cheering voice or ere I could pursue
> My voyage, resting else for ever there

Both MSS. must originally have contained considerably larger portions of Book I, as is clearly shown by the stubs of pages which have been cut out. Of passages to be found in later books of *The Prelude*, MS. 18*a* gives versions of the following: II. 322–41; V. 370–415 (including 'There was a Boy'); and both MSS. give drafts of IV. 363–502 (encounter with the discharged soldier) and XII. 194–201; also of *Nutting*, first intended for *The Prelude* but published separately in *Lyrical Ballads* 1800, and a long passage recognizable as an overflow of *Nutting* (*v.* note to *Prelude* XI. 214–21, p. 612 *infra*) 'I would not strike a flower'.

The version in the *Christabel* notebook of the lines beginning 'Was it for this' (*Prelude* I. 271 *et seq.*) is nearer than the text of 1805 to the version in MS. JJ and earlier than that of MSS. U and V. The version in MS. 18*a* of the skating-scene (*Prelude* I. 452–89) corresponds closely with D. W.'s copy in her letter to Coleridge from Goslar.

These two notebooks may possibly have been used first at Alfoxden but later than the *Alfoxden* notebook; more probably they were used chiefly in Germany, 1798–9, as a means of preserving short poems and passages of poems of which Wordsworth wished to keep a record. Naturally Wordsworth and D. W. continued to use them for a few entries after their return to England, at Sockburn and Grasmere in 1799 and 1800.

---

[1] Part II must have been copied in by M. H. after S. T. C.'s visit to Dove Cottage Oct. 4, 1800. Under that date D. W. writes in her *Journal*: 'Exceedingly delighted with the second part [of *Christabel*].'

## J

J is an oblong leather-bound notebook ($4\frac{7}{16} \times 7\frac{1}{4}$ in.) which contains D. W.'s *Journal* for May–December 1802. Leaves have been torn from the front of the book. The first eight pages contain passages of blank verse in Wordsworth's neatest handwriting. These are evidently lines intended for *Michael* or reflections arising out of its subject. The first fragment describes the sheep-fold —'There is a shapeless crowd of unhewn stones'; two others record reflections afterwards expanded in *The Prelude* VIII. 221–310; then drafts of four stanzas of *Ruth*, intended for the revised version of that poem in *Lyrical Ballads* 1802. After this D. W. resumes her diary. It is clear that Wordsworth wrote the verse into the book before D. W. appropriated it for her *Journal*, that is before May 1802; and it is more than probable that most of the blank verse is the work of October–December 1800, when the poet was engrossed with *Michael*.

## V, U, and RV

V and U are fair copies, based on the same MS., of Books I and II. Both lack the first 271 lines of Book I. V is made up of 40 pages ($8\frac{1}{4} \times 5\frac{3}{4}$ in.) with watermark 'Curteis & Sons, 1798'. It is in D.W.'s hand and is corrected and revised, generally by W. W. Two pages have been torn out at the beginning of Book II, so that it lacks ll. 1–$54\frac{1}{2}$, given in U.

U is a quarto vellum-bound notebook containing (1) *The Borderers*, (2) *The Prelude* I and II, (3) *The Beggar*,[1] MS. 2, all except the last in the careful hand of M. H. The transcript of *The Prelude* I and II is a straight copy with no intervention by Wordsworth.

Both these MSS. give the earliest extant draft of the bulk of Books I and II. Their contents follow the same order, the passages which finally found their place in Books I and II of the finished poem being interspersed with other episodes of the poet's childhood later transferred to other books. The order is as follows: I. 271–441 (442–51 in V only), 452–509, 535–70, 509–24; V. 450–72; XI. 258–316, 345–89; I. 571–663; II. 1–144 (1–$54\frac{1}{2}$ are missing in V), followed by lines on which VIII. [458–75] (1850 text) are based (*v.* notes, p. 582), followed by the rest of Book II. In MS. V, at the end of Book I, Wordsworth has inserted as an afterthought lines corresponding to ll. 525–33, and an alternative to ll. 520–3.

---

[1] *The Cumberland Beggar* was sent to the printer on Oct. 10, 1800 (*v.* D. W.'s *Journal*). The copy in U appears to have been made before this, since it has earlier readings than the first printed text.

RV (not mentioned by de Selincourt) is a fair copy of Book II
in the hands alternately of W. W. and D. W. with one passage,
ll. 92–208, written by S. H., on a number of sheets which have
been sewn into the notebook first used by M. W. for her fair copy
of *The Recluse*, Book I, MS. D. Between ll. 434 and 435 RV has
a passage not in U or V beginning

> By such communion was I early taught
> That what we see of forms and images

which corresponds substantially with a passage in W. W.'s hand
on a page of MS. 2 of *Peter Bell* (*v.* note to *Prelude* II. 434–5 *infra*).
Unlike U and V, RV does not include after II. 144 the lines on
which VIII. [458–75] (1850 text) are based. Otherwise RV follows
the order of Book II as in the 1805 text. There must have been
a companion copy of Book I which has been lost.

From internal evidence RV must be earlier than U and V:
passages are revised and rewritten, and where a correction or
addition is made between the lines or in the margin of the text the
corrected version is incorporated in the text of U and V.

The probable date of composition of these MSS. is 1800, between
January and October.

## *MS. W*

W is a small notebook covered in thin blue cardboard ($6\frac{1}{4} \times 3\frac{7}{8}$ in).
and consisting in its present state of 44 leaves. Leaves have been
torn out here and there. It was originally used by W. W. and
D. W. for copying out poems—first by W. W. for a copy of
Marvell's 'Horatian Ode', then by D. W., who transcribed a *Tale,
imitated from Gower*, and afterwards a number of W. W.'s sonnets
(*v. P.W.* iii. 418). W. W. must then have taken over the notebook
for drafts of *The Prelude*, which now fill up the blank spaces left
by the aforesaid transcripts. The drafts correspond to IV. 270–
304, 353–65, 304–45, 351–2; XIII. 66–119 (abortive passages);
XI. 224–57; V. 1–48, 445–515, 294–376, 591–4, 630–end. Then
comes the heading *5th Book*, and immediately under it lines corresponding to XIII. 1–135: of this ll. 1–65 is a fair copy by M. W.
followed by a long hitherto unpublished passage in W. W.'s hand
(*v.* notes, p. 623). After this XIII. 154–65; XI. 174–85, 123–8,
329–37, 317–28, 138–49, 316–37, 342–5, 199–223. The part of
the notebook devoted to *The Prelude* belongs to January–March
1804. For evidence of this and for the light which it throws on
the composition of the poem *v.* p. 1 *infra*.

## M

M is a stout vellum-bound volume ($6\frac{5}{8} \times 4\frac{1}{4}$ in.) containing fair copies of a miscellany of poems. It opens with *The Ruined Cottage* (*Excursion* I), copied by D. W., which is followed by sonnets and other short pieces (copied by D. W. and S. H.) composed after 1800 and for the most part included in the 1807 volumes. Then comes the *Ode: Intimations of Immortality*, &c., also first published in 1807, and *Peter Bell* (a copy made at a different time on pages of greater length folded at the bottom); finally, *The Prelude*, Books I–III, copied by S. H., and Books IV and V, copied by D. W. Books IV and V must have been entered after March 6, 1804, because at that date *The Prelude* was to be completed in five books which would have ended in the manner suggested in MS. W (*v.* p. 1 *infra*), whereas the version in M of Books IV and V is substantially that of *The Prelude* as we know it, with eight more books to follow. M is the first MS. to give ll. 1–271 of Book I. Though in the main the readings of A and M are identical, M preserves here and there an earlier reading. M would appear to be a duplicate of the copy written out for Coleridge to take abroad, if indeed it is not that very copy. D. W. writes to Mrs. Clarkson, March 24, 1804: 'We have been engaged, Mary and I, in making a complete copy of William's poems for poor Coleridge, to be his companions in Italy. . . . I ought to tell you that besides copying the verses for C. we have re-copied them entirely for ourselves as we went along.'[1] Wordsworth, in his letter to Coleridge on March 29, writes: 'The Poems were transcribed in a great hurry and I find on looking at our copy which was made at the same time that several lines have been overlooked here and there.[2] He notes two omissions in Book V which I find correspond with omissions in MS. M; but he notes a third which is *not* an omission in MS. M. This means that 'our copy' which he had in his hands was not M but another copy: the evidence points to its being that which was afterwards lost in December 1805 and found again in January 1806 (*v. E.L.* 550; *M.Y.* 2–3). It was soaked in the rain, and it has not survived.

The possibility that MS. M is (minus the pages of *Peter Bell*) the copy that Coleridge took with him to Malta must not be excluded. Professor MacGillivray has pointed out to me that the groups of pages in MS. M are numbered in obedience to Coleridge's instructions (*v.* letters of February 8 and 16, Griggs, ii. 1060 and

---

[1] *E.L.* 374.  [2] *E.L.* 380.

1065) that each packet sent must not weigh more than $2\frac{1}{4}$ or $2\frac{1}{2}$ oz. MS. M has the pages numbered in groups of seven to seventeen pages. The pages containing *The Prelude* are numbered 7 to 11; Book I numbered 7, eleven leaves; Book II numbered 8, eight leaves; Book III numbered 9, nine leaves; Book IV numbered 10, ten leaves; Book V numbered 11, thirteen leaves. Thus they make up five packets, each of suitable weight. This indicates either that MS. M is the very copy sent to Coleridge and finally returned to Wordsworth,[1] or that it is a copy kept at Dove Cottage which they had meant to send to him (and so numbered the pages in groups) but for which they decided in the end to send a substitute.

## X

A notebook similar to W, consisting in its present state of 40 leaves ($6\frac{1}{16} \times 3\frac{3}{4}$ in.). Some leaves have been torn out. It opens with a rough draft of passages from VII. 92–218 (two leaves have been torn out which may be assumed to have contained ll. 136–80) followed by a draft of *The Excursion* II. 241 ff. Then comes *The Prelude* VIII. 742–51, on which follows without a break VII. 75 to the end of VII. Some of this is copied by M. W., a little by D. W., and much by W. W.; but it is corrected throughout by W. W. It is mostly legible and shows few variations from A. This occupies half the book; the rest is given to a draft of *The Excursion* II probably added to the book later, for it begins with a passage used in Y for the opening of *Prelude* VIII.

The work on *The Prelude* contained in this book may be dated April and October or November 1804 (*v.* pp. li, lii).

## Y

A notebook similar to W and X ($6\frac{1}{4} \times 3\frac{7}{8}$ in.) consisting in its present state of 53 leaves. It is in very bad condition, for it has evidently been left out in the rain and then dried before a hot fire. In consequence the top half of many pages is illegible, and sometimes the top of the page has been scorched and has crumbled away. It is often possible, however, to read a word or two in an otherwise obliterated line and so to trace the sequence of the draft.

The first legible passage contains lines corresponding with VIII. 68–73; then, after an illegible page, there follows, more

---

[1] Its return to Wordsworth can be readily explained, for in the autumn of 1806 when Coleridge was with them once more, Wordsworth was preparing for the press the miscellany of poems published as *Poems in Two Volumes* in 1807, and would have been glad to have back Coleridge's MS. for the purpose of checking the text.

carefully written, IX. 293–519; after this a few pages have been torn out. The next page is only legible from the middle, but it appears to give a draft of the last lines of the opening passage of VII ending at l. 50. From here the MS. runs on into XIII. 333–67 (tributes to D. W. and Raisley Calvert). Was this possibly first intended as the opening of Book VIII ? What follows represents, probably, the first draft of that book, written in the autumn of 1804 (*v. infra*, p. lii). Its subject is that which is designated in the heading to Book VIII: *Retrospect. Love of Nature leading to Love of Man.* Its chief variations from the A version are:

1. In place of 1–61 stand lines afterwards adapted for *The Excursion* II. 1–25.
2. In place of 159–72 there is a long passage of 15 pages (*v.* notes, *infra*, pp. 569–78) tracing the development through Nature of man's mind and heart.
3. Between 497 and 498 is a deleted passage (*v.* notes, p. 581) afterwards utilized for *The Excursion* IV. 404–12˙ and IX. 437–48.
4. In place of 661–823 are $2\frac{1}{2}$ almost entirely illegible pages, and some pages have been torn out.
5. At the end of VIII follow lines related to XI. 9–14; XII. 112–227; and, after some illegible jottings, XIII. 374–85. All this may have been added later; but the lines might after all have been worked into a book entitled *Retrospect*.

## Z

Z consists of 22 leaves ($6\frac{5}{8} \times 4\frac{1}{8}$ in.) stitched together. It is a fair copy (written by M. W., and partly by W. W., all corrected by W. W.) of Books XI and XII [XII and XIII] headed *Book 12th*. Two leaves have been stitched on in front of the main body in place of others that have been cut away. They contain Book X. 690–711 ('O Pleasant exercise of hope and joy . . .'), followed by the words *Back again 9 leaves*, and XI. 1–41. After the stitched-on leaves the first page is headed *Book 12th* and begins: 'This history my friend has chiefly told' (XI. 42). On the top of the page Wordsworth has written: 'This whole book wants re touching, the subject is not sufficiently brought out.' But the main bulk of it is followed closely by A. The heading to the second part is *Book 13th*: 'From Nature doth emotion come . . . .'

The headings *Book 12th* and *Book 13th* suggest that originally Book X of A was divided into two as it was in 1850, and that the division found in D and E was a reversion to the older plan.

## § 2. 'The Prelude' and 'The Recluse'

Wordsworth's own account, in his Preface to *The Excursion*, 1814, of the origin of *The Prelude*, which he regarded as a subsidiary part of his great poem *The Recluse*, is undoubtedly misleading. He begins by stating that *The Excursion* is the second part of a long and laborious work which is to consist of three parts and is to be called *The Recluse*. He proceeds to explain the derivation of this title:

Several years ago, when the Author retired to his native Mountains, with the hope of being enabled to construct a literary Work that might live, it was a reasonable thing that he should take a review of his own Mind, and examine how far Nature and Education had qualified him for such employment. As subsidiary to this preparation, he undertook to record, in Verse, the origin and progress of his own powers, as far as he was acquainted with them. That Work, addressed to a dear Friend, most distinguished for his knowledge and genius, and to whom the Author's Intellect is deeply indebted, has been long finished ; and the result of the investigation which gave rise to it was a determination to compose a philosophical Poem, containing views of Man, Nature, and Society ; and to be entitled, 'The Recluse' ; as having for its principal subject the sensations and opinions of a Poet living in retirement.—The preparatory Poem is biographical, and conducts the history of the Author's mind to the point when he was emboldened to hope that his faculties were sufficiently matured for entering upon the arduous labour which he had proposed to himself; and the two Works have the same kind of relation to each other, if he may so express himself, as the Ante-chapel has to the body of a gothic Church.

He tells us here that he retired to his native mountains with the hope of constructing a work that might live, but then decided that, in preparation for this, he must investigate his qualifications, and thus was led on to write a poem recording the origin and progress of his powers (*The Prelude*): and the result was the resolve to compose a philosophical poem to be called *The Recluse*. As a statement of fact this will not stand. His retirement to his native mountains dates from December 20, 1799, when he and his sister moved into Dove Cottage, Grasmere; but as MSS. and letters show, the *idea* of the great philosophical poem was already fully fledged in March 1798,[1] and the first tentative beginnings of *The Prelude* itself date from the winter of 1798–9 in Germany.

Wordsworth was interested in origins, and we owe it to him to

---

[1] Wordsworth wrote on March 11, 1798, to James Losh: 'I have written 1300 lines of a poem which I hope to make of considerable utility. Its title will be *The Recluse*; or Views of Nature, Man and Society.'

trace as truly as we can the origin of *The Prelude*. We must start as far back as 1788, his second year at Cambridge, when he had his first prevision of some great poetic work.

> The Poet's soul was with me at that time
> . . . Those were the days
> Which also first encourag'd me to trust
> With firmness, hitherto but lightly touch'd
> With such a daring thought, that I might leave
> Some monument behind me which pure hearts
> Should reverence                    (*Prelude* VI. 55–69.)

This follows upon his dedication to poetry in the Long Vacation among the mountains (*Prelude* IV. 330–45). After Cambridge he spent four restless years, 1791–5, in London, in France, and on visits to friends in England, urged on by the desire to gain experience without chaining himself to a profession, convinced that his destiny was to be a poet. In January 1795 his friend Raisley Calvert died, leaving him a legacy of £900 'in the hope'[1]

> That I had some endowments by which good
> Might be promoted. . . . He [   ] did
> By a Bequest sufficient for my needs
> Enable me to pause for choice, and walk
> At large and unrestrain'd, nor damp'd too soon
> By mortal cares . . .
> He clear'd a passage for me, and the stream
> Flowed in the bent of Nature
>                    (*Prelude* (1805) XIII. 353–67.)

In the autumn of 1795 Wordsworth and his sister settled at Racedown in Dorset, and he was free to devote himself to his calling as poet. The first 54 lines of *The Prelude*, which appear in none of the early MSS. before MS. M (written in 1804), would appear to have been composed as a joyful extempore outpouring on his way to Racedown after his release from a long and tedious sojourn in London. In these lines beginning

> Oh there is blessing in this gentle breeze

he welcomes the breeze which greets him on his release and at the

---

[1] 'This bequest was from a young man with whom, though I call him friend, I had had but little connexion; and the act was done entirely from a confidence on his part that I had powers and attainments that might be of use to mankind.' Letter of W. W. to Sir G. Beaumont (Feb. 20, 1805).

same time heralds a quickening of his poetic life. As he approached
the cottage where he was to settle, he had

> assurance of some work
> Of glory, there forthwith to be begun,
> Perhaps too there perform'd

But the two years that followed at Racedown did not see the
initiation of his great work. It was not till the early months of
1798, after he had moved to Alfoxden, that Wordsworth determined, with Coleridge's enthusiastic encouragement, to compose
a great philosophical poem to be entitled '*The Recluse*, or Views
on Nature, Man and Society'.[1] The first draft of the famous lines
'On Man, on Nature and on human life', printed in his Preface to
'*The Excursion*, being a portion of *The Recluse*' in 1814, as a
'Prospectus of the design and scope of the whole Poem', may well
have been written in the first heat of this resolve.[2] He had already
written *The Ruined Cottage*, and other verse which would
naturally find a place in his comprehensive scheme. 'Indeed', he
wrote, 'I know not anything which will not come within the scope
of my plan.' In the eager confidence with which he embarked on
the enterprise he contemplated its completion in less than two
years. But the 'paramount impulse not to be withstood' soon gave
way to the doubts and misgivings which he so poignantly expresses in the first book of *The Prelude* (ll. 235–71). He tried in
vain to harness himself to his great task. It was in the autumn
and winter following (1798–9), in his keenly-felt exile in Germany,
that he began seriously to spur himself on to the writing of his
great poem by recalling, in passages of blank verse, what Nature
had done for him in childhood. These passages, which have survived in a notebook of Dorothy's (MS. JJ; *v.* Appendix, p. 633
*infra*), some of them also in a letter from Dorothy and William
to Coleridge of December–January 1798–9, were to form later the
substance of Book I of *The Prelude*. His theme is: Nature singled
me out and educated me to be a poet—was it for this—namely,
that I should fail in my calling ?

The first passage begins significantly:

> Was it for this
> That one, the fairest of all Rivers lov'd
> To blend his murmurs with my Nurse's song . . .
>                                    (*Prelude* I. 271.)

Passages that follow reiterate the thought:

> For this, when on the withered mountain slope . . .
>               (Cf. *Prelude* I. 311–18; JJ, p. 635.)

---

[1]  *v.* letters quoted pp. xlv, xlvi, *infra*.
[2]  *v.* notes to 'The Prospectus', *P.W.* v. 372.

> Ah not in vain, ye beings of the hills
>> (Cf. *Prelude* I. 428–34; JJ, p. 634.)
>
> Ah not for this, ye spirits of the Springs
>> (Cf. *Prelude* I. 490–2; JJ, p. 634.)

At the end of Book I in its complete form, reached later, he confesses:

> my hope has been that I might fetch
> Reproaches from my former years, whose power
> May spur me on . . .          (*Prelude* I. 648–52; MS. V.)

Amongst the reminiscences of his childhood in MS. JJ, there is a significant passage which suggests that he has always in mind the larger project of *The Recluse*:

> Nor while, though doubtíng yet not lost, I tread
> The mazes of this argument, and paint
> How Nature by collateral interest
> And by extrinsic passion peopled first
> My mind with beauteous objects, *may I well
> Forget what might demand a loftier song.*[1]

He has been spurred on to embark upon a record of his early preparation for his poetic calling: the loftier song, not to be forgotten, still awaits him.

In this MS. there is no allusion to Coleridge. It was perhaps not till the summer of 1799 that he conceived the happy idea of dedicating to Coleridge the autobiographic narrative on which he had started. The first we hear of this is in a letter of Coleridge to Wordsworth dated October 12, 1799, in which he writes:

> I long to see what you have been doing. O let it be the tailpiece of 'The Recluse', for of nothing but 'The Recluse' can I hear patiently. That it is to be addressed to me makes me more desirous that it should *not* be a poem of itself. To be addressed as a beloved man, by a thinker, *at the close* of such a poem as 'The Recluse' is the only event, I believe, capable of inciting in me an hour's vanity.

Wordsworth has, then, communicated his idea of composing a poem on the growth of his own mind which shall be dedicated to Coleridge, but he hesitates as to whether it should be an independent poem, or an appendix to *The Recluse*. Coleridge has made up his mind that it is to be a part of *The Recluse*, a tail-piece. Wordsworth later accepts the idea that it is to be attached to the main structure of the greater poem, but still without deciding how.

[1] *v.* Appendix, MS. JJ, p. 636.

Dorothy, writing in February 1804, refers to it as an appendix to *The Recluse*, but a little later as 'introductory to' and as 'a sort of portico to *The Recluse*, part of the same building'. In the Preface to the first edition of *The Excursion*, 1814, Wordsworth alludes to it as 'the preparatory Poem'. Coleridge persisted in calling it *The Recluse* until, after his return from Malta in 1806, he heard Wordsworth read the whole poem as it then stood: thereafter he referred to it in 'The Friend' as 'an unpublished Poem on the Growth and Revolutions of an Individual Mind'. As late as 1843 Wordsworth called it 'the poem on the growth of my own mind' (I. F. note to 'The Norman Boy') and 'the poem on my own poetical education' (I. F. note to 'There was a Boy'). In the Wordsworth household it had from the first been called 'the poem to Coleridge'. Only on its publication after his death did it receive from Mrs. Wordsworth its title of *The Prelude*.

Its independence of the larger poem followed naturally from its growth under his hand to a length he had not foreseen. His first plan, indicated in his letters of March 6, 1804, was for five books only (*v.* p. xlix) and its culminating episode was to be the consecration of his life to poetry on the heights above Hawkshead in his first Long Vacation (IV. 320–45). But he came to realize that his theme, the 'growth of his own mind', or his 'poetical education', would not be fully treated without going farther. The experiences of the next six years—his hopes and his despair for the Revolution in France, his life in London and in the country, homeless, and without means of livelihood, his sudden glad release from the bondage of circumstance, his settling down at Racedown with Dorothy, and his friendship with Coleridge—had all 'borne a part, and that a needful one', in making him the poet that he was. And eight more books were added.

But in writing thus fully of himself he encroached inevitably upon his first design. *The Recluse*, 'as having for its principal subject the sensations and opinions of a poet living in retirement', was itself essentially autobiographical—even in *The Excursion*, which was intended to be dramatic, not only the hero but also the Solitary and the Vicar were thinly veiled portraits of their author —and much of the poetry he wished to write would, in fact, be equally well suited to either work.[1] There can be no doubt that the wealth of *The Prelude* impoverished *The Recluse*. Coleridge's

---

[1] As a matter of fact several passages originally written for *The Excursion* were included in *The Prelude*, and vice versa. Cf. notes to II. 321–41; VII. 716–29; VIII. 1–61, 159–72, 497.

design for *The Recluse* is outlined in a passage of his recorded *Table Talk* (July 21, 1832). Wordsworth was to

assume the station of a man in mental repose, one whose principles were made up, and so prepared to deliver upon authority a system of philosophy. He was to treat man as man,—a subject of eye, ear, touch, and taste, in contact with external nature, and informing the senses from the mind, and not compounding a mind out of the senses; then he was to describe the pastoral and other states of society, assuming something of the Juvenalian spirit as he approached the high civilization of cities and towns, and opening a melancholy picture of the present state of degeneracy and vice; thence he was to infer and reveal the proof of, and necessity for, the whole state of man and society being subject to, and illustrative of, a redemptive process in operation, showing how this idea reconciled all the anomalies, and promised future glory and restoration. Something of this sort was, I think, agreed on. It is, in substance, what I have been all my life doing, in my system of philosophy.

But Wordsworth cannot have embraced the whole of this scheme; he certainly never adopted the idea of the redemptive process in any Coleridgean form. Parts I and III of the great philosophical poem which were to consist 'chiefly of meditations in the author's own person' (Preface to *The Excursion*, 1814) remained unwritten, burdening Wordsworth's conscience and engaging the hopes of his friends for at least the next twenty-five years.[1] In March 1804 he writes to De Quincey: 'Of this larger work [*The Recluse*] I have written one Book and several scattered fragments; it is a moral and philosophical Poem, the subject whatever I find most interesting in Nature, Man and Society. . . . To this work I mean to devote the prime of my life and the chief force of my mind.'[2] The words betray the amorphous nature of the poem, as it then hung fire in Wordsworth's mind. The subject is to be 'whatever he finds most interesting in Nature, Man and Society'; but what is to be the form? His difficulty was that he could not find the right form for it. The 'one book' that he succeeded in writing, *The Recluse*, Part First, Book First,[3] 'Home at Grasmere', is merely a personal introduction to Part I; the 'scattered fragments'[4] which survive in MS. are sketches of human characters, notes of scenes and images that impressed him, and

---

[1] *v. P.W.* v. 367.                              [2] *E.L.* 370.
[3] *P.W.* v. 313.
[4] *v.* quotations, pp. 525, 533, 566, 571–8, 581, 610, 612, 623, *infra*, and *P.W.*, v, Appendix B.

philosophical reflections arising out of both. There is no sign that he developed a constructive plan. It was not in him 'to deliver upon authority a system of philosophy', and even if he had achieved such a system it would not have given him a poetic form. The ambitious design of *The Recluse* demanded a philosophic and artistic unity which Coleridge might confidently anticipate but which Wordsworth could not supply: from the first it was doomed to failure. Its offshoot, *The Prelude*, had a unity which sprang from the poet's own inner life, and in it he produced a masterpiece.

As it stands *The Prelude* has not merely unity of design, it has something of epic character. It opens with an outburst of joy that after years of anxiety the poet is at last free to devote his life to its true vocation: its 'last word of personal concern' records his gratitude for the gift which brought him that freedom. Within this frame he places the history of his life from the seedtime of infancy to those days when, chaunting alternate songs with Coleridge as they roamed the Quantock hills together, he was first fully conscious that his genius was bearing fruit. Books I–IV lead up, through an account of his early life, to the first great climax, his poetic consecration; after which there is a pause in the narrative, whilst he reviews, in Book V, his early debt to literature. Books VI and VII resume his life's history, and carry it down to the moment before the second great climax—the awakening of his passionate interest in man (Book IX). But before this, the narrative pauses once more, whilst he gives a philosophic retrospect of his whole period of preparation in Book VIII. Book X leads up to and records thè catastrophe—the destruction of his hopes for man in so far as they were identified with the French Revolution, and his consequent despair of mind: Books XI–XIII give the reconciliation, his recovery from despair, the rebuilding of his hopes for man upon a sounder basis and, as a consequence, his entrance into his poetic heritage.

Wordsworth was in evident agreement with Milton on the true nature of the epic subject. Both of them repudiated military exploits, 'hitherto the only argument Heroic deemed', in the desire to bring within its confines a more spiritual conflict. 'O Heavens!' cries Wordsworth (*Prelude* III. 178),

> how awful is the might ʾof Souls,
> And what they do within themselves, while yet
> The yoke of earth is new to them . . .
> This is, in truth, heroic argument.

Only the pedant will dissent from their conception; and those who regard the mind of Wordsworth as both great in itself and essentially representative of the highest, the imaginative type of mind, will recognize its adventures as a fit theme for epic treatment. But Wordsworth himself, though he claimed this dignity for *The Recluse*, where his theme was the 'mind of man', was humbler in his comments on *The Prelude*. He admitted, indeed, that it was 'a thing unprecedented in literary history that a man should talk so much about himself'. 'It is not self-conceit', he wrote truly, 'that has induced me to do this, but real humility; I began the work because I was unprepared to treat any more arduous subject, and diffident of my own powers. Here, at least, I hoped that to a certain degree I should be sure of succeeding, as I had nothing to do but describe what I had felt and thought; therefore could not easily be bewildered. This might certainly have been done in narrower compass by a man of more address; but I have done my best.'[1] Yet, in truth, Wordsworth was never more eloquent than when he spoke of himself, and his best in *The Prelude* has never been rivalled in its own kind.

## § 3. *Preparation for writing 'The Prelude'*

For the task before him Wordsworth was well equipped by his wide knowledge of the literature of the past. The servant-maid at Rydal Mount, who told a visitor that her master's study was in the fields, touched unquestionably upon the main source of his inspiration, but her pretty epigram did not comprise the whole truth of the matter; and the poet who spoke of books as

> Powers
> For ever to be hallowed; only less
> For what we may become, and what we need,
> Than Nature's self, which is the breath of God . . .

was not likely to neglect them. Yet the superficial critic has always tended to underrate their influence upon him. *The Prelude* foresaw this error, but gave some countenance to it; for the section entitled 'Books' takes us no further than his school-days, and is rather a general discourse on the value of imaginative literature than a detailed account of his own reading. Yet it tells us, at least, that as a boy he read voraciously; and no habit acquired in childhood is easily discarded. As a matter of fact he retained the habit

---

[1] To Sir George Beaumont, May 1, 1805 (*E.L.* 489).

till his middle age, and only gave it up when his eyes declined their office. At Cambridge 'many books were skimmed, devoured, or studiously perused'—in Greek and Latin, Italian, French, and Spanish, as well as in his mother tongue—and not poetry alone, but history also. There is evidence that when he settled at Racedown he not only read widely, but was convinced that success in his art could not be acquired otherwise. In his search for a metaphysical basis to his theory of life he studied the philosophers of the eighteenth century:[1] De Quincey bore witness later to his extensive knowledge of ancient history. He had at all times a passion for the literature of travel, and insisted on its value in widening his outlook and enriching his experience. 'If', he wrote to a friend in March 1798, 'you could collect for me any books of travels, you would render me an essential service, as without much of such reading my present labours cannot be brought to a conclusion'; and the pages of *The Prelude* are studded with simile, metaphor, and allusion drawn from the narratives of famous navigators and explorers. But naturally his chief reading was in English poetry. Few poets could equal Wordsworth in a knowledge of their forerunners. Of his intimacy with the minor poets of the eighteenth century *The Evening Walk* and *Descriptive Sketches* bore painful witness : in *The Prelude* he was to show his true ancestry. 'When I began', he says, 'to give myself up to the profession of a poet for life, I was impressed with a conviction that there were four English poets whom I must have continually before me as examples—Chaucer, Shakespeare, Spenser and Milton. These I must study, and equal *if I could*: and I need not think of the rest.'[2] He was true to his conviction. The quintessence of Spenser's charm he could distil into two perfect lines:

> Sweet Spenser, moving through his clouded heaven
> With the moon's beauty and the moon's soft pace,

and the fragrance of Spenser is recalled on several pages of *The Prelude*. The poem abounds in reminiscence of Shakespearian scene and phrasing. Of Milton there is still more. It was his avowed ambition to be the Milton of his age ; nor, as Keats recognized,

---

[1] Cf. Beatty, *W. W.: His Doctrine and Art*. University of Wisconsin Studies, 1922.

[2] *Memoirs*, ii. 470. Cf. also letter to Alaric Watts, Nov. 16, 1824: 'I am disposed strenuously to recommend to your habitual perusal the great poets of our own country, who have stood the test of ages. Shakespeare I need not name, nor Milton, but Chaucer and Spenser are apt to be overlooked. It is almost painful to think how far these surpass all others.' (*L.Y.* 159.)

was that ambition ill founded. He had the same lofty conception of his art, the same passionate devotion to it, and like Milton, though in his own way, he strove 'to justify the ways of God to man'. Throughout *The Prelude* there are signs of devout Miltonic study. Not only does the style of the poem in its more eloquent passages take on a distinctly Miltonic manner, but constantly, in places where they would least be expected, Miltonic echoes can be heard. That Wordsworth himself was probably unconscious of them is only a proof of the completeness with which he had absorbed his master, so that Milton's phrase and cadence had become a natural and inseparable element in his own speech.

This study of the supreme artists was supported by prolonged meditation on both the principles and the technical minutiae of his art.[1] He chose the metre for his poem with a full consciousness of its pitfalls. It is significant to find copied into the notebook that contains the earliest fragments of *The Prelude* the warnings which Dr. Johnson had uttered on the peculiar dangers incident to the writing of blank verse.[2] From the contorted and unnatural phrasing of the *Descriptive Sketches* he was already in revolt. *The Prelude* was not written, like some of the *Lyrical Ballads*,[3] to illustrate a theory of poetic diction; yet it demonstrates clearly enough that 'a selection from the real language of men in a state of vivid sensation is adapted to the purposes of poetic pleasure'—at least when the man Wordsworth is addressing his closest friend. For its language is selected from the whole of his experience, and the style to which he moulds it rises with the character and the intensity of the emotion it has to express. And with Coleridge he had

---

[1] In Oct. 1831 J. S. Mill wrote (letter to John Sterling) that 'when you get Wordsworth on the subjects which are peculiarly his, such as the theory of his own art, no one can converse with him without feeling that he has advanced that great subject beyond any other man, being probably the first person who ever combined, with such eminent success in the practice of the art, such high powers of generalization and habits of meditation on its principles'. The foundations of this achievement were laid in 1797–8.

[2] 'Dr. Johnson observed, that in blank verse, the language suffered more distortion to keep it out of prose than any inconvenience to be apprehended from the shackles and circumspection of rhyme. This kind of distortion is the worst fault that poetry can have; for if once the natural order and connection of the words is broken, and the idiom of the language violated, the lines appear manufactured, and lose all that character of enthusiasm and inspiration, without which they become cold and vapid, how sublime soever the ideas and the images may be which they express.' *Alfoxden* MS. notebook, 1798.

[3] 'In these little poems . . . he wrote, at times, too much with a sectarian spirit, in a sort of bravado. But now he is at the helm of a noble bark; now

not only discussed the cardinal points of poetry,[1] but had argued upon matters of form and style. His main conclusions, despite occasional overstatement, the natural reaction from the false ideals of his youth, kept him, as Coleridge himself admitted, in the great tradition. The epithets 'simple' and 'natural', commonly applied to Wordsworth's poetry, alike for praise and blame, suggest a general ignorance of the intense study and careful artistry that lay behind it. But the popular view is in itself a tribute to the powerful originality of his mind and manner. His style is Wordsworthian as truly as Milton's is Miltonic.

### § 4. *Chronology of the Composition of 'The Prelude'*

Professor Garrod's acutely reasoned and illuminating essay on 'The Composition of The Prelude' (Garrod, pp. 186 ff.) carried our knowledge of the subject to the farthest point possible on the evidence available to him. An examination of the MSS. enables us to substantiate, sometimes to correct, and to fill out his account.

Wordsworth himself has provided a date for what he calls 'the glad preamble' to the narrative of *The Prelude*, the glad preamble being, as has been assumed, the opening lines (1–54) of Book I.

> Six changeful years have vanished since I first
> Poured out (saluted by that quickening breeze
> Which met me issuing from the City's walls)
> A glad preamble to this Verse . . .

(The version of 1805 reads 'Five years'. Wordsworth has corrected the date deliberately.)

So run the opening lines of Book VII, and Book VI is precisely dated by Wordsworth at ll. 61–62.

> Four years and thirty, told this very week,
> Have I been now a sojourner on earth

He was born on April 7, 1770. He is writing then in the second week of April 1804.

The editor of the first edition of *The Prelude*, published posthu-

he sails right onward; it is all open ocean and a steady breeze, and he drives before it, unfretted by short tacks, reefing and unreefing his sails, hauling and disentangling the ropes. His only disease is the having been out of his element; his return to it is food to famine; it is both the specific remedy and the condition of health.' Coleridge on *The Prelude*, *Anima Poetae*, p. 30.

[1] *Biographia Literaria*, chap. xiv. In July 1802 Coleridge told Southey that 'the Preface [i.e. of *The Lyrical Ballads*] is half a child of my own brain'.

mously in 1850, assumed that the city referred to in the lines just quoted, and in the opening of Book I, was Goslar, and the date of the poet's issuing from it February 1799.[1] Thomas Hutchinson first pointed out that the city must be London, and that 'the glad Preamble', which, as Wordsworth explicitly states,[2] was uttered extempore, must have been composed as he walked down to Racedown in September 1795. Professor Garrod has argued cogently for this interpretation. To get over the difficulty that ' six years' back[3] must refer to 1798 he suggests that the 'preamble' (I. 1–54) composed in 1795 should be regarded as a quotation standing in the forefront of the poem, and that Wordsworth has 'lapsed into an easily intelligible carelessness' in saying that six years have gone by since he began *The Prelude* itself, in the spring of 1798 at Alfoxden. Wordsworth's memory for dates is not always reliable, but his note at the end of MS. D of *The Prelude* is worth recording: 'The composition of this poem was finished early in 1805—it having been begun about 1798.'

Another explanation of what Wordsworth meant by the glad preamble is offered by Mr. H. M. Margoliouth.[4] The glad preamble, he thinks, must surely be the famous lines 'On Man, on Nature, and on Human Life', quoted by Wordsworth at the end of his Preface to *The Excursion* in 1814, as a kind of Prospectus of the design and scope of *The Recluse*—lines which have been credibly dated 1798—that is, six years before he wrote Books VI and VII of *The Prelude*. These great lines with their sustained exultant note undoubtedly fit his phrase 'dythyrambic fervour' in the MS. version:

> I sang
> Aloud, in Dythyrambic fervour, deep
> But short-liv'd uproar . . .
>
> *(Prelude (1805) VII. 4–6.)*

better than does the quiet opening passage of Book I:

> Oh there is blessing in this gentle breeze
> That blows from the green fields and from the clouds . . .

The suggestion may well hit the truth. We should suppose, then, that Wordsworth, as often, is running together in memory two cherished occasions: first the emergence from Bristol after a long

---

[1] *v. Prelude* (1850), p. 373.      [2] *Prelude* I. 55–59.

[3] *Prelude* VI. 61–62, with its reference to his birthday 34 years ago, April 7, 1770, indicates that he was composing the sixth book of *The Prelude* in April 1804; and we may infer from VII. 1–37 that he began to compose the seventh book, after an interval, in the autumn of the same year.

[4] *v. Wordsworth and Coleridge*, Home University Library.

tedious stay in London to walk down to Racedown in September 1795, secondly another emergence from Bristol after another stay in London, to walk down to Alfoxden on January 3, 1798. Did another breeze, a physical breeze again, promising a return to health and happiness, greet them as they headed once more for Alfoxden; or is he thinking even more of the irresistible quickening breeze that sets a poet's inner life in motion? Certainly this return to Alfoxden marked the opening of an unusually fruitful period of poetic composition. The first breeze would be associated in his mind with the extempore lines which so hopefully preluded his sojourn at Racedown, the second breeze with the constructive start made at Alfoxden to his great philosophic poem in the memorable lines 'On Man, on Nature, and on Human Life . . .'.

*The Prelude*, as we have seen, began to struggle into life as a part of the inchoate *Recluse*: in tracing the chronology of its composition we must start with the beginnings of *The Recluse*. Clues as to the dates at which the first portions of this poem were written can be gathered from the correspondence of Coleridge and the Wordsworths:

(1) *March 5th, 1798.* You desire me . . . to send you a copy of *The Ruined Cottage*. This is impossible for it has grown to the length of 900 lines. I will however send you a copy of that part which is immediately and solely connected with the Cottage. The Pedlar's character now makes a very, certainly the *most*, considerable part of the poem. . . . You have the rest to the end of Margaret's story. There is much more about the Pedlar. (D. W. to M. H.)

(2) *March 6th.* I have written 1300 lines of a poem in which I contrive to convey most of the knowledge of which I am possessed. My object is to give pictures of Nature, Man, and Society. Indeed I know not anything which will not come within the scope of my plan. . . . The work of composition is carved out for me, for at least a year and a half to come. (W. W. to James Tobin.)

(3) *March 8th.* He has written more than 1,200 lines of a blank verse, superior, I hesitate not to aver, to anything in our language which any way resembles it. Poole thinks of it as likely to benefit mankind much more than anything W. has yet written. (Coleridge to Joseph Cottle.)

(4) *March 11th.* I have been tolerably industrious within the last few weeks. I have written 1,300 lines of a poem which I hope to make of considerable utility. Its title will be *The Recluse*; or, *Views of Nature, Man, and Society*. (W. W. to James Losh.)

From (2) and (4) it is natural to suppose that he had written a draft of the lines already referred to 'On Man, on Nature, and on

Human Life' which voice his conception of the whole poem, *The Recluse*; and from the statement in (2) about its all-embracing scope, that most of the blank verse written at this time was intended for it. The *Alfoxden* notebook contains fragments of *The Old Cumberland Beggar*, and of the story of the discharged soldier (*Prelude* IV. 400–504), and some lines written for the character of the Pedlar, later appropriated to form part of the poet's own experience (*Prelude* II. 321–41; VII. 716–29). If we add 900 lines for *The Ruined Cottage*—greatly enlarged at this time as the MSS. show—we reach a total very near to the 1,300 lines to which Wordsworth refers.

Little more can have been written before the departure for Germany on September 16. In this intervening period Wordsworth composed more than half of the 140 pages which were his contribution to the *Lyrical Ballads*, also *Peter Bell*, a poem of 1,100 lines begun on April 20. In Goslar he fell to writing passage after passage of blank verse recalling experiences of his childhood, afterwards to form the substance of *The Prelude* Book I. Dorothy, in her letter to Coleridge, transcribing for him the skating-scene and the episode of the stolen boat, speaks of 'selecting from the mass of what William has written'.[1] In MS. JJ a large part of this mass is to be found.[2] To the Goslar period belong also a longer and more elaborate version of *Nutting*,[3] 'intended as a part of a poem on my own life but struck out as not being wanted there', and the lines beginning 'Wisdom and spirit of the Universe'.[4] Here then are the beginnings of 'the poem on my own life' which, breaking off from *The Recluse*, was to develop as a poem in its own right and to become *The Prelude*. The date of its inception as an independent poem is therefore the winter of 1798–9.

In notebooks used by D. W. and W. W. in 1798, 1799, and 1800, the *Christabel* MS. and MS. 18a, a large part of Book I has been copied and in MS. 18a after the end of Book I an abortive beginning of the next book, headed *2nd Part*,[5] follows. But no progress has been made with Book II. Coleridge is addressed in the last lines of Book I and in the few lines headed *2nd Part*: from these passages[5] we may infer that Wordsworth has come to a standstill at the end of Book I, is taking a rest, and is in danger of playing truant to the whole enterprise. At what date he was

---

[1] *E. L.* 209.  [2] *v. supra*, p. xxxv, and Appendix, *infra*, p. 633.
[3] *v.* I. F. note; *E.L.* 206; and *infra*, p. 610.
[4] *v. Prelude* I. 428–41; *Memoirs*, i. 136–7.
[5] *v.* I. 645 and II. 1 *app. crit.*

spurred on to write Book II and to make fair copies of both books it is difficult to determine precisely, but it must have been before October[1] 1800. The two books, copied in MS. U by M. H. and in MS. V by D. W., derive from a common original. A third MS. which I call RV (not noticed by E. de S.) contains, with no heading, Book II only, and gives an earlier text than that of MSS. V and U. It is a fair copy with one passage (ll. 99–208) in S. H.'s hand,[2] the rest in the hands of W. W. and D. W. alternately. The opening of Book II in this MS. corresponds closely with the text of 1805 and gives a backward limit to the date of its composition in ll. 36–38, where he speaks of his return to Hawkshead 'after long absence'. This can only refer to his visit with John Wordsworth and S. T. C. in November 1799. The lines would probably be written early in 1800. MS. U has these opening lines (which are absent accidentally from MS. V, two pages having been torn out) and it also provides an upward limit for date of composition, October 1800.[1] The farewell lines to Coleridge at the end of Book II would presumably have been written after Coleridge's return to London at the end of November 1799.

We must suppose that in the summer months of 1799 at Sockburn Wordsworth conceived the idea of an autobiographical poem dedicated to S. T. C.[3] as preliminary to the great philosophical poem so eagerly expected by him. In 1800, between January and October, he must have executed fair copies of Books I and II with the help of D. W. and M. H. In Book VII (ll. 9–11) he tells us that the stream of composition flowed awhile in strength, then stopped for years: that is to say that after a flow of composition starting in the Goslar winter of 1798–9, resulting, we suppose, in the execution and copying of Books I and II, in the early months of 1800, there was a halt of some years.[4] These books, occupied with the experiences of his boyhood, form one vital and self-contained whole.[5] When he had consigned them to fair copies, he failed to

---

[1] v. p. xxviii, note.

[2] S. H. may have transcribed this passage on Wordsworth's visit to Gallow Hill between May 14 and June 7, 1800; she did not visit Grasmere in 1800.

[3] v. p. xxxv, supra.

[4] Coleridge wrote in Feb. 1800: 'I grieve that The Recluse sleeps' (Memoirs, i. 160).

[5] There must have been at least one extra fair copy of these two books. Coleridge writes to Lady Beaumont in March 1804: 'I have left your Ladyship the first two parts of the biographical, or philosophical-biographical Poem to be prefixed or annexed to the Recluse' (March 26, 1804; v. Griggs, Letters of S. T. Coleridge, ii. 1104).

proceed: he failed even to compose the opening of Book I; for a strange anomaly meets us when we read the first lines of that book in the early MSS. The glad preamble (ll. 1–54) and the post-preamble (ll. 54–271) are not there; the text begins with a half-line, which presupposes an antecedent statement:

> Was it for this
> That one the fairest of all rivers . . .

It is not till 1804 that we find the opening lines (1–271) of the book entered in MS. M. In the interval there are only three references in D. W.'s *Journals* to his resuming work on the poem.

(1) *December 26, 1801.* William wrote part of the poem to Coleridge.

(2) *December 27, 1801.* Mary wrote some lines of the third part of William's poem (i.e. of Book III).

(3) *January 11, 1803.* William was working at his poem to Coleridge.

A beginning was made to Book III, but evidently there was little further progress. Coleridge continued to urge him to get on with *The Recluse*, and not to be led astray into writing short poems; at last in October 1803 he writes triumphantly to Poole: 'He has made a Beginning to his *Recluse*. . . . The habit too of writing such a multitude of small Poems was . . . hurtful to him. . . . I rejoice therefore with a deep and true Joy that he has at length yielded to my urgent and repeated—almost unremitting—requests and remonstrances,—and will go on with the *Recluse* exclusively A Great Work in which he will sail on an open Ocean and a steady wind.' It seems probable that Wordsworth braced himself now to make a constructive beginning to *The Prelude* (which Coleridge still calls the *Recluse*) and wrote in some coherent form the first 271 lines of Book I[1] which seem to comprise an early passage composed on the way to Racedown in 1795 (ll. 1–54), and a merging of reminiscences of perhaps three baffled periods of effort to get the great poem started—first at Racedown, then at Alfoxden, and later at Grasmere (ll. 46–271). Coleridge reports that *he has made a Beginning*, and Wordsworth himself tells us (*Prelude* (1805 text) VII. 12, 13) that he took up *The Prelude* again 'a little space Before last primrose-time', that is, he resumed the flow of composition in January or February 1804.

---

[1] On Nov. 13, 1803, D. W. writes: 'William has not yet done anything of importance at his great work.' Perhaps he had only managed to write the opening 271 lines of Book I, which had so long hung fire.

For the further composition of *The Prelude* (in 1804–5) we have the following external evidence:

(1) At a date shown by Professor Garrod to be between January 23 and February 18, 1804, Wordsworth wrote to Wrangham: At present I am engaged in a Poem on my own earlier life, which will take five parts, or books, to complete; three of which are nearly finished. (*E.L.* 355.)

(2) *Feb. 13, 1804.* William is chearfully engaged in composition, and goes on with great rapidity. He is writing the poem on his own early life, which is to be an appendix to the Recluse. (D. W. to C. Clarkson.)

(3) *March 6.* (*a*) [The poem] on my own life . . . is better than half complete, viz. four books, amounting to about 2,500 lines . . . . I have just finished that part in which I speak of my residence in the University. (W. W. to De Quincey.) (*b*) I finished five or six days ago another Book of my Poem, amounting to 650 lines. And now I am positively arrived at the subject I spoke of in my last. When this next book is done, which I shall begin in two or three days' time I shall consider the work as finished. (W. W. to Coleridge, *E.L.* 368.)

(4) *March 12.* I have been very busy during the last six weeks, and am advancing rapidly in a Poetical Work which though only introductory to another of greater importance will I hope be found not destitute of Interest. (W. W. to Sotheby, *E.L.* 372.)

(5) *March 24.* A great addition to the poem on my Brother's life he has made since C. left us (i.e. since January 10) 1,500 lines. (D. W. to C. Clarkson.)

(6) *March 29.* (*a*) William has begun another part of the Poem addressed to you. He has written some very affecting Lines which I wish you could have taken with you (i.e. to Malta). (D. W. to Coleridge.) (*b*) I am now, after a halt of near three weeks, started again; and I hope to go forward rapidly. (W. W. to Coleridge.)

Another part of the same letter proves that Coleridge was already in possession of Book V.

(7) *April 29.* I have been very busy these last ten weeks, having written between two and three thousand lines—accurately near three thousand—in that time: namely four books, and a third of another, of the Poem . . . on my own early life. I am at present in the seventh book. (W. W. to Sharp.)

(8) *Dec. 25.* I have written upwards of 2,000 verses during the last ten weeks. . . . I expect to have finished before the month of May. (W. W. to Sir George Beaumont.)

(9) *Feb. 1805* (first week). My Poem advances, quick or slow, as the fit comes. (W. W. to Sharp.)

(10) *May 1.* I have added 300 lines [to the Poem on my own life]

in the course of last week. Two books more will conclude it. It will not be much less than 9,000 lines. (W. W. to Beaumont.)

(11) *June 3.* I finished my poem about a fortnight ago. (W. W. to Beaumont.)

To this may be added the following internal evidence:

(12) Book VII. 1–13, from which we learn that after being 'stopped for years' the work had been resumed in the early months of 1804.

(13) Book VI. 61–62. Wordsworth is thirty-four years old this week (b. April 7, 1770).

(14) Book VII. 17–54. He has been at rest all the summer, but has resumed work in the autumn.

(15) Book X. 947–51 refer to Coleridge in Sicily. He was there from August to early November 1804.

(16) Book X. 933–4. A reference to the summons of the Pope to crown Napoleon (December 2, 1804).

The MS. notebooks W, X, and Y throw fresh light on the progress of composition. February and March 1804 were a time of rapid advance. Coleridge's imminent departure and his intense interest in the composition of Wordsworth's poem ('O! for one hour of the *Recluse*!', letter of S. T. C., February 8, 1804) supplied a strong stimulus. In late January or early February, as his letter to Wrangham shows (*v.* p. xlix above), Wordsworth had nearly finished three books, and would be starting upon the fourth, of a poem to be completed in five books. MS. W represents the next stage when (*a*) he was roughly putting together Book IV (none of it in its final form) with a combination of passages later to find their place in Books IV, V, XI, and XIII; and (*b*) he had made a start upon the supposedly final Book V (headed *5th book* in this MS.), which was to open with the Snowdon episode introducing the culminating argument about Imagination, his central theme. By March 6 (3) he must have completed a fair copy of Book IV (no MS. of this survives except for the few passages in W) combining matter afterwards used in IV and V, and was preparing to write the intended last book.[1] Soon after this he must have decided to enlarge the scope and scale of his poem so as to include his experience in France; thereby extending the work to perhaps twice the length originally intended.

This momentous decision must have been made and acted upon rapidly, for the copy of Book V dispatched to Coleridge about

---

[1] It is possible that, as Professor MacGillivray suggests, Wordsworth was on March 6 thinking rather of a poem of six books of which he had finished five.

March 17[1] is not in the form originally projected for a final Book V
(v. MS. W), but in that adopted after March 6 (v. MS. A), when
he had decided upon the enlarged form of the poem.[2] Between
March 6 and 17 he must have put together Book V as we know it
in MS. M and MS. A; he used 221 lines already written in MS. W
and 64 lines from two other passages written earlier ('There was
a Boy'—ll. 389–422 written in 1798, and 'Well do I call to mind'
—ll. 450–81 from MS. V), making a total of 285 lines at least, for
he may well have gathered in other passages dealing with his
youthful experience. Book V in MS. M contains 638 lines. Therefore he had at most only 353 lines to write before the halt of
'nearly three weeks' referred to on March 29 (5). If we allow for
a slight exaggeration on Wordsworth's part we may suppose that
the halt began about March 13, when he could have handed over
his new version of Book V for copying: this would be the last
pages transcribed for the miscellany of poems put together for
Coleridge in MS. M. Between March 6 and 'the halt'—say March 13
—he could have written the 353 lines. The reason of the halt at
this time of great activity is explained by Dorothy's letter of
March 24 where she relates that she and Mrs. W. have been making copies of William's poems, one for Coleridge and one for
themselves; 'for the manuscripts we took them from were in
such a wretched condition and so tedious to copy from—besides
requiring William's almost constant superintendence—that we considered it as almost necessary to save them alive that we should
re-copy them'. Our study of such manuscripts as survive fully
corroborates this statement: fresh composition was impossible
while the poet was employed in trying to read his own writing.

On March 29 he has begun another part of the poem (6), i.e.
Book VI. The 'very affecting lines' which Dorothy wishes Coleridge could take with him are doubtless the beautiful address to
his friend in ll. 246–331. In the next week he is writing ll. 55–69
(13). On April 29 he has written near 3,000 lines since February,
4⅓ books, and is at present in the seventh (7). Now Books IV, V,
and VI were clearly three of the four, but which was the other?
Notebooks X and Y come to our aid.

X opens with a rough draft of Book VII. 81–219, followed by a
page given up to The Excursion II. 742 ff., which obviously indicates

---

[1] v. D. W.'s letter of March 24.

[2] For clinching proof of this v. Wordsworth's letter to Coleridge March 29,
1804 (E.L. 380): the lines in Book V which he wishes to have corrected
occur in the version of MS. A.

a break in the composition of *The Prelude*. Then comes Book
VIII. 742–51 (a passage dealing with London, the subject of
Book VII, and first written for that book), and from VIII. 750
the manuscript runs without a break on to VII. 75, and so to the
end of that book. The rest of MS. X is given up to a version of
*The Excursion* II.

Notebook Y has at some time been left out in the rain, or
dropped into the lake, so that in places its writing is completely
washed out. Its first legible passage corresponds with VIII. 68–73;
then follows, more carefully written, and hence not a first draft,
Book IX. 293–520; and it is reasonable to suppose that the next
few pages, which have been torn out, contained more of IX. The
page, of which a facsimile is given, is only legible from the middle,
where can be read:

No[r is t]hat invitation thrown away,
The last night's genial feeling overflows
Upon this morning efficacious more
By reason that my Song must now return
If she desert not her appointed path
Back into Nature's bosom. Since the time
When with reluctance I withdrew from France

and so on, as XIII. 334–67. Then follows a continuous version of
Book VIII, introduced, however, not with the episode of Helvellyn
Fair, but with a draft of the first twenty-five lines of *The Excur-
sion* II.

Now the first two lines above quoted form the end of that
passage (VII. 12–54) which speaks of his resumption of work after
the summer's holiday; and of the preceding lines in the manuscript
enough words are legible here and there to identify the passage as a whole. Anything, therefore, entered in Y *before* these
lines must be the work of the spring. I conjecture, then, that as
soon as Wordsworth had finished Book VI (middle of April) he
plunged into the account of his life in France, intending his
London experiences to follow; and certainly the time spent in
London after his return from France, of which little is told in
*The Prelude*, was of greater importance to him than his previous
sojourn there; then, changing his mind, he broke off when he had
more or less completed one book on France, and wrote a part of
a book on London before he stopped work for the summer. The
4⅓ books, therefore, referred to in (6) will be IV, V, VI, IX, and
a part of VII, and the 'near 3,000 lines' will be IV, V, VI (as in A,
but *minus* about 200 lines written in 1797–8), i.e. 1645; of IX,

935 lines; of VII, some 250 lines, and the lines headed in MS. W *5th Book*, say 170; total 3,000.

We hear no more of *The Prelude* till December 25, 1804. But on that day 'upwards of 2,000 lines have been written in the last ten weeks'. What were they? Not, as we shall see later, the last three books. Clearly, therefore, they are two-thirds of VII, say 550 lines, VIII as in the A text (but omitting 90 lines copied in from J), 779 lines, and Book X (i.e. X and XI of 1850), 1,036 lines; total, 2,368 lines. If we add to this the passage found in Y but not included in A the total will be 2,608. It is impossible to determine the order in which this work was accomplished. It seems likely that after starting in Notebook Y with Book VIII Wordsworth would go some way with it, even if he did not finish it, before turning back to Notebook X and completing Book VII. But VII and VIII were probably more or less finished before he started upon X. Book X, ll. 933–4, could hardly have been written before December 2, when the coronation of Napoleon took place. It will be noted that X. 947–9 speaks of Coleridge in Syracuse, which he left early in November. But posts were not then as rapid as they are today. A letter from Coleridge, dated Malta, June 5, reached Keswick at the end of August; so that we can well believe that the close of Book X was not written till near the end of December. Ten weeks from December 25 takes us back to mid-October, and there is no reason to suppose that Wordsworth resumed work on *The Prelude* after the summer before then.[1] It would be a natural time for him to hear the choir of redbreasts (VII. 24), and if it may seem a little late for the glow-worm (*ibid.* 39) we may note that the poet himself seems to feel that the glow-worm is lingering beyond her usual time with a special message for him. Besides, the naturalist Hudson is our authority for the statement that the glow-worm shines long after it is dead (*v. Hampshire Days*, p. 78).

From the letter quoted as (10) we learn that Wordsworth did nothing to *The Prelude* between the first week in February 1805, when he heard of the death of his brother John, and the last week in April, when he added 300 lines, and had two more books to write to conclude the poem. In the first two weeks of May 1805 he wrote the last two books, or, rather, completed them; for, as we have seen, drafts of a considerable portion of them were already in existence. It is worth noting that Wordsworth approximated

[1] This is corroborated by D. W.'s letter to Mrs. Clarkson, dated Oct. 13: 'W. is quite well and goes on with his work again, but has had a long interruption from summer Company, Mary's confinement, *etc., etc.*'

more closely to the 9,000 lines mentioned in the letter to Beaumont (10) than has been supposed. For the A text contains 8,584 lines, as against 7,883 of the printed version, and if the extra passage found in Y (Book VIII) be included, the total amounts to 8,824.

## § 5. *'The Prelude' a posthumous work, but much revised throughout the poet's life*

Some time before *The Prelude* was finished Wordsworth had given up all idea of immediate publication. His high hopes in the poetic future that lay before him, and the spiritual history on which those hopes were founded, might indeed be confided to the friend who was his second self, but could not, without arrogance, be proclaimed to the world before he had given some solid earnest of their fulfilment. 'This Poem', he wrote to De Quincey (March 6, 1804), 'will not be published these many years, and never during my lifetime, till I have finished a larger and more important work to which it is tributary.'¹ Moreover, he was himself dissatisfied with it. 'When I looked back upon the performance', he wrote only a fortnight after its completion, 'it seemed to have a dead weight about it—the reality so far short of the expectation; it was the first long labour that I had finished, and the doubt whether I should ever live to write *The Recluse* and the sense which I had of this poem being so far below what I had seemed capable of executing, depressed me much.'² Nearly ten years later, as a first instalment of *The Recluse*, he published *The Excursion*, and there can be no doubt that his depression sank deeper, even as it was more fully justified. *The Prelude* had at least won the enthusiastic praise of Coleridge, but Coleridge made it quite clear that he was disappointed with *The Excursion*; and as Wordsworth read his friend's cool and measured commendation of this later work, and recalled the glowing tribute accorded to the earlier:

> an Orphic song indeed,
> To its own music chanted!

he had little heart to continue his great task. How soon the scheme of *The Recluse* was definitely abandoned we do not know;³ but its

---

¹ *E.L.* 370.  ² *E.L.* 497.
³ In March 1821 D. W. was evidently urging him to it, for she writes: 'W. is . . . very busy, though he has not looked at *The Recluse* or the poem on his own life; and this disturbs us. After fifty years of age there is no time to spare, and unfinished works should not, if it be possible, be left behind. This he feels, but the will never governs *his* labours. How different from

abandonment would only strengthen his resolve that *The Prelude* should remain in MS. till after his death.

*The Prelude* was not laid aside and forgotten. Though he thought it inferior to what it might have been, he was fully conscious of its worth. The vital intimacy of its theme, which, doubtless, had made him peculiarly sensitive to its shortcomings, made him all the more anxious to perfect it. His resolve that the poem was to appear posthumously did not lessen his interest, for he knew that the destiny of all his writings lay with posterity; it only gave him a larger leisure in which to review it. For thirty-five years he continually went back to *The Prelude*, retouching and revising. The poem which appeared in 1850 differed in many respects from that which he read to Coleridge in 1806. From the MSS., now for the first time examined in detail, we are able to note the nature and the extent of the alterations introduced into the text; and a fresh light is thrown, not only upon the changes which the poet's mind underwent, but also upon his principles and methods as an artist.

Even if Wordsworth had published *The Prelude* on its completion in 1805, it would not have appeared exactly as it is found in the A text; for no poet ever revised his work for press more meticulously than he. Writing in 1816 of some minor pieces which he had just composed he calls them 'effusions rather than Compositions, though in justice to myself I must say that upon the correction of the Style I have bestowed, as I always do, great Labour'.[1] 'The composition of verse',[2] he wrote later, 'is infinitely more of an art than men are prepared to believe; and absolute success in it depends on innumerable *minutiae*. . . . Milton talks of pouring "easy his unpremeditated verse". It would be harsh, untrue, and odious to say there is anything like cant in this, but it is not *true* to the letter, and tends to mislead.' He might have added that his own description of poetry as 'the spontaneous overflow of powerful feelings' was liable to the same misconstruction. For experience had taught him that this 'spontaneous over-

Southey, who can go as regularly as clockwork, from history to poetry, from poetry to criticism, and so on to biography, or anything else. If their minds could each spare a little to the other, how much better for both!' (*L.Y.* 28.) And again in Dec. 1824 she writes, 'My brother has not yet looked at *The Recluse*; he seems to feel the task so weighty that he shrinks from beginning with it, yet knows that he has now no time to loiter if another great work is to be accomplished by him' (*C.R.* 132–3). Wordsworth probably knew by this time that he would never go on with *The Recluse*, though his family still talked of its completion.        [1] *M.Y.* 713.        [2] *L.Y.* 586.

flow' was no more than the raw material of art. It was easy enough to give those feelings a loose impressionistic language adequate to record them for himself. But such language had not really expressed them, and could not transmit them to others. The poet, Wordsworth knew well, was a craftsman, who must toil with unremitting patience at every detail of his work, till it has gained a clearer outline, a fuller substance: not otherwise could it acquire that organic power which is the sure touchstone of art:

The vital spirit of a perfect form.[1]

The labour that Wordsworth bestowed on revision was at least equal to that of first composition, and was pursued when less scrupulous artists would have been well content to leave their work untouched. To Coleridge in 1798 *The Ruined Cottage* was 'superior to anything in our language which any way resembles it', yet three years later Wordsworth is found wearing himself out in trying to make it better. The slightness of the difference between many passages found in the rough notebooks, where they

[1] Cf. the following fragment of verse, found in an (unpunctuated) autograph manuscript belonging to 1798–1800 (MS. *Peter Bell*) (2), which shows how fully Wordsworth understood a principle underlying all great art:

> nor had my voice
> Been silent oftentimes, had I burst forth
> In verse which, with a strong and random light
> Touching an object in its prominent parts,
> Created a memorial which to me
> Was all sufficient, and, to my own mind
> Recalling the whole picture, seemed to speak
> An universal language: Scattering thus
> In passion many a desultory sound,
> I deemed that I had adequately cloathed
> Meanings at which I hardly hinted, thought
> And forms of which I scarcely had produced
> A monument and arbitrary sign.

[*There is a lacuna in the MS. here: the argument clearly requires some such words as* When I reviewed this random and desultory verse I saw its worthlessness, and came to realize that an artist reveals his true power only]

> In that considerate and laborious work
> That patience which, admitting no neglect,
> By slow creation, doth impart[s] to speach
> Outline and substance even, till it has given
> A function kindred to organic power,
> The vital spirit of a perfect form.

So, in a letter to Beaumont (July 20, 1804; *E.L.* 402), he praises Reynolds for his 'deep conviction of the necessity of unwearied labour and diligence, the reverence for the great men of his art'. Wordsworth's own reverence for the great masters, and his strenuous efforts to gain perfection of form, are not sufficiently realized. Cf. also VI. 600–5.

were jotted down in the hurry of immediate inspiration, and the
form they have assumed in the A text, affords ample proof that
Wordsworth was postponing correction rather than that he was
satisfied with his work as it stood. It is reasonable, therefore, to
suppose that had he prepared it for press in 1805 he would have
introduced into the text many of those changes which made their
first appearance at a much later date.[1]

### § 6. *Comparison of the texts in point of style:*
### *later improvements*

No one would doubt that the 1850 version is a better composition than the A text. Weak phrases are strengthened, and the
whole texture is more closely knit. The A text leaves often the
impression of a man writing rapidly, thinking aloud or talking to
his friend without waiting to shape his thought into the most concise and telling form, satisfied for the moment if he can put it into
metre by inverting the prose order of the words. It is not difficult
to point in A to halting lines, and to tame or diffuse expressions,
which called for drastic treatment. Thus tricks of speech, such as
'I mean', 'we might say', 'for instance', 'with regret sincere I
mention this', and the like, tend later to disappear. The awkward
circumlocution

> Yet do not deem, my Friend, though thus I speak
> Of Man as having taken in my mind
> A place thus early which might almost seem
> Pre-eminent, that it was really so,         (VIII. 472–5.)

is shortened to

> Yet deem not, Friend! that human kind with me
> Thus early took a place pre-eminent;

And in the same way the verbose

> Officers
> That to a Regiment appertain'd which then
> Was station'd in the City         (IX. 126–8.)

is later, with no loss to the sense, cut down to

> Officers, Then stationed in the city,

The 1850 version, while bracing the limp style of the earlier text,
often gives form and outline to a thought before but vaguely
suggested. The feeble statement

> Where good and evil never have that name,
> That which they ought to have, but wrong prevails,
> And vice at home         (IX. 359–61.)

---

[1] Cf. the statement made by D. W. on Nov. 29, 1805, quoted on p. xx.

is strengthened to
> Where good and evil interchange their names,
> And thirst for bloody spoils abroad is paired
> With vice at home.

Here he has carried to a further stage the idea which was at the back of his mind in 1805, but which never reached expression. Such changes as these exemplify no difference in theory of style, but simply the difference between good and bad writing. The desire for a more exact and vivid picture leads him more than twenty times in the poem to substitute, for the auxiliary 'to be', a verb with more definite meaning. No better example of this could be given than the description of the morning of his poetic dedication. In the first version it runs:

> Magnificent
> The morning was, a memorable pomp,
> More glorious than I ever had beheld.
> The Sea was laughing at a distance; all
> The solid Mountains were as bright as clouds,    (IV. 330–4.)

Many a poet would have rested satisfied with those lines as they stood, but no one can miss the gain in strength and vividness effected by the simple changes:

> Magnificent
> The morning rose, in memorable pomp,
> Glorious as e'er I had beheld—in front
> The sea lay laughing at a distance; near,
> The solid mountains shone, bright as the clouds,[1]

In the same way he gets rid of other auxiliaries which tend to weaken his sentence: of this the change from 'did soon become a patriot' to 'erelong became a patriot' is a typical example. Moreover, on re-reading his work, he detected many a jingle or inharmonious phrase, and for the sake of euphony altered 'betwixt' to 'between', 'itself' to 'herself', and 'which' to 'that', where it could be done without confusion to the sense. He noticed, too,

---

[1] A well-known example of the same change is found in the sonnet 'It is a beauteous evening', etc. (1802), where the line 'The gentleness of heaven broods o'er the sea' originally read 'is on' for 'broods o'er'. Wordsworth seems at this time to have had an almost mystical feeling for the verb 'to be'. Cf. a remark he makes on an early reading in Resolution and Independence. 'What is brought forward? A lonely place, "a Pond by which the old man was, far from all house or home;" not stood, nor sat, but was—the figure presented in the most naked simplicity possible.' But here as elsewhere 'naked simplicity' is resigned for the sake of vividness.

an unfortunate predilection for the words 'sweet' and 'beauteous', and banished them from many lines in favour of a more exactly appropriate epithet.[1] The cumulative effect of such changes, each one perhaps trifling in itself, cannot easily be over-estimated.

Wordsworth retained his critical acumen far longer than his creative energy: some of his best corrections, in *The Prelude* as in other poems, are among the last. And to the end he was capable of writing a superb line. Those who accept with too much literalness the obvious truth that what is greatest in Wordsworth belongs to a single decade (1798–1807), will do well to note that two lines on the statue of Newton

The marble index of a mind for ever
Voyaging through strange seas of Thought, alone,    (III. 62–63.)

were written when he was over sixty years of age, and that only about the same time a fine description of autumn in the Lake Country reached its climax in the lovely phrase

Clothed in the sunshine of the withering fern.    (VI. 11.)

To study the development of this and other passages[2] from their first conception is a lesson in the craftsmanship of letters.

*The Prelude*, as Wordsworth left it, had reached a high level of workmanship—so high, indeed, that the few remaining banalities, such as 'My drift, I fear, is scarcely obvious', or 'Alas, I fear that I am trifling', stand out conspicuous, making us wonder how they escaped his vigilance. Little survived that was slovenly or careless. Flats, of course, there are, such flats as are inevitable to so comprehensive a design as his; for some of the elements that went to make up the poet's mind were refractory to poetic handling. His lines drag their slow length along whilst he labours to express in exact intellectual terms a philosophic position which, when all is said, is more truly a faith than a philosophy. And there was a matter-of-fact side to his nature which no truthful autobiography could gloss over, and which would only be falsified by the coloured draperies of fancy. But alike from what is too abstract for poetry and from what is too commonplace, he can rise without effort to his noblest flights of song; and not seldom his most pregnant

---

[1] Hutchinson notes that in 1827 the word 'sweet' was removed from ten places in the poems; in 1836 from ten; in 1840 from one, in 1845 from three: = 24 in all.

[2] Note, e.g., the development through succeeding texts of VI. 63–64:
And yet the morning gladness is not gone
Which then was in my mind.

reflections spring from what seemed barren soil. Viewed as a
whole the style is adequate to its theme. It has often been falsely
judged. Wordsworth has been ridiculed for failing to attain to the
great manner when he was not attempting it, but was playing
upon his youthful foibles that gentle mockery which naturally
takes a mock-heroic form:[1] more often he has been attacked as
prosaic when his simple matter called for the plainest speech. His
first aim, as it was his great achievement, was sincerity; and the
main stylistic error of his later revision lies in a too generous
concession to the vulgar taste for poetical ornament.

### § 7. *Comparison of the texts in point of style: later deterioration*

In the years when his inspiration was flagging, Wordsworth
tended to fall back on that same abstract and artificial language
from which his own theories, and his own best practice, had been
a reaction. His true disciple, who has learnt from him to recognize
the unmistakable ring of sincerity in style, will be the first to
detect the false note in his master's work, the last to be cajoled
into the delusion that prose can be turned into poetry by the use
of unnatural diction or elaborate periphrasis. Nothing is gained
poetically by changing the word 'friend' into 'the partner of those
varied walks', nor 'human creature, be he who he may', to
'human creature howsoe'er endowed'. 'Thought and quietness'
is a more truly Wordsworthian phrase than 'meditative peace'.[2]
I find it hard to understand or to forgive the transformation of
'the Woman, and her garments vex'd and toss'd' (XI. 315) into
a 'female' [XII. 260]. The account of how, when he was 'dead to
deeper hope', he could yet rejoice in the life that is in nature:

> Plants, insects, beasts in field, and birds in bower,      (XI. 28.)

makes less impression upon us when the birds are pompously
described as
> boldly seeking pleasure nearer heaven
> On wings that navigate cerulean skies.

Such lines would have adorned *The Seasons*: *The Prelude* can
spare them. In the last version of the poem there is a fine but

---

[1] Cf. Book III. 15–54, and note on [17].

[2] [IV. 306]—and also more suited to the context, a description of his
state of feeling as a youth of eighteen.

somewhat mannered description of how, with his sister, he lay upon the battlements of Brougham Castle,

> Catching from tufts of grass and hare-bell flowers
> Their faintest whisper to the passing breeze,
> Given out while mid-day heat oppressed the plains;

but the voice of the authentic Wordsworth is more distinctly heard in the delicate simplicity of the rejected lines:

> Lay listening to the wild flowers and the grass,
> As they gave out their whispers to the wind.    (VI. 231–2.)

In the A text his encounter with the discharged soldier has this preface:

> A favourite pleasure hath it been with me,
> From time of earliest youth, to walk alone
> Along the public Way, when, for the night
> Deserted, in its silence it assumes
> A character of deeper quietness
> Than pathless solitudes.                         (IV. 363–8.)

The sentence opens lamely enough, though by the third line it has recovered; but as it stands, it is more in key with the bare impressive narrative that is to follow than is the grandiloquent exordium of the later version:

> When from our better selves we have too long
> Been parted by the hurrying world, and droop,
> Sick of its business, of its pleasures tired,[1]
> How gracious, how benign, is Solitude;

and so on, succeeded by far-sought similes of the watchman and the hermit—sixteen lines in all, of good but inappropriate writing, in the place of five and a half which needed but slight emendation to make them wholly adequate.[2] This anxiety to write up his poem, and give it a more definitely literary flavour, creates in places the impression of pompous phrase-making, which is farther removed than over-bald simplicity from the true Wordsworthian spirit.

---

[1] This line is, indeed, admirable in the antithetical style of the eighteenth century.

[2] This change in the text is all the more regrettable as it led to the omission of ll. 375–99, a passage of great beauty and penetrating psychology.

## § 8. *Changes in the text due to change of audience*

Other changes in the text, though in part matters of style, are more properly regarded as due to a change in the audience for whom the poem was destined. The A text was not merely dedicated to Coleridge, it was *addressed* to him, as to one

Who in my thoughts art ever at my side ;

its whole atmosphere is suggested by the parenthesis inserted in the tale of his sufferings during the Reign of Terror :

(I speak bare truth
As if to thee alone in private talk) ;

it has the tone of intimate conversation, or of a personal letter written without reserve, in the confidence that no detail will be accounted too trivial among friends 'who love as we do', that no confession about himself will be misconstrued as vain or empty egoism.[1] *The Prelude* never lost this intimate character ; but it was inevitable that when the poet reviewed it with an eye to publication, he should desire to tone down or to omit matter which, to a wider and less sympathetic audience, might seem irrelevant or superfluous. Thus the pronoun 'I', common in the A text, often gives way to a passive construction. In the A text we find a reference to his slender means in London, so that theatre-going, though a 'dear delight', was but a rare luxury with him ; we have an explicit statement of his reasons both for going to France and for returning to England ; we are told the name of the companion that he lost on the Penrith moor ; and we learn that the lake on which he had his momentous adventure in the stolen boat was not Esthwaite, as has so often been surmised, but Ullswater, for he was staying at the time at Patterdale, on his way home for the holidays. Throughout the later versions he tends to eliminate place-names. An early reviewer of *The Prelude* remarked, with some naïveté, that finding the place-names of his district unsuited for verse the poet was obliged 'to make up for this by descriptive circumlocution' ; but if Wordsworth could begin a sonnet with the name of Jones, he would hardly boggle at Cockermouth, or Patterdale, or Hawkshead, names endeared to

---

[1] Cf. also VI. 269–71 :

Throughout this narrative,
*Else sooner ended*, I have known full well
For whom I thus record *etc.* (The italics are mine.)

him by rich associations. Of a still deeper interest are those early readings which shed light upon his character. To Coleridge he can write lines protesting his innocence of the passions of envy and dissolute pleasure (III. 531-6), and allude more than once to that strain of constitutional melancholy (VI. 192; X. 869-70) which often destroyed his peace of mind; but while we appreciate the motives that led him to suppress these confidences, we may yet be glad to recover them. Poetically, indeed, much of this detail is nugatory, and some of it, as Wordsworth himself was inclined to think, 'beneath the dignity of verse'. But we value it in no spirit of mere vulgar curiosity. *The Prelude* is a great poem, but it is also the frank autobiography of a great man. It cannot be judged solely by poetic canons, any more than a letter can be judged by the same criteria as an essay: like a letter, it owes its peculiar charm to intimate revelation of the writer. Over many of his readers Wordsworth exerts a truly personal spell. To them he is not a poet only, but a friend; and among our friends the most trivial admissions are often welcomed because, in their very triviality, they seem to bring us nearer to the object of our love.

## § 9. *The ideal text of 'The Prelude'*

The ideal text of *The Prelude*, which the lover of Wordsworth may construct for himself from the material here presented to him, would follow no single manuscript. It would retain from the earliest version such familiar details as have any autobiographical significance. Of purely stylistic changes from that text, it would accept those only which Wordsworth might have made (and some he would certainly have made), had he prepared the poem for the press in his greatest period, changes designed to remove crudities of expression, and to develop or clarify his original meaning: but it would reject those later excrescences of a manner less pure, at times even meretricious, which are out of key with the spirit in which the poem was first conceived and executed. Most firmly would it reject all modifications of his original thought and attitude to his theme.

## § 10. *Changes of idea:* (a) *Life at Cambridge*

To the student of the poet's mind the first version of *The Prelude* is chiefly valuable because it presents us with the history of his spiritual growth as he saw it when his powers were still at their height, and when he was writing those poems on which his greatness rests most securely. No man is the same at seventy years of age as he was at thirty-five, and Wordsworth, perhaps, changed more than most of us; for though, like others, he descended into the vale of years, he descended from far more glorious heights.

The Wordsworth who, when the conversation turned upon Orleans, could say to his wife 'I wonder how I came to stay there so long, and at a period so exciting', was either a very different man from his younger self, or he had a keener sense of humour than is usually allowed him. When he wrote *The Prelude* he was gifted with a penetrative imagination that none of our poets, save Shakespeare, can surpass; but even then the gift came to him fitfully:

> I see by glimpses now, as age comes on
> May scarcely see at all.

The pathetic prophecy was fulfilled; as age came on, his sight was dimmed; and not only did he see less, but he tended to lose complete confidence in his earlier vision. He still towered above his fellows. As late as 1841 he could impress John Stuart Mill with the 'extensive range of his thoughts and the expansiveness of his feelings'. But compared with what he had once been he was narrow, and he was timid; and many of the later changes in the text of *The Prelude* are criticisms directed by a man of seventy winters against his own past.

It is not to be expected that he would find much to alter in his reminiscences of childhood; nor had he written anything of Cambridge that would seriously disquiet his more prudent age. He knew the darker side to the picture, for he told De Quincey that 'the manners of the young men were very frantic and dissolute at that time'; but to this he barely alludes in *The Prelude*. For there 'his tale was of himself', and the 'baser pleasures of the place' were 'by him unshared, and only now and then observed'. There could hardly be stronger testimony to the soundness of his early education and the strength of his character than that he could pass unscathed through the Cambridge of his day:

> For me, I grieve not; happy is the man,
> Who only misses what I miss'd, who falls
> No lower than I fell. (III. 504–6.)

The University had, in fact, little of academic worth to offer him; but the very apathy of those in authority, and the barren curriculum which they prescribed, had justified him in indulging his incorrigible passion for liberty. He had re-echoed in his heart the comment passed on Cambridge by his latest poetic predecessor—'If these are the profits of the place, give me the amusements of it'; but looking back from a maturer manhood, he saw little in this to regret. If his reading had been desultory, it had been far wider than is generally supposed. At Cambridge, too, he had learnt one of the supporting truths of his life, 'the spiritual presences of absent things'. Moreover he never ceased to recognize that he 'was not for that hour, Nor for that place'. But when he revised the book he made some slight concessions to the susceptibilities of his Alma Mater. He retained his attack on compulsory College chapel, but compensated for it by inserting here and there a few phrases which give the book a more religious flavour. He now defends his own idleness with less defiance, and exonerates his University from some of her responsibility for it. The later omission of lines, such as

> Why should I grieve ? I was a chosen Son . . .
> I was a Freeman; in the purest sense
> Was free, and to majestic ends was strong,

(III. 82–90.)

and the inclusion of others—

> Yet why take refuge in that plea ?—the fault
> This, I repeat, was mine; mine be the blame.

[VI. 188–9.]

sufficiently indicate a change of tone, befitting one who had sons of undergraduate age, and whose brother was Master of Trinity.

## § 11. *Changes of idea:* (b) *Attitude to the French Revolution*

From the first he was uncertain how he should deal with those fateful years that followed his departure from Cambridge. His original intention was to leave them out of *The Prelude* altogether and reserve all reflections upon the French Revolution for more dispassionate and impersonal treatment in *The Recluse*; and when he saw that to follow this course would leave the history of his mind's growth incomplete, he seems to have hesitated as to the amount of detail he should introduce. After recounting his return to England, the narrative, up to this point clear and consecutive, becomes involved and wavering; he goes backwards and forwards, so that the progress of events is not easy to trace. The order in which Books VII and IX were written suggests, at least, that at

one time the book devoted to London was to follow and not precede the account of his residence in France; had it done so it must
have included not merely the first impressions of an eager, bewildered stranger 'in the vast metropolis', but some details of
those exciting months when, with his Revolutionary ardour at its
height, he was associating with the English radical leaders; and
also of that later time when, in the bitter mood of disenchantment,
he clung to such straws of hope as he could clutch from the abstract principles of Godwin. There is no part of his life of which
we know so little as that which intervened between his departure
from France and his settlement at Racedown; there is none of
which we would fain know more.[1] His references to it in later
years were often vague and misleading; but even when he wrote
*The Prelude* he felt no inclination to say more of it than was barely
necessary to explain his recovery and release from it.

Critics who approach Wordsworth with a strong Revolutionary
bias have sometimes expected that the first version of *The Prelude*
would reveal a poet far more after their own heart than they have
found in the version of 1850. They forget that in the year 1804
he was already heart and soul with his own country in her struggle
with Napoleon, convinced that the cause of true liberty depended
on her ultimate triumph. Then, as later, in speaking of his Revolutionary ardour, 'juvenile errors' were his theme (X. 638). The
words with which in 1821 he met the charge of apostasy express
a conviction which he held as firmly when he wrote *The Prelude*:
' *You* have been deluded by *Places* and *Persons*, while I have stuck
to *Principles*. *I* abandoned France and her rulers when *they* abandoned the struggle for Liberty, gave themselves up to Tyranny,
and endeavoured to enslave the world.'[2] In point of fact his renunciation of France preceded the full blossoming of his poetic genius. All
later political changes came gradually, insensibly to himself. He
never regretted his enthusiasm for the Revolution in its early days
of promise, and retained to the last that democratic idealism, inherent in his nature, which had first attracted him to it. Nor was
he ever in theory the solid Tory that he became in practice. There
was always, he said, something of the Chartist in him. But with
the passage of years, as he himself admitted, he lost courage;
and his revision of *The Prelude* shows clear signs of his growing
conservatism.

[1] It has recently been revealed that he had several conversations with
Godwin between Feb. and Aug. 1795: *v*. Moorman, pp. 262–5.

[2] *L.Y.* 56. W. W. to James Losh.

Book IX, which relates his conversion, under the inspired guidance of Beaupuy, to the cause of France, he could leave almost untouched:[1] he revised more drastically those books which recorded a sympathy with the Revolution that seemed less justifiable. As time passed, he grew more severe upon France, more indulgent to English foreign policy, more apologetic for himself. _The Prelude_ records how the September massacres, though they appalled him, did not damp his ardour; for he was buoyed up by the faith that one great man might still save France from the Jacobins and restore her to her ideals. 'Enflamed with hope', the phrase with which he describes this faith in 1804, gives probably a truer impression of his emotion at the time than the more sober 'Cheered with this hope' which later he substituted for it. Moreover, in 1804 he could still endorse it in the pregnant words

> Creed which ten shameful years have not annulled. (X. 179.)

The removal of this line from his text not only points to a loss of faith, it removes the implication that his own country bore her part in the shame which those years brought forth. The originally bare account of his reluctant return homewards was elaborated into a passionately patriotic tribute to Albion's sacred shores, hardly expressing his sentiment at the time of which it was written. To the motives which he had given for the French declaration of a republic (September 1792) he now added others that were less worthy, and were quite foreign to his thoughts either then or in 1804; and though he admitted in later years to his sturdy radical friend, James Losh,[2] that he had 'disapproved of the war against France at its commencement, thinking, which was perhaps an error, that it might have been avoided' (note the 'perhaps', he is not sure of it even in 1821); he could not leave unmitigated the terms in which, in the A text, he had denounced it. In 1804 he had attributed it to 'the unhappy counsel of a few weak men', and laid greater stress on the extent of English sympathy with the Revolutionary cause, whilst his condemnation of the government for their persecution of the English radicals, severe, indeed, in the final text, was before at once more passionate and more contemptuous:

> Our Shepherds (this say merely) at that time
> Thirsted to make the guardian Crook of Law
> A tool of Murder; they who ruled the State,

---

[1] His omission of _Vaudracour and Julia_ from Book IX is discussed in the notes at the end of the volume (_v._ p. 592).  [2] _L.Y._ 57.

> Though with such awful proof before their eyes
> That he who would sow death, reaps death, or worse,
> And can reap nothing better, child-like long'd
> To imitate, not wise enough to avoid,
> Giants in their impiety alone,
> But, in their weapons and their warfare base
> As vermin working out of reach, they leagu'd
> Their strength perfidiously, to undermine
> Justice, and make an end of Liberty.          (X. 646–57.)

This is strong language to use against an English cabinet, and we cannot be surprised that it was modified upon revision.

But more significant, perhaps, is the introduction into Book VII, some time after 1820, of an enthusiastic tribute to Burke. There is no trace of this eulogy in the original text. Burke's oratory would, doubtless, have stirred the poet on his visits to London in either 1791 or 1793, but it would have stirred him to very different emotions from those which inspired the added lines. It is possible that even in 1804 he might have written them, but their insertion in the account of his early impressions of London, when he had lately returned from a holiday across a Europe which

> was thrilled with joy,
> France standing on the top of golden hours,
> And human nature seeming born again,

creates a misleading impression as to the state of his mind in that period of which the Book professes to be the record.

## § 12. *Changes of idea:* (c) *Philosophy of life and religion*

But most to be regretted are those alterations in the text which have obscured the statement of that religious faith which is reflected in all the poet's greatest work. When Wordsworth wrote *The Prelude* he had in nothing swerved from the faith that inspired the *Lines composed a few miles above Tintern Abbey.* This faith need only be referred to here in the barest outline. Starting from a fervid belief in the inherent goodness of human nature, Wordsworth attributes the growth of the whole moral and intellectual being—from infancy, through the stages of childhood and adolescence, to maturity—to impressions made upon the senses, bound together, reacting on one another, and ever growing in fullness and intensity by means of the law of association. The philosophical parentage of this conception is unmistakable; it is the direct offspring of the sensationalism of the eighteenth century, and in particular of David Hartley,

> he of mortal kind
> Wisest, he first who marked the ideal tribes
> Up the fine fibres through the sentient brain,[1]

but it is Hartley transcendentalized by Coleridge, and at once modified and exalted by Wordsworth's own mystical experience. For to him there was always this great paradox, that though it is through the proper exercise of eye and ear that man reaches his full moral and intellectual stature, so that he can recognize

> In nature and the language of the sense
> The anchor of my purest thoughts, the nurse,
> The guide, the guardian of my heart, and soul
> Of all my moral being,

yet revelation flashes upon him when 'the light of sense goes out'; and 'laid asleep in body', he becomes deeply conscious of the presence of God within him. In the highest mood of ecstasy this consciousness of complete oneness with God is so overwhelming, that his other attributes as man seem to fall from him, and he knows only that

> one interior life
> In which all beings live with god, themselves
> Are god, existing in the mighty whole,
> As undistinguishable as the cloudless east
> Is from the cloudless west, when all
> The hemisphere is one cerulean blue.[2]

How far this intense mystical experience is compatible with Christianity let theologians determine. Coleridge, whether, like a bee that draws its food from many different flowers, he took his nourishment from the Neo-Platonists, or Hartley, or Spinoza, or, as later, from the German metaphysicians, always contrived to give his honey some Christian flavour; and Wordsworth himself strayed no farther from orthodoxy than Coleridge had done in *Religious Musings* and *The Eolian Harp*. When Coleridge described

---

[1] Coleridge, *Religious Musings*. Wordsworth's debt to the philosophy of the eighteenth century has been exhaustively worked out by Professor Beatty in *W. W. : His Doctrine and Art*. Cf. also N. P. Stallknecht, *Strange Seas of Thought*, 1945.

[2] From a fragment found in a manuscript notebook containing *Peter Bell* (*v.* notes, p. 525).

his friend as a semi-atheist he was not objecting to his positive faith, but rather reflecting on what he regarded as its incompleteness. Certainly at this time Wordsworth's faith was in no way tinged with dogmatic Christianity. It is doubtful whether ever, except in that dark period of scepticism when he had wholly lost his bearings, he would have regarded himself as an opponent to Christianity: but Christianity in his early years had no special message for him. With Coleridge's attempt to fuse philosophy and religion he was wholly unconcerned. His philosophy, as far as he was a philosopher, *was* his religion; he never examined its logical implications, and any analysis that seemed to disturb its integrity he would have set down to 'that false secondary power By which we multiply distinctions', appealing against it to the tribunal of his own deepest experience. His faith was a passionate intuition of God present in the Universe and in the mind of man; his philosophy no more than the struggle of his reason to account for it. And to the end of his life this intuition remained the living centre of his creed; something

> Which neither listlessness nor mad endeavour,
> Nor all that is at enmity with joy,
> Can utterly abolish or destroy.

He always resented that cruder orthodoxy 'which considers the Supreme Being as bearing the same relation to the Universe as a watchmaker bears to a watch'. The Temple in which he worshipped most devoutly was still one not made with hands, the Bible in which he read the deepest lessons was still 'the Bible of the Universe, as it speaks to the ear of the intelligent, and as it lies open to the eyes of the humble-minded'. But later the vision grew dim, and though at times it was 'by miracle restored', it was no longer sufficient to meet his needs. Gradually, therefore, he turned more consciously to the Christian faith. This change was the almost inevitable outcome of his experience of life. The Wordsworth of 1798–1804 was the exultant champion of 'man's unconquerable mind': 'dignity', 'majesty', 'sovereignty' are words again and again applied to the human mind in the early *Prelude*, and again and again qualified in the later texts. Inspired by a passionate sense of the spiritual greatness of man, he forgot man's natural weakness. But the inevitable yoke brought by the years taught him the need of humility. We may resent in a passage which eulogizes man as 'of all visible natures crown' (VIII. 631–40) the intrusion of what seems the unnecessary reminder that he is 'born of dust and kindred to the worm'.[1] But the inserted phrase tells something that was essential to Wordsworth's later thought. Christian meekness had come to have a real meaning for him, and the more so because, of all the Christian virtues, it was for him the hardest to achieve.

Moreover, he felt a deep sense of responsibility as a teacher, and he had good reason to know that he was misunderstood. Both *Lines composed . . . above Tintern Abbey* and the *Ode: Intimations of Immortality* had proved a stumbling-block to many. He was accused, even by readers of *The Excursion*, of not distinguishing 'Nature as the work of God and God himself', and he felt it incumbent on him to remove from *The Prelude* all that might be interpreted as giving support to the heresy, and to bring that poem into accord with the later modifications of his faith. He took pains to relate, as far as possible, his naturalistic religion to a definitely Christian dogma. He toned down passages that savoured too much of independence. He inserted lines here and there which might lull asleep the watchful eye of the heresy-hunter. Sometimes these are merely what might be called pietistic embroidery, in no way affecting the argument, but creating, by the use of conventional phraseology, a familiar atmosphere of edification. In this spirit he adds a reference to matins and vespers [I. 45], includes among possible themes for poetic treatment 'Christian meekness hallowing faithful loves' [I. 185], changes the simple phrase 'as were a joy to hear of' into the more elaborate

> To which the silver wands of saints in Heaven
> Might point with rapturous joy,                    [X. 485–6.]

qualifies a statement that seems to him over-bold with the line

> So, with devout humility be it said,                    [X. 447.]

and adds, as a reason for the respect due to man as man, that he is

> Here placed to be the inheritor of heaven.    [VIII. 336.]

---

[1] Cf. also the lines:

> Dust as we are, the immortal spirit grows
> Like harmony in music.                    (I. 351 [340].)

which were first written (with no reference to our dusty origin):

> The mind of Man is fram'd even like the breath
> And harmony of music.

Here, unquestionably, the passage has gained by the fine contrast introduced between the body and the spirit of man.

These are small matters in themselves, but they give a new colour to his work, and are foreign to its original spirit.

He is, throughout, careful, by a small change in word or phrase, or the addition of a sentence, to cover up the traces of his early pantheism. Thus

> A soul divine which we participate,
> A deathless spirit                                 (V. 16–17.)

becomes

> As might appear to the eye of fleeting time,
> A deathless spirit

and

> God and nature's single sovereignty          (IX. 237.)

becomes

> presences of God's mysterious power
> Made manifest in Nature's sovereignty.

Most noticeable is his relapse from that religion of joy which springs from feeling, the reward of 'glad hearts without reproach or blot', to a less spontaneous, a disciplined emotion. The spirit of the early *Prelude* is that of one who, with God and nature communing,

> saw one life, and felt that it was joy.      (II. 430.)

But even to this simple utterance he adds the gloss

> Communing in this sort through earth and heaven
> With every form of creature, as it looked
> Towards the Uncreated with a countenance
> Of adoration, with an eye of love.

Nothing could be more significant than the change of

> I worshipp'd then among the depths of things
> As my soul bade me . . .
> I felt, and nothing else;                  (XI. 234–8.)

to

> Worshipping then among the depth of things
> As piety ordained . . .
> I felt, observed, and pondered;

(Of 'natural piety', indeed, the original *Prelude* is full: of what is ordinarily called piety there is nothing.)

In the same way

> The feeling of life endless, the great thought
> By which we live, Infinity and God.      (XIII. 183–4.)

becomes later

> Faith in life endless, the sustaining thought
> Of human Being, Eternity and God.

The highest achievement of that Power which he has learnt to reverence in Nature was, in the A text, that it 'lifts the Being into magnanimity', i.e. to that greatness of soul which raises us above our petty selves to realize the 'Godhead that is ours, as natural beings in the strength of nature'. In the later version this same power

> trains
> To meekness and exalts by humble faith.

And so, that imaginative rapture, that is 'balanced by a Reason which indeed Is reason' (XIII. 264–5), is later presented as

> balanced by pathetic truth, by trust
> In hopeful reason, leaning on the stay
> Of Providence,

and its lasting inspiration, 'sanctified by reason and by truth' (*ibid.* 443–4), is later

> sanctified by reason, blest by faith

By changes such as these, the last Book in particular, which is the philosophical conclusion of the whole matter, leaves a totally different impression from that created by the earlier text. The ideas he has introduced are from the brain that wrote the *Ecclesiastical Sonnets*; they were entirely alien to his thought and feeling, not only in that youth and early manhood of which *The Prelude* recounts the history, but in that maturer period when it was written; and they have no rightful place in the poem. Whether he ought to have felt them, or wished, when he was reviewing his work, that he had felt them, is another matter. The essential point for us to realize is that their intrusion has falsified our estimate of the authentic Wordsworth, the poet of the years 1798–1805.

The first signs of the change which dictated this revision are seen in the very months during which he was embarked upon the completion of the poem—in the *Ode to Duty*, where he renounces his reliance on the genial sense of youth

> When love is an unerring light
> And joy its own security,—

and in the second half of the 'immortal *Ode*'. But although he undoubtedly passed through a period of spiritual change, accentuated by his grief at the loss of his brother John—which indeed led to the suspension for a time of his work upon *The Prelude*—

yet he completed it in the spirit in which it had been begun, with
no sign of wavering from his early faith. In the first version of *The*
*Prelude* he wrote nothing that he might not have felt on that
eventful day when he revisited Tintern Abbey; and of 'that serene
and blessed mood' to which the lines then written give utterance,
Wordsworth is the inspired interpreter.

The revised *Prelude* represents another, less independent creed.
The position into which he had now withdrawn was not for him
a false position. He was sincere, now as ever. But if he was conscious of a change, as it is abundantly clear that he was, he
would surely have done better to leave as it stood what he had

first written for Coleridge, and, instead of disguising his former
faith, to have expounded in a book of *The Recluse*, or elsewhere,
the reasons that led him to move from it, and the manner in which
it could be reconciled with the tenets of an historic Church. In
truth that compromise, which provided so secure a haven for his
later years, was worthy of a finer exposition than he was ever able
to give it. It may have brought him peace, but it never stirred
him to that rapture of which great art is born. When his poetry
was commended for the purity of its moral he insisted that he,
on the other hand, valued it according to the powers of mind
which it presupposed in the writer and excited in the hearer.
That work of his which most triumphantly stands this test belongs
to the years 1798–1807; and of the vital source and hiding-places
of its power the original *Prelude* is the frankest and most direct
confession.

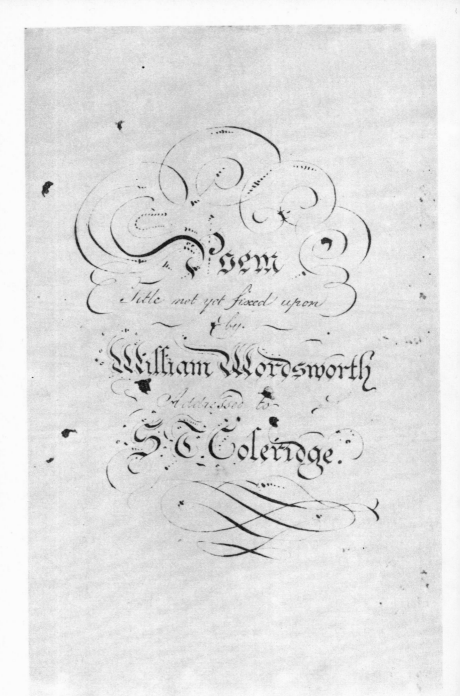

**MS. B. Title-page**

# THE PRELUDE,

## OR

# GROWTH OF A POET'S MIND;

### AN AUTOBIOGRAPHICAL POEM;

BY

## WILLIAM WORDSWORTH

LONDON:

EDWARD MOXON, DOVER STREET.

1850.

# BOOK FIRST

## INTRODUCTION—CHILDHOOD AND SCHOOL-TIME

OH there is blessing in this gentle breeze
That blows from the green fields and from the clouds
And from the sky: it beats against my cheek,
And seems half conscious of the joy it gives.
5 O welcome Messenger! O welcome Friend!
A captive greets thee, coming from a house
Of bondage, from yon City's walls set free,
A prison where he hath been long immured.
Now I am free, enfranchis'd and at large,
10 May fix my habitation where I will.
What dwelling shall receive me? In what Vale      [10]
Shall be my harbour? Underneath what grove
Shall I take up my home, and what sweet stream
Shall with its murmur lull me to my rest?
15 The earth is all before me: with a heart
Joyous, nor scar'd at its own liberty,      [15]
I look about, and should the guide I chuse
Be nothing better than a wandering cloud,
I cannot miss my way. I breathe again;
20 Trances of thought and mountings of the mind
Come fast upon me: it is shaken off,      [20]
As by miraculous gift 'tis shaken off,
That burthen of my own unnatural self,
The heavy weight of many a weary day
25 Not mine, and such as were not made for me.
Long months of peace (if such bold word accord
With any promises of human life),      [25]

[MSS. for Bk. I: J J Chr. 18a M A B C D E; for ll. 271–663 U V: for ll. 452–89 Letter to Coleridge, Dec.–Jan. 1798–9: also, for ll. 427–89 The Friend.]
Book First B: Part First A.
1–10 D reads as A 1-4 and goes on:
    O random Visitant who have to-day
    Thy task or favorite office thou soft Breeze
    Art welcome as a Messenger or Friend
    The first step greeting of a glad escape
    From yon vast City where too long hath pined

# BOOK FIRST

## INTRODUCTION—CHILDHOOD AND SCHOOL-TIME

O THERE is blessing in this gentle breeze,
A visitant that while it fans my cheek
Doth seem half-conscious of the joy it brings
From the green fields, and from yon azure sky.
Whate'er its mission, the soft breeze can come                   5
To none more grateful than to me; escaped
From the vast city, where I long had pined
A discontented sojourner: now free,
Free as a bird to settle where I will.
What dwelling shall receive me? in what vale                    10
Shall be my harbour? underneath what grove
Shall I take up my home? and what clear stream
Shall with its murmur lull me into rest?
The earth is all before me. With a heart
Joyous, nor scared at its own liberty,                          15
I look about; and should the chosen guide
Be nothing better than a wandering cloud,
I cannot miss my way. I breathe again!
Trances of thought and mountings of the mind
Come fast upon me: it is shaken off,                            20
That burthen of my own unnatural self,
The heavy weight of many a weary day
Not mine, and such as were not made for me.
Long months of peace (if such bold word accord
With any promises of human life),                               25

A discontented Sojourner now free,
Free as *etc. as* 1850. D² *reads*:
O random Visitant whate'er thy task
For whomsoe'er thy mission, thou, soft Breeze,
Doth come to none more grateful than to me
Escaped from yon vast City where I long
Have pined a discontented Sojourner
Delivered by a step as seems—at once
Free as *etc. as* 1850.

5 welcome] grateful A².          6 coming] issuing  A² C².
9 I am free] do I walk A² C².               14 murmur B D²: murmurs A C D.
14–49 D *stuck over*: D² *as* 1850.        17 guide I chuse] A² C² *as* 1850.
18 wandering] vagrant A² C².             23 *not in* M.

Long months of ease and undisturb'd delight
Are mine in prospect; whither shall I turn
30 By road or pathway or through open field,
Or shall a twig or any floating thing
Upon the river, point me out my course?                    [30]
   Enough that I am free; for months to come
May dedicate myself to chosen tasks;
35 May quit the tiresome sea and dwell on shore,
If not a Settler on the soil, at least
To drink wild water, and to pluck green herbs,
And gather fruits fresh from their native bough.
Nay more, if I may trust myself, this hour
40 Hath brought a gift that consecrates my joy;
For I, methought, while the sweet breath of Heaven
Was blowing on my body, felt within
A corresponding mild creative breeze,                      [35]
A vital breeze which travell'd gently on
45 O'er things which it had made, and is become
A tempest, a redundant energy
Vexing its own creation. 'Tis a power
That does not come unrecogniz'd, a storm,
Which, breaking up a long-continued frost                  [40]
50 Brings with it vernal promises, the hope
Of active days, of dignity and thought,
Of prowess in an honorable field,
Pure passions, virtue, knowledge, and delight,
The holy life of music and of verse.                       [45]

55    Thus far, O Friend! did I, not used to make
A present joy the matter of my Song,
Pour out, that day, my soul in measur'd strains
Even in the very words which I have here
Recorded: to the open fields I told                        [50]
60 A prophecy: poetic numbers came

29–32           Whither shall we turn
        Ye aery Spirits that attend my steps,
        Unseen though not inaudible impart
        Your wish in whispers, whither shall we turn
        By road? or pathway? or through open field?
        Yon upland shall we cross, or shall this wild
        And wandering Rivulet point me out my course? A² *deleted.*
33–34   Enough that I am free, embrace today
        An uncontroul'd enfranchisement; for months
        To come may live a life of chosen tasks M.

Long months of ease and undisturbed delight
Are mine in prospect; whither shall I turn,
By road or pathway, or through trackless field,
Up hill or down, or shall some floating thing
Upon the river point me out my course?                    30
  Dear Liberty! Yet what would it avail
But for a gift that consecrates the joy?
For I, methought, while the sweet breath of heaven
Was blowing on my body, felt within
A correspondent breeze, that gently moved              35
With quickening virtue, but is now become
A tempest, a redundant energy,
Vexing its own creation. Thanks to both,
And their congenial powers, that, while they join
In breaking up a long-continued frost,                    40
Bring with them vernal promises, the hope
Of active days urged on by flying hours,—
Days of sweet leisure, taxed with patient thought
Abstruse, nor wanting punctual service high,
Matins and vespers of harmonious verse!                45


    Thus far, O Friend! did I, not used to make
A present joy the matter of a song,
Pour forth that day my soul in measured strains
That would not be forgotten, and are here
Recorded: to the open fields I told                        50
A prophecy: poetic numbers came

**33–38** *in* D *and in* E (*with* pure waters *for* wild water).
**38** bough B A² C: tree A.
**33–52** A *has this deleted attempt at redrafting:*
    **33–37** Enough that I am free—relief more glad
        Feels not the sickly Mariner, allowed
        To quit the tiresome sea and dwell on shore
        Where he, long parched beneath a torrid clime,
        May drink clear water and may *etc.*
    **44–48** A vital breeze which quickened as it passed
        Smoothly along the surface of the mind
        Myriads of buds and blooms and is become
        A tempest a redundant energy
        Vexing its own creation. 'Tis a Power
        That agitates but injures not—a storm
    **51–52** Of active days and stirring thought, the love
        Of chearful labour in productive fields
**59** fields] Plains A².

Spontaneously, and cloth'd in priestly robe
My spirit, thus singled out, as it might seem,
For holy services: great hopes were mine;
My own voice chear'd me, and, far more, the mind's     [55]
65 Internal echo of the imperfect sound;
To both I listen'd, drawing from them both
A chearful confidence in things to come.


Whereat, being not unwilling now to give
A respite to this passion, I paced on       [60]
70 Gently, with careless steps; and came, erelong,
To a green shady place where down I sate
Beneath a tree, slackening my thoughts by choice,
And settling into gentler happiness.
'Twas Autumn, and a calm and placid day,      [65]
75 With warmth as much as needed from a sun
Two hours declin'd towards the west, a day
With silver clouds, and sunshine on the grass,
And, in the shelter'd grove where I was couch'd
A perfect stillness. On the ground I lay      [70]
80 Passing through many thoughts, yet mainly such
As to myself pertain'd. I made a choice
Of one sweet Vale whither my steps should turn
And saw, methought, the very house and fields
Present before my eyes: nor did I fail
85 To add, meanwhile, assurance of some work
Of glory, there forthwith to be begun,
Perhaps, too, there perform'd. Thus long I lay     [80]
Chear'd by the genial pillow of the earth
Beneath my head, sooth'd by a sense of touch
90 From the warm ground, that balanced me, else lost
Entirely, seeing nought, nought hearing, save
When here and there, about the grove of Oaks

62 it might seem] might appear B².       70 A C D: D² *as* 1850.
[71–77]              till fancy made
      Choice of a Vale whither my steps should turn.
      I saw methought the very house and fields.
      What picture of mere memory ever looked
      So fair, and while I gazed a higher Power    D: D² *as* 1850.
82 steps] feet A².
83       And saw methought the fields and very house
      Its porch, its casements, and its curling smoke A².
90 else] though M.

Spontaneously to clothe in priestly robe
A renovated spirit singled out,
Such hope was mine, for holy services.
My own voice cheered me, and, far more, the mind's          55
Internal echo of the imperfect sound;
To both I listened, drawing from them both
A cheerful confidence in things to come.


Content and not unwilling now to give
A respite to this passion, I paced on          60
With brisk and eager steps; and came, at length,
To a green shady place, where down I sate
Beneath a tree, slackening my thoughts by choice,
And settling into gentler happiness.
'Twas autumn, and a clear and placid day,          65
With warmth, as much as needed, from a sun
Two hours declined towards the west; a day
With silver clouds, and sunshine on the grass,
And in the sheltered and the sheltering grove
A perfect stillness. Many were the thoughts          70
Encouraged and dismissed, till choice was made
Of a known Vale, whither my feet should turn,
Nor rest till they had reached the very door
Of the one cottage which methought I saw.
No picture of mere memory ever looked          75
So fair; and while upon the fancied scene
I gazed with growing love, a higher power
Than Fancy gave assurance of some work
Of glory there forthwith to be begun,
Perhaps too there performed. Thus long I mused,          80
Nor e'er lost sight of what I mused upon,
Save when, amid the stately grove of oaks,
Now here, now there, an acorn, from its cup

91-93     Entirely, seeing nought else, lost mid the intense
          And absolute silence, hearing nothing, save
          When here and there within the grove of Oaks,
          The lightest of whose ripe and yellow leaves
          No zephyr stirred, an acorn *etc.* A².
          Of outward things nought seeing, hearing nought
          Save where, amid the grove, on that side now
          And now on this, an acorn from its cup  D: D² *as* 1850.
          Dislodged came rustling through sere leaves or dropped
          At once to earth and with a startling sound.  D E: E² *as* 1850.

Where was my bed, an acorn from the trees
Fell audibly, and with a startling sound.      [85]

95   Thus occupied in mind, I linger'd here
Contented, nor rose up until the sun
Had almost touch'd the horizon, bidding then
A farewell to the City left behind,
Even with the chance equipment of that hour
100 I journey'd towards the Vale that I had chosen.
It was a splendid evening; and my soul
Did once again make trial of the strength      [95]
Restored to her afresh; nor did she want
Eolian visitations; but the harp
105 Was soon defrauded, and the banded host
Of harmony dispers'd in straggling sounds
And, lastly, utter silence. 'Be it so,
It is an injury,' said I, 'to this day
To think of any thing but present joy.'      [100]
110 So like a Peasant I pursued my road
Beneath the evening sun, nor had one wish
Again to bend the sabbath of that time
To a servile yoke. What need of many words?      [105]
A pleasant loitering journey, through two days
115 Continued, brought me to my hermitage.
I spare to speak, my Friend, of what ensued,
The admiration and the love, the life
In common things; the endless store of things
Rare, or at least so seeming, every day      [110]
120 Found all about me in one neighbourhood,
The self-congratulation, the complete
Composure, and the happiness entire.
But speedily a longing in me rose
To brace myself to some determin'd aim,      [115]
125 Reading or thinking, either to lay up
New stores, or rescue from decay the old
By timely interference, I had hopes
Still higher, that with a frame of outward life,

93 trees] bough A².
99–100     Even on the strong temptation of that hour
          And with its chance equipment, I resolved
          To journey *etc.* B.
102 the A C: her B.     102–3 A C D: D² *as* 1850.
108–35 𝔄 C: *so* D, *but* too long *for* so long: D² *as* 1850.
109 joy 𝔄 C D: good D².
114 two 𝔄 C D E: *corr. in pencil to* three E².

Dislodged, through sere leaves rustled, or at once
To the bare earth dropped with a startling sound.          85
From that soft couch I rose not, till the sun
Had almost touched the horizon; casting then
A backward glance upon the curling cloud
Of city smoke, by distance ruralised;
Keen as a Truant or a Fugitive,                           90
But as a Pilgrim resolute, I took,
Even with the chance equipment of that hour,
The road that pointed toward the chosen Vale.
It was a splendid evening, and my soul
Once more made trial of her strength, nor lacked          95
Æolian visitations; but the harp
Was soon defrauded, and the banded host
Of harmony dispersed in straggling sounds,
And lastly utter silence! 'Be it so;
Why think of any thing but present good?'                 100
So, like a home-bound labourer I pursued
My way beneath the mellowing sun, that shed
Mild influence; nor left in me one wish
Again to bend the Sabbath of that time
To a servile yoke. What need of many words?               105
A pleasant loitering journey, through three days
Continued, brought me to my hermitage.
I spare to tell of what ensued, the life
In common things—the endless store of things,
Rare, or at least so seeming, every day                   110
Found all about me in one neighbourhood—
The self-congratulation, and, from morn
To night, unbroken cheerfulness serene.
But speedily an earnest longing rose
To brace myself to some determined aim,                   115
Reading or thinking; either to lay up
New stores, or rescue from decay the old
By timely interference: and therewith
Came hopes still higher, that with outward life

126-31    New stores, or animate the old conven'd
          Unto some common purpose. I had hopes
          Still higher, that I might give a life to shapes
          And phantoms which I long had marshall'd forth  M.
128-30    Still higher that I might with outward life
          Endue and station in a visible home.
          For discipline and honour a fair troop
          (For [*rational*] permanent communion a fair band  B³)
          Selected from those phantoms of conceit  B².

I might endue, might fix in a visible home
130 Some portion of those phantoms of conceit          [120]
That had been floating loose about so long,
And to such Beings temperately deal forth
The many feelings that oppress'd my heart.
But I have been discouraged; gleams of light
135 Flash often from the East, then disappear          [125]
And mock me with a sky that ripens not
Into a steady morning: if my mind,
Remembering the sweet promise of the past,
Would gladly grapple with some noble theme,
140 Vain is her wish; where'er she turns she finds          [130]
Impediments from day to day renew'd.

And now it would content me to yield up
Those lofty hopes awhile for present gifts
Of humbler industry. But, O dear Friend!
145 The Poet, gentle creature as he is,          [135]
Hath, like the Lover, his unruly times;
His fits when he is neither sick nor well,
Though no distress be near him but his own
Unmanageable thoughts. The mind itself
150 The meditative mind, best pleased, perhaps,          [140]
While she, as duteous as the Mother Dove,
Sits brooding, lives not always to that end,
But hath less quiet instincts, goadings on
That drive her as in trouble through the groves.
155 With me is now such passion, which I blame
No otherwise than as it lasts too long.          [145]

When, as becomes a man who would prepare
For such a glorious work, I through myself
Make rigorous inquisition, the report
160 Is often chearing; for I neither seem
To lack, that first great gift! the vital soul,          [150]
Nor general truths which are themselves a sort
Of Elements and Agents, Under-Powers,
Subordinate helpers of the living mind.
165 Nor am I naked in external things,
Forms, images; nor numerous other aids          [155]
Of less regard, though won perhaps with toil,
And needful to build up a Poet's praise.
Time, place, and manners; these I seek, and these

I might endue some airy phantasies                                    120
That had been floating loose about for years,
And to such beings temperately deal forth
The many feelings that oppressed my heart.
That hope hath been discouraged; welcome light
Dawns from the east, but dawns to disappear                           125
And mock me with a sky that ripens not
Into a steady morning: if my mind,
Remembering the bold promise of the past,
Would gladly grapple with some noble theme,
Vain is her wish; where'er she turns she finds                        130
Impediments from day to day renewed.

    And now it would content me to yield up
Those lofty hopes awhile, for present gifts
Of humbler industry. But, oh, dear Friend!
The Poet, gentle creature as he is,                                   135
Hath, like the Lover, his unruly times;
His fits when he is neither sick nor well,
Though no distress be near him but his own
Unmanageable thoughts: his mind, best pleased
While she as duteous as the mother dove                               140
Sits brooding, lives not always to that end,
But like the innocent bird, hath goadings on
That drive her as in trouble through the groves;
With me is now such passion, to be blamed
No otherwise than as it lasts too long.                               145

    When, as becomes a man who would prepare
For such an arduous work, I through myself
Make rigorous inquisition, the report
Is often cheering; for I neither seem
To lack that first great gift, the vital soul,                        150
Nor general Truths, which are themselves a sort
Of Elements and Agents, Under-powers,
Subordinate helpers of the living mind:
Nor am I naked of external things,
Forms, images, nor numerous other aids                               155
Of less regard, though won perhaps with toil
And needful to build up a Poet's praise.
Time, place, and manners do I seek, and these

149, 153 𝔄 C D: D² *as* 1850.　　　160 chearing] friendly  M.

170  I find in plenteous store; but nowhere such
     As may be singled out with steady choice;                    [160]
     No little Band of yet remember'd names
     Whom I, in perfect confidence, might hope
     To summon back from lonesome banishment
175  And make them inmates in the hearts of men
     Now living, or to live in times to come.                    [165]
     Sometimes, mistaking vainly, as I fear,
     Proud spring-tide swellings for a regular sea,
     I settle on some British theme, some old
180  Romantic tale, by Milton left unsung;
     More often resting at some gentle place                    [170]
     Within the groves of Chivalry, I pipe
     Among the Shepherds, with reposing Knights
     Sit by a Fountain-side, and hear their tales.
185  Sometimes, more sternly mov'd, I would relate
     How vanquish'd Mithridates northward pass'd,
     And, hidden in the cloud of years, became
     That Odin, Father of a Race, by whom
     Perish'd the Roman Empire: how the Friends                    [190]
190  And Followers of Sertorius, out of Spain
     Flying, found shelter in the Fortunate Isles;
     And left their usages, their arts, and laws,
     To disappear by a slow gradual death;
     To dwindle and to perish one by one                    [195]
195  Starved in those narrow bounds: but not the Soul
     Of Liberty, which fifteen hundred years

170 store] growth M.        171 As I can single out  M.
175 inmates 𝔄 C D: D² *as* 1850.
177 Sometimes the Power of choice mistaking vainly  D: D² *as* 1850.
181 resting at 𝔄 C D E: E² *as* 1850.
184                    and hear their Tales
          Of hard adventures brought to happy end
          And recompensed by faithful Lady's love. B (*added later*).
[173–85] D *stuck over*:
          Among the shepherds, mid reposing knights
          Sit by a fountain, then with eager hand
          Seizing the harp involve within a song
          Of war, or dangerous quest with spear and shield,
          Their Christian meekness and their patient zeal
          Their firm devotion to the God of Heaven
          'Their courteous courage and their loyal loves' D².
     *So* D³ E (*but* their undaunted truth *for* to the God of Heaven).
          To shepherd swains or seated harp in hand
          By a clear fountain mid reposing knights

Are found in plenteous store, but nowhere such
As may be singled out with steady choice;                160
No little band of yet remembered names
Whom I, in perfect confidence, might hope
To summon back from lonesome banishment,
And make them dwellers in the hearts of men
Now living, or to live in future years.                  165
Sometimes the ambitious Power of choice, mistaking
Proud spring-tide swellings for a regular sea,
Will settle on some British theme, some old
Romantic tale by Milton left unsung;
More often turning to some gentle place                  170
Within the groves of Chivalry, I pipe
To shepherd swains, or seated harp in hand,
Amid reposing knights by a river side
Or fountain, listen to the grave reports
Of dire enchantments faced and overcome                  175
By the strong mind, and tales of warlike feats,
Where spear encountered spear, and sword with sword
Fought, as if conscious of the blazonry
That the shield bore, so glorious was the strife;
Whence inspiration for a song that winds                 180
Through ever changing scenes of votive quest
Wrongs to redress, harmonious tribute paid
To patient courage and unblemished truth,
To firm devotion, zeal unquenchable,
And Christian meekness hallowing faithful loves.         185
Sometimes, more sternly moved, I would relate
How vanquished Mithridates northward passed,
And, hidden in the cloud of years, became
Odin, the Father of a race by whom
Perished the Roman Empire: how the friends               190
And followers of Sertorius, out of Spain
Flying, found shelter in the Fortunate Isles,
And left their usages, their arts and laws,
To disappear by a slow gradual death,
To dwindle and to perish one by one,                     195
Starved in those narrow bounds: but not the soul
Of Liberty, which fifteen hundred years

Their converse share and hear their sage reports
Of dire *etc.*  E²: E³ *as* 1850.
  In [181] E *has* Through ever varying scenes of perilous quest, *and in*
183] dauntless *for* patient: E² *as* 1850.

Surviv'd, and, when the European came
With skill and power that could not be withstood,
Did, like a pestilence, maintain its hold,                    [200]
200  And wasted down by glorious death that Race
Of natural Heroes: or I would record
How in tyrannic times some unknown Man,
Unheard of in the Chronicles of Kings,
Suffer'd in silence for the love of truth;                    [205]
205  How that one Frenchman, through continued force
Of meditation on the inhuman deeds
Of the first Conquerors of the Indian Isles,
Went single in his ministry across
The Ocean, not to comfort the Oppress'd,                      [210]
210  But, like a thirsty wind, to roam about,
Withering the Oppressor: how Gustavus found
Help at his need in Dalecarlia's Mines:
How Wallace fought for Scotland, left the name
Of Wallace to be found like a wild flower,                    [215]
215  All over his dear Country, left the deeds
Of Wallace, like a family of Ghosts,
To people the steep rocks and river banks,
Her natural sanctuaries, with a local soul
Of independence and stern liberty.                            [220]
220  Sometimes it suits me better to shape out
Some Tale from my own heart, more near akin
To my own passions and habitual thoughts,
Some variegated story, in the main
Lofty, with interchange of gentler things.                    [225]
225  But deadening admonitions will succeed
And the whole beauteous Fabric seems to lack
Foundation, and, withal, appears throughout
Shadowy and unsubstantial. Then, last wish,
My last and favourite aspiration! then
230  I yearn towards some philosophic Song
Of Truth that cherishes our daily life;                       [230]
With meditations passionate from deep
Recesses in man's heart, immortal verse
Thoughtfully fitted to the Orphean lyre;
235  But from this awful burthen I full soon
Take refuge, and beguile myself with trust                    [235]

203–6 𝔄 C D: D² *as* 1850.        205 Frenchman] Spaniard M.
212, 220 𝔄 C D: D² *as* 1850.     218 Their natural M.

Survived, and, when the European came
With skill and power that might not be withstood,
Did, like a pestilence, maintain its hold                        200
And wasted down by glorious death that race
Of natural heroes: or I would record
How, in tyrannic times, some high-souled man,
Unnamed among the chronicles of kings,
Suffered in silence for Truth's sake: or tell,                   205
How that one Frenchman, through continued force
Of meditation on the inhuman deeds
Of those who conquered first the Indian Isles,
Went single in his ministry across
The Ocean; not to comfort the oppressed,                         210
But, like a thirsty wind, to roam about
Withering the Oppressor: how Gustavus sought
Help at his need in Dalecarlia's mines;
How Wallace fought for Scotland; left the name
Of Wallace to be found, like a wild flower,                      215
All over his dear Country; left the deeds
Of Wallace, like a family of Ghosts,
To people the steep rocks and river banks,
Her natural sanctuaries, with a local soul
Of independence and stern liberty.                               220
Sometimes it suits me better to invent
A tale from my own heart, more near akin
To my own passions and habitual thoughts;
Some variegated story, in the main
Lofty, but the unsubstantial structure melts                     225
Before the very sun that brightens it,
Mist into air dissolving! Then a wish,
My best and favourite aspiration, mounts
With yearning toward some philosophic song
Of Truth that cherishes our daily life;                          230
With meditations passionate from deep
Recesses in man's heart, immortal verse
Thoughtfully fitted to the Orphean lyre;
But from this awful burthen I full soon
Take refuge and beguile myself with trust                        235

224-30 𝔄 C D: Lofty, but deadening admonitions lurk
              Near, and full soon the rising Fabric seems
                To lack foundation and appears throughout *etc. as* A, D²:
                D³ *as* 1850.

That mellower years will bring a riper mind
And clearer insight. Thus from day to day
I live, a mockery of the brotherhood
240 Of vice and virtue, with no skill to part
Vague longing that is bred by want of power
From paramount impulse not to be withstood,                    [240]
A timorous capacity from prudence;
From circumspection, infinite delay.
245 Humility and modest awe themselves
Betray me, serving often for a cloak
To a more subtle selfishness, that now                    [245]
Doth lock my functions up in blank reserve,
Now dupes me by an over-anxious eye
250 That with a false activity beats off
Simplicity and self-presented truth.
—Ah! better far than this, to stray about                    [250]
Voluptuously through fields and rural walks,
And ask no record of the hours, given up
255 To vacant musing, unreprov'd neglect
Of all things, and deliberate holiday;
Far better never to have heard the name                    [255]
Of zeal and just ambition, than to live
Thus baffled by a mind that every hour
260 Turns recreant to her task, takes heart again,
Then feels immediately some hollow thought
Hang like an interdict upon her hopes.                    [260]
This is my lot; for either still I find
Some imperfection in the chosen theme,
265 Or see of absolute accomplishment
Much wanting, so much wanting, in myself,
That I recoil and droop, and seek repose                    [265]
In listlessness from vain perplexity,
Unprofitably travelling towards the grave,
270 Like a false Steward who hath much received
And renders nothing back.—Was it for this
That one, the fairest of all Rivers, lov'd                    [270]
To blend his murmurs with my Nurse's song,
And from his alder shades and rocky falls,
275 And from his fords and shallows, sent a voice
That flow'd along my dreams? For this, didst Thou,
O Derwent! travelling over the green Plains                    [275]

241 that is 𝔄 C D: D² *as* 1850.    248–50, 254, 259 𝔄 C D: D² *as* 1850.

That mellower years will bring a riper mind
And clearer insight. Thus my days are past
In contradiction; with no skill to part
Vague longing, haply bred by want of power,
From paramount impulse not to be withstood,                240
A timorous capacity from prudence,
From circumspection, infinite delay.
Humility and modest awe themselves
Betray me, serving often for a cloak
To a more subtle selfishness; that now                     245
Locks every function up in blank reserve,
Now dupes me, trusting to an anxious eye
That with intrusive restlessness beats off
Simplicity and self-presented truth.
Ah! better far than this, to stray about                   250
Voluptuously through fields and rural walks,
And ask no record of the hours, resigned
To vacant musing, unreproved neglect
Of all things, and deliberate holiday.
Far better never to have heard the name                    255
Of zeal and just ambition, than to live
Baffled and plagued by a mind that every hour
Turns recreant to her task; takes heart again,
Then feels immediately some hollow thought
Hang like an interdict upon her hopes.                      260
This is my lot; for either still I find
Some imperfection in the chosen theme,
Or see of absolute accomplishment
Much wanting, so much wanting, in myself,
That I recoil and droop, and seek repose                   265
In listlessness from vain perplexity,
Unprofitably travelling toward the grave,
Like a false steward who hath much received
And renders nothing back.
                         Was it for this
That one, the fairest of all rivers, loved                 270
To blend his murmurs with my nurse's song,
And, from his alder shades and rocky falls,
And from his fords and shallows, sent a voice
That flowed along my dreams? For this, didst thou,
O Derwent! winding among grassy holms                      275

268 listlessness] indolence M.
276 That flow'd along] To intertwine JJ *Chr.*

Near my 'sweet Birthplace', didst thou, beauteous Stream,
Make ceaseless music through the night and day
280  Which with its steady cadence, tempering
Our human waywardness, compos'd my thoughts
To more than infant softness, giving me,
Among the fretful dwellings of mankind,
A knowledge, a dim earnest, of the calm
285  That Nature breathes among the hills and groves.        [281]
When, having left his Mountains, to the Towers
Of Cockermouth that beauteous River came,
Behind my Father's House he pass'd, close by,
Along the margin of our Terrace Walk.        [286]
290  He was a Playmate whom we dearly lov'd.
Oh! many a time have I, a five years' Child,
A naked Boy, in one delightful Rill,
A little Mill-race sever'd from his stream,
Made one long bathing of a summer's day,        [290]
295  Bask'd in the sun, and plunged, and bask'd again
Alternate all a summer's day, or cours'd
Over the sandy fields, leaping through groves
Of yellow grunsel, or when crag and hill,
The woods, and distant Skiddaw's lofty height,        [295]
300  Were bronz'd with a deep radiance, stood alone
Beneath the sky, as if I had been born
On Indian Plains, and from my Mother's hut
Had run abroad in wantonness, to sport,
A naked Savage, in the thunder shower.        [300]

305  Fair seed-time had my soul, and I grew up
Foster'd alike by beauty and by fear;
Much favor'd in my birthplace, and no less
In that beloved Vale to which, erelong,
I was transplanted. Well I call to mind        [305]
310  ('Twas at an early age, ere I had seen
Nine summers) when upon the mountain slope

279 Make ceaseless] Murmur perpetual JJ *Chr.*
279–81 𝔄 C D: D² *as* 1850.
284 knowledge 𝔄 V M C D: foretaste D² E.
285 hills] fields V M: among her woodland haunts JJ *Chr.*
286–90 D *stuck over*:
  When he had scarcely left those Norman towers
  That yet survive, a shattered Monument
  Of feudal pomp and power, the River passed *etc.* D²: D³ *as* 1850.
286–93 *not in* V, which *reads*:

Where I was looking on, a babe in arms,
Make ceaseless music that composed my thoughts
To more than infant softness, giving me
Amid the fretful dwellings of mankind
A foretaste, a dim earnest, of the calm             280
That Nature breathes among the hills and groves.
When he had left the mountains and received
On his smooth breast the shadow of those towers
That yet survive, a shattered monument
Of feudal sway, the bright blue river passed        285
Along the margin of our terrace walk;
A tempting playmate whom we dearly loved.
Oh, many a time have I, a five years' child,
In a small mill-race severed from his stream,
Made one long bathing of a summer's day;            290
Basked in the sun, and plunged and basked again
Alternate, all a summer's day, or scoured
The sandy fields, leaping through flowery groves
Of yellow ragwort; or when rock and hill,
The woods, and distant Skiddaw's lofty height,      295
Were bronzed with deepest radiance, stood alone
Beneath the sky, as if I had been born
On Indian plains, and from my mother's hut
Had run abroad in wantonness, to sport
A naked savage, in the thunder shower.              300

   Fair seed-time had my soul, and I grew up
Fostered alike by beauty and by fear:
Much favoured in my birth-place, and no less
In that beloved Vale to which erelong
We were transplanted—there were we let loose        305
For sports of wider range. Ere I had told
Ten birth-days, when among the mountain slopes

   Beloved Derwent, fairest of all streams,
   Was it for this that I, a four years child,
   A naked Boy among thy silent pools
289 Chafing his waves against our terrace walk M.
295 and plunged, *etc.*] or plunged into thy stream *Chr.* V.
297 leaping through groves] and dashed the flowers *Chr.* V.
298 crag 𝔄 C D: rock D².
299. The woods and all the distant mountain tops *Chr.*
304. Savage 𝔄 JJ U: Infant V M.   305–11 *Not in* V, *which reads*:
   Nor without kindred self reproach can I
   Recall to mind how in a later day
   Though early, when upon the mountain slope

The frost and breath of frosty wind had snapp'd
The last autumnal crocus, 'twas my joy
To wander half the night among the Cliffs
315 And the smooth Hollows, where the woodcocks ran
Along the open turf. In thought and wish
That time, my shoulder all with springes hung,                [310]
I was a fell destroyer. On the heights
Scudding away from snare to snare, I plied
320 My anxious visitation, hurrying on,
Still hurrying, hurrying onward; moon and stars
Were shining o'er my head; I was alone,                       [315]
And seem'd to be a trouble to the peace
That was among them. Sometimes it befel
325 In these night-wanderings, that a strong desire
O'erpower'd my better reason, and the bird
Which was the captive of another's toils                      [320]
Became my prey; and, when the deed was done
I heard among the solitary hills
330 Low breathings coming after me, and sounds
Of undistinguishable motion, steps
Almost as silent as the turf they trod.                       [325]
Nor less in springtime when on southern banks
The shining sun had from his knot of leaves
335 Decoy'd the primrose flower, and when the Vales
And woods were warm, was I a plunderer then
In the high places, on the lonesome peaks
Where'er, among the mountains and the winds,
The Mother Bird had built her lodge. Though mean
340 My object, and inglorious, yet the end
Was not ignoble. Oh! when I have hung                         [330]
Above the raven's nest, by knots of grass
And half-inch fissures in the slippery rock
But ill sustain'd, and almost, as it seem'd,
345 Suspended by the blast which blew amain,
Shouldering the naked crag; Oh! at that time,                 [335]
While on the perilous ridge I hung alone,
With what strange utterance did the loud dry wind

313–16 [309–12] D *stuck over*:      'twas my joy
                When the full moon shone brightly, to go forth
                With store *etc. as* 1850.
                And range the mountain heights *etc.*
                Along the *etc. as* 1850. D².

Frost, and the breath of frosty wind, had snapped
The last autumnal crocus, 'twas my joy
With store of springes o'er my shoulder hung                    310
To range the open heights where woodcocks run
Along the smooth green turf. Through half the night,
Scudding away from snare to snare, I plied
That anxious visitation;—moon and stars
Were shining o'er my head. I was alone,                          315
And seemed to be a trouble to the peace
That dwelt among them. Sometimes it befel
In these night wanderings, that a strong desire
O'erpowered my better reason, and the bird
Which was the captive of another's toil                         320
Became my prey; and when the deed was done
I heard among the solitary hills
Low breathings coming after me, and sounds
Of undistinguishable motion, steps
Almost as silent as the turf they trod.                         325
   Nor less when spring had warmed the cultured Vale,
Moved we as plunderers where the mother-bird
Had in high places built her lodge; though mean
Our object and inglorious, yet the end
Was not ignoble. Oh! when I have hung                           330
Above the raven's nest, by knots of grass
And half-inch fissures in the slippery rock
But ill sustained, and almost (so it seemed)
Suspended by the blast that blew amain,
Shouldering the naked crag, oh, at that time                    335
While on the perilous ridge I hung alone,
With what strange utterance did the loud dry wind

316 open 𝔄: moonlight  JJ V.
318–19    On the heights Scudding away] Gentle Powers
        Who give us happiness and call it peace.
        When scudding on  U: V (*deleted*).
321–6                onward, how my heart
    Panted among the scattered yew-trees and the crags
    That looked upon me how my bosom beat
    With expectation sometimes strong desire,
    Resistless overcame me and the bird U V.
336 Was I a plunderer V², 𝔄 C D: Roved we as plunderers D² E. *For*
plunderer V *has* rover.
338–40 Where'er . . . end]
    Among the mountains and the winds. Though mean
    And though inglorious were my views, the end V (*deleted*).
343 And 𝔄: Or V M.

Blow through my ears! the sky seem'd not a sky
350 Of earth, and with what motion mov'd the clouds!
The mind of man is fram'd even like the breath
And harmony of music. There is a dark                    [341]
Invisible workmanship that reconciles
Discordant elements, and makes them move
355 In one society. Ah me! that all
The terrors, all the early miseries                       [345]
Regrets, vexations, lassitudes, that all
The thoughts and feelings which have been infus'd
Into my mind, should ever have made up
360 The calm existence that is mine when I
Am worthy of myself! Praise to the end!                  [350]
Thanks likewise for the means! But I believe
That Nature, oftentimes, when she would frame
A favor'd Being, from his earliest dawn
365 Of infancy doth open out the clouds,
As at the touch of lightning, seeking him
With gentlest visitation; not the less,
Though haply aiming at the self-same end,
Does it delight her sometimes to employ
370 Severer interventions, ministry                       [355]
More palpable, and so she dealt with me.

One evening (surely I was led by her)
I went alone into a Shepherd's Boat,
A Skiff that to a Willow tree was tied
375 Within a rocky Cave, its usual home.
'Twas by the shores of Patterdale, a Vale
Wherein I was a Stranger, thither come
A School-boy Traveller, at the Holidays.
Forth rambled from the Village Inn alone
380 No sooner had I sight of this small Skiff,
Discover'd thus by unexpected chance,
Than I unloos'd her tether and embark'd.                  [360]

351–72   The mind of man is fashioned and built up
         Even as a strain of music: I believe
         That there are Spirits which, when they would form
         A favored being, from his very dawn
         Of infancy do open out the clouds
         As at the touch of lightning, seeking him
         With gentle visitation, quiet Powers!
         Retired and seldom recognized, yet kind

Blow through my ear! the sky seemed not a sky
Of earth—and with what motion moved the clouds!

Dust as we are, the immortal spirit grows                    340
Like harmony in music; there is a dark
Inscrutable workmanship that reconciles
Discordant elements, makes them cling together
In one society. How strange that all
The terrors, pains, and early miseries,                      345
Regrets, vexations, lassitudes interfused
Within my mind, should e'er have borne a part,
And that a needful part, in making up
The calm existence that is mine when I
Am worthy of myself! Praise to the end!                      350
Thanks to the means which Nature deigned to employ;
Whether her fearless visitings, or those
That came with soft alarm, like hurtless light
Opening the peaceful clouds; or she may use
Severer interventions, ministry                              355
More palpable, as best might suit her aim.

One summer evening (led by her) I found
A little boat tied to a willow tree
Within a rocky cave, its usual home.
Straight I unloosed her chain, and stepping in              360

And to the very meanest not unknown.
With me though rarely in my boyish days
They communed; others too there are who use
Yet haply aiming at the self-same end
Severer interventions, ministry
More palpable, and of their school was I.
They guided me: one evening led by them  V.
351–4 ... elements] D *as* 1850; 354–62 D as 𝔄, *followed by*
That Nature sometimes when her love would frame
A being destined for no common tasks
A favoured Being from his earliest dawn
Of life is prompt to open out the clouds  D² *as* 1850.
354–60 𝔄 C D (*but* D *has* life *for* mind): D² *as* 1850.
356–7 The medley of aversions and desires  V.
364 earliest day  U.
366–71 D *as* A, *followed by* A Pupil needing various discipline.
372–4, 380–4 D *as* A: D² *as* 1850.
376–82 *Not in* V (*text*), *but* 376–7 *added to* V *on separate page, and for*
377–82:       Where I was as a stranger thither come
              By chance in travel to my father's house:
              I from the village Inn had wander'd forth
              And finding this small vessel in its cave
              I had embarked without the owner's leave.  V².

The moon was up, the Lake was shining clear
Among the hoary mountains; from the Shore
385 I push'd, and struck the oars and struck again
In cadence, and my little Boat mov'd on
Even like a Man who walks with stately step
Though bent on speed. It was an act of stealth          [361]
And troubled pleasure; not without the voice
390 Of mountain-echoes did my Boat move on,
Leaving behind her still on either side
Small circles glittering idly in the moon,              [365]
Until they melted all into one track
Of sparkling light. A rocky Steep uprose
395 Above the Cavern of the Willow tree
And now, as suited one who proudly row'd
With his best skill, I fix'd a steady view
Upon the top of that same craggy ridge,                [370]
The bound of the horizon, for behind
400 Was nothing but the stars and the grey sky.
She was an elfin Pinnace; lustily
I dipp'd my oars into the silent Lake,
And, as I rose upon the stroke, my Boat
Went heaving through the water, like a Swan;           [375]
405 When from behind that craggy Steep, till then
The bound of the horizon, a huge Cliff,
As if with voluntary power instinct,
Uprear'd its head. I struck, and struck again,        [380]
And, growing still in stature, the huge Cliff
410 Rose up between me and the stars, and still,
With measur'd motion, like a living thing,
Strode after me. With trembling hands I turn'd,       [385]
And through the silent water stole my way
Back to the Cavern of the Willow tree.
415 There, in her mooring-place, I left my Bark,
And, through the meadows homeward went, with grave
And serious thoughts; and after I had seen            [390]
That spectacle, for many days, my brain
Work'd with a dim and undetermin'd sense
420 Of unknown modes of being; in my thoughts
There was a darkness, call it solitude,
Or blank desertion, no familiar shapes                [395]
Of hourly objects, images of trees,

387 Even like] Just like V: Even as V² M.

Pushed from the shore. It was an act of stealth
And troubled pleasure, nor without the voice
Of mountain-echoes did my boat move on;
Leaving behind her still, on either side,
Small circles glittering idly in the moon,                  365
Until they melted all into one track
Of sparkling light. But now, like one who rows,
Proud of his skill, to reach a chosen point
With an unswerving line, I fixed my view
Upon the summit of a craggy ridge,                          370
The horizon's utmost boundary; far above
Was nothing but the stars and the grey sky.
She was an elfin pinnace; lustily
I dipped my oars into the silent lake,
And, as I rose upon the stroke, my boat                     375
Went heaving through the water like a swan;
When, from behind that craggy steep till then
The horizon's bound, a huge peak, black and huge,
As if with voluntary power instinct.
Upreared its head. I struck and struck again,               380
And growing still in stature the grim shape
Towered up between me and the stars, and still,
For so it seemed, with purpose of its own
And measured motion like a living thing,
Strode after me. With trembling oars I turned,              385
And through the silent water stole my way
Back to the covert of the willow tree;
There in her mooring-place I left my bark,—
And through the meadows homeward went, in grave
And serious mood; but after I had seen                      390
That spectacle, for many days, my brain
Worked with a dim and undetermined sense
Of unknown modes of being; o'er my thoughts
There hung a darkness, call it solitude
Or blank desertion. No familiar shapes                      395
Remained, no pleasant images of trees,

394–407 D *stuck over*: D², *after correction, as* 1850.
399 for 𝔄 C D: far E.          401 lustily] twenty times V.
405 craggy 𝔄] rocky *Letter* V M.          407–9 *not in* B.
[381] grim D² E: huge D.
412 hands 𝔄 C D E : oars E².          414 cavern 𝔄 C D: covert D².
416 homeward *not in* B.          417, 423 𝔄 C D : D² *as* 1850.
420–1 in . . . was 𝔄 D E: o'er . . . hung E².

Of sea or sky, no colours of green fields;
425 But huge and mighty Forms that do not live
Like living men mov'd slowly through my mind
By day and were the trouble of my dreams.                    [400]

Wisdom and Spirit of the universe!
Thou Soul that art the Eternity of Thought!
430 That giv'st to forms and images a breath
And everlasting motion! not in vain,
By day or star-light thus from my first dawn               [405]
Of Childhood didst Thou intertwine for me
The passions that build up our human Soul,
435 Not with the mean and vulgar works of Man,
But with high objects, with enduring things,
With life and nature, purifying thus                        [410]
The elements of feeling and of thought,
And sanctifying, by such discipline,
440 Both pain and fear, until we recognize
A grandeur in the beatings of the heart.

Nor was this fellowship vouchsaf'd to me                    [415]
With stinted kindness. In November days,
When vapours, rolling down the valleys, made
445 A lonely scene more lonesome; among woods
At noon, and 'mid the calm of summer nights,
When, by the margin of the trembling Lake,                  [420]
Beneath the gloomy hills I homeward went
In solitude, such intercourse was mine;
450 'Twas mine among the fields both day and night,
And by the waters all the summer long.

And in the frosty season, when the sun                      [425]
Was set, and visible for many a mile
The cottage windows through the twilight blaz'd,
455 I heeded not the summons:—happy time
It was, indeed, for all of us; to me
It was a time of rapture: clear and loud                    [430]
The village clock toll'd six; I wheel'd about,
Proud and exulting, like an untired horse,
460 That cares not for its home.—All shod with steel,

426 my mind 𝔄 V MC: D E *as* 1850.
428-33            Ah! not in vain, ye Beings of the hills,
                  And ye that walk the woods and open heaths

Of sea or sky, no colours of green fields;
But huge and mighty forms, that do not live
Like living men, moved slowly through the mind
By day, and were a trouble to my dreams.                    400

    Wisdom and Spirit of the universe!
Thou Soul that art the eternity of thought,
That givest to forms and images a breath
And everlasting motion, not in vain
By day or star-light thus from my first dawn                405
Of childhood didst thou intertwine for me
The passions that build up our human soul;
Not with the mean and vulgar works of man,
But with high objects, with enduring things—
With life and nature, purifying thus                        410
The elements of feeling and of thought,
And sanctifying, by such discipline,
Both pain and fear, until we recognise
A grandeur in the beatings of the heart.
Nor was this fellowship vouchsafed to me                    415
With stinted kindness. In November days,
When vapours rolling down the valley made
A lonely scene more lonesome, among woods,
At noon and 'mid the calm of summer nights,
When, by the margin of the trembling lake,                  420
Beneath the gloomy hills homeward I went
In solitude, such intercourse was mine;
Mine was it in the fields both day and night,
And by the waters, all the summer long.

    And in the frosty season, when the sun            425
Was set, and visible for many a mile
The cottage windows blazed through twilight gloom,
I heeded not their summons: happy time
It was indeed for all of us—for me
It was a time of rapture! Clear and loud                    430
The village clock tolled six,—I wheeled about,
Proud and exulting like an untired horse
That cares not for his home. All shod with steel,

        By moon or starlight, thus from my first dawn
        Of childhood, did ye love to intertwine  V.
**436** enduring] eternal  V M.
**454, 464, 467, 469** 𝔄 C D: D² *as* 1850.
**455-7** happy . . . rapture] *added to* V.

We hiss'd along the polish'd ice, in games
Confederate, imitative of the chace                    [435]
And woodland pleasures, the resounding horn,
The Pack loud bellowing, and the hunted hare.
465 So through the darkness and the cold we flew,
And not a voice was idle; with the din,
Meanwhile, the precipices rang aloud,                    [440]
The leafless trees, and every icy crag
Tinkled like iron, while the distant hills
470 Into the tumult sent an alien sound
Of melancholy, not unnoticed, while the stars,
Eastward, were sparkling clear, and in the west                    [445]
The orange sky of evening died away.

Not seldom from the uproar I retired
475 Into a silent bay, or sportively
Glanced sideway, leaving the tumultuous throng,
To cut across the image of a star                    [450]
That gleam'd upon the ice: and oftentimes
When we had given our bodies to the wind,
480 And all the shadowy banks, on either side,
Came sweeping through the darkness, spinning still                    [455]
The rapid line of motion; then at once
Have I, reclining back upon my heels,
Stopp'd short, yet still the solitary Cliffs
485 Wheeled by me, even as if the earth had roll'd
With visible motion her diurnal round;                    [460]
Behind me did they stretch in solemn train
Feebler and feebler, and I stood and watch'd
Till all was tranquil as a dreamless sleep.

490      Ye Presences of Nature, in the sky
Or on the earth! Ye Visions of the hills!                    [465]
And Souls of lonely places! can I think
A vulgar hope was yours when Ye employ'd
Such ministry, when Ye through many a year

477 image  M 𝕬: shadow *Letter* 18a V.
478 [451] Image that flying still before me gleamed  D E: E² *as* 1850.
489 dreamless sleep] summer sea *Letter to S. T. C. Chr.* 18a V M *Friend*;
    B *leaves blank space.*
490-2   Ye Powers of earth, ye genii of the Springs
        And ye that have your voices in the clouds
        And ye that are familiars of the Lakes
        And standing pools, Ah, not for trivial ends
        Through snow and sunshine, through the sparkling plains

We hissed along the polished ice in games
Confederate, imitative of the chase                              435
And woodland pleasures,—the resounding horn,
The pack loud chiming, and the hunted hare.
So through the darkness and the cold we flew,
And not a voice was idle; with the din
Smitten, the precipices rang aloud;                             440
The leafless trees and every icy crag
Tinkled like iron; while far distant hills
Into the tumult sent an alien sound
Of melancholy not unnoticed, while the stars
Eastward were sparkling clear, and in the west              445
The orange sky of evening died away.
Not seldom from the uproar I retired
Into a silent bay, or sportively
Glanced sideway, leaving the tumultuous throng,
To cut across the reflex of a star                              450
That fled, and, flying still before me, gleamed
Upon the glassy plain; and oftentimes,
When we had given our bodies to the wind,
And all the shadowy banks on either side
Came sweeping through the darkness, spinning still          455
The rapid line of motion, then at once
Have I, reclining back upon my heels,
Stopped short; yet still the solitary cliffs
Wheeled by me—even as if the earth had rolled
With visible motion her diurnal round!                         460
Behind me did they stretch in solemn train,
Feebler and feebler, and I stood and watched
Till all was tranquil as a dreamless sleep.

Ye Presences of Nature in the sky
And on the earth! Ye Visions of the hills!                     465
And Souls of lonely places! can I think
A vulgar hope was yours when ye employed
Such ministry, when ye through many a year

Of moonlight frost and in the stormy day
Did ye with such assiduous love pursue
Your favorite and your joy. I may not think V.
*but the whole passage corr. to*
Ye winds ye voices that are in the clouds
Ye visions of the mountains and ye Souls
Of lonely places never may I think *Not in* U. *Blank space left.*

495  Haunting me thus among my boyish sports,
     On caves and trees, upon the woods and hills,                    [470]
     Impress'd upon all forms the characters
     Of danger or desire, and thus did make
     The surface of the universal earth
500  With triumph, and delight, and hope, and fear,
     Work like a sea?                                                 [475]
                    Not uselessly employ'd,
     I might pursue this theme through every change
     Of exercise and play, to which the year
     Did summon us in its delightful round.

505      We were a noisy crew, the sun in heaven
     Beheld not vales more beautiful than ours,                       [480]
     Nor saw a race in happiness and joy
     More worthy of the ground where they were sown.
     I would record with no reluctant voice
510  The woods of autumn and their hazel bowers
     With milk-white clusters hung; the rod and line,                 [485]
     True symbol of the foolishness of hope,
     Which with its strong enchantment led us on
     By rocks and pools, shut out from every star
515  All the green summer, to forlorn cascades
     Among the windings of the mountain brooks.                       [490]
     —Unfading recollections! at this hour
     The heart is almost mine with which I felt
     From some hill-top, on sunny afternoons
520  The Kite high up among the fleecy clouds
     Pull at its rein, like an impatient Courser,                     [495]
     Or, from the meadows sent on gusty days,
     Beheld her breast the wind, then suddenly
     Dash'd headlong; and rejected by the storm.

525      Ye lowly Cottages in which we dwelt,
     A ministration of your own was yours,                            [500]
     A sanctity, a safeguard, and a love!
     Can I forget you, being as ye were
     So beautiful among the pleasant fields

495      Thus by the agency of boyish sports  V: V² *as* 𝔄.
500      With meanings of delight, of hope and fear  V.
510 hazel 𝔄 V²: hidden  V M.        512, 513, 516 𝔄 C D:  D² *as* 1850.
514–15 shut . . . summer] where never summer star Impressed its shadow V.
517–19 *not in* V.

Haunting me thus among my boyish sports,
On caves and trees, upon the woods and hills,        470
Impressed upon all forms the characters
Of danger or desire; and thus did make
The surface of the universal earth
With triumph and delight, with hope and fear,
Work like a sea?        475
                    Not uselessly employed,
Might I pursue this theme through every change
Of exercise and play, to which the year
Did summon us in his delightful round.

We were a noisy crew; the sun in heaven
Beheld not vales more beautiful than ours;        480
Nor saw a band in happiness and joy
Richer, or worthier of the ground they trod.
I could record with no reluctant voice
The woods of autumn, and their hazel bowers
With milk-white clusters hung; the rod and line,        485
True symbol of hope's foolishness, whose strong
And unreproved enchantment led us on
By rocks and pools shut out from every star,
All the green summer, to forlorn cascades
Among the windings hid of mountain brook        490
—Unfading recollections! at this hour
The heart is almost mine with which I felt,
From some hill-top on sunny afternoons,
The paper kite high among fleecy clouds
Pull at her rein like an impetuous courser;        495
Or, from the meadows sent on gusty days,
Beheld her breast the wind, then suddenly
Dashed headlong, and rejected by the storm.

Ye lowly cottages wherein we dwelt,
A ministration of your own was yours;        500
Can I forget you, being as you were
So beautiful among the pleasant fields

520-3   The kite in sultry calms from some high hill
          Sent up, ascending thence till it was lost
          Among the fleecy clouds, in gusty days
          Launched from the lower grounds and suddenly V.
   524 V *introduces an episode here*: All these and more . . . *v.* p. 160 *infra,*
*app. crit.*
   527 safeguard] presence M. *This line deleted from* D.

530 In which ye stood ? Or can I here forget
    The plain and seemly countenance with which
    Ye dealt out your plain comforts ? Yet had ye          [505]
    Delights and exultations of your own.
    Eager and never weary we pursued
535 Our home amusements by the warm peat-fire
    At evening ; when with pencil and with slate,
    In square divisions parcell'd out, and all          [510]
    With crosses and with cyphers scribbled o'er,
    We schemed and puzzled, head opposed to head,
540 In strife too humble to be named in Verse.
    Or round the naked table, snow-white deal,
    Cherry or maple, sate in close array,          [515]
    And to the combat, Lu or Whist, led on
    A thick-ribbed Army ; not as in the world
545 Neglected and ungratefully thrown by
    Even for the very service they had wrought,
    But husbanded through many a long campaign.          [520]
    Uncouth assemblage was it, where no few
    Had changed their functions, some, plebeian cards,
550 Which Fate beyond the promise of their birth
    Had glorified, and call'd to represent
    The persons of departed Potentates.          [525]
    Oh! with what echoes on the Board they fell!
    Ironic Diamonds, Clubs, Hearts, Diamonds, Spades,
555 A congregation piteously akin.
    Cheap matter did they give to boyish wit,
    Those sooty knaves, precipitated down          [530]
    With scoffs and taunts, like Vulcan out of Heaven,
    The paramount Ace, a moon in her eclipse,
560 Queens, gleaming through their splendour's last decay,
    And Monarchs, surly at the wrongs sustain'd
    By royal visages. Meanwhile, abroad          [535]
    The heavy rain was falling, or the frost
    Raged bitterly, with keen and silent tooth,
565 And, interrupting oft the impassion'd game,
    From Esthwaite's neighbouring Lake the splitting ice,

533 Your own dear pastimes and your own delights  V.
536 and with ℥ C D: and smooth D².
543 Lu all MSS.: Loo 1850.
548 It was a motley host of which no few  M.
554–5    Ironic Diamonds, Clubs, Hearts, Spades, alike
        All furnish'd out in chimney-sweeper garb  M.

In which ye stood ? or can I here forget
The plain and seemly countenance with which
Ye dealt out your plain comforts ? Yet had ye     505
Delights and exultations of your own.
Eager and never weary we pursued
Our home-amusements by the warm peat-fire
At evening, when with pencil, and smooth slate
In square divisions parcelled out and all     510
With crosses and with cyphers scribbled o'er,
We schemed and puzzled, head opposed to head
In strife too humble to be named in verse:
Or round the naked table, snow-white deal,
Cherry or maple, sate in close array,     515
And to the combat, Loo or Whist, led on
A thick-ribbed army; not, as in the world,
Neglected and ungratefully thrown by
Even for the very service they had wrought,
But husbanded through many a long campaign.     520
Uncouth assemblage was it, where no few
Had changed their functions; some, plebeian cards
Which Fate, beyond the promise of their birth,
Had dignified, and called to represent
The persons of departed potentates.     525
Oh, with what echoes on the board they fell!
Ironic diamonds,—clubs, hearts, diamonds, spades,
A congregation piteously akin!
Cheap matter offered they to boyish wit,
Those sooty knaves, precipitated down     530
With scoffs and taunts, like Vulcan out of heaven:
The paramount ace, a moon in her eclipse,
Queens gleaming through their splendour's last decay,
And monarchs surly at the wrongs sustained
By royal visages. Meanwhile abroad     535
Incessant rain was falling, or the frost
Raged bitterly, with keen and silent tooth;
And, interrupting oft that eager game,
From under Esthwaite's splitting fields of ice

554 Ironic Diamonds, hearts of sable hue V: black funereal hearts V².
555–9 *not in* V.
561       Knaves wrapt in one assimilating gloom
         And Kings indignant at the shame incurr'd V.
563, 565 𝔄 C D: D² *as* 1850.
566–9 D *stuck over*: D² *as* 1850.

While it sank down towards the water, sent,
Among the meadows and the hills, its long　　　　　　[541]
And dismal yellings, like the noise of wolves
570　When they are howling round the Bothnic Main.

Nor, sedulous as I have been to trace
How Nature by extrinsic passion first　　　　　　[545]
Peopled my mind with beauteous forms or grand,
And made me love them, may I well forget
575　How other pleasures have been mine, and joys
Of subtler origin; how I have felt,
Not seldom, even in that tempestuous time,　　　　[550]
Those hallow'd and pure motions of the sense
Which seem, in their simplicity, to own
580　An intellectual charm, that calm delight
Which, if I err not, surely must belong
To those first-born affinities that fit　　　　　　[555]
Our new existence to existing things,
And, in our dawn of being, constitute
585　The bond of union betwixt life and joy.

Yes, I remember, when the changeful earth,
And twice five seasons on my mind had stamp'd　　[560]
The faces of the moving year, even then,
A Child, I held unconscious intercourse
590　With the eternal Beauty, drinking in
A pure organic pleasure from the lines
Of curling mist, or from the level plain　　　　　[565]
Of waters colour'd by the steady clouds.

The Sands of Westmoreland, the Creeks and Bays
595　Of Cumbria's rocky limits, they can tell
How when the Sea threw off his evening shade
And to the Shepherd's huts beneath the crags　　　[570]
Did send sweet notice of the rising moon,

569-70　　And frequent yellings imitative some
　　　　　　Of wolves that howl along the Bothnic Main.　V: V² *as* 𝔄.
　570　*In* B, *there follows*:
　　　　　　And sometimes not unlike the sound that issues
　　　　　　From out the deep chest of a lonely Bull
　　　　　　By no apparent enmity provoke(d)
　　　　　　To bend his head, and mutter with a tone
　　　　　　Sullenly answered by the hollow ground
　　　　　　So growled the frozen element, or yelled
　　　　　　Startling the valley and our bright fireside

The pent-up air, struggling to free itself,                       540
Gave out to meadow grounds and hills a loud
Protracted yelling, like the noise of wolves
Howling in troops along the Bothnic Main.

   Nor, sedulous as I have been to trace
How Nature by extrinsic passion first                             545
Peopled the mind with forms sublime or fair,
And made me love them, may I here omit
How other pleasures have been mine, and joys
Of subtler origin; how I have felt,
Not seldom even in that tempestuous time,                         550
Those hallowed and pure motions of the sense
Which seem, in their simplicity, to own
An intellectual charm; that calm delight
Which, if I err not, surely must belong
To those first-born affinities that fit                           555
Our new existence to existing things,
And, in our dawn of being, constitute
The bond of union between life and joy.

   Yes, I remember when the changeful earth,
And twice five summers on my mind had stamped                     560
The faces of the moving year, even then
I held unconscious intercourse with beauty
Old as creation, drinking in a pure
Organic pleasure from the silver wreaths
Of curling mist, or from the level plain                          565
Of waters coloured by impending clouds.

   The sands of Westmoreland, the creeks and bays
Of Cumbria's rocky limits, they can tell
How, when the Sea threw off his evening shade,
And to the shepherd's hut on distant hills                        570
Sent welcome notice of the rising moon,

*In* V *after 570 comes the line*:
        Nor with less willing heart would I rehearse
*followed by* 510–24 *and then by* Bk. V. 450–72, XI. 258–316, 345–89.
572–3     How Nature by collateral interest
         And by extrinsic passion peopled first
         My mind with forms or beautiful or grand V.
589, 591 𝔄 C D: D² *as* 1850.
597 huts] hut V M.
598 𝔄 C D: D² *as* 1850.

How I have stood, to fancies such as these,
600 Engrafted in the tenderness of thought,
A stranger, linking with the spectacle
No conscious memory of a kindred sight,
And bringing with me no peculiar sense                    [575]
Of quietness or peace, yet I have stood,
605 Even while mine eye has mov'd o'er three long leagues
Of shining water, gathering, as it seem'd,
Through every hair-breadth of that field of light,
New pleasure, like a bee among the flowers.               [580]

Thus, often in those fits of vulgar joy
610 Which, through all seasons, on a child's pursuits
Are prompt attendants, 'mid that giddy bliss
Which, like a tempest, works along the blood
And is forgotten; even then I felt                        [585]
Gleams like the flashing of a shield; the earth
615 And common face of Nature spake to me
Rememberable things; sometimes, 'tis true,
By chance collisions and quaint accidents
Like those ill-sorted unions, work suppos'd               [590]
Of evil-minded fairies, yet not vain
620 Nor profitless, if haply they impress'd
Collateral objects and appearances,
Albeit lifeless then, and doom'd to sleep
Until maturer seasons call'd them forth                   [595]
To impregnate and to elevate the mind.
625 —And if the vulgar joy by its own weight
Wearied itself out of the memory,
The scenes which were a witness of that joy
Remained, in their substantial lineaments                 [600]
Depicted on the brain, and to the eye
630 Were visible, a daily sight; and thus
By the impressive discipline of fear,
By pleasure and repeated happiness,
So frequently repeated, and by force                      [605]
Of obscure feelings representative
635 Of joys that were forgotten, these same scenes,
So beauteous and majestic in themselves,

599 fancies such as] images like V.          600 *not in* V *nor* JJ.
602 No body of associated forms V.          604 stood,] stood 𝔄.
607 every hair-breadth] the wide surface V.
609 𝔄 C D: D² *as* 1850.

How I have stood, to fancies such as these
A stranger, linking with the spectacle
No conscious memory of a kindred sight,
And bringing with me no peculiar sense                      575
Of quietness or peace; yet have I stood,
Even while mine eye hath moved o'er many a league
Of shining water, gathering as it seemed
Through every hair-breadth in that field of light
New pleasure like a bee among the flowers.                  580


    Thus oft amid those fits of vulgar joy
Which, through all seasons, on a child's pursuits
Are prompt attendants, 'mid that giddy bliss
Which, like a tempest, works along the blood
And is forgotten; even then I felt                          585
Gleams like the flashing of a shield;—the earth
And common face of Nature spake to me
Rememberable things; sometimes, 'tis true,
By chance collisions and quaint accidents
(Like those ill-sorted unions, work supposed               590
Of evil-minded fairies), yet not vain
Nor profitless, if haply they impressed
Collateral objects and appearances,
Albeit lifeless then, and doomed to sleep
Until maturer seasons called them forth                     595
To impregnate and to elevate the mind.
—And if the vulgar joy by its own weight
Wearied itself out of the memory,
The scenes which were a witness of that joy
Remained in their substantial lineaments                    600
Depicted on the brain, and to the eye
Were visible, a daily sight; and thus
By the impressive discipline of fear,
By pleasure and repeated happiness,
So frequently repeated, and by force                        605
Of obscure feelings representative
Of things forgotten, these same scenes so bright,
So beautiful, so majestic in themselves,

            617–20    By quaint associations, yet not vain
                        Nor profitless *etc.*  V.
        631 discipline] agency  V.

Though yet the day was distant, did at length
Become habitually dear, and all                            [610]
Their hues and forms were by invisible links
640 Allied to the affections.
                              I began
My story early, feeling as I fear,
The weakness of a human love, for days
Disown'd by memory, ere the birth of spring                [615]
Planting my snowdrops among winter snows.
645 Nor will it seem to thee, my Friend! so prompt
In sympathy, that I have lengthen'd out,
With fond and feeble tongue, a tedious tale.
Meanwhile, my hope has been that I might fetch            [620]
Invigorating thoughts from former years,
650 Might fix the wavering balance of my mind,
And haply meet reproaches, too, whose power
May spur me on, in manhood now mature,
To honorable toil. Yet should these hopes                  [625]
Be vain, and thus should neither I be taught
655 To understand myself, nor thou to know
With better knowledge how the heart was fram'd
Of him thou lovest, need I dread from thee
Harsh judgments, if I am so loth to quit                   [630]
Those recollected hours that have the charm
660 Of visionary things, and lovely forms
And sweet sensations that throw back our life
And almost make our Infancy itself
A visible scene, on which the sun is shining?              [635]

      One end hereby at least hath been attain'd,
665 My mind hath been revived, and if this mood
Desert me not, I will forthwith bring down,

637–43 𝔄 C D: D² E *as* 1850, *but in* 640 [612] Were tied and bound  to
the affections *and in* [613] hope *for* trust: [613] My story early I began not
misled I trust E² (*unmetrically*).
    643–4 [615–16]          ere the birth [birth *in all MSS.*] of spring
                Planting the flowers of spring mid winter snows  D² E.
    E *deletes and writes over the top*:
                          fancying flowers where none
              Not even the sweetest do or can survive
              For him at least whose dawning day they cheered.
    649–52   Reproaches from my former years, whose power
             May spur me on  V.
    650 *om.* B.

Though yet the day was distant, did become
Habitually dear, and all their forms                              610
And changeful colours by invisible links
Were fastened to the affections.
                                        I began
My story early—not misled, I trust,
By an infirmity of love for days
Disowned by memory—ere the breath of spring                       615
Planting my snowdrops among winter snows:
Nor will it seem to thee, O Friend! so prompt
In sympathy, that I have lengthened out
With fond and feeble tongue a tedious tale.
Meanwhile, my hope has been, that I might fetch                    620
Invigorating thoughts from former years;
Might fix the wavering balance of my mind,
And haply meet reproaches too, whose power
May spur me on, in manhood now mature,
To honourable toil. Yet should these hopes                        625
Prove vain, and thus should neither I be taught
To understand myself, nor thou to know
With better knowledge how the heart was framed
Of him thou lovest; need I dread from thee
Harsh judgments, if the song be loth to quit                      630
Those recollected hours that have the charm
Of visionary things, those lovely forms
And sweet sensations that throw back our life,
And almost make remotest infancy
A visible scene, on which the sun is shining?                     635

    One end at least hath been attained; my mind
Hath been revived, and if this genial mood
Desert me not, forthwith shall be brought down

653–4             Yet should it be
          That this is but an impotent desire
          That I by such inquiry am not taught  V.
662–3             And make our infancy a visible scene
          On which the sun is shining  V.
                    D *as* A:  D² *as* 1850.
[V *here goes on at* II. 55. *Two pages have been torn out.*]
663       On which the sun is shining? Here we pause
          Doubtful or lingering with a truant heart
          Slow and of stationary character
          Rarely adventurous, studious more of peace
          And soothing quiet which we here have found  18*a*.
666  A C D: D² *as* 1850.

Through later years, the story of my life.
The road lies plain before me; 'tis a theme          [640]
Single and of determined bounds; and hence
670 I chuse it rather at this time, than work
Of ampler or more varied argument.

[644–6] M D E: *added to* 𝔄 *later.*

Through later years the story of my life.
The road lies plain before me ;—'tis a theme          640
Single and of determined bounds ; and hence
I choose it rather at this time, than work
Of ampler or more varied argument,
Where I might be discomfited and lost:
And certain hopes are with me, that to thee          645
This labour will be welcome, honoured Friend!

# BOOK SECOND

## SCHOOL-TIME—(CONTINUED)

THUS far, O Friend! have we, though leaving much
Unvisited, endeavour'd to retrace
My life through its first years, and measured back
The way I travell'd when I first began
5 To love the woods and fields; the passion yet      [5]
Was in its birth, sustain'd, as might befal,
By nourishment that came unsought; for still,
From week to week, from month to month, we liv'd
A round of tumult: duly were our games
10 Prolong'd in summer till the day-light fail'd;      [10]
No chair remain'd before the doors, the bench
And threshold steps were empty; fast asleep
The Labourer, and the Old Man who had sate,
A later lingerer, yet the revelry
15 Continued, and the loud uproar: at last,      [15]
When all the ground was dark, and the huge clouds
Were edged with twinkling stars, to bed we went,
With weary joints, and with a beating mind.
Ah! is there one who ever has been young,
20 And needs a monitory voice to tame      [20]
The pride of virtue, and of intellect?
And is there one, the wisest and the best
Of all mankind, who does not sometimes wish
For things which cannot be, who would not give,
25 If so he might, to duty and to truth      [25]
The eagerness of infantine desire?
A tranquillizing spirit presses now
On my corporeal frame: so wide appears
The vacancy between me and those days,
30 Which yet have such self-presence in my mind      [30]

[MSS. for Bk. II: RV U M A B C D E; *for ll.* 54—*end* V; *for* 321–41 *Alf.*
and 18a.
   1 MS. 18a *has an abortive beginning of this book headed* 2nd Part:
        Friend of my heart and genius we had reach'd
        A small green island which I was well pleased
        To pass not lightly by for though I felt
        Strength unabated yet I seem'd to need
        Thy cheering voice or ere I could pursue
        My voyage, resting else for ever there.

# BOOK SECOND

## SCHOOL·TIME—(CONTINUED)

Thus far, O Friend! have we, though leaving much
Unvisited, endeavoured to retrace
The simple ways in which my childhood walked;
Those chiefly that first led me to the love
Of rivers, woods, and fields. The passion yet          5
Was in its birth, sustained as might befal
By nourishment that came unsought; for still
From week to week, from month to month, we lived
A round of tumult. Duly were our games
Prolonged in summer till the day-light failed:          10
No chair remained before the doors; the bench
And threshold steps were empty; fast asleep
The labourer, and the old man who had sate
A later lingerer; yet the revelry
Continued and the loud uproar: at last,          15
When all the ground was dark, and twinkling stars
Edged the black clouds, home and to bed we went,
Feverish with weary joints and beating minds.
Ah! is there one who ever has been young,
Nor needs a warning voice to tame the pride          20
Of intellect and virtue's self-esteem?
One is there, though the wisest and the best
Of all mankind, who covets not at times
Union that cannot be;—who would not give,
If so he might, to duty and to truth          25
The eagerness of infantine desire?
A tranquillising spirit presses now
On my corporeal frame, so wide appears
The vacancy between me and those days
Which yet have such self-presence in my mind,          30

3 𝔄 C D: A² B² D³ *as* 1850.
4 𝔄 C: And shew'd by what inducement I began  A² B²; Shewing *etc*. A³.
[3–5]  The simple ways that led me first to love
    The woods and fields; the kindly passion yet  D²: D³ *as* 1850.
13 had B: hade (*sic*) A.
18–24 𝔄 C D: D² *as* 1850.
30 mind] heart  RV M.

That, sometimes, when I think of them, I seem
Two consciousnesses, conscious of myself
And of some other Being. A grey Stone
Of native rock, left midway in the Square
35 Of our small market Village, was the home
And centre of these joys, and when, return'd      [36]
After long absence, thither I repair'd,
I found that it was split, and gone to build
A smart Assembly-room that perk'd and flar'd
40 With wash and rough-cast elbowing the ground
Which had been ours. But let the fiddle scream,      [40]
And be ye happy! yet, my Friends! I know
That more than one of you will think with me
Of those soft starry nights, and that old Dame
45 From whom the Stone was nam'd who there had sate
And watch'd her Table with its huckster's wares      [45]
Assiduous, thro' the length of sixty years.

     We ran a boisterous race; the year span round
With giddy motion. But the time approach'd
50 That brought with it a regular desire
For calmer pleasures, when the beauteous forms      [50]
Of Nature were collaterally attach'd
To every scheme of holiday delight,
And every boyish sport, less grateful else,
55 And languidly pursued.
                When summer came
 It was the pastime of our afternoons      [55]
To beat along the plain of Windermere
With rival oars, and the selected bourne
Was now an Island musical with birds
60 That sang for ever; now a Sister Isle
Beneath the oaks' umbrageous covert, sown      [60]
With lillies of the valley, like a field;
And now a third small Island where remain'd
An old stone Table, and a moulder'd Cave,

31 them B A² C: it A.
33 grey Stone] rude mass A² D²: grey mass D.
37 repair'd,] repair'd 𝔄.
38       Gone was the old grey stone; that 'Stone of Rowe'
           Split into fragments which had helped to rear A².
           Split at the Builder's call and gone to rear A³.
40 With wash and rough-cast] In snow-white splendour A².
41 But] There A².

That, musing on them, often do I seem
Two consciousnesses, conscious of myself
And of some other Being. A rude mass
Of native rock, left midway in the square
Of our small market village, was the goal                    35
Or centre of these sports; and when, returned
After long absence, thither I repaired,
Gone was the old grey stone, and in its place
A smart Assembly-room usurped the ground
That had been ours. There let the fiddle scream,             40
And be ye happy! Yet, my Friends! I know
That more than one of you will think with me
Of those soft starry nights, and that old Dame
From whom the stone was named, who there had sate,
And watched her table with its huckster's wares             45
Assiduous, through the length of sixty years.

We ran a boisterous course; the year span round
With giddy motion. But the time approached
That brought with it a regular desire
For calmer pleasures, when the winning forms                 50
Of Nature were collaterally attached
To every scheme of holiday delight
And every boyish sport, less grateful else
And languidly pursued.
                          When summer came,
Our pastime was, on bright half-holidays,                    55
To sweep along the plain of Windermere
With rival oars; and the selected bourne
Was now an Island musical with birds
That sang and ceased not; now a Sister Isle
Beneath the oaks' umbrageous covert, sown                    60
With lilies of the valley like a field;
And now a third small Island, where survived
In solitude the ruins of a shrine
Once to Our Lady dedicate, and served

45 there had sate] had sate thereon A².      56, 57 𝔄 C D: D² *as* 1850.
59-60    . . . populous with birds
       That dwell in unmolested solitude
       A darkling Choir whose notes of love and joy
       Cheared the blank waters; now a Sister Isle   A² B².
[64, 65]     Once to the holy Virgin dedicate
       And served with punctual rites   D: D² *as* 1850.

65 A Hermit's history. In such a race,　　　　[65]
　　So ended, disappointment could be none,
　　Uneasiness, or pain, or jealousy:
　　We rested in the shade, all pleas'd alike,
　　Conquer'd and Conqueror. Thus the pride of strength,
70 And the vain-glory of superior skill　　　　[70]
　　Were interfus'd with objects which subdu'd
　　And temper'd them, and gradually produc'd
　　A quiet independence of the heart.
　　And to my Friend, who knows me, I may add,
75 Unapprehensive of reproof, that hence
　　Ensu'd a diffidence and modesty,　　　　[75]
　　And I was taught to feel, perhaps too much,
　　The self-sufficing power of solitude.

　　　No delicate viands sapp'd our bodily strength;
80 More than we wish'd we knew the blessing then
　　Of vigorous hunger, for our daily meals　　　　[80]
　　Were frugal, Sabine fare! and then, exclude
　　A little weekly stipend, and we lived
　　Through three divisions of the quarter'd year
85 In pennyless poverty. But now, to School
　　Return'd, from the half-yearly holidays,　　　　[85]
　　We came with purses more profusely fill'd,
　　Allowance which abundantly suffic'd
　　To gratify the palate with repasts
90 More costly than the Dame of whom I spake,
　　That ancient Woman, and her board supplied.
　　Hence inroads into distant Vales, and long
　　Excursions far away among the hills,
　　Hence rustic dinners on the cool green ground,
95 Or in the woods, or near a river side,　　　　[90]
　　Or by some shady fountain, while soft airs
　　Among the leaves were stirring, and the sun
　　Unfelt, shone sweetly round us in our joy.

　　　Nor is my aim neglected, if I tell
100 How twice in the long length of those half-years　　[95]
　　We from our funds, perhaps, with bolder hand
　　Drew largely, anxious for one day, at least,
　　To feel the motion of the galloping Steed;

　69 Conquer'd or conqueror. Thus our selfishness
　　Was mellowed down and thus the pride of strength  V.

Daily with chaunted rites. In such a race                    65
So ended, disappointment could be none,
Uneasiness, or pain, or jealousy:
We rested in the shade, all pleased alike,
Conquered and conqueror. Thus the pride of strength,
And the vain-glory of superior skill,                        70
Were tempered; thus was gradually produced
A quiet independence of the heart;
And to my Friend who knows me I may add,
Fearless of blame, that hence for future days
Ensued a diffidence and modesty,                             75
And I was taught to feel, perhaps too much,
The self-sufficing power of Solitude.

Our daily meals were frugal, Sabine fare!
More than we wished we knew the blessing then
Of vigorous hunger—hence corporeal strength                  80
Unsapped by delicate viands; for, exclude
A little weekly stipend, and we lived
Through three divisions of the quartered year
In penniless poverty. But now to school
From the half-yearly holidays returned,                      85
We came with weightier purses, that sufficed
To furnish treats more costly than the Dame
Of the old grey stone, from her scant board, supplied.
Hence rustic dinners on the cool green ground,
Or in the woods, or by a river side                          90
Or shady fountains, while among the leaves
Soft airs were stirring, and the mid-day sun
Unfelt shone brightly round us in our joy.
Nor is my aim neglected if I tell
How sometimes, in the length of those half-years,            95
We from our funds drew largely;—proud to curb,
And eager to spur on, the galloping steed;

75 𝔄 C D: D² *as* 1850.          78 solitude] loneliness B².
[87] Costlier repasts to furnish than the Dame D: D² *as* 1850.
92, 93 𝔄 C D: D² *deletes.*
96            Or fountain, festive banquet that provoked
              The languid action of a natural scene
              By pleasure of corporeal appetite V: V² *as* A.
              fountain 𝔄 C D: fountains E.
96–98 𝔄 C D: D² *as* 1850.          98 shone sweetly] was shining B².
100 𝔄 C D: D² *as* 1850.          102 day, at least] happy day A² B².
103 feel] enjoy A²: prove B².

And with the good old Inn-keeper, in truth,
105 On such occasion sometimes we employ'd
Sly subterfuge; for the intended bound                [100]
Of the day's journey was too distant far
For any cautious man, a Structure famed
Beyond its neighbourhood, the antique Walls
110 Of that large Abbey which within the Vale
Of Nightshade, to St. Mary's honour built,
Stands yet, a mouldering Pile, with fractured Arch,   [105]
Belfry, and Images, and living Trees,
A holy Scene! along the smooth green turf
115 Our Horses grazed: to more than inland peace
Left by the Sea wind passing overhead
(Though wind of roughest temper) trees and towers     [110]
May in that Valley oftentimes be seen,
Both silent and both motionless alike;
120 Such is the shelter that is there, and such
The safeguard for repose and quietness.


Our steeds remounted, and the summons given,          [115]
With whip and spur we by the Chauntry flew
In uncouth race, and left the cross-legg'd Knight,
125 And the stone-Abbot, and that single Wren
Which one day sang so sweetly in the Nave
Of the old Church, that, though from recent showers   [120]
The earth was comfortless, and, touch'd by faint
Internal breezes, sobbings of the place,
130 And respirations, from the roofless walls
The shuddering ivy dripp'd large drops, yet still,
So sweetly 'mid the gloom the invisible Bird          [125]
Sang to itself, that there I could have made
My dwelling-place, and liv'd for ever there
135 To hear such music. Through the Walls we flew
And down the valley, and a circuit made

104 good old] friendly D: cautious D².
104–5 in truth *etc.*]                    that Friend
Whose unambitious Stud supplied our want
Full oft on such occasion we employ'd A² B² C.
105 I needs must say that sometimes we have used V M.
110–12 Of a large abbey with its fractured arch V M RV.
116 West wind sweeping A² B².

And with the courteous inn-keeper, whose stud
Supplied our want, we haply might employ
Sly subterfuge, if the adventure's bound          100
Were distant: some famed temple where of yore
The Druids worshipped, or the antique walls
Of that large abbey, where within the Vale
Of Nightshade, to St. Mary's honour built,
Stands yet a mouldering pile with fractured arch,    105
Belfry, and images, and living trees,
A holy scene! Along the smooth green turf
Our horses grazed. To more than inland peace
Left by the west wind sweeping overhead
From a tumultuous ocean, trees and towers          110
In that sequestered valley may be seen,
Both silent and both motionless alike;
Such the deep shelter that is there, and such
The safeguard for repose and quietness.

Our steeds remounted and the summons given,        115
With whip and spur we through the chauntry flew
In uncouth race, and left the cross-legged knight,
And the stone-abbot, and that single wren
Which one day sang so sweetly in the nave
Of the old church, that—though from recent showers  120
The earth was comfortless, and touched by faint
Internal breezes, sobbings of the place
And respirations, from the roofless walls
The shuddering ivy dripped large drops—yet still
So sweetly 'mid the gloom the invisible bird        125
Sang to herself, that there I could have made
My dwelling-place, and lived for ever there
To hear such music. Through the walls we flew
And down the valley, and, a circuit made

116–17 Left by the winds that overpass the Vale
              In that sequester'd ruin, trees and towers  RV: A² B² D *as* 1850,
*but in* 117 Even when that wind is roughest. D² *as* 1850.
118 ℨ C: Within that winding valley may be seen A²: B² *as* 1850.
              In that deep valley often D: D² *as* 1850.
120–1 Such perfect shelter there is found *etc.* D: A² B² D² *as* 1850. *For
these lines* RV V M *have*
              Hear all day long the murmuring sea that beats
              Incessantly upon a craggy shore.
129–30 Internal breezes from its roofless walls V: M *as* A, *but* Uncertain
*for* Internal.
130 respirations] inward breathings M.

In wantonness of heart, through rough and smooth　　[130]
We scamper'd homeward. Oh! ye Rocks and Streams,
And that still Spirit of the evening air!
140 Even in this joyous time I sometimes felt
Your presence, when with slacken'd step we breath'd
Along the sides of the steep hills, or when,　　　　[135]
Lighted by gleams of moonlight from the sea,
We beat with thundering hoofs the level sand.


145 　Upon the Eastern Shore of Windermere,
Above the crescent of a pleasant Bay,
There stood an Inn, no homely-featured Shed,　　　[140]
Brother of the surrounding Cottages,
But 'twas a splendid place, the door beset
150 With Chaises, Grooms, and Liveries, and within
Decanters, Glasses, and the blood-red Wine.
In ancient times, or ere the Hall was built　　　　[145]
On the large Island, had this Dwelling been
More worthy of a Poet's love, a Hut,
155 Proud of its one bright fire, and sycamore shade.
But though the rhymes were gone which once inscribed
The threshold, and large golden characters　　　　[150]
On the blue-frosted Signboard had usurp'd
The place of the old Lion, in contempt
160 And mockery of the rustic painter's hand,
Yet to this hour the spot to me is dear
With all its foolish pomp. The garden lay　　　　[155]
Upon a slope surmounted by the plain
Of a small Bowling-green; beneath us stood
165 A grove; with gleams of water through the trees
And over the tree-tops; nor did we want
Refreshment, strawberries and mellow cream.　　　[160]
And there, through half an afternoon, we play'd
On the smooth platform, and the shouts we sent
170 Made all the mountains ring. But ere the fall
Of night, when in our pinnace we return'd　　　　[165]

139 of the 𝕬 C D: shed from D².
140. What wonder if I then had other joys
　　　Than what ye give. Yet did I sometimes feel *del.* RV.
143 Lighted] Lightened RV M.
144 *followed in* V *by passage corresponding to* VIII [458–75]. *v. note,*
p. 582.

In wantonness of heart, through rough and smooth　　130
We scampered homewards. Oh, ye rocks and streams,
And that still spirit shed from evening air!
Even in this joyous time I sometimes felt
Your presence, when with slackened step we breathed
Along the sides of the steep hills, or when　　135
Lighted by gleams of moonlight from the sea
We beat with thundering hoofs the level sand.

Midway on long Winander's eastern shore,
Within the crescent of a pleasant bay,
A tavern stood; no homely-featured house,　　140
Primeval like its neighbouring cottages,
But 'twas a splendid place, the door beset
With chaises, grooms, and liveries, and within
Decanters, glasses, and the blood-red wine.
In ancient times, and ere the Hall was built　　145
On the large island, had this dwelling been
More worthy of a poet's love, a hut
Proud of its own bright fire and sycamore shade.
But—though the rhymes were gone that once inscribed
The threshold, and large golden characters,　　150
Spread o'er the spangled sign-board, had dislodged
The old Lion and usurped his place, in slight
And mockery of the rustic painter's hand—
Yet, to this hour, the spot to me is dear
With all its foolish pomp. The garden lay　　155
Upon a slope surmounted by a plain
Of a small bowling-green; beneath us stood
A grove, with gleams of water through the trees
And over the tree-tops; nor did we want
Refreshment, strawberries and mellow cream.　　160
There, while through half an afternoon we played
On the smooth platform, whether skill prevailed
Or happy blunder triumphed, bursts of glee
Made all the mountains ring. But, ere night-fall,
When in our pinnace we returned at leisure　　165

145–8 𝔄 C D: D² *as* 1850.　　　152 or 𝔄 C D: and E.
155 one 𝔄 C D: own E.
158–9 𝔄 C D: On the blue sign-board had usurp'd the place
　　　　　　Of the old Lion, why, but in contempt D² E: E² *as* 1850.
169 and the shouts we sent] fitful bursts of glee D: D² *as* 1850.
170–2 𝔄 C D: D² *as* 1850.

        Over the dusky Lake, and to the beach
        Of some small Island steer'd our course with one,
        The Minstrel of our troop, and left him there,
175     And row'd off gently, while he blew his flute
        Alone upon the rock; Oh! then the calm                    [170]
        And dead still water lay upon my mind
        Even with a weight of pleasure, and the sky
        Never before so beautiful, sank down
180     Into my heart, and held me like a dream.


        Thus daily were my sympathies enlarged,                   [175]
        And thus the common range of visible things
        Grew dear to me: already I began
        To love the sun, a Boy I lov'd the sun,
185     Not as I since have lov'd him, as a pledge
        And surety of our earthly life, a light                   [180]
        Which while we view we feel we are alive;
        But, for this cause, that I had seen him lay
        His beauty on the morning hills, had seen
190     The western mountain touch his setting orb,               [185]
        In many a thoughtless hour, when, from excess

172 dusky 𝔄 C D: shadowy D².
181 Thus day by day my sympathies increas'd V.
181-3 Thus daily . . . dear to me: *At end of Book*, B *adds three drafts
expanding this passage*:
        (1)              by which propitious course
            The daring instincts and the brooding powers
            Were mutually sustained, the mind was fill'd
        (2)                      already I began
            To follow with my eyes the sailing clouds
            In conscious admiration, nor less pleased
            To stand beneath the universal vault
            Of the blue vacant firmament whose fair
            Yet gloomy depth I strove to penetrate
            Whose texture fancy toil'd to comprehend
            Boy as I was I loved the glorious sun
        (3) Thus daily were my sympathies enlarged
            Refined or strengthened; by such gracious course
            The daring instincts and the brooding Powers
            Were mutually upheld, the senses trained
            To nice observance and the mind to thought.
            And thus the common range of visible things
            Grew dear to me; not only those huge heights,
            My native region's own peculiar boast,
            And headlong torrents, but the lowly plains
            With flowers besprent and unassuming brooks
            And warm green fields by sheltering woods embraced

Over the shadowy lake, and to the beach
Of some small island steered our course with one,
The Minstrel of the Troop, and left him there,
And rowed off gently, while he blew his flute
Alone upon the rock—oh, then, the calm                              170
And dead still water lay upon my mind
Even with a weight of pleasure, and the sky,
Never before so beautiful, sank down
Into my heart, and held me like a dream!
Thus were my sympathies enlarged, and thus                          175
Daily the common range of visible things
Grew dear to me: already I began
To love the sun; a boy I loved the sun,
Not as I since have loved him, as a pledge
And surety of our earthly life, a light                             180
Which we behold and feel we are alive;
Nor for his bounty to so many worlds—
But for this cause, that I had seen him lay
His beauty on the morning hills, had seen
The western mountain touch his setting orb,                         185
In many a thoughtless hour, when, from excess

> And nature's universal aspect, seen
> In earth or sky. Already I began
> To follow with my eyes the sailing clouds
> In conscious admiration; loved to watch
> Their shifting colours and their changeful forms,
> And with a curious patience of regard
> Laboured the subtile process to detect
> By which, like thoughts within the mind itself,
> They rose as if from nothing, and dissolved
> Insensibly; see with the lofty winds
> These hurrying out of sight in troops, while that,
> A lonely One upon the mountain top,
> Resteth in sedentary quietness,
> Faint answers yielding as my thoughts inquired
> By what subjection he was fix'd, what law
> Stay'd him, and why alone he linger'd there
> Crowning that regal hill, or like a spirit
> Whispering angelic tidings; and in turn
> To records listening of primeval [days] hours
> And the dread labours of the earth, ere form
> From the conflicting [shocks] powers of flood and fire
> Escaped, stood fixed in permanence serene.
> Nor was I unaccustom'd with a heart
> As pleas'd to stand beneath th' impending cope
> Of the blue etc. as (2)

181–2, 187 D as 𝔄: D² as 1850.          [182] added to D.

Of happiness, my blood appear'd to flow
With its own pleasure, and I breath'd with joy.
And from like feelings, humble though intense,
195 To patriotic and domestic love                        [190]
Analogous, the moon to me was dear;
For I would dream away my purposes,
Standing to look upon her while she hung
Midway between the hills, as if she knew
200 No other region; but belong'd to thee,                [195]
Yea, appertain'd by a peculiar right
To thee and thy grey huts, my darling Vale!

Those incidental charms which first attach'd
My heart to rural objects, day by day
205 Grew weaker, and I hasten on to tell                  [200]
How Nature, intervenient till this time,
And secondary, now at length was sought
For her own sake. But who shall parcel out
His intellect, by geometric rules,
210 Split, like a province, into round and square?        [205]
Who knows the individual hour in which
His habits were first sown, even as a seed,
Who that shall point, as with a wand, and say,
'This portion of the river of my mind                     [209]
215 Came from yon fountain?' Thou, my Friend! art one
More deeply read in thy own thoughts; to thee
Science appears but, what in truth she is,
Not as our glory and our absolute boast,
But as a succedaneum, and a prop
220 To our infirmity. Thou art no slave                   [215]
Of that false secondary power, by which,
In weakness, we create distinctions, then
Deem that our puny boundaries are things
Which we perceive, and not which we have made.
225 To thee, unblinded by these outward shows,            [220]
The unity of all has been reveal'd
And thou wilt doubt with me, less aptly skill'd
Than many are to class the cabinet
Of their sensations, and, in voluble phrase,              [225]
230 Run through the history and birth of each,

202 my darling 𝔄 C D: my native RV U: my [     ] V.
216–20 to thee . . . art] *added to* V.          216 thoughts] mind RV.
[215] officious D²: timid D.      223 Deem that 𝔄 V²: Believe RV V.

Of happiness, my blood appeared to flow
For its own pleasure, and I breathed with joy.
And, from like feelings, humble though intense,
To patriotic and domestic love                                    190
Analogous, the moon to me was dear;
For I could dream away my purposes,
Standing to gaze upon her while she hung
Midway between the hills, as if she knew
No other region, but belonged to thee,                            195
Yea, appertained by a peculiar right
To thee and thy grey huts, thou one dear Vale!

Those incidental charms which first attached
My heart to rural objects, day by day
Grew weaker, and I hasten on to tell                              200
How Nature, intervenient till this time
And secondary, now at length was sought
For her own sake. But who shall parcel out
His intellect by geometric rules,
Split like a province into round and square?                     205
Who knows the individual hour in which
His habits were first sown, even as a seed?
Who that shall point as with a wand and say
'This portion of the river of my mind
Came from yon fountain?' Thou, my Friend! art one    210
More deeply read in thy own thoughts; to thee
Science appears but what in truth she is,
Not as our glory and our absolute boast,
But as a succedaneum, and a prop
To our infirmity. No officious slave                             215
Art thou of that false secondary power
By which we multiply distinctions, then
Deem that our puny boundaries are things
That we perceive, and not that we have made.
To thee, unblinded by these formal arts,                         220
The unity of all hath been revealed,
And thou wilt doubt, with me less aptly skilled
Than many are to range the faculties
In scale and order, class the cabinet
Of their sensations, and in voluble phrase                       225
Run through the history and birth of each

225 outward shows 𝔄 C D: formal arts D².
227–59 *stuck over in* D: 239, 240, 242–3 D² *as* 𝔄: D³ *as* 1850.

As of a single independent thing.
Hard task to analyse a soul, in which,
Not only general habits and desires,
But each most obvious and particular thought,
235 Not in a mystical and idle sense,                               [230]
But in the words of reason deeply weigh'd,
Hath no beginning.
                         Bless'd the infant Babe,
(For with my best conjectures I would trace
The progress of our being) blest the Babe,
240 Nurs'd in his Mother's arms, the Babe who sleeps          [235]
Upon his Mother's breast, who, when his soul
Claims manifest kindred with an earthly soul,
Doth gather passion from his Mother's eye!
Such feelings pass into his torpid life
245 Like an awakening breeze, and hence his mind
Even [in the first trial of its powers]
Is prompt and watchful, eager to combine
In one appearance, all the elements
And parts of the same object, else detach'd
250 And loth to coalesce. Thus, day by day,
Subjected to the discipline of love,
His organs and recipient faculties
Are quicken'd, are more vigorous, his mind spreads,
Tenacious of the forms which it receives.
255 In one beloved Presence, nay and more,
In that most apprehensive habitude
And those sensations which have been deriv'd
From this beloved Presence, there exists
A virtue which irradiates and exalts
260 All objects through all intercourse of sense.                 [240]
No outcast he, bewilder'd and depress'd;
Along his infant veins are interfus'd
The gravitation and the filial bond
Of nature, that connect him with the world.                   [244]

244–7     This passion is the awakening breeze of life
          Thus stirred in the first trial of its powers
          [*Stirred up by constant sensibility*]
          His mind is prompt and eager to combine  RV.
   246 Even in the first trial of its powers  RV V M: 𝔄 C *leave line blank
after* Even.         260 𝔄 C D: D² *as* 1850.         261 bewilder'd] abandon'd  RV.
   [244–57] D *has several deleted drafts of this passage.* (1) *shows very little
change from* A, *but between* 264 *and* 265 *has*

As of a single independent thing.
Hard task, vain hope, to analyse the mind,
If each most obvious and particular thought,
Not in a mystical and idle sense,                                    230
But in the words of Reason deeply weighed,
Hath no beginning.
                        Blest the infant Babe,
(For with my best conjecture I would trace
Our Being's earthly progress,) blest the Babe,
Nursed in his Mother's arms, who sinks to sleep                       235
Rocked on his Mother's breast; who with his soul
Drinks in the feelings of his Mother's eye!
For him, in one dear Presence, there exists
A virtue which irradiates and exalts
Objects through widest intercourse of sense.                          240
No outcast he, bewildered and depressed:
Along his infant veins are interfused
The gravitation and the filial bond
Of nature that connect him with the world.
Is there a flower, to which he points with hand                       245
Too weak to gather it, already love
Drawn from love's purest earthly fount for him
Hath beautified that flower; already shades
Of pity cast from inward tenderness
Do fall around him upon aught that bears                              250
Unsightly marks of violence or harm.

       From the new earth of man and his concerns
       Up to the silent wilderness of stars.
(2) *after* world, (264) *goes on*:
       Among whose elements he breathes with signs
       And symbols for instruction and delight
       Before, beneath, about him, and above,
       From the green earth up to the sparkling stars.
*then continues as* E . . . harm [251], *and goes on*:
       Man beast or bird or even on some sad tree
       That haply stands with arms lopt off among
       Its leafy brethren, mangled and deformed.
*These three lines are then deleted for*:
       And O! the bliss of gratitude that burns
       Within his heart bright as a household fire
       Tended by careful hands when winds blow keen
*and after* universe [254]   Love as his place of refuge, love the source
[255–8]     For feeling has imparted thought and power
       Of animation for his opening mind
       That like an Agent of the one great Mind
       Creates *etc.* D³ *as* 1850.

265  Emphatically such a Being lives,
     An inmate of this *active* universe;
     From nature largely he receives; nor so
     Is satisfied, but largely gives again,
     For feeling has to him imparted strength,          [255]
270  And powerful in all sentiments of grief,
     Of exultation, fear, and joy, his mind,
     Even as an agent of the one great mind,
     Creates, creator and receiver both,
     Working but in alliance with the works
275  Which it beholds.—Such, verily, is the first       [260]
     Poetic spirit of our human life;
     By uniform controul of after years
     In most abated or suppress'd, in some,
     Through every change of growth or of decay,
280  Pre-eminent till death.                            [265]
                            From early days,
     Beginning not long after that first time
     In which, a Babe, by intercourse of touch,
     I held mute dialogues with my Mother's heart
     I have endeavour'd to display the means
285  Whereby the infant sensibility,                    [270]
     Great birthright of our Being, was in me
     Augmented and sustain'd. Yet is a path
     More difficult before me, and I fear
     That in its broken windings we shall need
290  The chamois' sinews, and the eagle's wing:         [275]
     For now a trouble came into my mind
     From unknown causes. I was left alone,
     Seeking the visible world, nor knowing why.
     The props of my affections were remov'd,
295  And yet the building stood, as if sustain'd        [280]
     By its own spirit! All that I beheld
     Was dear to me, and from this cause it came,
     That now to Nature's finer influxes
     My mind lay open, to that more exact
300  And intimate communion which our hearts
     Maintain with the minuter properties
     Of objects which already are belov'd,
     And of those only. Many are the joys
     Of youth; but oh! what happiness to live           [285]
305  When every hour brings palpable access

Emphatically such a Being lives,
Frail creature as he is, helpless as frail,
An inmate of this active universe.
For feeling has to him imparted power                    255
That through the growing faculties of sense
Doth like an agent of the one great Mind
Create, creator and receiver both,
Working but in alliance with the works
Which it beholds.—Such, verily, is the first            260
Poetic spirit of our human life,
By uniform control of after years,
In most, abated or suppressed; in some,
Through every change of growth and of decay,
Pre-eminent till death.                                 265
                              From early days,
Beginning not long after that first time
In which, a Babe, by intercourse of touch
I held mute dialogues with my Mother's heart,
I have endeavoured to display the means
Whereby this infant sensibility,                        270
Great birthright of our being, was in me
Augmented and sustained. Yet is a path
More difficult before me; and I fear
That in its broken windings we shall need
The chamois' sinews, and the eagle's wing:              275
For now a trouble came into my mind
From unknown causes. I was left alone
Seeking the visible world, nor knowing why.
The props of my affections were removed,
And yet the building stood, as if sustained             280
By its own spirit! All that I beheld
Was dear, and hence to finer influxes
The mind lay open to a more exact
And close communion. Many are our joys
In youth, but oh! what happiness to live                285
When every hour brings palpable access

274 alliance with] the spirit of RV.
285 the infant 𝔄 C: this infant RV V C².
292 unknown] obscure *del.* RV: *left blank* V.
303–21 And of those only. I would walk alone  RV, *which adds the inter-*
*vening lines in margin.*

Of knowledge, when all knowledge is delight,
And sorrow is not there.  The seasons came,
And every season to my notice brought
A store of transitory qualities                                    [290]
310 Which, but for this most watchful power of love
Had been neglected, left a register
Of permanent relations, else unknown,
Hence life, and change, and beauty, solitude
More active, even, than 'best society',                            [295]
315 Society made sweet as solitude
By silent inobtrusive sympathies,
And gentle agitations of the mind
From manifold distinctions, difference
Perceived in things, where to the common eye,                      [300]
320 No difference is; and hence, from the same source
Sublimer joy; for I would walk alone,
In storm and tempest, or in star-light nights
Beneath the quiet Heavens; and, at that time,
Have felt whate'er there is of power in sound
325 To breathe an elevated mood, by form                           [305]
Or image unprofaned; and I would stand,
Beneath some rock, listening to sounds that are
The ghostly language of the ancient earth,
Or make their dim abode in distant winds.                          [310]
330 Thence did I drink the visionary power.
I deem not profitless those fleeting moods
Of shadowy exultation: not for this,
That they are kindred to our purer mind
And intellectual life; but that the soul,                          [315]
335 Remembering how she felt, but what she felt
Remembering not, retains an obscure sense
Of possible sublimity, to which
With growing faculties she doth aspire,
With faculties still growing, feeling still                        [320]
340 That whatsoever point they gain, they still
Have something to pursue.
                              And not alone,
In grandeur and in tumult, but no less

308  did to notice bring M.
308–9   And every season brought a countless store
            Of modes and temporary qualities RV V: D *as* 𝔄: D² *as* 1850.
316  𝔄 C D: By inward concords, silent, inobtrusive D² E.

Of knowledge, when all knowledge is delight,
And sorrow is not there! The seasons came,
And every season wheresoe'er I moved
Unfolded transitory qualities,                              290
Which, but for this most watchful power of love,
Had been neglected; left a register
Of permanent relations, else unknown.
Hence life, and change, and beauty, solitude
More active even than 'best society'—                      295
Society made sweet as solitude
By silent inobtrusive sympathies,
And gentle agitations of the mind
From manifold distinctions, difference
Perceived in things, where, to the unwatchful eye,          300
No difference is, and hence, from the same source,
Sublimer joy; for I would walk alone,
Under the quiet stars, and at that time
Have felt whate'er there is of power in sound
To breathe an elevated mood, by form                       305
Or image unprofaned; and I would stand,
If the night blackened with a coming storm,
Beneath some rock, listening to notes that are
The ghostly language of the ancient earth,
Or make their dim abode in distant winds.                  310
Thence did I drink the visionary power;
And deem not profitless those fleeting moods
Of shadowy exultation: not for this,
That they are kindred to our purer mind
And intellectual life; but that the soul,                  315
Remembering how she felt, but what she felt
Remembering not, retains an obscure sense
Of possible sublimity, whereto
With growing faculties she doth aspire,
With faculties still growing, feeling still                320
That whatsoever point they gain, they yet
Have something to pursue.
      And not alone,
'Mid gloom and tumult, but no less 'mid fair

320–8 *Stuck over in* D: D² *as* 1850.
322–3      and beneath the beam
    Of quiet moons. *Alf.* MS. 18*a.*
324 Have felt] Would feel RV V.
331 those] these RV.    342–3 ℈ C D: D² *as* 1850.

In tranquil scenes, that universal power
And fitness in the latent qualities                        [325]
345 And essences of things, by which the mind
Is mov'd by feelings of delight, to me
Came strengthen'd with a superadded soul,
A virtue not its own. My morning walks
Were early; oft, before the hours of School     [330]
350 I travell'd round our little Lake, five miles
Of pleasant wandering, happy time! more dear
For this, that one was by my side, a Friend
Then passionately lov'd; with heart how full
Will he peruse these lines, this page, perhaps
355 A blank to other men! for many years           [335]
Have since flow'd in between us; and our minds,
Both silent to each other, at this time
We live as if those hours had never been.
Nor seldom did I lift our cottage latch
360 Far earlier, and before the vernal thrush
Was audible, among the hills I sate
Alone, upon some jutting eminence
At the first hour of morning, when the Vale        .
Lay quiet in an utter solitude.                          [345]
365 How shall I trace the history, where seek
The origin of what I then have felt?
Oft in those moments such a holy calm
Did overspread my soul, that I forgot
That I had bodily eyes, and what I saw           [350]
370 Appear'd like something in myself, a dream,
A prospect in my mind.
                            'Twere long to tell
What spring and autumn, what the winter snows,
And what the summer shade, what day and night,
The evening and the morning, what my dreams   [355]
375 And what my waking thoughts supplied, to nurse
That spirit of religious love in which
I walked with Nature. But let this, at least
Be not forgotten, that I still retain'd
My first creative sensibility,                          [360]
380 That by the regular action of the world

433 tranquil] humbler B². 347 soul] power V. 360–5 *Stuck over in* D.
[341–3]  the vernal thrush . . . Alone] the thrush, high-perched,
              Piped to the woods his shrill reveillé, sate
              Alone A² (*deleted*) D E.

And tranquil scenes, that universal power
And fitness in the latent qualities                         325
And essences of things, by which the mind
Is moved with feelings of delight, to me
Came, strengthened with a superadded soul,
A virtue not its own. My morning walks
Were early;—oft before the hours of school                  330
I travelled round our little lake, five miles
Of pleasant wandering. Happy time! more dear
For this, that one was by my side, a Friend,
Then passionately loved; with heart how full
Would he peruse these lines! For many years                 335
Have since flowed in between us, and, our minds
Both silent to each other, at this time
We live as if those hours had never been.
Nor seldom did I lift our cottage latch
Far earlier, ere one smoke-wreath had risen                 340
From human dwelling, or the vernal thrush
Was audible; and sate among the woods
Alone upon some jutting eminence,
At the first gleam of dawn-light, when the Vale,
Yet slumbering, lay in utter.solitude.                      345
How shall I seek the origin? where find
Faith in the marvellous things which then I felt?
Oft in these moments such a holy calm
Would overspread my soul, that bodily eyes
Were utterly forgotten, and what I saw                      350
Appeared like something in myself, a dream,
A prospect in the mind.
                              'Twere long to tell
What spring and autumn, what the winter snows,
And what the summer shade, what day and night,
Evening and morning, sleep and waking, thought              355
From sources inexhaustible, poured forth
To feed the spirit of religious love
In which I walked with Nature. But let this
Be not forgotten, that I still retained
My first creative sensibility;                              360
That by the regular action of the world

369 That I had bodily eyes M 𝔄: The agency of sight RV.
[355] sleep and waking thought, D: dreams and waking thought, D².

My soul was unsubdu'd. A plastic power
Abode with me, a forming hand, at times
Rebellious, acting in a devious mood,
A local spirit of its own, at war                    [365]
385 With general tendency, but for the most
Subservient strictly to the external things
With which it commun'd. An auxiliar light
Came from my mind which on the setting sun
Bestow'd new splendor, the melodious birds,          [370]
390 The gentle breezes, fountains that ran on,
Murmuring so sweetly in themselves, obey'd
A like dominion; and the midnight storm
Grew darker in the presence of my eye.
Hence my obeisance, my devotion hence,               [375]
395 And hence my transport.
                              Nor should this, perchance,
Pass unrecorded, that I still had lov'd
The exercise and produce of a toil
Than analytic industry to me
More pleasing, and whose character I deem            [380]
400 Is more poetic as resembling more
Creative agency. I mean to speak
Of that interminable building rear'd
By observation of affinities
In objects where no brotherhood exists               [385]
405 To common minds. My seventeenth year was come
And, whether from this habit, rooted now
So deeply in my mind, or from excess
Of the great social principle of life,
Coercing all things into sympathy,                   [390]
410 To unorganic natures I transferr'd
My own enjoyments, or, the power of truth
Coming in revelation, I convers'd
With things that really are, I, at this time
Saw blessings spread around me like a sea.           [395]
415 Thus did my days pass on, and now at length
From Nature and her overflowing soul
I had receiv'd so much that all my thoughts
Were steep'd in feeling; I was only then
Contented when with bliss ineffable                  [400]

395–407 *Added in the margin* RV.
405 common 𝔄 C D: passive D².

My soul was unsubdued. A plastic power
Abode with me; a forming hand, at times
Rebellious, acting in a devious mood;
A local spirit of his own, at war                                365
With general tendency, but, for the most,
Subservient strictly to external things
With which it communed. An auxiliar light
Came from my mind, which on the setting sun
Bestowed new splendour; the melodious birds,                     370
The fluttering breezes, fountains that run on
Murmuring so sweetly in themselves, obeyed
A like dominion, and the midnight storm
Grew darker in the presence of my eye:
Hence my obeisance, my devotion hence,                           375
And hence my transport.
      Nor should this, perchance,
Pass unrecorded, that I still had loved
The exercise and produce of a toil,
Than analytic industry to me
More pleasing, and whose character I deem                        380
Is more poetic as resembling more
Creative agency. The song would speak
Of that interminable building reared
By observation of affinities
In objects where no brotherhood exists                           385
To passive minds. My seventeenth year was come;
And, whether from this habit rooted now
So deeply in my mind, or from excess
In the great social principle of life
Coercing all things into sympathy,                               390
To unorganic natures were transferred
My own enjoyments; or the power of truth
Coming in revelation, did converse
With things that really are; I, at this time,
Saw blessings spread around me like a sea.                       395
Thus while the days flew by, and years passed on,
From Nature and her overflowing soul,
I had received so much, that all my thoughts
Were steeped in feeling; I was only then
Contented, when with bliss ineffable                             400

415 𝔄 C D E (*but* D E the *for* my): E² *as* 1850.
416 and her overflowing soul] overflowing on [in E²] my soul D E.

420  I felt the sentiment of Being spread
     O'er all that moves, and all that seemeth still,
     O'er all, that, lost beyond the reach of thought
     And human knowledge, to the human eye
     Invisible, yet liveth to the heart,                                    [405]
425  O'er all that leaps, and runs, and shouts, and sings,
     Or beats the gladsome air, o'er all that glides
     Beneath the wave, yea, in the wave itself
     And mighty depth of waters. Wonder not
     If such my transports were; for in all things                          [410]
430  I saw one life, and felt that it was joy.
     One song they sang, and it was audible,                                [415]
     Most audible then when the fleshly ear,
     O'ercome by grosser prelude of that strain,
     Forgot its functions, and slept undisturb'd.

435      If this be error, and another faith
     Find easier access to the pious mind,                                  [420]
     Yet were I grossly destitute of all
     Those human sentiments which make this earth
     So dear, if I should fail, with grateful voice
440  To speak of you, Ye Mountains and Ye Lakes,
     And sounding Cataracts! Ye Mists and Winds                             [425]
     That dwell among the hills where I was born.
     If, in my youth, I have been pure in heart,
     If, mingling with the world, I am content
445  With my own modest pleasures, and have liv'd,
     With God and Nature communing, remov'd                                 [430]
     From little enmities and low desires,
     The gift is yours; if in these times of fear,
     This melancholy waste of hopes o'erthrown,
450  If, 'mid indifference and apathy
     And wicked exultation, when good men,                                  [435]
     On every side fall off we know not how,
     To selfishness, disguis'd in gentle names
     Of peace, and quiet, and domestic love,
455  Yet mingled, not unwillingly, with sneers
     On visionary minds; if in this time                                    [440]
     Of dereliction and dismay, I yet

429 all things 𝔄 C M: all things now D E.
429–30 𝔄 C D E (*but* D E *as above*): E² *as* 1850 [410–14].
449 waste 𝔄 V²: world RV V.

I felt the sentiment of Being spread
O'er all that moves and all that seemeth still;
O'er all that, lost beyond the reach of thought
And human knowledge, to the human eye
Invisible, yet liveth to the heart;                               405
O'er all that leaps and runs, and shouts and sings,
Or beats the gladsome air; o'er all that glides
Beneath the wave, yea, in the wave itself,
And mighty depth of waters. Wonder not
If high the transport, great the joy I felt,                      410
Communing in this sort through earth and heaven
With every form of creature, as it looked
Towards the Uncreated with a countenance
Of adoration, with an eye of love.
One song they sang, and it was audible,                           415
Most audible, then, when the fleshly ear,
O'ercome by humblest prelude of that strain,
Forgot her functions, and slept undisturbed.

    If this be error, and another faith
Find easier access to the pious mind,                             420
Yet were I grossly destitute of all
Those human sentiments that make this earth
So dear, if I should fail with grateful voice
To speak of you, ye mountains, and ye lakes
And sounding cataracts, ye mists and winds                        425
That dwell among the hills where I was born.
If in my youth I have been pure in heart,
If, mingling with the world, I am content
With my own modest pleasures, and have lived
With God and Nature communing, removed                            430
From little enmities and low desires,
The gift is yours; if in these times of fear,
This melancholy waste of hopes o'erthrown,
If, 'mid indifference and apathy,
And wicked exultation when good men                               435
On every side fall off, we know not how,
To selfishness, disguised in gentle names
Of peace and quiet and domestic love,
Yet mingled not unwillingly with sneers
On visionary minds; if, in this time                              440
Of dereliction and dismay, I yet

Despair not of our nature; but retain
A more than Roman confidence, a faith
460 That fails not, in all sorrow my support,
The blessing of my life, the gift is yours,                              [445]
Ye mountains! thine, O Nature! Thou hast fed
My lofty speculations; and in thee,
For this uneasy heart of ours I find
465 A never-failing principle of joy,                                      [450]
And purest passion.
                        Thou, my Friend! wert rear'd
In the great City, 'mid far other scenes;
But we, by different roads at length have gain'd
The self-same bourne. And for this cause to Thee
470 I speak, unapprehensive of contempt,                                  [455]
The insinuated scoff of coward tongues,
And all that silent language which so oft
In conversation betwixt man and man
Blots from the human countenance all trace
475 Of beauty and of love. For Thou hast sought                          [460]
The truth in solitude, and Thou art one,
The most intense of Nature's worshippers,
In many things my Brother, chiefly here                                 [465]
In this my deep devotion.
                        Fare Thee well!
480 Health, and the quiet of a healthful mind
Attend thee! seeking oft the haunts of men,
And yet more often living with Thyself,
And for Thyself, so haply shall thy days                                [470]
Be many, and a blessing to mankind.

461/462 Ye mists and sounding cataracts 'tis yours B².
466 wert rear'd] wast bred RV.
476–9 The truth . . . devotion 𝔄 D E: E² *as* 1850.
480–1 Be happy seeking oft . . . RV *del.*

Despair not of our nature, but retain
A more than Roman confidence, a faith
That fails not, in all sorrow my support,
The blessing of my life; the gift is yours,                445
Ye winds and sounding cataracts! 'tis yours,
Ye mountains! thine, O Nature! Thou hast fed
My lofty speculations; and in thee,
For this uneasy heart of ours, I find
A never-failing principle of joy                            450
And purest passion.
                        Thou, my Friend! wert reared
In the great city, 'mid far other scenes;
But we, by different roads, at length have gained
The self-same bourne. And for this cause to thee
I speak, unapprehensive of contempt,                        455
The insinuated scoff of coward tongues,
And all that silent language which so oft
In conversation between man and man
Blots from the human countenance all trace
Of beauty and of love. For thou hast sought               460
The truth in solitude, and, since the days
That gave thee liberty, full long desired
To serve in Nature's temple, thou hast been
The most assiduous of her ministers;
In many things my brother, chiefly here                     465
In this our deep devotion.
                        Fare thee well!
Health and the quiet of a healthful mind
Attend thee! seeking oft the haunts of men,
And yet more often living with thyself,
And for thyself, so haply shall thy days                    470
Be many, and a blessing to mankind.

# BOOK THIRD

## RESIDENCE AT CAMBRIDGE

I T was a dreary morning when the Chaise
Roll'd over the flat Plains of Huntingdon
And, through the open windows, first I saw
The long-back'd Chapel of King's College rear
5  His pinnacles above the dusky groves.           [5]

    Soon afterwards, we espied upon the road,
A student cloth'd in Gown and tassell'd Cap;
He pass'd; nor was I master of my eyes
Till he was left a hundred yards behind.
10  The Place, as we approach'd, seem'd more and more
To have an eddy's force, and suck'd us in
More eagerly at every step we took.
Onward we drove beneath the Castle, down        [15]
By Magdalene Bridge we went and cross'd the Cam,
15  And at the *Hoop* we landed, famous Inn.
    My spirit was up, my thoughts were full of hope;
Some Friends I had, acquaintances who there
Seem'd Friends, poor simple Schoolboys, now hung round

[MSS. for Bk. III: M A B C D E.]
1–5       No sunshine cheared the morning and our course
            Over a champaign flat and and objectless
            Was wearisome, till classic Cambridge showed
            The long roofed *etc. as* 𝔄. D.
1–2 *as* 𝔄; 3–4 And on we went uncheared, till first we saw
                The long roofed *etc.* D².
            No sunshine cheared the morning and the way
            Was dull and wearisome till Cambridge shew'd
            The long roof'd chapel of King's College rearing
            Its pinnacles above a boundary line
            Of dusky groves broken by low hung clouds D³.
5–6 *Left blank in* C.        6 Soon afterwards] Advancing A² B².
9 *foll.* Till he who strode indifferently along
          With youthful pace was left as far behind
          As ere at sunset stretched his spindling shade. A².
10–12 Nearer and nearer as we drew the Place
           More strongly wrought upon me and appeared
           To suck us in as with an eddy's force
           At every instant more perceptible
13–15 Onward we drove beneath the Castle—down
           To Magdalene Bridge whirl'd rapidly, there saw

# BOOK THIRD

## RESIDENCE AT CAMBRIDGE

It was a dreary morning when the wheels
Rolled over a wide plain o'erhung with clouds,
And nothing cheered our way till first we saw
The long-roofed chapel of King's College lift
Turrets and pinnacles in answering files,          5
Extended high above a dusky grove.

   Advancing, we espied upon the road
A student clothed in gown and tasselled cap,
Striding along as if o'ertasked by Time,
Or covetous of exercise and air;                   10
He passed—nor was I master of my eyes
Till he was left an arrow's flight behind.
As near and nearer to the spot we drew,
It seemed to suck us in with an eddy's force.
Onward we drove beneath the Castle; caught,        15
While crossing Magdalene Bridge, a glimpse of Cam;
And at the *Hoop* alighted, famous Inn.
   My spirit was up, my thoughts were full of hope;
Some friends I had, acquaintances who there
Seemed friends, poor simple school-boys, now hung round  20

      And cross'd the sleepy Cam, pursued our way
      By antique gateways, (*crowded*) rattling streets
      And at the *Hoop* alighted *etc.* A².
10–12 Muse whom I serve, bear witness that the Place
      The venerable place as we approached
      So wrought upon my mind that it appeared *etc. as* A², A³.
13–15 A³ *has* swept *for* drove *and for* And crossed . . . streets *has*
      And crossed on rattling wheels the sleepy Cam,
      Through antique gateways caught a transient glimpse,
10–14 The place as we approached seemed more and more
      To have an eddy's force; onward we drove
      Beneath the Castle, crossed the sleepy Cam D.
      The place on our approach had seemed to gain
      An eddy's force nor failed to suck us in
      More and more eagerly at every step
      Onward we drove beneath the Castle mound
      Caught as we crossed the Bridge a glimpse of Cam, D². D³ E *as*
        1850, *but in* [15] That quickened not our pace, but soon we
        caught

With honour and importance; in a world
20 Of welcome faces up and down I rov'd;
Questions, directions, counsel and advice
Flow'd in upon me from all sides, fresh day
Of pride and pleasure! to myself I seem'd                    [25]
A man of business and expense, and went
25 From shop to shop about my own affairs,
To Tutors or to Tailors, as befel,
From Street to Street with loose and careless heart.

I was the Dreamer, they the Dream; I roam'd          [30]
Delighted, through the motley spectacle;
30 Gowns grave or gaudy, Doctors, Students, Streets,
Lamps, Gateways, Flocks of Churches, Courts and Towers:
Strange transformation for a mountain Youth,
A northern Villager. As if by word                          [35]
Of magic or some Fairy's power, at once
35 Behold me rich in monies, and attir'd
In spendid clothes, with hose of silk, and hair
Glittering like rimy trees when frost is keen.
My lordly Dressing-gown I pass it by,                       [40]
With other signs of manhood which supplied
40 The lack of beard.—The weeks went roundly on,
With invitations, suppers, wine, and fruit,
Smooth housekeeping within, and all without
Liberal and suiting Gentleman's array!                      [45]

The Evangelist St. John my Patron was,
45 Three gloomy Courts are his; and in the first
Was my abiding-place, a nook obscure!
Right underneath, the College kitchens made
A humming sound, less tuneable than bees,                   [50]
But hardly less industrious; with shrill notes
50 Of sharp command and scolding intermix'd.
Near me was Trinity's loquacious Clock,
Who never let the Quarters, night or day,
Slip by him unproclaim'd, and told the hours                [55]

20 up and down] here and there A².
21 counsel 𝕬 C D E: warnings E².        27 *Not in* M.
31 Lamps, Gateways] Groves, Cloisters, A² B². D *as* A: D² *as* 1850.
32 Most strange migration and therewith as strange
    A transformation for a mountain youth D E: E² *as* 1850.
36 clothes 𝕬 C D: garb A² B² D².        37 Glittering 𝕬 C D: Powdered D².
45 gloomy 𝕬 C D: gothic D².

With honour and importance: in a world
Of welcome faces up and down I roved;
Questions, directions, warnings and advice,
Flowed in upon me, from all sides; fresh day
Of pride and pleasure! to myself I seemed          25
A man of business and expense, and went
From shop to shop about my own affairs,
To Tutor or to Tailor, as befel,
From street to street with loose and careless mind.

I was the Dreamer, they the Dream; I roamed        30
Delighted through the motley spectacle;
Gowns grave, or gaudy, doctors, students, streets,
Courts, cloisters, flocks of churches, gateways, towers:
Migration strange for a stripling of the hills,
A northern villager.                               35
                    As if the change
Had waited on some Fairy's wand, at once
Behold me rich in monies, and attired
In splendid garb, with hose of silk, and hair
Powdered like rimy trees, when frost is keen.
My lordly dressing-gown, I pass it by,             40
With other signs of manhood that supplied
The lack of beard.—The weeks went roundly on,
With invitations, suppers, wine and fruit,
Smooth housekeeping within, and all without
Liberal, and suiting gentleman's array.            45

The Evangelist St. John my patron was:
Three Gothic courts are his, and in the first
Was my abiding-place, a nook obscure;
Right underneath, the College kitchens made
A humming sound, less tuneable than bees,          50
But hardly less industrious; with shrill notes
Of sharp command and scolding intermixed.
Near me hung Trinity's loquacious clock,
Who never let the quarters, night or day,
Slip by him unproclaimed, and told the hours       55

51   And to me nearer than to most of those
       Whom he was destined specially to serve
       Thy clock O stately Trinity kept watch
       A Monitor importunately (superfluously A³) strict A²
       Near me the Clock of Trinity kept watch A Monitor *etc.*  B².

Twice over with a male and female voice.
55 Her pealing organ was my neighbour too;
And, from my Bedroom, I in moonlight nights
Could see, right opposite, a few yards off,
The Antechapel, where the Statue stood                    [60]
Of Newton, with his Prism and silent Face.

60    Of College labours, of the Lecturer's Room,
All studded round, as thick as chairs could stand,        [65]
With loyal Students, faithful to their books,
Half-and-half Idlers, hardy Recusants,
And honest Dunces;—of important Days,
65 Examinations, when the Man was weigh'd
As in the balance!—of excessive hopes,                    [70]
Tremblings withal, and commendable fears,
Small jealousies, and triumphs good or bad
I make short mention; things they were which then
70 I did not love, nor do I love them now.
Such glory was but little sought by me,
And little won.  But it is right to say
That even so early, from the first crude days            [75]
Of settling-time in this my new abode,
75 Not seldom I had melancholy thoughts,
From personal and family regards,
Wishing to hope without a hope; some fears
About my future worldly maintenance,
And, more than all, a strangeness in my mind,            [80]
80 A feeling that I was not for that hour,
Nor for that place. But wherefore be cast down?
Why should I grieve? I was a chosen Son.
For hither I had come with holy powers

56–58 And in deep midnight when          And from my pillow I had power
    the moon shone fair                     to mark
  Or even by dimmer influence         Solemnly pressed upon my sted-
    of the stars                            fast gaze
  In wakeful vision rapt I could      By glimmering starlight or with
    behold                                  mellow gleams
  Solemnly near and pressing          Of moonshine on the branchy
    on my sight                             windows playing
  The Antechapel A².                  The Antechapel B².
56–63 *Stuck over in* D: D² *as* 1850.
   69–76 D *as* 𝔄 C, *but* 72–73 *as* 1850, *and in* 70 I did not prize, and scarcely
prize them now; D² *as* 1850.
   81–108 *page stuck over in* D, *followed by page of erasures.* D³ *as* 1850.
   82 I was] who was A² B².

Twice over with a male and female voice.
Her pealing organ was my neighbour too;
And from my pillow, looking forth by light
Of moon or favouring stars, I could behold
The antechapel where the statue stood          60
Of Newton with his prism and silent face,
The marble index of a mind for ever
Voyaging through strange seas of Thought, alone.

Of College labours, of the Lecturer's room
All studded round, as thick as chairs could stand,          65
With loyal students faithful to their books,
Half-and-half idlers, hardy recusants,
And honest dunces—of important days,
Examinations, when the man was weighed
As in a balance! of excessive hopes,          70
Tremblings withal and commendable fears,
Small jealousies, and triumphs good or bad,
Let others that know more speak as they know.
Such glory was but little sought by me,
And little won. Yet from the first crude days          75
Of settling time in this untried abode,
I was disturbed at times by prudent thoughts,
Wishing to hope without a hope, some fears
About my future worldly maintenance,
And, more than all, a strangeness in the mind,          80
A feeling that I was not for that hour,
Nor for that place. But wherefore be cast down?
For (not to speak of Reason and her pure
Reflective acts to fix the moral law
Deep in the conscience, nor of Christian Hope,          85
Bowing her head before her sister Faith
As one far mightier), hither I had come,
Bear witness Truth, endowed with holy powers

82–93 A *makes two attempts to recast*:
  (1) A youthful Druid taught in shady groves
      Primeval mysteries, a Bard elect
      To celebrate in sympathetic verse
      Magnanimous exploits, nor unprepared,
      If high occasions called, to act or suffer
      As from the invisible shrine within the breast
      Nature might urge, or antient story taught.
      Why should he grieve who was a chosen Son
      Why should he languish with a student's gown
      Depress'd, who would more fitly have been clad
      In vernal green, like an Aspirant Youth          *[continued overleaf*

    And faculties, whether to work or feel:         [89]
85  To apprehend all passions and all moods
    Which time, and place, and season do impress
    Upon the visible universe, and work
    Like changes there by force of my own mind.
    I was a Freeman; in the purest sense
90  Was free, and to majestic ends was strong.
    I do not speak of learning, moral truth,
    Or understanding; 'twas enough for me
    To know that I was otherwise endow'd.
    When the first glitter of the show was pass'd,
95  And the first dazzle of the taper light,
    As if with a rebound my mind return'd
    Into its former self. Oft did I leave
    My Comrades, and the Crowd, Buildings and Groves,    [92]
    And walked along the fields, the level fields,
100  With Heaven's blue concave rear'd above my head;
    And now it was, that, from such change entire
    And this first absence from those shapes sublime
    Wherewith I had been conversant, my mind       [95]
    Seem'd busier in itself than heretofore;
105  At least, I more directly recognised
    My powers and habits: let me dare to speak
    A higher language, say that now I felt       [100]
    The strength and consolation which were mine.
    As if awaken'd, summon'd, rous'd, constrain'd,
110  I look'd for universal things; perused
    The common countenance of earth and heaven;    [110]
    And, turning the mind in upon itself,
    Pored, watch'd, expected, listen'd; spread my thoughts
    And spread them with a wider creeping; felt
115  Incumbences more awful, visitings
    Of the Upholder of the tranquil Soul,       [120]

    (2) What need that aught of self-respecting fear
       Should plague the young Initiate who had seen
       Thrice sacred mysteries mid Druid groves
       Or where grey Temples stood on native Hills?
       Why should he droop who fitliest had been clad
       Like an Aspirant in cerulean Robes
       Address'd to celebrate with harp and voice
       Magnanimous exploits, nor unprepared

85–90  Ⱥ C D²; *but* D² characters and *for* passions and all; *deleted* D³.
87  work] make A².      [88] endowed E²: had come D² E.
[90]  Oft when those novelties had lost by use Their power D²: D³ *as* 1850.
91  learning A C: knowledge M B.      91–93 A *deletes*.

And faculties, whether to work or feel.
Oft when the dazzling show no longer new                    90
Had ceased to dazzle, ofttimes did I quit
My comrades, leave the crowd, buildings and groves,
And as I paced alone the level fields
Far from those lovely sights and sounds sublime
With which I had been conversant, the mind                  95
Drooped not; but there into herself returning,
With prompt rebound seemed fresh as heretofore.
At least I more distinctly recognized
Her native instincts: let me dare to speak
A higher language, say that now I felt                      100
What independent solaces were mine,
To mitigate the injurious sway of place
Or circumstance, how far soever changed
In youth, or *to* be changed in manhood's prime;
Or for the few who shall be called to look                  105
On the long shadows in our evening years,
Ordained precursors to the night of death.
As if awakened, summoned, roused, constrained,
I looked for universal things; perused
The common countenance of earth and sky:                    110
Earth, nowhere unembellished by some trace
Of that first Paradise whence man was driven;
And sky, whose beauty and bounty are expressed
By the proud name she bears—the name of Heaven.
I called on both to teach me what they might;               115
Or turning the mind in upon herself
Pored, watched, expected, listened, spread my thoughts
And spread them with a wider creeping; felt
Incumbencies more awful, visitings
Of the Upholder of the tranquil soul,                       120

95 dazzle] dazzling M.
110/111 With busier glance and more attentive gaze B.
111/112 *Between these lines is added to* A:
    Earth partially embellish'd as becomes
    The fix'd abiding place of fallen mankind
    And sky whose infinite bounty is express'd
    By the proud name she bears—the name of Heaven.
    I called on both to teach me what they might,
      D *omits* partially . . . The *and reads* beauty *and for* infinite. D² *as*
      1850.
115 Incumbences 𝔄 C: Incumbencies D.

Which underneath all passion lives secure
A steadfast life. But peace! it is enough
To notice that I was ascending now                              [125]
120 To such community with highest truth.

A track pursuing not untrod before,
From deep analogies by thought supplied,
Or consciousnesses not to be subdued,
To every natural form, rock, fruit or flower,                  [130]
125 Even the loose stones that cover the high-way,
I gave a moral life, I saw them feel,
Or link'd them to some feeling: the great mass
Lay bedded in a quickening soul, and all
That I beheld respired with inward meaning.                     [135]
130 Thus much for the one Presence, and the Life
Of the great whole; suffice it here to add
That whatsoe'er of Terror or of Love,
Or Beauty, Nature's daily face put on
From transitory passion, unto this
135 I was as wakeful, even, as waters are
To the sky's motion; in a kindred sense                        [140]
Of passion was obedient as a lute
That waits upon the touches of the wind.
So was it with me in my solitude;
140 So often among multitudes of men.
Unknown, unthought of, yet I was most rich,
I had a world about me; 'twas my own,
I made it; for it only liv'd to me,                            [145]
And to the God who look'd into my mind.
145 Such sympathies would sometimes shew themselves
By outward gestures and by visible looks.
Some call'd it madness: such, indeed, it was,
If child-like fruitfulness in passing joy,                     [150]
If steady moods of thoughtfulness, matur'd
150 To inspiration, sort with such a name;
If prophesy be madness; if things view'd
By Poets of old time, and higher up
By the first men, earth's first inhabitants,                   [155]

117–18      Which regulates the motions of all life
            And tolerates the indignities of time
            Till time shall cease. But peace, A².
    D as 𝔄 C: D² E *as* 1850, *except that for* In glory immutable [124] *they*
*read* Secure, a steadfast life. E² *as* 1850.

That tolerates the indignities of Time,
And, from the centre of Eternity
All finite motions overruling, lives
In glory immutable. But peace! enough
Here to record that I was mounting now                    125
To such community with highest truth—
A track pursuing, not untrod before,
From strict analogies by thought supplied
Or consciousnesses not to be subdued.
To every natural form, rock, fruit or flower,            130
Even the loose stones that cover the high-way,
I gave a moral life: I saw them feel,
Or linked them to some feeling: the great mass
Lay bedded in a quickening soul, and all
That I beheld respired with inward meaning.              135
Add that whate'er of Terror or of Love
Or Beauty, Nature's daily face put on
From transitory passion, unto this
I was as sensitive as waters are
To the sky's influence in a kindred mood                 140
Of passion; was obedient as a lute
That waits upon the touches of the wind.
Unknown, unthought of, yet I was most rich—
I had a world about me—'twas my own;
I made it, for it only lived to me,                       145,
And to the God who sees into the heart.
Such sympathies, though rarely, were betrayed
By outward gestures and by visible looks:
Some called it madness—so indeed it was,
If child-like fruitfulness in passing joy,               150
If steady moods of thoughtfulness matured
To inspiration, sort with such a name;
If prophecy be madness; if things viewed
By poets in old time, and higher up
By the first men, earth's first inhabitants,             155

119 𝔄 C D: D² E *as* 1850: Here to record I had ascended now E².
130–2 A² *as* 1850.
135 as wakeful even as] more sensitive than B²: as watchful even as D:
D² *as* 1850.
136 motion 𝔄 C D: influence D² E; sense 𝔄 C D E: tone B²: mood E².
136–7 motion; . . . passion 𝔄 C: motion: . . . passion, D: influence: . . .
passion, D²: influence, . . . passion, E.
144 look'd . . . mind] looked . . . heart B² D: looks . . . heart E: sees E².
145 shew themselves] be revealed A².

May in these tutor'd days no more be seen
155 With undisorder'd sight: but leaving this
It was no madness: for I had an eye
Which in my strongest workings, evermore
Was looking for the shades of difference      [160]
As they lie hid in all exterior forms,
160 Near or remote, minute or vast, an eye
Which from a stone, a tree, a wither'd leaf,
To the broad ocean and the azure heavens,
Spangled with kindred multitudes of stars,      [165]
Could find no surface where its power might sleep,
165 Which spake perpetual logic to my soul,
And by an unrelenting agency
Did bind my feelings, even as in a chain.

And here, O Friend! have I retrac'd my life      [170]
Up to an eminence, and told a tale
170 Of matters which, not falsely, I may call
The glory of my youth. Of Genius, Power,
Creation and Divinity itself
I have been speaking, for my theme has been      [175]
What pass'd within me. Not of outward things
175 Done visibly for other minds, words, signs,
Symbols or actions; but of my own heart
Have I been speaking, and my youthful mind.
O Heavens! how awful is the might of Souls,      [180]
And what they do within themselves, while yet
180 The yoke of earth is new to them, the world
Nothing but a wild field where they were sown.
This is, in truth, heroic argument,
And genuine prowess; which I wish'd to touch      [185]
With hand however weak; but in the main
185 It lies far hidden from the reach of words.
Points have we all of us within our souls,
Where all stand single; this I feel, and make
Breathings for incommunicable powers.      [190]
Yet each man is a memory to himself,
190 And, therefore, now that I must quit this theme,
I am not heartless; for there's not a man
That lives who hath not had his godlike hours,

157–9 That mid these blendings did not cease to look
      For shades of difference in external things D: D² *as* 1850.
173 speaking] treating B².

May in these tutored days no more be seen
With undisordered sight. But leaving this,
It was no madness, for the bodily eye
Amid my strongest workings evermore
Was searching out the lines of difference                    160
As they lie hid in all external forms,
Near or remote, minute or vast, an eye
Which from a tree, a stone, a withered leaf,
To the broad ocean and the azure heavens
Spangled with kindred multitudes of stars,                   165
Could find no surface where its power might sleep;
Which spake perpetual logic to my soul,
And by an unrelenting agency
Did bind my feelings even as in a chain.

And here, O Friend! have I retraced my life               170
Up to an eminence, and told a tale
Of matters which not falsely may be called
The glory of my youth. Of genius, power,
Creation and divinity itself
I have been speaking, for my theme has been               175
' What passed within me. Not of outward things
Done visibly for other minds, words, signs,
Symbols or actions, but of my own heart
Have I been speaking, and my youthful mind.
O Heavens! how awful is the might of souls,               180
And what they do within themselves while yet
The yoke of earth is new to them, the world
Nothing but a wild field where they were sown.
This is, in truth, heroic argument,
This genuine prowess, which I wished to touch             185
With hand however weak, but in the main
It lies far hidden from the reach of words.
Points have we all of us within our souls
Where all stand single; this I feel, and make
Breathings for incommunicable powers;                     190
But is not each a memory to himself,
And, therefore, now that we must quit this theme,
I am not heartless, for there's not a man
That lives who hath not known his god-like hours,

189 Yet each Man is 𝔄 C D E: E² *as* 1850.
192 had] told A².

And knows not what majestic sway we have,                    [195]
As natural beings in the strength of nature.


195    Enough: for now into a populous Plain
We must descend.—A Traveller I am,
And all my Tale is of myself; even so,
So be it, if the pure in heart delight                    [200]
To follow me; and Thou, O honor'd Friend!
200  Who in my thoughts art ever at my side,
Uphold, as heretofore, my fainting steps.


It hath been told already, how my sight
Was dazzled by the novel show, and how,                    [205]
Erelong, I did into myself return.
205  So did it seem, and so, in truth, it was.
Yet this was but short liv'd: thereafter came
Observance less devout. I had made a change
In climate; and my nature's outward coat
Changed also, slowly and insensibly.
210  To the deep quiet and majestic thoughts                    [210]
Of loneliness succeeded empty noise
And superficial pastimes; now and then
Forced labour; and, more frequently, forced hopes;
And, worse than all, a treasonable growth
215  Of indecisive judgments that impair'd                    [215]
And shook the mind's simplicity. And yet
This was a gladsome time. Could I behold,
Who less insensible than sodden clay
On a sea River's bed at ebb of tide,
220  Could have beheld with undelighted heart,                    [220]
So many happy Youths, so wide and fair
A congregation, in its budding-time
Of health, and hope, and beauty; all at once
So many divers samples of the growth
225  Of life's sweet season, could have seen unmov'd                    [225]
That miscellaneous garland of wild flowers
Upon the matron temples of a Place
So famous through the world? To me, at least,

193 majestic sway we have 𝔄 C: high sway we exercise A².
197 A² as 1850.        201 Uphold] Support A².
202 It hath been said how much my youthful sight A².
[205] With which I looked upon D: D² as 1850.        205 A D delete.

And feels not what an empire we inherit                   195
As natural beings in the strength of Nature.

    No more: for now into a populous plain
We must descend. A Traveller I am,
Whose tale is only of himself; even so,
So be it, if the pure of heart be prompt                  200
To follow, and if thou, my honoured Friend!
Who in these thoughts art ever at my side,
Support, as heretofore, my fainting steps.

    It hath been told, that when the first delight
That flashed upon me from this novel show               205
Had failed, the mind returned into herself;
Yet true it is, that I had made a change
In climate, and my nature's outward coat
Changed also slowly and insensibly.
Full oft the quiet and exalted thoughts                   210
Of loneliness gave way to empty noise
And superficial pastimes; now and then
Forced labour, and more frequently forced hopes;
And, worst of all, a treasonable growth
Of indecisive judgments, that impaired                    215
And shook the mind's simplicity.—And yet
This was a gladsome time. Could I behold—
Who, less insensible than sodden clay
In a sea-river's bed at ebb of tide,
Could have beheld,—with undelighted heart,               220
So many happy youths, so wide and fair
A congregation in its budding-time
Of health, and hope, and beauty, all at once
So many divers samples from the growth
Of life's sweet season—could have seen unmoved          225
That miscellaneous garland of wild flowers
Decking the matron temples of a place
So famous through the world ? To me, at least,

207 A less devout observance, visits paid
      Remissly, at chance seasons, to a Friend
      Unsettled in the heart by cozenage
      Of new affections. I had made a change M.
210–11 𝔄 C D: D² *as* 1850.
227 Upon D: Decking D².
228 So famous through 𝔄 C D E²: Famous throughout D² E.

It was a goodly prospect: for, through youth,
230 Though I had been train'd up to stand unpropp'd,                    [230]
And independent musings pleased me so
That spells seem'd on me when I was alone,
Yet could I only cleave to solitude
In lonesome places; if a throng was near
235 That way I lean'd by nature; for my heart                    [235]
Was social, and lov'd idleness and joy.

Not seeking those who might participate
My deeper pleasures (nay I had not once,
Though not unused to mutter lonesome songs,
240 Even with myself divided such delight,                    [240]
Or looked that way for aught that might be cloath'd
In human language), easily I pass'd
From the remembrances of better things,
And slipp'd into the weekday works of youth,
245 Unburthen'd, unalarm'd, and unprofan'd.                    [245]
Caverns there were within my mind, which sun
Could never penetrate, yet did there not
Want store of leafy arbours where the light
Might enter in at will. Companionships,
250 Friendships, acquaintances, were welcome all;                    [250]
We saunter'd, play'd, we rioted, we talk'd
Unprofitable talk at morning hours,
Drifted about along the streets and walks,
Read lazily in lazy books, went forth
255 To gallop through the country in blind zeal                    [255]
Of senseless horsemanship, or on the breast
Of Cam sail'd boisterously; and let the stars
Come out, perhaps without one quiet thought.

Such was the tenor of the opening act
260 In this new life. Imagination slept,                    [260]
And yet not utterly: I could not print
Ground where the grass had yielded to the steps
Of generations of illustrious Men,

229–31 for through youth *etc.* M 𝔄 C: for though trained
          To stand unpropp'd, habituated to work
          In singleness of spirit and of mind
          By independent musings so enthralled A².
  250/1 *Between these lines* M *has:*
          The meanest found some leaf or wither'd bough
          To shine upon, and aid the gladsome shew.

It was a goodly prospect: for, in sooth,
Though I had learnt betimes to stand unpropped,          230
And independent musings pleased me so
That spells seemed on me when I was alone,
Yet could I only cleave to solitude
In lonely places; if a throng was near
That way I leaned by nature; for my heart          235
Was social, and loved idleness and joy.

    Not seeking those who might participate
My deeper pleasures (nay, I had not once,
Though not unused to mutter lonesome songs,
Even with myself divided such delight,          240
Or looked that way for aught that might be clothed
In human language), easily I passed
From the remembrances of better things,
And slipped into the ordinary works
Of careless youth, unburthened, unalarmed.          245
*Caverns* there were within my mind which sun
Could never penetrate, yet did there not
Want store of leafy *arbours* where the light
Might enter in at will. Companionships,
Friendships, acquaintances, were welcome all.          250
We sauntered, played, or rioted; we talked
Unprofitable talk at morning hours;
Drifted about along the streets and walks,
Read lazily in trivial books, went forth
To gallop through the country in blind zeal          255
Of senseless horsemanship, or on the breast
Of Cam sailed boisterously, and let the stars
Come forth, perhaps without one quiet thought.

    Such was the tenor of the second act
In this new life. Imagination slept,          260
And yet not utterly. I could not print
Ground where the grass had yielded to the steps
Of generations of illustrious men,

257–8 the stars *etc.*]                                   the stars
      From day's imperial custody released  ·
      Commence their vigils without one calm thought. A².
259 opening 𝔄 C D: second D².
260–1 In this new life. And yet I could not print M.

Unmov'd; I could not always lightly pass
265 Through the same Gateways; sleep where they had slept,
Wake where they wak'd, range that enclosure old
That garden of great intellects undisturb'd.
Place also by the side of this dark sense
Of nobler feeling, that those spiritual Men,
270 Even the great Newton's own etherial Self,                    [270]
Seem'd humbled in these precincts; thence to be
The more belov'd; invested here with tasks
Of life's plain business, as a daily garb;
Dictators at the plough, a change that left
275 All genuine admiration unimpair'd.                    [277]

Beside the pleasant Mills of Trompington
I laugh'd with Chaucer; in the hawthorn shade
Heard him (while birds were warbling) tell his tales                    [280]
Of amorous passion. And that gentle Bard,
280 Chosen by the Muses for their Page of State,
Sweet Spenser, moving through his clouded heaven
With the moon's beauty and the moon's soft pace,
I call'd him Brother, Englishman, and Friend.                    [285]
Yea, our blind Poet, who, in his later day,
285 Stood almost single, uttering odious truth,
Darkness before, and danger's voice behind;
Soul awful! if the earth has ever lodg'd
An awful Soul, I seem'd to see him here                    [290]
Familiarly, and in his Scholar's dress
290 Bounding before me, yet a stripling Youth,
A Boy, no better, with his rosy cheeks
Angelical, keen eye, courageous look,
And conscious step of purity and pride.                    [295]

Among the band of my Compeers was one
295 My Class-fellow at School, whose chance it was
To lodge in the Apartments which had been,
Time out of mind, honor'd by Milton's name;
The very shell reputed of the abode
Which he had tenanted. O temperate Bard!
300 One afternoon, the first time I set foot

269 nobler 𝔄 C D: noble E.        spiritual Men] earthborn spirits A².
272–4 Beloved as men.—Invested on this ground
          With life's plain business as a daily garb
          Their memory underwent a change that left  A².

Unmoved. I could not always lightly pass
Through the same gateways, sleep where they had slept,  265
Wake where they waked, range that inclosure old,
That garden of great intellects, undisturbed.
Place also by the side of this dark sense
Of noble feeling, that those spiritual men,
Even the great Newton's own ethereal self,          270
Seemed humbled in these precincts thence to be
The more endeared. Their several memories here
(Even like their persons in their portraits clothed
With the accustomed garb of daily life)
Put on a lowly and a touching grace               275
Of more distinct humanity, that left
All genuine admiration unimpaired.

   Beside the pleasant Mill of Trompington
I laughed with Chaucer in the hawthorn shade;
Heard him, while birds were warbling, tell his tales  280
Of amorous passion. And that gentle Bard,
Chosen by the Muses for their Page of State—
Sweet Spenser, moving through his clouded heaven
With the moon's beauty and the moon's soft pace,
I called him Brother, Englishman, and Friend!       285
Yea, our blind Poet, who, in his later day,
Stood almost single; uttering odious truth—
Darkness before, and danger's voice behind,
Soul awful—if the earth has ever lodged
An awful soul—I seemed to see him here             290
Familiarly, and in his scholar's dress
Bounding before me, yet a stripling youth—
A boy, no better, with his rosy cheeks
Angelical, keen eye, courageous look,
And conscious step of purity and pride.            295
Among the band of my compeers was one
Whom chance had stationed in the very room
Honoured by Milton's name. O temperate Bard!
Be it confest that, for the first time, seated

     The more beloved; their precious memory
     With life's plain business as a daily garb
     Invested, underwent a change that left D: D² *as* 1850.
277 Chaucer; shade A: Chaucer, shade B C D: Chaucer  shade, E.
291 In years a very Boy, with rosy cheeks A².
300      Forgive me for the first time *etc.* A².
      I must confess that when I first set foot A³.

In this thy innocent Nest and Oratory,                    [300]
Seated with others in a festive ring
Of common-place convention, I to thee
Pour'd out libations, to thy memory drank,
305  Within my private thoughts, till my brain reel'd
Never so clouded by the fumes of wine
Before that hour, or since. Thence forth I ran          [305]
From that assembly, through a length of streets,
Ran, Ostrich-like, to reach our Chapel Door
310  In not a desperate or opprobrious time,
Albeit long after the importunate Bell
Had stopp'd, with wearisome Cassandra voice            [310]
No longer haunting the dark winter night.
Call back, O Friend! a moment to thy mind,
315  The place itself and fashion of the rites.
Up-shouldering in a dislocated lump,
With shallow ostentatious carelessness,
My Surplice, gloried in, and yet despised,
I clove in pride through the inferior throng            [315]
320  Of the plain Burghers, who in audience stood
On the last skirts of their permitted ground,
Beneath the pealing Organ. Empty thoughts!
I am ashamed of them; and that great Bard,
And thou, O Friend! who in thy ample mind              [320]
325  Hast station'd me for reverence and love,
Ye will forgive the weakness of that hour
In some of its unworthy vanities,
Brother of many more.
                              In this mix'd sort
The months pass'd on, remissly, not given up           [325]
330  To wilful alienation from the right,
Or walks of open scandal; but in vague
And loose indifference, easy likings, aims
Of a low pitch; duty and zeal dismiss'd,
Yet nature, or a happy course of things                [330]
335  Not doing in their stead the needful work.
The memory languidly revolv'd, the heart
Repos'd in noontide rest; the inner pulse
Of contemplation almost fail'd to beat.                [334]
Rotted as by a charm, my life became

304-6 𝔄 C D:                  to thy memory drank
            Glad and more glad, until exulting pride

Within thy innocent lodge and oratory,                       300
One of a festive circle, I poured out
Libations, to thy memory drank, till pride
And gratitude grew dizzy in a brain
Never excited by the fumes of wine
Before that hour, or since. Then, forth I ran            305
From the assembly; through a length of streets,
Ran, ostrich-like, to reach our chapel door
In not a desperate or opprobrious time,
Albeit long after the importunate bell
Had stopped, with wearisome Cassandra voice            310
No longer haunting the dark winter night.
Call back, O Friend! a moment to thy mind
The place itself and fashion of the rites.
With careless ostentation shouldering up
My surplice, through the inferior throng I clove       315
Of the plain Burghers, who in audience stood
On the last skirts of their permitted ground,
Under the pealing organ. Empty thoughts!
I am ashamed of them: and that great Bard,
And thou, O Friend! who in thy ample mind              320
Hast placed me high above my best deserts,
Ye will forgive the weakness of that hour,
In some of its unworthy vanities,
Brother to many more.
                    In this mixed sort
The months passed on, remissly, not given up          325
To wilful alienation from the right,
Or walks of open scandal, but in vague
And loose indifference, easy likings, aims
Of a low pitch—duty and zeal dismissed,
Yet Nature, or a happy course of things                330
Not doing in their stead the needful work.
The memory languidly revolved, the heart
Reposed in noontide rest, the inner pulse
Of contemplation almost failed to beat.
Such life might not inaptly be compared                335

                    Shook hands with dizzy gratitude in a mind
                    Never excited *etc.* D² E: E² *as* 1850.
312–13                    with accent tiresome as the voice
                    Of her who prophesied the doom of Troy A².
315 fashion] custom M.
325 𝔄 C D: D² *as* 1850.          336–7 the heart . . . rest] *om.* M.

340  A floating island, an amphibious thing,
     Unsound, of spungy texture, yet withal,
     Not wanting a fair face of water-weeds
     And pleasant flowers.—The thirst of living praise,
     A reverence for the glorious Dead, the sight          [340]
345  Of those long Vistos, Catacombs in which
     Perennial minds lie visibly entomb'd,
     Have often stirr'd the heart of youth, and bred
     A fervent love of rigorous discipline.
     Alas! such high commotion touch'd not me;             [345]
350  No look was in these walls to put to shame
     My easy spirits, and discountenance
     Their light composure, far less to instil
     A calm resolve of mind, firmly address'd
     To puissant efforts. Nor was this the blame           [350]
355  Of others but my own; I should, in truth,
     As far as doth concern my single self
     Misdeem most widely, lodging it elsewhere.
     For I, bred up in Nature's lap, was even
     As a spoil'd Child; and rambling like the wind        [355]
360  As I had done in daily intercourse
     With those deliciòus rivers, solemn heights,
     And mountains; ranging like a fowl of the air,
     I was ill tutor'd for captivity,
     To quit my pleasure, and from month to month,         [360]
365  Take up a station calmly on the perch
     Of sedentary peace. Those lovely forms
     Had also left less space within my mind,
     Which, wrought upon instinctively, had found
     A freshness in those objects of its love,             [365]
370  A winning power, beyond all other power.
     Not that I slighted Books; that were to lack
     All sense; but other passions had been mine,
     More fervent, making me less prompt, perhaps,
     To in-door study than was wise or well                [370]
375  Or suited to my years. Yet I could shape
     The image of a Place which, sooth'd and lull'd
     As I had been, train'd up in paradise
     Among sweet garlands and delightful sounds,

345 Vistos 𝔄 C D: Vistas E.        347 These oft have stirr'd M.
348 A love of unremitting discipline. M.
349 commotion 𝔄 C D: emotion D².        350 𝔄 C D: D² *as* 1850.

To a floating island, an amphibious spot
Unsound, of spongy texture, yet withal
Not wanting a fair face of water weeds
And pleasant flowers. The thirst of living praise,
Fit reverence for the glorious Dead, the sight          340
Of those long vistas, sacred catacombs,
Where mighty *minds* lie visibly entombed,
Have often stirred the heart of youth, and bred
A fervent love of rigorous discipline.—
Alas! such high emotion touched not me.          345
Look was there none within these walls to shame
My easy spirits, and discountenance
Their light composure, far less to instil
A calm resolve of mind, firmly addressed
To puissant efforts. Nor was this the blame          350
Of others but my own; I should, in truth,
As far as doth concern my single self,
Misdeem most widely, lodging it elsewhere:
For I, bred up 'mid Nature's luxuries,
Was a spoiled child, and rambling like the wind,          355
As I had done in daily intercourse
With those crystalline rivers, solemn heights,
And mountains, ranging like a fowl of the air,
I was ill-tutored for captivity;
To quit my pleasure, and, from month to month,          360
Take up a station calmly on the perch
Of sedentary peace. Those lovely forms
Had also left less space within my mind,
Which, wrought upon instinctively, had found
A freshness in those objects of her love,          365
A winning power, beyond all other power.
Not that I slighted books,—that were to lack
All sense,—but other passions in me ruled,
Passions more fervent, making me less prompt
To in-door study than was wise or well,          370
Or suited to those years. Yet I, though used
In magisterial liberty to rove,
Culling such flowers of learning as might tempt
A random choice, could shadow forth a place

353 A calm resolve] A patient strength M.
361 delicious 𝔄 C D: crystalline D².
375–8 𝔄 C D: D² *as* 1850.          375–6 I . . . which] A *deletes.*

Accustom'd in my loneliness to walk
380 With Nature magisterially, yet I,
Methinks, could shape the image of a Place
Which with its aspect should have bent me down          [376]
To instantaneous service, should at once
Have made me pay to science and to arts
385 And written lore, acknowledg'd my liege Lord,
A homage, frankly offer'd up, like that                [380]
Which I had paid to Nature. Toil and pains
In this recess which I have bodied forth
Should spread from heart to heart; and stately groves,
390 Majestic edifices, should not want
A corresponding dignity within.                        [385]
The congregating temper, which pervades
Our unripe years, not wasted, should be made
To minister to works of high attempt,
395 Which the enthusiast would perform with love;
Youth should be aw'd, possess'd, as with a sense       [390]
Religious, of what holy joy there is
In knowledge, if it be sincerely sought
For its own sake, in glory, and in praise,
400 If but by labour won, and to endure.
The passing Day should learn to put aside              [395]
Her trappings here, should strip them off, abash'd
Before antiquity, and stedfast truth,
And strong book-mindedness; and over all
405 Should be a healthy, sound simplicity,
A seemly plainness, name it as you will,               [400]
Republican or pious.
                              If these thoughts
Be a gratuitous emblazonry
That does but mock this recreant age, at least
410 Let Folly and False-seeming, we might say,
Be free to affect whatever formal gait
Of moral or scholastic discipline                      [405]
Shall raise them highest in their own esteem;

379–84 D *stuck over*: D² *as* 1850.
380–1 yet I, Methinks] methinks That I A².
388 Whatever be believed, in this Recess
     Whose composition stands before my mind A².
396–400 𝔄 C D: D² *as* 1850.
     400–1 endure. The passing Day 𝔄 C D: endure  The passing day,  E
(*comma added later*).        401 put] lay M.
     402 should strip them off] she should retire  M.

(If now I yield not to a flattering dream)                     375
Whose studious aspect should have bent me down
To instantaneous service; should at once
Have made me pay to science and to arts
And written lore, acknowledged my liege lord,
A homage frankly offered up, like that                         380
Which I had paid to Nature. Toil and pains
In this recess, by thoughtful Fancy built,
Should spread from heart to heart; and stately groves,
Majestic edifices, should not want
A corresponding dignity within.                                385
The congregating temper that pervades
Our unripe years, not wasted, should be taught
To minister to works of high attempt—
Works which the enthusiast would perform with love.
Youth should be awed, religiously possessed                    390
With a conviction of the power that waits
On knowledge, when sincerely sought and prized
For its own sake, on glory and on praise
If but by labour won, and fit to endure
The passing day; should learn to put aside                     395
Her trappings here, should strip them off abashed
Before antiquity and stedfast truth
And strong book-mindedness; and over all
A healthy sound simplicity should reign,
A seemly plainness, name it what you will,                     400
Republican or pious.
                        If these thoughts
Are a gratuitous emblazonry
That mocks the recreant age *we* live in, then
Be Folly and False-seeming free to affect
Whatever formal gait of discipline                             405
Shall raise them highest in their own esteem—

405 A rigorous firm simplicity should rule A².
409 𝔄 C D: D² *as* 1850.
411-24  Wear not the vizard of the ancient time
        Upon a modern face: fling to the ground
        Thy monkish Caul; and run no more abroad,
        A grey Beard Masquerader, dizen'd out
        In Superstition's cast-off garb; and jingling
        The holy Toy thou carri'st in thy hand
        A Bell as noisy as a common Crier's,
        Dull thoughted mummery! that brings disgrace M.

Let them parade, among the Schools, at will;
415 But spare the House of God. Was ever known
The witless Shepherd who would drive his Flock
With serious repetition to a pool                                    [409]
Of which 'tis plain to sight they never taste ?
A weight must surely hang on days begun
420 And ended with worst mockery: be wise,
Ye Presidents and Deans, and to your Bells
Give seasonable rest; for 'tis a sound                               [416]
Hollow as ever vex'd the tranquil air;
And your officious doings bring disgrace
425 On the plain Steeples of our English Church,
Whose worship 'mid remotest village trees                           [420]
Suffers for this. Even Science, too, at hand
In daily sight of such irreverence,
Is smitten thence with an unnatural taint,
430 Loses her just authority, falls beneath
Collateral suspicion, else unknown.                                 [425]
This obvious truth did not escape me then,
Unthinking as I was, and I confess
That, having in my native hills given loose
435 To a Schoolboy's dreaming, I had rais'd a pile
Upon the basis of the coming time,
Which now before me melted fast away,
Which could not live, scarcely had life enough
To mock the Builder. Oh! what joy it were                           [430]
440 To see a Sanctuary for our Country's Youth,
With such a spirit in it as might be
Protection for itself, a Virgin grove,
Primaeval in its purity and depth;
Where, though the shades were fill'd with chearfulness,
445 Nor indigent of songs, warbled from crowds                      [435]
In under-coverts, yet the countenance
Of the whole place should wear a stamp of awe;
A habitation sober and demure
For ruminating creatures, a domain
450 For quiet things to wander in, a haunt                          [440]

420 𝕬 C: And closed with worst hypocrisy A²: And ended with [like
*del.*] hypocrisy D: with hypocrisy D² E: with such mockery E².
421 [413–15] Deans, and to your Bells 𝕬 C D E: E² *as* 1850.
426 worship] altars M.          427 Suffer M.
432-3 M 𝕬 C, *but in* M, homespun (432) *for* obvious: A² *as* 1850.
                    This obvious truth did not escape me then

Let them parade among the Schools at will,
But spare the House of God. Was ever known
The witless shepherd who persists to drive
A flock that thirsts not to a pool disliked ?    410
A weight must surely hang on days begun
And ended with such mockery. Be wise,
Ye Presidents and Deans, and, till the spirit
Of ancient times revive, and youth be trained
At home in pious service, to your bells    415
Give seasonable rest, for 'tis a sound
Hollow as ever vexed the tranquil air ;
And your officious doings bring disgrace
On the plain steeples of our English Church,
Whose worship, 'mid remotest village trees,    420
Suffers for this. Even Science, too, at hand
In daily sight of this irreverence,
Is smitten thence with an unnatural taint,
Loses her just authority, falls beneath
Collateral suspicion, else unknown.    425
This truth escaped me not, and I confess,
That having 'mid my native hills given loose
To a schoolboy's vision, I had raised a pile
Upon the basis of the coming time,
That fell in ruins round me. Oh, what joy    430
To see a sanctuary for our country's youth
Informed with such a spirit as might be
Its own protection ; a primeval grove,
Where, though the shades with cheerfulness were filled,
Nor indigent of songs warbled from crowds    435
In under-coverts, yet the countenance
Of the whole place should bear a stamp of awe ;
A habitation sober and demure
For ruminating creatures ; a domain
For quiet things to wander in ; a haunt    440

Though careless of the injury, and I own A².
And for unsoundness manifest elsewhere
I could not chuse but grieve, and will confess A³.
437–9 M 𝔄: Which could not now support itself but fell
        In ruins round me. Oh what joy it were A² C.
        That did not imperceptibly dissolve
        But fell in ruins round me Oh what joy D : D² as 1850.
441–2 Staid, venerable, a wide Virgin Grove M.
441–4 A² C as 1850.
447 wear a stamp 𝔄 C D² : wear a face D : bear a stamp E.

In which the Heron might delight to feed
By the shy rivers, and the Pelican
Upon the cypress spire in lonely thought
Might sit and sun himself. Alas! alas!
455 　In vain for such solemnity we look;　　　　　　　　　[445]
　Our eyes are cross'd by Butterflies, our ears
　Hear chattering Popinjays; the inner heart
　Is trivial, and the impresses without
　Are of a gaudy region.
　　　　　　　　　　　　Different sight
460 　Those venerable Doctors saw of old　　　　　　　　　[450]
　When all who dwelt within these famous Walls
　Led in abstemiousness a studious life,
　When, in forlorn and naked chambers coop'd
　And crowded, o'er their ponderous Books they sate
465 　Like caterpillars eating out their way　　　　　　　　[455]
　In silence, or with keen devouring noise
　Not to be track'd or father'd. Princes then
　At matins froze, and couch'd at curfew-time,
　Train'd up, through piety and zeal, to prize
470 　Spare diet, patient labour, and plain weeds.　　　　　[460]
　O Seat of Arts! renown'd throughout the world,
　Far different service in those homely days
　The Nurslings of the Muses underwent
　From their first childhood; in that glorious time,
475 　When Learning, like a Stranger come from far,　　　　[465]
　Sounding through Christian Lands her Trumpet, rouz'd
　The Peasant and the King; when Boys and Youths,
　The growth of ragged villages and huts,
　Forsook their homes, and, errant in the quest
480 　Of Patron, famous School or friendly Nook,　　　　　　[470]
　Where, pension'd, they in shelter might sit down,
　From Town to Town and through wide-scatter'd Realms
　Journeyed with their huge folios in their hands;
　And often, starting from some covert place,
485 　Saluted the chance-comer on the road,　　　　　　　　[475]
　Crying, 'an obolus, a penny give
　To a poor Scholar'; when illustrious Men,
　Lovers of truth, by penury constrain'd,
　Bucer, Erasmus, or Melancthon read

　　　455-9 𝔄 C D: D² as 1850.　　　　464 sate] hung A² C.
　　　473 𝔄 C D: D² as 1850.　　　477-8 𝔄 C D: D² as 1850.

In which the heron should delight to feed
By the shy rivers, and the pelican
Upon the cypress spire in lonely thought
Might sit and sun himself.—Alas! Alas!
In vain for such solemnity I looked;                          445
Mine eyes were crossed by butterflies, ears vexed
By chattering popinjays; the inner heart
Seemed trivial, and the impresses without
Of a too gaudy region.
                              Different sight
Those venerable Doctors saw of old,                          450
When all who dwelt within these famous walls
Led in abstemiousness a studious life;
When, in forlorn and naked chambers cooped
And crowded, o'er the ponderous books they hung
Like caterpillars eating out their way                       455
In silence, or with keen devouring noise
Not to be tracked or fathered. Princes then
At matins froze, and couched at curfew-time,
Trained up through piety and zeal to prize
Spare diet, patient labour, and plain weeds.                 460
O seat of Arts! renowned throughout the world!
Far different service in those homely days
The Muses' modest nurslings underwent
From their first childhood: in that glorious time
When Learning, like a stranger come from far,               465
Sounding through Christian lands her trumpet, roused
Peasant and king; when boys and youths, the growth
Of ragged villages and crazy huts,
Forsook their homes, and, errant in the quest
Of Patron, famous school or friendly nook,                  470
Where, pensioned, they in shelter might sit down,
From town to town and through wide scattered realms
Journeyed with ponderous folios in their hands;
And often, starting from some covert place,
Saluted the chance comer on the road,                       475
Crying, 'An obolus, a penny give
To a poor scholar!'—when illustrious men,
Lovers of truth, by penury constrained,
Bucer, Erasmus, or Melancthon, read

483 their huge M 𝔄: ponderous A² C.      488 *om.* M.

490  Before the doors or windows of their Cells                        [480]
     By moonshine, through mere lack of taper light.


       But peace to vain regrets! We see but darkly
     Even when we look behind us; and best things
     Are not so pure by nature that they needs
495  Must keep to all, as fondly all believe,                          [485]
     Their highest promise. If the Mariner,
     When at reluctant distance he hath pass'd
     Some fair enticing Island, did but know
     What fate might have been his, could he have brought
500  His Bark to land upon the wished-for spot,                        [490]
     Good cause full often would he have to bless
     The belt of churlish Surf that scared him thence,
     Or haste of the inexorable wind.
     For me, I grieve not; happy is the man,
505  Who only misses what I miss'd, who falls                          [495]
     No lower than I fell.
                          I did not love,
     As hath been notic'd heretofore, the guise
     Of our scholastic studies; could have wish'd
     The river to have had an ampler range,
510  And freer pace; but this I tax not; far                           [500]
     Far more I griev'd to see among the Band
     Of those who in the field of contest stood
     As combatants, passions that did to me
     Seem low and mean; from ignorance of mine,
515  In part, and want of just forbearance, yet
     My wiser mind grieves now for what I saw.
     Willingly did I part from these, and turn
     Out of their track, to travel with the shoal                      [506]
     Of more unthinking Natures; easy Minds
520  And pillowy; and not wanting love that makes
     The day pass lightly on, when foresight sleeps,
     And wisdom, and the pledges interchanged                          [510]
     With our own inner being are forgot.


       To Books, our daily fare prescrib'd, I turn'd
525  With sickly appetite, and when I went,
     At other times, in quest of my own food,
     I chaced not steadily the manly deer,
     But laid me down to any casual feast

Before the doors or windows of their cells                    480
By moonshine through mere lack of taper light.

　　　But peace to vain regrets! We see but darkly
Even when we look behind us, and best things
Are not so pure by nature that they needs
Must keep to all, as fondly all believe,                      485
Their highest promise. If the mariner
When at reluctant distance he hath passed
Some tempting island, could but know the ills
That must have fallen upon him had he brought
His bark to land upon the wished-for shore,                   490
Good cause would oft be his to thank the surf
Whose white belt scared him thence, or wind that blew
Inexorably adverse: for myself
I grieve not; happy is the gownèd youth,
Who only misses what I missed, who falls                      495
No lower than I fell.
　　　　　　　I did not love,
Judging not ill perhaps, the timid course
Of our scholastic studies; could have wished
To see the river flow with ampler range
And freer pace; but more, far more, I grieved                 500
To see displayed among an eager few,
Who in the field of contest persevered,
Passions unworthy of youth's generous heart
And mounting spirit, pitiably repaid,
When so disturbed, whatever palms are won.                    505
From these I turned to travel with the shoal
Of more unthinking natures, easy minds
And pillowy; yet not wanting love that makes
The day pass lightly on, when foresight sleeps,
And wisdom and the pledges interchanged                       510
With our own inner being are forgot.

498–504 D *stuck over*: D² *as* 1850.        501 he have 𝔄 C: be his D.
507 noticed heretofore *etc.* M 𝔄: said erewhile the frame and guise A² C.
509 A² C *as* 1850.        510 𝔄 C D E: E² *as* 1850.
511 see 𝔄: note A² C D E: E² *as* 1850.
512–18 𝔄 C D: D² *as* 1850, *omitting* [504–5] *which are in* E².
524–41 M 𝔄, *not in* C D E. *Against these lines in* A, *Wordsworth has
written* 'out'.

Of wild wood-honey; or, with truant eyes
530 Unruly, peep'd about for vagrant fruit.
And, as for what pertains to human life,
The deeper passions working round me here,
Whether of envy, jealousy, pride, shame,
Ambition, emulation, fear, or hope,
535 Or those of dissolute pleasure, were by me
Unshar'd; and only now and then observ'd,
So little was their hold upon my being,
As outward things that might administer
To knowledge or instruction. Hush'd, meanwhile,
540 Was the under soul, lock'd up in such a calm,
That not a leaf of the great nature stirr'd.

Yet was this deep vacation not given up
To utter waste. Hitherto I had stood
In my own mind remote from human life,
545 At least from what we commonly so name,                    [515]
Even as a shepherd on a promontory,
Who, lacking occupation, looks far forth
Into the endless sea, and rather makes
Than finds what he beholds. And sure it is
550 That this first transit from the smooth delights,          [520]
And wild outlandish walks of simple youth,
To something that resembled an approach
Towards mortal business; to a privileg'd world
Within a world, a midway residence
555 With all its intervenient imagery,                         [525]
Did better suit my visionary mind,
Far better, than to have been bolted forth,
Thrust out abruptly into Fortune's way
Among the conflicts of substantial life;
560 By a more just gradation did lead on                       [530]
To higher things, more naturally matur'd,
For permanent possession, better fruits
Whether of truth or virtue, to ensue.

In playful zest of fancy did we note,                         [535]
565 (How could we less?) the manners and the ways
Of those who in the livery were array'd
Of good or evil fame; of those with whom
By frame of academic discipline
Perforce we were connected, men whose sway                    [540]

    Yet was this deep vacation not given up
To utter waste. Hitherto I had stood
In my own mind remote from social life,
(At least from what we commonly so name,)        515
Like a lone shepherd on a promontory
Who lacking occupation looks far forth
Into the boundless sea, and rather makes
Than finds what he beholds. And sure it is,
That this first transit from the smooth delights      520
And wild outlandish walks of simple youth
To something that resembles an approach
Towards human business, to a privileged world
Within a world, a midway residence
With all its intervenient imagery,        525
Did better suit my visionary mind,
Far better, than to have been bolted forth,
Thrust out abruptly into Fortune's way
Among the conflicts of substantial life;
By a more just gradation did lead on        530
To higher things; more naturally matured,
For permanent possession, better fruits,
Whether of truth or virtue, to ensue.
In serious mood, but oftener, I confess,
With playful zest of fancy did we note        535
(How could we less ?) the manners and the ways
Of those who lived distinguished by the badge
Of good or ill report; or those with whom
By frame of Academic discipline
We were perforce connected, men whose sway    540

536 Unshar'd: nay more, were scarcely even observ'd M.
540 soul] mind M.    544 human 𝔄 C D E: social E².
564–70 𝔄 C D: D² *as* 1850.

570 And whose authority of Office serv'd
    To set our minds on edge, and did no more.
    Nor wanted we rich pastime of this kind,
    Found everywhere; but chiefly, in the ring
    Of the grave Elders, Men unscour'd, grotesque        [545]
575 In character; trick'd out like aged trees
    Which, through the lapse of their infirmity,
    Give ready place to any random seed
    That chuses to be rear'd upon their trunks.

    Here on my view, confronting as it were            [550]
580 Those Shepherd Swains whom I had lately left,
    Did flash a different image of old age;
    How different! yet both withal alike,
    A Book of rudiments for the unpractis'd sight,
    Objects emboss'd! and which with sedulous care       [554]
585 Nature holds up before the eye of Youth
    In her great School; with further view, perhaps,
    To enter early on her tender scheme
    Of teaching comprehension with delight,             [560]
    And mingling playful with pathetic thoughts.

590    The surfaces of artificial life
    And manners finely spun, the delicate race
    Of colours, lurking, gleaming up and down
    Through that state arras woven with silk and gold;   [565]
    This wily interchange of snaky hues,
595 Willingly and unwillingly reveal'd
    I had not learn'd to watch, and at this time
    Perhaps, had such been in my daily sight
    I might have been indifferent thereto
    As Hermits are to tales of distant things.
600 Hence for these rarities elaborate
    Having no relish yet, I was content
    With the more homely produce, rudely pil'd
    In this our coarser warehouse. At this day          [570]
    I smile in many a mountain solitude
606 At passages and fragments that remain
    Of that inferior exhibition, play'd
    By wooden images, a theatre

582–3 alike, A Book] supplying
    Fit specimens to illustrate and to adorn
    A Book A² C.

And known authority of office served
To set our minds on edge, and did no more.
Nor wanted we rich pastime of this kind,
Found everywhere, but chiefly in the ring
Of the grave Elders, men unscoured, grotesque          545
In character, tricked out like aged trees
Which through the lapse of their infirmity
Give ready place to any random seed
That chooses to be reared upon their trunks.

Here on my view, confronting vividly          550
Those shepherd swains whom I had lately left,
Appeared a different aspect of old age;
How different! yet both distinctly marked,
Objects embossed to catch the general eye,
Or portraitures for special use designed,          555
As some might seem, so aptly do they serve
To illustrate Nature's book of rudiments—
That book upheld as with maternal care
When she would enter on her tender scheme
Of teaching comprehension with delight,          560
And mingling playful with pathetic thoughts.

The surfaces of artificial life
And manners finely wrought, the delicate race
Of colours, lurking, gleaming up and down
Through that state arras woven with silk and gold:          565
This wily interchange of snaky hues,
Willingly or unwillingly revealed,
I neither knew nor cared for; and as such
Were wanting here, I took what might be found
Of less elaborate fabric. At this day          570
I smile, in many a mountain solitude
Conjuring up scenes as obsolete in freaks
Of character, in points of wit as broad,
As aught by wooden images performed

582-8 D *stuck over*: D² *as* 1850.
591 finely spun 𝔄 C D: smooth'd and trim'd M: D² *as* 1850.
596-607 D *stuck over*: D² *as* 1850.
597-9     Had such appear'd before me, might have been
          To their attractions as indifferent
          As a lone Hermit to luxurious fare. A² C.
605 that remain] in my mind M.

For Wake or Fair. And oftentimes do flit                        [576]
Remembrances before me of old Men,
610 Old Humourists who have been long in their graves,
And having almost in my mind put off
Their human names, have into Phantoms pass'd          [580]
Of texture midway betwixt life and books.

I play the loiterer: 'tis enough to note
615 That here, in dwarf proportions, were express'd
The limbs of the great world, its goings-on
Collaterally pourtray'd, as in mock fight,                    [585]
A Tournament of blows, some hardly dealt,
Though short of mortal combat; and whate'er
620 Might of this pageant be suppos'd to hit
A simple Rustic's notice, this way less,
More that way, was not wasted upon me.                    [590]
—And yet this spectacle may well demand
A more substantial name, no mimic shew,
625 Itself a living part of a live whole,
A creek of the vast sea. For all Degrees
And Shapes of spurious fame and short-liv'd praise    [595]
Here sate in state, and fed with daily alms
Retainers won away from solid good;
630 And here was Labour, his own Bond-slave, Hope
That never set the pains against the prize,
Idleness, halting with his weary clog,                        [600]
And poor misguided Shame, and witless Fear,
And simple Pleasure, foraging for Death,
635 Honour misplaced, and Dignity astray;
Feuds, Factions, Flatteries, Enmity, and Guile;
Murmuring Submission, and bald Government;          [605]
The Idol weak as the Idolater;
And Decency and Custom starving Truth;
640 And blind Authority, beating with his Staff
The Child that might have led him; Emptiness
Followed, as of good omen; and meek Worth           [610]
Left to itself unheard of, and unknown.

Of these and other kindred notices
645 I cannot say what portion is in truth

616 goings-on 𝔄 C D: D² *as* 1850.
621 A simple 𝔄 C D: An artless D².

For entertainment of the gaping crowd                    575
At wake or fair. And oftentimes do flit
Remembrances before me of old men—
Old humourists, who have been long in their graves,
And having almost in my mind put off
Their human names, have into phantoms passed         580
Of texture midway between life and books.

    I play the loiterer: 'tis enough to note
That here in dwarf proportions were expressed
The limbs of the great world; its eager strifes
Collaterally pourtrayed, as in mock fight,              585
A tournament of blows, some hardly dealt
Though short of mortal combat; and whate'er
Might in this pageant be supposed to hit
An artless rustic's notice, this way less,
More that way, was not wasted upon me—                 590
And yet the spectacle may well demand
A more substantial name, no mimic show,
Itself a living part of a live whole,
A creek in the vast sea; for, all degrees
And shapes of spurious fame and short-lived praise     595
Here sate in state, and fed with daily alms
Retainers won away from solid good;
And here was Labour, his own bond-slave; Hope,
That never set the pains against the prize;
Idleness halting with his weary clog,                  600
And poor misguided Shame, and witless Fear,
And simple Pleasure foraging for Death;
Honour misplaced, and Dignity astray;
Feuds, factions, flatteries, enmity, and guile
Murmuring submission, and bald government,             605
(The idol weak as the idolator,)
And Decency and Custom starving Truth,
And blind Authority beating with his staff
The child that might have led him; Emptiness
Followed as of good omen, and meek Worth               610
Left to herself unheard of and unknown.

    Of these and other kindred notices
I cannot say what portion is in truth

636–7 Guile; Murmuring 𝔄 C D: guile Murmuring E.

The naked recollection of that time,
And what may rather have been call'd to life          [615]
By after-meditation. But delight,
That, in an easy temper lull'd asleep,
650 Is still with innocence its own reward,
This surely was not wanting. Carelessly
I gaz'd, roving as through a Cabinet                  [620]
Or wide Museum (throng'd with fishes, gems,
Birds, crocodiles, shells) where little can be seen
655 Well understood, or naturally endear'd,
Yet still does every step bring something forth
That quickens, pleases, stings; and here and there
A casual rarity is singled out,
And has its brief perusal, then gives way
660 To others, all supplanted in their turn.
Meanwhile, amid this gaudy Congress, fram'd
Of things, by nature, most unneighbourly,            [625]
The head turns round, and cannot right itself;
And, though an aching and a barren sense
665 Of gay confusion still be uppermost,
With few wise longings and but little love,
Yet something to the memory sticks at last,          [630]
Whence profit may be drawn in times to come.

Thus in submissive idleness, my Friend,
670 The labouring time of Autumn, Winter, Spring,
Nine months, roll'd pleasingly away; the tenth
Return'd me to my native hills again.                 [635]

The naked recollection of that time,
And what may rather have been called to life          615
By after-meditation. But delight
That, in an easy temper lulled asleep,
Is still with Innocence its own reward,
This was not wanting. Carelessly I roamed
As through a wide museum from whose stores          620
A casual rarity is singled out
And has its brief perusal, then gives way
To others, all supplanted in their turn;
Till 'mid this crowded neighbourhood of things
That are by nature most unneighbourly,          625
The head turns round and cannot right itself;
And though an aching and a barren sense
Of gay confusion still be uppermost,
With few wise longings and but little love,
Yet to the memory something cleaves at last,          630
Whence profit may be drawn in times to come.

  Thus in submissive idleness, my Friend!
The labouring time of autumn, winter, spring,
Eight months! rolled pleasingly away; the ninth
Came and returned me to my native hills.          635

    647-8 And what more recent coinage. But delight M.
    651-7, 661, 662, 667 𝔄 C D: D² *as* 1850.
    669 submissive] unburthen'd M.
    671 Eight . . . ninth 𝔄 C D: Nine . . . tenth D².
    672 𝔄 C D: D² *as* 1850.

# BOOK FOURTH

## SUMMER VACATION

A PLEASANT sight it was when, having clomb
The Heights of Kendal, and that dreary Moor
Was cross'd, at length, as from a rampart's edge,
I overlook'd the bed of Windermere.                    [5]
5 I bounded down the hill, shouting amain
A lusty summons to the farther shore
For the old Ferryman; and when he came                 [13]
I did not step into the well-known Boat
Without a cordial welcome. Thence right forth
10 I took my way, now drawing towards home,
To that sweet Valley where I had been rear'd;
'Twas but a short hour's walk ere, veering round,      [20]
I saw the snow-white Church upon its hill
Sit like a thronèd Lady, sending out
15 A gracious look all over its domain.
Glad greetings had I, and some tears, perhaps,         [27]
From my old Dame, so motherly and good;
While she perus'd me with a Parent's pride.
The thoughts of gratitude shall fall like dew          [30]
20 Upon thy grave, good Creature! While my heart
Can beat I never will forget thy name.
Heaven's blessing be upon thee where thou liest,

[MSS. for Book IV: M A B C D E; *for ll.* 270–365 W; *for ll.* 450–81 *Alf.*;
*for ll.* 363–504 MS. 18a *and Chr.*]
Book Fourth. Summer Vacation B C: *no heading in* A.
1 A pleasant sight] Moment of joy A² B² C.
1–4 D *stuck over*: D² *as* 1850.
4–5 *Between these lines* A² B² C *add* [6–11].
    *After* bays [8] And bordering groves and cottages and woods, A² B².
           Saw from that height, beneath the ethereal Vault A² B² C.
7–8      For the old Ferryman, the rocks replied,
         The waveless lake was friendly to the shout
         And soon as measuring with well-tim'd oars
         And leisurely despatch his beaten course
         The Ferryman had reached the jutting pier
         I did not step A² C.
         And when the Charon of the flood with oars
         Deliberate had reached the jutting pier
         I did not step D: D² *as* 1850.
9–10 [17–18] A C D: D² *as* 1850.

# BOOK FOURTH

## SUMMER VACATION

BRIGHT was the summer's noon when quickening steps
Followed each other till a dreary moor
Was crossed, a bare ridge clomb, upon whose top
Standing alone, as from a rampart's edge,
I overlooked the bed of Windermere,                           5
Like a vast river, stretching in the sun.
With exultation, at my feet I saw
Lake, islands, promontories, gleaming bays,
A universe of Nature's fairest forms
Proudly revealed with instantaneous burst,                   10
Magnificent, and beautiful, and gay.
I bounded down the hill shouting amain
For the old Ferryman; to the shout the rocks
Replied, and when the Charon of the flood
Had staid his oars, and touched the jutting pier,            15
I did not step into the well-known boat
Without a cordial greeting. Thence with speed
Up the familiar hill I took my way
Towards that sweet Valley where I had been reared;
'Twas but a short hour's walk, ere veering round             20
I saw the snow-white church upon her hill
Sit like a thronèd Lady, sending out
A gracious look all over her domain.
Yon azure smoke betrays the lurking town;
With eager footsteps I advance and reach                     25
The cottage threshold where my journey closed.
Glad welcome had I, with some tears, perhaps,
From my old Dame, so kind and motherly,
While she perused me with a parent's pride.
The thoughts of gratitude shall fall like dew                30
Upon thy grave, good creature! While my heart
Can beat never will I forget thy name.
Heaven's blessing be upon thee where thou liest

[24–26] *Not in* 𝔄: *added* A², *but with* That *for* Yon *and* quickening *for*
eager. *So* C D E: E² *as* 1850.
16–17 greetings . . . and . . . motherly and good 𝔄 C D: D² *as* 1850.

After thy innocent and busy stir
In narrow cares, thy little daily growth                                    [35]
25  Of calm enjoyments, after eighty years,
And more than eighty, of untroubled life,
Childless, yet by the strangers to thy blood
Honour'd with little less than filial love.
Great joy was mine to see thee once again,                                  [40]
30  Thee and thy dwelling; and a throng of things
About its narrow precincts all belov'd,
And many of them seeming yet my own.
Why should I speak of what a thousand hearts
Have felt, and every man alive can guess?                                   [45]
35  The rooms, the court, the garden were not left
Long unsaluted, and the spreading Pine
And broad stone Table underneath its boughs,
Our summer seat in many a festive hour;
And that unruly Child of mountain birth,                                    [50]
40  The froward Brook, which soon as he was box'd
Within our Garden, found himself at once,
As if by trick insidious and unkind,
Stripp'd of his voice, and left to dimple down
Without an effort and without a will,                                       [55]
45  A channel pavèd by the hand of man.
I look'd at him, and smil'd, and smil'd again,
And in the press of twenty thousand thoughts,
'Ha,' quoth I, 'pretty Prisoner, are you there!'                           [59]
And now, reviewing soberly that hour,
50  I marvel that a fancy did not flash
Upon me, and a strong desire, straitway,
At sight of such an emblem that shew'd forth
So aptly my late course of even days
And all their smooth enthralment, to pen down
55  A satire on myself. My aged Dame
Was with me, at my side: She guided me;                                     [65]
I willing, nay—nay—wishing to be led.
—The face of every neighbour whom I met
Was as a volume to me: some I hail'd

26 life,] life 𝔄 C.          29 Great 𝔄 C D: True D² E: What E².
30 throng 𝔄 C D: crowd D².          40 froward 𝔄 C D: famous E.
45 pavèd A²: paved 𝔄.
49–52          Pleasure and satisfaction filled the heart
                Else how could playful fancy have forborne
                At sight etc. A² C.

After thy innocent and busy stir
In narrow cares, thy little daily growth　　　　35
Of calm enjoyments, after eighty years,
And more than eighty, of untroubled life,
Childless, yet by the strangers to thy blood
Honoured with little less than filial love.
What joy was mine to see thee once again,　　　　40
Thee and thy dwelling, and a crowd of things
About its narrow precincts all beloved,
And many of them seeming yet my own!
Why should I speak of what a thousand hearts
Have felt, and every man alive can guess?　　　　45
The rooms, the court, the garden were not left
Long unsaluted, nor the sunny seat
Round the stone table under the dark pine,
Friendly to studious or to festive hours;
Nor that unruly child of mountain birth,　　　　50
The famous brook, who, soon as he was boxed
Within our garden, found himself at once,
As if by trick insidious and unkind,
Stripped of his voice and left to dimple down
(Without an effort and without a will)　　　　55
A channel paved by man's officious care.
I looked at him and smiled, and smiled again,
And in the press of twenty thousand thoughts,
'Ha,' quoth I, 'pretty prisoner, are you there!'
Well might sarcastic Fancy then have whispered,　　　　60
'An emblem here behold of thy own life;
In its late course of even days with all
Their smooth enthralment;' but the heart was full,
Too full for that reproach. My aged Dame
Walked proudly at my side: she guided me;　　　　65
I willing, nay—nay, wishing to be led.
—The face of every neighbour whom I met
Was like a volume to me: some were hailed

[60–62]　　　How could sarcastic fancy then abstain
　　　　　　From whispering 'Lo! an emblem of thyself
　　　　　　Of thy late course of even days with all D.
　　　　　　Strange that sarcastic fancy then forebore
　　　　　　To whisper Lo an emblem of thy life
　　　　　　In its late course of *etc.* D² E: E² *as* 1850.
[64] that reproach D² E: such a thought D.

60  Far off, upon the road, or at their work,
    Unceremonious greetings, interchang'd                        [70]
    With half the length of a long field between.
    Among my Schoolfellows I scatter'd round
    A salutation that was more constrain'd,
65  Though earnest, doubtless with a little pride,
    But with more shame, for my habiliments,                     [75]
    The transformation, and the gay attire.

        Delighted did I take my place again
    At our domestic Table; and, dear Friend!
70  Relating simply as my wish hath been
    A Poet's history, can I leave untold                         [80]
    The joy with which I laid me down at night
    In my accustomed Bed, more welcome now
    Perhaps, than if it had been more desir'd
75  Or been more often thought of with regret;
    That Bed whence I had heard the roaring wind                 [85]
    And clamorous rain, that Bed where I, so oft,
    Had lain awake, on breezy nights, to watch
    The moon in splendour couch'd among the leaves
80  Of a tall Ash, that near our cottage stood,
    Had watch'd her with fix'd eyes, while to and fro            [90]
    In the dark summit of the moving Tree
    She rock'd with every impulse of the wind.

        Among the faces which it pleas'd me well
85  To see again, was one, by ancient right
    Our Inmate, a rough Terrier of the hills,                    [95]
    By birth and call of Nature pre-ordain'd
    To hunt the badger, and unearth the fox,
    Among the impervious crags; but, having been
90  From youth our own adopted, he had pass'd
    Into a gentler service. And when first                       [100]
    The boyish spirit flagg'd, and day by day
    Along my veins I kindled with the stir,
    The fermentation and the vernal heat
95  Of Poesy, affecting private shades
    Like a sick lover, then this Dog was used                    [105]
    To watch me, an attendant and a friend

60 Pacing the public road, others at their work  D: D² *as* 1850.
64, 65, 67 𝔄 C D: D² *as* 1850.

Upon the road, some busy at their work,
Unceremonious greetings interchanged                          70
With half the length of a long field between.
Among my schoolfellows I scattered round
Like recognitions, but with some constraint
Attended, doubtless, with a little pride,
But with more shame, for my habiliments,                      75
The transformation wrought by gay attire.
Not less delighted did I take my place
At our domestic table: and, dear Friend!
In this endeavour simply to relate
A Poet's history, may I leave untold                          80
The thankfulness with which I laid me down
In my accustomed bed, more welcome now
Perhaps than if it had been more desired
Or been more often thought of with regret;
That lowly bed whence I had heard the wind                    85
Roar and the rain beat hard, where I so oft
Had lain awake on summer nights to watch
The moon in splendour couched among the leaves
Of a tall ash, that near our cottage stood;
Had watched her with fixed eyes while to and fro              90
In the dark summit of the waving tree
She rocked with every impulse of the breeze.

Among the favourites whom it pleased me well
To see again, was one by ancient right
Our inmate, a rough terrier of the hills;                     95
By birth and call of nature pre-ordained
To hunt the badger and unearth the fox
Among the impervious crags, but having been
From youth our own adopted, he had passed
Into a gentler service. And when first                        100
The boyish spirit flagged, and day by day
Along my veins I kindled with the stir,
The fermentation, and the vernal heat
Of poesy, affecting private shades
Like a sick Lover, then this dog was used                     105
To watch me, an attendant and a friend,

71–73 A C D:        be one word given
To the delight which met me once again
Entering my humble chamber, now more priz'd D²: D³ *as* 1850.
76–77 A² C *as* 1850.        79 leaves] trees M.        85 see] meet B².

Obsequious to my steps, early and late,
Though often of such dilatory walk
100  Tired, and uneasy at the halts I made.
A hundred times when, in these wanderings,                    [110]
I have been busy with the toil of verse,
Great pains and little progress, and at once
Some fair enchanting image in my mind
105  Rose up, full-form'd, like Venus from the sea
Have I sprung forth towards him, and let loose               [115]
My hand upon his back with stormy joy,
Caressing him again, and yet again.
And when, in the public roads at eventide
110  I saunter'd, like a river murmuring
And talking to itself, at such a season                      [120]
It was his custom to jog on before;
But, duly, whensoever he had met
A passenger approaching, would he turn
115  To give me timely notice, and straitway,
Punctual to such admonishment, I hush'd                      [125]
My voice, composed my gait, and shap'd myself
To give and take a greeting that might save
My name from piteous rumours, such as wait
120  On men suspected to be craz'd in brain.                  [130]


Those walks, well worthy to be priz'd and lov'd,
Regretted! that word, too, was on my tongue,
But they were richly laden with all good,
And cannot be remember'd but with thanks
125  And gratitude, and perfect joy of heart,                 [135]
Those walks did now, like a returning spring,
Come back on me again. When first I made
Once more the circuit of our little Lake
If ever happiness hath lodg'd with man,
130  That day consummate happiness was mine,                  [140]

99 dilatory] desultory M.
  101 in these wanderings] wandering in this sort B²: roving high and low
A² C.
  101–2 A hundred times when, with my shaggy friend
          Thus roving through the mountains high and low
          I have been harassed by the toil of verse A³.
  104 𝔄 C D: D² as 1850.
  105–6     Appeared full-formed, as Venus from the sea
            Rising, have I sprung forward D: D² as 1850.

Obsequious to my steps early and late,
Though often of such dilatory walk
Tired, and uneasy at the halts I made.
A hundred times when, roving high and low,                110
I have been harassed with the toil of verse,
Much pains and little progress, and at once
Some lovely Image in the song rose up
Full-formed, like Venus rising from the sea;
Then have I darted forwards to let loose                115
My hand upon his back with stormy joy,
Caressing him again and yet again.
And when at evening on the public way
I sauntered, like a river murmuring
And talking to itself when all things else                120
Are still, the creature trotted on before;
Such was his custom; but whene'er he met
A passenger approaching, he would turn
To give me timely notice, and straightway,
Grateful for that admonishment, I hushed                125
My voice, composed my gait, and, with the air
And mien of one whose thoughts are free, advanced
To give and take a greeting that might save
My name from piteous rumours, such as wait
On men suspected to be crazed in brain.                130

Those walks well worthy to be prized and loved—
Regretted!—that word, too, was on my tongue,
But they were richly laden with all good,
And cannot be remembered but with thanks
And gratitude, and perfect joy of heart—                135
Those walks in all their freshness now came back
Like a returning Spring. When first I made
Once more the circuit of our little lake,
If ever happiness hath lodged with man,
That day consummate happiness was mine,                140

106–7    Have I sprung forward and let loose my hand
              Upon the Creature's back with stormy joy A²
111  at such a season] at such still season A² D: D² *as* 1850.
111–13  𝔄 C D: D² *as* 1850.
116  Punctual to 𝔄 C D E: Grateful for E².
117–18  shap'd myself To give 𝔄: A² C *as* 1850.
121  priz'd 𝔄 C E²; praised D E.
126–7  𝔄 C D: D² *as* 1850 [136], *but* new (*error for* their new (?)) *for* all
their. *So* E, *but* E² *as* 1850.

Wide-spreading, steady, calm, contemplative.
The sun was set, or setting, when I left
Our cottage door, and evening soon brought on
A sober hour, not winning or serene,
135 For cold and raw the air was, and untun'd:                    [145]
But, as a face we love is sweetest then
When sorrow damps it, or, whatever look
It chance to wear is sweetest if the heart
Have fulness in itself, even so with me
140 It fared that evening. Gently did my soul                     [150]
Put off her veil, and, self-transmuted, stood
Naked as in the presence of her God.
As on I walked, a comfort seem'd to touch
A heart that had not been disconsolate,
145 Strength came where weakness was not known to be,    [155]
At least not felt; and restoration came,
Like an intruder, knocking at the door
Of unacknowledg'd weariness. I took
The balance in my hand and weigh'd myself.
150 I saw but little, and thereat was pleas'd;                    [161]
Little did I remember, and even this
Still pleas'd me more; but I had hopes and peace
And swellings of the spirits, was rapt and soothed,
Convers'd with promises, had glimmering views
155 How Life pervades the undecaying mind,                       [165]
How the immortal Soul with God-like power
Informs, creates, and thaws the deepest sleep
That time can lay upon her; how on earth,
Man, if he do but live within the light
160 Of high endeavours, daily spreads abroad                     [170]
His being with a strength that cannot fail.
Nor was there want of milder thoughts, of love,
Of innocence, and holiday repose;
And more than pastoral quiet, in the heart
165 Of amplest projects; and a peaceful end                      [175]
At last, or glorious, by endurance won.
Thus musing, in a wood I sate me down,
Alone, continuing there to muse: meanwhile
The mountain heights were slowly overspread

148 weariness B²: weakness M 𝔄.
149 𝔄 C D: D² as 1850.
[160] D²: Of the external world that round me lay: *added in* B, *not in* C.

Wide-spreading, steady, calm, contemplative.
The sun was set, or setting, when I left
Our cottage door, and evening soon brought on
A sober hour, not winning or serene,
For cold and raw the air was, and untuned;                145
But as a face we love is sweetest then
When sorrow damps it, or, whatever look
It chance to wear, is sweetest if the heart
Have fulness in herself; even so with me
It fared that evening. Gently did my soul                150
Put off her veil, and, self-transmuted, stood
Naked, as in the presence of her God.
While on I walked, a comfort seemed to touch
A heart that had not been disconsolate:
Strength came where weakness was not known to be,        155
At least not felt; and restoration came
Like an intruder knocking at the door
Of unacknowledged weariness. I took
The balance, and with firm hand weighed myself.
—Of that external scene which round me lay,              160
Little, in this abstraction, did I see;
Remembered less; but I had inward hopes
And swellings of the spirit, was rapt and soothed,
Conversed with promises, had glimmering views
How life pervades the undecaying mind;                   165
How the immortal soul with God-like power
Informs, creates, and thaws the deepest sleep
That time can lay upon her; how on earth,
Man, if he do but live within the light
Of high endeavours, daily spreads abroad                 170
His being armed with strength that cannot fail.
Nor was there want of milder thoughts, of love
Of innocence, and holiday repose;
And more than pastoral quiet, 'mid the stir
Of boldest projects, and a peaceful end                  175
At last, or glorious, by endurance won.
Thus musing, in a wood I sate me down
Alone, continuing there to muse: the slopes
And heights meanwhile were slowly overspread

153 spirits M 𝔄 C: spirit *with final* s *erased* D.  rapt B² D²: **wrapp'd**
M 𝔄 C D.
161–80 𝔄 C D: D² *as* 1850.

170  With darkness, and before a rippling breeze          [180]
     The long Lake lengthen'd out its hoary line;
     And in the shelter'd coppice where I sate,
     Around me, from among the hazel leaves,
     Now here, now there, stirr'd by the straggling wind,
175  Came intermittingly a breath-like sound,              [185]
     A respiration short and quick, which oft,
     Yea, might I say, again and yet again,
     Mistaking for the panting of my Dog,
     The off-and-on Companion of my walk,
180  I turn'd my head, to look if he were there.          [189]

         A freshness also found I at this time
     In human Life, the life I mean of those
     Whose occupations really I lov'd.
     The prospect often touch'd me with surprize,
185  Crowded and full, and chang'd, as seem'd to me,
     Even as a garden in the heat of Spring,              [195]
     After an eight-days' absence. For (to omit
     The things which were the same and yet appear'd
     So different) amid this solitude,
190  The little Vale where was my chief abode,
     'Twas not indifferent to a youthful mind             [200]
     To note, perhaps, some shelter'd Seat in which
     An old Man had been used to sun himself,
     Now empty; pale-fac'd Babes whom I had left
195  In arms, known children of the neighbourhood,
     Now rosy prattlers, tottering up and down;          [205]
     And growing Girls whose beauty, filch'd away
     With all its pleasant promises, was gone
     To deck some slighted Playmate's homely cheek.

200      Yes, I had something of another eye,
     And often, looking round, was mov'd to smiles,      [210]
     Such as a delicate work of humour breeds.
     I read, without design, the opinions, thoughts
     Of those plain-living People, in a sense
205  Of love and knowledge; with another eye
     I saw the quiet Woodman in the Woods,               [215]
     The Shepherd on the Hills. With new delight,

189  A C D: D² *as* 1850.
192  To note some shelter'd seat, in which erewhile B².

With darkness, and before a rippling breeze  180
The long lake lengthened out its hoary line,
And in the sheltered coppice where I sate,
Around me from among the hazel leaves,
Now here, now there, moved by the straggling wind,
Came ever and anon a breath-like sound,  185
Quick as the pantings of the faithful dog,
The off and on companion of my walk;
And such, at times, believing them to be,
I turned my head to look if he were there;
Then into solemn thought I passed once more.  190

A freshness also found I at this time
In human Life, the daily life of those
Whose occupations really I loved;
The peaceful scene oft filled me with surprise
Changed like a garden in the heat of spring  195
After an eight-days' absence. For (to omit
The things which were the same and yet appeared
Far otherwise) amid this rural solitude,
A narrow Vale where each was known to all,
'Twas not indifferent to a youthful mind  200
To mark some sheltering bower or sunny nook,
Where an old man had used to sit alone,
Now vacant; pale-faced babes whom I had left
In arms, now rosy prattlers at the feet
Of a pleased grandame tottering up and down;  205
And growing girls whose beauty, filched away
With all its pleasant promises, was gone
To deck some slighted playmate's homely cheek.

Yes, I had something of a subtler sense,
And often looking round was moved to smiles  210
Such as a delicate work of humour breeds;
I read, without design, the opinions, thoughts,
Of those plain-living people now observed
With clearer knowledge; with another eye
I saw the quiet woodman in the woods,  215
The shepherd roam the hills. With new delight,

192–4 To note a shelter'd and a sunny seat
        Where some old Man had used to sit alone
        Now vacant A². *So* D. *but* nook *for* seat; D³ *as* 1850.
200, 204–5, 207–8 𝔄 C D: D² *as.*1850.

This chiefly, did I view my grey-hair'd Dame,
Saw her go forth to Church, or other work
210 Of state, equipp'd in monumental trim,
Short Velvet Cloak (her Bonnet of the like)                [220]
A Mantle such as Spanish Cavaliers
Wore in old time. Her smooth domestic life,
Affectionate without uneasiness,
215 Her talk, her business pleas'd me, and no less
Her clear though shallow stream of piety,                  [225]
That ran on Sabbath days a fresher course.
With thoughts unfelt till now, I saw her read
Her Bible on the Sunday afternoons;
220 And lov'd the book, when she had dropp'd asleep,
And made of it a pillow for her head.                      [230]

        Nor less do I remember to have felt
Distinctly manifested at this time
A dawning, even as of another sense,
225 A human-heartedness about my love
For objects hitherto the gladsome air
Of my own private being, and no more;                      [235]
Which I had loved, even as a blessed Spirit
Or Angel, if he were to dwell on earth,
230 Might love, in individual happiness.
But now there open'd on me other thoughts,
Of change, congratulation, and regret,                     [240]
A new-born feeling. It spread far and wide;
The trees, the mountains shared it, and the brooks;
235 The stars of Heaven, now seen in their old haunts,
White Sirius, glittering o'er the southern crags,
Orion with his belt, and those fair Seven,                 [245]
Acquaintances of every little child,
And Jupiter, my own beloved Star.
240 Whatever shadings of mortality
Had fallen upon these objects heretofore                   [250]
Were different in kind; not tender: strong,
Deep, gloomy were they and severe; the scatterings
Of Childhood; and, moreover, had given way,

214 uneasiness 𝔄: disquietude A² B² C.
219 the 𝔄 C D: hot D².
224 A dawning *etc.* 𝔄 C D, *but* D *deletes*.
226 gladsome air 𝔄: absolute wealth A² C: absolute joy B².

This chiefly, did I note my grey-haired Dame;
Saw her go forth to church or other work
Of state, equipped in monumental trim;
Short velvet cloak, (her bonnet of the like),          220
A mantle such as Spanish Cavaliers
Wore in old time. Her smooth domestic life,
Affectionate without disquietude,
Her talk, her business, pleased me; and no less
Her clear though shallow stream of piety             225
That ran on Sabbath days a fresher course;
With thoughts unfelt till now I saw her read
Her Bible on hot Sunday afternoons,
And loved the book, when she had dropped asleep
And made of it a pillow for her head.                230

  Nor less do I remember to have felt,
Distinctly manifested at this time,
A human-heartedness about my love
For objects hitherto the absolute wealth
Of my own private being and no more:                 235
Which I had loved, even as a blessed spirit
Or Angel, if he were to dwell on earth,
Might love in individual happiness.
But now there opened on me other thoughts
Of change, congratulation or regret,                 240
A pensive feeling! It spread far and wide;
The trees, the mountains shared it, and the brooks,
The stars of Heaven, now seen in their old haunts—
White Sirius glittering o'er the southern crags,
Orion with his belt, and those fair Seven,           245
Acquaintances of every little child,
And Jupiter, my own beloved star!
Whatever shadings of mortality,
Whatever imports from the world of death
Had come among these objects heretofore,             250
Were, in the main, of mood less tender: strong,
Deep, gloomy were they, and severe; the scatterings
Of awe or tremulous dread, that had given way

233 new-born 𝔄 C D: pensive D².
240 A² B² *add line here* Drawn from the pure imaginative soul. *So* C.
[249] *added to* D.        241 fallen upon 𝔄 C D: come among D².
242 not tender 𝔄 C: less tender M.

245    In later youth, to beauty, and to love
       Enthusiastic, to delight and joy.                    [255]

          As one who hangs down-bending from the side
       Of a slow-moving Boat, upon the breast
       Of a still water, solacing himself
250    With such discoveries as his eye can make,
       Beneath him, in the bottom of the deeps,            [260]
       Sees many beauteous sights, weeds, fishes, flowers,
       Grots, pebbles, roots of trees, and fancies more;
       Yet often is perplex'd, and cannot part
255    The shadow from the substance, rocks and sky,
       Mountains and clouds, from that which is indeed     [265]
       The region, and the things which there abide
       In their true dwelling; now is cross'd by gleam
       Of his own image, by a sunbeam now,
260    And motions that are sent he knows not whence,
       Impediments that make his task more sweet;          [270]
       —Such pleasant office have we long pursued
       Incumbent o'er the surface of past time
       With like success; nor have we often look'd
265    On more alluring shows (to me, at least,)
       More soft, or less ambiguously descried,
       Than those which now we have been passing by,       [275]
       And where we still are lingering. Yet, in spite
       Of all these new employments of the mind,
270    There was an inner falling-off. I loved,
       Loved deeply, all that I had loved before,
       More deeply even than ever; but a swarm             [280]
       Of heady thoughts jostling each other, gawds,
       And feast, and dance, and public revelry,
275    And sports and games (less pleasing in themselves,
       Than as they were a badge glossy and fresh          [285]
       Of manliness and freedom) these did now

253 Pebbles or roots M.
255 Shadow from substance, rocks from azure sky B².
256–7 that which is indeed The region, and *not in* M: A² B² C *as* 1850.
260 motions that are] tremulous motions A² C.
263 Incumbent o'er] Floating upon A² B² C.
264–8                              nor often in the abyss
          Have we discover'd more alluring shows
          More soft, or less ambiguously descried,
          Than those, my Friend, which we have lately passed,
          And which do still detain us A² B² C: D *stuck over*: D² *as* 1850.

In later youth to yearnings of a love
Enthusiastic, to delight and hope.                                255

    As one who hangs down-bending from the side
Of a slow-moving boat, upon the breast
Of a still water, solacing himself
With such discoveries as his eye can make
Beneath him in the bottom of the deep,                            260
Sees many beauteous sights—weeds, fishes, flowers,
Grots, pebbles, roots of trees, and fancies more,
Yet often is perplexed and cannot part
The shadow from the substance, rocks and sky,
Mountains and clouds, reflected in the depth                      265
Of the clear flood, from things which there abide
In their true dwelling; now is crossed by gleam
Of his own image, by a sun-beam now,
And wavering motions sent he knows not whence,
Impediments that make his task more sweet;                        270
Such pleasant office have we long pursued
Incumbent o'er the surface of past time
With like success, nor often have appeared
Shapes fairer or less doubtfully discerned
Than these to which the Tale, indulgent Friend!                   275
Would now direct thy notice. Yet in spite
Of pleasure won, and knowledge not withheld,
There was an inner falling off—I loved,
Loved deeply all that had been loved before,
More deeply even than ever: but a swarm                           280
Of heady schemes jostling each other, gawds,
And feast and dance, and public revelry,
And sports and games (too grateful in themselves,
Yet in themselves less grateful, I believe,
Than as they were a badge glossy and fresh                        285
Of manliness and freedom) all conspired

270 falling-off] weakness. Much M. W *begins here, thus*:
        Auspicious was this outset and the days
        That follow'd march'd in flattering symphony
        With such a fair presage; but 'twas not long
        Ere fallings off and indirect desires
        Told of an inner weakness. Much I lov'd
272 swarm 𝔄 C D: throng W: D² *as* 1850.
275 [283–4] A² C D *as* 1850, *but* D *has* pleasing *for* grateful: grateful D².
277 manliness and] manhood and of W.

Seduce me from the firm habitual quest
Of feeding pleasures, from that eager zeal,
280 Those yearnings which had every day been mine,
A wild unworldly-minded Youth, given up                    [290]
To Nature and to Books, or, at the most,
From time to time, by inclination shipp'd,
One among many, in societies,
285 That were, or seem'd, as simple as myself.
But now was come a change; it would demand
Some skill, and longer time than may be spared,
To paint, even to myself, these vanities,
And how they wrought. But, sure it is that now
290 Contagious air did oft environ me
Unknown among these haunts in former days.
The very garments that I wore appear'd                    [295]
To prey upon my strength, and stopp'd the course
And quiet stream of self-forgetfulness.
295 Something there was about me that perplex'd
Th' authentic sight of reason, press'd too closely
On that religious dignity of mind,
That is the very faculty of truth;
Which wanting, either, from the very first,
300 A function never lighted up, or else
Extinguish'd, Man, a creature great and good,
Seems but a pageant plaything with vile claws
And this great frame of breathing elements
A senseless Idol.
                          That vague heartless chace
305 Of trivial pleasures was a poor exchange
For Books and Nature at that early age.
'Tis true, some casual knowledge might be gain'd                    [300]
Of character or life; but at that time
Of manners put to school I took small note;
310 And all my deeper passions lay elsewhere.
Far better had it been to exalt the mind
By solitary study; to uphold                    [305]
Intense desire by thought and quietness.
And yet, in chastisement of these regrets,
315 The memory of one particular hour
Doth here rise up against me. In a throng,
A festal company of Maids and Youths,
Old Men, and Matrons staid, promiscuous rout,                    [310]

To lure my mind from firm habitual quest
Of feeding pleasures, to depress the zeal
And damp those yearnings which had once been mine—
A wild, unworldly-minded youth, given up　　　　290
To his own eager thoughts. It would demand
Some skill, and longer time than may be spared,
To paint these vanities, and how they wrought
In haunts where they, till now, had been unknown.
It seemed the very garments that I wore　　　　295
Preyed on my strength, and stopped the quiet stream
Of self-forgetfulness.

　　　　　　　　　Yes, that heartless chase
Of trivial pleasures was a poor exchange
For books and nature at that early age.
'Tis true, some casual knowledge might be gained　　　300
Of character or life; but at that time,
Of manners put to school I took small note,
And all my deeper passions lay elsewhere.
Far better had it been to exalt the mind
By solitary study, to uphold　　　　305
Intense desire through meditative peace;
And yet, for chastisement of these regrets,
The memory of one particular hour
Doth here rise up against me. 'Mid a throng
Of maids and youths, old men, and matrons staid,　　　310

279-82 𝔄 C D: D² *as* 1850, *but with* those daily yearnings (*hyper-metrically*). *So* E.
282-6 or, at the most, . . . change] A B *delete*: *not in* C.
288 paint] unfold W.
296-7 press'd too closely On] interfered With W.
299-300 Which wanting, either from the first, a function
　　　　Not lighted up, or one by hapless doom A² B² C. *So* D, *but with*
　　　　by untoward *for* one by hapless
299-301 either . . . Extinguish'd] *not in* W.
302 Seems but a piece of fearful mechanism
　　Vile as the Tyger's which the barbarous East
　　Constructs, to lodge within her palace walls, A² C. *So* B², *but in*
　　*place of last two lines reads*
　　An oriental plaything with vile claws.
　　D *reads* Vile as the Tygers, which, with skill perverse
　　　　　And monstrous, Tyrants of the barbarous East
　　　　　Construct to growl *etc.*
304 This flitting idleness, this giddy chase W.
　　A senseless Idol. Such vague M A² C.
307 gain'd] glean'd W.
309 Of outside manners I took little note W.

A medley of all tempers, I had pass'd
320 The night in dancing, gaiety and mirth;
With din of instruments, and shuffling feet,
And glancing forms, and tapers glittering,
And unaim'd prattle flying up and down,
Spirits upon the stretch, and here and there     [316]
325 Slight shocks of young love-liking interspers'd,
That mounted up like joy into the head,
And tingled through the veins. Ere we retired,
The cock had crow'd, the sky was bright with day.     [320]
Two miles I had to walk along the fields
330 Before I reached my home. Magnificent
The morning was, a memorable pomp,
More glorious than I ever had beheld.     [325]
The Sea was laughing at a distance; all
The solid Mountains were as bright as clouds,
335 Grain-tinctured, drench'd in empyrean light;
And, in the meadows and the lower grounds,
Was all the sweetness of a common dawn,     [330]
Dews, vapours, and the melody of birds,
And Labourers going forth into the fields.
340 —Ah! need I say, dear Friend, that to the brim
My heart was full; I made no vows, but vows
Were then made for me; bond unknown to me     [335]
Was given, that I should be, else sinning greatly,
A dedicated Spirit. On I walk'd
345 In blessedness, which even yet remains.

Strange rendezvous my mind was at that time,
A party-colour'd show of grave and gay,     [340]
Solid and light, short-sighted and profound,
Of inconsiderate habits and sedate,
350 Consorting in one mansion unreprov'd.
I knew the worth of that which I possess'd,
Though slighted and misus'd. Besides, in truth,     [345]
That Summer, swarming as it did with thoughts

324 Like pauses in a fight and here and there W.
    Bustle and spirits strain'd and here and there W².
326 A² C *as* 1850.     328 D *as* 𝔄, *but* dawn *for* day.
329–30 Through woods and pleasant fields the pathway wound
       That led towards my home. A² C D: D² *as* 1850.
331 was, a] M U 𝔄: was, in 𝔄²: rose, in C.
332–4, 345 𝔄 C D: D² *as* 1850.
345 remains 𝔄 C D: survives D².

A medley of all tempers, I had passed
The night in dancing, gaiety, and mirth,
With din of instruments and shuffling feet,
And glancing forms, and tapers glittering,
And unaimed prattle flying up and down;                          315
Spirits upon the stretch, and here and there
Slight shocks of young love-liking interspersed,
Whose transient pleasure mounted to the head,
And tingled through the veins. Ere we retired,
The cock had crowed, and now the eastern sky                     320
Was kindling, not unseen, from humble copse
And open field, through which the pathway wound,
And homeward led my steps. Magnificent
The morning rose, in memorable pomp,
Glorious as e'er I had beheld—in front,                          325
The sea lay laughing at a distance; near,
The solid mountains shone, bright as the clouds,
Grain-tinctured, drenched in empyrean light;
And in the meadows and the lower grounds
Was all the sweetness of a common dawn—                          330
Dews, vapours, and the melody of birds,
And labourers going forth to till the fields.

Ah! need I say, dear Friend! that to the brim
My heart was full; I made no vows, but vows
Were then made for me; bond unknown to me                        335
Was given, that I should be, else sinning greatly,
A dedicated Spirit. On I walked
In thankful blessedness, which yet survives.

Strange rendezvous! My mind was at that time
A parti-coloured show of grave and gay,                          340
Solid and light, short-sighted and profound;
Of inconsiderate habits and sedate,
Consorting in one mansion unreproved.
The worth I knew of powers that I possessed,
Though slighted and too oft misused. Besides,                    345
That summer, swarming as it did with thoughts

346 rendezvous my . . . time, 𝔄 C D: rendezvous my . . . time E.
351 𝔄 C D: D² *as* 1850.
353–7      That summer was not seldom interspersed
           With primitive hours when by these hindrances
           Uncross'd I recogniz'd within myself
           Conformity *etc.* W.

Transient and loose, yet wanted not a store
355 Of primitive hours, when, by these hindrances
Unthwarted, I experienc'd in myself
Conformity as just as that of old [350]
To the end and written spirit of God's works,
Whether held forth in Nature or in Man.

360 From many wanderings that have left behind
Remembrances not lifeless, I will here
Single out one, then pass to other themes.

A favorite pleasure hath it been with me,
From time of earliest youth, to walk alone
365 Along the public Way, when, for the night
Deserted, in its silence it assumes
A character of deeper quietness
Than pathless solitudes. At such an hour
Once, ere these summer months were pass'd away, [370]
370 I slowly mounted up a steep ascent [380]
Where the road's watry surface, to the ridge
Of that sharp rising, glitter'd in the moon,
And seem'd before my eyes another stream
Creeping with silent lapse to join the brook
375 That murmur'd in the valley. On I went [384]
Tranquil, receiving in my own despite
Amusement, as I slowly pass'd along,
From such near objects as from time to time,
Perforce intruded on the listless sense
380 Quiescent, and dispos'd to sympathy,
With an exhausted mind, worn out by toil,
And all unworthy of the deeper joy
Which waits on distant prospect, cliff, or sea,
The dark blue vault, and universe of stars.

[354–88] D *stuck over*: D² *as* 1850, *but in* [360] centre—anchorite (*as* E)
*for* human centre—hermit (E² *as* 1850), *and in* [362–3] Cathedral's silent
space *for* Cathedral, where . . . seen.
363–4 I love to walk *Chr.* 18a.
    It was a habit form'd in early youth
    And is a favorite pleasure with me now
    Dear Friend, as well thou knowest, to walk alone  A².
    A favorite pleasure was it of my youth
    Such is it now, dear friend, *etc.* A³ C.
364 Even from the time of earliest youth to walk W.
374 Creeping 𝔄 C: Stealing *Chr.* 18a M D² E.

Transient and idle, lacked not intervals
When Folly from the frown of fleeting Time
Shrunk, and the mind experienced in herself
Conformity as just as that of old                               350
To the end and written spirit of God's works,
Whether held forth in Nature or in Man,
Through pregnant vision, separate or conjoined.

When from our better selves we have too long
Been parted by the hurrying world, and droop,                   355
Sick of its business, of its pleasures tired,
How gracious, how benign, is Solitude;
How potent a mere image of her sway;
Most potent when impressed upon the mind
With an appropriate human centre—hermit,                        360
Deep in the bosom of the wilderness;
Votary (in vast cathedral, where no foot
Is treading, where no other face is seen)
Kneeling at prayers; or watchman on the top
Of lighthouse, beaten by Atlantic waves;                        365
Or as the soul of that great Power is met
Sometimes embodied on a public road,
When, for the night deserted, it assumes
A character of quiet more profound
Than pathless wastes.                                           370
                    Once, when those summer months
Were flown, and autumn brought its annual show
Of oars with oars contending, sails with sails,
Upon Winander's spacious breast, it chanced
That—after I had left a flower-decked room
(Whose in-door pastime, lighted up, survived                    375
To a late hour), and spirits overwrought
Were making night do penance for a day
Spent in a round of strenuous idleness—
My homeward course led up a long ascent,
Where the road's watery surface, to the top                     380
Of that sharp rising, glittered to the moon
And bore the semblance of another stream
Stealing with silent lapse to join the brook
That murmured in the vale. All else was still;

376–8    Receiving as I slowly passed along
            Amusement from near objects that perf[orce] A².
380 sympathy,] sympathy A C.

385 Thus did I steal along that silent road,
    My body from the stillness drinking in
    A restoration like the calm of sleep
    But sweeter far. Above, before, behind,
    Around me, all was peace and solitude,
390 I look'd not round, nor did the solitude
    Speak to my eye; but it was heard and felt.
    O happy state! what beauteous pictures now
    Rose in harmonious imagery—they rose
    As from some distant region of my soul
395 And came along like dreams; yet such as left
    Obscurely mingled with their passing forms
    A consciousness of animal delight,
    A self-possession felt in every pause
    And every gentle movement of my frame.
400     While thus I wander'd, step by step led on,
    It chanc'd a sudden turning of the road                    [388]
    Presented to my view an uncouth shape                      [387]
    So near, that, slipping back into the shade
    Of a thick hawthorn, I could mark him well,                [390]
405 Myself unseen. He was of stature tall,
    A foot above man's common measure tall,
    Stiff in his form, and upright, lank and lean,
    A man more meagre, as it seem'd to me,
    Was never seen abroad by night or day.
410 His arms were long, and bare his hands; his mouth         [395]
    Shew'd ghastly in the moonlight; from behind
    A milestone propp'd him, and his figure seem'd
    Half-sitting, and half-standing. I could mark
    That he was clad in military garb,
415 Though faded, yet entire. He was alone,
    Had no attendant, neither Dog, nor Staff,                  [400]
    Nor knapsack; in his very dress appear'd
    A desolation, a simplicity
    That seem'd akin to solitude. Long time
420 Did I peruse him with a mingled sense
    Of fear and sorrow. From his lips, meanwhile,
    There issued murmuring sounds, as if of pain               [405]
    Or of uneasy thought; yet still his form
    Kept the same steadiness; and at his feet
425 His shadow lay, and mov'd not. In a Glen
    Hard by, a Village stood, whose roofs and doors

No living thing appeared in earth or air,　　　385
And, save the flowing water's peaceful voice,
Sound there was none—but, lo! an uncouth shape,
Shown by a sudden turning of the road,
So near that, slipping back into the shade
Of a thick hawthorn, I could mark him well,　　　390
Myself unseen. He was of stature tall,
A span above man's common measure, tall,
Stiff, lank, and upright; a more meagre man
Was never seen before by night or day.
Long were his arms, pallid his hands; his mouth　　　395
Looked ghastly in the moonlight: from behind,
A mile-stone propped him; I could also ken
That he was clothed in military garb,
Though faded, yet entire. Companionless,
No dog attending, by no staff sustained,　　　400
He stood, and in his very dress appeared
A desolation, a simplicity,
To which the trappings of a gaudy world
Make a strange back-ground. From his lips, ere long,
Issued low muttered sounds, as if of pain　　　405
Or some uneasy thought; yet still his form
Kept the same awful steadiness—at his feet
His shadow lay, and moved not. From self-blame

390 not round] around M.　　　410 Long were his arms A² C.
411 Shew'd 𝔄 C D: Look'd M.
412–39 D *as* A² (*but omitting* 428):  D² *as* 1850.
419 seem'd] *So* M *but del.*; was M².
424 Kept the same awful steadiness—at his feet A² C D.

Were visible among the scatter'd trees,
Scarce distant from the spot an arrow's flight;
I wish'd to see him move; but he remain'd
430 Fix'd to his place, and still from time to time
Sent forth a murmuring voice of dead complaint,
Groans scarcely audible. Without self-blame
I had not thus prolong'd my watch; and now,
Subduing my heart's specious cowardise                         [410]
435 I left the shady nook where I had stood,
And hail'd him. Slowly from his resting-place
He rose, and with a lean and wasted arm
In measur'd gesture lifted to his head,
Return'd my salutation; then resum'd                           [415]
440 His station as before: and when, erelong,
I ask'd his history, he in reply
Was neither slow nor eager; but unmov'd,
And with a quiet, uncomplaining voice,
A stately air of mild indifference,                           [420]
445 He told, in simple words, a Soldier's Tale,
That in the Tropic Islands he had serv'd,
Whence he had landed, scarcely ten days past,
That on his landing he had been dismiss'd,
And now was travelling to his native home.                    [425]
450 At this, I turn'd and looked towards the Village
But all were gone to rest; the fires all out;
And every silent window to the Moon
Shone with a yellow glitter. 'No one there,'
Said I, 'is waking, we must measure back
455 The way which we have come: behind yon wood
A Labourer dwells; and, take it on my word
He will not murmur should we break his rest;
And with a ready heart will give you food
And lodging for the night.' At this he stoop'd,
460 And from the ground took up an oaken Staff,                 [428]
By me yet unobserv'd, a Traveller's Staff;
Which, I suppose, from his slack hand had dropp'd,
And lain till now neglected in the grass.                     [430]

Towards the Cottage without more delay
465 We shap'd our course; as it appear'd to me,
He travell'd without pain, and I beheld                       [432]
With ill-suppress'd astonishment his tall
And ghastly figure moving at my side;

Not wholly free, I watched him thus; at length
Subduing my heart's specious cowardice,  410
I left the shady nook where I had stood
And hailed him. Slowly from his resting-place
He rose, and with a lean and wasted arm
In measured gesture lifted to his head
Returned my salutation; then resumed  415
His station as before; and when I asked
His history, the veteran, in reply,
Was neither slow nor eager; but, unmoved,
And with a quiet uncomplaining voice,
A stately air of mild indifference,  420
He told in few plain words a soldier's tale—
That in the Tropic Islands he had served,
Whence he had landed scarcely three weeks past;
That on his landing he had been dismissed,
And now was travelling towards his native home.  425
This heard, I said, in pity, 'Come with me.'
He stooped, and straightway from the ground took up
An oaken staff by me yet unobserved—
A staff which must have dropt from his slack hand
And lay till now neglected in the grass.  430
Though weak his step and cautious, he appeared
To travel without pain, and I beheld,
With an astonishment but ill suppressed,
His ghostly figure moving at my side;

428 flight; M: flight, 𝔄 C.
445 simple] few plain A² C; a Soldier's Tale] a simple fact  18*a* M.
447 ten days 𝔄 C D: three weeks D².
450–2  I turn'd and through the open trees
Look'd down into the village. All were gone
To rest nor hearth nor taper-light appear'd
But every *etc. Alf.*
450–60 D *as* 𝔄 C, *but* traveller's *for* oaken (460): D² *as* 1850.
456 A labourer dwells an honest man and kind  *Alf.*
458–66  And he shall give you food, if food you need
And lodging for the night, so back we turnd
And to the cottage bent our steps. He appear'd
To travel  *Alf.*
465–6 course; as it appeared to me, He travell'd] course together. He
appeared To travel A² C.
467–8 𝔄 C D: D² *as* 1850 (*but* ghostly).

Nor, while we journey'd thus could I forbear    [435]
470 To question him of what he had endur'd
From hardship, battle, or the pestilence.
He, all the while, was in demeanor calm,    [440]
Concise in answer; solemn and sublime
He might have seem'd, but that in all he said
475 There was a strange half-absence, and a tone
Of weakness and indifference, as of one
Remembering the importance of his theme    [444]
But feeling it no longer. We advanced
Slowly, and, ere we to the wood were come
480 Discourse had ceas'd. Together on we pass'd,    [445-6]
In silence, through the shades, gloomy and dark;
Then, turning up along an open field
We gain'd the Cottage. At the door I knock'd,    [449]
Calling aloud 'my Friend, here is a Man
485 By sickness overcome; beneath your roof
This night let him find rest, and give him food,
If food he need, for he is faint and tired.'
Assur'd that now my Comrade would repose
In comfort, I entreated that henceforth
490 He would not linger in the public ways    [455]
But ask for timely furtherance and help
Such as his state requir'd. At this reproof,
With the same ghastly mildness in his look
He said 'my trust is in the God of Heaven
495 And in the eye of him that passes me.'    [460]
    The Cottage door was speedily unlock'd,
And now the Soldier touch'd his hat again
With his lean hand; and in a voice that seem'd
To speak with a reviving interest,
500 Till then unfelt, he thank'd me; I return'd    [465]
The blessing of the poor unhappy Man;
And so we parted. Back I cast a look,
And linger'd near the door a little space;
Then sought with quiet heart my distant home.

469 Nor, while we thus were journeying, did I fail M.
470-3 D *stuck over*: D² *as* 1850.        471 hardship,] War or 18a M.
475-81 D *as* A, *but* still *for* dark (481): D² *as* 1850.
482 Upturning, then,  A² C.
483 gain'd the  𝔄 C D: reached a D².
484-7 And to the charitable care of those
        Who dwelt within, commended him as one
        Belated, and by sickness overcome. A² C D:  D² *as* 1850.
488 my Comrade 𝔄 C D: the traveller D².

Nor could I, while we journeyed thus, forbear                     435
To turn from present hardships to the past,
And speak of war, battle, and pestilence,
Sprinkling this talk with questions, better spared,
On what he might himself have seen or felt.
He all the while was in demeanour calm,                           440
Concise in answer; solemn and sublime
He might have seemed, but that in all he said
There was a strange half-absence, as of one
Knowing too well the importance of his theme,
But feeling it no longer. Our discourse                           445
Soon ended, and together on we passed
In silence through a wood gloomy and still.
Up-turning, then, along an open field,
We reached a cottage. At the door I knocked,
And earnestly to charitable care                                  450
Commended him as a poor friendless man,
Belated and by sickness overcome.
Assured that now the traveller would repose
In comfort, I entreated that henceforth
He would not linger in the public ways,                           455
But ask for timely furtherance and help
Such as his state required. At this reproof,
With the same ghastly mildness in his look,
He said, 'My trust is in the God of Heaven,
And in the eye of him who passes me!'                             460

The cottage door was speedily unbarred,
And now the soldier touched his hat once more
With his lean hand, and in a faltering voice,
Whose tone bespake reviving interests
Till then unfelt, he thanked me; I returned                       465
The farewell blessing of the patient man,
And so we parted. Back I cast a look,
And lingered near the door a little space,
Then sought with quiet heart my distant home.

491 timely] proper M.
                    But at the door of cottage or of inn
                    Demand the succour that his state required
                    And needful furtherance. A² *deleted.*
496 unlock'd 𝔄 C D: unbarred D².
*At end of Book,* D *and* E *add three lines* (*marked with a query*):
                    This passed, and he who deigns to mark with care
                    By what rules governed, with what end in view
                    This work proceeds, *he* will not wish for more.

# BOOK FIFTH

## BOOKS

EVEN in the steadiest mood of reason, when
All sorrow for thy transitory pains
Goes out, it grieves me for thy state, O Man,
Thou paramount Creature! and thy race, while ye
5  Shall sojourn on this planet; not for woes       [5]
Which thou endur'st; that weight, albeit huge,
I charm away; but for those palms atchiev'd
Through length of time, by study and hard thought,    [10]
The honours of thy high endowments, there
10  My sadness finds its fuel. Hitherto,
In progress through this Verse, my mind hath look'd
Upon the speaking face of earth and heaven
As her prime Teacher, intercourse with man
Establish'd by the sovereign Intellect,           [15]
15  Who through that bodily Image hath diffus'd
A soul divine which we participate,
A deathless spirit. Thou also, Man, hast wrought,
For commerce of thy nature with itself,
Things worthy of unconquerable life;          [20]

[MSS. for Bk. V: M A B C D E; *for ll.* 1–48, 294–376, 445–515, 590–4,
630–7 W; *ll.* 370–415 18*a*; *ll.* 450–72 V.]
  Book Fifth. Books B C: 5 A.
    1–2 Even in the steadiest quiet which the soul
        Attains by reason and exalted thought
        Then, when all sorrow for thy transient pains  B².
    1–3 When Contemplation's tranquillizing power
        Hath stricken deep into the soul, and spread
        Wide, like the night-calm over sea and land
        Oft doth it grieve me for thy state, O man  A² C.
   1–10 Even in the steadiest quiet which the soul
        Attains by reason or by faith spread wide
        And striking deep, it grieves me for thy state
        O Man, thou paramount Creature and thy race
        While ye on earth shall sojourn. Not for woes
        Which thou must bear, that heavy weight doth oft
        Mount like a cloud touched with a light from Heaven,
        Or melts away, but for those palms atchieved
        Through length of time by study and hard thought
        Precious reward of high endowments; there
        My sadness finds its fuel. Hitherto  D.

# BOOK FIFTH

## BOOKS

WHEN Contemplation, like the night-calm felt
Through earth and sky, spreads widely, and sends deep
Into the soul its tranquillizing power,
Even then I sometimes grieve for thee, O Man,
Earth's paramount Creature! not so much for woes     5
That thou endurest; heavy though that weight be,
Cloud-like it mounts, or touched with light divine
Doth melt away; but for those palms achieved,
Through length of time, by patient exercise
Of study and hard thought; there, there, it is     10
That sadness finds its fuel. Hitherto,
In progress through this Verse, my mind hath looked
Upon the speaking face of earth and heaven
As her prime teacher, intercourse with man
Established by the sovereign Intellect,     15
Who through that bodily image hath diffused,
As might appear to the eye of fleeting time,
A deathless spirit. Thou also, man! hast wrought,
For commerce of thy nature with herself,
Things that aspire to unconquerable life;     20

> Even in the steadiest calm to which the soul
> By any power less than religious faith
> Can rise, it grieves me for thy lot, O Man,
> While thou on earth shalt sojourn: not for woes
> And pains to which the happiest of thy kind
> Are born; that burthen, heavy though it be
> Mounts etc. as D, D².
> When Contemplation's tranquillizing power
> Has stricken deep into the soul, even then
> I grieve not seldom for thy lot, O Man,
> Thou paramount Creature and thy Race while ye
> On Earth shall sojourn; not for pain and woe
> Which all must by inevitable doom
> Partake, that burthen heavy though it be,
> Mounts like a cloud or touched with light from Heaven
> Doth melt away; but for those palms achieved
> Thro' length of time, by study and hard thought
> Guerdon of sage and high endeavours, there
> The sadness D³: D⁴ as 1850: not in E (v. note).

7 I charm] Is charmed A² C.     11 Verse 𝔄 C D: work D² E.
16 𝔄 C D: A soul divine not doubtfully perceived D² E: E² as 1850.

20 And yet we feel, we cannot chuse but feel
     That these must perish. Tremblings of the heart
     It gives, to think that the immortal being
     No more shall need such garments; and yet Man,
     As long as he shall be the Child of Earth,      [25]
25 Might almost 'weep to have' what he may lose,
     Nor be himself extinguish'd; but survive
     Abject, depress'd, forlorn, disconsolate.
     A thought is with me sometimes, and I say,
     Should earth by inward throes be wrench'd throughout,
30 Or fire be sent from far to wither all
     Her pleasant habitations, and dry up
     Old Ocean in his bed left sing'd and bare,
     Yet would the living Presence still subsist
     Victorious; and composure would ensue,      [35]
35 And kindlings like the morning; presage sure,
     Though slow, perhaps, of a returning day.
     But all the meditations of mankind,
     Yea, all the adamantine holds of truth,
     By reason built, or passion, which itself      [40]
40 Is highest reason in a soul sublime;
     The consecrated works of Bard and Sage,
     Sensuous or intellectual, wrought by men,
     Twin labourers and heirs of the same hopes,
     Where would they be? Oh! why hath not the mind      [45]
45 Some element to stamp her image on
     In nature somewhat nearer to her own?
     Why, gifted with such powers to send abroad
     Her spirit, must it lodge in shrines so frail?

     One day, when in the hearing of a Friend,      [50]
50 I had given utterance to thoughts like these,
     He answer'd with a smile that, in plain truth
     'Twas going far to seek disquietude;
     But on the front of his reproof, confess'd
     That he, at sundry seasons, had himself      [55]

29 Should earth's whole frame be wrenched by inward throes A² B² C.
33–34      Yet would the vital spirit of her frame
          Subsist victoriously and peace ensue W.
36         Of day returning—and of life revived A² C.
37 mankind] man's mind W.
38–43      The adamantine holds of quiet thought
          Or passionate where Bards and Sages dwell,

And yet we feel—we cannot choose but feel—
That they must perish. Tremblings of the heart
It gives, to think that our immortal being
No more shall need such garments; and yet man,
As long as he shall be the child of earth,                          25
Might almost 'weep to have' what he may lose,
Nor be himself extinguished, but survive,
Abject, depressed, forlorn, disconsolate.
A thought is with me sometimes, and I say,—
Should the whole frame of earth by inward throes                    30
Be wrenched, or fire come down from far to scorch
Her pleasant habitations, and dry up
Old Ocean, in his bed left singed and bare,
Yet would the living Presence still subsist
Victorious, and composure would ensue,                             35
And kindlings like the morning—presage sure
Of day returning and of life revived.
But all the meditations of mankind,
Yea, all the adamantine holds of truth
By reason built, or passion, which itself                          40
Is highest reason in a soul sublime;
The consecrated works of Bard and Sage,
Sensuous or intellectual, wrought by men,
Twin labourers and heirs of the same hopes;
Where would they be? Oh! why hath not the Mind                     45
Some element to stamp her image on
In nature somewhat nearer to her own?
Why, gifted with such powers to send abroad
Her spirit, must it lodge in shrines so frail?


One day, when from my lips a like complaint                        50
Had fallen in presence of a studious friend,
He with a smile made answer, that in truth
'Twas going far to seek disquietude;
But on the front of his reproof confessed
That he himself had oftentimes given way                           55

             Twin builders up of consecrated truth
             Sensuous or intellectual work of those
             Exempt from all external injury  W.
49–50        One day when I had uttered thoughts like these
             In hearing of a Philosophic Friend  A² C.
51 A² C *as* 1850.              54–55 (. . . hauntings) 𝕬 C D:  D² *as* 1850.

55 Yielded to kindred hauntings. And forthwith
   Added, that once upon a summer's noon,
   While he was sitting in a rocky cave
   By the sea-side, perusing, as it chanced,
   The famous History of the Errant Knight          [60]
60 Recorded by Cervantes, these same thoughts
   Came to him; and to height unusual rose
   While listlessly he sate, and having closed
   The Book, had turned his eyes towards the Sea.
   On Poetry and geometric Truth,                   [65]
65 The knowledge that endures, upon these two,
   And their high privilege of lasting life,
   Exempt from all internal injury,
   He mused; upon these chiefly: and at length,
   His senses yielding to the sultry air,
70 Sleep seiz'd him, and he pass'd into a dream.    [70]
   He saw before him an Arabian Waste,
   A Desart; and he fancied that himself
   Was sitting there in the wide wilderness,
   Alone, upon the Sands. Distress of mind
75 Was growing in him when, behold! at once
   To his great joy a Man was at his side,
   Upon a dromedary, mounted high.                  [76]
   He seem'd an Arab of the Bedouin Tribes,
   A Lance he bore, and underneath one arm
80 A Stone; and, in the opposite hand, a Shell
   Of a surpassing brightness. Much rejoic'd        [80]
   The dreaming Man that he should have a Guide
   To lead him through the Desart; and he thought,
   While questioning himself what this strange freight
85 Which the Newcomer carried through the Waste     [85]
   Could mean, the Arab told him that the Stone,
   To give it in the language of the Dream,
   Was Euclid's Elements; 'and this,' said he,
   'This other,' pointing to the Shell, 'this Book
90 Is something of more worth.' And, at the word,
   The Stranger, said my Friend continuing,
   Stretch'd forth the Shell towards me, with command   [90]

[56–57] And that once, In the deep *etc.* D: D² *as* 1850.
57–88 He . . . him . . . his 𝔄 C D: I . . . me . . . my D².
61 Came to] Beset A² B² C.

To kindred hauntings. Whereupon I told,
That once in the stillness of a summer's noon,
While I was seated in a rocky cave
By the sea-side, perusing, so it chanced,
The famous history of the errant knight           60
Recorded by Cervantes, these same thoughts
Beset me, and to height unusual rose,
While listlessly I sate, and, having closed
The book, had turned my eyes toward the wide sea.
On poetry and geometric truth,                    65
And their high privilege of lasting life,
From all internal injury exempt,
I mused, upon these chiefly: and at length,
My senses yielding to the sultry air,
Sleep seized me, and I passed into a dream.       70
I saw before me stretched a boundless plain
Of sandy wilderness, all black and void,
And as I looked around, distress and fear
Came creeping over me, when at my side,
Close at my side, an uncouth shape appeared       75
Upon a dromedary, mounted high.
He seemed an Arab of the Bedouin tribes:
A lance he bore, and underneath one arm
A stone, and in the opposite hand, a shell
Of a surpassing brightness. At the sight          80
Much I rejoiced, not doubting but a guide
Was present, one who with unerring skill
Would through the desert lead me; and while yet
I looked and looked, self-questioned what this freight
Which the new-comer carried through the waste     85
Could mean, the Arab told me that the stone
(To give it in the language of the dream)
Was 'Euclid's Elements;' and 'This,' said he,
'Is something of more worth;' and at the word
Stretched forth the shell, so beautiful in shape,  90
In colour so resplendent, with command

71–76 D *stuck over*: D² E *as* 1850, *but* [74] lo! at once *for* at my side: E²
*as* 1850.
    76 was] is A².        81–82 Much . . . man 𝔄 C D: D² *as* 1850.
    82 that he should have a Guide] most thankful to have gained Thus
unexpectedly a practised Guide A² C.
    83–84 D *stuck over*: D² *as* 1850.        86 Could mean] Imported A² C.
    91 D *deletes*.

That I should hold it to my ear; I did so,
And heard that instant in an unknown Tongue,
95 Which yet I understood, articulate sounds,
A loud prophetic blast of harmony,                    [95]
An Ode, in passion utter'd, which foretold
Destruction to the Children of the Earth,
By deluge now at hand. No sooner ceas'd
100 The Song, but with calm look, the Arab said
That all was true; that it was even so
As had been spoken; and that he himself              [100]
Was going then to bury those two Books:
The one that held acquaintance with the stars,
105 And wedded man to man by purest bond
Of nature, undisturbed by space or time;             [105]
Th' other that was a God, yea many Gods,
Had voices more than all the winds, and was
A joy, a consolation, and a hope.
110 My Friend continued, 'strange as it may seem,    [110]
I wonder'd not, although I plainly saw
The one to be a Stone, th' other a Shell,
Nor doubted once but that they both were Books,
Having a perfect faith in all that pass'd.
115 A wish was now ingender'd in my fear
To cleave unto this Man, and I begg'd leave          [116]
To share his errand with him. On he pass'd
Not heeding me; I follow'd, and took note
That he look'd often backward with wild look,
120 Grasping his twofold treasure to his side.
—Upon a Dromedary, Lance in rest,                   [120]
He rode, I keeping pace with him, and now

100–2 𝔄 C D: D² *as* 1850.
105 man to man by] soul to soul by  A² C D.          by] in  D².
106 nature] Reason  A² C.
108–9 and was . . . hope]                  with power
            To exhilarate the spirit and soothe the heart
            Of human kind, in every clime of earth
            Raising the mortal Creature to divine  A².
                             with power
            To irradiate the spirit with a light
            Piercing and vital as the solar beams
            Whence joy and hope, and solace to mankind  A³.
                             with power
            To exhilarate the spirit and to soothe
            The heart of human-kind, through every zone

That I should hold it to my ear. I did so,
And heard that instant in an unknown tongue,
Which yet I understood, articulate sounds,
A loud prophetic blast of harmony;                              95
An Ode, in passion uttered, which foretold
Destruction to the children of the earth
By deluge, now at hand. No sooner ceased
The song, than the Arab with calm look declared
That all would come to pass of which the voice                 100
Had given forewarning, and that he himself
Was going then to bury those two books:
The one that held acquaintance with the stars,
And wedded soul to soul in purest bond
Of reason, undisturbed by space or time;                       105
The other that was a god, yea many gods,
Had voices more than all the winds, with power
To exhilarate the spirit, and to soothe,
Through every clime, the heart of human kind.
While this was uttering, strange as it may seem,               110
I wondered not, although I plainly saw
The one to be a stone, the other a shell;
Nor doubted once but that they both were books,
Having a perfect faith in all that passed.
Far stronger, now, grew the desire I felt                      115
To cleave unto this man; but when I prayed
To share his enterprise, he hurried on
Reckless of me: I followed, not unseen,
For oftentimes he cast a backward look,
Grasping his twofold treasure.—Lance in rest,                  120
He rode, I keeping pace with him; and now

By which the habitable sphere is marked
Raising, *etc.* A⁴ C.
               with power
To exhilarate the spirit while it soothed
Thro' every clime the heart of human kind,
Raising, *etc.* D: D² *as* 1850.
110 In vivid recollection of his dream
    My Friend continued 'strange as may appear
    The assurance, yet, while he was speaking thus A² C.
115 Far stronger was the wish which now I felt D: Far stronger now
was the desire I felt D² E: E² *as* 1850.
117 pass'd] went M.
118 Not heeding] Reckless of A² C.
118–23 and took note . . . Knight 𝔄 C D: D² *as* 1850.

I fancied that he was the very Knight
Whose Tale Cervantes tells, yet not the Knight,
125 But was an Arab of the Desart, too;
    Of these was neither, and was both at once.                    [125]
    His countenance, meanwhile, grew more disturb'd,
    And, looking backwards when he look'd, I saw
    A glittering light, and ask'd him whence it came.
130 "It is," said he, "the waters of the deep                    [130]
    Gathering upon us," quickening then his pace
    He left me: I call'd after him aloud;
    He heeded not; but with his twofold charge
    Beneath his arm, before me full in view                    [135]
135 I saw him riding o'er the Desart Sands,
    With the fleet waters of the drowning world
    In chase of him, whereat I wak'd in terror,
    And saw the Sea before me; and the Book,
    In which I had been reading, at my side.'                    [140]

140     Full often, taking from the world of sleep
    This Arab Phantom, which my Friend beheld,
    This Semi-Quixote, I to him have given
    A substance, fancied him a living man,
    A gentle Dweller in the Desart, craz'd                    [145]
145 By love and feeling and internal thought,
    Protracted among endless solitudes;
    Have shap'd him, in the oppression of his brain,
    Wandering upon this quest, and thus equipp'd.
    And I have scarcely pitied him; have felt
150 A reverence for a Being thus employ'd;                    [150]
    And thought that in the blind and awful lair
    Of such a madness, reason did lie couch'd.
    Enow there are on earth to take in charge
    Their Wives, their Children, and their virgin Loves,
155 Or whatsoever else the heart holds dear;                    [155]
    Enow to think of these; yea, will I say,
    In sober contemplation of the approach
    Of such great overthrow, made manifest
    By certain evidence, that I, methinks,

129 A bright refulgence on the distant plain
    A bed of glittering light, and asked the cause. A² C D (*but* strong *for*
    bright): D² *as* 1850.

He, to my fancy, had become the knight
Whose tale Cervantes tells; yet not the knight,
But was an Arab of the desert too;
Of these was neither, and was both at once.          125
His countenance, meanwhile, grew more disturbed;
And, looking backwards when he looked, mine eyes
Saw, over half the wilderness diffused,
A bed of glittering light: I asked the cause:
'It is,' said he, 'the waters of the deep           130
Gathering upon us;' quickening then the pace
Of the unwieldly creature he bestrode,
He left me: I called after him aloud;
He heeded not; but, with his twofold charge
Still in his grasp, before me, full in view,        135
Went hurrying o'er the illimitable waste,
With the fleet waters of a drowning world
In chase of him; whereat I waked in terror,
And saw the sea before me, and the book,
In which I had been reading, at my side.            140

    Full often, taking from the world of sleep
This Arab phantom, which I thus beheld,
This semi-Quixote, I to him have given
A substance, fancied him a living man,
A gentle dweller in the desert, crazed              145
By love and feeling, and internal thought
Protracted among endless solitudes;
Have shaped him wandering upon this quest!
Nor have I pitied him; but rather felt
Reverence was due to a being thus employed;         150
And thought that, in the blind and awful lair
Of such a madness, reason did lie couched.
Enow there are on earth to take in charge
Their wives, their children, and their virgin loves,
Or whatsoever else the heart holds dear;            155
Enow to stir for these; yea, will I say,
Contemplating in soberness the approach
Of an event so dire, by signs in earth
Or heaven made manifest, that I could share

131 A C D: D² as 1850 [131-2].        134-5 D as A: D² as 1850.
135 riding] hurrying A² C D.        141 my Friend A C D: I thus D².
148 A C D: And so equipped wandering upon this quest D².

160    Could share that Maniac's anxiousness, could go                [160]
       Upon like errand. Oftentimes, at least,
       Me hath such deep entrancement half-possess'd,
       When I have held a volume in my hand
       Poor earthly casket of immortal Verse!
165    Shakespeare, or Milton, Labourers divine!                      [165]
          Mighty indeed, supreme must be the power
       Of living Nature, which could thus so long
       Detain me from the best of other thoughts.
       Even in the lisping time of Infancy,                           [170]
170    And later down, in prattling Childhood, even
       While I was travelling back among those days,
       How could I ever play an ingrate's part?
       Once more should I have made those bowers resound,
       And intermingled strains of thankfulness                      [175]
175    With their own thoughtless melodies; at least,
       It might have well beseem'd me to repeat
       Some simply fashion'd tale; to tell again,
       In slender accents of sweet Verse, some tale
       That did bewitch me then, and soothes me now.                 [180]
180    O Friend! O Poet! Brother of my soul,
       Think not that I could ever pass along
       Untouch'd by these remembrances; no, no,
       But I was hurried forward by a stream,
       And could not stop. Yet wherefore should I speak,
185    Why call upon a few weak words to say
       What is already written in the hearts                         [185]
       Of all that breathe? what in the path of all
       Drops daily from the tongue of every Child,
       Wherever Man is found. The trickling tear
190    Upon the cheek of listening Infancy
       Tells it, and the insuperable look                            [190]
       That drinks as if it never could be full.

          That portion of my Story I shall leave
       There register'd: whatever else there be
195    Of power or pleasure, sown or foster'd thus,
       Peculiar to myself, let that remain                           [195]
       Where it lies hidden in its endless home
       Among the depths of time. And yet it seems
       That here, in memory of all books which lay

[160] That simple maniac's anxiousness, and go  D:  D² *as* 1850.
162 half-possess'd] overcome  A² C.

That maniac's fond anxiety, and go                          160
Upon like errand. Oftentimes at least
Me hath such strong entrancement overcome,
When I have held a volume in my hand,
Poor earthly casket of immortal verse,
Shakespeare, or Milton, labourers divine!                   165
    Great and benign, indeed, must be the power
Of living nature, which could thus so long
Detain me from the best of other guides
And dearest helpers, left unthanked, unpraised,
Even in the time of lisping infancy;                        170
And later down, in prattling childhood even,
While I was travelling back among those days,
How could I ever play an ingrate's part?
Once more should I have made those bowers resound,
By intermingling strains of thankfulness                    175
With their own thoughtless melodies; at least
It might have well beseemed me to repeat
Some simply fashioned tale, to tell again,
In slender accents of sweet verse, some tale
That did bewitch me then, and soothes me now.               180
O Friend! O Poet! brother of my soul,
Think not that I could pass along untouched
By these remembrances. Yet wherefore speak?
Why call upon a few weak words to say
What is already written in the hearts                       185
Of all that breathe?—what in the path of all
Drops daily from the tongue of every child,
Wherever man is found? The trickling tear
Upon the cheek of listening Infancy
Proclaims it, and the insuperable look                      190
That drinks as if it never could be full.

    That portion of my story I shall leave
There registered: whatever else of power
Or pleasure sown, or fostered thus, may be
Peculiar to myself, let that remain                         195
Where still it works, though hidden from all search
Among the depths of time. Yet is it just
That here, in memory of all books which lay

166–70 D *stuck over*: D² *as* 1850.        170 prattling] budding  M.
191 Tells] Proclaims A² B² C.        196 𝔄 C D: D² *as* 1850.

200 Their sure foundations in the heart of Man;
     Whether by native prose or numerous verse,                    [200]
     That in the name of all inspirèd Souls,
     From Homer, the great Thunderer; from the voice
     Which roars along the bed of Jewish Song;
205 And that, more varied and elaborate,
     Those trumpet-tones of harmony that shake                     [205]
     Our Shores in England; from those loftiest notes
     Down to the low and wren-like warblings, made
     For Cottagers and Spinners at the wheel,
210 And weary Travellers when they rest themselves
     By the highways and hedges; ballad tunes,                     [210]
     Food for the hungry ears of little Ones,
     And of old Men who have surviv'd their joy;
     It seemeth, in behalf of these, the works
215 And of the Men who fram'd them, whether known,
     Or sleeping nameless in their scatter'd graves,               [215]
     That I should here assert their rights, attest
     Their honours; and should, once for all, pronounce
     Their benediction; speak of them as Powers
220 For ever to be hallowed; only less,
     For what we may become, and what we need,                     [220]
     Than Nature's self, which is the breath of God.


     Rarely, and with reluctance, would I stoop
     To transitory themes; yet I rejoice,
225 And, by these thoughts admonish'd, must speak out             [225]
     Thanksgivings from my heart, that I was rear'd
     Safe from an evil which these days have laid
     Upon the Children of the Land, a pest
     That might have dried me up, body and soul.
230 This Verse is dedicate to Nature's self,                       [230]
     And things that teach as Nature teaches, then
     Oh where had been the Man, the Poet where?
     Where had we been, we two, beloved Friend,
     If we, in lieu of wandering, as we did,                       [235]
235 Through heights and hollows, and bye-spots of tales

204 roars 𝔄 C D²: pours D.
     210 𝔄 C: And travellers when they rest their weary limbs B²: D *as* 𝔄,
*but* their limbs *for* themselves. D² *as* 1850.
     211, 221, 223, 224 𝔄 C D: D² *as* 1850.
     222 which is the breath 𝔄 C D E²: the pregnant work D² E.

Their sure foundations in the heart of man,
Whether by native prose, or numerous verse,                    200
That in the name of all inspirèd souls,
From Homer the great Thunderer, from the voice
That roars along the bed of Jewish song,
And that more varied and elaborate,
Those trumpet-tones of harmony that shake                    205
Our shores in England,—from those loftiest notes
Down to the low and wren-like warblings, made
For cottagers and spinners at the wheel,
And sun-burnt travellers resting their tired limbs,
Stretched under wayside hedge-rows, ballad tunes,                    210
Food for the hungry ears of little ones,
And of old men who have survived their joys:
'Tis just that in behalf of these, the works,
And of the men that framed them, whether known,
Or sleeping nameless in their scattered graves,                    215
That I should here assert their rights, attest
Their honours, and should, once for all, pronounce
Their benediction; speak of them as Powers
For ever to be hallowed; only less,
For what we are and what we may become,                    220
Than Nature's self, which is the breath of God,
Or His pure Word by miracle revealed.

Rarely and with reluctance would I stoop
To transitory themes; yet I rejoice,
And, by these thoughts admonished, will pour out                    225
Thanks with uplifted heart, that I was reared
Safe from an evil which these days have laid
Upon the children of the land, a pest
That might have dried me up, body and soul.
This verse is dedicate to Nature's self,                    230
And things that teach as Nature teaches: then,
Oh! where had been the Man, the Poet where,
Where had we been, we two, beloved Friend!
If in the season of unperilous choice,
In lieu of wandering, as we did, through vales                    235

[222] Or God's own will D. *Not in* 𝔄, *added to* C, *as* Or God's own Will *etc.*:
D² *as* 1850.
    235–7 of tales *etc.*]                    bye-spots of old
        Indigenous tales, a pasture ranged at will  M.

Rich with indigenous produce, open ground
Of Fancy, happy pastures rang'd at will!
Had been attended, follow'd, watch'd, and noos'd,
Each in his several melancholy walk
240 String'd like a poor man's Heifer, at its feed                    [240]
Led through the lanes in forlorn servitude;
Or rather like a stalled Ox shut out
From touch of growing grass; that may not taste
A flower till it have yielded up its sweets
245 A prelibation to the mower's scythe.                    [245]

Behold the Parent Hen amid her Brood,
Though fledged and feather'd, and well pleased to part
And straggle from her presence, still a Brood,
And she herself from the maternal bond
250 Still undischarged; yet doth she little more                    [250]
Than move with them in tenderness and love,
A centre of the circle which they make;
And, now and then, alike from need of theirs,
And call of her own natural appetites,
255 She scratches, ransacks up the earth for food                    [255]
Which they partake at pleasure. Early died
My honour'd Mother; she who was the heart
And hinge of all our learnings and our loves:
She left us destitute, and as we might
260 Trooping together. Little suits it me                    [260]
To break upon the sabbath of her rest
With any thought that looks at others' blame,
Nor would I praise her but in perfect love.
Hence am I check'd: but I will boldly say,
265 In gratitude, and for the sake of truth,                    [265]
Unheard by her, that she, not falsly taught,
Fetching her goodness rather from times past
Than shaping novelties from those to come,
Had no presumption, no such jealousy;
270 Nor did by habit of her thoughts mistrust                    [270]
Our Nature; but had virtual faith that he,
Who fills the Mother's breasts with innocent milk,
Doth also for our nobler part provide,
Under his great correction and controul,
275 As innocent instincts, and as innocent food.                    [275]

242 shut out] debarred A² C.          264 I will 𝔄 C D: let me D².

Rich with indigenous produce, open ground
Of Fancy, happy pastures ranged at will,
We had been followed, hourly watched, and noosed,
Each in his several melancholy walk
Stringed like a poor man's heifer at its feed,                    240
Led through the lanes in forlorn servitude;
Or rather like a stallèd ox debarred
From touch of growing grass, that may not taste
A flower till it have yielded up its sweets
A prelibation to the mower's scythe.                    245


    Behold the parent hen amid her brood,
Though fledged and feathered, and well pleased to part
And straggle from her presence, still a brood,
And she herself from the maternal bond
Still undischarged; yet doth she little more                    250
Than move with them in tenderness and love,
A centre to the circle which they make;
And now and then, alike from need of theirs
And call of her own natural appetites,
She scratches, ransacks up the earth for food,                    255
Which they partake at pleasure. Early died
My honoured Mother, she who was the heart
And hinge of all our learnings and our loves:
She left us destitute, and, as we might,
Trooping together. Little suits it me                    260
To break upon the sabbath of her rest
With any thought that looks at others' blame;
Nor would I praise her but in perfect love.
Hence am I checked: but let me boldly say,
In gratitude, and for the sake of truth,                    265
Unheard by her, that she, not falsely taught,
Fetching her goodness rather from times past,
Than shaping novelties for times to come,
Had no presumption, no such jealousy,
Nor did by habit of her thoughts mistrust                    270
Our nature, but had virtual faith that He
Who fills the mother's breast with innocent milk,
Doth also for our nobler part provide,
Under His great correction and control,
As innocent instincts, and as innocent food;                    275

This was her creed, and therefore she was pure
From feverish dread of error or mishap                    [280]
And evil, overweeningly so call'd;
Was not puff'd up by false unnatural hopes;
280 Nor selfish with unnecessary cares;
Nor with impatience from the season ask'd
More than its timely produce; rather lov'd                    [285]
The hours for what they are than from regards
Glanced on their promises in restless pride.
285 Such was she; not from faculties more strong
Than others have, but from the times, perhaps,
And spot in which she liv'd, and through a grace                    [290]
Of modest meekness, simple-mindedness,
A heart that found benignity and hope,
290 Being itself benign.
                    My drift hath scarcely,
I fear, been obvious; for I have recoil'd
From showing as it is the monster birth
Engender'd by these too industrious times.
Let few words paint it: 'tis a Child, no Child,
295 But a dwarf Man; in knowledge, virtue, skill;
In what he is not, and in what he is,
The noontide shadow of a man complete;
A worshipper of worldly seemliness,
Not quarrelsome; for that were far beneath                    [300]
300 His dignity; with gifts he bubbles o'er
As generous as a fountain; selfishness
May not come near him, gluttony or pride;
The wandering Beggars propagate his name,                    [305]
Dumb creatures find him tender as a Nun.
305 Yet deem him not for this a naked dish

[276–8] *Not in* 𝔄 C.
          Or teaches minds left free to trust in Him
          Thro' the simplicities of early life
          To suck sweet honey out of dreaded weeds. D E.  E² *as* 1850.
277 feverish dread 𝔄 C D: anxious fear A² D² E. or B: and A.
290–1 My drift . . . obvious] M *as* 1850.
290–8 My drift . . . seemliness]      On different objects
          The admiration of these days is fixed
          Their *discipline* pursues a higher aim
          The child which *that* would fashion early learns
          A due respect for worldly seemliness A² C.
290–360 [293–340] D² *as* 1850: D [291–304], [328–30] *stuck over.*
305–30 [307 *ff.*] And natural or supernatural fear
Unless it leap upon him in a dream

Or draws for minds that are left free to trust
In the simplicities of opening life
Sweet honey out of spurned or dreaded weeds.
This was her creed, and therefore she was pure
From anxious fear of error or mishap,                           280
And evil, overweeningly so called;
Was not puffed up by false unnatural hopes,
Nor selfish with unnecessary cares,
Nor with impatience from the season asked
More than its timely produce; rather loved                      285
The hours for what they are, than from regard
Glanced on their promises in restless pride.
Such was she—not from faculties more strong
Than others have, but from the times, perhaps,
And spot in which she lived, and through a grace                290
Of modest meekness, simple-mindedness,
A heart that found benignity and hope,
Being itself benign.
                 My drift I fear
Is scarcely obvious; but, that common sense
May try this modern system by its fruits,                       295
Leave let me take to place before her sight
A specimen pourtrayed with faithful hand.
Full early trained to worship seemliness,
This model of a child is never known
To mix in quarrels; that were far beneath                       300
Its dignity; with gifts he bubbles o'er
As generous as a fountain; selfishness
May not come near him, nor the little throng
Of flitting pleasures tempt him from his path;
The wandering beggars propagate his name,                       305
Dumb creatures find him tender as a nun,
And natural or supernatural fear,

Touches him not. To enhance the wonder see
How arch his notices, how nice his sense
Of the ridiculous: deceit and guile
Meanness and falsehood he detects, can treat
With apt and graceful laughter, nor is blind
To the broad follies of the licens'd world,
Yet innocent himself withal, though shrewd.
The moral part is perfect, and in books
He is a prodigy. The outward signs
Of that extensive Empire which he holds
A miracle of scientific lore A². *So* C, *but omitting* The moral . . . he holds

Of goodness merely, he is garnish'd out.
Arch are his notices, and nice his sense
Of the ridiculous; deceit and guile
Meanness and falsehood he detects, can treat
310 With apt and graceful laughter; nor is blind
To the broad follies of the licens'd world;                    [312]
Though shrewd, yet innocent himself withal
And can read lectures upon innocence.
He is fenc'd round, nay arm'd, for aught we know
315 In panoply complete; and fear itself,
Natural or supernatural alike,                    [307]
Unless it leap upon him in a dream,
Touches him not. Briefly, the moral part
Is perfect, and in learning and in books
320 He is a prodigy. His discourse moves slow,
Massy and ponderous as a prison door,
Tremendously emboss'd with terms of art;
Rank growth of propositions overruns
The Stripling's brain; the path in which he treads
325 Is chok'd with grammars; cushion of Divine
Was never such a type of thought profound
As is the pillow where he rests his head.
The Ensigns of the Empire which he holds,
The globe and sceptre of his royalties
330 Are telescopes, and crucibles, and maps.
Ships he can guide across the pathless sea,                    [316]
And tell you all their cunning; he can read
The inside of the earth, and spell the stars;
He knows the policies of foreign Lands;
335 Can string you names of districts, cities, towns,                    [320]
The whole world over, tight as beads of dew
Upon a gossamer thread; he sifts, he weighs;
Takes nothing upon trust. His Teachers stare;
The Country People pray for God's good grace,
340 And tremble at his deep experiments.
All things are put to question; he must live
Knowing that he grows wiser every day,
Or else not live at all; and seeing, too,                    [325]
Each little drop of wisdom as it falls
345 Into the dimpling cistern of his heart;                    [327]

316*om.* M.

Unless it leap upon him in a dream,
Touches him not. To enhance the wonder, see
How arch his notices, how nice his sense                310
Of the ridiculous; nor blind is he
To the broad follies of the licensed world,
Yet innocent himself withal, though shrewd,
And can read lectures upon innocence;
A miracle of scientific lore,                           315
Ships he can guide across the pathless sea,
And tell you all their cunning; he can read
The inside of the earth, and spell the stars;
He knows the policies of foreign lands;
Can string you names of districts, cities, towns,      320
The whole world over, tight as beads of dew
Upon a gossamer thread; he sifts, he weighs;
All things are put to question; he must live
Knowing that he grows wiser every day
Or else not live at all, and seeing too                325
Each little drop of wisdom as it falls
Into the dimpling cistern of his heart:
For this unnatural growth the trainer blame,
Pity the tree.—Poor human vanity,
Wert thou extinguished, little would be left           330

323–4   With propositions are the younker's brains
        Filled to the brim, the path in which he treads  W.
        Nurs'd in his brain do propositions thrive,
        As in their native home; the path he treads  M.
330 maps  W²: prisms  W.
337                        thread, boundless th' embrace
        Of his intelligence, he sifts *etc. Letter* 29 Mar. 04.
340 tremble] shudder  M W.  *After* experiments A² *reads*:
        Blush Common-sense, thou modest, sacred Power!
        Blush for the growth of too industrious times
        Monstrous as China's vegetable Dwarfs
        Where Nature is subjected to such freaks
        Of human care industriously perverse
        Here to advance the work and there retard
        That the proportions of the full-grown oak
        Its roots, its trunk, its boughs and foliage, all
        Appear in living miniature expressed
        The oak beneath whose umbrage, freely spread
        Within its native fields, whole herds repose.
        By this preposterous Mimicry of Man *etc. as* A 341–5, *followed by*
Vanity is the soul of all he seeks, *and* 357–62, 346–9.  *So* C.  *A version of this*
*passage* (Blush . . . repose), *deleted from the text of* D, *is found in* D *and* E *as*
*an* 'Overflow' (*v. note to ll.* 291–349).

Meanwhile old Grandame Earth is grieved to find     [337]
The playthings which her love design'd for him
Unthought of: in their woodland beds the flowers
Weep, and the river-sides are all forlorn.     [340]

350     Now this is hollow, 'tis a life of lies
From the beginning, and in lies must end.
Forth bring him to the air of common sense,
And, fresh and shewy as it is, the Corps
Slips from us into powder. Vanity
355 That is his soul, there lives he, and there moves;
It is the soul of every thing he seeks;
That gone, nothing is left which he can love.
Nay, if a thought of purer birth should rise
To carry him towards a better clime
360 Some busy helper still is on the watch
To drive him back and pound him like a Stray     [335]
Within the pinfold of his own conceit;
Which is his home, his natural dwelling-place.
Oh! give us once again the Wishing-Cap
365 Of Fortunatus, and the invisible Coat
Of Jack the Giant-killer, Robin Hood,
And Sabra in the Forest with St. George!
The Child, whose love is here, at least, doth reap     [345]
One precious gain, that he forgets himself.

370     These mighty workmen of our later age
Who with a broad highway have overbridged
The froward chaos of futurity,
Tam'd to their bidding; they who have the art     [350]
To manage books, and things, and make them work
375 Gently on infant minds, as does the sun
Upon a flower; the Tutors of our Youth
The Guides, the Wardens of our faculties,
And Stewards of our labour, watchful men
And skilful in the usury of time,
380 Sages, who in their prescience would controul     [355]
All accidents, and to the very road
Which they have fashion'd would confine us down,
Like engines, when will they be taught
That in the unreasoning progress of the world
385 A wiser Spirit is at work for us,     [360]

Which he could truly love; but how escape?
For, ever as a thought of purer birth
Rises to lead him toward a better clime,
Some intermeddler still is on the watch
To drive him back, and pound him, like a stray,            335
Within the pinfold of his own conceit.
Meanwhile old grandame earth is grieved to find
The playthings, which her love designed for him,
Unthought of: in their woodland beds the flowers
Weep, and the river sides are all forlorn.                 340
Oh! give us once again the wishing cap
Of Fortunatus, and the invisible coat
Of Jack the Giant-killer, Robin Hood,
And Sabra in the forest with St. George!
The child, whose love is here, at least, doth reap         345
One precious gain, that he forgets himself.

   These mighty workmen of our later age,
Who, with a broad highway, have overbridged
The froward chaos of futurity,
Tamed to their bidding; they who have the skill            350
To manage books, and things, and make them act
On infant minds as surely as the sun
Deals with a flower; the keepers of our time,
The guides and wardens of our faculties,
Sages who in their prescience would control               355
All accidents, and to the very road
Which they have fashioned would confine us down,
Like engines; when will their presumption learn,
That in the unreasoning progress of the world
A wiser spirit is at work for us,                          360

376-444                        the tutors of our youth
        Though falling short, far short of what we dreamt
        Of Childhood . . . (*rest of line illegible, then goes on to* 445). W.
383 A² B² C *as* 1850.
384-7 D *stuck over*: To reverence th' invisible eye that still
      Is watching over us: when will they perceive
      That in the unreasoning progress of the world
      A spirit works most prodigal of blessings
      And evermore most studious of our good  D² E:  E² *as* 1850.

A better eye than theirs, more prodigal
Of blessings, and more studious of our good,
Even in what seem our most unfruitful hours ?

    There was a Boy, ye knew him well, ye Cliffs
390 And Islands of Winander! many a time                    [365]
    At evening, when the stars had just begun
    To move along the edges of the hills,
    Rising or setting, would he stand alone
    Beneath the trees, or by the glimmering Lake,
395 And there, with fingers interwoven, both hands         [370]
    Press'd closely, palm to palm, and to his mouth
    Uplifted, he, as through an instrument,
    Blew mimic hootings to the silent owls
    That they might answer him.—And they would shout
400 Across the watry Vale, and shout again,                [375]
    Responsive to his call, with quivering peals,
    And long halloos, and screams, and echoes loud
    Redoubled and redoubled; concourse wild
    Of mirth and jocund din! And when it chanced
405 That pauses of deep silence mock'd his skill,          [380]
    Then sometimes, in that silence, while he hung
    Listening, a gentle shock of mild surprize
    Has carried far into his heart the voice
    Of mountain torrents; or the visible scene
410 Would enter unawares into his mind                     [385]
    With all its solemn imagery, its rocks,
    Its woods, and that uncertain Heaven, receiv'd
    Into the bosom of the steady Lake.

    This Boy was taken from his Mates, and died
415 In childhood, ere he was full ten years old.           [390]
    —Fair are the woods, and beauteous is the spot,
    The Vale where he was born; the Churchyard hangs
    Upon a Slope above the Village School,
    And there, along that bank, when I have pass'd
420 At evening, I believe that oftentimes                  [395]

388 hours?] hours. 𝔄.
391 stars had just begun 𝔄 1800–5: earliest stars began A² C 1815.
401                his call. Alternate now
      And regular one solitary cry
      Came back to him; then quivering peals were heard 18a.
403 concourse wild] a wild scene JJ 18a: a concourse wild M.

A better eye than theirs, most prodigal
Of blessings, and most studious of our good,
Even in what seem our most unfruitful hours ?

　There was a Boy: ye knew him well, ye cliffs
And islands of Winander!—many a time　　　　　　365
At evening, when the earliest stars began
To move along the edges of the hills,
Rising or setting, would he stand alone
Beneath the trees or by the glimmering lake,
And there, with fingers interwoven, both hands　　370
Pressed closely palm to palm, and to his mouth
Uplifted, he, as through an instrument,
Blew mimic hootings to the silent owls,
That they might answer him; and they would shout
Across the watery vale, and shout again,　　　　　375
Responsive to his call, with quivering peals,
And long halloos and screams, and echoes loud,
Redoubled and redoubled, concourse wild
Of jocund din; and, when a lengthened pause
Of silence came and baffled his best skill,　　　　380
Then sometimes, in that silence while he hung
Listening, a gentle shock of mild surprise
Has carried far into his heart the voice
Of mountain torrents; or the visible scene
Would enter unawares into his mind,　　　　　　385
With all its solemn imagery, its rocks,
Its woods, and that uncertain heaven, received
Into the bosom of the steady lake.

　This Boy was taken from his mates, and died
In childhood, ere he was full twelve years old.　　390
Fair is the spot, most beautiful the vale
Where he was born; the grassy churchyard hangs
Upon a slope above the village school,
And through that churchyard when my way has led
On summer evenings, I believe that there　　　　395

404–5, 420, 423 𝔄 C D: D² *as* 1850.
405, 408, 410 my *for* his JJ.　　　406. I *for* he JJ.
414–22 18a *om. ll.* 414–15 *and for ll.* 420–2 *reads*
　　　　　At evening, I believe that near his grave
　　　　　A full half-hour together I have stood
　　　　　Mute,—for he died when he was ten years old.
415 ten] twelve A² C.

A full half-hour together I have stood
Mute—looking at the Grave in which he lies.

Even now, methinks, I have before my sight
That self-same Village Church; I see her sit,
425 The thronèd Lady spoken of erewhile,                    [400]
On her green hill; forgetful of this Boy
Who slumbers at her feet; forgetful, too,
Of all her silent neighbourhood of graves,
And listening only to the gladsome sounds
430 That, from the rural School ascending, play              [405]
Beneath her and about her. May she long
Behold a race of young Ones like to those
With whom I herded! (easily, indeed,
We might have fed upon a fatter soil
435 Of Arts and Letters, but be that forgiven)              [410]
A race of real children, not too wise,
Too learned, or too good; but wanton, fresh,
And bandied up and down by love and hate,
Fierce, moody, patient, venturous, modest, shy;           [415]
440 Mad at their sports like wither'd leaves in winds;
Though doing wrong, and suffering, and full oft
Bending beneath our life's mysterious weight
Of pain and fear; yet still in happiness
Not yielding to the happiest upon earth.                   [420]
445 Simplicity in habit, truth in speech,
Be these the daily strengtheners of their minds!
May books and nature be their early joy!
And knowledge, rightly honor'd with that name,
Knowledge not purchas'd with the loss of power!           [425]

450    Well do I call to mind the very week
When I was first entrusted to the care
Of that sweet Valley; when its paths, its shores,
And brooks, were like a dream of novelty

450–56 *In* V *this episode follows* Bk. I. 524, *and is thus introduced*:
All these and more with rival claims demand
Grateful acknowledgement. It were a song
Venial and such as if I rightly judge
I might protract unblamed, but I perceive
That much is overlooked and we should ill
Attain our object if from delicate fears
Of breaking in upon the unity
Of this my argument I should omit

A long half hour together I have stood
Mute, looking at the grave in which he lies!
Even now appears before the mind's clear eye
That self-same village church; I see her sit
(The thronèd Lady whom erewhile we hailed)                    400
On her green hill, forgetful of this Boy
Who slumbers at her feet,—forgetful, too,
Of all her silent neighbourhood of graves,
And listening only to the gladsome sounds
That, from the rural school ascending, play                    405
Beneath her and about her. May she long
Behold a race of young ones like to those
With whom I herded!—(easily, indeed,
We might have fed upon a fatter soil
Of arts and letters—but be that forgiven)—                    410
A race of real children; not too wise,
Too learned, or too good; but wanton, fresh,
And bandied up and down by love and hate;
Not unresentful where self-justified;
Fierce, moody, patient, venturous, modest, shy;                    415
Mad at their sports like withered leaves in winds;
Though doing wrong and suffering, and full oft
Bending beneath our life's mysterious weight
Of pain, and doubt, and fear, yet yielding not
In happiness to the happiest upon earth.                    420
Simplicity in habit, truth in speech,
Be these the daily strengtheners of their minds;
May books and Nature be their early joy!
And knowledge, rightly honoured with that name—
Knowledge not purchased by the loss of power!                    425

    Well do I call to mind the very week
When I was first intrusted to the care
Of that sweet Valley; when its paths, its shores,
And brooks were like a dream of novelty

> To speak of such effects as cannot here
> Be regularly classed, yet tend no less
> To the same point, the growth of mental powers
> And love of Nature's works. Ere I had seen
> Eight summers (and 'twas in the very week
> When I was first transplanted to thy Vale
> Beloved Hawkshead! when thy paths, thy shores
> And brooks were like a dream of novelty
> To my half infant mind) I chanced to cross . . .

To my half-infant thoughts; that very week                    [430]
455 While I was roving up and down alone,
Seeking I knew not what, I chanced to cross
One of those open fields, which, shaped like ears,
Make green peninsulas on Esthwaite's Lake:
Twilight was coming on; yet through the gloom,               [435]
460 I saw distinctly on the opposite Shore
A heap of garments, left, as I suppos'd,
By one who there was bathing; long I watch'd,
But no one own'd them; meanwhile the calm Lake
Grew dark, with all the shadows on its breast,              [440]
465 And, now and then, a fish up-leaping, snapp'd
The breathless stillness. The succeeding day,
(Those unclaimed garments telling a plain Tale)            [443]
Went there a Company, and, in their Boat
Sounded with grappling irons, and long poles.              [447]
470 At length, the dead Man, 'mid that beauteous scene
Of trees, and hills and water, bolt upright
Rose with his ghastly face; a spectre shape                 [450]
Of terror even! and yet no vulgar fear,
Young as I was, a Child not nine years old,
475 Possess'd me; for my inner eye had seen
Such sights before, among the shining streams
Of Fairy Land, the Forests of Romance:                     [455]
Thence came a spirit hallowing what I saw
With decoration and ideal grace;
480 A dignity, a smoothness, like the works
Of Grecian Art, and purest Poesy.

I had a precious treasure at that time                      [460]

460 I saw] Appeared A² C. *In* V *follows the line* Beneath a tree, and close
by the lakeside,
461–2                                      garments as if left by one
           Who there was bathing. Half an hour I watched  V.
           Who there, perchance, was bathing  D: D² *as* 1850.
465 a leaping fish disturb'd V.          467 *not in* V.
466        The breathless stillness. Soon as I reach'd home
           I to our little household of the sight
           Made casual mention. The succeeding day.  W (*but deletes* Soon
. . . mention).
467–9      Those unclaimed garments drew an anxious crowd
           Of friends and neighbours to the fatal spot.
           In passive expectation on the shore
           These stood, while others sounded, from a Boat,
           The deep—with grappling irons and long poles  A² C.

To my half-infant thoughts; that very week,                    430
While I was roving up and down alone,
Seeking I knew not what, I chanced to cross
One of those open fields, which, shaped like ears,
Make green peninsulas on Esthwaite's Lake:
Twilight was coming on, yet through the gloom                    435
Appeared distinctly on the opposite shore
A heap of garments, as if left by one
Who might have there been bathing. Long I watched,
But no one owned them; meanwhile the calm lake
Grew dark with all the shadows on its breast,                    440
And, now and then, a fish up-leaping snapped
The breathless stillness. The succeeding day,
Those unclaimed garments telling a plain tale
Drew to the spot an anxious crowd; some looked
In passive expectation from the shore,                    445
While from a boat others hung o'er the deep,
Sounding with grappling irons and long poles.
At last, the dead man, 'mid that beauteous scene
Of trees and hills and water, bolt upright
Rose, with his ghastly face, a spectre shape                    450
Of terror; yet no soul-debasing fear,
Young as I was, a child not nine years old,
Possessed me, for my inner eye had seen
Such sights before, among the shining streams
Of faëry land, the forest of romance.                    455
Their spirit hallowed the sad spectacle
With decoration of ideal grace;
A dignity, a smoothness, like the works
Of Grecian art, and purest poesy.

A precious treasure had I long possessed,                    460

469 Sounded with iron hooks and with long poles  V.
472 Rose with his ghastly face. I might advert
    To numerous accidents in flood or field
    Quarry or moor, or 'mid the winter snows
    Distresses and disasters, tragic facts
    Of rural history that impressed my mind
    With images to which in following years
    Far other feelings were attached; with forms
    That yet exist with independent life
    And, like their archetypes, know no decay.
*So* V.  V *then goes on to* XI. 258 [XII. 208].
474 not nine] of eight  W.
482 𝔄 C D:  A precious treasure long had been my own  D² E: E² *as* 1850.

A little, yellow canvas-cover'd Book,
A slender abstract of the Arabian Tales;
485 And when I learn'd, as now I first did learn,
From my Companions in this new abode,
That this dear prize of mine was but a block
Hewn from a mighty quarry; in a word,                          [465]
That there were four large Volumes, laden all
490 With kindred matter, 'twas, in truth, to me
A promise scarcely earthly. Instantly
I made a league, a covenant with a Friend
Of my own age, that we should lay aside                        [470]
The monies we possess'd, and hoard up more,
495 Till our joint savings had amass'd enough
To make this Book our own. Through several months
Religiously did we preserve that vow,
And spite of all temptation, hoarded up
And hoarded up; but firmness fail'd at length                  [475]
500 Nor were we ever masters of our wish.

     And afterwards, when to my Father's House
Returning at the holidays, I found
That golden store of books which I had left
Open to my enjoyment once again
505 What heart was mine! Full often through the course          [480]
Of those glad respites in the summer-time
When, arm'd with rod and line we went abroad
For a whole day together, I have lain
Down by thy side, O Derwent! murmuring Stream,
510 On the hot stones and in the glaring sun,                   [485]
And there have read, devouring as I read,
Defrauding the day's glory, desperate!
Till, with a sudden bound of smart reproach,
Such as an Idler deals with in his shame,
515 I to my sport betook myself again.                          [490]

     A gracious Spirit o'er this earth presides,
And o'er the heart of man: invisibly
It comes, directing those to works of love
Who care not, know not, think not what they do:                [495]

485–7 𝔄 C D E: E² *as* 1850.
488–9 Hewn out of four large volumes, laden all  D E:  E² *as* 1850.
491–3                                        On the spot
        With him who gave the tidings was I bound

A little yellow, canvas-covered book,
A slender abstract of the Arabian tales;
And, from companions in a new abode,
When first I learnt, that this dear prize of mine
Was but a block hewn from a mighty quarry—               465
That there were four large volumes, laden all
With kindred matter, 'twas to me, in truth,
A promise scarcely earthly. Instantly,
With one not richer than myself, I made
A covenant that each should lay aside                     470
The moneys he possessed, and hoard up more,
Till our joint savings had amassed enough
To make this book our own. Through several months,
In spite of all temptation, we preserved
Religiously that vow; but firmness failed,                475
Nor were we ever masters of our wish.

   And when thereafter to my father's house
The holidays returned me, there to find
That golden store of books which I had left,
What joy was mine! How often in the course              480
Of those glad respites, though a soft west wind
Ruffled the waters to the angler's wish
For a whole day together, have I lain
Down by thy side, O Derwent! murmuring stream,
On the hot stones, and in the glaring sun,              485
And there have read, devouring as I read,
Defrauding the day's glory, desperate!
Till with a sudden bound of smart reproach,
Such as an idler deals with in his shame,
I to the sport betook myself again.                     490

   A gracious spirit o'er this earth presides,
And o'er the heart of man: invisibly
It comes, to works of unreproved delight,
And tendency benign, directing those
Who care not, know not, think not what they do.         495

By covenant that we should lay aside
The money each possessed and hoard up more  D E:  E² *as* 1850.
497–9  A² C *as* 1850.
505  heart 𝔄 C D: joy D².   Full] How A² C.
506–7  in the summer time . . . abroad] tho' a soft west wind
      Promised continuance to [of E] the angler's sport  D E:  E² *as* 1850.
518  𝔄 C D E:  E² *as* 1850 [493–4].

520 The Tales that charm away the wakeful night
In Araby, Romances, Legends, penn'd
For solace, by the light of monkish Lamps;
Fictions for Ladies, of their Love, devis'd
By youthful Squires; adventures endless, spun [500]
525 By the dismantled Warrior in old age,
Out of the bowels of those very thoughts
In which his youth did first extravagate,
These spread like day, and something in the shape
Of these, will live till man shall be no more. [505]
530 Dumb yearnings, hidden appetites are ours,
And they must have their food: our childhood sits,
Our simple childhood sits upon a throne
That hath more power than all the elements.
I guess not what this tells of Being past, [510]
535 Nor what it augurs of the life to come;
But so it is; and in that dubious hour,
That twilight when we first begin to see
This dawning earth, to recognise, expect;
And in the long probation that ensues, [515]
540 The time of trial, ere we learn to live
In reconcilement with our stinted powers,
To endure this state of meagre vassalage;
Unwilling to forego, confess, submit,
Uneasy and unsettled; yoke-fellows [520]
545 To custom, mettlesome, and not yet tam'd
And humbled down, oh! then we feel, we feel,
We know when we have Friends. Ye dreamers, then,
Forgers of lawless tales! we bless you then,
Impostors, drivellers, dotards, as the ape [525]
550 Philosophy will call you: then we feel
With what, and how great might ye are in league,
Who make our wish our power, our thought a deed,
An empire, a possession; Ye whom Time
And Seasons serve; all Faculties; to whom [530]
555 Earth crouches, th' elements are potter's clay,
Space like a Heaven fill'd up with Northern lights;
Here, nowhere, there, and everywhere at once.

It might demand a more impassion'd strain

547 when 𝔄: where A² C.     548 lawless 𝔄 C D: daring E.

The tales that charm away the wakeful night
In Araby, romances; legends penned
For solace by dim light of monkish lamps;
Fictions, for ladies of their love, devised
By youthful squires; adventures endless, spun          500
By the dismantled warrior in old age,
Out of the bowels of those very schemes
In which his youth did first extravagate;
These spread like day, and something in the shape
Of these will live till man shall be no more.          505
Dumb yearnings, hidden appetites, are ours,
And *they must* have their food. Our childhood sits,
Our simple childhood, sits upon a throne
That hath more power than all the elements.
I guess not what this tells of Being past,             510
Nor what it augurs of the life to come;
But so it is, and, in that dubious hour,
That twilight when we first begin to see
This dawning earth, to recognise, expect,
And in the long probation that ensues,                 515
The time of trial, ere we learn to live
In reconcilement with our stinted powers;
To endure this state of meagre vassalage,
Unwilling to forego, confess, submit,
Uneasy and unsettled, yoke-fellows                     520
To custom, mettlesome, and not yet tamed
And humbled down; oh! then we feel, we feel,
We know where we have friends. Ye dreamers, then,
Forgers of daring tales! we bless you then,
Impostors, drivellers, dotards, as the ape             525
Philosophy will call you: *then* we feel
With what, and how great might ye are in league,
Who make our wish, our power, our thought a deed,
An empire, a possession,—ye whom time
And seasons serve; all Faculties to whom               530
Earth crouches, the elements are potter's clay,
Space like a heaven filled up with northern lights,
Here, nowhere, there, and everywhere at once.

   Relinquishing this lofty eminence

[534–5] Relinquishing this glorious eminence
    For humbler ground yet not the less a tract  D:  D² *as* 1850.

To tell of later pleasures, link'd to these,                    [535]
560 A tract of the same isthmus which we cross
In progress from our native continent
To earth and human life: I mean to speak
Of that delightful time of growing youth
When cravings for the marvellous relent,                    [540]
565 And we begin to love what we have seen;
And sober truth, experience, sympathy,
Take stronger hold of us; and words themselves
Move us with conscious pleasure.                    [545]
                                        I am sad
At thought of raptures, now for ever flown,
570 Even unto tears, I sometimes could be sad
To think of, to read over, many a page,
Poems withal of name, which at that time
Did never fail to entrance me, and are now                    [550]
Dead in my eyes as is a theatre
575 Fresh emptied of spectators. Thirteen years
Or haply less, I might have seen, when first
My ears began to open to the charm
Of words in tuneful order, found them sweet                    [555]
For *their own sakes*, a passion and a power;
580 And phrases pleas'd me, chosen for delight,
For pomp, or love. Oft in the public roads,
Yet unfrequented, while the morning light
Was yellowing the hill-tops, with that dear Friend,                    [560]
The same whom I have mention'd heretofore,
585 I went abroad, and for the better part
Of two delightful hours we stroll'd along
By the still borders of the misty Lake,
Repeating favorite verses with one voice,
Or conning more; as happy as the birds                    [565]
590 That round us chaunted. Well might we be glad,
Lifted above the ground by airy fancies
More bright than madness or the dreams of wine,
And, though full oft the objects of our love
Were false, and in their splendour overwrought,                    [570]
595 Yet, surely, at such time no vulgar power
Was working in us, nothing less, in truth,
Than that most noble attribute of man,

564–7 𝔄 C D: D² *as* 1850.          575 Thirteen 𝔄: Twice five A² C.

For ground, though humbler, not the less a tract          535
Of the same isthmus, which our spirits cross
In progress from their native continent
To earth and human life, the Song might dwell
On that delightful time of growing youth,
When craving for the marvellous gives way               540
To strengthening love for things that we have seen;
When sober truth and steady sympathies,
Offered to notice by less daring pens,
Take firmer hold of us, and words themselves
Move us with conscious pleasure.                        545
                              I am sad
At thought of raptures now for ever flown;
Almost to tears I sometimes could be sad
To think of, to read over, many a page,
Poems withal of name, which at that time
Did never fail to entrance me, and are now              550
Dead in my eyes, dead as a theatre
Fresh emptied of spectators. Twice five years
Or less I might have seen, when first my mind
With conscious pleasure opened to the charm
Of words in tuneful order, found them sweet             555
For their own *sakes*, a passion, and a power;
And phrases pleased me chosen for delight,
For pomp, or love. Oft, in the public roads
Yet unfrequented, while the morning light
Was yellowing the hill tops, I went abroad              560
With a dear friend, and for the better part
Of two delightful hours we strolled along
By the still borders of the misty lake,
Repeating favourite verses with one voice,
Or conning more, as happy as the birds                  565
That round us chaunted. Well might we be glad,
Lifted above the ground by airy fancies,
More bright than madness or the dreams of wine;
And, though full oft the objects of our love
Were false, and in their splendour overwrought,         570
Yet was there surely then no vulgar power
Working within us,—nothing less, in truth,
Than that most noble attribute of man,

576–7 𝔄 C D: D² *as* 1850.

Though yet untutor'd and inordinate,
That wish for something loftier, more adorn'd,        [575]
600 Than is the common aspect, daily garb
Of human life. What wonder then if sounds
Of exultation echoed through the groves!
For images, and sentiments, and words,
And every thing with which we had to do        [580]
605 In that delicious world of poesy,
Kept holiday; a never-ending show,
With music, incense, festival and flowers!

Here must I pause: this only will I add,
From heart-experience, and in humblest sense        [585]
610 Of modesty, that he, who, in his youth
A wanderer among the woods and fields,
With living Nature hath been intimate,
Not only in that raw unpractis'd time
Is stirr'd to ecstasy, as others are,        [590]
615 By glittering verse; but, he doth furthermore,
In measure only dealt out to himself,
Receive enduring touches of deep joy
From the great Nature that exists in works
Of mighty Poets. Visionary Power        [595]
620 Attends upon the motions of the winds
Embodied in the mystery of words.
There darkness makes abode, and all the host
Of shadowy things do work their changes there,
As in a mansion like their proper home:        [600]
625 Even forms and substances are circumfus'd
By that transparent veil with light divine;
And through the turnings intricate of Verse,
Present themselves as objects recognis'd,
In flashes, and with a glory scarce their own.        [605]

630      Thus far a scanty record is deduced
Of what I owed to Books in early life;

598 Though yet inordinate and unmatur'd  M.
604 with which we had to do] presented to the soul  A² C.
608 I] we  A² C.          611 𝕬 C D: D² *as* 1850.
615-17 A² C *as* 1850.
    619 Visionary Power] M *underlines* Visionary *and adds in margin* (a sub-
sensuous).
    623 𝕬 C D:  D² *as* 1850.

Though yet untutored and inordinate,
That wish for something loftier, more adorned,                575
Than is the common aspect, daily garb,
Of human life. What wonder, then, if sounds
Of exultation echoed through the groves!
For, images, and sentiments, and words,
And everything encountered or pursued                          580
In that delicious world of poesy,
Kept holiday, a never-ending show,
With music, incense, festival, and flowers!


   Here must we pause: this only let me add,
From heart-experience, and in humblest sense                   585
Of modesty, that he, who in his youth
A daily wanderer among woods and fields
With living Nature hath been intimate,
Not only in that raw unpractised time
Is stirred to extasy, as others are,                           590
By glittering verse; but further, doth receive,
In measure only dealt out to himself,
Knowledge and increase of enduring joy
From the great Nature that exists in works
Of mighty Poets. Visionary power                               595
Attends the motions of the viewless winds,
Embodied in the mystery of words:
There, darkness makes abode, and all the host
Of shadowy things work endless changes,—there,
As in a mansion like their proper home,                        600
Even forms and substances are circumfused
By that transparent veil with light divine,
And, through the turnings intricate of verse,
Present themselves as objects recognised,
In flashes, and with glory not their own.                      605


624 like their proper home:] kindred to their own; M.
629 A² C *as* 1850.          630–7 𝔄 C D E.
630 deduced] brought down M.
630–2 Thus far by tedious Retrospect I fear
     Have I my Friend endeavoured to bring down
     The Register of what I owed to Books
     In early life, their later Gifts do yet
     Remain untold.
     The record of my early debt to Books *variants in* W.

Their later influence yet remains untold ;
But as this work was taking in my thoughts
Proportions that seem'd larger than had first
635 Been meditated, I was indisposed
To any further progress at a time
When these acknowledgements were left unpaid.

632–7 Their later gifts do yet remain untold
      But as this meditative History
      Was calling me to a far different work
      Which lies before us, yet untouch'd, I mean
      To speak of an abasement in my mind
      Not altogether wrought without the help
      Of Books ill-chosen, I was loth to think
      Of such ungracious office, at a time
      When these acknowledgements were yet unpaid. M.
633 thoughts] mind D.

# BOOK SIXTH

## CAMBRIDGE AND THE ALPS

THE leaves were yellow when to Furness Fells,
The haunt of Shepherds, and to cottage life
I bade adieu; and, one among the Flock
Who by that season are conven'd, like birds
5  Trooping together at the Fowler's lure,                    [5]
Went back to Granta's cloisters; not so fond,
Or eager, though as gay and undepress'd
In spirit, as when I thence had taken flight
A few short months before. I turn'd my face
10  Without repining from the mountain pomp                  [10]
Of Autumn, and its beauty enter'd in
With calmer Lakes, and louder Streams; and You,
Frank-hearted Maids of rocky Cumberland,
You and your not unwelcome days of mirth                     [15]
15  I quitted, and your nights of revelry,
And in my own unlovely Cell sate down
In lightsome mood; such privilege has Youth,
That cannot take long leave of pleasant thoughts.

We need not linger o'er the ensuing time,
20  But let me add at once that, now the bonds
Of indolent and vague society                                [20]
Relaxing in their hold, I liv'd henceforth
More to myself, read more, reflected more,
Felt more, and settled daily into habits
25  More promising. Two winters may be pass'd
Without a separate notice; many books
Were read in process of this time, devour'd,
Tasted or skimm'd, or studiously perus'd,

[MSS. for Book VI: A B C D E.]
Book Sixth. Cambridge and the Alps  B C: 6 A.
1 yellow . . . Furness Fells] A² C *as* 1850.
3 Flock] youth A² C.
4-5        By summer's vacant season scatter'd wide
           And reassembling now like kindred birds
           That troop *etc.*  A² C.
8 spirit ꟻ D: mind A² C D².

# BOOK SIXTH

## CAMBRIDGE AND THE ALPS

THE leaves were fading when to Esthwaite's banks
And the simplicities of cottage life
I bade farewell; and, one among the youth
Who, summoned by that season, reunite
As scattered birds troop to the fowler's lure,      5
Went back to Granta's cloisters, not so prompt
Or eager, though as gay and undepressed
In mind, as when I thence had taken flight
A few short months before. I turned my face
Without repining from the coves and heights      10
Clothed in the sunshine of the withering fern;
Quitted, not loth, the mild magnificence
Of calmer lakes and louder streams; and you,
Frank-hearted maids of rocky Cumberland,
You and your not unwelcome days of mirth,      15
Relinquished, and your nights of revelry,
And in my own unlovely cell sate down
In lightsome mood—such privilege has youth
That cannot take long leave of pleasant thoughts.

    The bonds of indolent society      20
Relaxing in their hold, henceforth I lived
More to myself. Two winters may be passed
Without a separate notice: many books
Were skimmed, devoured, or studiously perused,

10–12                from the beauty and pomp
      Of Autumn, entering under azure skies
      To mountains clothe(d) in golden robe of fire,
      To calmer lakes
11–12  Of Autumn azure skies and mountains clothed
      In [crested ?] fire with mild magnificence
      Of calmer lakes *alternatives added in* B.
11–12  Of Autumn, undisturbed by ruffling winds
      And entering with the mild magnificence
      Of calmer Lakes *etc.* A² C.
11–12  In the soft sunshine of their golden fern
      Attired; from Autumn's mild magnificence
      Her calmer Lakes  D: D² *as* 1850.
19–21  A² C *as* 1850.
23–25  read more . . . promising] A *deletes; not in* C.

Yet with no settled plan. I was detached [25]
30 Internally from academic cares,
From every hope of prowess and reward,
And wish'd to be a lodger in that house
Of Letters, and no more: and should have been
Even such, but for some personal concerns
35 That hung about me in my own despite
Perpetually, no heavy weight, but still
A baffling and a hindrance, a controul
Which made the thought of planning for myself
A course of independent study seem
40 An act of disobedience towards them
Who lov'd me, proud rebellion and unkind.
This bastard virtue, rather let it have [30]
A name it more deserves, this cowardice,
Gave treacherous sanction to that overlove
45 Of freedom planted in me from the very first
And indolence, by force of which I turn'd
From regulations even of my own,
As from restraints and bonds. And who can tell, [35]
Who knows what thus may have been gain'd both then
50 And at a later season, or preserv'd;
What love of nature, what original strength
Of contemplation, what intuitive truths
The deepest and the best, and what research [40]
Unbiass'd, unbewilder'd, and unaw'd?

55     The Poet's soul was with me at that time,
Sweet meditations, the still overflow
Of happiness and truth. A thousand hopes
Were mine, a thousand tender dreams, of which [45]
No few have since been realiz'd, and some
60 Do yet remain, hopes for my future life.
Four years and thirty, told this very week,
Have I been now a sojourner on earth,
And yet the morning gladness is not gone
Which then was in my mind. Those were the days
65 Which also first encourag'd me to trust
With firmness, hitherto but lightly touch'd
With such a daring thought, that I might leave [55]

32-37 A *deletes*; *not in* C.     38 Which made] Yet did A² C.
43 more *all MSS.*: now 1850.

But with no settled plan. I was detached                  25
Internally from academic cares;
Yet independent study seemed a course
Of hardy disobedience toward friends
And kindred, proud rebellion and unkind.
This spurious virtue, rather let it bear                  30
A name it now deserves, this cowardice,
Gave treacherous sanction to that over-love
Of freedom which encouraged me to turn
From regulations even of my own
As from restraints and bonds. Yet who can tell—           35
Who knows what thus may have been gained, both then
And at a later season, or preserved;
What love of nature, what original strength
Of contemplation, what intuitive truths,
The deepest and the best, what keen research,            40
Unbiassed, unbewildered, and unawed?

The Poet's soul was with me at that time;
Sweet meditations, the still overflow
Of present happiness, while future years
Lacked not anticipations, tender dreams,                  45
No few of which have since been realised;
And some remain, hopes for my future life.
Four years and thirty, told this very week,
Have I been now a sojourner on earth,
By sorrow not unsmitten; yet for me                       50
Life's morning radiance hath not left the hills,
Her dew is on the flowers. Those were the days
Which also first emboldened me to trust
With firmness, hitherto but lightly touched
By such a daring thought, that I might leave             55

45 very first 𝕬: B *deletes* very: A² *as* 1850.
45–46 A² C *as* 1850.          48 And] Yet  A² B² C.
52–54                 what intuitive research
          Unbiassed . . . unawed  E:  E² *as* 1850.
53 and what  𝕬 C D:  what keen  E².
57–60  𝕬 C.
     Of happiness from beauty and (from) truth
     Proceeding; while the future did not want
     Anticipations, tender dreams, of which (*etc. as* A)  D:  D² *as* 1850.
63 gladness] radiance  A² C.          64 then was in] gladden'd then  A² C.
[51–52] Life's morning . . . Her dew  E²:  The morning . . . The dew  D E.
65 encourag'd] emboldened  A² C.

Some monument behind me which pure hearts
Should reverence. The instinctive humbleness,
70 Upheld even by the very name and thought
Of printed books and authorship, began
To melt away, and further, the dread awe                    [60]
Of mighty names was soften'd down, and seem'd
Approachable, admitting fellowship
75 Of modest sympathy. Such aspect now,
Though not familiarly, my mind put on;
I lov'd, and I enjoy'd, that was my chief
And ruling business, happy in the strength
And loveliness of imagery and thought.
80 All winter long, whenever free to take
My choice, did I at night frequent our Groves
And tributary walks, the last, and oft
The only one, who had been lingering there
Through hours of silence, till the Porter's Bell,          [70]
85 A punctual follower on the stroke of nine,
Rang with its blunt unceremonious voice,
Inexorable summons. Lofty Elms,
Inviting shades of opportune recess,
Did give composure to a neighbourhood                      [75]
90 Unpeaceful in itself. A single Tree
There was, no doubt yet standing there, an Ash
With sinuous trunk, boughs exquisitely wreath'd;
Up from the ground and almost to the top                   [80]
The trunk and master branches everywhere
95 Were green with ivy; and the lightsome twigs
And outer spray profusely tipp'd with seeds
That hung in yellow tassels and festoons,
Moving or still, a Favourite trimm'd out
By Winter for himself, as if in pride,
100 And with outlandish grace. Oft have I stood               [85]
Foot-bound, uplooking at this lovely Tree
Beneath a frosty moon. The hemisphere
Of magic fiction, verse of mine perhaps
May never tread; but scarcely Spenser's self
105 Could have more tranquil visions in his youth,           [90]
More bright appearances could scarcely see

77–78  I lov'd to observe, to admire and to enjoy,
          Such passion ruled me  A² C.
[65] achieve] admire  D E:  achieve 1850 *clearly a mistake.*

Some monument behind me which pure hearts
Should reverence. The instinctive humbleness,
Maintained even by the very name and thought
Of printed books and authorship, began
To melt away; and further, the dread awe                      60
Of mighty names was softened down and seemed
Approachable, admitting fellowship
Of modest sympathy. Such aspect now,
Though not familiarly, my mind put on,
Content to observe, to achieve, and to enjoy.                 65

    All winter long, whenever free to choose,
Did I by night frequent the College groves
And tributary walks; the last, and oft
The only one, who had been lingering there
Through hours of silence, till the porter's bell,             70
A punctual follower on the stroke of nine,
Rang with its blunt unceremonious voice,
Inexorable summons! Lofty elms,
Inviting shades of opportune recess,
Bestowed composure on a neighbourhood                          75
Unpeaceful in itself. A single tree
With sinuous trunk, boughs exquisitely wreathed,
Grew there; an ash which Winter for himself
Decked as in pride, and with outlandish grace:
Up from the ground, and almost to the top,                    80
The trunk and every master branch were green
With clustering ivy, and the lightsome twigs
And outer spray profusely tipped with seeds
That hung in yellow tassels, while the air
Stirred them, not voiceless. Often have I stood               85
Foot-bound uplooking at this lovely tree
Beneath a frosty moon. The hemisphere
Of magic fiction, verse of mine perchance
May never tread; but scarcely Spenser's self
Could have more tranquil visions in his youth,               90
Or could more bright appearances create

[67] Alone by night did I frequent our groves D : D² *as* 1850.
91 There stood, and doubtless yet survives, an Ash  A² C.
94–95 Green were the trunk and master branches, green
        With flourishing ivy  B². *So* A² (*but second* green *deleted*); C *as* A².
[82] flourishing  D E: clustering  E².
97 Clustered in yellow tassels as they hung  A² C.
[84] Pendent in yellow tassels, and, if air  D: D² *as* 1850.

Of human Forms and superhuman Powers,
Than I beheld, standing on winter nights
Alone, beneath this fairy work of earth.
110 'Twould be a waste of labour to detail
The rambling studies of a truant Youth,                    [95]
Which further may be easily divin'd,
What, and what kind they were. My inner knowledge,
(This barely will I note) was oft in depth
115 And delicacy like another mind
Sequester'd from my outward taste in books,
And yet the books which then I lov'd the most
Are dearest to me now; for, being vers'd                    [100]
In living Nature, I had there a guide
120 Which open'd frequently my eyes, else shut,
A standard which was usefully applied,
Even when unconsciously, to other things
Which less I understood. In general terms,
I was a better judge of thoughts than words,                    [106]
125 Misled as to these latter, not alone
By common inexperience of youth
But by the trade in classic niceties,
Delusion to young Scholars incident,
And old ones also, by that overpriz'd
130 And dangerous craft of picking phrases out                    [110]
From languages that want the living voice
To make of them a nature to the heart,
To tell us what is passion, what is truth,
What reason, what simplicity and sense.

135   Yet must I not entirely overlook                    [115]
The pleasure gather'd from the elements
Of geometric science. I had stepp'd
In these inquiries but a little way,
No farther than the threshold; with regret                    [119]
140 Sincere I mention this; but there I found
Enough to exalt, to chear me and compose.
With Indian awe and wonder, ignorance

107 Forms and ℑ C: Forms with D.
110–13 'Twould be . . . they were]
              The rambling studies of a truant Youth
              'Twere idle to detail. A² C.
[97] This barely may be noted, did full oft
        Differ as widely D² E (D *illegible*): E² *as* 1850.

Of human forms with superhuman powers,
Than I beheld loitering on calm clear nights
Alone, beneath this fairy work of earth.
    On the vague reading of a truant youth                    95
'Twere idle to descant. My inner judgment
Not seldom differed from my taste in books,
As if it appertained to another mind,
And yet the books which then I valued most
Are dearest to me *now*; for, having scanned,               100
Not heedlessly, the laws, and watched the forms
Of Nature, in that knowledge I possessed
A standard, often usefully applied,
Even when unconsciously, to things removed
From a familiar sympathy.—In fine,                          105
I was a better judge of thoughts than words,
Misled in estimating words, not only
By common inexperience of youth,
But by the trade in classic niceties,
The dangerous craft of culling term and phrase              110
From languages that want the living voice
To carry meaning to the natural heart;
To tell us what is passion, what is truth,
What reason, what simplicity and sense.

Yet may we not entirely overlook                            115
The pleasure gathered from the rudiments
Of geometric science. Though advanced
In these inquiries, with regret I speak,
No farther than the threshold, there I found
Both elevation and composed delight:                        120
With Indian awe and wonder, ignorance pleased

119–20 In living nature's countenance, and her laws
        For the mind's private service I possess'd  A² C.
122–3 to other things . . . terms] to things removed For (From ?) my
familiar sympathy—in fine  A² C.
128–30 A *deletes*; A² C *as* 1850.
132 [112] 𝔄 C D: nature for B²: E *as* 1850.
135 must I not] may we not  A² C.
136 elements 𝔄 C D: rudiments  D².
137 I had stepp'd] Though advanced  A² C.
139–40 with regret . . . but] A *deletes*; *not in* C.
[120–8] D *stuck over*: D² E *as* 1850, *but* [125] agents  D³ E²:  creatures
D² E.

Which even was cherish'd, did I meditate
Upon the alliance of those simple, pure
145 Proportions and relations with the frame
And laws of Nature, how they would become
Herein a leader to the human mind,
And made endeavours frequent to detect
The process by dark guesses of my own.
150 Yet from this source more frequently I drew
A pleasure calm and deeper, a still sense                    [130]
Of permanent and universal sway
And paramount endowment in the mind,
An image not unworthy of the one
155 Surpassing Life, which out of space and time,             [135]
Nor touch'd by welterings of passion, is
And hath the name of God. Transcendent peace
And silence did await upon these thoughts                    [140]
That were a frequent comfort to my youth.

160     And as I have read of one by shipwreck thrown
With fellow Sufferers whom the waves had spar'd
Upon a region uninhabited
An island of the Deep, who having brought
To land a single Volume and no more,                         [145]
165 A treatise of Geometry, was used,
Although of food and clothing destitute,
And beyond common wretchedness depress'd,
To part from company and take this book,
Then first a self-taught pupil in those truths,             [150]
170 To spots remote and corners of the Isle
By the sea side, and draw his diagrams
With a long stick upon the sand, and thus
Did oft beguile his sorrow, and almost
Forget his feeling; even so, if things
175 Producing like effect, from outward cause                 [155]
So different, may rightly be compar'd,
So was it with me then, and so will be
With Poets ever. Mighty is the charm

151–3 A C D: D² *as* 1850.        155–7 A² C *as* 1850.
162–3 Upon a desart coast, who, having brought  A² C.
169–70                    in the lore
     Of scientific truth, to spots remote  A² C.
170 Isle  B: Island  A.
172 stick] staff  A² C.

With its own struggles, did I meditate
On the relation those abstractions bear
To Nature's laws, and by what process led,
Those immaterial agents bowed their heads           125
Duly to serve the mind of earth-born man;
From star to star, from kindred sphere to sphere,
From system on to system without end.

More frequently from the same source I drew
A pleasure quiet and profound, a sense            130
Of permanent and universal sway,
And paramount belief; there, recognised
A type, for finite natures, of the one
Supreme Existence, the surpassing life
Which—to the boundaries of space and time,        135
Of melancholy space and doleful time,
Superior, and incapable of change,
Nor touched by welterings of passion—is,
And hath the name of, God.  Transcendent peace
And silence did await upon these thoughts         140
That were a frequent comfort to my youth.

'Tis told by one whom stormy waters threw,
With fellow-sufferers by the shipwreck spared,
Upon a desert coast, that having brought
To land a single volume, saved by chance,         145
A treatise of Geometry, he wont,
Although of food and clothing destitute,
And beyond common wretchedness depressed,
To part from company and take this book
(Then first a self-taught pupil in its truths)    150
To spots remote, and draw his diagrams
With a long staff upon the sand, and thus
Did oft beguile his sorrow, and almost
Forget his feeling: so (if like effect
From the same cause produced, 'mid outward things 155
So different, may rightly be compared),
So was it then with me, and so will be
With Poets ever. Mighty is the charm

175–6 Producing . . . different]
        By kindly action of the self-same cause
        Inwardly wrought, mid outward circumstance
        So different  A² C.

Of those abstractions to a mind beset
180 With images, and haunted by itself;                    [160]
And specially delightful unto me
Was that clear Synthesis built up aloft
So gracefully, even then when it appear'd
No more than as a plaything, or a toy
185 Embodied to the sense, not what it is                   [165]
In verity, an independent world
Created out of pure Intelligence.

Such dispositions then were mine, almost
Through grace of Heaven and inborn tenderness.        [170]
190 And not to leave the picture of that time
Imperfect, with these habits I must rank
A melancholy from humours of the blood
In part, and partly taken up, that lov'd
A pensive sky, sad days, and piping winds,
195 The twilight more than dawn, Autumn than Spring;    [175]
A treasur'd and luxurious gloom, of choice
And inclination mainly, and the mere
Redundancy of youth's contentedness.
Add unto this a multitude of hours
200 Pilfer'd away by what the Bard who sang              [180]
Of the Enchanter Indolence hath call'd
'Good-natured lounging,' and behold a map
Of my Collegiate life, far less intense
Than Duty call'd for, or without regard
205 To Duty, might have sprung up of itself              [185]
By change of accidents, or even, to speak
Without unkindness, in another place.

In summer among distant nooks I rov'd
Dovedale, or Yorkshire Dales, or through bye-tracts
210 Of my own native region, and was blest               [195]
Between these sundry wanderings with a joy

185 𝔄 C D: D² *as* 1850.
188–9 𝔄 C: inborn tenderness  D: inward aptitudes  D² E: E² *as* 1850.
192 from humours of the blood] native to my frame  A² C.
199 A² C *as* 1850.
[188–90] D *stuck over.*
[189] Was wholly mine, mine only be the blame  D² E: D³ E² *as* 1850.
208–9 In summer making eager quest of scenes
          For beauty famed I left not unexplor'd
          That stream whose azure current works its way

Of those abstractions to a mind beset
With images, and haunted by herself,                        160
And specially delightful unto me
Was that clear synthesis built up aloft
So gracefully; even then when it appeared
Not more than a mere plaything, or a toy
To sense embodied: not the thing it is                      165
In verity, an independent world,
Created out of pure intelligence.

    Such dispositions then were mine unearned
By aught, I fear, of genuine desert—
Mine, through heaven's grace and inborn aptitudes.          170
And not to leave the story of that time
Imperfect, with these habits must be joined,
Moods melancholy, fits of spleen, that loved
A pensive sky, sad days, and piping winds,
The twilight more than dawn, autumn than spring;            175
A treasured and luxurious gloom of choice
And inclination mainly, and the mere
Redundancy of youth's contentedness.
—To time thus spent, add multitudes of hours
Pilfered away, by what the Bard who sang                    180
Of the Enchanter Indolence hath called
'Good-natured lounging,' and behold a map
Of my collegiate life—far less intense
Than duty called for, or, without regard
To duty, *might* have sprung up of itself                   185
By change of accidents, or even, to speak
Without unkindness, in another place.
Yet why take refuge in that plea ?—the fault,
This I repeat, was mine; mine be the blame.

    In summer, making quest for works of art,                190
Or scenes renowned for beauty, I explored
That streamlet whose blue current works its way
Between romantic Dovedale's spiry rocks;
Pried into Yorkshire dales, or hidden tracts
Of my own native region, and was blest                      195
Between these sundry wanderings with a joy

    Between romantic Dovedale's spiry rocks:
    Roamed with swift foot through Yorkshire's splendid Vales
    Or loitered, prying into hidden tracts   A² C.

Above all joys, that seem'd another morn
Risen on mid noon, the presence, Friend, I mean
Of that sole Sister, she who hath been long
215 Thy Treasure also, thy true friend and mine,                    [200]
Now, after separation desolate
Restor'd to me, such absence that she seem'd
A gift then first bestow'd. The gentle Banks
Of Emont, hitherto unnam'd in Song,
220 And that monastic Castle, on a Flat                    [205]
Low-standing by the margin of the Stream,
A Mansion not unvisited of old
By Sidney, where, in sight of our Helvellyn,
Some snatches he might pen, for aught we know,
225 Of his Arcadia, by fraternal love                    [210]
Inspir'd; that River and that mouldering Dome
Have seen us sit in many a summer hour,
My sister and myself, when having climb'd
In danger through some window's open space,
230 We look'd abroad, or on the Turret's head
Lay listening to the wild flowers and the grass,
As they gave out their whispers to the wind.
Another Maid there was, who also breath'd
A gladness o'er that season, then to me                    [225]
235 By her exulting outside look of youth
And placid under-countenance, first endear'd,
That other Spirit, Coleridge, who is now .
So near to us, that meek confiding heart,
So reverenced by us both. O'er paths and fields                    [230]

213 A² C *as* 1850.          214 she *all MSS.*: her 1850.
220 on a Flat]                         mid tall trees
          Embowered, and on a level meadow ground A² C.
222–4 A² C *as* 1850.
226–30          that River and that
mouldering Dome                         Pile D: Tower D².
Have seen us sit in many a          oftentimes in summer hours D E.
summer hour
When having mounted by the          (228–31) D *stuck over*)
darksome stair
Or crept along the ridge of fractured wall
In danger, through some window's          Not without trembling we in safety
open space                                   stood
Looking abroad; we gathered          Where through some gothic win-
with one mind                                   dow's open space

Above all joys, that seemed another morn
Risen on mid noon; blest with the presence, Friend!
Of that sole Sister, her who hath been long
Dear to thee also, thy true friend and mine,                    200
Now, after separation desolate,
Restored to me—such absence that she seemed
A gift then first bestowed. The varied banks
Of Emont, hitherto unnamed in song,
And that monastic castle, 'mid tall trees,                      205
Low-standing by the margin of the stream,
A mansion visited (as fame reports)
By Sidney, where, in sight of our Helvellyn,
Or stormy Cross-fell, snatches he might pen
Of his Arcadia, by fraternal love                              210
Inspired;—that river and those mouldering towers
Have seen us side by side, when, having clomb
The darksome windings of a broken stair,
And crept along a ridge of fractured wall,
Not without trembling, we in safety looked                     215
Forth, through some Gothic window's open space,
And gathered with one mind a rich reward
From the far-stretching landscape, by the light
Of morning beautified, or purple eve;
Or, not less pleased, lay on some turret's head,               220
Catching from tufts of grass and hare-bell flowers
Their faintest whisper to the passing breeze,
Given out while mid-day heat oppressed the plains.

    Another maid there was, who also shed
A gladness o'er that season, then to me,                        225
By her exulting outside look of youth
And placid under-countenance, first endeared;
That other spirit, Coleridge! who is now
So near to us, that meek confiding heart,
So reverenced by us both. O'er paths and fields                230

| | |
|---|---|
| Rich recompense from all that we beheld | We gathered (*etc. as* 1850) D² E. |
| Of the surrounding landscape by the light | From the  D² E. |
| Of morning beautified or shadowy [*alt. to* purple] eve | |
| Or on the turret's head, a happy pair,  A² C. | E² *throughout as* 1850. |
| 233 breath'd] shed  A² C. | |

240 In all that neighbourhood, through narrow lanes
Of eglantine, and through the shady woods,
And o'er the Border Beacon, and the Waste
Of naked Pools, and common Crags that lay
Expos'd on the bare Fell, was scatter'd love, [235]
245 A spirit of pleasure and youth's golden gleam.
O Friend! we had not seen thee at that time;
And yet a power is on me and a strong
Confusion, and I seem to plant Thee there.
Far art Thou wander'd now in search of health, [240]
250 And milder breezes, melancholy lot!
But Thou art with us, with us in the past,
The present, with us in the times to come:
There is no grief, no sorrow, no despair,
No languor, no dejection, no dismay, [245]
255 No absence scarcely can there be for those
Who love as we do. Speed Thee well! divide
Thy pleasure with us, thy returning strength
Receive it daily as a joy of ours;
Share with us thy fresh spirits, whether gift [250]
260 Of gales Etesian, or of loving thoughts.

I, too, have been a Wanderer; but, alas!
How different is the fate of different men
Though Twins almost in genius and in mind!
Unknown unto each other, yea, and breathing
265 As if in different elements, we were framed [255]
To bend at last to the same discipline,
Predestin'd, if two Beings ever were,
To seek the same delights, and have one health,
One happiness. Throughout this narrative,
270 Else sooner ended, I have known full well [260]
For whom I thus record the birth and growth
Of gentleness, simplicity, and truth,
And joyous loves that hallow innocent days
Of peace and self-command. Of Rivers, Fields,
275 And Groves, I speak to Thee, my Friend; to Thee, [265]
Who, yet a liveried School-Boy, in the depths
Of the huge City, on the leaded Roof
Of that wide Edifice, thy Home and School,

245 𝔄 C D: A spirit of gladness D²: Joy bearing fragrance D³: And gladness, sparkling in Youth's golden gleam D⁴ E: E² *as* 1850.

In all that neighbourhood, through narrow lanes
Of eglantine, and through the shady woods
And o'er the Border Beacon, and the waste
Of naked pools, and common crags that lay
Exposed on the bare fell, were scattered love,          235
The spirit of pleasure, and youth's golden gleam.
O Friend! we had not seen thee at that time,
And yet a power is on me, and a strong
Confusion, and I seem to plant thee there.
Far art thou wandered now in search of health          240
And milder breezes,—melancholy lot!
But thou art with us, with us in the past,
The present, with us in the times to come.
There is no grief, no sorrow, no despair,
No languor, no dejection, no dismay,          245
No absence scarcely can there be, for those
Who love as we do. Speed thee well! divide
With us thy pleasure; thy returning strength,
Receive it daily as a joy of ours;
Share with us thy fresh spirits, whether gift          250
Of gales Etesian or of tender thoughts.

    I, too, have been a wanderer; but, alas!
How different the fate of different men.
Though mutually unknown, yea nursed and reared
As if in several elements, we were framed          255
To bend at last to the same discipline,
Predestined, if two beings ever were,
To seek the same delights, and have one health,
One happiness. Throughout this narrative,
Else sooner ended, I have borne in mind          260
For whom it registers the birth, and marks the growth,
Of gentleness, simplicity, and truth,
And joyous loves, that hallow innocent days
Of peace and self-command. Of rivers, fields,
And groves I speak to thee, my Friend! to thee,          265
Who, yet a liveried schoolboy, in the depths
Of the huge city, on the leaded roof
Of that wide edifice, thy school and home,

263–5 𝔄 C D: D² *as* 1850.
270–1 𝔄 C D: Else sooner closed: I have borne in mind for whom
        I register the birth, and mark the growth  D² E: E² *as* 1850.

      Wast used to lie and gaze upon the clouds
280 Moving in Heaven; or hàply, tired of this,       [270]
      To shut thine eyes, and by internal light
      See trees, and meadows, and thy native Stream
      Far distant, thus beheld from year to year
      Of thy long exile. Nor could I forget
285 In this late portion of my argument       [275]
      That scarcely had I finally resign'd
      My rights among those academic Bowers
      When Thou wert thither guided. From the heart
      Of London, and from Cloisters there Thou cam'st,
290 And didst sit down in temperance and peace,       [280]
      A rigorous Student. What a stormy course
      Then follow'd. Oh! it is a pang that calls
      For utterance, to think how small a change
      Of circumstances might to thee have spared
295 A world of pain, ripen'd ten thousand hopes       [285]
      For ever wither'd. Through this retrospect
      Of my own College life I still have had
      Thy after sojourn in the self-same place
      Present before my eyes; I have play'd with times,
300 (I speak of private business of the thought)
      And accidents as children do with cards,       [290]
      Or as a Man, who, when his house is built,
      A frame lock'd up in wood and stone, doth still,
      In impotence of mind, by his fireside
305 Rebuild it to his liking. I have thought
      Of Thee, thy learning, gorgeous eloquence,       [295]
      And all the strength and plumage of thy youth,
      Thy subtle speculations, toils abstruse
      Among the Schoolmen, and platonic forms
310 Of wild ideal pageantry, shap'd out
      From things well-match'd, or ill, and words for things, [300]
      The self-created sustenance of a mind
      Debarr'd from Nature's living images,
      Compell'd to be a life unto itself,
315 And unrelentingly possess'd by thirst
      Of greatness, love, and beauty. Not alone,       [305]
      Ah! surely not in singleness of heart

  280 𝔄 C D: D² *as* 1850.
  284–5 𝔄 C D: Of a long banishment. Nor could the Muse
          In this late portion of her task forget D² E: E² *as* 1850.

Wert used to lie and gaze upon the clouds
Moving in heaven; or, of that pleasure tired,                     270
To shut thine eyes, and by internal light
See trees, and meadows, and thy native stream,
Far distant, thus beheld from year to year
Of a long exile. Nor could I forget,
In this late portion of my argument,                             275
That scarcely, as my term of pupilage
Ceased, had I left those academic bowers
When thou wert thither guided. From the heart
Of London, and from cloisters there, thou camest,
And didst sit down in temperance and peace,                      280
A rigorous student. What a stormy course
Then followed. Oh! it is a pang that calls
For utterance, to think what easy change
Of circumstances might to thee have spared
A world of pain, ripened a thousand hopes,                       285
For ever withered. Through this retrospect
Of my collegiate life I still have had
Thy after-sojourn in the self-same place
Present before my eyes, have played with times
And accidents as children do with cards,                         290
Or as a man, who, when his house is built,
A frame locked up in wood and stone, doth still,
As impotent fancy prompts, by his fireside,
Rebuild it to his liking. I have thought
Of thee, thy learning, gorgeous eloquence,                       295
And all the strength and plumage of thy youth,
Thy subtle speculations, toils abstruse
Among the schoolmen, and Platonic forms
Of wild ideal pageantry, shaped out
From things well-matched or ill, and words for things,           300
The self-created sustenance of a mind
Debarred from Nature's living images,
Compelled to be a life unto herself,
And unrelentingly possessed by thirst
Of greatness, love, and beauty. Not alone,                       305
Ah! surely not in singleness of heart

286–7 𝔄 C D E: E² *as* 1850.                    293 A² C *as* 1850.
295 ten thousand 𝔄 C D E: a thousand E².
297 own College] collegiate A² C.               300 A *deletes*; *not in* C.
304 𝔄 C D: D² *as* 1850.                        308 subtle A: subtile B.

Should I have seen the light of evening fade
Upon the silent Cam, if we had met,
320   Even at that early time: I needs must hope,
Must feel, must trust, that my maturer age,          [310]
And temperature less willing to be mov'd,
My calmer habits and more steady voice
Would with an influence benign have sooth'd
325   Or chas'd away the airy wretchedness
That batten'd on thy youth. But thou hast trod,
In watchful meditation thou hast trod
A march of glory, which doth put to shame          [315]
These vain regrets; health suffers in thee; else
330   Such grief for Thee would be the weakest thought
That ever harbour'd in the breast of Man.


A passing word erewhile did lightly touch
On wanderings of my own; and now to these          [320]
My Poem leads me with an easier mind.
335   The employments of three winters when I wore
A student's gown have been already told,
Or shadow'd forth, as far as there is need.
When the third summer brought its liberty
A Fellow Student and myself, he, too,
340   A Mountaineer, together sallied forth
And, Staff in hand, on foot pursu'd our way          [325]
Towards the distant Alps. An open slight
Of College cares and study was the scheme,
Nor entertain'd without concern for those
345   To whom my worldly interests were dear:          [332]
But Nature then was sovereign in my heart,
And mighty forms seizing a youthful Fancy
Had given a charter to irregular hopes.          [335]

319 𝔄 C D: D² *as* 1850.          320-3 A² C *as* 1850.
335-8 𝔄 C D: D² *as* 1850.
339 A Fellow Student, a bold Mountaineer D: D² *as* 1850.
339-45 A Fellow student, rear'd on Clwyd's banks
          'Mid Cambrian Hills, accepted from my voice
          Bold invitation with no timid mind;
          And sallying forth on foot, we took our way
          Towards the distant Alps. The scheme implied
          An open slight of academic cares
          At a most urgent season (for we then
          Were near the close of our Novitiate)
          Nor was it, I acknowledge, framed by me (*etc. as* 1850)  A² C.

Should I have seen the light of evening fade
From smooth Cam's silent waters: had we met,
Even at that early time, needs must I trust
In the belief, that my maturer age,                    310
My calmer habits, and more steady voice,
Would with an influence benign have soothed,
Or chased away, the airy wretchedness
That battened on thy youth. But thou hast trod
A march of glory, which doth put to shame             315
These vain regrets; health suffers in thee, else
Such grief for thee would be the weakest thought
That ever harboured in the breast of man.

A passing word erewhile did lightly touch
On wanderings of my own, that now embraced           320
With livelier hope a region wider far.

When the third summer freed us from restraint,
A youthful friend, he too a mountaineer,
Not slow to share my wishes, took his staff,
And sallying forth, we journeyed side by side,        325
Bound to the distant Alps. A hardy slight
Did this unprecedented course imply
Of college studies and their set rewards;
Nor had, in truth, the scheme been formed by me
Without uneasy forethought of the pain,               330
The censures, and ill-omening of those
To whom my worldly interests were dear.
But Nature then was sovereign in my mind,
And mighty forms, seizing a youthful fancy,
Had given a charter to irregular hopes.               335

342–5            an open slight                    An open slight
Did this unprecedented scheme        Was this adventure of scholastic
express                                   cares
Of College Studies and those        Nor entertained without concern
urgent care(s)                            for all
Expected from us, being at that      To whom our worldly interests were
time                                      dear  D: D² *as* 1850.
Near to the close of our noviciate
Nor was it form'd by me without
some fears
And some uneasy forethought of
the pain
The censures and ill omening of
those
To whom my worldly interests
were dear  B².

In any age, without an impulse sent
350 From work of Nations, and their goings-on,
I should have been possessed by like desire:
But 'twas a time when Europe was rejoiced,
France standing on the top of golden hours,          [340]
And human nature seeming born again.
355 Bound, as I said, to the Alps, it was our lot
To land at Calais on the very Eve                    [345]
Of that great federal Day; and there we saw,
In a mean City, and among a few,
How bright a face is worn when joy of one
360 Is joy of tens of millions. Southward thence
We took our way direct through Hamlets, Towns,       [350]
Gaudy with reliques of that Festival,
Flowers left to wither on triumphal Arcs,
And window-Garlands. On the public roads,
365 And, once, three days successively, through paths.
By which our toilsome journey was abridg'd,          [355]
Among sequester'd villages we walked,
And found benevolence and blessedness
Spread like a fragrance everywhere, like Spring
370 That leaves no corner of the land untouch'd.
Where Elms, for many and many a league, in files,    [360]
With their thin umbrage, on the stately roads
Of that great Kingdom, rustled o'er our heads,
For ever near us as we paced along,
375 'Twas sweet at such a time, with such delights
On every side, in prime of youthful strength,        [365]
To feed a Poet's tender melancholy
And fond conceit of sadness, to the noise
And gentle undulation which they made.
380 Unhous'd, beneath the Evening Star we saw          [370]
Dances of Liberty, and, in late hours
Of darkness, dances in the open air.

349–51 A² C *as* 1850.
352 𝕬 C D: D² *as* 1850.
355 Bound to th' Helvetian Alps it was our lot  A² C.
[342–3]  Lightly equipped with scarcely one brief look
            Cast backward on our native shore  D.
[343–4]  Upon the white cliffs of our native shore
            Cast backward from the vessel's deck  D² E:  E² *as* 1850.
361 took] held  A² C.        369–70 𝕬 C D: D² *as* 1850.
373–4 waved above our heads, Or rustled near us while we  A² C.

In any age of uneventful calm
Among the nations, surely would my heart
Have been possessed by similar desire;
But Europe at that time was thrilled with joy,
France standing on the top of golden hours,    340
And human nature seeming born again.

   Lightly equipped, and but a few brief looks
Cast on the white cliffs of our native shore
From the receding vessel's deck, we chanced
To land at Calais on the very eve    345
Of that great federal day; and there we saw,
In a mean city, and among a few,
How bright a face is worn when joy of one
Is joy for tens of millions. Southward thence
We held our way, direct through hamlets, towns,    350
Gaudy with reliques of that festival,
Flowers left to wither on triumphal arcs,
And window-garlands. On the public roads,
And, once, three days successively, through paths
By which our toilsome journey was abridged,    355
Among sequestered villages we walked
And found benevolence and blessedness
Spread like a fragrance everywhere, when spring
Hath left no corner of the land untouched:
Where elms for many and many a league in files    360
With their thin umbrage, on the stately roads
Of that great kingdom, rustled o'er our heads,
For ever near us as we paced along:
How sweet at such a time, with such delight
On every side, in prime of youthful strength,    365
To feed a Poet's tender melancholy
And fond conceit of sadness, with the sound
Of undulations varying as might please
The wind that swayed them; once, and more than once,
Unhoused beneath the evening star we saw    370
Dances of liberty, and, in late hours
Of darkness, dances in the open air
Deftly prolonged, though grey-haired lookers on
Might waste their breath in chiding.

       373–83 D *stuck over*: D² *as* 1850.

Among the vine-clad Hills of Burgundy, [375]
Upon the bosom of the gentle Soane
385 We glided forward with the flowing stream:
Swift Rhone, thou wert the wings on which we cut
Between thy lofty rocks! Enchanting show [380]
Those woods, and farms, and orchards did present,
And single Cottages, and lurking Towns,
390 Reach after reach, procession without end
Of deep and stately Vales. A lonely Pair
Of Englishmen we were, and sail'd along [385]
Cluster'd together with a merry crowd
Of those emancipated, with a host
395 Of Travellers, chiefly Delegates, returning
From the great Spousals newly solemniz'd
At their chief City in the sight of Heaven. [390]
Like bees they swarm'd, gaudy and gay as bees;
Some vapour'd in the unruliness of joy
400 And flourish'd with their swords, as if to fight
The saucy air. In this blithe Company
We landed, took with them our evening Meal, [395]
Guests welcome almost as the Angels were
To Abraham of old. The Supper done,
405 With flowing cups elate, and happy thoughts,
We rose at signal giv'n, and form'd a ring
And, hand in hand, danced round and round the Board; [400]
All hearts were open, every tongue was loud
With amity and glee; we bore a name
410 Honour'd in France, the name of Englishmen,
And hospitably did they give us hail
As their forerunners in a glorious course, [405]
And round, and round the Board they danced again.
With this same Throng our voyage we pursu'd
415 At early dawn; the Monastery Bells
Made a sweet jingling in our youthful ears;
The rapid River flowing without noise, [410]
And every Spire we saw among the rocks
Spake with a sense of peace, at intervals
420 Touching the heart amid the boisterous Crew [413]
With which we were environ'd. Having parted

384 Soane *all MSS.*: Saone 1850.
[379] In A² *added in W. W.'s hand*: C D E.
390 procession] succession A² C.     414 𝔄 C D: D² *as* 1850.

Under hills—
The vine-clad hills and slopes of Burgundy,               375
Upon the bosom of the gentle Saone
We glided forward with the flowing stream.
Swift Rhone! thou wert the *wings* on which we cut
A winding passage with majestic ease
Between thy lofty rocks. Enchanting show              380
Those woods and farms and orchards did present,
And single cottages and lurking towns,
Reach after reach, succession without end
Of deep and stately vales! A lonely pair
Of strangers, till day closed, we sailed along,          385
Clustered together with a merry crowd
Of those emancipated, a blithe host
Of travellers, chiefly delegates returning
From the great spousals newly solemnised
At their chief city, in the sight of Heaven.            390
Like bees they swarmed, gaudy and gay as bees;
Some vapoured in the unruliness of joy,
And with their swords flourished as if to fight
The saucy air. In this proud company
We landed—took with them our evening meal,           395
Guests welcome almost as the angels were
To Abraham of old. The supper done,
With flowing cups elate and happy thoughts
We rose at signal given, and formed a ring
And, hand in hand, danced round and round the board;  400
All hearts were open, every tongue was loud
With amity and glee; we bore a name
Honoured in France, the name of Englishmen,
And hospitably did they give us hail,
As their forerunners in a glorious course;            405
And round and round the board we danced again.
With these blithe friends our voyage we renewed
At early dawn. The monastery bells
Made a sweet jingling in our youthful ears;
The rapid river flowing without noise,               410
And each uprising or receding spire
Spake with a sense of peace, at intervals
Touching the heart amid the boisterous crew
By whom we were encompassed. Taking leave

421-5 𝔄 C D: D² *as* 1850, *but* Attained [418] D² E *for* Beheld

From this glad Rout, the Convent of Chartreuse
Received us two days afterwards, and there
We rested in an awful Solitude;                              [419]
425  Thence onward to the Country of the Swiss.

A² *interposes the following passage*:

[Yes, for no other than a lonesome place                     [420]
A soul-affecting Solitude appeared
That region's circuit, though our eyes beheld,
As we approached the Convent, flash of arms
5    And military glare of riotous men
Commissioned to expel and overturn                          [425]
With senseless rapine. For ourselves we trod,
In sympathetic reverence we trod,                           [475]
The floor of those dim cloisters, from the day
10   Of their foundation till that rueful change
Approached with awe and strangers to the presence
Of unrestricted and unthinking man.
Abroad how chearingly the sunshine lay
Upon the open lawns; Vallombre's groves                     [480]
15   Entering, we fed the Soul with darkness, thence
Issued, and with uplifted eyes beheld
In every quarter of the bending sky
The cross of Jesus stand erect, as if
By angels planted on the aerial rock
20   And by the storm full surely reverenced, yet           [485]
From desperate blasphemers insecure,
And too obnoxious to the sweeping rage
Of rash destroyers.—'Stay your impious hands,'
Such was the vain injunction of that hour
25   By Nature uttered from her Alpine Throne,               [431]
'Oh leave in quiet this transcendent frame
Of social Being, this embodied dream
This substance by which mortal men have clothed,
Humanly clothed, the ghostliness of things
30   In silence visible and perpetual calm.
Let this one Temple last; be this one spot
Of earth devoted to Eternity.'                              [435]
A radiant Cloud upon a spiry rock
Through the still bosom of the azure sky
35   Descended, and abstracted from my trance
I heard no more. But as the sea prolongs
Her agitation though the wind which first
Call'd up the surges from the peaceful deep
Be spent or intermitted, so my mind
40   Continued still to heave within herself.
The radiant cloud forsook its spiry seat
And while Saint Bruno's wood before me waved
Her piny top, not silent as it waved,
And while below along their several beds

Of this glad throng, foot-travellers side by side,                    415

Measuring our steps in quiet, we pursued

Our journey, and ere twice the sun had set

Beheld the Convent of Chartreuse, and there

Rested within an awful *solitude*:

Yes, for even then no other than a place                              420

Of soul-affecting *solitude* appeared

That far-famed region, though our eyes had seen,

As toward the sacred mansion we advanced,

Arms flashing, and a military glare

Of riotous men commissioned to expel                                 425

The blameless inmates, and belike subvert

That frame of social being, which so long

Had bodied forth the ghostliness of things

In silence visible and perpetual calm.

—'Stay, stay your sacrilegious hands!'—The voice                     430

Was Nature's, uttered from her Alpine throne;

I heard it then and seem to hear it now—

'Your impious work forbear, perish what may,

Let this one temple last, be this one spot

Of earth devoted to eternity!'                                       435

She ceased to speak, but while St. Bruno's pines

Waved their dark tops, not silent as they waved,

And while below, along their several beds,

[430–1] hands!' exclaim'd The voice of Nature  D:  D² *as* 1850.
[436] I heard no more but  D:  D² *as* 1850.

45 Murmured the sister streams of Life and Death, [439]
 The voice commingling with those sounds returned
 Upon my inward ear, and thus the strains
 Proceeded 'Honour to the patriot's zeal,
 Glory and pride to new-born Liberty,
50 Hail to the mighty passions of the time,
 The vengeance and the transport and the hope,
 The gay or stern delight of this big hour!
 But spare, if past and future be the wings
 On whose support harmoniously conjoined
55 Moves the great Spirit of human knowledge, spare [450]
 This House, these Courts of Mystery, where a step
 Between the portals of the shadowy rocks
 Leaves far behind the vanities of life,
 Where if a Peasant enter or a King
60 One holy thought, a single holy thought
 Has power to initiate; let it be redeemed
 With all its blameless priesthood, for the sake
 Of faith and meditative reason resting
 Upon the word of heaven-imparted truth [460]
65 Triumphantly assured; for humbler claim
 Of that imaginative impulse sent
 From these majestic floods—those shining cliffs,
 The untransmuted shapes of many worlds,
 Cerulean Ether's pure inhabitants, [465]
70 These forests unapproachable by death,
 That shall endure, as long as man endures
 To think, to hope, to worship and to feel,
 To struggle, to be lost within himself
 In trepidation, from the blank abyss [470]
75 To look with bodily eyes and be consoled.'
  We left this desecrated spot with pain
  And hastened to the Country of the Swiss.]

C *as* A²; D, *with some variants (recorded below), as* 1850. *Pasted into* A *is a version intermediary between* C *and* D.
 B *has three, probably the earliest, drafts of the opening of this passage:*

 (i) In sympathetic quietness we paced
  The (*circuit*) floor of those [ ] cloisters from the day
  Of their foundation hallowed by a law
  Of silence for the Grey-rob'd brotherhood
  And till the lamentable change which now
  We witnessed not obnoxious to the (? view)
  Of unrestricted and unthinking men.
 (ii) That floor we trod in sympathetic peace
  Abroad (*etc. as* A² 13–21); *then goes on*:
  Alas for what we saw, the flash of arms
 (iii) The last, we two perchance the very last
  Of strangers destined to repose their limbs
  Within those modest walls, or in their hearts
  Receive a comfort from those (*awful*) holy Spires.

Murmured the sister streams of Life and Death,
Thus by conflicting passions pressed, my heart          440
Responded; 'Honour to the patriot's zeal!
Glory and hope to new-born Liberty!
Hail to the mighty projects of the time!
Discerning sword that Justice wields, do thou
Go forth and prosper; and, ye purging fires,           445
Up to the loftiest towers of Pride ascend,
Fanned by the breath of angry Providence.
But oh! if Past and Future be the wings
On whose support harmoniously conjoined
Moves the great spirit of human knowledge, spare       450
These courts of mystery, where a step advanced
Between the portals of the shadowy rocks
Leaves far behind life's treacherous vanities,
For penitential tears and trembling hopes
Exchanged—to equalise in God's pure sight             455
Monarch and peasant: be the house redeemed
With its unworldly votaries, for the sake
Of conquest over sense, hourly achieved
Through faith and meditative reason, resting
Upon the word of heaven-imparted truth,                460
Calmly triumphant; and for humbler claim
Of that imaginative impulse sent
From these majestic floods, yon shining cliffs,
The untransmuted shapes of many worlds,
Cerulean ether's pure inhabitants,                     465
These forests unapproachable by death,
That shall endure as long as man endures,
To think, to hope, to worship, and to feel,
To struggle, to be lost within himself
In trepidation, from the blank abyss                   470
To look with bodily eyes, and be consoled.'
Not seldom since that moment have I wished
That thou, O Friend! the trouble or the calm
Hadst shared, when, from profane regards apart,
In sympathetic reverence we trod                       475
The floors of those dim cloisters, till that hour,
From their foundation, strangers to the presence
Of unrestricted and unthinking man.

[450] spare D E²: then Let them be spared, for ever undisturbed D² E.
[453] life's treacherous vanities E²: the vanities of life D E.

[*Variants continued on pp. 202–3*

O grief for what we saw the flash of arms
And military glare of riotous men
Commissioned to expel and overturn
With senseless rapine. 'Stay your impious hands *etc. as* A² 24–32; *then*
*goes on:*
I heard or seemed to hear and thus the voice
Commingled with the murmur of the breeze
That swept along St. Bruno's waving wood
And down the sister streams of life and death
And thus my thoughts proceed, yet with that stream
According. Honour to the Patriot's zeal *etc. as* A² *to* time (50).
*On another page* B *starts with* A² 62–75 (With all the blameless · .con-
soled) *and goes on:*
Yes, I was moved and to this hour am moved.
*then goes on as* A² 8–21, 76–77.

## 1805–6

'Tis not my present purpose to retrace
That variegated journey step by step:                     [490]
A march it was of military speed,
And earth did change her images and forms
430   Before us, fast as clouds are chang'd in Heaven.
Day after day, up early and down late,
From vale to vale, from hill to hill we went              [495]
From Province on to Province did we pass,
Keen Hunters in a chace of fourteen weeks
435   Eager as birds of prey, or as a Ship
Upon the stretch when winds are blowing fair.
Sweet coverts did we cross of pastoral life,             [500]
Enticing Vallies, greeted them, and left
Too soon, while yet the very flash and gleam
440   Of salutation were not pass'd away.
Oh! sorrow for the Youth who could have seen
Unchasten'd, unsubdu'd, unaw'd, unrais'd               [505]
To patriarchal dignity of mind,
And pure simplicity of wish and will,
445   Those sanctified abodes of peaceful Man.

[454] trembling hopes D² E: holy thoughts D.
[456] be the house E²: let it be  D E.
60  One penitential tear or holy thought  A² *corr.*
[457] votaries D² E: priesthood D.
[461] Calmly triumphant and  E²: Victoriously assured  D E.
[472] Not seldom  D² E: How often  D.
[476–7] till that hour, From  E²: since the day Of  D E.
[484–5] stand erect as if Hands of  E²: stand firm and erect As if  D E.
[484–7] As if it there had first been fix'd by hands

Abroad, how cheeringly the sunshine lay
Upon the open lawns! Vallombre's groves                    480
Entering, we fed the soul with darkness; thence
Issued, and with uplifted eyes beheld,
In different quarters of the bending sky,
The cross of Jesus stand erect, as if
Hands of angelic powers had fixed it there,               485
Memorial reverenced by a thousand storms;
Yet then, from the undiscriminating sweep
And rage of one State-whirlwind, insecure.

'Tis not my present purpose to retrace
That variegated journey step by step.                     490
A march it was of military speed,
And Earth did change her images and forms
Before us, fast as clouds are changed in heaven.
Day after day, up early and down late,
From hill to vale we dropped, from vale to hill           495
Mounted—from province on to province swept,
Keen hunters in a chase of fourteen weeks,
Eager as birds of prey, or as a ship
Upon the stretch, when winds are blowing fair:
Sweet coverts did we cross of pastoral life,              500
Enticing valleys, greeted them and left
Too soon, while yet the very flash and gleam
Of salutation were not passed away.
Oh! sorrow for the youth who could have seen
Unchastened, unsubdued, unawed, unraised                  505
To patriarchal dignity of mind,
And pure simplicity of wish and will,
Those sanctified abodes of peaceful man,
Pleased (though to hardship born, and compassed round
With danger, varying as the seasons change),              510
Pleased with his daily task, or, if not pleased,
Contented, from the moment that the dawn
(Ah! surely not without attendant gleams
Of soul-illumination) calls him forth
To industry, by glistenings flung on rocks,               515

      Of Angels, hovering round the aerial Cliff
      Type by a thousand tempests reverenced, yet
      From desperate blasphemers insecure D *deleted.*
432–3 𝔄 C D: D² *as* 1850.
444–68 D *stuck over*: D² E [523–8] *as* A: E² *as* 1850.

My heart leap'd up when first I did look down
On that which was first seen of those deep haunts,
A green recess, an aboriginal vale
Quiet, and lorded over and possess'd                              [520]
450 By naked huts, wood-built, and sown like tents
Or Indian cabins over the fresh lawns,
And by the river side. That day we first
Beheld the summit of Mont Blanc, and griev'd                      [525]
To have a soulless image on the eye
455 Which had usurp'd upon a living thought
That never more could be: the wondrous Vale
Of Chamouny did, on the following dawn,
With its dumb cataracts and streams of ice,                       [530]
A motionless array of mighty waves,
460 Five rivers broad and vast, make rich amends,
And reconcil'd us to realities.
There small birds warble from the leafy trees,
The Eagle soareth in the element;                                 [535]
There doth the Reaper bind the yellow sheaf,
465 The Maiden spread the haycock in the sun,
While Winter like a tamed Lion walks
Descending from the mountain to make sport
Among the cottages by beds of flowers.                            [540]

      Whate'er in this wide circuit we beheld,
470 Or heard, was fitted to our unripe state
Of intellect and heart. By simple strains
Of feeling, the pure breath of real life,
We were not left untouch'd. With such a book
Before our eyes, we could not chuse but read
475 A frequent lesson of sound tenderness,                        [545]
The universal reason of mankind,
The truth of Young and Old. Nor, side by side
Pacing, two brother Pilgrims, or alone
Each with his humour, could we fail to abound
480 (Craft this which hath been hinted at before)

446 My heart leap'd up] How leap'd my heart  A² C.
454 soulless  Є E²: spiritless  D² E.
460–1   Five chasmy rivers bordered by smooth fields
        Where jocund Reapers bind the yellow sheaf
        And Maidens spread the haycock to the sun
        Made for that recent shock of disappointment
        That sudden blank of soul most rich amends
        And reconciled us to reality.  D² E: E³ *as* 1850.

Whose evening shadows lead him to repose.

Well might a stranger look with bounding heart
Down on a green recess, the first I saw
Of those deep haunts, an aboriginal vale,
Quiet and lorded over and possessed                    520
By naked huts, wood-built, and sown like tents
Or Indian cabins over the fresh lawns
And by the river side.
     That very day,
From a bare ridge we also first beheld
Unveiled the summit of Mont Blanc, and grieved         525
To have a soulless image on the eye
That had usurped upon a living thought
That never more could be. The wondrous Vale
Of Chamouny stretched far below, and soon
With its dumb cataracts and streams of ice,            530
A motionless array of mighty waves,
Five rivers broad and vast, made rich amends,
And reconciled us to realities;
There small birds warble from the leafy trees,
The eagle soars high in the element,                   535
There doth the reaper bind the yellow sheaf,
The maiden spread the haycock in the sun,
While Winter like a well-tamed lion walks,
Descending from the mountain to make sport
Among the cottages by beds of flowers.                 540

Whate'er in this wide circuit we beheld,
Or heard, was fitted to our unripe state
Of intellect and heart. With such a book
Before our eyes, we could not choose but read
Lessons of genuine brotherhood, the plain             545
And universal reason of mankind,
The truths of young and old. Nor, side by side
Pacing, two social pilgrims, or alone
Each with his humour, could we fail to abound

  Made for that sudden blank of soul, that shock
  And recent disappointment rich amends *etc.* E².
466–7 A D E:  While Winter like a Lion that had issued
    In threats and anger from his darksome cave
    Among the mountains, to a gentler mood
    Is won as he descends, and maketh sport  A² C.
471–3 By ... untouch'd D *deletes.*

In dreams and fictions pensively compos'd,                    [550]
Dejection taken up for pleasure's sake,
And gilded sympathies; the willow wreath,
Even among those solitudes sublime,
485   And sober posies of funereal flowers,
Cull'd from the gardens of the Lady Sorrow,                    [555]
Did sweeten many a meditative hour.

Yet still in me, mingling with these delights
Was something of stern mood, an under-thirst
490   Of vigour, never utterly asleep.                        [559]
Far different dejection once was mine,
A deep and genuine sadness then I felt;
The circumstances I will here relate
Even as they were. Upturning with a Band
495   Of Travellers, from the Valais we had clomb
Along the road that leads to Italy;
A length of hours, making of these our Guides
Did we advance, and having reach'd an Inn
Among the mountains, we together ate
500   Our noon's repast, from which the Travellers rose,
Leaving us at the Board. Ere long we follow'd,
Descending by the beaten road that led
Right to a rivulet's edge, and there broke off.
The only track now visible was one                             [570]
505   Upon the further side, right opposite,
And up a lofty Mountain. This we took
After a little scruple, and short pause,
And climb'd with eagerness, though not, at length             [575]
Without surprise, and some anxiety
510   On finding that we did not overtake
Our Comrades gone before. By fortunate chance,

[554] Gathered E²: Cull'd even D E.
488–9 A C D: mingled with these delights Something of sterner mood
D² E: E² *as* 1850.
492–4 A deep a genuine sadness, that day, fill'd
        My heart and soul. A² C.
494–502 Upturning with a Band of Muleteers
          Along the steep and rugged road that leads
          Over the Simplon Pass to Italy
          We clomb, and when the ridge was crossed soon reached
          The wished for Inn where all together took
          Their noon-tide meal; in haste the Travellers rose
          Leaving *us* at the Board. Ere long we followed
          Descending by the beaten road that led E: E² *as* 1850.

In dreams and fictions, pensively composed:                550
Dejection taken up for pleasure's sake,
And gilded sympathies, the willow wreath,
And sober posies of funereal flowers,
Gathered among those solitudes sublime
From formal gardens of the lady Sorrow,                    555
Did sweeten many a meditative hour.


  Yet still in me with those soft luxuries
Mixed something of stern mood, an under-thirst
Of vigour seldom utterly allayed.
And from that source how different a sadness               560
Would issue, let one incident make known.
When from the Vallais we had turned, and clomb
Along the Simplon's steep and rugged road,
Following a band of muleteers, we reached
A halting-place, where all together took                   565
Their noon-tide meal. Hastily rose our guide,
Leaving us at the board; awhile we lingered,
Then paced the beaten downward way that led
Right to a rough stream's edge, and there broke off;
The only track now visible was one                         570
That from the torrent's further brink held forth
Conspicuous invitation to ascend
A lofty mountain. After brief delay
Crossing the unbridged stream, that road we took,
And clomb with eagerness, till anxious fears               575
Intruded, for we failed to overtake
Our comrades gone before. By fortunate chance,

497–500  A length of hours thus guided we advanced
         And reached a seasonable halting-place
         Where we together ate our noon's repast
         From which the more impatient Travellers rose,  A² C.
505–10  That from the Streamlet's farther bank held forth
         Conspicuous invitation to ascend
         A lofty mountain. This bold path we chose
         After brief pause, of scrupulous delay,
         And clomb with eagerness, though not at length
         Without intrusion of some anxious thoughts
         On finding that we failed to overtake  A².  *So* A³ C, *but for* This
bold . . . delay *they read* After brief delay
         By prudent scruples bred, this path we chose
*and for* though not at length Without *they read* but soon were check'd By the
509      Without surprise, and some foreboding thoughts  B².

While every moment now encreas'd our doubts,
A Peasant met us, and from him we learn'd
That to the place which had perplex'd us first          [580]
515 We must descend, and there should find the road
Which in the stony channel of the Stream
Lay a few steps, and then along its Banks;
And further, that thenceforward all our course
Was downwards, with the current of that Stream.          [585]
520 Hard of belief, we question'd him again,
And all the answers which the Man return'd
To our inquiries, in their sense and substance,
Translated by the feelings which we had          [590]
Ended in this; *that we had cross'd the Alps.*


525     Imagination! lifting up itself
Before the eye and progress of my Song
Like an unfather'd vapour; here that Power,
In all the might of its endowments, came
Athwart me; I was lost as in a cloud,
530 Halted, without a struggle to break through.          [597]
And now recovering, to my Soul I say
I recognise thy glory; in such strength
Of usurpation, in such visitings
Of awful promise, when the light of sense          ⌈600⌉
535 Goes out in flashes that have shewn to us
The invisible world, doth Greatness make abode.
There harbours whether we be young or old.
Our destiny, our nature, and our home
Is with infinitude, and only there;          [605]
540 With hope it is, hope that can never die,
Effort, and expectation, and desire,
And something evermore about to be.
The mind beneath such banners militant
Thinks not of spoils or trophies, nor of aught          [610]

520–1  Hard of belief we question'd him again
         But every answer which the Peasant gave  D E:  E² *as* 1850.
[592–4] *seq.* Imagination—here that awful Power
         Before the retrospective Song rose up  D E.
         Imagination at that moment rose
         The awful Power before my mental eye
         Then suddenly depressed before me rose  E²: E³ *as* 1850.
527–8  Like an unfather'd vapour that bestows

While every moment added doubt to doubt,
A peasant met us, from whose mouth we learned
That to the spot which had perplexed us first          580
We must descend, and there should find the road,
Which in the stony channel of the stream
Lay a few steps, and then along its banks;
And, that our future course, all plain to sight,
Was downwards, with the current of that stream.          585
Loth to believe what we so grieved to hear,
For still we had hopes that pointed to the clouds,
We questioned him again, and yet again;
But every word that from the peasant's lips
Came in reply, translated by our feelings,          590
Ended in this,—*that we had crossed the Alps.*

Imagination—here the Power so called
Through sad incompetence of human speech,
That awful Power rose from the mind's abyss
Like an unfathered vapour that enwraps,          595
At once, some lonely traveller. I was lost;
Halted without an effort to break through;
But to my conscious soul I now can say—
'I recognise thy glory:' in such strength
Of usurpation, when the light of sense          600
Goes out, but with a flash that has revealed
The invisible world, doth greatness make abode,
There harbours; whether we be young or old,
Our destiny, our being's heart and home,
Is with infinitude, and only there;          605
With hope it is, hope that can never die,
Effort, and expectation, and desire,
And something evermore about to be.
Under such banners militant, the soul
Seeks for no trophies, struggles for no spoils          610

Its presence on some solitary place
Here in the might of *etc.*  A² C.
                    that enwraps
    A waywor(n) traveller on a lonely Moor  A³.
531 But to my conscious Soul I now can say  A² C.
533–4 in such visitings Of awful promise A *deletes*; *not in* C.
535 us] Man A² C: Goes out in glimpse and flash that have revealed
A³ D: D² *as* 1850.          536–7 abode, old. A C D: abode   old E.
543 [609] The soul beneath such banners militant D E: E² *as* 1850.
544 A² C *as* 1850.

545 That may attest its prowess, blest in thoughts
    That are their own perfection and reward,
    Strong in itself, and in the access of joy
    Which hides it like the overflowing Nile.

    The dull and heavy slackening that ensued                    [617]
550 Upon those tidings by the Peasant given
    Was soon dislodg'd; downwards we hurried fast,
    And enter'd with the road which we had miss'd              [620]
    Into a narrow chasm; the brook and road
    Were fellow-travellers in this gloomy Pass,
555 And with them did we journey several hours
    At a slow step. The immeasurable height
    Of woods decaying, never to be decay'd,                    [625]
    The stationary blasts of water-falls,
    And every where along the hollow rent
560 Winds thwarting winds, bewilder'd and forlorn,
    The torrents shooting from the clear blue sky,
    The rocks that mutter'd close upon our ears,              [630]
    Black drizzling crags that spake by the way-side
    As if a voice were in them, the sick sight
565 And giddy prospect of the raving stream,
    The unfetter'd clouds, and region of the Heavens,
    Tumult and peace, the darkness and the light             [635]
    Were all like workings of one mind, the features
    Of the same face, blossoms upon one tree,
570 Characters of the great Apocalypse,
    The types and symbols of Eternity,
    Of first and last, and midst, and without end.           [640]

[614–16] Which hides her like the fertilizing Nile
         That overflows the whole Egyptian plain. E: E² *as* 1850.
549 dull and heavy 𝕬: melancholy A² C.
559 And mid the labyrinths of the hollow rent A² C D E: E² *as* 1850.
560 forlorn 𝕬 D² E: oppresst A² B² C D.
562 *foll.* The rocks that muttered close upon our ears,
         *With dull reverberation never ceasing*
         *Audibly to attend the astounding uproar*
         *Of the vex'd flood, by drizzling crags beset,*
         Black drizzling crags that spake by the wayside
         As if a voice were in them, the sick sight
         And giddy prospect of the raving stream,
         *And ever as we halted, or crept on,*
         *Huge fragments of primœval mountain spread*
         *In powerless ruin, blocks as huge aloft*
         *Impending, nor permitted yet to fall,*
         *The sacred Death-cross, monument forlorn*

That may attest her prowess, blest in thoughts
That are their own perfection and reward,
Strong in herself and in beatitude
That hides her, like the mighty flood of Nile
Poured from his fount of Abyssinian clouds                615
To fertilise the whole Egyptian plain.

    The melancholy slackening that ensued
Upon those tidings by the peasant given
Was soon dislodged. Downwards we hurried fast,
And, with the half-shaped road which we had missed,       620
Entered a narrow chasm. The brook and road
Were fellow-travellers in this gloomy strait,
And with them did we journey several hours
At a slow pace. The immeasurable height
Of woods decaying, never to be decayed,                   625
The stationary blasts of waterfalls,
And in the narrow rent at every turn
Winds thwarting winds, bewildered and forlorn,
The torrents shooting from the clear blue sky,
The rocks that muttered close upon our ears,              630
Black drizzling crags that spake by the way-side
As if a voice were in them, the sick sight
And giddy prospect of the raving stream,
The unfettered clouds and region of the Heavens,
Tumult and peace, the darkness and the light—             635
Were all like workings of one mind, the features
Of the same face, blossoms upon one tree;
Characters of the great Apocalypse,
The types and symbols of Eternity,
Of first, and last, and midst, and without end.           640

      *Though frequent of the perish'd Traveller,*
      The unfettered clouds, *etc.*
*Italicized lines added to* A *and* B. C *omits* Audibly . . . beset: D *for* With
dull . . . wayside *has*
      With dull reverberation, solid crags
      Drizzling and black that spake by the wayside, *and deletes* And ever
. . . Traveller. B[3], *after* crept on, *has*
      Faint voices muttering close upon our ears
      Reverberations plaintive of the sound
      From the vex'd flood incessantly received
      By masses of primeval mountain spread
      In powerless ruin, or from blocks as huge *etc.*
      Reverberations close upon our ear
      A plaintive undersong that did not cease B[4].
  572–6 D *stuck over*: D[2] *as* E.

That night our lodging was an Alpine House,
An Inn, or Hospital, as they are nam'd,
575 Standing in that same valley by itself,
And close upon the confluence of two Streams;
A dreary Mansion, large beyond all need,                    [645]
With high and spacious rooms, deafen'd and stunn'd
By noise of waters, making innocent Sleep
580 Lie melancholy among weary bones.

Upris'n betimes, our journey we renew'd,
Led by the Stream, ere noon-day magnified                   [650]
Into a lordly River, broad and deep,
Dimpling along in silent majesty,
585 With mountains for its neighbours, and in view
Of distant mountains and their snowy tops,
And thus proceeding to Locarno's Lake,                      [655]
Fit resting-place for such a Visitant.
—Locarno, spreading out in width like Heaven,
590 And Como, thou, a treasure by the earth                 [660]
Kept to itself, a darling bosom'd up
In Abyssinian privacy, I spake
Of thee, thy chestnut woods, and garden plots
Of Indian corn tended by dark-eyed Maids,
595 Thy lofty steeps, and pathways roof'd with vines        [665]
Winding from house to house, from town to town,
Sole link that binds them to each other, walks
League after league, and cloistral avenues
Where silence is, if music be not there:
600 While yet a Youth, undisciplin'd in Verse,              [670]
Through fond ambition of my heart, I told
Your praises; nor can I approach you now
Ungreeted by a more melodious Song,
Where tones of learned Art and Nature mix'd
605 May frame enduring language. Like a breeze              [675]

574 An Hospital, (such name those Structures bear)  A² C.
575–6 Where falling from aloft, a torrent swelled
        The rapid flood whose margin we had trod  A².
575 𝔄 C D² E: E² *as* 1850.
588 Proud to receive the stately Visitant  A³ C.
590–2                              whom the earth
      Keeps to herself embosomed  { in the depths Of  A².
                                  { and confined In  A³.
591–2 Embosomed and confined as of a depth Of  A⁴.
        C *leaves* 591 *blank*.

That night our lodging was a house that stood
Alone within the valley, at a point
Where, tumbling from aloft, a torrent swelled
The rapid stream whose margin we had trod;
A dreary mansion, large beyond all need,　　645
With high and spacious rooms, deafened and stunned
By noise of waters, making innocent sleep
Lie melancholy among weary bones.

Uprisen betimes, our journey we renewed,
Led by the stream, ere noon-day magnified　　650
Into a lordly river, broad and deep,
Dimpling along in silent majesty,
With mountains for its neighbours, and in view
Of distant mountains and their snowy tops,
And thus proceeding to Locarno's Lake,　　655
Fit resting-place for such a visitant.
Locarno! spreading out in width like Heaven,
How dost thou cleave to the poetic heart,
Bask in the sunshine of the memory;
And Como! thou, a treasure whom the earth　　660
Keeps to herself, confined as in a depth
Of Abyssinian privacy. I spake
Of thee, thy chestnut woods, and garden plots
Of Indian corn tended by dark-eyed maids;
Thy lofty steeps, and pathways roofed with vines,　　665
Winding from house to house, from town to town,
Sole link that binds them to each other; walks,
League after league, and cloistral avenues,
Where silence dwells if music be not there:
While yet a youth undisciplined in verse,　　670
Through fond ambition of that hour, I strove
To chant your praise; nor can approach you now
Ungreeted by a more melodious Song,
Where tones of Nature smoothed by learned Art
May flow in lasting current. Like a breeze　　675

599 is 𝔄 C: rests D: dwells D² E.
600 While yet a Youth undisciplin'd in Verse,
　　Though most familiar then with noblest works
　　Of poesy, and by the heavenly Muse
　　Internally encouraged and inspired. A² C D: D *deletes last three lines*.
601–10 D *stuck over*: D² *as* 1850, *but* [674] *as* 𝔄 *and in* [679–80] *and yet*
sweet *for* yet endowed . . . sweet: D³ *as* 1850.

Or sunbeam over your domain I pass'd
In motion without pause; but Ye have left
Your beauty with me, an impassion'd sight
Of colours and of forms, whose power is sweet     [680]
610 And gracious, almost might I dare to say,
As virtue is, or goodness, sweet as love
Or the remembrance of a noble deed,
Or gentlest visitations of pure thought
When God, the Giver of all joy, is thank'd
615 Religiously, in silent blessedness,     [686]
Sweet as this last herself; for such it is.

    Through those delightful pathways we advanc'd,
Two days, and still in presence of the Lake,
Which, winding up among the Alps, now chang'd     [690]
620 Slowly its lovely countenance, and put on
A sterner character. The second night,
In eagerness, and by report misled
Of those Italian clocks that speak the time
In fashion different from ours, we rose
625 By moonshine, doubting not that day was near,     [695]
And that, meanwhile, coasting the Water's edge
As hitherto, and with as plain a track
To be our guide, we might behold the scene
In its most deep repose.—We left the Town
630 Of Gravedona with this hope; but soon     [700]
Were lost, bewilder'd among woods immense,
Where, having wander'd for a while, we stopp'd
And on a rock sate down, to wait for day.
An open place it was, and overlook'd,
635 From high, the sullen water underneath,
On which a dull red image of the moon     [705]
Lay bedded, changing oftentimes its form
Like an uneasy snake: long time we sate,
For scarcely more than one hour of the night,
640 Such was our error, had been gone, when we
Renew'd our journey. On the rock we lay
And wish'd to sleep but could not, for the stings     [711]

616 Sweet 𝔄 D² E: Pure A² C D.         618 A² C *as* 1850.
  622–4 By the church clock awakened, and misled
     By its report, for then we had not learn'd
     That in this land the course of time doth bear
     A measure different A² C.

Or sunbeam over your domain I passed
In motion without pause; but ye have left
Your beauty with me, a serene accord
Of forms and colours, passive, yet endowed
In their submissiveness with power as sweet          680
And gracious, almost might I dare to say,
As virtue is, or goodness; sweet as love,
Or the remembrance of a generous deed,
Or mildest visitations of pure thought,
When God, the giver of all joy, is thanked          685
Religiously, in silent blessedness;
Sweet as this last herself, for such it is.

With those delightful pathways we advanced,
For two days' space, in presence of the Lake,
That, stretching far among the Alps, assumed        690
A character more stern. The second night,
From sleep awakened, and misled by sound
Of the church clock telling the hours with strokes
Whose import then we had not learned, we rose
By moonlight, doubting not that day was nigh,       695
And that meanwhile, by no uncertain path,
Along the winding margin of the lake,
Led, as before, we should behold the scene
Hushed in profound repose. We left the town
Of Gravedona with this hope; but soon               700
Were lost, bewildered among woods immense,
And on a rock sate down, to wait for day.
An open place it was, and overlooked,
From high, the sullen water far beneath,
On which a dull red image of the moon               705
Lay bedded, changing oftentimes its form
Like an uneasy snake. From hour to hour
We sate and sate, wondering, as if the night
Had been ensnared by witchcraft. On the rock
At last we stretched our weary limbs for sleep,     710
But *could not* sleep, tormented by the stings

*In middle lines* B² *has* for Strangers in that land
        We had not learnd that there the time is told
622–9 D *stuck over*: D² *as* 1850.
642–4 And wish'd to sleep, but wish'd to sleep in vain
        From ceaseless persecution by the stings A² C.

Of insects, which with noise like that of noon
Fill'd all the woods; the cry of unknown birds,
645 The mountains, more by darkness visible
And their own size, than any outward light,                    [715]
The breathless wilderness of clouds, the clock
That told with unintelligible voice
The widely-parted hours, the noise of streams
650 And sometimes rustling motions nigh at hand
Which did not leave us free from personal fear,               [720]
And lastly the withdrawing Moon, that set
Before us, while she still was high in heaven,
These were our food, and such a summer's night
655 Did to that pair of golden days succeed,
With now and then a doze and snatch of sleep,
On Como's Banks, the same delicious Lake.                     [725]

But here I must break off, and quit at once,                  [727]
Though loth, the record of these wanderings,
660 A theme which may seduce me else beyond
All reasonable bounds. Let this alone
Be mention'd as a parting word, that not
In hollow exultation, dealing forth
Hyperboles of praise comparative,
665 Not rich one moment to be poor for ever,                   [735]
Not prostrate, overborn, as if the mind
Itself were nothing, a mean pensioner
On outward forms, did we in presence stand
Of that magnificent region. On the front
670 Of this whole Song is written that my heart                [740]
Must in such temple needs have offer'd up
A different worship. Finally whate'er
I saw, or heard, or felt, was but a stream
That flow'd into a kindred stream, a gale                     [744]
675 That help'd me forwards, did administer
To grandeur and to tenderness, to the one
Directly, but to tender thoughts by means
Less often instantaneous in effect;                           [750]
Conducted me to these along a path

645 darkness 𝕬 C D: D² *as* 1850.          653 yet A: still B.
655–7 𝕬 C D: D² *as* 1850.
   659–61 these wanderings . . . bounds.] that ardent quest **Curious and
intricate** A² C. *So* B², *which adds* and every day **Pregnant with new delight**
*and reads* course *for* quest.          659 D *stuck over*: D² *as* 1850.

Of insects, which, with noise like that of noon,
Filled all the woods; the cry of unknown birds;
The mountains more by blackness visible
And their own size, than any outward light;    **715**
The breathless wilderness of clouds; the clock
That told, with unintelligible voice,
The widely parted hours; the noise of streams,
And sometimes rustling motions nigh at hand,
That did not leave us free from personal fear;    **720**
And, lastly, the withdrawing moon, that set
Before us, while she still was high in heaven;—
These were our food; and such a summer's night
Followed that pair of golden days that shed
On Como's Lake, and all that round it lay,    **725**
Their fairest, softest, happiest influence.

But here I must break off, and bid farewell
To days, each offering some new sight, or fraught
With some untried adventure, in a course
Prolonged till sprinklings of autumnal snow    **730**
Checked our unwearied steps. Let this alone
Be mentioned as a parting word, that not
In hollow exultation, dealing out
Hyperboles of praise comparative;
Not rich one moment to be poor for ever;    **735**
Not prostrate, overborne, as if the mind
Herself were nothing, a mere pensioner
On outward forms—did we in presence stand
Of that magnificent region. On the front
Of this whole Song is written that my heart    **740**
Must, in such Temple, needs have offered up
A different worship. Finally, whate'er
I saw, or heard, or felt, was but a stream
That flowed into a kindred stream; a gale,
Confederate with the current of the soul,    **745**
To speed my voyage; every sound or sight,
In its degree of power, administered
To grandeur or to tenderness,—to the one
Directly, but to tender thoughts by means
Less often instantaneous in effect;    **750**
Led me to these by paths that, in the main,

679–80 [751–3], 687 𝔄 C D:  D² *as* 1850.

680  Which in the main was more circuitous.

    Oh! most beloved Friend, a glorious time
A happy time that was; triumphant looks                    [755]
Were then the common language of all eyes:
As if awak'd from sleep, the Nations hail'd
685  Their great expectancy: the fife of War
Was then a spirit-stirring sound indeed,
A Blackbird's whistle in a vernal grove.                    [760]
We left the Swiss exulting in the fate
Of their near Neighbours, and when shortening fast
690  Our pilgrimage, nor distant far from home,
We cross'd the Brabant Armies on the fret
For battle in the cause of Liberty.                         [765]
A Stripling, scarcely of the household then
Of social life, I look'd upon these things
695  As from a distance, heard, and saw, and felt,
Was touch'd, but with no intimate concern;
I seem'd to move among them as a bird                       [770]
Moves through the air, or as a fish pursues
Its business, in its proper element;
700  I needed not that joy, I did not need
Such help; the ever-living Universe,                        [774]
And independent spirit of pure youth
Were with me at that season, and delight
Was in all places spread around my steps
705  As constant as the grass upon the fields.

        699 business 𝔄 C D: sport, and feeds D².
        700 need 𝔄 C D: want D².

Were more circuitous, but not less sure
Duly to reach the point marked out by Heaven.

    Oh, most belovèd Friend! a glorious time,
A happy time that was; triumphant looks                    755
Were then the common language of all eyes;
As if awaked from sleep, the Nations hailed
Their great expectancy: the fife of war
Was then a spirit-stirring sound indeed,
A black-bird's whistle in a budding grove.                 760
We left the Swiss exulting in the fate
Of their near neighbours; and, when shortening fast
Our pilgrimage, nor distant far from home,
We crossed the Brabant armies on the fret
For battle in the cause of Liberty.                        765
A stripling, scarcely of the household then
Of social life, I looked upon these things
As from a distance; heard, and saw, and felt,
Was touched, but with no intimate concern;
I seemed to move along them, as a bird                     770
Moves through the air, or as a fish pursues
Its sport, or feeds in its proper element;
I wanted not that joy, I did not need
Such help; the ever-living universe,
Turn where I might, was opening out its glories,           775
And the independent spirit of pure youth
Called forth, at every season, new delights
Spread round my steps like sunshine o'er green fields.

702–5 D *stuck over*: D² *as* E.
[778] Spread round my steps like grass o'er sunny fields  D² E: E² *as* 1850.

# BOOK SEVENTH

## RESIDENCE IN LONDON

FIVE years are vanish'd since I first pour'd out
Saluted by that animating breeze
Which met me issuing from the City's Walls,
A glad preamble to this Verse: I sang
5  Aloud, in Dythyrambic fervour, deep           [5]
But short-liv'd uproar, like a torrent sent
Out of the bowels of a bursting cloud
Down Scafell, or Blencathra's rugged sides,
A waterspout from Heaven. But 'twas not long
10  Ere the interrupted stream broke forth once more,
And flow'd awhile in strength, then stopp'd for years;  [10]
Not heard again until a little space
Before last primrose-time. Beloved Friend,
The assurances then given unto myself,
15  Which did beguile me of some heavy thoughts
At thy departure to a foreign Land,
Have fail'd; for slowly doth this work advance.      [15]
Through the whole summer have I been at rest,
Partly from voluntary holiday
20  And part through outward hindrance. But I heard,
After the hour of sunset yester even,
Sitting within doors betwixt light and dark,      [20]
A voice that stirr'd me. 'Twas a little Band,
A Quire of Redbreasts gather'd somewhere near
25  My threshold, Minstrels from the distant woods
And dells, sent in by Winter to bespeak
For the Old Man a welcome, to announce,
With preparation artful and benign,
Yea the most gentle music of the year,
30  That their rough Lord had left the surly North    [25]
And hath begun his journey. A delight,
At this unthought of greeting, unawares

[MSS. for Bk. VII: A B C D E: *for ll.* 75–*end* X.]
BOOK SEVENTH. Residence in London B C: 7 A.
1–2 𝕬 C D: D² *as* 1850.     5 A² C *as* 1850.
6 uproar A: transport A² B C.
6–10  Of short lived transport, like a torrent bursting

# BOOK SEVENTH

## RESIDENCE IN LONDON

SIX changeful years have vanished since I first
Poured out (saluted by that quickening breeze
Which met me issuing from the City's walls)
A glad preamble to this Verse: I sang
Aloud, with fervour irresistible                                   5
Of short-lived transport, like a torrent bursting,
From a black thunder-cloud, down Scafell's side
To rush and disappear. But soon broke forth
(So willed the Muse) a less impetuous stream,
That flowed awhile with unabating strength,                        10
Then stopped for years; not audible again
Before last primrose-time. Belovèd Friend!
The assurance which then cheered some heavy thoughts
On thy departure to a foreign land
Has failed; too slowly moves the promised work.                    15
Through the whole summer have I been at rest,
Partly from voluntary holiday,
And part through outward hindrance. But I heard,
After the hour of sunset yester-even,
Sitting within doors between light and dark,                       20
A choir of redbreasts gathered somewhere near
My threshold,—minstrels from the distant woods
Sent in on Winter's service, to announce,
With preparation artful and benign,
That the rough lord had left the surly North                       25
On his accustomed journey. The delight,
Due to this timely notice, unawares

> From out the bowels of a cloud to rush
> Down Scawfell, or Blencathra's rugged sides
> With momentary sweep. But soon broke forth
> (So willed the Muse) a less impetuous stream  A² C.
> 6-7  Though short lived transport like a torrent sent
>       From out the bowels of a bursting cloud  B².
> 10    But soon broke forth a less impetuous stream  B² (*omitting l.* 9).
> 12 heard again 𝔄: audible  A² B² C.
> 20 hindrance A² B: indolence A.
> 23 *deleted from* A B; *not in* C.      26-27  A² C *as* 1850.
> 26 Sent in on Winter's service  A² B² C.  A² *deletes l.* 27, C *retains.*

Smote me, a sweetness of the coming time,
And listening, I half whispered, 'We will be
35 Ye heartsome Choristers, ye and I will be
Brethren, and in the hearing of bleak winds            [30]
Will chaunt together.' And, thereafter, walking
By later twilight on the hills, I saw
A Glow-worm from beneath a dusky shade
40 Or canopy of yet unwithered fern,
Clear-shining, like a Hermit's taper seen            [35]
Through a thick forest; silence touch'd me here
No less than sound had done before; the Child
Of Summer, lingering, shining by itself,
45 The voiceless Worm on the unfrequented hills,
Seem'd sent on the same errand with the Quire            [40]
Of Winter that had warbled at my door,
And the whole year seem'd tenderness and love.

The last Night's genial feeling overflow'd
50 Upon this morning, and my favourite Grove,
Now tossing its dark boughs in sun and wind            [45]
Spreads through me a commotion like its own,
Something that fits me for the Poet's task,
Which we will now resume with chearful hope,
55 Nor check'd by aught of tamer argument            [50]
That lies before us, needful to be told.

Return'd from that excursion, soon I bade
Farewell for ever to the private Bowers
Of gownèd Students, quitted these, no more            [54]
60 To enter them, and pitch'd my vagrant tent,
A casual Dweller and at large, among
The unfenc'd regions of society.

Yet undetermin'd to what plan of life
I should adhere, and seeming thence to have
65 A little space of intermediate time            [60]
Loose and at full command, to London first

34 And listening thus I whisper'd my resolve A²: thus I whisper'd 'we will be' A³ B² C.
37–38                    Straitway to the hills
        Gone forth, as twilight deepened, I espied D: D² *as* 1850.
48 seem'd] breathed A² B² C.
51 𝔄 C D: D² *as* 1850.

Smote me, and, listening, I in whispers said,
'Ye heartsome Choristers, ye and I will be
Associates, and, unscared by blustering winds,    30
Will chant together.' Thereafter, as the shades
Of twilight deepened, going forth, I spied
A glow-worm underneath a dusky plume
Or canopy of yet unwithered fern,
Clear-shining, like a hermit's taper seen    35
Through a thick forest. Silence touched me here
No less than sound had done before; the child
Of Summer, lingering, shining, by herself,
The voiceless worm on the unfrequented hills,
Seemed sent on the same errand with the choir    40
Of Winter that had warbled at my door,
And the whole year breathed tenderness and love.

The last night's genial feeling overflowed
Upon this morning, and my favourite grove,
Tossing in sunshine its dark boughs aloft,    45
As if to make the strong wind visible,
Wakes in me agitations like its own,
A spirit friendly to the Poet's task,
Which we will now resume with lively hope,
Nor checked by aught of tamer argument    50
That lies before us, needful to be told.

Returned from that excursion, soon I bade
Farewell for ever to the sheltered seats
Of gownèd students, quitted hall and bower,
And every comfort of that privileged ground,    55
Well pleased to pitch a vagrant tent among
The unfenced regions of society.

Yet, undetermined to what course of life
I should adhere, and seeming to possess
A little space of intermediate time    60
At full command, to London first I turned,

52–53 Awakens agitations like its own
        Friendly as music to the Poet's task  D: D² *as* 1850.
58–59 [53–54] A² B² C *as* 1850.        [55] every D²: all the  D.
60 [55] No more to tread that consecrated ground
        With privileged steps, and pitch'd my vagrant tent  A² B² C.
64 thence to have] to possess  A² B² C.
66–67 A² B² C *as* 1850.

I turn'd, if not in calmness, nevertheless
In no disturbance of excessive hope,
At ease from all ambition personal,
70 Frugal as there was need, and though self-will'd,      [64]
Yet temperate and reserv'd, and wholly free
From dangerous passions. 'Twas at least two years
Before this season when I first beheld
That mighty place, a transient vistant:
75 And now it pleas'd me my abode to fix                 [69]
Single in the wide waste, to have a house
It was enough (what matter for a home ?)
That own'd me; living chearfully abroad,
With fancy on the stir from day to day,               [75]
80 And all my young affections out of doors.

There was a time when whatsoe'er is feign'd
Of airy Palaces, and Gardens built
By Genii of Romance, or hath in grave
Authentic History been set forth of Rome,             [80]
85 Alcairo, Babylon, or Persepolis,
Or given upon report by Pilgrim-Friars
Of golden Cities ten months' journey deep
Among Tartarian wilds, fell short, far short,
Of that which I in simpleness believed                [85]
90 And thought of London; held me by a chain
Less strong of wonder, and obscure delight.
I know not that herein I shot beyond
The common mark of childhood; but I well
Remember that among our flock of Boys                 [90]
95 Was one, a Cripple from his birth, whom chance
Summon'd from School to London, fortunate
And envied Traveller! and when he return'd,
After short absence, and I first set eyes
Upon his person, verily, though strange
100 The thing may seem, I was not wholly free           [95]
From disappointment to behold the same

69 𝔄 C D: D² *as* 1850.
72–74                         I had felt the shock
    Of that huge Town's first presence heretofore
    And paced her streets A² B² C D: D² *as* 1850.
[70–71] pleasure . . . And] *not in* D: D² *as* 1850.
79 𝔄 C D: A² D² *as* 1850.        80 my 𝔄 C D E²: his D² E.
89 I in simpleness] my simplicity A² B² C.

In no disturbance of excessive hope,
By personal ambition unenslaved,
Frugal as there was need, and, though self-willed,
From dangerous passions free. Three years had flown    65
Since I had felt in heart and soul the shock
Of the huge town's first presence, and had paced
Her endless streets, a transient visitant:
Now, fixed amid that concourse of mankind
Where Pleasure whirls about incessantly,    70
And life and labour seem but one, I filled
An idler's place; an idler well content
To have a house (what matter for a home ?)
That owned him; living cheerfully abroad
With unchecked fancy ever on the stir,    75
And all my young affections out of doors.


There was a time when whatsoe'er is feigned
Of airy palaces, and gardens built
By Genii of romance; or hath in grave
Authentic history been set forth of Rome,    80
Alcairo, Babylon, or Persepolis;
Or given upon report by pilgrim friars,
Of golden cities ten months' journey deep
Among Tartarian wilds—fell short, far short,
Of what my fond simplicity believed    85
And thought of London—held me by a chain
Less strong of wonder and obscure delight.
Whether the bolt of childhood's Fancy shot
For me beyond its ordinary mark,
'Twere vain to ask; but in our flock of boys    90
Was One, a cripple from his birth, whom chance
Summoned from school to London; fortunate
And envied traveller! When the Boy returned,
After short absence, curiously I scanned
His mien and person, nor was free, in sooth,    95
From disappointment, not to find some change

92–94 ℧ C D: D² *as* 1850.
96–98    Summoned from School and homely rural scenes
         To Britain's capital city, fortunate
         And envied traveller—scarcely did a Month
         Elapse, ere to our Valley he returned
         And in the moment when I first set eyes  A² B² C.

Appearance, the same body, not to find
Some change, some beams of glory brought away
From that new region. Much I question'd him,
105 And every word he utter'd, on my ears
Fell flatter than a cagèd Parrot's note,                    [100]
That answers unexpectedly awry,
And mocks the Prompter's listening. Marvellous things
My fancy had shap'd forth, of sights and shows,
110 Processions, Equipages, Lords and Dukes,
The King, and the King's Palace, and not last
Or least, heaven bless him! the renown'd Lord Mayor:
Dreams hardly less intense than those which wrought
A change of purpose in young Whittington,
115 When he in friendlessness, a drooping Boy,
Sate on a Stone, and heard the Bells speak out
Articulate music. Above all, one thought                    [115]
Baffled my understanding, how men lived
Even next-door neighbours, as we say, yet still
120 Strangers, and knowing not each other's names.

Oh wond'rous power of words, how sweet they are
According to the meaning which they bring!                    [120]
Vauxhall and Ranelagh, I then had heard
Of your green groves, and wilderness of lamps,
125 Your gorgeous Ladies, fairy cataracts,                    [124]
And pageant fireworks; nor must we forget
Those other wonders different in kind,
Though scarcely less illustrious in degree,
The River proudly bridged, the giddy top
130 And Whispering Gallery of St. Paul's, the Tombs                    [130]

102–3    Appearance, not to find some obvious trace
              Of transformation wrought upon his frame
              Or countenance—some beams of glory fetch'd  A² B² C.
109–14  A² B² C D *as* 1850; *but* fond *for* quick [103], fancied *for* pictured
[107], *and* did beget *for* once begat [111].
115–16  When he a solitary, friendless boy
              Upon a stone sate drooping, till the bells
              Chiming far off in sympathetic tones
              Repeated deliver'd to his ear  A² C.
117–18                              Above all it seem'd
              A thought unfathomable how men could live  X:  X² *as* 1850.
118 *followed in* A² C *by the line* In that metropolis from year to year
120 [118]  A C D: nor knowing each the other's name  D² E: not *etc.* 1850.
123 *followed in* X *by the line* Among our distant mountain dales had
heard

In look and air, from that new region brought,
As if from Fairy-land. Much I questioned him;
And every word he uttered, on my ears
Fell flatter than a cagèd parrot's note,                         100
That answers unexpectedly awry,
And mocks the prompter's listening. Marvellous things
Had vanity (quick Spirit that appears
Almost as deeply seated and as strong
In a Child's heart as fear itself) conceived               105
For my enjoyment. Would that I could now
Recal what then I pictured to myself
Of mitred Prelates, Lords in ermine clad,
The King, and the King's Palace, and, not last,
Nor least, Heaven bless him! the renowned Lord Mayor: 110
Dreams not unlike to those which once begat
A change of purpose in young Whittington,
When he, a friendless and a drooping boy,
Sate on a stone, and heard the bells speak out
Articulate music. Above all, one thought                   115
Baffled my understanding: how men lived
Even next-door neighbours, as we say, yet still
Strangers, not knowing each the other's name.

O, wond'rous power of words, by simple faith
Licensed to take the meaning that we love!                 120
Vauxhall and Ranelagh! I then had heard
Of your green groves, and wilderness of lamps
Dimming the stars, and fireworks magical,
And gorgeous ladies, under splendid domes,
Floating in dance, or warbling high in air                 125
The songs of spirits! Nor had Fancy fed
With less delight upon that other class
Of marvels, broad-day wonders permanent:
The River proudly bridged; the dizzy top
And Whispering Gallery of St. Paul's; the tombs            130

124  wilderness  𝔄 X²: labyrinth  X.
126  And pageant fireworks, and had wings been mine
      I surely should have taken flight and been
      Your Visitant; nor must I overlook  X.
126-7                        nor unnoticed leave
      The class of broad-day wonders permanent  D:  D² as 1850

Of Westminster, the Giants of Guildhall,
Bedlam, and the two figures at its Gates,
Streets without end, and Churches numberless,
Statues, with flowery Gardens in vast Squares,                    [135]
135  The Monument, and Armoury of the Tower.

These fond imaginations of themselves                       [142]
Had long before given way in season due,
Leaving a throng of others in their stead;
And now I looked upon the real scene,
140  Familiarly perus'd it day by day                            [145]
With keen and lively pleasure even there
Where disappointment was the strongest, pleas'd
Through courteous self-submission, as a tax
Paid to the object by prescriptive right,                   [148]
145  A thing that ought to be. Shall I give way,
Copying the impression of the memory,
Though things unnumber'd idly do half seem
The work of fancy, shall I, as the mood
Inclines me, here describe, for pastime's sake
150  Some portion of that motley imagery,
A vivid pleasure of my Youth, and now
Among the lonely places that I love
A frequent day-dream for my riper mind.
—And first the look and aspect of the place
155  The broad high-way appearance, as it strikes
On Strangers of all ages, the quick dance
Of colours, lights and forms, the Babel din            [155]
The endless stream of men, and moving things,
From hour to hour the illimitable walk
160  Still among Streets with clouds and sky above,
The wealth, the bustle and the eagerness,
The glittering Chariots with their pamper'd Steeds,
Stalls, Barrows, Porters; midway in the Street
The Scavenger, who begs with hat in hand,
165  The labouring Hackney Coaches, the rash speed
Of Coaches travelling far, whirl'd on with horn

131–3 Of Westminster, Streets, Churches numberless  X.
132 Bedlam, and the [those  B] two Maniacs carved in stone
        Perpetually recumbent at her gates  A² B² C.
135 [136–41] The Monument and that chamber of the Tower
        Where England's Sovereigns sit in long array,
        Their Steeds bestriding, and each mimic shape

Of Westminster; the Giants of Guildhall;
Bedlam, and those carved maniacs at the gates,
Perpetually recumbent; Statues—man,
And the horse under him—in gilded pomp
Adorning flowery gardens, 'mid vast squares;              135
The Monument, and that Chamber of the Tower
Where England's sovereigns sit in long array,
Their steeds bestriding,—every mimic shape
Cased in the gleaming mail the monarch wore,
Whether for gorgeous tournament addressed,              140
Or life or death upon the battle-field.
Those bold imaginations in due time
Had vanished, leaving others in their stead:
And now I looked upon the living scene;
Familiarly perused it; oftentimes,                    145
In spite of strongest disappointment, pleased
Through courteous self-submission, as a tax
Paid to the object by prescriptive right.

   Rise up, thou monstrous ant-hill on the plain
Of a too busy world! Before me flow,                   150
Thou endless stream of men and moving things!
Thy every-day appearance, as it strikes—
With wonder heightened, or sublimed by awe—
On strangers, of all ages; the quick dance
Of colours, lights, and forms; the deafening din;       155

Cased in the very suit of gleaming mail
    Which in his time the living Monarch wore
    For Tournament addressed or deadly fight
    Mid thickest conflict on the ensanguin'd field. A² C. *So* D, *but*
[140–1] Whether for shock of gaudy tournament
    Addressed, or conflict on the ensanguined field. D² *as* 1850.
136 fond] vague A² C.          137 given way] withdrawn A² C.
136–8 A *deletes*.
    142–53 𝔄 C D; *but* A² D, *for* 148–9, The work of fancy shall I here
describe; D² 150–3, *after many corrections*,
    Some portion of those lively images
    That charmed my youth, and may be now to thousands
    Of my coevals scatter'd through the world (*or* all climes)
    A frequent day-dream for the riper mind. D³ *as* 1850.
    145–55 A thing that ought to be, with slight regard
    I pass the first blunt aspect of the place | The broad *etc.* X.
    154–62 𝔄 C D; *but* A² C D every day *for* broad highway *and* D deafen-
ing *for* Babel. D *omits* 159–61.
    163–71 A B *deletes*; *not in* C.          163–4  *not in* D.
    [151] Thou swarming Wilderness of brick and stone! D (*deleted*).

     Loud blowing, and the sturdy Drayman's Team,
     Ascending from some Alley of the Thames
     And striking right across the crowded Strand
170 Till the fore Horse veer round with punctual skill:
     Here there and everywhere a weary Throng
     The Comers and the Goers face to face,         [156]
     Face after face; the string of dazzling Wares,
     Shop after shop, with Symbols, blazon'd Names,
175 And all the Tradesman's honours overhead;
     Here, fronts of houses, like a title-page        [160]
     With letters huge inscribed from top to toe;
     Station'd above the door, like guardian Saints,
     There, allegoric shapes, female or male;
180 Or physiognomies of real men,
     Land-Warriors, Kings, or Admirals of the Sea,   [165]
     Boyle, Shakspear, Newton, or the attractive head
     Of some Scotch doctor, famous in his day.

     Meanwhile the roar continues, till, at length,
185 Escaped as from an enemy, we turn
     Abruptly into some sequester'd nook        [170]
     Still as a shelter'd place when winds blow loud:
     At leisure thence, through tracts of thin resort,
     And sights and sounds that come at intervals,
190 We take our way: a raree-show is here
     With Children gather'd round, another Street   [175]
     Presents a company of dancing Dogs,
     Or Dromedary, with an antic pair
     Of Monkies on his back, a minstrel Band
195 Of Savoyards, or, single and alone,
     An English Ballad-singer. Private Courts,     [180]
     Gloomy as Coffins, and unsightly Lanes
     Thrill'd by some female Vender's scream, belike
     The very shrillest of all London Cries,
200 May then entangle us awhile,
     Conducted through those labyrinths unawares   [185]
     To privileg'd Regions and inviolate,
     Where from their airy lodges studious Lawyers
     Look out on waters, walks, and gardens green.

205    Thence back into the throng, until we reach,
     Following the tide that slackens by degrees,    [190]

The comers and the goers face to face,
Face after face; the string of dazzling wares,
Shop after shop, with symbols, blazoned names,
And all the tradesman's honours overhead:
Here, fronts of houses, like a title-page,　　　160
With letters huge inscribed from top to toe,
Stationed above the door, like guardian saints;
There, allegoric shapes, female or male,
Or physiognomies of real men,
Land-warriors, kings, or admirals of the sea,　　　165
Boyle, Shakespeare, Newton, or the attractive head
Of some quack-doctor, famous in his day.

Meanwhile the roar continues, till at length,
Escaped as from an enemy, we turn
Abruptly into some sequestered nook,　　　170
Still as a sheltered place when winds blow loud!
At leisure, thence, through tracts of thin resort,
And sights and sounds that come at intervals,
We take our way. A raree-show is here,
With children gathered round; another street　　　175
Presents a company of dancing dogs,
Or dromedary, with an antic pair
Of monkeys on his back; a minstrel band
Of Savoyards; or, single and alone,
An English ballad-singer. Private courts,　　　180
Gloomy as coffins, and unsightly lanes
Thrilled by some female vendor's scream, belike
The very shrillest of all London cries,
May then entangle our impatient steps;
Conducted through those labyrinths, unawares,　　　185
To privileged regions and inviolate,
Where from their airy lodges studious lawyers
Look out on waters, walks, and gardens green.

Thence back into the throng, until we reach,
Following the tide that slackens by degrees,　　　190

177–8 toe; Saints, 𝔄 C D: toe, Saints E.
183 some Scotch X A: Scottish B²: some Quack- A² C.
200 𝔄 C D: Perhaps entangle us awhile at length (at length *deleted*) X:
D² *as* 1850.

Some half-frequented scene where wider Streets
Bring straggling breezes of suburban air;
Here files of ballads dangle from dead walls,
210 Advertisements of giant-size, from high
Press forward in all colours on the sight;                    [195]
These, bold in conscious merit; lower down
That, fronted with a most imposing word,
Is, peradventure, one in masquerade.
215 As on the broadening Causeway we advance,
Behold a Face turn'd up toward us, strong                    [200]
In lineaments, and red with over-toil;
'Tis one perhaps, already met elsewhere,
A travelling Cripple, by the trunk cut short,
220 And stumping with his arms: in Sailor's garb
Another lies at length beside a range                    [205]
Of written characters, with chalk inscrib'd
Upon the smooth flat stones: the Nurse is here,
The Bachelor that loves to sun himself,
225 The military Idler, and the Dame,
That field-ward takes her walk in decency.                    [210]

Now homeward through the thickening hubbub, where
See, among less distinguishable Shapes,
The Italian, with his frame of Images                    [215]
230 Upon his head; with Basket at his waist
The Jew; the stately and slow-moving Turk
With freight of slippers piled beneath his arm.
Briefly, we find, if tired of random sights
And haply to that search our thoughts should turn,
235 Among the crowd, conspicuous less or more,                    [221]
As we proceed, all specimens of Man
Through all the colours which the sun bestows,
And every character of form and face,
The Swede, the Russian; from the genial South,
240 The Frenchman and the Spaniard; from remote                    [225]

213–17 That peradventure, one in masquerade
         Inviting is the leading word, a bait
         Which cannot be resisted, at the close
         The simple reader, if he laugh not, looks
         Blank as an April fool.  Behold a face
         Turn'd up towards us strong in lineaments,
         Heated and red as if with overtoil.  X² *deleted*: X³ *as* 𝔄.
218 A C D:  D² *as* 1850.          222 written 𝔄 C D:  well-formed D².

Some half-frequented scene, where wider streets
Bring straggling breezes of suburban air.
Here files of ballads dangle from dead walls;
Advertisements, of giant-size, from high
Press forward, in all colours, on the sight;     195
These, bold in conscious merit, lower down;
*That*, fronted with a most imposing word,
Is, peradventure, one in masquerade.
As on the broadening causeway we advance,
Behold, turned upwards, a face hard and strong     200
In lineaments, and red with over-toil.
'Tis one encountered here and everywhere;
A travelling cripple, by the trunk cut short,
And stumping on his arms. In sailor's garb
Another lies at length, beside a range     205
Of well-formed characters, with chalk inscribed
Upon the smooth flat stones: the Nurse is here,
The Bachelor, that loves to sun himself,
The military Idler, and the Dame,
That field-ward takes her walk with decent steps.     210

Now homeward through the thickening hubbub, where
See, among less distinguishable shapes,
The begging scavenger, with hat in hand;
The Italian, as he thrids his way with care,
Steadying, far-seen, a frame of images     215
Upon his head; with basket at his breast
The Jew; the stately and slow-moving Turk,
With freight of slippers piled beneath his arm!

Enough;—the mighty concourse I surveyed
With no unthinking mind, well pleased to note     220
Among the crowd all specimens of man,
Through all the colours which the sun bestows,
And every character of form and face:
The Swede, the Russian; from the genial south,
The Frenchman and the Spaniard; from remote     225

226 in decency 𝔄: with decent steps A² B² C.
232 With pile of slippers underneath his arm X: grasped beneath X².
233–6 Briefly . . . proceed 𝔄:
> Enough, a mighty concourse was before me
> Which I surveyed with no unthinking mind
> Well pleased to note conspicuous less or more
> Among the crowd A² B² C D: D² *as* 1850.

America, the Hunter-Indian; Moors,
Malays, Lascars, the Tartar and Chinese,
And Negro Ladies in white muslin gowns.

At leisure let us view, from day to day,
245  As they present themselves, the Spectacles
Within doors, troops of wild Beasts, birds and beasts     [230]
Of every nature, from all Climes conven'd;
And, next to these, those mimic sights that ape
The absolute presence of reality,
250  Expressing, as in mirror, sea and land,
And what earth is, and what she has to shew;              [235]
I do not here allude to subtlest craft,
By means refin'd attaining purest ends,
But imitations fondly made in plain
255  Confession of Man's weakness, and his loves.
Whether the Painter fashioning a work                    [240]
To Nature's circumambient scenery,
And with his greedy pencil taking in
A whole horizon on all sides with power,
260  Like that of Angels or commission'd Spirits,
Plant us upon some lofty Pinnacle,
Or in a Ship on Waters, with a world                     [245]
Of life, and life-like mockery, to East,
To West, beneath, behind us, and before;
265  Or more mechanic Artist represent
By scale exact, in Model, wood or clay,
From shading colours also borrowing help,                [250]
Some miniature of famous spots and things
Domestic, or the boast of foreign Realms;
270  The Firth of Forth, and Edinburgh throned
On crags, fit empress of that mountain Land;
St. Peter's Church; or, more aspiring aim,
In microscopic vision, Rome itself;
Or else perhaps, some rural haunt, the Falls
275  Of Tivoli, and high upon that steep                       [255]
The Temple of the Sibyl, every tree
Through all the landscape, tuft, stone, scratch minute,
And every Cottage, lurking in the rocks,
All that the Traveller sees when he is there.

280     Add to these exhibitions mute and still               [260]

America, the Hunter-Indian; Moors,
Malays, Lascars, the Tartar, the Chinese,
And Negro Ladies in white muslin gowns.

At leisure, then, I viewed, from day to day,
The spectacles within doors,—birds and beasts          230
Of every nature, and strange plants convened
From every clime; and, next, those sights that ape
The absolute presence of reality,
Expressing, as in mirror, sea and land,
And what earth is, and what she has to shew.           235
I do not here allude to subtlest craft,
By means refined attaining purest ends,
But imitations, fondly made in plain
Confession of man's weakness and his loves.
Whether the Painter, whose ambitious skill            240
Submits to nothing less than taking in
A whole horizon's circuit, do with power,
Like that of angels or commissioned spirits,
Fix us upon some lofty pinnacle,
Or in a ship on waters, with a world                  245
Of life, and life-like mockery beneath,
Above, behind, far stretching and before;
Or more mechanic artist represent
By scale exact, in model, wood or clay,
From blended colours also borrowing help,             250
Some miniature of famous spots or things,—
St. Peter's Church; or, more aspiring aim,
In microscopic vision, Rome herself;
Or, haply, some choice rural haunt,—the Falls
Of Tivoli; and, high upon that steep,                 255
The Sibyl's mouldering Temple! every tree,
Villa, or cottage, lurking among rocks
Throughout the landscape; tuft, stone scratch minute—
All that the traveller sees when he is there.

And to these exhibitions, mute and still,             260

243 gowns 𝔄 D E: robes A² C.      244–6 A² B² C *as* 1850.
247–8 𝔄 C D: D² *as* 1850.      256–9 𝔄 C D: D² *as* 1850.
263–4 A² C *as* 1850.
269–71 Domestic . . . Land: A B *delete*; *not in* C.
274 [254] A² B² C *as* 1850.
275 Of Tivoli and dim Frescati's (*sic*) bowers
    And high upon the steep that mouldring fane  X: A² B² C *as* 1850
    (*v. note*).

Others of wider scope, where living men,
Music, and shifting pantomimic scenes,
Together join'd their multifarious aid
To heighten the allurement. Need I fear
285 To mention by its name, as in degree
    Lowest of these, and humblest in attempt,         [265]
    Though richly graced with honours of its own,
    Half-rural Sadler's Wells ? Though at that time
    Intolerant, as is the way of Youth
290 Unless itself be pleased, I more than once
    Here took my seat, and, maugre frequent fits     [270]
    Of irksomeness, with ample recompense
    Saw Singers, Rope-dancers, Giants and Dwarfs,
    Clowns, Conjurors, Posture-masters, Harlequins,
295 Amid the uproar of the rabblement,
    Perform their feats. Nor was it mean delight
    To watch crude nature work in untaught minds,   [275]
    To note the laws and progress of belief;
    Though obstinate on this way, yet on that
300 How willingly we travel, and how far!
    To have, for instance, brought upon the scene
    The Champion Jack the Giant-killer, Lo!
    He dons his Coat of Darkness; on the Stage     [281]
    Walks, and atchieves his wonders, from the eye
305 Of living mortal safe as is the moon
    'Hid in her vacant interlunar cave'
    Delusion bold! and faith must needs be coy;    [285]
    How is it wrought ? His garb is black, the word
    INVISIBLE flames forth upon his Chest.

310    Nor was it unamusing here to view
    Those samples as of the ancient Comedy
    And Thespian times, dramas of living Men,
    And recent things, yet warm with life; a Sea-fight,
    Shipwreck, or some domestic incident
315 The fame of which is scatter'd through the Land;
    Such as this daring Brotherhood of late
    Set forth, too holy theme for such a place,     [295]
    And doubtless treated with irreverence,
    Albeit with their very best of skill,
320 I mean, O distant Friend! a Story drawn
    From our own ground, the Maid of Buttermere,

Others of wider scope, where living men,
Music, and shifting pantomimic scenes,
Diversified the allurement. Need I fear
To mention by its name, as in degree,
Lowest of these and humblest in attempt,                          265
Yet richly graced with honours of her own,
Half-rural Sadler's Wells? Though at that time
Intolerant, as is the way of youth
Unless itself be pleased, here more than once
Taking my seat, I saw (nor blush to add,                          270
With ample recompense) giants and dwarfs,
Clowns, conjurors, posture-masters, harlequins,
Amid the uproar of the rabblement,
Perform their feats. Nor was it mean delight
To watch crude Nature work in untaught minds;                     275
To note the laws and progress of belief;
Though obstinate on this way, yet on that
How willingly we travel, and how far!
To have, for instance, brought upon the scene
The champion, Jack the Giant-killer: Lo!                          280
He dons his coat of darkness; on the stage
Walks, and achieves his wonders, from the eye
Of living Mortal covert, 'as the moon
Hid in her vacant interlunar cave.'
Delusion bold! and how can it be wrought?                         285
The garb he wears is black as death, the word
'*Invisible*' flames forth upon his chest.

Here, too, were 'forms and pressures of the time,'
Rough, bold, as Grecian comedy displayed
When Art was young; dramas of living men,                         290
And recent things yet warm with life; a sea-fight,
Shipwreck, or some domestic incident
Divulged by Truth and magnified by Fame,
Such as the daring brotherhood of late
Set forth, too serious theme for that light place—                295
I mean, O distant Friend! a story drawn
From our own ground,—the Maid of Buttermere,—

288 Half-rural] Illustrious  X.
290-3 𝔄 C D: D² *as* 1850.          315 A² C *as* 1850.
316 Such as of late this bold adventurer  X.
318 A *deletes*; *not in* C.
319 Albeit treated with their best of skill  A² C.

    And how the Spoiler came, 'a bold bad Man'
    To God unfaithful, Children, Wife, and Home,
    And wooed the artless Daughter of the hills,       [300]
325 And wedded her, in cruel mockery
    Of love and marriage bonds. O Friend! I speak
    With tender recollection of that time
    When first we saw the Maiden, then a name
    By us unheard of; in her cottage Inn       [305]
330 Were welcomed, and attended on by her,
    Both stricken with one feeling of delight,
    An admiration of her modest mien,
    And carriage, mark'd by unexampled grace.
    Not unfamiliarly we since that time
335 Have seen her; her discretion have observ'd,       [310]
    Her just opinions, female modesty,
    Her patience, and retiredness of mind
    Unsoil'd by commendation, and the excess
    Of public notice. This memorial Verse
340 Comes from the Poet's heart, and is her due.
    For we were nursed, as almost might be said,
    On the same mountains; Children at one time
    Must haply often on the self-same day
    Have from our several dwellings gone abroad
345 To gather daffodils on Coker's Stream.

        These last words utter'd, to my argument
    I was returning, when, with sundry Forms
    Mingled, that in the way which I must tread
    Before me stand, thy image rose again,
350 Mary of Buttermere! She lives in peace       [320]
    Upon the ground where she was born and rear'd;
    Without contamination does she live
    In quietness, without anxiety:
    Beside the mountain-Chapel sleeps in earth
355 Her new-born Infant, fearless as a lamb       [325]
    That thither comes, from some unsheltered place,
    To rest beneath the little rock-like Pile
    When storms are blowing. Happy are they both
    Mother and Child! These feelings, in themselves
360 Trite, do yet scarcely seem so when I think       [330]
    Of those ingenuous moments of our youth,

        [298] a virtuous D²: an honoured D.

And how, unfaithful to a virtuous wife
Deserted and deceived, the spoiler came
And wooed the artless daughter of the hills,                    300
And wedded her, in cruel mockery
Of love and marriage bonds. These words to thee
Must needs bring back the moment when we first,
Ere the broad world rang with the maiden's name,
Beheld her serving at the cottage inn,                          305
Both stricken, as she entered or withdrew,
With admiration of her modest mien
And carriage, marked by unexampled grace.
We since that time not unfamiliarly
Have seen her,—her discretion have observed,                   310
Her just opinions, delicate reserve,
Her patience, and humility of mind
Unspoiled by commendation and the excess
Of public notice—an offensive light
To a meek spirit suffering inwardly.                            315

From this memorial tribute to my theme
I was returning, when, with sundry forms
Commingled—shapes which met me in the way
That we must tread—thy image rose again,
Maiden of Buttermere! She lives in peace                        320
Upon the spot where she was born and reared;
Without contamination doth she live
In quietness, without anxiety:
Beside the mountain chapel, sleeps in earth
Her new-born infant, fearless as a lamb                         325
That, thither driven from some unsheltered place,
Rests underneath the little rock-like pile
When storms are raging. Happy are they both—
Mother and child!—These feelings, in themselves
Trite, do yet scarcely seem so when I think                     330
On those ingenuous moments of our youth

[309–15] *Against this passage is written in* E, Revise this page and the next (*i.e. down to* [350]).
330 A B *delete*: *not in* C.       331 𝔄 C D: D² *as* 1850.
334 *All MSS. as* 𝔄.       336 Her delicacy, female modesty, X.
348–9 𝔄 C D: D² *as* 1850.       350 Mary 𝔄: Maiden A² B² C.
351 ground A: spot A² B C.       356–7 𝔄 C D: D² *as* 1850.
358 blowing 𝔄 C D: gathering D²: raging D³ E.
359 Mother and Child X²: Alas how many women now alive Might envy them X.       361–74 D² *stuck over*: D² *as* 1850.

Ere yet by use we have learn'd to slight the crimes
And sorrows of the world. Those days are now
My theme; and, mid the numerous scenes which they    [334]
365 Have left behind them, foremost I am cross'd
Here by remembrance of two figures, One
A rosy Babe, who, for a twelvemonth's space
Perhaps, had been of age to deal about
Articulate prattle, Child as beautiful
370 As ever sate upon a Mother's knee;
The other was the Parent of that Babe;
But on the Mother's cheek the tints were false,
A painted bloom. 'Twas at a Theatre
That I beheld this Pair; the Boy had been
375 The pride and pleasure of all lookers-on
In whatsoever place; but seem'd in this
A sort of Alien scatter'd from the clouds.          [350]
Of lusty vigour, more than infantine,
He was in limbs; in face a cottage rose
380 Just three parts blown; a Cottage Child, but ne'er
Saw I, by Cottage or elsewhere, a Babe             [355]
By Nature's gifts so honor'd. Upon a Board
Whence an attendant of the Theatre
Serv'd out refreshments, had this Child been plac'd,
385 And there he sate, environ'd with a Ring
Of chance Spectators, chiefly dissolute men        [360]
And shameless women; treated and caress'd,
Ate, drank, and with the fruit and glasses play'd,
While oaths, indecent speech, and ribaldry
390 Were rife about him as are songs of birds
In spring-time after showers. The Mother, too,     [365]
Was present! but of her I know no more
Than hath been said, and scarcely at this time
Do I remember her. But I behold
395 The lovely Boy as I beheld him then,
Among the wretched and the falsely gay,
Like one of those who walk'd with hair unsinged

368 Perhaps 𝔄: I guess A² C: Not more A³.
373–4 'Twas at a Theatre *etc.*] By lamp and taper light
        Within the walls of Drury's splendid house
        Did I behold  A² C.
374 That I beheld this pair, and at the time
        Which now my tale hath reached. The Boy had been  X.
377–8 clouds, A miracle. An infant Hercules  X.

Ere we have learnt by use to slight the crimes
And sorrows of the world. Those simple days
Are now my theme; and, foremost of the scenes,
Which yet survive in memory, appears                        335
One, at whose centre sate a lovely Boy,
A sportive infant, who, for six months' space,
Not more, had been of age to deal about
Articulate prattle—Child as beautiful
As ever clung around a mother's neck,                       340
Or father fondly gazed upon with pride.
There, too, conspicuous for stature tall
And large dark eyes, beside her infant stood
The mother; but, upon her cheeks diffused,
False tints too well accorded with the glare               345
From play-house lustres thrown without reserve
On every object near. The Boy had been
The pride and pleasure of all lookers-on
In whatsoever place, but seemed in this
A sort of alien scattered from the clouds.                  350
Of lusty vigour, more than infantine
He was in limb, in cheek a summer rose
Just three parts blown—a cottage-child—if e'er,
By cottage-door on breezy mountain side,
Or in some sheltering vale, was seen a babe                355
By Nature's gifts so favoured. Upon a board
Decked with refreshments had this child been placed,
*His* little stage in the vast theatre,
And there he sate surrounded with a throng
Of chance spectators, chiefly dissolute men                360
And shameless women, treated and caressed;
Ate, drank, and with the fruit and glasses played,
While oaths and laughter and indecent speech
Were rife about him as the songs of birds
Contending after showers. The mother now                   365
Is fading out of memory, but I see
The lovely Boy as I beheld him then
Among the wretched and the falsely gay,
Like one of those who walked with hair unsinged

379–83 D *stuck over*: D² *as* 1850.
384–6 Serv'd cakes liqueurs and wines he sate begirt With chance *etc.* **X.**
393 Than may be gathered from this fact, and what
    Hath been already said, and scarcely now **X.**

Amid the fiery furnace. He hath since                     [370]
Appear'd to me oft-times as if embalm'd
400 By Nature; through some special privilege,            [375]
Stopp'd at the growth he had; destined to live,
To be, to have been, come and go, a Child
And nothing more, no partner in the years
That bear us forward to distress and guilt,
405 Pain and abasement, beauty in such excess
Adorn'd him in that miserable place.
So have I thought of him a thousand times,
And seldom otherwise. But he perhaps
Mary! may now have liv'd till he could look
410 With envy on thy nameless Babe that sleeps           [380]
Beside the mountain Chapel, undisturb'd!


    It was but little more than three short years
Before the season which I speak of now
When first, a Traveller from our pastoral hills,
415 Southward two hundred miles I had advanced,
And for the first time in my life did hear
The voice of Woman utter blasphemy;                      [385]
Saw Woman as she is to open shame
Abandon'd and the pride of public vice.
420 Full surely from the bottom of my heart
I shudder'd; but the pain was almost lost,
Absorb'd and buried in the immensity
Of the effect: a barrier seem'd at once
Thrown in, that from humanity divorced
425 The human Form, splitting the race of Man            [390]
In twain, yet leaving the same outward shape.
Distress of mind ensued upon this sight
And ardent meditation; afterwards
A milder sadness on such spectacles
430 Attended; thought, commiseration, grief              [395]
For the individual, and the overthrow


398–408 Amid the fiery furnace. We have heard
        Of potent spells by which the kindly growth
        Of Nature hath maliciously been check'd.
        Ah, with how different spirit might a prayer
        Have been preferred that on this opening flower
        A hindrance might be laid, that this fair Creature

Amid the fiery furnace. Charms and spells                                370
Muttered on black and spiteful instigation
Have stopped, as some believe, the kindliest growths.
Ah, with how different spirit might a prayer
Have been preferred, that this fair creature, checked
By special privilege of Nature's love,                                   375
Should in his childhood be detained for ever!
But with its universal freight the tide
Hath rolled along, and this bright innocent,
Mary! may now have lived till he could look
With envy on thy nameless babe that sleeps,                              380
Beside the mountain chapel, undisturbed.


Four rapid years had scarcely then been told
Since, travelling southward from our pastoral hills,
I heard, and for the first time in my life,
The voice of woman utter blasphemy—                                      385
Saw woman as she is, to open shame
Abandoned, and the pride of public vice;
I shuddered, for a barrier seemed at once
Thrown in, that from humanity divorced
Humanity, splitting the race of man                                      390
In twain, yet leaving the same outward form.
Distress of mind ensued upon the sight
And ardent meditation. Later years
Brought to such spectacle a milder sadness,
Feelings of pure commiseration, grief                                    395
For the individual and the overthrow


By special privilege of Nature's hand
Might in his Childhood be detained for ever!
Not subject to the motion of those years
That bear us forward to distress and guilt
Pain and abasement, wretchedness and fear
But with *etc. as* [377–8] A² B² C.
412       It was but little short of four long years  X.
412–15    Not four brief years were numbered at that time
          Since first a traveller from our pastoral hills
          Southward through town and village far advanced D: D²*as* 1850.
428–30                        Later years
          Brought milder sadness on such spectacles
          Attendant, thought *etc.* D: D² *as* 1850.

Of her soul's beauty; farther at that time
Than this I was but seldom led; in truth
The sorrow of the passion stopp'd me here.

435     I quit this painful theme; enough is said         [400]
To shew what thoughts must often have been mine
At theatres, which then were my delight,
A yearning made more strong by obstacles
Which slender funds imposed. Life then was new,
440 The senses easily pleased; the lustres, lights,
The carving and the gilding, paint and glare,
And all the mean upholstery of the place,
Wanted not animation in my sight:         [410]
Far less the living Figures on the Stage,
445 Solemn or gay: whether some beauteous Dame
Advanced in radiance through a deep recess
Of thick-entangled forest, like the Moon         [415]
Opening the clouds; or sovereign King, announced
With flourishing Trumpets, came in full-blown State
450 Of the world's greatness, winding round with Train
Of Courtiers, Banners, and a length of Guards;
Or Captive led in abject weeds, and jingling         [420]
His slender manacles; or romping Girl
Bounced, leapt, and paw'd the air; or mumbling Sire,
455 A scare-crow pattern of old Age, patch'd up
Of all the tatters of infirmity,
All loosely put together, hobbled in,         [425]
Stumping upon a Cane, with which he smites,
From time to time, the solid boards, and makes them
460 Prate somewhat loudly of the whereabout
Of one so overloaded with his years.
But what of this! the laugh, the grin, grimace,         [430]

432-4                 farther at that time
          Than this I was but seldom led, untaught
          At these appearances habitually
          To feel that such division has no place
          And cannot have; that in society
          [As light with light, worst evil to best good
          Can give a taint, that in society]
          There are no gaps, that vice whatever shape
          It may put on a breathing object is
          No statue, and doth momently send forth
          Her respirations to be blown about
          At random by the universal air. X.

Of her soul's beauty; farther I was then
But seldom led, or wished to go; in truth
The sorrow of the passion stopped me there.

But let me now, less moved, in order take                     400
Our argument. Enough is said to show
How casual incidents of real life,
Observed where pastime only had been sought,
Outweighed, or put to flight, the set events
And measured passions of the stage, albeit                    405
By Siddons trod in the fulness of her power.
Yet was the theatre my dear delight;
The very gilding, lamps and painted scrolls,
And all the mean upholstery of the place,
Wanted not animation, when the tide                           410
Of pleasure ebbed but to return as fast
With the ever-shifting figures of the scene,
Solemn or gay: whether some beauteous dame
Advanced in radiance through a deep recess
Of thick entangled forest, like the moon                      415
Opening the clouds; or sovereign king, announced
With flourishing trumpet, came in full-blown state
Of the world's greatness, winding round with train
Of courtiers, banners, and a length of guards;
Or captive led in abject weeds, and jingling                  420
His slender manacles; or romping girl
Bounced, leapt, and pawed the air; or mumbling sire,
A scare-crow pattern of old age dressed up
In all the tatters of infirmity
All loosely put together, hobbled in,                         425
Stumping upon a cane with which he smites,
From time to time, the solid boards, and makes them
Prate somewhat loudly of the whereabout
Of one so overloaded with his years.
But what of this! the laugh, the grin, grimace,               430

432–3 𝔄 C D: D² *as* 1850.

435–44 𝔄 C: A² *has first draft of* 1850 [400–12], *but* ordered passions of
the stage; though trod By Siddons in the zenith of her power [405–6] *and*
The lustres carving gilding *etc.* [408]. *After* [407] Life then was new, the
sense was easily pleased.

[410–11] Lacked not their animation could the tide
         Of pleasure ebb but to return as fast. A²: D *stuck over*; D² *as*
A²: D³ *as* 1850.

455–6 patch'd up Of] composed From A² B² C D: D² *as* 1850.

And all the antics and buffoonery,
The least of them not lost, were all received
465 With charitable pleasure. Through the night,
Between the show, and many-headed mass
Of the Spectators, and each little nook                    [435]
That had its fray or brawl, how eagerly,
And with what flashes, as it were, the mind
470 Turn'd this way, that way! sportive and alert
And watchful, as a Kitten when at play,
While winds are blowing round her, among grass            [440]
And rustling leaves. Enchanting age and sweet!
Romantic almost, looked at through a space,
475 How small of intervening years! For then,
Though surely no mean progress had been made
In meditations holy and sublime,                          [445]
Yet something of a girlish child-like gloss
Of novelty surviv'd for scenes like these;
480 Pleasure that had been handed down from times
When, at a Country-Playhouse, having caught,             [449]
In summer, through the fractur'd wall, a glimpse
Of daylight, at the thought of where I was
I gladden'd more than if I had beheld
485 Before me some bright Cavern of Romance,                 [455]
Or than we do, when on our beds we lie
At night, in warmth, when rains are beating hard.

The matter that detains me now will seem,
To many neither dignified enough
490 Nor arduous; and is, doubtless, in itself                [460]
Humble and low; yet not to be despis'd
By those who have observ'd the curious props
By which the perishable hours of life
Rest on each other, and the world of thought
495 Exists and is sustain'd. More lofty Themes,              [465]
Such as, at least, do wear a prouder face,

463–5, 467 𝔄 C D: D² *as* 1850.        468 A² B² C *as* 1850.
472, 480 𝔄 C D: D² *as* 1850.
481–3 𝔄 C D:                    if I caught
          On summer evenings through the fractured wall
          A glimpse of daylight, thought of where I was D² E: E² *as* 1850.
486–7 [456] A² C D *as* 1850, *but* occupied in *for* busy among: D² *as* 1850.
488–9 The matter which detains me at this time
          Will (like that string of figures which erewhile

The antics striving to outstrip each other,
Were all received, the least of them not lost,
With an unmeasured welcome. Through the night,
Between the show, and many-headed mass
Of the spectators, and each several nook                    435
Filled with its fray or brawl, how eagerly
And with what flashes, as it were, the mind
Turned this way—that way! sportive and alert
And watchful, as a kitten when at play,
While winds are eddying round her, among straws             440
And rustling leaves. Enchanting age and sweet!
Romantic almost, looked at through a space,
How small, of intervening years! For then,
Though surely no mean progress had been made
In meditations holy and sublime,                            445
Yet something of a girlish child-like gloss
Of novelty survived for scenes like these;
Enjoyment haply handed down from times
When at a country-playhouse, some rude barn
Tricked out for that proud use, if I perchance              450
Caught, on a summer evening through a chink
In the old wall, an unexpected glimpse
Of daylight, the bare thought of where I was
Gladdened me more than if I had been led
Into a dazzling cavern of romance,                          455
Crowded with Genii busy among works
Not to be looked at by the common sun.

      The matter that detains us now may seem,
To many, neither dignified enough
Nor arduous, yet will not be scorned by them,               460
Who, looking inward, have observed the ties
That bind the perishable hours of life
Each to the other, and the curious props
By which the world of memory and thought
Exists and is sustained. More lofty themes,                 465
Such as at least do wear a prouder face,

      We threaded as we pass'd along the streets
      An Indian toy of many coloured beads)
      Appear to some not dignified enough  X.
491–5 𝔄 C: yet safe from their contempt, Who *etc. as* 1850 [461–5],
A² D: D² *as* 1850.

Might here be spoken of; but when I think
Of these, I feel the imaginative Power
Languish within me; even then it slept
500 When, wrought upon by tragic sufferings,                [470]
The heart was full; amid my sobs and tears
It slept, even in the season of my youth:
For though I was most passionately moved
And yielded to the changes of the scene
505 With most obsequious feeling, yet all this              [475]
Pass'd not beyond the suburbs of the mind:
If aught there were of real grandeur here
'Twas only then when gross realities,
The incarnation of the Spirits that mov'd
510 Amid the Poet's beauteous world, call'd forth,          [480]
With that distinctness which a contrast gives
Or opposition, made me recognize
As by a glimpse, the things which I had shap'd
And yet not shaped, had seen, and scarcely seen,
515 Had felt, and thought of in my solitude.               [485]

     Pass we from entertainments that are such
Professedly to others titled higher,
Yet in the estimate of youth at least,
More near akin to these than names imply,
520 I mean the brawls of Lawyers in their Courts           [490]
Before the ermined Judge, or that great Stage
Where Senators, tongue-favor'd Men, perform,
Admir'd and envied. Oh! the beating heart!
When one among the prime of these rose up,
525 One, of whose name from Childhood we had heard         [495]
Familiarly, a household term, like those,
The Bedfords, Glocesters, Salisburys of old,
Which the fifth Harry talks of. Silence! hush!
This is no trifler, no short-flighted Wit,
530 No stammerer of a minute, painfully                    [500]
Deliver'd. No! the Orator hath yoked
The Hours, like young Aurora, to his Car;
O Presence of delight, can patience e'er
Grow weary of attending on a track
535 That kindles with such glory? Marvellous!              [505]

500–1, 505 𝔄 C D: D² *as* 1850.        502, 507–10 A² *as* 1850.
511–15 𝔄 C D: D² *as* 1850 [481–5].

Solicit our regard; but when I think
Of these, I feel the imaginative power
Languish within me; even then it slept,
When, pressed by tragic sufferings, the heart                470
Was more than full; amid my sobs and tears
It slept, even in the pregnant season of youth.
For though I was most passionately moved
And yielded to all changes of the scene
With an obsequious promptness, yet the storm               475
Passed not beyond the suburbs of the mind;
Save when realities of act and mien,
The incarnation of the spirits that move
In harmony amid the Poet's world,
Rose to ideal grandeur, or, called forth                   480
By power of contrast, made me recognise,
As at a glance, the things which I had shaped,
And yet not shaped, had seen and scarcely seen,
When, having closed the mighty Shakspeare's page,
I mused, and thought, and felt, in solitude.               485

Pass we from entertainments, that are such
Professedly, to others titled higher,
Yet, in the estimate of youth at least,
More near akin to those than names imply,—
I mean the brawls of lawyers in their courts               490
Before the ermined judge, or that great stage
Where senators, tongue-favoured men, perform,
Admired and envied. Oh! the beating heart,
When one among the prime of these rise up,—
One, of whose name from childhood we had heard            495
Familiarly, a household term, like those,
The Bedfords, Glosters, Salsburys, of old
Whom the fifth Harry talks of. Silence! hush!
This is no trifler, no short-flighted wit,
No stammerer of a minute, painfully                        500
Delivered. No! the Orator hath yoked
The Hours, like young Aurora, to his car:
Thrice welcome Presence! how can patience e'er
Grow weary of attending on a track
That kindles with such glory! All are charmed,             505

532  to his Car] X *adds line* And stands he not most radiant in his seat?
533 Ａ C D:  D² *as* 1850.

917.40                              Y

The enchantment spreads and rises; all are rapt
Astonish'd; like a Hero in Romance
He winds away his never-ending horn,
Words follow words, sense seems to follow sense;
540 What memory and what logic! till the Strain
Transcendent, superhuman as it is,            [510]
Grows tedious even in a young Man's ear.

These are grave follies: other public Shows
The capital City teems with, of a kind
545 More light, and where but in the holy Church?

541 Transcendent etc.] Work, as it seems, of superhuman power X.
[512–43] not in 𝔄 C. First draft, written into A, runs:
  i  Genius of Burke! forgive the pen seduced
    By specious wonders, and too slow to tell
    Of what the ingenuous and the sensitive,
    All wise men wishing to grow wiser caught
  v  Rapt auditors! from thy most eloquent tongue—
    Now mute, forever mute in the cold grave.
    I see thee stand, stricken with many years
    Stand like an oak whose stag-horn boughs start forth
    Out of his leafy brows, the more to awe
  x  His younger brethren of the grove. Who sits
    Listening beside thee—no—no longer near
    Yet still in heart thy friend. Illustrious Fox
    Thy grateful Pupil. In the power of words
    Thundering and light(e)ning when his turn shall come
 xv  A British Pericles. The times were big
    With change that nightly failed not to provoke
    Keen struggles, and black clouds of passion raised.
    Yet Wisdom like the Goddess from Jove's brain
    Broke forth in armour of resplendent words.
 xx  Who, above all if he were young, and one
    In ancient story versed, whose breast had heaved
    Under the weight of ancient eloquence,
    Could sit, see, hear, ungrateful, uninspired?
x–xxiii stuck over in D: D² as A², but in xiii–xiv reads
      Thy grateful pupil in his turn to rise,
      Thunder, and scatter lightning thro' the realm
which is corr. to who in turn shall rise, Thunder, and etc. And in xvi
      With fearful change that night by night provoked:
D³ E as 1850, except that for [523–32] (launches forth . . . Murmur) they
read:
                  or insists
      Upon the paramount force of social rights
      And that allegiance to which men are born
      Murmur: E² as 1850.
After uninspired: draft in A goes on
      Yet then and there parade of follies, grave
      Or light, grew rank, while other public shews
543 public shows 𝔄 X: spectacles X².      [544–50] stuck in to D.

Astonished; like a hero in romance,
He winds away his never-ending horn;
Words follow words, sense seems to follow sense:
What memory and what logic! till the strain
Transcendent, superhuman, as it seemed,　　510
Grows tedious even in a young man's ear.

Genius of Burke! forgive the pen seduced
By specious wonders, and too slow to tell
Of what the ingenuous, what bewildered men,
Beginning to mistrust their boastful guides,　　515
And wise men, willing to grow wiser, caught,
Rapt auditors! from thy most eloquent tongue—
Now mute, for ever mute in the cold grave.
I see him,—old, but vigorous in age,—
Stand like an oak whose stag-horn branches start　　520
Out of its leafy brow, the more to awe
The younger brethren of the grove. But some—
While he forewarns, denounces, launches forth,
Against all systems built on abstract rights,
Keen ridicule; the majesty proclaims　　525
Of Institutes and Laws, hallowed by time;
Declares the vital power of social ties
Endeared by Custom; and with high disdain,
Exploding upstart Theory, insists
Upon the allegiance to which men are born—　　530
Some—say at once a froward multitude—
Murmur (for truth is hated, where not loved)
As the winds fret within the Æolian cave,
Galled by their monarch's chain. The times were big
With ominous change, which, night by night, provoked
Keen struggles, and black clouds of passion raised;
But memorable moments intervened,　　537
When Wisdom, like the Goddess from Jove's brain,
Broke forth in armour of resplendent words,
Startling the Synod. Could a youth, and one　　540
In ancient story versed, whose breast had heaved
Under the weight of classic eloquence,
Sit, see, and hear, unthankful, uninspired?

Nor did the Pulpit's oratory fail
To achieve its higher triumph. Not unfelt　　545
Were its admonishments, nor lightly heard

There have I seen a comely Bachelor,                    [551]
Fresh from a toilette of two hours, ascend
The Pulpit, with seraphic glance look up,
And, in a tone elaborately low
550 Beginning, lead his voice through many a maze,      [555]
A minuet course, and winding up his mouth,
From time to time into an orifice
Most delicate, a lurking eyelet, small
And only not invisible, again
555 Open it out, diffusing thence a smile               [560]
Of rapt irradiation exquisite.
Meanwhile the Evangelists, Isaiah, Job,
Moses, and he who penn'd the other day
The Death of Abel, Shakspear, Doctor Young,
560 And Ossian, (doubt not, 'tis the naked truth)
Summon'd from streamy Morven, each and all
Must in their turn lend ornament and flowers
To entwine the Crook of eloquence with which         [570]
This pretty Shepherd, pride of all the Plains,
565 Leads up and down his captivated Flock.

I glance but at a few conspicuous marks,
Leaving ten thousand others, that do each,
In Hall or Court, Conventicle, or Shop,               [575]
In public Room or private, Park or Street,
570 With fondness rear'd on his own Pedestal,
Look out for admiration. Folly, vice,
Extravagance in gesture, mien, and dress,
And all the strife of singularity,                    [580]
Lies to the ear, and lies to every sense,
575 Of these, and of the living shapes they wear,
There is no end. Such Candidates for regard,
Although well pleased to be where they were found,
I did not hunt after, or greatly prize,               [585]
Nor made unto myself a secret boast
580 Of reading them with quick and curious eye;
But as a common produce, things that are

[549] domineering, oft E²: paramount there, full oft  D² E.
558 the other day  A D²: in these our days  A² C D.
559 Doctor Young 𝔄: and the Bard Of night who spangled . . . stars *as*
1850, A² C D:  D² *as* 1850.
563–5  A² C *as* 1850.       567–71 𝔄 C D:  D² *as* 1850.
573 Vain boasting affectation [       ] X:  X² *as* 𝔄.

The awful truths delivered thence by tongues
Endowed with various power to search the soul;
Yet ostentation, domineering, oft
Poured forth harangues, how sadly out of place!—   550
There have I seen a comely bachelor,
Fresh from a toilette of two hours, ascend
His rostrum, with seraphic glance look up,
And, in a tone elaborately low
Beginning, lead his voice through many a maze   555
A minuet course; and, winding up his mouth,
From time to time, into an orifice
Most delicate, a lurking eyelet, small,
And only not invisible, again
Open it out, diffusing thence a smile   560
Of rapt irradiation, exquisite.
Meanwhile the Evangelists, Isaiah, Job,
Moses, and he who penned, the other day,
The Death of Abel, Shakspeare, and the Bard
Whose genius spangled o'er a gloomy theme   565
With fancies thick as his inspiring stars,
And Ossian (doubt not, 'tis the naked truth)
Summoned from streamy Morven—each and all
Would, in their turns, lend ornaments and flowers
To entwine the crook of eloquence that helped   570
This pretty Shepherd, pride of all the plains,
To rule and guide his captivated flock.

    I glance but at a few conspicuous marks,
Leaving a thousand others, that, in hall,
Court, theatre, conventicle, or shop,   575
In public room or private, park or street,
Each fondly reared on his own pedestal,
Looked out for admiration. Folly, vice,
Extravagance in gesture, mien, and dress,
And all the strife of singularity,   580
Lies to the ear, and lies to every sense—
Of these, and of the living shapes they wear,
There is no end. Such candidates for regard,
Although well pleased to be where they were found,
I did not hunt after, nor greatly prize,   585
Nor made unto myself a secret boast
Of reading them with quick and curious eye;
But, as a common produce, things that are

To-day, to-morrow will be, took of them

Such willing note as, on some errand bound　　　　[590]

Of pleasure or of Love some Traveller might,

585 Among a thousand other images,

Of sea-shells that bestud the sandy beach,

Or daisies swarming through the fields in June.


But foolishness, and madness in parade,

Though most at home in this their dear domain,　　[595]

590 Are scatter'd everywhere, no rarities,

Even to the rudest novice of the Schools.　　　　[597]

O Friend! one feeling was there which belong'd

To this great City, by exclusive right;

How often in the overflowing Streets,　　　　　　[626]

595 Have I gone forward with the Crowd, and said

Unto myself, the face of every one

That passes by me is a mystery.


584–5 𝔄 C: A² *as* 1850.

592–3 𝔄 C D E: E² *deletes and adds* [598–625]; *cf.* VIII. 839–59.

594 A sentiment that stood far far aloof

　　From all obtrusive individual sights

　　And every petty effort that cried out

　　For notice. Oft in the overflowing streets X: X² *illegible*: X³ *as* 𝔄.

[598–9] Well might it please me more to mark and keep

　　In Memory, how that vast abiding-place

　　Of human creatures turn where I might was sown

　　Profusely sown with individual sights E: E² *as* 1850.

To-day, to-morrow will be, took of them
Such willing note, as, on some errand bound          590
That asks not speed, a Traveller might bestow
On sea-shells that bestrew the sandy beach,
Or daisies swarming through the fields of June.

But foolishness and madness in parade,
Though most at home in this their dear domain,          595
Are scattered everywhere, no rarities,
Even to the rudest novice of the Schools.
Me, rather, it employed, to note, and keep
In memory, those individual sights
Of courage, or integrity, or truth,          600
Or tenderness, which there, set off by foil,
Appeared more touching. One will I select;
A Father—for he bore that sacred name—
Him saw I, sitting in an open square,
Upon a corner-stone of that low wall,          605
Wherein were fixed the iron pales that fenced
A spacious grass-plot; there, in silence, sate
This One Man, with a sickly babe outstretched
Upon his knee, whom he had thither brought
For sunshine, and to breathe the fresher air.          610
Of those who passed, and me who looked at him,
He took no heed; but in his brawny arms
(The Artificer was to the elbow bare,
And from his work this moment had been stolen)
He held the child, and, bending over it,          615
As if he were afraid both of the sun
And of the air, which he had come to seek,
Eyed the poor babe with love unutterable.

As the black storm upon the mountain top
Sets off the sunbeam in the valley, so          620
That huge fermenting mass of human-kind
Serves as a solemn back-ground, or relief,
To single forms and objects, whence they draw,
For feeling and contemplative regard,
More than inherent liveliness and power.          625
How oft, amid those overflowing streets,
Have I gone forward with the crowd, and said
Unto myself, 'The face of every one
That passes by me is a mystery!'

Thus have I look'd, nor ceas'd to look, oppress'd     [630]
By thoughts of what, and whither, when and how,
600 Until the shapes before my eyes became
A second-sight procession, such as glides
Over still mountains, or appears in dreams;
And all the ballast of familiar life,
The present, and the past; hope, fear; all stays,
605 All laws of acting, thinking, speaking man
Went from me, neither knowing me, nor known.
And once, far-travell'd in such mood, beyond     [635]
The reach of common indications, lost
Amid the moving pageant, 'twas my chance
610 Abruptly to be smitten with the view
Of a blind Beggar, who, with upright face,
Stood propp'd against a Wall, upon his Chest     [640]
Wearing a written paper, to explain
The story of the Man, and who he was.
615 My mind did at this spectacle turn round
As with the might of waters, and it seem'd
To me that in this Label was a type,
Or emblem, of the utmost that we know,     [645]
Both of ourselves and of the universe;
620 And, on the shape of the unmoving man,
His fixèd face and sightless eyes, I look'd
As if admonish'd from another world.


Though rear'd upon the base of outward things,     [650]
These, chiefly, are such structures as the mind
625 Builds for itself. Scenes different there are,
Full-form'd, which take, with small internal help,
Possession of the faculties; the peace
Of night, for instance, the solemnity     [655]
Of nature's intermediate hours of rest,
630 When the great tide of human life stands still,
The business of the day to come unborn,
Of that gone by, lock'd up as in the grave;
The calmness, beauty, of the spectacle,     [660]
Sky, stillness, moonshine, empty streets, and sounds
635 Unfrequent as in desarts; at late hours

603–6 𝔄: A *deletes*, B *queries*; *not in* C.

Thus have I looked, nor ceased to look, oppressed            630
By thoughts of what and whither, when and how,
Until the shapes before my eyes became
A second-sight procession, such as glides
Over still mountains, or appears in dreams;
And once, far-travelled in such mood, beyond            635
The reach of common indication, lost
Amid the moving pageant, I was smitten
Abruptly, with the view (a sight not rare)
Of a blind Beggar, who, with upright face,
Stood, propped against a wall, upon his chest            640
Wearing a written paper, to explain
His story, whence he came, and who he was.
Caught by the spectacle my mind turned round
As with the might of waters; an apt type
This label seemed of the utmost we can know,            645
Both of ourselves and of the universe;
And, on the shape of that unmoving man,
His steadfast face and sightless eyes, I gazed,
As if admonished from another world.


Though reared upon the base of outward things,            650
Structures like these the excited spirit mainly
Builds for herself; scenes different there are,
Full-formed, that take, with small internal help,
Possession of the faculties,—the peace
That comes with night; the deep solemnity            655
Of nature's intermediate hours of rest,
When the great tide of human life stands still;
The business of the day to come, unborn,
Of that gone by, locked up, as in the grave;
The blended calmness of the heavens and earth,            660
Moonlight and stars, and empty streets, and sounds
Unfrequent as in deserts; at late hours

609–10 𝔄 C D E: E² *as* 1850.
615-21 𝔄 C: A² D E *as* 1850, *but* look'd *for* gazed (E²).
624-5 𝔄 C D: D² E *as* 1850, *but* doth mainly Build: E² *as* 1850.
628 Of night for instance, the solemnity 𝔄 C: Of drowsy night, the deep
solemnity A² D: D² *as* 1850.
628–9 Of midnight, nature's intermediate rest  X: X² *as* 1850.
633-4 𝔄 C D: D² *as* 1850.

Of winter evenings when unwholesome rains
Are falling hard, with people yet astir,
The feeble salutation from the voice          [665]
Of some unhappy Woman, now and then
640 Heard as we pass; when no one looks about,
Nothing is listen'd to. But these, I fear,
Are falsely catalogu'd, things that are, are not,
Even as we give them welcome, or assist,          [670]
Are prompt, or are remiss. What say you then,
645 To times, when half the City shall break out
Full of one passion, vengeance, rage, or fear,
To executions, to a Street on fire,
Mobs, riots, or rejoicings? From these sights          [675]
Take one, an annual Festival, the Fair
650 Holden where Martyrs suffer'd in past time,
And named of Saint Bartholomew; there see
A work that's finish'd to our hands, that lays,
If any spectacle on earth can do,          [680]
The whole creative powers of man asleep!
655 For once the Muse's help will we implore,
And she shall lodge us, wafted on her wings,
Above the press and danger of the Crowd,
Upon some Showman's platform: what a hell          [685]
For eyes and ears! what anarchy and din
660 Barbarian and infernal! 'tis a dream,
Monstrous in colour, motion, shape, sight, sound.
Below, the open space, through every nook
Of the wide area, twinkles, is alive          [690]
With heads; the midway region and above
665 Is throng'd with staring pictures, and huge scrolls,
Dumb proclamations of the prodigies;
And chattering monkeys dangling from their poles,
And children whirling in their roundabouts;          [695]
With those that stretch the neck, and strain the eyes,
670 And crack the voice in rivalship, the crowd
Inviting; with buffoons against buffoons
Grimacing, writhing, screaming; him who grinds
The hurdy-gurdy, at the fiddle weaves;          [700]
Rattles the salt-box, thumps the kettle-drum,

643–5 Just as we give them welcome or assist
         Prompt or remiss. What say you then to times
         When half the populous City shall break out  A² D:  D² *as* 1850.

Of winter evenings, when unwholesome rains
Are falling hard, with people yet astir,
The feeble salutation from the voice                          665
Of some unhappy woman, now and then
Heard as we pass, when no one looks about,
Nothing is listened to. But these, I fear,
Are falsely catalogued; things that are, are not,
As the mind answers to them, or the heart                     670
Is prompt, or slow, to feel. What say you, then,
To times, when half the city shall break out
Full of one passion, vengeance, rage, or fear?
To executions, to a street on fire,
Mobs, riots, or rejoicings? From these sights                 675
Take one,—that ancient festival, the Fair,
Holden where martyrs suffered in past time,
And named of St. Bartholomew; there, see
A work completed to our hands, that lays,
If any spectacle on earth can do,                             680
The whole creative powers of man asleep!—
For once, the Muse's help will we implore,
And she shall lodge us, wafted on her wings,
Above the press and danger of the crowd,
Upon some showman's platform. What a shock                    685
For eyes and ears! what anarchy and din,
Barbarian and infernal,—a phantasma,
Monstrous in colour, motion, shape, sight, sound!
Below, the open space, through every nook
Of the wide area, twinkles, is alive                          690
With heads; the midway region, and above,
Is thronged with staring pictures and huge scrolls,
Dumb proclamations of the Prodigies;
With chattering monkeys dangling from their poles,
And children whirling in their roundabouts;                   695
With those that stretch the neck and strain the eyes,
And crack the voice in rivalship, the crowd
Inviting; with buffoons against buffoons
Grimacing, writhing, screaming,—him who grinds
The hurdy-gurdy, at the fiddle weaves,                        700
Rattles the salt-box, thumps the kettle-drum,

649 annual 𝔄 C D: ancient E.
652 that's finish'd 𝔄: completed A² B² C.
658 hell] shock A² B² C.          660 'tis a dream] a phantasma A² C.

675   And him who at the trumpet puffs his cheeks,
      The silver collar'd Negro with his timbrel,
      Equestrians, Tumblers, Women, Girls, and Boys,
      Blue-breech'd, pink-vested, and with towering plumes.
      —All moveables of wonder from all parts,                          [706]
680   Are here, Albinos, painted Indians, Dwarfs,
      The Horse of Knowledge, and the learned Pig,
      The Stone-eater, the Man that swallows fire,
      Giants, Ventriloquists, the Invisible Girl,                       [710]
      The Bust that speaks, and moves its goggling eyes,
685   The Wax-work, Clock-work, all the marvellous craft
      Of modern Merlins, wild Beasts, Puppet-shows,
      All out-o'-th'-way, far-fetch'd, perverted things,
      All freaks of Nature, all Promethean thoughts                     [715]
      Of Man; his dulness, madness, and their feats,
690   All jumbled up together to make up
      This Parliament of Monsters. Tents and Booths
      Meanwhile, as if the whole were one vast Mill,
      Are vomiting, receiving, on all sides,                            [720]
      Men, Women, three-years' Children, Babes in arms.

695     Oh, blank confusion! and a type not false
      Of what the mighty City is itself
      To all except a Straggler here and there,
      To the whole Swarm of its inhabitants;
      An undistinguishable world to men,
700   The slaves unrespited of low pursuits,
      Living amid the same perpetual flow                               [725]
      Of trivial objects, melted and reduced
      To one identity, by differences
      That have no law, no meaning, and no end;
705   Oppression under which even highest minds
      Must labour, whence the strongest are not free;                   [730]
      But though the picture weary out the eye,
      By nature an unmanageable sight,
      It is not wholly so to him who looks
710   In steadiness, who hath among least things
      An under-sense of greatest; sees the parts                        [735]
      As parts, but with a feeling of the whole.

                 690 make up 𝔄 C D E: compose A² B² D² E².
                 695 a type not false 𝔄 C D: true epitome D².
                    Oh blank confusion strange reality

And him who at the trumpet puffs his cheeks,
The silver-collared Negro with his timbrel,
Equestrians, tumblers, women, girls, and boys,
Blue-breeched, pink-vested, with high-towering plumes.  705
All moveables of wonder, from all parts,
Are here—Albinos, painted Indians, Dwarfs,
The Horse of knowledge, and the learned Pig,
The Stone-eater, the man that swallows fire,
Giants, Ventriloquists, the Invisible Girl,                 710
The Bust that speaks and moves its goggling eyes,
The Wax-work, Clock-work, all the marvellous craft
Of modern Merlins, Wild Beasts, Puppet-shows,
All out-o'-the-way, far-fetched, perverted things,
All freaks of nature, all Promethean thoughts            715
Of man, his dullness, madness, and their feats
All jumbled up together, to compose
A Parliament of Monsters. Tents and Booths
Meanwhile, as if the whole were one vast mill,
Are vomiting, receiving on all sides,                       720
Men, Women, three-years Children, Babes in arms.

Oh, blank confusion! true epitome
Of what the mighty City is herself
To thousands upon thousands of her sons,
Living amid the same perpetual whirl                       725
Of trivial objects, melted and reduced
To one identity, by differences
That have no law, no meaning, and no end—
Oppression, under which even highest minds
Must labour, whence the strongest are not free.          730
But though the picture weary out the eye,
By nature an unmanageable sight,
It is not wholly so to him who looks
In steadiness, who hath among least things
An under-sense of greatest; sees the parts                735
As parts, but with a feeling of the whole.

Surpassing aught that wildest Fancy e'er
Conceived or grasp'd in a distemper'd [   ?   ] B².
696 itself 𝔄: herself B².
697–700 To thousands and ten thousands of her sons  D E: E² *as* 1850.
*In* E *follows line* 700, *against which is written in pencil* out
698 𝔄: To the main flock of her B².
701 flow 𝔄 C D: strife D² E: whirl E².

This, of all acquisitions first, awaits
On sundry and most widely different modes
715 Of education; nor with least delight
On that through which I pass'd. Attention comes,        [740]
And comprehensiveness and memory,
From early converse with the works of God
Among all regions; chiefly where appear
720 Most obviously simplicity and power.                   [744]
By influence habitual to the mind
The mountain's outline and its steady form
Gives a pure grandeur, and its presence shapes
The measure and the prospect of the soul              [755]
725 To majesty; such virtue have the forms
Perennial of the ancient hills; nor less
The changeful language of their countenances
Gives movement to the thoughts, and multitude,
With order and relation. This, if still,               [761]
730 As hitherto, with freedom I may speak,
And the same perfect openness of mind,
Not violating any just restraint,
As I would hope, of real modesty,
This did I feel in that vast receptacle.               [765]
735 The Spirit of Nature was upon me here;
The Soul of Beauty and enduring life
Was present as a habit, and diffused,
Through meagre lines and colours, and the press
Of self-destroying, transitory things                  [770]
740 Composure and ennobling Harmony.

734 𝔄 C D:  D² *as* 1850.
            This I had cause to feel tho' then I took
            No note thereof in that vast receptacle  X.
736 enduring] eternal  X.
737 A² C *as* 1850.

This, of all acquisitions, first awaits
On sundry and most widely different modes
Of education, nor with least delight
On that through which I passed. Attention springs, 740
And comprehensiveness and memory flow,
From early converse with the works of God
Among all regions; chiefly where appear
Most obviously simplicity and power.
Think, how the everlasting streams and woods, 745
Stretched and still stretching far and wide, exalt
The roving Indian, on his desert sands:
What grandeur not unfelt, what pregnant show
Of beauty, meets the sun-burnt Arab's eye:
And, as the sea propels, from zone to zone, 750
Its currents; magnifies its shoals of life
Beyond all compass; spreads, and sends aloft
Armies of clouds,—even so, its powers and aspects
Shape for mankind, by principles as fixed,
The views and aspirations of the soul 755
To majesty. Like virtue have the forms
Perennial of the ancient hills; nor less
The changeful language of their countenances
Quickens the slumbering mind, and aids the thoughts,
However multitudinous, to move 760
With order and relation. This, if still,
As hitherto, in freedom I may speak,
Not violating any just restraint,
As may be hoped, of real modesty,—
This did I feel, in London's vast domain. 765
The Spirit of Nature was upon me there;
The soul of Beauty and enduring Life
Vouchsafed her inspiration, and diffused,
Through meagre lines and colours, and the press
Of self-destroying, transitory things, 770
Composure, and ennobling Harmony.

[745–60] D *stuck over.*
[747–9] Indian, . . . Arab's eye E[2]: Indian. On his desart sands
　　　　What grandeur meets the sunburnt Arab's eye D[2] E.
　[753] even so, its powers and aspects D[3] E[2]: God's visible presence there
D[2] E.

# BOOK EIGHTH

## RETROSPECT.—LOVE OF NATURE LEADING TO LOVE OF MANKIND

WHAT sounds are those, Helvellyn, which are heard
Up to thy summit? Through the depth of air
Ascending, as if distance had the power
To make the sounds more audible: what Crowd
5 Is yon, assembled in the gay green Field?                    [5]
Crowd seems it, solitary Hill! to thee,
Though but a little Family of Men,
Twice twenty, with their Children and their Wives,
And here and there a Stranger interspers'd.                    [10]
10 It is a summer festival, a Fair,
Such as, on this side now, and now on that,
Repeated through his tributary Vales,
Helvellyn, in the silence of his rest,
Sees annually, if storms be not abroad,                        [15]
15 And mists have left him an unshrouded head.
Delightful day it is for all who dwell
In this secluded Glen, and eagerly
They give it welcome. Long ere heat of noon                    [20]
Behold the cattle are driven down; the sheep
20 That have for traffic been cull'd out are penn'd
In cotes that stand together on the Plain
Ranged side by side; the chaffering is begun.
The Heifer lows uneasy at the voice
Of a new Master, bleat the Flocks aloud;
25 Booths are there none; a Stall or two is here,               [25]
A lame Man, or a blind, the one to beg,
The other to make music; hither, too,
From far, with Basket, slung upon her arm,

[MSS. for Bk. VIII: A B C D E: *for ll.* 68–*end* Y; *for ll.* 221–310 J.]
BOOK EIGHTH: Retrospect *etc.* B. Book Eighth C. 8 A.
3 had the 𝔄 C D E²: lacked not D² E.
5, 6 𝔄 C D: What crowd is yonder, in the gay green croft
    Espied, crowd seems it, solitary hill, to thee D² E.
    Behold we yonder *deleted* E²: E³ *as* 1850.
  8 Twice twenty, 𝔄 C: Attended by A²: Mere shepherds C² D: D² E *as*
1850. Children and their wives 𝔄 C D E²: wives and little ones E.

# BOOK EIGHTH

## RETROSPECT.—LOVE OF NATURE LEADING TO LOVE OF MAN

WHAT sounds are those, Helvellyn, that are heard
Up to thy summit, through the depth of air
Ascending, as if distance had the power
To make the sounds more audible ? What crowd
Covers, or sprinkles o'er, yon village green ?                    5
Crowd seems it, solitary hill ! to thee,
Though but a little family of men,
Shepherds and tillers of the ground—betimes
Assembled with their children and their wives,
And here and there a stranger interspersed.                       10
They hold a rustic fair—a festival,
Such as, on this side now, and now on that,
Repeated through his tributary vales,
Helvellyn, in the silence of his rest,
Sees annually, if clouds towards either ocean                     15
Blown from their favourite resting-place, or mists
Dissolved, have left him an unshrouded head.
Delightful day it is for all who dwell
In this secluded glen, and eagerly
They give it welcome. Long ere heat of noon,                      20
From byre or field the kine were brought ; the sheep
Are penned in cotes ; the chaffering is begun.
The heifer lows, uneasy at the voice
Of a new master ; bleat the flocks aloud.
Booths are there none ; a stall or two is here ;                  25
A lame man or a blind, the one to beg,
The other to make music ; hither, too,
From far, with basket, slung upon her arm,

10 It is a Festival, a rustic fair  A².
   They hold a rustic fair—a festival  D E².
   Amid the throng they hold a rustic fair  D² E.
14–15 𝔄 C D E: D² E² *as* 1850.
16 Delightful day for those whose lives are past  A².
16–18 It is a summer Festival, a Fair,
       The only one which that secluded Glen
       Has to be proud of. Long ere heat of noon *Letter* June–July 1805.
19 A C D E: E² *as* 1850.
20–21 That have for this day's traffic been cull'd out
       Are penn'd in cotes together on the Plain A² C.

Of Hawker's Wares, books, pictures, combs, and pins,
30 Some aged Woman finds her way again,                    [30]
Year after year a punctual Visitant!
The Showman with his Freight upon his Back,
And once, perchance, in lapse of many years
Prouder Itinerant, Mountebank, or He                    [35]
35 Whose Wonders in a cover'd Wain lie hid.
But One is here, the loveliest of them all,
Some sweet Lass of the Valley, looking out
For gains, and who that sees her would not buy?
Fruits of her Father's Orchard, apples, pears,          [40]
40 (On that day only to such office stooping)
She carries in her Basket, and walks round
Among the crowd, half pleas'd with, half ashamed
Of her new calling, blushing restlessly.
The Children now are rich, the old Man now
45 Is generous; so gaiety prevails                        [45]
Which all partake of, Young and Old. Immense           [55]
Is the Recess, the circumambient World
Magnificent, by which they are embraced.
They move about upon the soft green field:
50 How little They, they and their doings seem,
Their herds and flocks about them, they themselves,
And all that they can further or obstruct!              [60]
Through utter weakness pitiably dear
As tender Infants are: and yet how great!
55 For all things serve them; them the Morning light
Loves as it glistens on the silent rocks,
And them the silent Rocks, which now from high          [65]
Look down upon them; the reposing Clouds,
The lurking Brooks from their invisible haunts,
60 And Old Helvellyn, conscious of the stir,

29 pins, C: pins 𝔄.
32 The showman on his back bearing [    ] D: The stout man bent under
his raree show D² (*deleted*): D³ *as* 1850.      33 𝔄 C D: D² *as* 1850.
39–41 𝔄 C D (*but* on that day *for* apples, pears, D): D² *as* 1850.
45–48 𝔄 C D E.
                    Is generous or haply if the sire
                    Content with looking on should sit apart
                    'A cheerful smile *etc, as* 1850  E².
                              . . . sit apart
                    And single, or in converse with his mate
                    Memory's dear partner, hope's unfailing stay
                    'A cheerful smile *etc.*  E³: E⁴ *as* 1850.

Of hawker's wares—books, pictures, combs, and pins—
Some aged woman finds her way again,                    30
Year after year, a punctual visitant!
There also stands a speech-maker by rote,
Pulling the strings of his boxed raree-show;
And in the lapse of many years may come
Prouder itinerant, mountebank, or he                    35
Whose wonders in a covered wain lie hid.
But one there is, the loveliest of them all,
Some sweet lass of the valley, looking out
For gains, and who that sees her would not buy?
Fruits of her father's orchard, are her wares,          40
And with the ruddy produce, she walks round
Among the crowd, half pleased with half ashamed
Of her new office, blushing restlessly.
The children now are rich, for the old to-day
Are generous as the young; and, if content             45
With looking on, some ancient wedded pair
Sit in the shade together, while they gaze,
'A cheerful smile unbends the wrinkled brow,
The days departed start again to life,
And all the scenes of childhood reappear,               50
Faint, but more tranquil, like the changing sun
To him who slept at noon and wakes at eve.'
Thus gaiety and cheerfulness prevail,
Spreading from young to old, from old to young,
And no one seems to want his share.—Immense            55
Is the recess, the circumambient world
Magnificent, by which they are embraced:
They move about upon the soft green turf:
How little they, they and their doings, seem,
And all that they can further or obstruct!              60
Through utter weakness pitiably dear,
As tender infants are: and yet how great!
For all things serve them: them the morning light
Loves, as it glistens on the silent rocks;
And them the silent rocks, which now from high          65
Look down upon them; the reposing clouds;
The wild brooks prattling from invisible haunts;
And old Helvellyn, conscious of the stir

49 field 𝔄 C D: fields E: turf E².
59 from 𝔄 E²: mid A² C D E.

And the blue Sky that roofs their calm abode.

With deep devotion, Nature, did I feel                    [70]
In that great City what I owed to thee,
High thoughts of God and Man, and love of Man,
65  Triumphant over all those loathsome sights
Of wretchedness and vice; a watchful eye,
Which with the outside of our human life
Not satisfied, must read the inner mind;
For I already had been taught to love
70  My Fellow-beings, to such habits train'd
Among the woods and mountains, where I found
In thee a gracious Guide, to lead me forth
Beyond the bosom of my Family,
My Friends and youthful Playmates. 'Twas thy power
75  That rais'd the first complacency in me,
And noticeable kindliness of heart,                    [124]
Love human to the Creature in himself
As he appear'd, a stranger in my path,
Before my eyes a Brother of this world;
80  Thou first didst with those motions of delight
Inspire me.—I remember, far from home
Once having stray'd, while yet a very Child,
I saw a sight, and with what joy and love!
It was a day of exhalations, spread
85  Upon the mountains, mists and steam-like fogs
Redounding everywhere, not vehement,
But calm and mild, gentle and beautiful,
With gleams of sunshine on the eyelet spots
And loop-holes of the hills, wherever seen,
90  Hidden by quiet process, and as soon
Unfolded, to be huddled up again:
Along a narrow Valley and profound
I journey'd, when, aloft above my head,
Emerging from the silvery vapours, lo!
95  A Shepherd and his Dog! in open day:
Girt round with mists they stood and look'd about
From that enclosure small, inhabitants
Of an aerial Island floating on,
As seem'd, with that Abode in which they were,
100  A little pendant area of grey rocks,
By the soft wind breath'd forward. With delight

Which animates this day their calm abode.

With deep devotion, Nature, did I feel,                    70
In that enormous City's turbulent world
Of men and things, what benefit I owed
To thee, and those domains of rural peace,

55–61 A *supplies this alternative version*:
        For all things serve them, serve them for delight
        Or profit from the moment when the dawn
        Ah surely not without attendant gleams
        Of heart illumination strikes the sense
        With its first glistening on the silent rock
        Whose evening shadows led them to repose
        And doubt ye that these solitudes are paced
        By tutelary Powers more safely versed
        In weal and woe than aught that fabling Greece
        Invented, Spirits gentle and benign
        Who now perhaps from yon reposing cloud
        Look down upon them or frequent the ridge
        Of old Helvellyn listening to the stir
        That with this ancient Festival returns
        To animate and chear their calm abode.

61 [69] A̶ C D E: E² *as* 1850.

64 love of] hope in A² C.

71–72 Amid those regions where in thee I found
        A guide that led the young affections forth A².

[70–87] D *stuck over*: D² *as* 1850.

74–83 My friends and playmates, ne'er shall I forget
        The kindliness a simple pastoral sight
        Raised in me once while yet a very child
        On careless pastime bent and far from home A³.

81–85                        I remember, on a day
        Of summer, while the mountains were involved
        With exhalations, mists, *etc.* A² C (*but* C *omits* involved).

85 steam-like fogs] fogs like smoke Y.

*After* 86 Y *has extra line*:
        Like those which have been recently described

93 I journey'd on, when high above my head Y.

96–97 and looked about] ... and forth did look B². A *deletes* and **looked
about** ... small: *not in* C.

98 Of an aerial and a floating Isle A² C.

99 A *deletes*: *not in* C.

As bland almost, one Evening I beheld,
And at as early age (the spectacle
Is common, but by me was then first seen)
105 A Shepherd in the bottom of a Vale
Towards the centre standing, who with voice,
And hand waved to and fro as need required
Gave signal to his Dog, thus teaching him
To chace along the mazes of steep crags
110 The Flock he could not see: and so the Brute
Dear Creature! with a Man's intelligence
Advancing, or retreating on his steps,
Through every pervious strait, to right or left,
Thridded a way unbaffled; while the Flock
115 Fled upwards from the terror of his Bark
Through rocks and seams of turf with liquid gold
Irradiate, that deep farewell light by which
The setting sun proclaims the love he bears
To mountain regions.
                    Beauteous the domain
120 Where to the sense of beauty first my heart
Was open'd, tract more exquisitely fair                    [75]
Than is that Paradise of ten thousand Trees,
Or Gehol's famous Gardens, in a Clime
Chosen from widest Empire, for delight
125 Of the Tartarian Dynasty composed;
(Beyond that mighty Wall, not fabulous,
China's stupendous mound!) by patient skill                    [80]
Of myriads, and boon Nature's lavish help;
Scene link'd to scene, an evergrowing change,
130 Soft, grand, or gay! with Palaces and Domes
Of Pleasure spangled over, shady Dells                    [85]
For Eastern Monasteries, sunny Mounds
With Temples crested, Bridges, Gondolas,
Rocks, Dens, and Groves of foliage taught to melt
135 Into each other their obsequious hues
Going and gone again, in subtile chace,                    [90]
Too fine to be pursued; or standing forth
In no discordant opposition, strong
And gorgeous as the colours side by side
140 Bedded among rich plumes of Tropic Birds;
And mountains over all embracing all;                    [95]
And all the landscape endlessly enrich'd

Where to the sense of beauty first my heart
Was opened; tract more exquisitely fair                     75
Than that famed paradise of ten thousand trees,
Or Gehol's matchless gardens, for delight
Of the Tartarian dynasty composed
(Beyond that mighty wall, not fabulous,
China's stupendous mound) by patient toil                   80
Of myriads and boon nature's lavish help;
There, in a clime from widest empire chosen,
Fulfilling (could enchantment have done more?)
A sumptuous dream of flowery lawns, with domes
Of pleasure sprinkled over, shady dells                     85
For eastern monasteries, sunny mounts
With temples crested, bridges, gondolas,
Rocks, dens, and groves of foliage taught to melt
Into each other their obsequious hues,
Vanished and vanishing in subtle chase,                     90
Too fine to be pursued; or standing forth
In no discordant opposition, strong
And gorgeous as the colours side by side
Bedded among rich plumes of tropic birds;
And mountains over all, embracing all;                      95
And all the landscape, endlessly enriched

103–4 A *deletes*, C *retains*.
108 thus teaching him 𝔄: instructed thus A² B² C.
111 *not in* C: With his own speed and Man's intelligence A².
114 a way Y B²: his way B³: away 𝔄 C.
134 Rocks dens and caves and forests taught to melt Y: Y² *as* 𝔄.
136 Going and gone again A C: Vanished and vanishing A².

With waters running, falling, or asleep.

But lovelier far than this the Paradise
145 Where I was rear'd; in Nature's primitive gifts
Favor'd no less, and more to every sense                    [100]
Delicious, seeing that the sun and sky,
The elements and seasons in their change
Do find their dearest Fellow-labourer there,
150 The heart of Man, a district on all sides
The fragrance breathing of humanity,
Man free, man working for himself, with choice
Of time, and place, and object; by his wants,                [105]
His comforts, native occupations, cares,
155 Conducted on to individual ends
Or social, and still followed by a train
Unwoo'd, unthought-of even, simplicity,
And beauty, and inevitable grace.                            [110]

Yea, doubtless, at an age when but a glimpse
160 Of those resplendent Gardens, with their frame
Imperial, and elaborate ornaments,
Would to a child be transport over-great,
When but a half-hour's roam through such a place
Would leave behind a dance of images
165 That shall break in upon his sleep for weeks;             [115]
Even then the common haunts of the green earth,
With the ordinary human interests
Which they embosom, all without regard
As both may seem, are fastening on the heart
170 Insensibly, each with the other's help,                   [120]
So that we love, not knowing that we love,
And feel, not knowing whence our feeling comes.

Such league have these two principles of joy
In our affections. I have singled out
175 Some moments, the earliest that I could, in which
Their several currents blended into one,
Weak yet, and gathering imperceptibly,
Flow'd in by gushes. My first human love,
As hath been mention'd, did incline to those
180 Whose occupations and concerns were most
Illustrated by Nature and adorn'd,                           [127]
And Shepherds were the men who pleas'd me first.

With waters running, falling, or asleep.

But lovelier far than this, the paradise
Where I was reared; in Nature's primitive gifts
Favoured no less, and more to every sense                    100
Delicious, seeing that the sun and sky,
The elements, and seasons as they change,
Do find a worthy fellow-labourer there—
Man free, man working for himself, with choice
Of time, and place, and object; by his wants,                105
His comforts, native occupations, cares,
Cheerfully led to individual ends
Or social, and still followed by a train
Unwooed, unthought-of even—simplicity,
And beauty, and inevitable grace.                            110

Yea, when a glimpse of those imperial bowers
Would to a child be transport over-great,
When but a half-hour's roam through such a place
Would leave behind a dance of images,
That shall break in upon his sleep for weeks;               115
Even then the common haunts of the green earth,
And ordinary interests of man,
Which they embosom, all without regard
As both may seem, are fastening on the heart
Insensibly, each with the other's help.                     120
For me, when my affections first were led
From kindred, friends, and playmates, to partake
Love for the human creature's absolute self,
That noticeable kindliness of heart
Sprang out of fountains, there abounding most               125
Where sovereign Nature dictated the tasks
And occupations which her beauty adorned,
And Shepherds were the men that pleased me first;

149 their dearest] a worthy A² C.        150–1 A *deletes*; *not in* C.
159–72 *For alternative passage in* Y *v. notes.*
167 With the ordinary interests of man D E: E² *as* 1850.
171–91 C *has some rough pencillings of later version, which in* D *is stuck over earlier version. In place of* [122] D² E *read* Beyond the bosom of my family My friends and playmates, to participate (D³ E² *as* 1850), *and after* [123] E *has* As he appeared a stranger in my path (*marked* 'out'): [125] From casual fountains flowed, abounding there D² E: E² *as* 1850. *After* [128] D² E *have* Not such, tho' imagination played around them: [136] D² wind; D³ fate.

Not such as in Arcadian Fastnesses
Sequester'd, handed down among themselves,
185 So ancient Poets sing, the golden Age;
Nor such, a second Race, allied to these,
As Shakespeare in the Wood of Arden plac'd
Where Phoebe sigh'd for the false Ganymede,                    [141]
Or there where Florizel and Perdita
190 Together danc'd, Queen of the Feast and King;
Nor such as Spenser fabled. True it is,
That I had heard (what he perhaps had seen)                    [145]
Of Maids at sunrise bringing in from far
Their May-bush, and along the Streets, in flocks,
195 Parading with a Song of taunting Rhymes,
Aim'd at the Laggards slumbering within doors;
Had also heard, from those who yet remember'd,                    [150]
Tales of the May-pole Dance, and flowers that deck'd
The Posts and the Kirk-pillars, and of Youths,
200 That each one with his Maid, at break of day,
By annual custom issued forth in troops,
To drink the waters of some favorite well,
And hang it round with Garlands. This, alas!
Was but a dream; the times had scatter'd all
205 These lighter graces, and the rural ways
And manners which it was my chance to see                    [160]
In childhood were severe and unadorn'd,
The unluxuriant produce of a life
Intent on little but substantial needs,

183 Not such as in the depths of Arcady  Y.
183–5 Not such as by the changes of the world
    Unbreath'd upon, preserv'd from sire to son
    Among Arcadian fastnesses, so sing
    The bards of ancient Greece, the golden age  A² C.
186–7 Nor such as by the changes of the world
    Unbreath'd upon or wishing so to be
    Among the wide spread woods of Arden dwelt  B².
188–90 Where wayward Phoebe, scorning Sylvius, made
    To the false Ganymede her suit, or there
    Where Florizel and beauteous Perdita
    Together danced, King of the Feast, and Queen.  A² C.
194–6 In celebration of thy birth, sweet May!
    A branch of flowery hawthorn, and, in shoals
    And mirthful companies, from street to street
    Parading with a song of taunting Rhymes [rymes A², *W. W.'s hand*]
    Aimed at the laggards slumbering within doors,
    Heedless of spring and morning's pure delight.  A² C.

Not such as Saturn ruled 'mid Latian wilds,
With arts and laws so tempered, that their lives        130
Left, even to us toiling in this late day,
A bright tradition of the golden age;
Not such as, 'mid Arcadian fastnesses
Sequestered, handed down among themselves
Felicity, in Grecian song renowned;        135
Nor such as, when an adverse fate had driven,
From house and home, the courtly band whose fortunes
Entered, with Shakespeare's genius, the wild woods
Of Arden, amid sunshine or in shade,
Culled the best fruits of Time's uncounted hours,        140
Ere Phoebe sighed for the false Ganymede;
Or there where Perdita and Florizel
Together danced, Queen of the feast, and King;
Nor such as Spenser fabled. True it is,
That I had heard (what he perhaps had seen)        145
Of maids at sunrise bringing in from far
Their May-bush, and along the street in flocks
Parading with a song of taunting rhymes,
Aimed at the laggards slumbering within doors;
Had also heard, from those who yet remembered,        150
Tales of the May-pole dance, and wreaths that decked
Porch, door-way, or kirk-pillar; and of youths,
Each with his maid, before the sun was up,
By annual custom, issuing forth in troops,
To drink the waters of some sainted well,        155
And hang it round with garlands. Love survives;
But, for such purpose, flowers no longer grow:
The times, too sage, perhaps too proud, have dropped
These lighter graces; and the rural ways
And manners which my childhood looked upon        160
Were the unluxuriant produce of a life
Intent on little but substantial needs,

203–7                    Garlands. Love survives
          But for such purpose flowers no longer grow.
          The times too wise, or shall we say too proud
          Have dropped these lighter graces, and the shows
          Of rural manners which I chanced to see
          In childhood *etc.* A³ C.
205 ways 𝔄: customs A².
205–7 These graces and the aspect which I saw
          In child(hood) was severe and unadorn'd Y.

210 Yet beautiful, and beauty that was felt.
But images of danger and distress,
And suffering, these took deepest hold of me,
Man suffering among awful Powers, and Forms;     [165]
Of this I heard and saw enough to make
215 The imagination restless; nor was free
Myself from frequent perils; nor were tales
Wanting, the tragedies of former times,
Or hazards and escapes, which in my walks        [170]
I carried with me among crags and woods
220 And mountains; and of these may here be told
One, as recorded by my Household Dame.

    At the first falling of autumnal snow
A Shepherd and his Son one day went forth
(Thus did the Matron's Tale begin) to seek
225 A Straggler of their Flock. They both had rang'd
Upon this service the preceding day
All over their own pastures and beyond,
And now, at sun-rise sallying out again
Renew'd their search begun where from Dove Crag,
230 Ill home for bird so gentle, they look'd down
On Deep-dale Head, and Brothers-water, named
From those two Brothers that were drown'd therein,
Thence, northward, having pass'd by Arthur's Seat,
To Fairfield's highest summit; on the right
235 Leaving St. Sunday's Pike, to Grisdale Tarn
They shot, and over that cloud-loving Hill,
Seat Sandal, a fond lover of the clouds;
Thence up Helvellyn, a superior Mount
With prospect underneath of Striding-Edge,
240 And Grisdale's houseless Vale, along the brink
Of Russet Cove, and those two other Coves,
Huge skeletons of crags, which from the trunk
Of old Helvellyn spread their arms abroad,
And make a stormy harbour for the winds.
245 Far went those Shepherds in their devious quest,
From mountain ridges peeping as they pass'd
Down into every Glen: at length the Boy
Said, 'Father, with your leave I will go back,

*Between* 209 *and* 210 Y *has*
        Set off by Nature's weekday help alone.
210 beautiful, and 𝔄 C D: rich in beauty E.

Yet rich in beauty, beauty that was felt.
But images of danger and distress,
Man suffering among awful Powers and Forms;          165
Of this I heard, and saw enough to make
Imagination restless; nor was free
Myself from frequent perils; nor were tales
Wanting,—the tragedies of former times,
Hazards and strange escapes, of which the rocks          170
Immutable and everflowing streams,
Where'er I roamed, were speaking monuments.

211–13 But 'twas the image of a danger in them
       And suffering man that took most [       ]
       Man suffering among *etc.*  Y.
218–20 A³ C *as* 1850.
220–311 A B *delete*; *not in* C (242–94 *cut out of* B).
221 *followed in* Y *by*
       The story of a child a Shepherd boy
       Whose perilous adventure pleas'd me much
       To hear while I myself was yet a child  Y.
222 th' autumnal snows  J.
223–6 A shepherd and his son one day went forth
       In search of a stray sheep—It was the time
       When from the heights our shepherds drive their flocks
       To gather all their mountain family
       Into the homestalls, ere they send them back
       There to defend themselves the winter long.
       Old Michael for this purpose had driven down
       His flock into the Vale, but as it chanced,
       A single sheep was wanting. They had sought
       The straggler during the preceding day  J².
224–6 Thus did the matron's narrative begin
       In search of a stray sheep. The flock had all
       By custom of the season been driven down
       To the homestalls: the whole mountain family
       Gather'd together, but a single sheep
       As it befell was missing *etc. as* J², J.
228 And sallying forth before the sun was up  J.
228–9 And now at sunrise sallying forth again
       Far did they go that morning: with their search
       Beginning towards the south, where from Dove Crag  J² Y:  Y²
       *as* A.
233 having pass'd] did they pass  J Y.          235 Pike] crag  J Y.
247 Glen] nook  J.
247–9 And far did they look forth. At length said Luke
       Father 'tis loss of labour *etc. as*  J², *but* 249 Up to the ground
       which we have search'd before  J.
248–50 Said Father, 'tis lost labour with your leave
       I will go back and range a second time
       The grounds which we have hunted through before.
       So saying, homeward  J² Y:  Y² *as* A.

And range the ground which we have search'd before.'
250 So speaking, southward down the hill the Lad
Sprang like a gust of wind, crying aloud
'I know where I shall find him.' 'For take note,
Said here my grey-hair'd Dame, that tho' the storm
Drive one of those poor Creatures miles and miles,
255 If he can crawl he will return again
To his own hills, the spots where, when a Lamb,
He learn'd to pasture at his Mother's side.'
After so long a labour, suddenly
Bethinking him of this, the Boy
260 Pursued his way towards a brook whose course
Was through that unfenced tract of mountain-ground
Which to his Father's little Farm belong'd,
The home and ancient Birth-right of their Flock.
Down the deep channel of the Stream he went,
265 Prying through every nook; meanwhile the rain
Began to fall upon the mountain tops,
Thick storm and heavy which for three hours' space
Abated not; and all that time the Boy
Was busy in his search until at length
270 He spied the Sheep upon a plot of grass,
An Island in the Brook. It was a place
Remote and deep, piled round with rocks where foot
Of man or beast was seldom used to tread;
But now, when everywhere the summer grass
275 Had fail'd, this one Adventurer, hunger-press'd,
Had left his Fellows, and made his way alone
To the green plot of pasture in the Brook.
Before the Boy knew well what he had seen
He leapt upon the Island with proud heart
280 And with a Prophet's joy. Immediately
The Sheep sprang forward to the further Shore
And was borne headlong by the roaring flood.
At this the Boy look'd round him, and his heart
Fainted with fear; thrice did he turn his face
285 To either brink; nor could he summon up
The courage that was needful to leap back
Cross the tempestuous torrent; so he stood,
A Prisoner on the Island, not without
More than one thought of death and his last hour.
290 Meanwhile the Father had return'd alone

251-4    wind: and with a heart
Brimful of glory said within himself
I know where I shall find him,
    though the storm
Have driven him twenty miles be-
    fore this time J.

            wind: his heart was full
Of confidence that he should quickly
    find
What they had sought so long; for
    ye must know
Said here *etc. as* A 252-3. J² Y.

259 These thoughts thus working in his mind, the Lad J
    Bethinking him of this again the boy J².
275 Began to fail, this sheep by hunger pressed J: J² *as* A.
276 made his way J² A: had gone J.
290 the Father J² A: old Michael J.

To his own house; and now at the approach
Of evening he went forth to meet his Son,
Conjecturing vainly for what cause the Boy
Had stay'd so long. The Shepherd took his way
295 Up his own mountain grounds, where, as he walk'd
Along the Steep that overhung the Brook,
He seem'd to hear a voice, which was again
Repeated, like the whistling of a kite.
At this, not knowing why, as oftentimes
300 Long afterwards he has been heard to say,
Down to the Brook he went, and track'd its course
Upwards among the o'erhanging rocks; nor thus
Had he gone far, ere he espied the Boy
Where on that little plot of ground he stood
305 Right in the middle of the roaring Stream,
Now stronger every moment and more fierce.
The sight was such as no one could have seen
Without distress and fear. The Shepherd heard
The outcry of his Son, he stretch'd his Staff
310 Towards him, bade him leap, which word scarce said
The Boy was safe within his Father's arms.

Smooth life had Flock and Shepherd in old time,
Long Springs and tepid Winters on the Banks
Of delicate Galesus; and no less                    [175]
315 Those scatter'd along Adria's myrtle Shores:
Smooth life the Herdsman and his snow-white Herd
To Triumphs and to sacrificial Rites
Devoted, on the inviolable Stream
Of rich Clitumnus; and the Goat-herd liv'd           [180]
320 As sweetly, underneath the pleasant brows
Of cool Lucretilis, where the Pipe was heard
Of Pan, the invisible God, thrilling the rocks
With tutelary music, from all harm
The Fold protecting. I myself, mature                [185]
325 In manhood then, have seen a pastoral Tract
Like one of these, where Fancy might run wild,
Though under skies less generous and serene;
Yet there, as for herself, had Nature fram'd
A Pleasure-ground, diffused a fair expanse           [190]
330 Of level Pasture, islanded with Groves
And bank'd with woody Risings; but the Plain

Smooth life had flock and shepherd in old time,
Long springs and tepid waters, on the banks
Of delicate Galesus; and no less                              175
Those scattered along Adria's myrtle shores:
Smooth life had herdsman, and his snow-white herd
To triumphs and to sacrificial rites
Devoted, on the inviolable stream
Of rich Clitumnus; and the goat-herd lived                    180
As calmly, underneath the pleasant brows
Of cool Lucretilis, where the pipe was heard
Of Pan, Invisible God, thrilling the rocks
With tutelary music, from all harm
The fold protecting. I myself, mature                         185
In manhood then, have seen a pastoral tract
Like one of these, where Fancy might run wild,
Though under skies less generous, less serene:
There, for her own delight had Nature framed
A pleasure-ground, diffused a fair expanse                    190
Of level pasture, islanded with groves
And banked with woody risings; but the Plain

293 Conjecturing vainly . . . cause] Nor could he guess the cause for
which J.
300 The old man afterwards was heard to say  J.        306 *Not in* J.
307–8 Without alarm and trouble, Michael heard  J:  J² *as* A.
311 his Father's  J² A:  the old man's J.
315 Those scatter'd along]
         To kindly Jupiter owed they, who dwelt
         Scattered along warm  D:  D² *as* 1850.
316 the] had  A² C.        320 sweetly  𝔄:  calmly  A² C.
328 A² C *as* 1850 [189].

Endless; here opening widely out, and there
Shut up in lesser lakes or beds of lawn
And intricate recesses, creek or bay                    [195]
335  Shelter'd within a shelter, where at large
The Shepherd strays, a rolling hut his home:
Thither he comes with spring-time, there abides
All summer, and at sunrise ye may hear
His flute or flagelet resounding far;
340  There's not a Nook or Hold of that vast space,
Nor Strait where passage is, but it shall have
In turn its Visitant, telling there his hours
In unlaborious pleasure, with no task                    [205]
More toilsome than to carve a beechen bowl
345  For Spring or Fountain, which the Traveller finds
When through the region he pursues at will
His devious course. A glimpse of such sweet life
I saw when, from the melancholy Walls                    [210]
Of Goslar, once Imperial! I renew'd
350  My daily walk along that chearful Plain,
Which, reaching to her Gates, spreads East and West
And Northwards, from beneath the mountainous verge
Of the Hercynian forest. Yet hail to You,                    [215]
Your rocks and precipices, Ye that seize
355  The heart with firmer grasp! your snows and streams
Ungovernable, and your terrifying winds,                    [220]
That howl'd so dismally when I have been
Companionless, among your solitudes.
There 'tis the Shepherd's task the winter long
360  To wait upon the storms: of their approach
Sagacious, from the height he drives his Flock                    [225]
Down into sheltering coves, and feeds them there
Through the hard time, long as the storm is *lock'd*,
(So do they phrase it) bearing from the stalls
365  A toilsome burden up the craggy ways,
To strew it on the snow. And when the Spring

339  His liquid flute or flageolet from far  D:  D² *as* 1850.
340–1  A² B² C *as* 1850.
347  devious 𝔄 C D: dubious E: *query* devious E².
350–1  A² C *as* 1850.          353–4  𝔄 C D, *but* D huge *for* Ye: D² *as* 1850.
354  rocks] crags  Y.
357–8                              when I have trod,
          Companionless, your awful solitudes  A² C.

Endless, here opening widely out, and there
Shut up in lesser lakes or beds of lawn
And intricate recesses, creek or bay                    195
Sheltered within a shelter, where at large
The shepherd strays, a rolling hut his home.
Thither he comes with spring-time, there abides
All summer, and at sunrise ye may hear
His flageolet to liquid notes of love                   200
Attuned, or sprightly fife resounding far.
Nook is there none, nor tract of that vast space
Where passage opens, but the same shall have
In turn its visitant, telling there his hours
In unlaborious pleasure, with no task                   205
More toilsome than to carve a beechen bowl
For spring or fountain, which the traveller finds,
When through the region he pursues at will
His devious course. A glimpse of such sweet life
I saw when, from the melancholy walls                   210
Of Goslar, once imperial, I renewed
My daily walk along that wide champaign,
That, reaching to her gates, spreads east and west,
And northwards, from beneath the mountainous verge
Of the Hercynian forest. Yet, hail to you              215
Moors, mountains, headlands, and ye hollow vales,
Ye long deep channels for the Atlantic's voice,
Powers of my native region! Ye that seize
The heart with firmer grasp! Your snows and streams
Ungovernable, and your terrifying winds,                220
That howl so dismally for him who treads
Companionless your awful solitudes!
There, 'tis the shepherd's task the winter long
To wait upon the storms: of their approach
Sagacious, into sheltering coves he drives              225
His flock, and thither from the homestead bears
A toilsome burden up the craggy ways,
And deals it out, their regular nourishment
Strewn on the frozen snow. And when the spring

361 Flock] charge Y.
361–5 𝔄 C. *So* D, *but omitting* feeds . . . bearing *and adding*, after 365, He
duly bears their welcome nourishment. D² *as* 1850.
362 Downwards and feeds them among sheltering coves A².
[228] regular E²: punctual D E.

Looks out, and all the mountains dance with lambs,        [230]
He through the enclosures won from the steep Waste,
And through the lower Heights hath gone his rounds;
370  And when the Flock with warmer weather climbs
Higher and higher, him his office leads
To range among them, through the hills dispers'd,
And watch their goings, whatsoever track
Each Wanderer chuses for itself; a work
375  That lasts the summer through. He quits his home
At day-spring, and no sooner doth the sun          [235]
Begin to strike him with a fire-like heat
Than he lies down upon some shining place
And breakfasts with his Dog; when he hath stay'd,
380  As for the most he doth, beyond his time,          [239]
He springs up with a bound, and then away!
Ascending fast with his long Pole in hand,
Or winding in and out among the crags.
What need to follow him through what he does          [250]
385  Or sees in his day's march? He feels himself
In those vast regions where his service is
A Freeman; wedded to his life of hope
And hazard, and hard labour interchang'd
With that majestic indolence so dear          [255]
390  To native Man. A rambling Schoolboy, thus
Have I beheld him, without knowing why
Have felt his presence in his own domain,
As of a Lord and Master; or a Power
Or Genius, under Nature, under God,
395  Presiding; and severest solitude          [260]
Seem'd more commanding oft when he was there.
Seeking the raven's nest, and suddenly
Surpriz'd with vapours, or on rainy days
When I have angled up the lonely brooks

367 mountains 𝕬 C D: pastures D².
378 place] rock A² C.
380–5 As he is wont, beyond the allotted time
          From his hard couch he starts *etc. to* turf [244] *as* 1850.
                          with beauty how profuse
          The lingering dews smoke round him—On he hies
          His staff portending like a hunter's spear *etc. to* [251] *as* 1850. A² C.
386 is 𝕬: lies A² C.        396 A² C² *as* 1850.
397 While seeking the Kite's nest Y: Y² *as* 𝕬.

Looks out, and all the pastures dance with lambs,                    230
And when the flock, with warmer weather, climbs
Higher and higher, him his office leads
To watch their goings, whatsoever track
The wanderers choose. For this he quits his home
At day-spring, and no sooner doth the sun                    235
Begin to strike him with a fire-like heat,
Than he lies down upon some shining rock,
And breakfasts with his dog. When they have stolen,
As is their wont, a pittance from strict time,
For rest not needed or exchange of love,                    240
Then from his couch he starts; and now his feet
Crush out a livelier fragrance from the flowers
Of lowly thyme, by Nature's skill enwrought
In the wild turf: the lingering dews of morn
Smoke round him, as from hill to hill he hies,                    245
His staff protending like a hunter's spear,
Or by its aid leaping from crag to crag,
And o'er the brawling beds of unbridged streams.
Philosophy, methinks, at Fancy's call,
Might deign to follow him through what he does                    250
Or sees in his day's march; himself he feels,
In those vast regions where his service lies,
A freeman, wedded to his life of hope
And hazard, and hard labour interchanged
With that majestic indolence so dear                    255
To native man. A rambling school-boy, thus
I felt his presence in his own domain,
As of a lord and master, or a power,
Or genius, under Nature, under God,
Presiding; and severest solitude                    260
Had more commanding looks when he was there.
When up the lonely brooks on rainy days
Angling I went, or trod the trackless hills
By mists bewildered, suddenly mine eyes

397–400 How oft when angling up the lonely brooks
          On rainy days, or suddenly surpriz'd
          With vapour, when I sought the raven's nest
          Have I beheld him, distant a few steps A².
          When I have angled up the lonely brooks
          On rainy days, or trod the trackless hills
          By mists bewildered suddenly mine eyes
          Have glanced upon him distant a few steps A³ C.

400  Mine eyes have glanced upon him, few steps off,              [265]
     In size a giant, stalking through the fog,
     His Sheep like Greenland Bears; at other times
     When round some shady promontory turning,
     His Form hath flash'd upon me, glorified
405  By the deep radiance of the setting sun:                     [270]
     Or him have I descried in distant sky,
     A solitary object and sublime,
     Above all height! like an aerial Cross,
     As it is stationed on some spiry Rock
410  Of the Chartreuse, for worship. Thus was Man                 [275]
     Ennobled outwardly before mine eyes,
     And thus my heart at first was introduc'd
     To an unconscious love and reverence
     Of human Nature; hence the human form
415  To me was like an index of delight,                          [280]
     Of grace and honour, power and worthiness.
     Meanwhile, this Creature, spiritual almost
     As those of Books; but more exalted far,
     Far more of an imaginative form,
420  Was not a Corin of the groves, who lives                     [285]
     For his own fancies, or to dance by the hour
     In coronal, with Phillis in the midst,
     But, for the purposes of kind, a Man
     With the most common; Husband, Father; learn'd,
425  Could teach, admonish, suffer'd with the rest                [290]
     From vice and folly, wretchedness and fear;
     Of this I little saw, car'd less for it,
     But something must have felt.
                              Call ye these appearances
     Which I beheld of Shepherds in my youth,
430  This sanctity of Nature given to Man                         [295]
     A shadow, a delusion, ye who are fed
     By the dead letter, not the spirit of things,
     Whose truth is not a motion or a shape
     Instinct with vital functions, but a Block
435  Or waxen Image which yourselves have made,                   [300]
     And ye adore. But blessed be the God
     Of Nature and of Man that this was so,
     That Men did at the first present themselves
     Before my untaught eyes thus purified,

     409 A² C *as* 1850.        415 was like] became A² C.

Have glanced upon him distant a few steps,                    265
In size a giant, stalking through thick fog,
His sheep like Greenland bears; or, as he stepped
Beyond the boundary line of some hill-shadow,
His form hath flashed upon me, glorified
By the deep radiance of the setting sun:                    270
Or him have I descried in distant sky,
A solitary object and sublime,
Above all height! like an aerial cross
Stationed alone upon a spiry rock
Of the Chartreuse, for worship. Thus was man                    275
Ennobled outwardly before my sight,
And thus my heart was early introduced
To an unconscious love and reverence
Of human nature; hence the human form
To me became an index of delight,                    280
Of grace and honour, power and worthiness.
Meanwhile this creature—spiritual almost
As those of books, but more exalted far;
Far more of an imaginative form
Than the gay Corin of the groves, who lives                    285
For his own fancies, or to dance by the hour,
In coronal, with Phyllis in the midst—
Was, for the purposes of kind, a man
With the most common; husband, father; learned,
Could teach, admonish; suffered with the rest                    290
From vice and folly, wretchedness and fear;
Of this I little saw, cared less for it,
But something must have felt.
                              Call ye these appearances—
Which I beheld of shepherds in my youth,
This sanctity of Nature given to man—                    295
A shadow, a delusion, ye who pore
On the dead letter, miss the spirit of things;
Whose truth is not a motion or a shape
Instinct with vital functions, but a block
Or waxen image which yourselves have made,                    300
And ye adore! But blessed be the God
Of Nature and of Man that this was so;
That men before my inexperienced eyes
Did first present themselves thus purified,

431-2 𝔄 C D: D² *as* 1850.        438-9 A² C *as* 1850.

440 Remov'd, and at a distance that was fit.                    [305]
    And so we all of us in some degree
    Are led to knowledge, whencesoever led,
    And howsoever; were it otherwise,
    And we found evil fast as we find good
445 In our first years, or think that it is found,              [310]
    How could the innocent heart bear up and live!
    But doubly fortunate my lot; not here
    Alone, that something of a better life
    Perhaps was round me than it is the privilege
450 Of most to move in, but that first I look'd               [315]
    At Man through objects that were great and fair,
    First commun'd with him by their help. And thus
    Was founded a sure safeguard and defence
    Against the weight of meanness, selfish cares,
455 Coarse manners, vulgar passions, that beat in             [320]
    On all sides from the ordinary world
    In which we traffic. Starting from this point,
    I had my face towards the truth, began
    With an advantage; furnish'd with that kind
460 Of prepossession without which the soul                   [325]
    Receives no knowledge that can bring forth good,
    No genuine insight ever comes to her:
    Happy in this, that I with nature walk'd,                  [330]
    Not having a too early intercourse
465 With the deformities of crowded life,
    And those ensuing laughters and contempts
    Self-pleasing, which if we would wish to think
    With admiration and respect of man                        [335]
    Will not permit us; but pursue the mind
470 That to devotion willingly would be rais'd
    Into the Temple and the Temple's heart.

        Yet do not deem, my Friend, though thus I speak
    Of Man as having taken in my mind                         [340]
    A place thus early which might almost seem
475 Pre-eminent, that it was really so.
    Nature herself was at this unripe time,
    But secondary to my own pursuits

    459 furnish'd with Ⓐ C D: rising from A²: founded on A³: furnished
by D².
    [328-9] *added to* D *and* E *in Wordsworth's hand.*

Removed, and to a distance that was fit:                305
And so we all of us in some degree
Are led to knowledge, wheresoever led,
And howsoever; were it otherwise,
And we found evil fast as we find good
In our first years, or think that it is found,          310
How could the innocent heart bear up and live!
But doubly fortunate my lot; not here
Alone, that something of a better life
Perhaps was round me than it is the privilege
Of most to move in, but that first I looked             315
At Man through objects that were great or fair;
First communed with him by their help. And thus
Was founded a sure safeguard and defence
Against the weight of meanness, selfish cares,
Coarse manners, vulgar passions, that beat in           320
On all sides from the ordinary world
In which we traffic. Starting from this point
I had my face turned toward the truth, began
With an advantage furnished by that kind
Of prepossession, without which the soul                325
Receives no knowledge that can bring forth good,
No genuine insight ever comes to her.
From the restraint of over-watchful eyes
Preserved, I moved about, year after year,
Happy, and now most thankful that my walk               330
Was guarded from too early intercourse
With the deformities of crowded life,
And those ensuing laughters and contempts,
Self-pleasing, which, if we would wish to think
With a due reverence on earth's rightful lord,          335
Here placed to be the inheritor of heaven,
Will not permit us; but pursue the mind,
That to devotion willingly would rise,
Into the temple and the temple's heart.

      Yet deem not, Friend! that human kind with me     340
Thus early took a place pre-eminent;
Nature herself was, at this unripe time,
But secondary to my own pursuits

 468 𝕬 C D: D² *as* 1850 [335–6].          470 be raised 𝕬 C D: rise D².

And animal activities, and all
Their trivial pleasures; and long afterwards          [345]
480 When those had died away, and Nature did
For her own sake become my joy, even then
And upwards through late youth, until not less
Than three and twenty summers had been told
Was man in my affections and regards                 [350]
485 Subordinate to her; her awful forms
And viewless agencies: a passion, she!
A rapture often, and immediate joy,
Ever at hand; he distant, but a grace
Occasional, an accidental thought,                   [355]
490 His hour being not yet come. Far less had then
The inferior Creatures, beast or bird, attun'd
My spirit to that gentleness of love,
Won from me those minute obeisances                  [360]
Of tenderness, which I may number now
495 With my first blessings. Nevertheless, on these
The light of beauty did not fall in vain,
Or grandeur circumfuse them to no end.               [364]


Why should I speak of Tillers of the soil?
The Ploughman and his Team; or Men and Boys
500 In festive summer busy with the rake,
Old Men and ruddy Maids, and Little Ones
All out together, and in sun and shade
Dispers'd among the hay-grounds alder-fringed,
The Quarry-man, far heard! that blasts the rock,
505 The Fishermen in pairs, the one to row,
And one to drop the Net, plying their trade
''Mid tossing lakes and tumbling boats' and winds
Whistling; the Miner, melancholy Man!
That works by taper light, while all the hills
510 Are shining with the glory of the day.


But when that first poetic Faculty                   [365]
Of plain imagination and severe,
No longer a mute Influence of the soul,
An Element of the nature's inner self,

479–80 and . . . away] A² C as 1850.     483 three 𝔄 C D: two D².
485 awful 𝔄 C D: visible D².

And animal activities, and all
Their trivial pleasures; and when these had drooped          345
And gradually expired, and Nature, prized
For her own sake, became my joy, even then—
And upwards through late youth, until not less
Than two-and-twenty summers had been told—
Was Man in my affections and regards                        350
Subordinate to her, her visible forms
And viewless agencies: a passion, she,
A rapture often, and immediate love
Ever at hand; he, only a delight
Occasional, an accidental grace,                            355
His hour being not yet come. Far less had then
The inferior creatures, beast or bird, attuned
My spirit to that gentleness of love
(Though they had long been carefully observed),
Won from me those minute obeisances                         360
Of tenderness, which I may number now
With my first blessings. Nevertheless, on these
The light of beauty did not fall in vain,
Or grandeur circumfuse them to no end.


But when that first poetic faculty                          365
Of plain Imagination and severe,
No longer a mute influence of the soul,
Ventured, at some rash Muse's earnest call,

488 he distant, but a grace 𝔄 C D: he only, a delight D²: *he* only a
delight E.
489 thought 𝔄 C D: grace D² E.
[359] *added to* D *in Wordsworth's hand.*
497 Or] Nor Y.
502–3 In sun and shade promiscuously dispers'd
          Among the meadowy hay-grounds, alder fring'd, A².
504 The Quarry Man whose thunders all day long
      Break forth at intervals and chase the sleep
      Of Echo. She is ris'n and hurries round
      And round the amplest circuit of the Hills.
      Mark'd ye that step? a fainter could not fall
      Though the last effort of exhausted powers—
      That pause—it is the prelude of a course
      Bolder and bolder. Thus the nymph bemocks
      Her sister Silence mid those aery haunts
      Where both abide in shadowy loneliness
      Preserv'd while pass successively away
      The feeble generations of mankind. A².

515   Began to have some promptings to put on
     A visible shape, and to the works of art,
     The notions and the images of books              [370]
     Did knowingly conform itself, by these
     Enflamed, and proud of that her new delight,
520   There came among those shapes of human life
     A wilfulness of fancy and conceit
     Which gave them new importance to the mind;
     And Nature and her objects beautified
     These fictions, as in some sort in their turn      [375]
525   They burnish'd her. From touch of this new power
     Nothing was safe: the Elder-tree that grew
     Beside the well-known Charnel-house had then
     A dismal look; the Yew-tree had its Ghost,
     That took its station there for ornament:      [380]
530   Then common death was none, common mishap,
     But matter for this humour everywhere,
     The tragic super-tragic, else left short.
     Then, if a Widow, staggering with the blow
     Of her distress, was known to have made her way   [385]
535   To the cold grave in which her Husband slept,
     One night, or haply more than one, through pain
     Or half-insensate impotence of mind
     The fact was caught at greedily, and there
     She was a Visitant the whole year through,     [390]
540   Wetting the turf with never-ending tears,
     And all the storms of Heaven must beat on her.

     Through wild obliquities could I pursue
     Among all objects of the fields and groves
     These cravings; when the Foxglove, one by one,
545   Upwards through every stage of its tall stem,
     Had shed its bells, and stood by the wayside     [395]
     Dismantled, with a single one, perhaps,
     Left at the ladder's top, with which the Plant
     Appeared to stoop, as slender blades of grass   [398]
550   Tipp'd with a bead of rain or dew, behold!

515–20  Began to have some promptings to put on
       A visible clothing of harmonious words,
       The notions and the images of books
       And art did knowingly conform itself,
       There came among *etc.* D: D² *as* 1850.
522  mind;] mind 𝔄 C D: D *deletes the line.*

To try her strength among harmonious words;
And to book-notions and the rules of art                       370
Did knowingly conform itself; there came
Among the simple shapes of human life
A wilfulness of fancy and conceit;
And Nature and her objects beautified
These fictions, as in some sort, in their turn,                375
They burnished her. From touch of this new power
Nothing was safe: the elder-tree that grew
Beside the well-known charnel-house had then
A dismal look: the yew-tree had its ghost,
That took his station there for ornament:                      380
The dignities of plain occurrence then
Were tasteless, and truth's golden mean, a point
Where no sufficient pleasure could be found.
Then, if a widow, staggering with the blow
Of her distress, was known to have turned her steps           385
To the cold grave in which her husband slept,
One night, or haply more than one, through pain
Or half-insensate impotence of mind,
The fact was caught at greedily, and there
She must be visitant the whole year through,                   390
Wetting the turf with never-ending tears.

     Through quaint obliquities I might pursue
These cravings; when the fox-glove, one by one,
Upwards through every stage of the tall stem,
Had shed beside the public way its bells,                      395
And stood of all dismantled, save the last
Left at the tapering ladder's top, that seemed
To bend as doth a slender blade of grass
Tipped with a rain-drop, Fancy loved to seat,

530–2 Fact, simple fact, and plain occurrence *etc. as* 1850, A² C.
534 made her way 𝔄 C D: D² *as* 1850.
536–7 In storm and darkness faithful to her past
      A monumental effigy of love A³.
541 A *deletes; not in* C.
542 Through most fantastic windings could I trace Y.
543 A *and* C *delete.* Among all objects of the changeful years A².
546–7 A² C *as* 1850.
548–9 Left to adorn the tapering ladder's top
      That bent or seem'd to bend beneath the weight A².
549 To (*bend*) droop beneath the weight as blades of grass A³.
550–7 *stuck over in* D: D² *as* 1850.

If such a sight were seen, would Fancy bring
Some Vagrant thither with her Babes, and seat her
Upon the turf beneath the stately Flower
Drooping in sympathy, and making so
555 A melancholy Crest above the head
Of the lorn Creature, while her Little-Ones,
All unconcerned with her unhappy plight,
Were sporting with the purple cups that lay          [405]
Scatter'd upon the ground.
                              There was a Copse
560 An upright bank of wood and woody rock
That opposite our rural Dwelling stood,
In which a sparkling patch of diamond light
Was in bright weather duly to be seen
On summer afternoons, within the wood
565 At the same place. 'Twas doubtless nothing more
Than a black rock, which, wet with constant springs
Glister'd far seen from out its lurking-place
As soon as ever the declining sun
Had smitten it. Beside our Cottage hearth,          [410]
570 Sitting with open door, a hundred times
Upon this lustre have I gaz'd, that seem'd
To have some meaning which I could not find;
And now it was a burnished shield, I fancied,
Suspended over a Knight's Tomb, who lay             [415]
575 Inglorious, buried in the dusky wood;
An entrance now into some magic cave
Or Palace for a Fairy of the rock;
Nor would I, though not certain whence the cause
Of the effulgence, thither have repair'd
580 Without a precious bribe, and day by day
And month by month I saw the spectacle,
Nor ever once have visited the spot                 [420]
Unto this hour. Thus sometimes were the shapes
Of wilful fancy grafted upon feelings
585 Of the imagination, and they rose
In worth accordingly. My present Theme
Is to retrace the way that led me on
Through Nature to the love of Human Kind;
Nor could I with such object overlook
590 The influence of this Power which turn'd itself
Instinctively to human passions, things            [425]

Beneath the plant despoiled, but crested still 400
With this last relic, soon itself to fall,
Some vagrant mother, whose arch little ones,
All unconcerned by her dejected plight,
Laughed as with rival eagerness their hands
Gathered the purple cups that round them lay, 405
Strewing the turf's green slope.

               A diamond light
(Whene'er the summer sun, declining, smote
A smooth rock wet with constant springs) was seen
Sparkling from out a copse-clad bank that rose
Fronting our cottage. Oft beside the hearth 410
Seated, with open door, often and long
Upon this restless lustre have I gazed,
That made my fancy restless as itself.
'Twas now for me a burnished silver shield
Suspended over a knight's tomb, who lay 415
Inglorious, buried in the dusky wood:
An entrance now into some magic cave
Or palace built by fairies of the rock;
Nor could I have been bribed to disenchant
The spectacle, by visiting the spot. 420
Thus wilful Fancy, in no hurtful mood,
Engrafted far-fetched shapes on feelings bred
By pure Imagination: busy Power
She was, and with her ready pupil turned
Instinctively to human passions, then 425

556 Creature] wanderer A² C.
559-69         A copse-clad bank
  There was which opposite our Dwelling rose
  Where in bright weather duly might be seen
  On summer afternoons, a radiant speck
  A stationary patch of diamond light
  Sparkling, far-kenn'd from out its lurking place,
  In the green wood. Beside our cottage hearth A² (*but* copse-clad bank
    *and* Sparkling *are corrections of* shaggy steep *and* Glancing). *So* C,
    *but* C *omits* far-kenn'd . . . place.
565-6         The object which produced
  The appearance was the surface of a rock
  Abrupt and smooth which wet *etc.* A².
570 a hundred times] how oft and long A² C.
571-3 𝔄 C D: D² *as* 1850.
575 the A: a B.
577 𝔄 C: A² *as* 1850.       588 Kind] life Y.

Least understood; of this adulterate Power,
For so it may be call'd, and without wrong,
When with that first compar'd. Yet in the midst
595 Of these vagaries, with an eye so rich
As mine was, through the chance, on me not wasted
Of having been brought up in such a grand
And lovely region, I had forms distinct
To steady me; these thoughts did oft revolve          [430]
600 About some centre palpable, which at once
Incited them to motion, and control'd,
And whatsoever shape the fit might take,
And whencesoever it might come, I still
At all times had a real solid world
605 Of images about me; did not pine
As one in cities bred might do; as Thou,
Beloved Friend! hast told me that thou didst,
Great Spirit as thou art, in endless dreams          [435]
Of sickliness, disjoining, joining things
610 Without the light of knowledge. Where the harm,
If, when the Woodman languish'd with disease
From sleeping night by night among the woods
Within his sod-built Cabin, Indian-wise,          [440]
I call'd the pangs of disappointed love
615 And all the long Etcetera of such thought
To help him to his grave? Meanwhile the Man,
If not already from the woods retir'd
To die at home, was haply, as I knew,          [445]
Pining alone among the gentle airs,
620 Birds, running Streams, and Hills so beautiful
On golden evenings, while the charcoal Pile
Breath'd up its smoke, an image of his ghost
Or spirit that was soon to take its flight.          [450]

[428] As mine was through the favourable chance
        Of having been brought up in such a grand  D: D² *as* 1850.
[430] To steady me: these thoughts did each revolve  D: D² *as* 1850.
[434] As thou, dear Friend, hast told me thou didst pine  D: D² *as* 1850.
612 𝔄 C D: D² *as* 1850.
613–14 Within his cabin Indian-wise I called Perhaps *etc.* Y.
615 such thought 𝔄: such thoughts C: the wrong D.
619 Pining] Withering A² C.        620–35 D *stuck over.*

Least understood. Yet, 'mid the fervent swarm
Of these vagaries, with an eye so rich
As mine was through the bounty of a grand
And lovely region, I had forms distinct
To steady me: each airy thought revolved                    430
Round a substantial centre, which at once
Incited it to motion, and controlled.
I did not pine like one in cities bred,
As was thy melancholy lot, dear Friend!
Great Spirit as thou art, in endless dreams                    435
Of sickliness, disjoining, joining, things
Without the light of knowledge. Where the harm,
If, when the woodman languished with disease
Induced by sleeping nightly on the ground
Within his sod-built cabin, Indian-wise,                    440
I called the pangs of disappointed love,
And all the sad etcetera of the wrong,
To help him to his grave. Meanwhile the man,
If not already from the woods retired
To die at home, was haply, as I knew,                    445
Withering by slow degrees, 'mid gentle airs,
Birds, running streams, and hills so beautiful
On golden evenings, while the charcoal pile
Breathed up its smoke, an image of his ghost
Or spirit that full soon must take her flight.                    450

There came a time of greater dignity
625 Which had been gradually prepar'd, and now
Rush'd in as if on wings, the time in which
The pulse of Being everywhere was felt,                    [480]
When all the several frames of things, like stars
Through every magnitude distinguishable,
630 Were half confounded in each other's blaze,
One galaxy of life and joy. Then rose                      [485]
Man, inwardly contemplated, and present
In my own being, to a loftier height;
As of all visible natures crown; and first
635 In capability of feeling what

[451-75] *No counterpart in* 𝔄 C: *stuck in to* D. D E *read*:
  With casual outward hints by Nature given
  Thus Fancy deigned to play—that she might serve
  The Boy for the Man's sake. Nor may I here
  Forget like influence exercised by her
  Over one motion of my opening mind
  In character more dignified—While gazing
  On golden beams flung from the setting sun
  As they reposed upon the naked ridge
  Of a high eastern hill, I sighed and said
  (Then first beginning with a yielding heart
  To catch well-pleased the dim similitudes
  That link our feelings with external forms)
  In whatsoever region life should close
  Her journey, I would think dear Native Hills
  On you, on you would cast a backward look
  Even as *etc.* . . . E² *as* 1850 [471 *ff.*]: D *has also two deleted versions of*
    [451 *ff.*]:
    (i) These, tho' not idly find a record here
        As notices subservient to our aim
        Are but the freaks of Fancy. Pause we then
        In our main road, and with a moment's leave
        Given for her sake, her influence let me tell
        Over one motion of a boyish mind.
    (ii) These are but fancy's toys: more fit it were
        For her sweet sake her influence to tell
        Over one motion of a boyish mind
        Pensive yet sound in character,—while watching
        From under an old Sycamore's wide spread shade
        The golden *etc.*
(*for lines in* V *on which* [458-75] *are based v.* notes).
  [476] humble arguments E²: petty offices D: such quaint offices D²:
    minor offices E.
  [478] made known D²: disclosed D.   624-37 D *stuck over*: D² *as* 1850.
  625-6 For which I had been gradually prepared,
          Yet it rushed in as if on wings, for now A².
  635-6 A² C *as* 1850.

Nor shall we not be tending towards that point
Of sound humanity to which our Tale
Leads, though by sinuous ways, if here I shew
How Fancy, in a season when she wove
Those slender cords, to guide the unconscious Boy          455
For the Man's sake, could feed at Nature's call
Some pensive musings which might well beseem
Maturer years.
             A grove there is whose boughs
Stretch from the western marge of Thurston-mere,
With length of shade so thick, that whoso glides          460
Along the line of low-roofed water, moves
As in a cloister. Once—while, in that shade
Loitering, I watched the golden beams of light
Flung from the setting sun, as they reposed
In silent beauty on the naked ridge                       465
Of a high eastern hill—thus flowed my thoughts
In a pure stream of words fresh from the heart;
Dear native Regions, wheresoe'er shall close
My mortal course, there will I think on you;
Dying, will cast on you a backward look;                  470
Even as this setting sun (albeit the Vale
Is no where touched by one memorial gleam)
Doth with the fond remains of his last power
Still linger, and a farewell lustre sheds
On the dear mountain-tops where first he rose.            475


    Enough of humble arguments; recal,
My Song! those high emotions which thy voice
Has heretofore made known; that bursting forth
Of sympathy, inspiring and inspired,
When everywhere a vital pulse was felt,                   480
And all the several frames of things, like stars,
Through every magnitude distinguishable,
Shone mutually indebted, or half lost
Each in the other's blaze, a galaxy
Of life and glory. In the midst stood Man,                485
Outwardly, inwardly contemplated,
As, of all visible natures, crown, though born
Of dust, and kindred to the worm; a Being,
Both in perception and discernment, first

Was to be felt; in being rapt away                    [490]
By the divine effect of power and love,
As, more than anything we know instinct
With Godhead, and by reason and by will
640  Acknowledging dependency sublime.

Erelong transported hence as in a dream        [495]
I found myself begirt with temporal shapes
Of vice and folly thrust upon my view,
Objects of sport, and ridicule, and scorn,
645  Manners and characters discriminate,
And little busy passions that eclips'd,        [500]
As well they might, the impersonated thought,
The idea or abstraction of the Kind.
An Idler among academic Bowers,
650  Such was my new condition, as at large
Hath been set forth; yet here the vulgar light        [505]
Of present actual superficial life,
Gleaming through colouring of other times,
Old usages and local privilege,
655  Thereby was soften'd, almost solemnized,
And render'd apt and pleasing to the view;
This notwithstanding, being brought more near        [510]
As I was now, to guilt and wretchedness,
I trembled, thought of human life at times
660  With an indefinite terror and dismay
Such as the storms and angry elements
Had bred in me, but gloomier far, a dim        [515]
Analogy to uproar and misrule,
Disquiet, danger, and obscurity.

665      It might be told (but wherefore speak of things
Common to all?) that seeing, I essay'd
To give relief, began to deem myself
A moral agent, judging between good        [520]
And evil, not as for the mind's delight
670  But for her safety, one who was to act,
As sometimes, to the best of my weak means,
I did, by human sympathy impell'd;

641 *left blank in* B, *added later to* A.        in] by  Y.
641–3 𝔄 C: Erelong I was begirt with temporal shapes *etc.* D: D² *as*
1850.

In every capability of rapture,                              490
Through the divine effect of power and love;
As, more than anything we know, instinct
With godhead, and, by reason and by will,
Acknowledging dependency sublime.

    Ere long, the lonely mountains left, I moved,     495
Begirt, from day to day, with temporal shapes
Of vice and folly thrust upon my view,
Objects of sport, and ridicule, and scorn,
Manners and characters discriminate,
And little bustling passions that eclipse,                  500
As well they might, the impersonated thought,
The idea, or abstraction of the kind.

    An idler among academic bowers,
Such was my new condition, as at large
Has been set forth; yet here the vulgar light              505
Of present, actual, superficial life,
Gleaming through colouring of other times,
Old usages and local privilege,
Was welcome, softened, if not solemnised.
This notwithstanding, being brought more near             510
To vice and guilt, forerunning wretchedness,
I trembled,—thought, at times, of human life
With an indefinite terror and dismay,
Such as the storms and angry elements
Had bred in me; but gloomier far, a dim                   515
Analogy to uproar and misrule,
Disquiet, danger, and obscurity.

    It might be told (but whereof speak of things
Common to all?) that, seeing, I was led
Gravely to ponder—judging between good                    520
And evil, not as for the mind's delight
But for her guidance—one who was to *act*,
As sometimes to the best of feeble means
I did, by human sympathy impelled:

643 thrust upon] pressing on  Y.          646 busy] 𝔄 C: bustling A².
655 A *deletes* : *not in C*.        656 And] Was  A² C D :  D² *as* 1850.
658-9 To guilt and wretchedness, I trembled—thought
     Of mortal destiny and human life  D :  D² *as* 1850.
666-71 𝔄 C D :  D² *as* 1850.

And through dislike and most offensive pain                    [525]
Was to the truth conducted; of this faith
675 Never forsaken, that by acting well
And understanding, I should learn to love
The end of life and every thing we know.

Preceptress stern, that did instruct me next,                    [530]
London! to thee I willingly return.
680 Erewhile my Verse play'd only with the flowers
Enwrought upon thy mantle; satisfied
With this amusement, and a simple look                    [535]
Of child-like inquisition, now and then
Cast upwards on thine eye to puzzle out
685 Some inner meanings, which might harbour there.
Yet did I not give way to this light mood                    [539]
Wholly beguiled, as one incapable
Of higher things, and ignorant that high things
Were round me. Never shall I forget the hour
690 The moment rather say when having thridded
The labyrinth of suburban Villages,
At length I did unto myself first seem
To enter the great City. On the roof
Of an itinerant Vehicle I sate
695 With vulgar Men about me, vulgar forms                    [545]
Of houses, pavement, streets, of men and things,
Mean shapes on every side: but, at the time,
When to myself it fairly might be said,
The very moment that I seem'd to know
700 The threshold now is overpass'd, Great God!
That aught *external* to the living mind                    [550]
Should have such mighty sway! yet so it was
A weight of Ages did at once descend
Upon my heart; no thought embodied, no
705 Distinct remembrances; but weight and power,
Power growing with the weight: alas! I feel                    [555]
That I am trifling: 'twas a moment's pause.
All that took place within me, came and went
As in a moment, and I only now

678 𝕬 C D: D² *as* 1850 [530–1].
680 only 𝕬 C D: idly D² E.          684 A² C *as* 1850.
686 give way to this] indulge in such  A² C.
686–9 𝕬 C D: D² *as* 1850 [539–40].

And, through dislike and most offensive pain,                    525
Was to the truth conducted; of this faith
Never forsaken, that, by acting well,
And understanding, I should learn to love
The end of life, and every thing we know.

    Grave Teacher, stern Preceptress! for at times        530
Thou canst put on an aspect most severe;
London, to thee I willingly return.
Erewhile my verse played idly with the flowers
Enwrought upon thy mantle; satisfied
With that amusement, and a simple look                    535
Of child-like inquisition now and then
Cast upwards on thy countenance, to detect
Some inner meanings which might harbour there.
But how could I in mood so light indulge,
Keeping such fresh remembrance of the day,                    540
When, having thridded the long labyrinth
Of the suburban villages, I first
Entered thy vast dominion? On the roof
Of an itinerant vehicle I sate,
With vulgar men about me, trivial forms                    545
Of houses, pavement, streets, of men and things,—
Mean shapes on every side: but, at the instant,
When to myself it fairly might be said,
The threshold now is overpast, (how strange
That aught external to the living mind                    550
Should have such mighty sway! yet so it was),
A weight of ages did at once descend
Upon my heart; no thought embodied, no
Distinct remembrances, but weight and power,—
Power growing under weight: alas! I feel                    555
That I am trifling: 'twas a moment's pause,—
All that took place within me came and went
As in a moment; yet with Time it dwells,

692–3 At length . . . great City]
        Too slowly for my eager wish I first
        Did enter the great City. A² C D: D² *as* 1850.
695 vulgar forms] trivial forms  A² C.
696 things,  B: things; D E.
697 time] moment  A² D: instant  D².
699 A *deletes*: *not in* C.
700 Great God  𝕬 C D: —how strange  D² E.
706 with the  𝕬 C D: under  D².       709–10  𝕬 C D: D² *as* 1850.

710 Remember that it was a thing divine.

As when a Traveller hath from open day      [560]
    With torches pass'd into some Vault of Earth,
    The Grotto of Antiparos, or the Den
    Of Yordas among Craven's mountain tracts;
715 He looks and sees the cavern spread and grow,
    Widening itself on all sides, sees, or thinks      [565]
    He sees, erelong, the roof above his head,
    Which instantly unsettles and recedes
    Substance and shadow, light and darkness, all
720 Commingled, making up a Canopy
    Of Shapes and Forms and Tendencies to Shape      [570]
    That shift and vanish, change and interchange
    Like Spectres, ferment quiet and sublime;
    Which, after a short space, works less and less,
725 Till every effort, every motion gone,
    The scene before him lies in perfect view,      [575]
    Exposed and lifeless, as a written book.
    But let him pause awhile, and look again
    And a new quickening shall succeed, at first
730 Beginning timidly, then creeping fast
    Through all which he beholds; the senseless mass,      [580]
    In its projections, wrinkles, cavities,
    Through all its surface, with all colours streaming,
    Like a magician's airy pageant, parts,
735 Unites, embodying everywhere some pressure
    Or image, recognis'd or new, some type
    Or picture of the world; forests and lakes,
    Ships, Rivers, Towers, the Warrior clad in Mail,      [585]
    The prancing Steed, the Pilgrim with his Staff,
740 The mitred Bishop and the throned King,
    A Spectacle to which there is no end.

No otherwise had I at first been moved      [590]

712 Vault of Earth] spacious vault A².
714–15 Of Yordas . . . grow]
      Of Yordas; he looks round and sees the cave A².
723 quiet 𝔄 C D E: silent E²
726 lies 𝔄 C D E: stands E².
732–41 Busies the eye with images and forms
      Boldly assembled—here is shadowed forth
      A variegated landscape—there the shape
      Of some gigantic Warrior clad in mail.

And grateful memory, as a thing divine.

    The curious traveller, who, from open day,       560
Hath passed with torches into some huge cave,
The Grotto of Antiparos, or the Den
In old time haunted by that Danish Witch,
Yordas; he looks around and sees the vault
Widening on all sides; sees, or thinks he sees,      565
Erelong, the massy roof above his head,
That instantly unsettles and recedes,—
Substance and shadow, light and darkness, all
Commingled, making up a canopy
Of shapes and forms and tendencies to shape      570
That shift and vanish, change and interchange
Like spectres,—ferment silent and sublime!
That after a short space works less and less,
Till, every effort, every motion gone,
The scene before him stands in perfect view      575
Exposed, and lifeless as a written book!—
But let him pause awhile, and look again,
And a new quickening shall succeed, at first
Beginning timidly, then creeping fast,
Till the whole cave, so late a senseless mass,      580
Busies the eye with images and forms
Boldly assembled,—here is shadowed forth
From the projections, wrinkles, cavities,
A variegated landscape,—there the shape
Of some gigantic warrior clad in mail,      585
The ghostly semblance of a hooded monk,
Veiled nun, or pilgrim resting on his staff:
Strange congregation! yet not slow to meet
Eyes that perceive through minds that can inspire.

    Even in such sort had I at first been moved,      590

      A pilgrim with his Staff, or throned king,
      Strange spectacle to which there is no end.  A[2] C.
      With a diversity of colours streaming
      Here shadows forth a Landscape—there the tubes
      Of a mute organ, further on the shape
      Of some gigantic warrior clad in mail:
      A mitred Bishop or a throned King.  A[3].
*Between* [582] *and* [583] D *has* Half seen, created half with wanton power.
  738–41 D *stuck over*: D[2] *as* 1850.
  742–51 *These lines appear in* X *text, but in* 750 seat *for* home.

With such a swell of feeling, follow'd soon
By a blank sense of greatness pass'd away
745 And afterwards continu'd to be mov'd
In presence of that vast Metropolis,
The Fountain of my Country's destiny
And of the destiny of Earth itself,
That great Emporium, Chronicle at once
750 And Burial-place of passions and their home          [595]
Imperial and chief living residence.

With strong Sensations, teeming as it did
Of past and present, such a place must needs
Have pleas'd me, in those times; I sought not then
755 Knowledge; but craved for power, and power I found  [600]
In all things; nothing had a circumscribed
And narrow influence; but all objects, being
Themselves capacious, also found in me               [605]
Capaciousness and amplitude of mind;
760 Such is the strength and glory of our Youth.
The Human nature unto which I felt
That I belong'd, and which I lov'd and reverenc'd,
Was not a punctual Presence, but a Spirit            [610]
Living in time and space, and far diffus'd.
765 In this my joy, in this my dignity
Consisted; the external universe,
By striking upon what is found within,
Had given me this conception, with the help
Of Books, and what they picture and record.          [616]

770     'Tis true the History of my native Land,
With those of Greece compar'd and popular Rome,
Events not lovely nor magnanimous,
But harsh and unaffecting in themselves
And in our high-wrought modern narratives
775 Stript of their harmonising soul, the life
Of manners and familiar incidents,                   [621]
Had never much delighted me. And less
Than other minds I had been used to owe
The pleasure which I found in place or thing
780 To extrinsic transitory accidents,

746–8 By each particular sight that met my eye
      As I explored the vast metropolis
      Fountain of England's destiny and the world's  A².

Nor otherwise continued to be moved,
As I explored the vast metropolis,
Fount of my country's destiny and the world's;
That great emporium, chronicle at once
And burial-place of passions, and their home          595
Imperial, their chief living residence.


With strong sensations teeming as it did
Of past and present, such a place must needs
Have pleased me, seeking knowledge at that time
Far less than craving power; yet knowledge came,      600
Sought or unsought, and influxes of power
Came, of themselves, or at her call derived
In fits of kindliest apprehensiveness,
From all sides, when whate'er was in itself
Capacious found, or seemed to find, in me             605
A correspondent amplitude of mind;
Such is the strength and glory of our youth!
The human nature unto which I felt
That I belonged, and reverenced with love,
Was not a punctual presence, but a spirit             610
Diffused through time and space, with aid derived
Of evidence from monuments, erect,
Prostrate, or leaning towards their common rest
In earth, the widely scattered wreck sublime
Of vanished nations, or more clearly drawn            615
From books and what they picture and record.


'Tis true, the history of our native land,
With those of Greece compared and popular Rome,
And in our high-wrought modern narratives
Stript of their harmonising soul, the life            620
Of manners and familiar incidents,
Had never much delighted me. And less
Than other intellects had mine been used
To lean upon extrinsic circumstance

754-5 in those times . . . power, 𝔄 C: A² *as* 1850.
755-65 D *stuck over*: D² E *as* 1850, *but in* [611] not without aid *for* with
aid derived E².
765-6 In this . . . consisted 𝔄 C: God's glorious work A².
778-80 𝔄 C: A² *as* 1850, *but* accident *for* circumstance.

To records or traditions; but a sense                    [625]
Of what had been here done, and suffer'd here
Through ages, and was doing, suffering, still
Weigh'd with me, could support the test of thought,
785 Was like the enduring majesty and power             [631]
Of independent nature; and not seldom
Even individual remembrances,
By working on the Shapes before my eyes,
Became like vital functions of the soul;
790 And out of what had been, what was, the place
Was throng'd with impregnations, like those wilds
In which my early feelings had been nurs'd,
And naked valleys, full of caverns, rocks,                [635]
And audible seclusions, dashing lakes,
795 Echoes and Waterfalls, and pointed crags
That into music touch the passing wind.

 Thus here imagination also found
An element that pleas'd her, tried her strength,         [640]
Among new objects simplified, arranged,
800 Impregnated my knowledge, made it live,
And the result was elevating thoughts
Of human Nature. Neither guilt nor vice,                 [645]
Debasement of the body or the mind,
Nor all the misery forced upon my sight,
805 Which was not lightly passed, but often scann'd
Most feelingly, could overthrow my trust
In what we may become, induce belief                     [650]
That I was ignorant, had been falsely taught,
A Solitary, who with vain conceits
810 Had been inspired, and walk'd about in dreams.
When from that awful prospect overcast
And in eclipse, my meditations turn'd,
Lo! everything that was indeed divine                    [655]
Retain'd its purity inviolate
815 And unencroach'd upon, nay, seem'd brighter far
For this deep shade in counterview, that gloom
Of opposition, such as shew'd itself
To the eyes of Adam, yet in Paradise,
Though fallen from bliss, when in the East he saw        [660]

781–6 but a sense . . . nature 𝔄 C D: *but* A² D  Rival'd *for* Was like D² *as*
1850.
793 And naked 𝔄 C D: Bare hills and D².

Of record or tradition; but a sense                              625
Of what in the Great City had been done
And suffered, and was doing, suffering, still,
Weighed with me, could support the test of thought;
And, in despite of all that had gone by,
Or was departing never to return,                               630
There I conversed with majesty and power
Like independent natures. Hence the place
Was thronged with impregnations like the Wilds
In which my early feelings had been nursed—
Bare hills and valleys, full of caverns, rocks,                 635
And audible seclusions, dashing lakes,
Echoes and waterfalls, and pointed crags
That into music touch the passing wind.
Here then my young imagination found
No uncongenial element; could here                              640
Among new objects serve or give command,
Even as the heart's occasions might require,
To forward reason's else too scrupulous march.
The effect was, still more elevated views
Of human nature. Neither vice nor guilt,                        645
Debasement undergone by body or mind,
Nor all the misery forced upon my sight,
Misery not lightly passed, but sometimes scanned
Most feelingly, could overthrow my trust
In what we *may* become; induce belief                          650
That I was ignorant, had been falsely taught,
A solitary, who with vain conceits
Had been inspired, and walked about in dreams.
From those sad scenes when meditation turned,
Lo! every thing that was indeed divine                          655
Retained its purity inviolate,
Nay brighter shone, by this portentous gloom
Set off; such opposition as aroused
The mind of Adam, yet in Paradise
Though fallen from bliss, when in the East he saw               660

797–802 𝕬 C D: *but* 800 Impregnated 𝕬 C: Inspirited A² D: D² *as*
1850.
    811–12 When from that prospect meditation turned A².
    815–18 Nay brighter seemed set off by contrast such
            As roused attention, damped at once and cheared
            The mind of Adam *etc*. D: D² *as* 1850.
    817–18 shew'd itself To the eyes] did appall The mind A² C.

820  Darkness ere day's mid course, and morning light
     More orient in the western cloud, that drew
     ' O'er the blue firmament a radiant white,
     Descending slow with something heavenly fraught.'

     Add also, that among the multitudes           [665]
825  Of that great City, oftentimes was seen
     Affectingly set forth, more than elsewhere
     Is possible, the unity of man,
     One spirit over ignorance and vice
     Predominant, in good and evil hearts         [670]
830  One sense for moral judgements, as one eye
     For the sun's light. When strongly breath'd upon
     By this sensation, whencesoe'er it comes
     Of union or communion doth the soul
     Rejoice as in her highest joy: for there,
835  There chiefly, hath she feeling whence she is,
     And, passing through all Nature rests with God.

     And is not, too, that vast Abiding-place
     Of human Creatures, turn where'er we may,
     Profusely sown with individual sights
840  Of courage, and integrity, and truth,         [VII. 600]
     And tenderness, which, here set off by foil,
     Appears more touching. In the tender scenes    [VII. 602]
     Chiefly was my delight, and one of these
     Never will be forgotten. 'Twas a Man,
845  Whom I saw sitting in an open Square
     Close to an iron paling that fenced in      [VII. 605]
     The spacious Grass-plot; on the corner stone
     Of the low wall in which the pales were fix'd
     Sate this one Man, and with a sickly babe
850  Upon his knee, whom he had thither brought
     For sunshine, and to breathe the fresher air.    [VII. 610]
     Of those who pass'd, and me who look'd at him,
     He took no note; but in his brawny Arms
     (The Artificer was to the elbow bare,
855  And from his work this moment had been stolen)
     He held the Child, and, bending over it,     [VII. 615]
     As if he were afraid both of the sun
     And of the air which he had come to seek,
     He eyed it with unutterable love.

Darkness ere day's mid course, and morning light
More orient in the western cloud, that drew
O'er the blue firmament a radiant white,
Descending slow with something heavenly fraught.

Add also, that among the multitudes                    **665**
Of that huge city, oftentimes was seen
Affectingly set forth, more than elsewhere
Is possible, the unity of man,
One spirit over ignorance and vice
Predominant, in good and evil hearts;                    **670**
One sense for moral judgments, as one eye
For the sun's light. The soul when smitten thus
By a sublime *idea*, whencesoe'er
Vouchsafed for union or communion, feeds
On the pure bliss, and takes her rest with God.                    **675**

[Me, rather, it employed, to note, and keep                    [VII. 598]
In memory, those individual sights
Of courage, or integrity, or truth,
Or tenderness, which there, set off by foil,
Appeared more touching. One will I select;                    [VII. 602]
A Father—for he bore that sacred name—
Him saw I, sitting in an open square,
Upon a corner-stone of that low wall,                    [VII. 605]
Wherein were fixed the iron pales that fenced
A spacious grass-plot; there, in silence, sate
This One Man, with a sickly babe outstretched
Upon his knee, whom he had thither brought
For sunshine, and to breathe the fresher air.                    [VII. 610]
Of those who passed, and me who looked at him,
He took no heed; but in his brawny arms
(The Artificer was to the elbow bare,
And from his work this moment had been stolen)
He held the child, and, bending over it,                    [VII. 615]
As if he were afraid both of the sun
And of the air, which he had come to seek,
Eyed the poor babe with love unutterable.]

831–6 𝔄 C: A² *as* 1850.
833–6                                        hath my Soul
        Been still accustom'd to rejoice, for there
        There chiefly, did she find her destiny. Y.
837–59 *Transferred in* E *to* Book VII [598–618]. D *retains here.*
842–6, 849 A² D *as* 1850.
849–50 He sate and with a sickly child, a babe
        Upon his knees whom thither he had brought Y.
859 A² D *as* 1850.

860    Thus from a very early age, O Friend!
       My thoughts had been attracted more and more        [676]
       By slow gradations towards human kind
       And to the good and ill of human life;
       Nature had led me on, and now I seem'd
865  To travel independent of her help,                    [681]
       As if I had forgotten her; but no,
       My Fellow beings still were unto me
       Far less than she was, though the scale of love
       Were filling fast, 'twas light, as yet, compared     [685]
870  With that in which her mighty objects lay.

      860–2  B A² C: Thus were my thoughts attracted more and more
                    By slow gradations  A.

Thus from a very early age, O Friend!
My thoughts by slow gradations had been drawn
To human-kind, and to the good and ill
Of human life: Nature had led me on;
And oft amid the 'busy hum' I seemed                    680
To travel independent of her help,
As if I had forgotten her; but no,
The world of human-kind outweighed not hers
In my habitual thoughts; the scale of love,
Though filling daily, still was light, compared         685
With that in which *her* mighty objects lay.

867–9 𝕬 C D:  D² *as* 1850.

# BOOK NINTH

## RESIDENCE IN FRANCE

As oftentimes a River, it might seem,
Yielding in part to old remembrances,
Part sway'd by fear to tread an onward road
That leads direct to the devouring sea
5  Turns, and will measure back his course, far back,    [5]
Towards the very regions which he cross'd
In his first outset; so have we long time
Made motions retrograde, in like pursuit
Detain'd. But now we start afresh; I feel
10  An impulse to precipitate my Verse.
Fair greetings to this shapeless eagerness,
Whene'er it comes, needful in work so long,    [20]
Thrice needful to the argument which now
Awaits us; Oh! how much unlike the past!
15  One which though bright the promise, will be found
Ere far we shall advance, ungenial, hard
To treat of, and forbidding in itself.

Free as a colt at pasture on the hill,
I ranged at large, through the Metropolis
20  Month after month. Obscurely did I live,    [25]
Not courting the society of Men
By literature, or elegance, or rank
Distinguish'd; in the midst of things, it seem'd,
Looking as from a distance on the world
25  That mov'd about me; yet insensibly
False preconceptions were corrected thus
And errors of the fancy rectified,
Alike with reference to men and things,
And sometimes from each quarter were pour'd in
30  Novel imaginations and profound.

[MSS. for Bk. IX: A B C D E; *for ll.* 293–520 Y.]
Book Ninth, Residence in France B: 9 A: Book Ninth C.
1–3 𝔄 C D: D² *as* 1850.
15–17                   will full soon
      Darken, presenting in exchange for peace
      Among mankind, and concord's golden chain

# BOOK NINTH

## RESIDENCE IN FRANCE

EVEN as a river,—partly (it might seem)
Yielding to old remembrances, and swayed
In part by fear to shape a way direct,
That would engulph him soon in the ravenous sea—
Turns, and will measure back his course, far back,    .5
Seeking the very regions which he crossed
In his first outset; so have we, my Friend!
Turned and returned with intricate delay.
Or as a traveller, who has gained the brow
Of some aerial Down, while there he halts    10
For breathing-time, is tempted to review
The region left behind him; and, if aught
Deserving notice have escaped regard,
Or been regarded with too careless eye,
Strives, from that height, with one and yet one more    15
Last look, to make the best amends he may:
So have we lingered. Now we start afresh
With courage, and new hope risen on our toil.
Fair greetings to this shapeless eagerness,
Whene'er it comes! needful in work so long,    20
Thrice needful to the argument which now
Awaits us! Oh, how much unlike the past!

    Free as a colt at pasture on the hill,
I ranged at large, through London's wide domain,
Month after month. Obscurely did I live,    25
Not seeking frequent intercourse with men,
By literature, or elegance, or rank,
Distinguished. Scarcely was a year thus spent
Ere I forsook the crowded solitude,
With less regret for its luxurious pomp,    30

    Distraction,—and for amity fierce hate
    Of all that Reason sanctifies and loves. A² C.
19 the Metropolis] London's wide domain A² C: L's vast domain B².
23–25 Distinguish'd; looking on the busy world
    As from a distance, yet insensibly A² C.
26 Erroneous preconceptions were displaced A², *deleting* 27: C *as* A.

A year thus spent, this field (with small regret  
Save only for the Book-stalls in the streets,       [32]  
Wild produce, hedge-row fruit, on all sides hung  
To tempt the sauntering traveller from his track)  
35   I quitted, and betook myself to France,  
Led thither chiefly by a personal wish  
To speak the language more familiarly,  
With which intent I chose for my abode  
A City on the Borders of the Loire.       [41]


40      Through Paris lay my readiest path, and there  
I sojourn'd a few days, and visited  
In haste each spot of old and recent fame  
The latter chiefly, from the Field of Mars  
Down to the Suburbs of St. Anthony,  
45   And from Mont Martyr southward, to the Dome  
Of Geneviève. In both her clamorous Halls,  
The National Synod and the Jacobins  
I saw the revolutionary Power       [50]  
Toss like a Ship at anchor, rock'd by storms;  
50   The Arcades I traversed in the Palace huge  
Of Orleans, coasted round and round the line  
Of Tavern, Brothel, Gaming-house, and Shop,  
Great rendezvous of worst and best, the walk       [55]  
Of all who had a purpose, or had not;  
55   I star'd and listen'd with a stranger's ears  
To Hawkers and Haranguers, hubbub wild!  
And hissing Factionists with ardent eyes,  
In knots, or pairs, or single, ant-like swarms       [60]  
Of Builders and Subverters, every face


31–39   A year of independent ease thus spent  
       The crowded solitude, (with less regret  
       For its luxurious pomps, the shows of art  
       And all the nicely guarded stores of wealth  
       Than for the humble Bookstalls in the streets)  
       I quitted and was speedily conveyed  
       To that attractive land which I had crossed  
       Erewhile in journey towards the snowclad Alps  
*etc. as* 1850 [36–41], A³ C (*for* A² v. *notes*).  
   [33] *not in D: added to* E.       34 from his track A: aside B.  
   [34] realm E²: land D E.       40 path] course A² C.  
   41 sojourn'd] tarried A² C D: D² *as* 1850.

And all the nicely-guarded shows of art,
Than for the humble book-stalls in the streets,
Exposed to eye and hand where'er I turned.

France lured me forth; the realm that I had crossed
So lately, journeying toward the snow-clad Alps.    35
But now, relinquishing the scrip and staff,
And all enjoyment which the summer sun
Sheds round the steps of those who meet the day
With motion constant as his own, I went
Prepared to sojourn in a pleasant town,    40
Washed by the current of the stately Loire.

Through Paris lay my readiest course, and there
Sojourning a few days, I visited,
In haste, each spot of old or recent fame,
The latter chiefly; from the field of Mars    45
Down to the suburbs of St. Antony,
And from Mont Martyr southward to the Dome
Of Geneviève. In both her clamorous Halls,
The National Synod and the Jacobins,
I saw the Revolutionary Power    50
Toss like a ship at anchor, rocked by storms;
The Arcades I traversed, in the Palace huge
Of Orleans; coasted round and round the line
Of Tavern, Brothel, Gaming-house, and Shop,
Great rendezvous of worst and best, the walk    55
Of all who had a purpose, or had not;
I stared and listened, with a stranger's ears,
To Hawkers and Haranguers, hubbub wild!
And hissing Factionists with ardent eyes,
In knots, or pairs, or single. Not a look    60
Hope takes, or Doubt or Fear is forced to wear,

58–62    single. Much dismay'd
But more astonish'd often did I gaze
With dizzy sight upon those ant-like
    swarms
Of builders and subverters—every
    look
That hope or apprehension could
    put on,
Joy, anger and vexation, face to face
And side by side with dissolute Idle-
    ness. A² C.

single, ant-like forms
Of Builders and Subverters dizzily
Heaped on each other Helped and
    Helper plagued
With mutual condemnation; every
    look
Hope takes, or doubt and dread are
    forced to use
And every gesture uncontrolable
Of anger *etc. as* 1850 A³.

60 That hope or apprehension could put on,
Joy, anger, and vexation in the midst
Of gaiety and dissolute idleness.                    [66]

   Where silent zephyrs sported with the dust
Of the Bastile, I sate in the open sun,
65 And from the rubbish gather'd up a stone
And pocketed the relick in the guise                 [70]
Of an Enthusiast, yet, in honest truth
Though not without some strong incumbences;
And glad, (could living man be otherwise)
70 I look'd for something that I could not find,
Affecting more emotion than I felt,
For 'tis most certain that the utmost force          [74]
Of all these various objects which may shew
The temper of my mind as then it was
75 Seem'd less to recompense the Traveller's pains,
Less mov'd me, gave me less delight than did
Among other sights, the Magdalene of le Brun,
A Beauty exquisitely wrought, fair face
And rueful, with its ever-flowing tears.             [80]

80     But hence to my more permanent residence
I hasten; there, by novelties in speech
Domestic manners, customs, gestures, looks,
And all the attire of ordinary life,
Attention was at first engross'd; and thus,          [85]
85 Amused and satisfied, I scarcely felt
The shock of these concussions, unconcerned,
Tranquil, almost, and careless as a flower
Glassed in a Green-house, or a Parlour shrub
When every bush and tree, the country through,       [90]
90 Is shaking to the roots; indifference this
Which may seem strange; but I was unprepared
With needful knowledge, had abruptly pass'd
Into a theatre, of which the stage

68 incumbences B: incumbencies A C.
68–69 𝔄 C D: D *deletes*.
76–77 Less mov'd me, gave my spirit less delight
       Than one famed product of the pencil's skill
       A single picture merely, hunted out
       Among other sights, *etc.* A² C.
[79–80] rueful cheek Pale and bedropped D² C:
       pallid cheek Rueful with drops D.

But seemed there present; and I scanned them all,
Watched every gesture uncontrollable,
Of anger, and vexation, and despite,
All side by side, and struggling face to face,        65
With gaiety and dissolute idleness.


Where silent zephyrs sported with the dust
Of the Bastille, I sate in the open sun,
And from the rubbish gathered up a stone,
And pocketed the relic, in the guise        70
Of an enthusiast; yet, in honest truth,
I looked for something that I could not find,
Affecting more emotion than I felt;
For 'tis most certain, that these various sights,
However potent their first shock, with me        75
Appeared to recompense the traveller's pains
Less than the painted Magdalene of Le Brun,
A beauty exquisitely wrought, with hair
Dishevelled, gleaming eyes, and rueful cheek
Pale and bedropped with everflowing tears.        80


But hence to my more permanent abode
I hasten; there, by novelties in speech,
Domestic manners, customs, gestures, looks,
And all the attire of ordinary life,
Attention was engrossed; and, thus amused,        85
I stood, 'mid those concussions, unconcerned,
Tranquil almost, and careless as a flower
Glassed in a green-house, or a parlour shrub
That spreads its leaves in unmolested peace,
While every bush and tree, the country through,        90
Is shaking to the roots: indifference this
Which may seem strange: but I was unprepared
With needful knowledge, had abruptly passed
Into a theatre, whose stage was filled

80 residence] abode  A² B² C.
84-89 Attention was engross'd, and thus amused
        And satisfied I scarcely felt the shock
        Of those concussions, yea might it be said
        Remained almost as tranquil as a flower
        Glassed in a Greenhouse or a Parlour shrub
        That spreads its leaves in unmolested calm  A² C.

Was busy with an action far advanced.                    [95]
95  Like others I had read, and eagerly
Sometimes, the master Pamphlets of the day;
Nor wanted such half-insight as grew wild
Upon that meagre soil, help'd out by Talk
And public News; but having never chanced          [100]
100 To see a regular Chronicle which might shew,
(If any such indeed existed then)
Whence the main Organs of the Public Power
Had sprung, their transmigrations when and how
Accomplish'd, giving thus unto events
105 A form and body, all things were to me            [105]
Loose and disjointed, and the affections left
Without a vital interest. At that time,
Moreover, the first storm was overblown,
And the strong hand of outward violence
110 Lock'd up in quiet. For myself, I fear             [110]
Now in connection with so great a Theme
To speak (as I must be compell'd to do)
Of one so unimportant: a short time
I loiter'd, and frequented night by night
115 Routs, card-tables, the formal haunts of Men,
Whom in the City privilege of birth               [115]
Sequester'd from the rest, societies
Where, through punctilios of elegance
And deeper causes, all discourse, alike
120 Of good and evil in the time, was shunn'd
With studious care; but 'twas not long ere this    [120]
Proved tedious, and I gradually withdrew
Into a noisier world; and thus did soon
Become a Patriot, and my heart was all
125 Given to the People, and my love was theirs.

A knot of military Officers,                         [125]
That to a Regiment appertain'd which then
Was station'd in the City, were the chief
Of my associates: some of these wore Swords
130 Which had been seasoned in the Wars, and all
Were men well-born, at least laid claim to such
Distinction, as the Chivalry of France.

95–96 A² C as 1850.       102 Organs B A² C: objects A.
110 Locked 𝔄 C D: Looked E.       113 short time 𝔄: brief while A² C.

And busy with an action far advanced.                          95
Like others, I had skimmed, and sometimes read
With care, the master pamphlets of the day;
Nor wanted such half-insight as grew wild
Upon that meagre soil, helped out by talk
And public news; but having never seen                        100
A chronicle that might suffice to show
Whence the main organs of the public power
Had sprung, their transmigrations, when and how
Accomplished, giving thus unto events
A form and body; all things were to me                        105
Loose and disjointed, and the affections left
Without a vital interest. At that time,
Moreover, the first storm was overblown,
And the strong hand of outward violence
Locked up in quiet. For myself, I fear                        110
Now in connection with so great a theme
To speak (as I must be compelled to do)
Of one so unimportant; night by night
Did I frequent the formal haunts of men,
Whom, in the city, privilege of birth                         115
Sequestered from the rest; societies
Polished in arts, and in punctilio versed;
Whence, and from deeper causes, all discourse
Of good and evil of the time was shunned
With scrupulous care; but these restrictions soon             120
Proved tedious, and I gradually withdrew
Into a noisier world, and thus ere long
Became a patriot; and my heart was all
Given to the people, and my love was theirs.

    A band of military Officers,                        125
Then stationed in the city, were the chief
Of my associates: some of these wore swords
That had been seasoned in the wars, and all
Were men well-born; the chivalry of France.

117–18 Sequester'd from their fellows, circles where
      Through nice punctilios of society  A² C.
117–19           circles versed
     In nice punctilios of society
     Whence, and from deeper causes, all discourse  A³.
121 studious] scrupulous  A² C.     126 knot] band  A² C.
127 A *deletes*: *not in* C.    128 Was] Then  A² C.

In age and temper differing, they had yet                [130]
One spirit ruling in them all, alike
135  (Save only one, hereafter to be nam'd)
Were bent upon undoing what was done:
This was their rest, and only hope, therewith
No fear had they of bad becoming worse,               [135]
For worst to them was come, nor would have stirr'd,
140  Or deem'd it worth a moment's while to stir,
In anything, save only as the act
Look'd thitherward. One, reckoning by years,
Was in the prime of manhood, and erewhile            [140]
He had sate Lord in many tender hearts,
145  Though heedless of such honours now, and chang'd:
His temper was quite master'd by the times,
And they had blighted him, had eat away
The beauty of his person, doing wrong                 [145]
Alike to body and to mind: his port,
150  Which once had been erect and open, now
Was stooping and contracted, and a face,
By nature lovely in itself, express'd                 [150]
As much as any that was ever seen,
A ravage out of season, made by thoughts
155  Unhealthy and vexatious. At the hour,
The most important of each day, in which
The public News was read, the fever came,            [155]
A punctual visitant, to shake this Man,
Disarm'd his voice, and fann'd his yellow cheek
160  Into a thousand colours; while he read,
Or mused, his sword was haunted by his touch
Continually, like an uneasy place                     [160]
In his own body. 'Twas in truth an hour
Of universal ferment; mildest men
165  Were agitated; and commotions, strife
Of passion and opinion fill'd the walls
Of peaceful houses with unquiet sounds.               [165]
The soil of common life was at that time
Too hot to tread upon; oft said I then,
170  And not then only, 'what a mockery this
Of history, the past and that to come!
Now do I feel how I have been deceived,               [170]

140  while] thought  A² C.        147  eat *all MSS.*:  eaten 1850.

In age and temper differing, they had yet          130
One spirit ruling in each heart; alike
(Save only one, hereafter to be named)
Were bent upon undoing what was done:
This was their rest and only hope; therewith
No fear had they of bad becoming worse,          135
For worst to them was come; nor would have stirred,
Or deemed it worth a moment's thought to stir,
In any thing, save only as the act
Looked thitherward. One, reckoning by years,
Was in the prime of manhood, and erewhile          140
He had sate lord in many tender hearts;
Though heedless of such honours now, and changed:
His temper was quite mastered by the times,
And they had blighted him, had eaten away
The beauty of his person, doing wrong          145
Alike to body and to mind: his port,
Which once had been erect and open, now
Was stooping and contracted, and a face,
Endowed by Nature with her fairest gifts
Of symmetry and light and bloom, expressed,          150
As much as any that was ever seen,
A ravage out of season, made by thoughts
Unhealthy and vexatious. With the hour,
That from the press of Paris duly brought
Its freight of public news, the fever came,          155
A punctual visitant, to shake this man,
Disarmed his voice and fanned his yellow cheek
Into a thousand colours; while he read,
Or mused, his sword was haunted by his touch
Continually, like an uneasy place          160
In his own body. 'Twas in truth an hour
Of universal ferment; mildest men
Were agitated; and commotions, strife
Of passion and opinion, filled the walls
Of peaceful houses with unquiet sounds.          165
The soil of common life, was, at that time,
Too hot to tread upon. Oft said I then,
And not then only, 'What a mockery this
Of history, the past and that to come!
Now do I feel how all men are deceived,          170

152 By nature admirably fair, expressed A² C: Erewhile enriched with
nature's fairest gifts D: D² *as* 1850.

Reading of Nations and their works, in faith,
Faith given to vanity and emptiness;
175 Oh! laughter for the Page that would reflect
To future times the face of what now is!'
The land all swarm'd with passion, like a Plain    [175]
Devour'd by locusts, Carra, Gorsas, add
A hundred other names, forgotten now,
180 Nor to be heard of more, yet were they Powers,
Like earthquakes, shocks repeated day by day,
And felt through every nook of town and field.    [180]

The Men already spoken óf as chief
Of my Associates were prepared for flight
185 To augment the band of Emigrants in Arms
Upon the borders óf the Rhine, and leagued
With foreign Foes mustered for instant war.    [185]
This was their undisguis'd intent, and they
Were waiting with the whole of their desires
190 The moment to depart.
                 An Englishman,
Born in a Land, the name of which appear'd
To license some unruliness of mind,    [190]
A Stranger, with Youth's further privilege,
And that indulgence which a half-learn'd speech
195 Wins from the courteous, I who had been else
Shunn'd and not tolerated freely lived
With these Defenders of the Crown, and talk'd    [195]
And heard their notions, nor did they disdain
The wish to bring me over to their cause.

200    But though untaught by thinking or by books
To reason well of polity or law
And nice distinctions, then on every tongue,    [200]
Of natural rights and civil, and to acts
Of Nations, and their passing interests,
205 (I speak comparing these with other things)
Almost indifferent, even the Historian's Tale
Prizing but little otherwise than I priz'd    [205]
Tales of the Poets, as it made my heart
Beat high and fill'd my fancy with fair forms,
210 Old Heroes and their sufferings and their deeds;

[176] Gorcas 1850: Gorsas 1851.      183–4 A² C *as* 1850.

Reading of nations and their works, in faith,
Faith given to vanity and emptiness;
Oh! laughter for the page that would reflect
To future times the face of what now is!'
The land all swarmed with passion, like a plain          175
Devoured by locusts,—Carra, Gorcas,—add
A hundred other names, forgotten now,
Nor to be heard of more; yet, they were powers,
Like earthquakes, shocks repeated day by day,
And felt through every nook of town and field.          180

    Such was the state of things. Meanwhile the chief
Of my associates stood prepared for flight
To augment the band of emigrants in arms
Upon the borders of the Rhine, and leagued
With foreign foes mustered for instant war.          185
This was their undisguised intent, and they
Were waiting with the whole of their desires
The moment to depart.
               An Englishman,
Born in a land whose very name appeared
To license some unruliness of mind;          190
A stranger, with youth's further privilege,
And the indulgence that a half-learnt speech
Wins from the courteous; I, who had been else
Shunned and not tolerated, freely lived
With these defenders of the Crown, and talked,          195
And heard their notions; nor did they disdain
The wish to bring me over to their cause.

    But though untaught by thinking or by books
To reason well of polity or law,
And nice distinctions, then on every tongue,          200
Of natural rights and civil; and to acts
Of nations and their passing interests,
(If with unworldly ends and aims compared)
Almost indifferent, even the historian's tale
Prizing but little otherwise than I prized          205
Tales of the poets, as it made the heart
Beat high, and filled the fancy with fair forms,
Old heroes and their sufferings and their deeds;

186 Rhine A² B² C; Loire ꓥ.      191 ꓫ C: B² *as* 1850.

Yet in the regal Sceptre, and the pomp
Of Orders and Degrees, I nothing found                    [210]
Then, or had ever, even in crudest youth,
That dazzled me; but rather what my soul
215 Mourn'd for, or loath'd, beholding that the best
Rul'd not, and feeling that they ought to rule.


For, born in a poor District, and which yet          [215]
Retaineth more of ancient homeliness,
Manners erect, and frank simplicity,
220 Than any other nook of English Land,
It was my fortune scarcely to have seen
Through the whole tenor of my School-day time
The face of one, who, whether Boy or Man,          [220]
Was vested with attention or respect
225 Through claims of wealth or blood; nor was it least
Of many debts which afterwards I owed
To Cambridge, and an academic life
That something there was holden up to view          [225]
Of a Republic, where all stood thus far
230 Upon equal ground, that they were brothers all
In honour, as in one community,
Scholars and Gentlemen, where, furthermore,
Distinction lay open to all that came,          [230]
And wealth and titles were in less esteem
235 Than talents and successful industry.
Add unto this, subservience from the first
To God and Nature's single sovereignty,          [235]
Familiar presences of awful Power
And fellowship with venerable books
240 To sanction the proud workings of the soul,
And mountain liberty. It could not be
But that one tutor'd thus, who had been form'd
To thought and moral feeling in the way
This story hath described, should look with awe
245 Upon the faculties of Man, receive          [240]
Gladly the highest promises, and hail
As best the government of equal rights
And individual worth. And hence, O Friend!
If at the first great outbreak I rejoiced
250 Less than might well befit my youth, the cause          [245]
In part lay here, that unto me the events

Yet in the regal sceptre, and the pomp
Of orders and degrees, I nothing found                     210
Then, or had ever, even in crudest youth,
That dazzled me, but rather what I mourned
And ill could brook, beholding that the best
Ruled not, and feeling that they ought to rule.

For, born in a poor district, and which yet                215
Retaineth more of ancient homeliness,
Than any other nook of English ground,
It was my fortune scarcely to have seen,
Through the whole tenor of my school-day time,
The face of one, who, whether boy or man,                  220
Was vested with attention or respect
Through claims of wealth or blood; nor was it least
Of many benefits, in later years
Derived from academic institutes
And rules, that they held something up to view             225
Of a Republic, where all stood thus far
Upon equal ground; that we were brothers all
In honour, as in one community,
Scholars and gentlemen; where, furthermore,
Distinction open lay to all that came,                     230
And wealth and titles were in less esteem
Than talents, worth, and prosperous industry.
Add unto this, subservience from the first
To presences of God's mysterious power
Made manifest in Nature's sovereignty,                     235
And fellowship with venerable books, *
To sanction the proud workings of the soul,
And mountain liberty. It could not be
But that one tutored thus should look with awe
Upon the faculties of man, receive                         240
Gladly the highest promises, and hail,
As best, the government of equal rights
And individual worth. And hence, O Friend!
If at the first great outbreak I rejoiced
Less than might well befit my youth, the cause            245
In part lay here, that unto me the events

218 Retaineth more of moral virtue, more
        Of shrewd discernment, ancient homeliness  A² C.
227 To the institutes of academic life
        And to my sojourn on the banks of Cam  A² C.
233 lay open *all MSS.*: open lay 1850.

Seem'd nothing out of nature's certain course,
A gift that rather was come late than soon.
No wonder, then, if advocates like these [249]
255 Whom I have mention'd, at this riper day
Were impotent to make my hopes put on
The shape of theirs, my understanding bend
In honour to their honour, zeal which yet
Had slumber'd, now in opposition burst [255]
260 Forth like a Polar Summer; every word
They utter'd was a dart, by counter-winds
Blown back upon themselves, their reason seem'd
Confusion-stricken by a higher power
Than human understanding, their discourse [260]
265 Maim'd, spiritless, and in their weakness strong
I triumph'd.
         Meantime, day by day, the roads
(While I consorted with these Royalists)
Were crowded with the bravest Youth of France,
And all the promptest of her Spirits, link'd
270 In gallant Soldiership, and posting on [265]
To meet the War upon her Frontier Bounds.
Yet at this very moment do tears start
Into mine eyes; I do not say I weep,
I wept not then, but tears have dimm'd my sight,
275 In memory of the farewells of that time, [270]
Domestic severings, female fortitude
At dearest separation, patriot love
And self-devotion, and terrestrial hope
Encourag'd with a martyr's confidence;
280 Even files of Strangers merely, seen but once, [275]
And for a moment, men from far with sound
Of music, martial tunes, and banners spread
Entering the City, here and there a face
Or person singled out among the rest,
285 Yet still a Stranger and belov'd as such, [280]
Even by these passing spectacles my heart
Was oftentimes uplifted, and they seem'd
Like arguments from Heaven, that 'twas a cause
Good, and which no one could stand up against
290 Who was not lost, abandon'd, selfish, proud, [285]

       255 A² C *as* 1850.      267 A *deletes*; *not in* C.

Seemed nothing out of nature's certain course,
A gift that was come rather late than soon.
No wonder, then, if advocates like these,
Inflamed by passion, blind with prejudice,   250
And stung with injury, at this riper day,
Were impotent to make my hopes put on
The shape of theirs, my understanding bend
In honour to their honour: zeal, which yet
Had slumbered, now in opposition burst   255
Forth like a Polar summer: every word
They uttered was a dart, by counter-winds
Blown back upon themselves; their reason seemed
Confusion-stricken by a higher power
Than human understanding, their discourse   260
Maimed, spiritless; and, in their weakness strong,
I triumphed.
           Meantime, day by day, the roads
Were crowded with the bravest youth of France,
And all the promptest of her spirits, linked
In gallant soldiership, and posting on   265
To meet the war upon her frontier bounds.
Yet at this very moment do tears start
Into mine eyes: I do not say I weep—
I wept not then,—but tears have dimmed my sight,
In memory of the farewells of that time,   270
Domestic severings, female fortitude
At dearest separation, patriot love
And self-devotion, and terrestrial hope,
Encouraged with a martyr's confidence;
Even files of strangers merely seen but once,   275
And for a moment, men from far with sound
Of music, martial tunes, and banners spread,
Entering the city, here and there a face,
Or person singled out among the rest,
Yet still a stranger and beloved as such;   280
Even by these passing spectacles my heart
Was oftentimes uplifted, and they seemed
Arguments sent from Heaven to prove the cause
Good, pure, which no one could stand up against,
Who was not lost, abandoned, selfish, proud,   ·285

274 tears have dimm'd 𝕬 C D E: moisture dims A².

Mean, miserable, wilfully deprav'd,
Hater perverse of equity and truth.

Among that band of Officers was one
Already hinted at, of other mold,
295 A Patriot, thence rejected by the rest                    [290]
And with an oriental loathing spurn'd,
As of a different Cast. A meeker Man
Than this liv'd never, or a more benign
Meek, though enthusiastic to the height
300 Of highest expectation. Injuries
Made *him* more gracious, and his nature then              [295]
Did breathe its sweetness out most sensibly
As aromatic flowers on alpine turf
When foot hath crush'd them. He thro' the events
305 Of that great change wander'd in perfect faith,
As through a Book, an old Romance or Tale                  [300]
Of Fairy, or some dream of actions wrought
Behind the summer clouds. By birth he rank'd
With the most noble, but unto the poor
310 Among mankind he was in service bound
As by some tie invisible, oaths profess'd                  [305]
To a religious Order. Man he lov'd
As Man; and to the mean and the obscure
And all the homely in their homely works
315 Transferr'd a courtesy which had no air
Of condescension, but did rather seem                      [310]
A passion and a gallantry, like that
Which he, a Soldier, in his idler day
Had pay'd to Woman; somewhat vain he was,
320 Or seem'd so, yet it was not vanity
But fondness, and a kind of radiant joy                    [315]
That cover'd him about when he was bent
On works of love or freedom, or revolved
Complacently the progress of a cause,
325 Whereof he was a part; yet this was meek
And placid, and took nothing from the Man                  [320]
That was delightful: oft in solitude
With him did I discourse about the end
Of civil government, and its wisest forms,
330 Of ancient prejudice, and chartered rights,

293 Among] Amid  Y.        297 Cast *all MSS*.: caste 1850.

Mean, miserable, wilfully depraved,
Hater perverse of equity and truth.

Among that band of Officers was one,
Already hinted at, of other mould—
A patriot, thence rejected by the rest,                    290
And with an oriental loathing spurned,
As of a different caste. A meeker man
Than this lived never, nor a more benign,
Meek though enthusiastic. Injuries
Made *him* more gracious, and his nature then              295
Did breathe its sweetness out most sensibly,
As aromatic flowers on Alpine turf,
When foot hath crushed them. He through the events
Of that great change wandered in perfect faith,
As through a book, an old romance, or tale                 300
Of Fairy, or some dream of actions wrought
Behind the summer clouds. By birth he ranked
With the most noble, but unto the poor
Among mankind he was in service bound,
As by some tie invisible, oaths professed                  305
To a religious order. Man he loved
As man; and, to the mean and the obscure,
And all the homely in their homely works,
Transferred a courtesy which had no air
Of condescension; but did rather seem                      310
A passion and a gallantry, like that
Which he, a soldier, in his idler day
Had paid to woman: somewhat vain he was,
Or seemed so, yet it was not vanity,
But fondness, and a kind of radiant joy                    315
Diffused around him, while he was intent
On works of love or freedom, or revolved
Complacently the progress of a cause,
Whereof he was a part: yet this was meek
And placid, and took nothing from the man                  320
That was delightful. Oft in solitude
With him did I discourse about the end
Of civil government, and its wisest forms;
Of ancient loyalty, and chartered rights,

301 *him* A C: him B.        307 Fairy] Faery  Y.
322 A² C *as* 1850.        330 prejudice] loyalty  A² C.

Allegiance, faith, and law by time matured,
Custom and habit, novelty and change,                    [325]
Of self-respect, and virtue in the Few
For patrimonial honour set apart,
335 And ignorance in the labouring Multitude.
For he, an upright Man and tolerant,
Balanced these contemplations in his mind                [330]
And I, who at that time was scarcely dipp'd
Into the turmoil, had a sounder judgment
340 Than afterwards, carried about me yet
With less alloy to its integrity
The experience of past ages, as through help            [335]
Of Books and common life it finds its way
To youthful minds, by objects over near
345 Not press'd upon, nor dazzled or misled
By struggling with the crowd for present ends.

But though not deaf and obstinate to find              [340]
Error without apology on the side
Of those who were against us, more delight
350 We took, and let this freely be confess'd,
In painting to ourselves the miseries
Of royal Courts, and that voluptuous life              [345]
Unfeeling, where the Man who is of soul
The meanest thrives the most, where dignity,
355 True personal dignity, abideth not,
A light and cruel world, cut off from all
The natural inlets of just sentiment,                  [350]
From lowly sympathy, and chastening truth,
Where good and evil never have that name,
360 That which they ought to have, but wrong prevails,
And vice at home. We added dearest themes,
Man and his noble nature, as it is                      [355]
The gift of God and lies in his own power,
His blind desires and steady faculties
365 Capable of clear truth, the one to break
Bondage, the other to build Liberty
On firm foundations, making social life,               [360]

331 A *deletes*: *not in* C.
336 A² C *as* 1850: For he by nature tolerant and subdued  Y.
339 had] bore A² C.        judgment 𝕬 C D E: mind  Y.
343 finds its way 𝕬 C D: makes sure way  D².

Custom and habit, novelty and change;                    325
Of self-respect, and virtue in the few
For patrimonial honour set apart,
And ignorance in the labouring multitude.
For he, to all intolerance indisposed,
Balanced these contemplations in his mind;               330
And I, who at that time was scarcely dipped
Into the turmoil, bore a sounder judgment
Than later days allowed; carried about me,
With less alloy to its integrity,
The experience of past ages, as, through help            335
Of books and common life, it makes sure way
To youthful minds, by objects over near
Not pressed upon, nor dazzled or misled
By struggling with the crowd for present ends.

But though not deaf, nor obstinate to find               340
Error without excuse upon the side
Of them who strove against us, more delight
We took, and let this freely be confessed,
In painting to ourselves the miseries
Of royal courts, and that voluptuous life                345
Unfeeling, where the man who is of soul
The meanest thrives the most; where dignity,
True personal dignity, abideth not;
A light, a cruel, and vain world cut off
From the natural inlets of just sentiment,               350
From lowly sympathy and chastening truth;
Where good and evil interchange their names,
And thirst for bloody spoils abroad is paired
With vice at home. We added dearest themes—
Man and his noble nature, as it is                       355
The gift which God has placed within his power,
His blind desires and steady faculties
Capable of clear truth, the one to break
Bondage, the other to build liberty
On firm foundations, making social life,                 360

349 who were] who strove  A² C.
359–61 Where Good and Evil interchange their names
    ·    Whence Evil irresistibly prevails
         The senseless thirst of bloody spoils abroad
         And vice  A² C.  Y *as* 𝔄 359–60, *followed by* The senseless thirst
*etc. as* A².

Through knowledge spreading and imperishable,
As just in regulation, and as pure
370 As individual in the wise and good.
We summon'd up the honorable deeds
Of ancient Story, thought of each bright spot                    [365]
That could be found in all recorded time
Of truth preserv'd and error pass'd away,
375 Of single Spirits that catch the flame from Heaven,
And how the multitude of men will feed
And fan each other, thought of Sects, how keen                   [370]
They are to put the appropriate nature on,
Triumphant over every obstacle
380 Of custom, language, Country, love and hate,
And what they do and suffer for their creed,
How far they travel, and how long endure,                        [375]
How quickly mighty Nations have been form'd
From least beginnings, how, together lock'd
385 By new opinions, scatter'd tribes have made
One body spreading wide as clouds in heaven.
To aspirations then of our own minds                             [380]
Did we appeal; and finally beheld
A living confirmation of the whole
390 Before us in a People risen up
Fresh as the morning Star: elate we look'd                       [385]
Upon their virtues, saw in rudest men
Self-sacrifice the firmest, generous love
And continence of mind, and sense of right
395 Uppermost in the midst of fiercest strife.

Oh! sweet it is, in academic Groves,                             [390]
Or such retirement, Friend! as we have known
Among the mountains, by our Rotha's Stream,
Greta or Derwent, or some nameless Rill,
400 To ruminate with interchange of talk
On rational liberty, and hope in Man,                            [395]
Justice and peace; but far more sweet such toil,
Toil say I, for it leads to thoughts abstruse
If Nature then be standing on the brink
405 Of some great trial, and we hear the voice
Of One devoted, one whom circumstance                            [400]

373 could] *all MSS.*        387 minds 𝔄 C D E: souls A² B².
390–1 People . . . star A²: C *as* 1850.        398 A² C *as* 1850.

Through knowledge spreading and imperishable,
As just in regulation, and as pure
As individual in the wise and good.

    We summoned up the honourable deeds
Of ancient Story, thought of each bright spot,       **365**
That would be found in all recorded time,
Of truth preserved and error passed away;
Of single spirits that catch the flame from Heaven,
And how the multitudes of men will feed
And fan each other; thought of sects, how keen     **370**
They are to put the appropriate nature on,
Triumphant over every obstacle
Of custom, language, country, love, or hate,
And what they do and suffer for their creed;
How far they travel, and how long endure;      **375**
How quickly mighty Nations have been formed,
From least beginnings; how, together locked
By new opinions, scattered tribes have made
One body, spreading wide as clouds in heaven.
To aspirations then of our own minds       **380**
Did we appeal; and, finally, beheld
A living confirmation of the whole
Before us, in a people from the depth
Of shameful imbecility uprisen,
Fresh as the morning star. Elate we looked     **385**
Upon their virtues; saw, in rudest men,
Self-sacrifice the firmest; generous love,
And continence of mind, and sense of right,
Uppermost in the midst of fiercest strife.

    Oh, sweet it is, in academic groves,      **390**
Or such retirement, Friend! as we have known
In the green dales beside our Rotha's stream,
Greta, or Derwent, or some nameless rill,
To ruminate, with interchange of talk,
On rational liberty, and hope in man,       **395**
Justice and peace. But far more sweet such toil—
Toil, say I, for it leads to thoughts abstruse—
If nature then be standing on the brink
Of some great trial, and we hear the voice
Of one devoted,—one whom circumstance     **400**

404 brink] edge Y.    405 trial ... hear 𝔄 Y²: task ... should hear Y.

Hath call'd upon to embody his deep sense
In action, give it outwardly a shape,
And that of benediction to the world ;
410 Then doubt is not, and truth is more than truth,
A hope it is and a desire, a creed                          [405]
Of zeal by an authority divine
Sanction'd of danger, difficulty or death.
Such conversation under Attic shades
415 Did Dion hold with Plato, ripen'd thus
For a Deliverer's glorious task, and such,                  [410]
He, on that ministry already bound,
Held with Eudemus and Timonides,
Surrounded by Adventurers in Arms,
420 When those two Vessels with their daring Freight
For the Sicilian Tyrant's overthrow                         [415]
Sail'd from Zacynthus, philosophic war
Led by Philosophers. With harder fate,
Though like ambition, such was he, O Friend!
425 Of whom I speak, so Beaupuis (let the Name
Stand near the worthiest of Antiquity)                      [420]
Fashion'd his life, and many a long discourse
With like persuasion honor'd we maintain'd,
He on his part accoutred for the worst.
430 He perish'd fighting in supreme command
Upon the Borders of the unhappy Loire                       [425]
For Liberty against deluded Men,
His Fellow-countrymen, and yet most bless'd
In this, that he the fate of later times
435 Lived not to see, nor what we now behold
Who have as ardent hearts as he had then.                   [430]


Along that very Loire, with Festivals
Resounding at all hours, and innocent yet
Of civil slaughter was our frequent walk
440 Or in wide Forests of the neighbourhood,
High woods and over-arch'd with open space                  [435]
On every side, and footing many a mile,
Inwoven roots and moss smooth as the sea,
A solemn region. Often in such place

424 he, O Friend!] he my Friend Y.
437 Festivals 𝔄: festivals Y: festal joy B²: festal mirth A² C.

Hath called upon to embody his deep sense
In action, give it outwardly a shape,
And that of benediction, to the world.
Then doubt is not, and truth is more than truth,—
A hope it is, and a desire; a creed                    405
Of zeal, by an authority Divine
Sanctioned, of danger, difficulty, or death.
Such conversation, under Attic shades,
Did Dion hold with Plato; ripened thus
For a Deliverer's glorious task,—and such              410
He, on that ministry already bound,
Held with Eudemus and Timonides,
Surrounded by adventurers in arms,
When these two vessels with their daring freight,
For the Sicilian Tyrant's overthrow,                   415
Sailed from Zacynthus,—philosophic war,
Led by Philosophers. With harder fate,
Though like ambition, such was he, O Friend!
Of whom I speak. So Beaupuis (let the name
Stand near the worthiest of Antiquity)                 420
Fashioned his life; and many a long discourse,
With like persuasion honoured, we maintained:
He on his part, accoutred for the worst.
He perished fighting, in supreme command,
Upon the borders of the unhappy Loire,                 425
For liberty, against deluded men,
His fellow country-men; and yet most blessed
In this, that he the fate of later times
Lived not to see, nor what we now behold,
Who have as ardent hearts as he had then.              430

Along that very Loire, with festal mirth
Resounding at all hours, and innocent yet
Of civil slaughter, was our frequent walk;
Or in wide forests of continuous shade,
Lofty and over-arched, with open space                 435
Beneath the trees, clear footing many a mile—
A solemn region. Oft amid those haunts,

440–2  A² C as 1850, but smooth for clear.
442–3                   and footing without end
                Of intermingled roots and lawny moss  Y.
444 in such place 𝔄 C: in such haunts  A².

445 From earnest dialogues I slipp'd in thought
And let remembrance steal to other times [439]
When Hermits from their sheds and caves forth stray'd
Walk'd by themselves, so met in shades like these,
And if a devious Traveller was heard [447]
450 Approaching from a distance, as might chance,
With speed and echoes loud of trampling hoofs
From the hard floor reverberated, then [450]
It was Angelica thundering through the woods
Upon her Palfrey, or that gentler Maid
455 Erminia, fugitive as fair as She.
Sometimes I saw, methought, a pair of Knights
Joust underneath the trees, that, as in storm, [455]
Did rock above their heads; anon the din
Of boisterous merriment and music's roar,
460 With sudden Proclamation, burst from haunt
Of Satyrs in some viewless glade, with dance
Rejoicing o'er a Female in the midst, [460]
A mortal Beauty, their unhappy Thrall;
The width of those huge Forests, unto me
465 A novel scene, did often in this way
Master my fancy, while I wander'd on
With that revered Companion. And sometimes [465]
When to a Convent in a meadow green
By a brook-side we came, a roofless Pile,
470 And not by reverential touch of Time
Dismantled, but by violence abrupt,
In spite of those heart-bracing colloquies, [470]
In spite of real fervour, and of that
Less genuine and wrought up within myself
475 I could not but bewail a wrong so harsh,
And for the matin Bell to sound no more
Griev'd, and the evening Taper, and the Cross [475]
High on the topmost Pinnacle, a sign
Admonitory to the Traveller
480 First seen above the woods.
                              And when my Friend

[446–50] D *stuck over*: D² *as* 1850.        449 And] But A² C.
450 A² C *as* 1850.        460 With] Gave Y.
477 evening 𝔄 C: twilight B² C².        479 to] by Y.
478–80 High station'd on the topmost pinnacle
            For reverential notice; and a sign
            (How welcome . . . rest. (*as* 1850)
            And when the honoured partner of my walks  A² C.

From earnest dialogues I slipped in thought,
And let remembrance steal to other times,
When, o'er those interwoven roots, moss-clad,        440
And smooth as marble or a waveless sea,
Some Hermit, from his cell forth-strayed, might pace
In sylvan meditation undisturbed;
As on the pavement of a Gothic church
Walks a lone Monk, when service hath expired,        445
In peace and silence.  But if e'er was heard,—
Heard, though unseen,—a devious traveller,
Retiring or approaching from afar
With speed and echoes loud of trampling hoofs
From the hard floor reverberated, then        450
It was Angelica thundering through the woods
Upon her palfrey, or that gentle maid
Erminia, fugitive as fair as she.
Sometimes methought I saw a pair of knights
Joust underneath the trees, that as in storm        455
Rocked high above their heads; anon, the din
Of boisterous merriment, and music's roar,
In sudden proclamation, burst from haunt
Of Satyrs in some viewless glade, with dance
Rejoicing o'er a female in the midst,        460
A mortal beauty, their unhappy thrall.
The width of those huge forests, unto me
A novel scene, did often in this way
Master my fancy while I wandered on
With that revered companion.  And sometimes—        465
When to a convent in a meadow green,
By a brook-side, we came, a roofless pile,
And not by reverential touch of Time
Dismantled, but by violence abrupt—
In spite of those heart-bracing colloquies,        470
In spite of real fervour, and of that
Less genuine and wrought up within myself—
I could not but bewail a wrong so harsh,
And for the Matin-bell to sound no more
Grieved, and the twilight taper, and the cross        475
High on the topmost pinnacle, a sign
(How welcome to the weary traveller's eyes!)
Of hospitality and peaceful rest.
And when the partner of those varied walks

Pointed upon occasion to the Site [480]
Of Romorentin, home of ancient Kings,
To the imperial Edifice of Blois
Or to that rural Castle, name now slipp'd
485 From my remembrance, where a Lady lodg'd
By the first Francis wooed, and bound to him [485]
In chains of mutual passion; from the Tower,
As a Tradition of the Country tells,
Practis'd to commune with her Royal Knight
490 By cressets and love-beacons, intercourse
'Twixt her high-seated Residence and his [490]
Far off at Chambord on the Plain beneath:
Even here, though less than with the peaceful House
Religious, 'mid these frequent monuments
495 Of Kings, their vices and their better deeds,
Imagination, potent to enflame [495]
At times with virtuous wrath and noble scorn,
Did also often mitigate the force
Of civic prejudice, the bigotry,
500 So call it, of a youthful Patriot's mind,
And on these spots with many gleams I look'd [500]
Of chivalrous delight. Yet not the less,
Hatred of absolute rule, where will of One
Is law for all, and of that barren pride
505 In those who, by immunities unjust,
Betwixt the Sovereign and the People stand, [505]
His helpers and not theirs, laid stronger hold
Daily upon me, mix'd with pity too
And love; for where hope is there love will be
510 For the abject multitude. And when we chanc'd
One day to meet a hunger-bitten Girl, [510]
Who crept along, fitting her languid self
Unto a Heifer's motion, by a cord
Tied to her arm, and picking thus from the lane
515 Its sustenance, while the Girl with her two hands
Was busy knitting, in a heartless mood [515]
Of solitude, and at the sight my Friend
In agitation said, ''Tis against *that*

492 beneath:] beneath A: beneath. B C D E.
494 monuments] vestiges Y.    498 mitigate ℨ Y²· mellow down Y.
512 self ℨ C: gait C².
515 her two ℨ: two lean B²: pallid A² C.

Pointed upon occasion to the site                           480
Of Romorentin, home of ancient kings,
To the imperial edifice of Blois,
Or to that rural castle, name now slipped
From my remembrance, where a lady lodged,
By the first Francis wooed, and bound to him              485
In chains of mutual passion, from the tower,
As a tradition of the country tells,
Practised to commune with her royal knight
By cressets and love-beacons, intercourse
'Twixt her high-seated residence and his                    490
Far off at Chambord on the plain beneath;
Even here, though less than with the peaceful house
Religious, 'mid those frequent monuments
Of Kings, their vices and their better deeds,
Imagination, potent to inflame                              495
At times with virtuous wrath and noble scorn,
Did also often mitigate the force
Of civic prejudice, the bigotry,
So call it, of a youthful patriot's mind;
And on these spots with many gleams I looked             500
Of chivalrous delight. Yet not the less,
Hatred of absolute rule, where will of one
Is law for all, and of that barren pride
In them who, by immunities unjust,
Between the sovereign and the people stand,              505
His helper and not theirs, laid stronger hold
Daily upon me, mixed with pity too
And love; for where hope is, there love will be
For the abject multitude. And when we chanced
One day to meet a hunger-bitten girl,                      510
Who crept along fitting her languid gait
Unto a heifer's motion, by a cord
Tied to her arm, and picking thus from the lane
Its sustenance, while the girl with pallid hands
Was busy knitting in a heartless mood                      515
Of solitude, and at the sight my friend
In agitation said, ' 'Tis against *that*

515–16          while th' attendant with her hands
       Was busied  Y.
518–19  Said with emotion, 'Against that it is Which we are fighting' Y.
There is it, there, That which we fight against  A² C.

Which we are fighting,' I with him believed
520 Devoutly that a spirit was abroad
     Which could not be withstood, that poverty       [520]
     At least like this, would in a little time
     Be found no more, that we should see the earth
     Unthwarted in her wish to recompense
525 The industrious, and the lowly Child of Toil,
     All institutes for ever blotted out       [525]
     That legalized exclusion, empty pomp
     Abolish'd, sensual state and cruel power
     Whether by edict of the one or few,
530 And finally, as sum and crown of all,
     Should see the People having a strong hand       [530]
     In making their own Laws, whence better days
     To all mankind. But, these things set apart,
     Was not the single confidence enough
535 To animate the mind that ever turn'd
     A thought to human welfare, that henceforth       [535]
     Captivity by mandate without law
     Should cease, and open accusation lead
     To sentence in the hearing of the world
540 And open punishment, if not the air
     Be free to breathe in, and the heart of Man       [540]
     Dread nothing. Having touch'd this argument
     I shall not, as my purpose was, take note
     Of other matters which detain'd us oft
545 In thought or conversation, public acts,
     And public persons, and the emotions wrought
     Within our minds by the ever-varying wind       [545]
     Of Record and Report which day by day
     Swept over us; but I will here instead
550 Draw from obscurity a tragic Tale
     Not in its spirit singular indeed
     But haply worth memorial, as I heard
     The events related by my patriot Friend
     And others who had borne a part therein.

520 Devoutly that a 𝔄 C: That a benignant A².
521 could 𝔄 C: might A².
522 At least like 𝔄 C: Abject like A² C².
525 The industrious and lowly 𝔄 C: A² as 1850.
532 making] framing A² C.
542 argument] sacred theme A² C.       547 our minds] the breast A².
549 Swept over] Broke in upon A² C.
550 obscurity] domestic life A² C.

That we are fighting,' I with him believed
That a benignant spirit was abroad
Which might not be withstood, that poverty                    520
Abject as this would in a little time
Be found no more, that we should see the earth
Unthwarted in her wish to recompense
The meek, the lowly, patient child of toil.
All institutes for ever blotted out                          525
That legalised exclusion, empty pomp
Abolished, sensual state and cruel power,
Whether by edict of the one or few;
And finally, as sum and crown of all,
Should see the people having a strong hand                   530
In framing their own laws; whence better days
To all mankind. But, these things set apart,
Was not this single confidence enough
To animate the mind that ever turned
A thought to human welfare? That henceforth                  535
Captivity by mandate without law
Should cease; and open accusation lead
To sentence in the hearing of the world,
And open punishment, if not the air
Be free to breathe in, and the heart of man                  540
Dread nothing. From this height I shall not stoop
To humbler matter that detained us oft
In thought or conversation, public acts,
And public persons, and emotions wrought
Within the breast, as ever-varying winds                     545
Of record or report swept over us;
But I might here, instead, repeat a tale,
Told by my Patriot friend, of sad events,
That prove to what low depth had struck the roots,
How widely spread the boughs, of that old tree               550
Which, as a deadly mischief, and a foul
And black dishonour, France was weary of.

551 Not in its spirit singularly fraught
     With tyranny and suffering undeserved  A².
     With the dire exercise of lawless power
     Fraught, though alas not singularly fraught  A³ C.
[551-2] D *stuck over*: D² *as* 1850.
554 By others too who having chanced to bear
     No wish'd for part therein with tears confirmed
     The truth their lips unwillingly rehears'd.  A² C.

555    Oh! happy time of youthful Lovers! thus
    My Story may begin, Oh! balmy time
    In which a Love-knot on a Lady's brow                                [555]
    Is fairer than the fairest Star in heaven!
    To such inheritance of blessedness                                    [5]
560    Young Vaudracour was brought by years that had
    A little overstepp'd his stripling prime.
    A Town of small repute in the heart of France                        [10]
    Was the Youth's Birth-place: there he vow'd his love
    To Julia, a bright Maid, from Parents sprung
565    Not mean in their condition; but with rights
    Unhonour'd of Nobility, and hence
    The Father of the young Man, who had place
    Among that order, spurn'd the very thought
    Of such alliance. From their cradles up,
570    With but a step between their several homes                            [20]
    The pair had thriven together year by year,
    Friends, Playmates, Twins in pleasure, after strife
    And petty quarrels had grown fond again,                              [22]
    Each other's advocate, each other's help,
575    Nor ever happy if they were apart:
    A basis this for deep and solid love,
    And endless constancy, and placid truth;
    But whatsoever of such treasures might,
    Beneath the outside of their youth, have lain
580    Reserv'd for mellower years, his present mind
    Was under fascination; he beheld
    A vision, and he lov'd the thing he saw.

560–1 Even such, the noble Vaudracour was brought
      By years that had a little overstepp'd *etc. as* 1820 A² C.
564–8 To a bright Maid—what boots it that no gem
      To princely courts exalted from the mine
      Glitters with such a witchery of light
      No field-flower blooms a thousandth part as sweet
      Plebeian *etc. as* 1820 [15] A² C.
574 help] stay A² C.
575 And strangers to content if long apart
      . . . each others sight *as* 1820 [24–29] A² C.
576–7 An earnest this of love imperishable
      Unclouded constancy, unblemished truth
      Peace without flaw—content without alloy C.
578 But whatsoe'er of such enjoyments might A².
578–80 But whatsoe'er of such rare treasure lay
      Beneath the surface of their youthful prime
      Reserv'd, had fate permitted, for support
      Of their remotest years, his present mind C.

Oh, happy time of youthful lovers, (thus
The story might begin). Oh, balmy time,
In which a love-knot, on a lady's brow,                    555

---

## VAUDRACOUR AND JULIA (1820)

O happy time of youthful lovers (thus
My story may begin) O balmy time,
In which a love-knot on a lady's brow
Is fairer than the fairest star in heaven!
To such inheritance of blessed fancy                       5
(Fancy that sports more desperately with minds
Than ever fortune hath been known to do)
The high-born Vaudracour was brought, by years
Whose progress had a little overstepped
His stripling prime. A town of small repute,              10
Among the vine-clad mountains of Auvergne,
Was the Youth's birth-place. There he woo'd a Maid
Who heard the heart-felt music of his suit
With answering vows. Plebeian was the stock,
Plebeian, though ingenuous, the stock,                     15
From which her graces and her honours sprung
And hence the father of the enamoured Youth,
With haughty indignation, spurned the thought
Of such alliance.—From their cradles up,
With but a step between their several homes,               20
Twins had they been in pleasure; after strife
And petty quarrels, had grown fond again;
Each other's advocate, each other's stay;
And strangers to content if long apart,
Or more divided than a sportive pair                       25
Of sea-fowl, conscious both that they are hovering
Within the eddy of a common blast,
Or hidden only by the concave depth
Of neighbouring billows from each other's sight.
    Thus, not without concurrence of an age                30
Unknown to memory, was an earnest given,
By ready nature, for a life of love,
For endless constancy and placid truth;
But whatsoe'er of such rare treasure lay
Reserved, had fate permitted, for support                 35
Of their maturer years, his present mind
Was under fascination;—he beheld
A vision, and adored the thing he saw.

>          580 mellower] distant A².
>          582 he lov'd] adored C.

Arabian Fiction never fill'd the world
With half the wonders that were wrought for him.    [40]

585 Earth liv'd in one great presence of the spring,
Life turn'd the meanest of her implements
Before his eyes to price above all gold,
The house she dwelt in was a sainted shrine,
Her chamber-window did surpass in glory    [45]

590 The portals of the East, all paradise
Could by the simple opening of a door
Let itself in upon him, pathways, walks,
Swarm'd with enchantment till his spirit sank    [49]
Beneath the burthen, overbless'd for life.

595 This state was theirs, till whether through effect
Of some delirious hour, or that the Youth,
Seeing so many bars betwixt himself
And the dear haven where he wish'd to be
In honorable wedlock with his love    [60]

600 Without a certain knowledge of his own,
Was inwardly prepared to turn aside
From law and custom, and entrust himself
To Nature for a happy end of all;
And thus abated of that pure reserve

605 Congenial to his loyal heart, with which
It would have pleas'd him to attend the steps
Of Maiden so divinely beautiful
I know not, but reluctantly must add
That Julia, yet without the name of Wife    [66]

610 Carried about her for a secret grief
The promise of a Mother.
                     To conceal
The threaten'd shame the Parents of the Maid
Found means to hurry her away by night    [70]
And unforewarn'd, that in a distant Town

615 She might remain shrouded in privacy,

[557–end] D *stuck over*: D² *as* 1850.
585 liv'd] breath'd C.        590 East] dawn C.
594 Surcharged *etc.* . . . mortality! *as* 1820 [50–53] A² C.
595–7 This state . . . himself] So years pass'd on till . . . restraint [56] *as*
1820, *followed by*
                 or that the Youth who saw
          So many bars *etc. as* 1820 A².
          Thus time pass'd on *etc.* . . . . state *as* 1820 [54–58] A³ C.
600 Without a certain knowledge] Without a shaped intention C.

Is fairer than the fairest star in Heaven!
So might—and with that prelude *did* begin
The record; and, in faithful verse, was given

---

## VAUDRACOUR AND JULIA (1820)

Arabian fiction never filled the world
With half the wonders that were wrought for him.                40
Earth breathed in one great presence of the spring;
Life turn'd the meanest of her implements,
Before his eyes, to price above all gold;
The house she dwelt in was a sainted shrine;
Her chamber window did surpass in glory                        45
The portals of the dawn; all paradise
Could, by the simple opening of a door,
Let itself in upon him; pathways, walks,
Swarm'd with enchantment, till his spirit sank
Surcharged within him,—overblest to move                      50
Beneath a sun that wakes a weary world
To its dull round of ordinary cares;
A man too happy for mortality!
  So passed the time, till, whether through effect
Of some unguarded moment that dissolved                       55
Virtuous restraint—ah, speak it, think it not!
Deem rather that the fervent Youth, who saw
So many bars between his present state
And the dear haven where he wished to be
In honourable wedlock with his Love,                          60
Was inwardly prepared to turn aside
From law and custom, and entrust his cause
To nature for a happy end of all;
Deem that by such fond hope the Youth was swayed,
And bear with their transgression, when I add                 65
That Julia, wanting yet the name of wife,
Carried about her for a secret grief
The promise of a mother.
              To conceal
The threatened shame, the parents of the Maid
Found means to hurry her away by night                        70
And unforewarned, that in some distant spot
She might remain shrouded in privacy,

604 pure] strict C.
607–8 so divinely beautiful . . . add] not more beautiful than pure
      More bright than spotless;—this believe and add
      With the reluctance due to painful truth, A² C.
611 promise] burthen C.
614 a distant Town] some distant spot C.

Until the Babe was born. When morning came
The Lover thus bereft, stung with his loss
And all uncertain whither he should turn                          [75]
Chafed like a wild beast in the toils; at length,
620 Following as his suspicions led, he found
O joy! sure traces of the fugitives,
Pursu'd them to the Town where they had stopp'd,
And lastly to the very House itself
Which had been chosen for the Maid's retreat.
625 The sequel may be easily divined,                             [79]
Walks backwards, forwards, morning, noon and night
When decency and caution would allow
And Julia, who, whenever to herself
She happen'd to be left a moment's space,
630 Was busy at her casement, as a Swallow
About its nest, ere long did thus espy
Her Lover, thence a stolen interview                             [85]
By night accomplish'd, with a ladder's help.

I pass the raptures of the Pair; such theme
635 Hath by a hundred Poets been set forth
In more delightful verse than skill of mine
Could fashion, chiefly by that darling Bard                      [90]
Who told of Juliet and her Romeo,
And of the Lark's note heard before its time,
640 And of the streaks that lac'd the severing clouds
In the unrelenting East. 'Tis mine to tread                      [94]
The humbler province of plain history,
And, without choice of circumstance, submissively
Relate what I have heard. The Lovers came
645 To this resolve, with which they parted, pleas'd
And confident, that Vaudracour should hie

623 Their flight, and lastly to the very House A² C.
625 easily] readily C.
626–31 Walks to and fro, and watchings at all hours  A²
          And the fair Captive who whene'er she might
          Was busy etc. . . . . swallow  A².
*So* C, *but* watchings at every hour *for* and watchings at all hours, may *for*
might *and* Is *for* Was. *After* Swallow C *goes on*:
          Fluttering in sight, nay almost within reach
          About that pendent edifice where rests
          A callow brood, did thus erelong espy
   635 Innumerable poets have described A², A³ *as* 1820, *but* sung *for*
touched [88]: C *as* 1820.

The doleful sequel.

But our little bark
On a strong river boldly hath been launched;    560

---

## VAUDRACOUR AND JULIA (1820)

Until the babe was born. When morning came
The Lover, thus bereft, stung with his loss,
And all uncertain whither he should turn,    75
Chafed like a wild beast in the toils; but soon
Discovering traces of the fugitives,
Their steps he followed to the Maid's retreat.
The sequel may be easily divined,—
Walks to and fro—watchings at every hour;    80
And the fair Captive, who, whene'er she may,
Is busy at her casement as the swallow
Fluttering its pinions, almost within reach,
About the pendant nest; did thus espy
Her Lover!—thence a stolen interview,    85
Accomplished under friendly shade of night.
    I pass the raptures of the Pair;—such theme
Is, by innumerable poets, touched
In more delightful verse than skill of mine
Could fashion, chiefly by that darling bard    90
Who told of Juliet and her Romeo,
And of the lark's note heard before its time,
And of the streaks that laced the severing clouds
In the unrelenting east.—Through all her courts
The vacant City slept; the busy winds,    95

641–50 'Tis mine *etc*. . . . take flight] Through all her courts *etc*. . . . .
filament! *as* 1820 [94–101], *followed by*
        Elate with hopeful courage from the arms
        Of his beloved, generous Vaudracour
        Springs like an arrow from the strict embrace
        Of bow and archer launch'd into the air
        Conspicuous, yet with doubtful import charg'd
        Of gladness; or festivity, or death.
        Lo! he hath reach'd the natal threshold—there
        To make (as in their hearts' simplicity
        The Lovers at their Parting had agreed)
        A sacrifice if nothing less may serve
        Of birthright, from the Father to obtain
        His final portion in a sum of gold,
        Which granted *etc. as* 1820 [107 *ff*.] C.
644–8 The Lovers *etc*. . . . obtain] They parted, pleased
        In their simplicity with this resolve
        That Vaudracour should seek his Father's house
        And though with sacrifice of rights and claims
        Endeavour to obtain *etc*. A².

    Back to his Father's house, and there employ
    Means aptest to obtain a sum of gold,
    A final portion, even, if that might be,          [106]
650 Which done, together they could then take flight
    To some remote and solitary place
    Where they might live with no one to behold     [110]
    Their happiness, or to disturb their love.
    Immediately, and with this mission charg'd
655 Home to his Father's House the Youth return'd
    And there remain'd a while without hint given
    Of his design; but if a word were dropp'd
    Touching the matter of his passion, still
    In hearing of his Father, Vaudracour         [115]
660 Persisted openly that nothing less
    Than death should make him yield up hope to be
    A blessed Husband of the Maid he loved.

    Incensed at such obduracy and slight
    Of exhortations and remonstrances
665 The Father threw out threats that by a mandate
    Bearing the private signet of the State
    He should be baffled of his mad intent,         [120]
    And that should cure him. From this time the Youth
    Conceiv'd a terror, and by night or day
670 Stirr'd nowhere without Arms. Soon afterwards
    His Parents to their Country Seat withdrew     [125]
    Upon some feign'd occasion; and the Son
    Was left with one Attendant in the house.
    Retiring to his Chamber for the night,
675 While he was entering at the door, attempts
    Were made to seize him by three armed Men,    [129]

653 Far less disturb their unambitious joy. C.
654–8 When with this mission charged the Youth had reached
    His Father's house he ventured not to speak
    In furtherance of his scheme but if a word
    Were dropt that touched upon his passion, still A².
654–62 C *as* 1820 [112–19], *but* intrusive *for* obtrusive [113].
663–8 Incensed . . . cure him] You shall be baffled in your mad intent
    And by a private signet of the State
    Muttered the Father A²; C *as* 1820 [120–2].
670–1 Soon afterwards . . . withdrew] While he was thus
    Harass'd in mind yet hoping in his fear
    His parents to their country seat withdrew A².
                  To their country seat
    Meanwhile his Parents artfully withdrew C.

And from the driving current should we turn
To loiter wilfully within a creek,
Howe'er attractive, Fellow voyager!

---

## VAUDRACOUR AND JULIA (1820)

That keep no certain intervals of rest,
Mov'd not; meanwhile the galaxy display'd
Her fires, that like mysterious pulses beat
Aloft;—momentous but uneasy bliss!
To their full hearts the universe seemed hung          100
On that brief meeting's slender filament!
   They parted; and the generous Vaudracour
Reached speedily the native threshold, bent
On making (so the Lovers had agreed)
A sacrifice of birth-right, to attain              105
A final portion from his Father's hand;
Which granted, Bride and Bridegroom then would flee
To some remote and solitary place,
Shady as night, and beautiful as heaven,
Where they may live, with no one to behold          110
Their happiness, or to disturb their love.
But *now* of this no whisper; not the less,
If ever an obtrusive word were dropped
Touching the matter of his passion, still,
In his stern Father's hearing, Vaudracour          115
Persisted openly that death alone
Should abrogate his human privilege
Divine, of swearing everlasting truth,
Upon the altar, to the Maid he loved.
   'You shall be baffled in your mad intent          120
If there be justice in the Court of France,'
Muttered the Father.—From this time the Youth
Conceived a terror,—and, by night or day,
Stirred no where without arms. To their rural seat,
Meanwhile, his Parents artfully withdrew          125
Upon some feigned occasion, and the Son
Remained with one attendant. At midnight
When to his chamber he retired, attempt
Was made to seize him by three armed men,

673–81  in the house . . . resigned]  At midnight . . . resigned *as* 1820
[127–35] C.  *So* A², *but* The passive instruments of ruffian power *for* Acting
. . . state [130–1].

The instruments of ruffian power; the Youth
In the first impulse of his rage, laid one
Dead at his feet, and to the second gave
680 A perilous wound, which done, at sight
Of the dead Man, he peacefully resign'd                [135]
His Person to the Law, was lodged in prison,
And wore the fetters of a Criminal.

Through three weeks' space, by means which love devis'd,
685 The Maid in her seclusion had received
Tidings of Vaudracour, and how he sped
Upon his enterprize. Thereafter came
A silence, half a circle did the moon
Complete, and then a whole, and still the same
690 Silence; a thousand thousand fears and hopes
Stirr'd in her mind; thoughts waking, thoughts of sleep
Entangled in each other, and at last
Self-slaughter seem'd her only resting-place.
So did she fare in her uncertainty.

695    At length, by interference of a Friend,          [151]
One who had sway at Court, the Youth regain'd
His liberty, on promise to sit down
Quietly in his Father's House, nor take
One step to reunite himself with her
700 Of whom his Parents disapproved: hard law
To which he gave consent only because
His freedom else could nowise be procured.
Back to his Father's house he went, remain'd
Eight days, and then his resolution fail'd:
705 He fled to Julia, and the words with which         [155]
He greeted her were these. 'All right is gone,
Gone from me. Thou no longer now art mine,            [160]

677–81 One with ungovernable hand the Youth
        Assailed and slew, and to the second gave
        A perilous wound—He shuddered at the sight
        Of the pale corse *etc.* A³.
684–94 C *as* 1820 [138–50], *but for* [146–7] *reads*:
        Tormented, then your memory doth possess
        Images which if sympathy be yours
        For this lost Pair, may help you to conceive
        The vex'd condition of each mind: ah no!
693 only resting-place] sorrow's only cure A².
695–710 C *as* 1820 [151–63]:
        For him by private interest at the Court

Would'st thou not chide ? Yet deem not my pains lost:
For Vaudracour and Julia (so were named                    565
The ill-fated pair) in that plain tale will draw

---

## VAUDRACOUR AND JULIA (1820)

Acting, in furtherance of the Father's will,                130
Under a private signet of the State.
One, did the Youth's ungovernable hand
Assault and slay ;—and to a second gave
A perilous wound,—he shuddered to behold
The breathless corse ; then peacefully resigned             135
His person to the law, was lodged in prison,
And wore the fetters of a criminal.
   Have you beheld a tuft of winged seed
That, from the dandelion's naked stalk
Mounted aloft, is suffered not to use                       140
Its natural gifts for purposes of rest,
Driven by the autumnal whirlwind to and fro
Through the wide element ? or have you marked
The heavier substance of a leaf-clad bough,
Within the vortex of a foaming flood,                       145
Tormented ? by such aid you may conceive
The perturbation of each mind ;—ah, no !
Desperate the Maid,—the Youth is stained with blood !
But as the troubled seed and tortured bough
Is man, subjected to despotic sway.                         150
   For him, by private influence with the Court,
Was pardon gained, and liberty procured ;
But not without exaction of a pledge
Which liberty and love dispersed in air.
He flew to her from whom they would divide him—             155
He clove to her who could not give him peace—
Yea, his first word of greeting was,—'All right
Is gone from me ; my lately-towering hopes,
To the least fibre of their lowest root,
Are withered ;—thou no longer canst be mine,                160

    His deed was pardoned and the Youth regained
    His liberty on promise to abjure
    All effort to unite himself with her
    Of whom his Parents disapproved hard law
    But freedom could not otherwise be gained.
    Full speedily his resolution failed
    He flew to Julia and his lips pronounced
    These words in greeting her 'All right is gone, *etc. as* 1820 [157–
      63] A².

I thine; a Murderer, Julia, cannot love
An innocent Woman; I behold thy face
710 I see thee and my misery is complete.'
She could not give him answer; afterwards
She coupled with his Father's name some words      [166]
Of vehement indignation; but the Youth
Check'd her, nor would he hear of this; for thought
715 Unfilial, or unkind, had never once
Found harbour in his breast. The Lovers thus
United once again together lived
For a few days, which were to Vaudracour
Days of dejection, sorrow and remorse
720 For that ill deed of violence which his hand
Had hastily committed: for the Youth
Was of a loyal spirit, a conscience nice
And over tender for the trial which
His fate had call'd him to. The Father's mind,
725 Meanwhile, remain'd unchanged, and Vaudracour
Learn'd that a mandate had been newly issued
To arrest him on the spot. Oh pain it was
To part! he could not—and he linger'd still
To the last moment of his time, and then,
730 At dead of night with snow upon the ground,
He left the City, and in Villages
The most sequester'd of the neighbourhood
Lay hidden for the space of several days
Until the horseman bringing back report
735 That he was nowhere to be found, the search
Was ended. Back return'd the ill-fated Youth,
And from the House where Julia lodg'd (to which
He now found open ingress, having gain'd
The affection of the family, who lov'd him
740 Both for his own, and for the Maiden's sake)
One night retiring, he was seiz'd—But here
A portion of the Tale may well be left      [177]
In silence, though my memory could add
Much how the Youth, and in short space of time,
745 Was travers'd from without, much, too, of thoughts
By which he was employ'd in solitude
Under privation and restraint, and what      [182]
Through dark and shapeless fear of things to come,
         711–41 C *as* 1820 [164–76].

Tears from the hearts of others, when their own
Shall beat no more. Thou, also, there mayst read,
At leisure, how the enamoured youth was driven,

---

## VAUDRACOUR AND JULIA (1820)

I thine—the conscience-stricken must not woo
The unruffled Innocent,—I see thy face,
Behold thee, and my misery is complete!'
   'One, are we not?' exclaim'd the Maiden—'One,
For innocence and youth, for weal and woe?'                165
Then, with the Father's name she coupled words
Of vehement indignation; but the Youth
Check'd her with filial meekness; for no thought
Uncharitable, no presumptuous rising
Of hasty censure, modelled in the eclipse                  170
Of true domestic loyalty, did e'er
Find place within his bosom.—Once again
The persevering wedge of tyranny
Achieved their separation;—and once more
Were they united,—to be yet again,                         175
Disparted—pitiable lot! But here
A portion of the Tale may well be left
In silence, though my memory could add
Much how the Youth, in scanty space of time,
Was traversed from without; much, too, of thoughts         180
That occupied his days in solitude
Under privation and restraint; and what,
Through dark and shapeless fear of things to come,

711–12 She answered not nor spake until impelled To couple *etc.*  A²;
C *as* 1820.
716–18                The Lovers, thus
     United once again, within those doors
     (Where now he found prompt ingress, having gained
     The affections of the Family who loved him
     Both for his own and for the Maiden's sake)
     Dwelt a few days that were to Vaudracour  A².
723–4 And of a heart too tender for the trials Which fate *etc.*  A².
     And over tender—O that he had weigh'd
     Untremblingly their wicked institutes
     And taken his repose upon the breast
     Of Nature and of God. The Father's mind  A³.
730 while snow was on the ground  A²: while snow enwrapp'd the
ground  A³.
731–2 in villages . . . neighbourhood] in haunts obscure  A².
737–41 to which . . . here] One night, Retiring, he was seized once more—
But here  A².
744 and in short] in scanty  C.
746 By which he was employed] That occupied his time  A²: C *as* 1820.

And what through strong compunction for the past
750 He suffer'd breaking down in heart and mind.     [185]
Such grace, if grace it were, had been vouchsafed
Or such effect had through the Father's want
Of power, or through his negligence ensued
That Vaudracour was suffer'd to remain,
755 Though under guard and without liberty,
In the same City with the unhappy Maid
From whom he was divided. So they fared
Objects of general concern, till, moved
With pity for their wrongs, the Magistrate,
760 The same who had plac'd the Youth in custody,
By application to the Minister
Obtain'd his liberty upon condition
That to his Father's house he should return.

He left his Prison almost on the eve
765 Of Julia's travail; she had likewise been
As from the time indeed, when she had first
Been brought for secrecy to this abode,
Though treated with consoling tenderness,
Herself a Prisoner, a dejected one,
770 Fill'd with a Lover's and a Woman's fears,
And whensoe'er the Mistress of the House
Enter'd the Room for the last time at night
And Julia with a low and plaintive voice
Said 'You are coming then to lock me up'
775 The Housewife when these words, always the same,
Were by her Captive languidly pronounced
Could never hear them utter'd without tears.

A day or two before her Child-bed time
Was Vaudracour restored to her, and soon
780 As he might be permitted to return
Into her Chamber after the Child's birth
The Master of the Family begg'd that all
The household might be summon'd, doubting not
But that they might receive impressions then
785 Friendly to human kindness. Vaudracour
(This heard I from one present at the time)
Held up the new-born Infant in his arms
And kiss'd, and bless'd, and cover'd it with tears,

By public power abased, to fatal crime,                          570
Nature's rebellion against monstrous law;
How, between heart and heart, oppression thrust

---

## VAUDRACOUR AND JULIA (1820)

And what, through strong compunction for the past,
He suffered—breaking down in heart and mind!         185
   Doomed to a third and last captivity,
His freedom he recovered on the eve
Of Julia's travail. When the babe was born

750 mind ℧ C: soul A².
751–98 C *as* 1820 [186–90].
755 without liberty] rigorously confined A².
759–62 By pity and indignant sense of wrong
        A Magistrate, by earnest suit, obtained
        The Lover's Liberty on promise given  A².
766–9  As from the time when she to this Abode
        Was brought a Prisoner, *etc.* A².
772–4  for the last . . . up] ere she retired to rest
        And Julia said with plaintive voice 'You come
        To close the cage upon a sleepless Bird' A².
777 never] seldom A².
778–85 A day . . . Vaudracour] The Child was born; and Vaudracour
that day A².

Uttering a prayer that he might never be
790 As wretched as his Father; then he gave
The Child to her who bare it, and she too
Repeated the same prayer, took it again
And muttering something faintly afterwards
He gave the Infant to the Standers-by,
795 And wept in silence upon Julia's neck.

Two months did he continue in the House,
And often yielded up himself to plans
Of future happiness. 'You shall return,                    [190]
Julia,' said he, 'and to your Father's House
800 Go with your Child, you have been wretched, yet
It is a town where both of us were born,
None will reproach you, for our loves are known;
With ornaments the prettiest you shall dress
Your Boy, as soon as he can run about,
805 And when he thus is at his play my Father                 [205]
Will see him from the window, and the Child
Will by his beauty move his Grandsire's heart,            [210]
So that it shall be soften'd, and our loves
End happily, as they began.' These gleams
810 Appear'd but seldom; oftener was he seen
Propping a pale and melancholy face
Upon the Mother's bosom, resting thus                     [215]
His head upon one breast, while from the other
The Babe was drawing in its quiet food.
815 At other times, when he, in silence, long
And fixedly had look'd upon her face,
He would exclaim, 'Julia, how much thine eyes
Have cost me!' During day-time when the Child

793–4 something . . . Infant] some faint accents he restored The sleeping
Infant A².
796–7 Not heedless of his promise, yet, in mind
        Irresolute, he lingered, lingered on
        And often yielded up himself to schemes  A².
800–1 C *as* 1820 [192–7].
802 loves are known] faith is known  C, *followed by* 1820 [199–200].
804–5 Your Boy when time enables him to walk
        And gambol like a Lambkin in the fields
        And while he thus pursues his play, my Father  A².
803–6 C *as* 1820 [201–9].
815–61 C *as* 1820 [218–41], *but in place of* [224–32],  C *reads*
        Of her affections ? Stand astonish'd ye
        That are too happy in your course of life

Her mandates, severing whom true love had joined,
Harassing both; until he sank and pressed
The couch his fate had made for him; supine,      575

---

## VAUDRACOUR AND JULIA (1820)

Its presence tempted him to cherish schemes
Of future happiness. 'You shall return,      190
Julia,' said he, 'and to your Father's house
Go with the Child.—You have been wretched, yet
The silver shower, whose reckless burthen weighs
Too heavily upon the lily's head,
Oft leaves a saving moisture at its root.      195
Malice, beholding you, will melt away.
Go!—'tis a Town where both of us were born;
None will reproach you, for our truth is known;
And if, amid those once-bright bowers, our fate
Remain unpitied, pity is not in man.      200
With ornaments—the prettiest, nature yields
Or art can fashion, shall you deck your Boy,
And feed his countenance with your own sweet looks
Till no one can resist him.—Now, even now,
I see him sporting on the sunny lawn;      205
My Father from the window sees him too;
Startled, as if some new-created Thing
Enriched the earth, or Faery of the woods
Bounded before him;—but the unweeting Child
Shall by his beauty win his Grandsire's heart      210
So that it shall be softened, and our loves
End happily—as they began!' These gleams
Appeared but seldom: oftener was he seen
Propping a pale and melancholy face
Upon the Mother's bosom; resting thus      215
His head upon one breast, while from the other
The Babe was drawing in its quiet food.

    To have known the depths of things. The word he hears
    Gathers it up in calm despondency
    Compos'd and silent, without visible sign
    Of even the least emotion. Noting this
    When Julia scatter'd an upbraiding speech
    Upon his slackness, he thereto return'd
817–18 He started greeting the blank air with words
    Forc'd from him partly by his own sad thoughts
    Partly by heavenly sight of her dear eyes
    Words which I know and could by living voice
    Repeat the same, but have not heart to trust
    Their tender meaning to this lifeless pen.
    And often during daytime. A².

Lay in its cradle, by its side he sate,
820 Not quitting it an instant. The whole Town
In his unmerited misfortunes now
Took part, and if he either at the door
Or window for a moment with his Child
Appear'd, immediately the Street was throng'd
825 While others frequently without reserve
Pass'd and repass'd before the house to steal
A look at him. Oft at this time he wrote
Requesting, since he knew that the consent
Of Julia's Parents never could be gain'd
830 To a clandestine marriage, that his Father
Would from the birthright of an eldest Son
Exclude him, giving but, when this was done,
A sanction to his nuptials: vain request,
To which no answer was return'd. And now
835 From her own home the Mother of his Love
Arrived to apprise the Daughter of her fix'd
And last resolve, that, since all hope to move
The old Man's heart prov'd vain, she must retire
Into a Convent, and be there immured.
840 Julia was thunderstricken by these words,
And she insisted on a Mother's rights
To take her Child along with her, a grant
Impossible, as she at last perceived;
The Persons of the house no sooner heard
845 Of this decision upon Julia's fate
Than everyone was overwhelm'd with grief
Nor could they frame a manner soft enough
To impart the tidings to the Youth; but great
Was their astonishment when they beheld him
850 Receive the news in calm despondency,
Composed and silent, without outward sign
Of even the least emotion; seeing this                    [230]
When Julia scatter'd some upbraiding words
Upon his slackness he thereto return'd
855 No answer, only took the Mother's hand
Who lov'd him scarcely less than her own Child,
And kissed it, without seeming to be press'd          [235]
By any pain that 'twas the hand of one
Whose errand was to part him from his Love
860 For ever. In the city he remain'd                      [241]

Save when the stings of viperous remorse,
Trying their strength, enforced him to start up,
Aghast and prayerless. Into a deep wood

---

## VAUDRACOUR AND JULIA (1820)

—That pillow is no longer to be thine,
Fond Youth! that mournful solace now must pass
Into the list of things that cannot be!                          220
Unwedded Julia, terror-smitten, hears
The sentence, by her Mother's lip pronounced,
That dooms her to a Convent.—Who shall tell,
Who dares report, the tidings to the Lord
Of her affections? So they blindly asked                         225
Who knew not to what quiet depths a weight
Of agony had press'd the sufferer down;—
The word, by others dreaded, he can hear
Composed and silent, without visible sign
Of even the least emotion. Noting this                           230
When the impatient Object of his love
Upbraided him with slackness, he returned
No answer, only took the Mother's hand
And kissed it—seemingly devoid of pain,
Or care, that what so tenderly he pressed,                       235
Was a dependant upon the obdurate heart
Of One who came to disunite their lives
For ever—sad alternative! preferred,
By the unbending Parents of the Maid,
To secret 'spousals meanly disavowed.—                           240
—So be it!
          In the city he remained

---

826 Pass'd and repass'd to steal a look at him A², *which deletes* 827–35
*and goes on*:
          And now the Mother of his Love arrived
          And to her terror-stricken daughter spake
          Her last resolve *etc.*
840–3 A² *deletes.*
844 Persons of] Dwellers in  A².
856 A² *deletes.*
859 part him from his Love] disunite their lives  A².
860–910 C *as* 1820 [241–84]; *but between* hill-top *and* His eyes [254] C *has*
                    And is the curtain fallen?
          For the relief of aching sympathy
          Would that it were!

A season after Julia had retired
And in the Convent taken up her home
To the end that he might place his Infant Babe
With a fit Nurse, which done, beneath the roof
865 Where now his little One was lodg'd, he pass'd
The day entire, and scarcely could at length
Tear himself from the cradle to return
Home to his Father's House, in which he dwelt
Awhile, and then came back that he might see
870 Whether the Babe had gain'd sufficient strength
To bear removal. He quitted this same Town
For the last time, attendant by the side                    [246]
Of a close chair, a Litter or Sedan,
In which the Child was carried. To a hill,
875 Which rose at a League's distance from the Town,
The Family of the house where he had lodged
Attended him, and parted from him there,
Watching below till he had disappear'd
On the hill top. His eyes he scarcely took,
880 Through all that journey, from the Chair in which          [255]
The Babe was carried; and at every Inn
Or place at which they halted or reposed
Laid him upon his knees, nor would permit                    [260]
The hands of any but himself to dress
885 The Infant or undress. By one of those
Who bore the Chair these facts, at his return,
Were told, and in relating them he wept.

This was the manner in which Vaudracour
Departed with his Infant; and thus reach'd
890 His Father's House, where to the innocent Child            [265]
Admittance was denied. The young Man spake
No words of indignation or reproof,
But of his Father begg'd, a last request,
That a retreat might be assign'd to him,
895 A house where in the Country he might dwell                [270]
With such allowance as his wants required
And the more lonely that the Mansion was
'Twould be more welcome. To a lodge that stood
Deep in a Forest, with leave given, at the age

863–71 A Foster-mother for the Child was found
        It grew in health and strength and when the time

He fled, to shun the haunts of human kind;
There dwelt, weakened in spirit more and more;        580
Nor could the voice of Freedom, which through France

---

## VAUDRACOUR AND JULIA (1820)

A season after Julia had withdrawn
To those religious walls. He, too, departs—
Who with him?—even the senseless Little-one!
With that sole Charge he pass'd the city-gates,        245
For the last time, attendant by the side
Of a close chair, a litter, or sedan,
In which the Babe was carried. To a hill,
That rose a brief league distant from the town,
The Dwellers in that house where he had lodged        250
Accompanied his steps, by anxious love
Impell'd:—they parted from him there, and stood
Watching below, till he had disappeared
On the hill-top. His eyes he scarcely took,
Throughout that journey, from the vehicle        255
(Slow-moving ark of all his hopes!) that veiled
The tender Infant: and at every inn,
And under every hospitable tree
At which the Bearers halted or reposed,
Laid him with timid care upon his knees,        260
And looked, as mothers ne'er were known to look,
Upon the Nursling which his arms embraced.
    —This was the manner in which Vaudracour
Departed with his Infant; and thus reached
His Father's house, where to the innocent Child        265
Admittance was denied. The young Man spake
No words of indignation or reproof,
But of his Father begged, a last request,
That a retreat might be assigned to him
Where in forgotten quiet he might dwell,        270
With such allowance as his wants required;
For wishes he had none. To a Lodge that stood
Deep in a forest, with leave given, at the age

    Was come that to the impatient Father gave
    Courage to undertake a Charge so young
    Then did he quit this melancholy Town  A².
876-7 The Dwellers in that house where he was lodged
    Accompanied his steps with anxious love
    And parted from him there, and there they stood  A².
880-1 Chair . . . carried] Chair that held The hapless Infant  A².
882-7 A² *as* 1820 [257-62].        895, 897-8, 905  A² *as* 1820.

900  Of four and twenty summers he retir'd;
     And thither took with him his Infant Babe,                        [275]
     And one Domestic for their common needs,
     An aged woman. It consoled him here
     To attend upon the Orphan and perform
905  The office of a Nurse to his young Child
     Which after a short time by some mistake                          [280]
     Or indiscretion of the Father, died.
     The Tale I follow to its last recess
     Of suffering or of peace, I know not which;
910  Theirs be the blame who caused the woe, not mine.

          From that time forth he never utter'd word                  [285]
     To any living. An Inhabitant
     Of that same Town in which the Pair had left
     So lively a remembrance of their griefs
915  By chance of business coming within reach
     Of his retirement to the spot repair'd                           [290]
     With the intent to visit him: he reach'd
     The House and only found the Matron there,
     Who told him that his pains were thrown away,
920  For that her Master never utter'd word
     To living soul—not even to her. Behold                           [295]
     While they were speaking, Vaudracour approach'd;
     But, seeing some one there, just as his hand
     Was stretch'd towards the garden-gate, he shrunk,
925  And like a shadow glided out of view.
     Shock'd at his savage outside, from the place                    [300]
     The Visitor retired.
                         Thus liv'd the Youth
     Cut off from all intelligence with Man,
     And shunning even the light of common day;
930  Nor could the voice of Freedom, which through France
     Soon afterwards resounded, public hope,                          [305]
     Or personal memory of his own deep wrongs,
     Rouze him: but in those solitary shades
     His days he wasted, an imbecile mind.

          911–12  From this time forth he never spared a smile
                    To mortal Creature  A² C.
          921  To living soul] To aught alive  A²: To [   ]  C.
          931  Soon afterwards] Full speedily  A² C.

Full speedily resounded, public hope,
Or personal memory of his own worst wrongs,
Rouse him; but, hidden in those gloomy shades,
His days he wasted,—an imbecile mind.                585

---

## VAUDRACOUR AND JULIA (1820)

Of four-and-twenty summers he withdrew;
And thither took with him his infant Babe,            275
And one Domestic, for their common needs,
An aged Woman. It consoled him here
To attend upon the Orphan, and perform
Obsequious service to the precious Child,
Which, after a short time, by some mistake,           280
Or indiscretion of the Father, died.—
The Tale I follow to its last recess
Of suffering or of peace, I know not which;
Theirs be the blame who caused the woe, not mine!
  From this time forth he never shared a smile        285
With mortal creature. An Inhabitant
Of that same Town, in which the Pair had left
So lively a remembrance of their griefs,
By chance of business, coming within reach
Of his retirement, to the spot repaired              290
With an intent to visit him. He reached
The house, and only found the Matron there,
Who told him that his pains were thrown away,
For that her Master never uttered word
To living Thing—not even to her.—Behold!             295
While they were speaking, Vaudracour approached;
But, seeing some one near, even as his hand
Was stretched towards the garden gate, he shrunk—
And, like a shadow, glided out of view.
Shocked at his savage aspect, from the place          300
The Visitor retired.
                    Thus lived the Youth
Cut off from all intelligence with man,
And shunning even the light of common day;
Nor could the voice of Freedom, which through France
Full speedily resounded, public hope,                305
Or personal memory of his own deep wrongs,
Rouse him: but in those solitary shades
His days he wasted, an imbecile mind!

# BOOK TENTH

## RESIDENCE IN FRANCE AND FRENCH REVOLUTION

IT was a beautiful and silent day
That overspread the countenance of earth,
Then fading, with unusual quietness,     [3]
When from the Loire I parted, and through scenes
5  Of vineyard, orchard, meadow-ground and tilth,
Calm waters, gleams of sun, and breathless trees
Towards the fierce Metropolis turn'd my steps
Their homeward way to England. From his Throne     [11]
The King had fallen; the congregated Host,
10  Dire cloud upon the front of which was written
The tender mercies of the dismal wind
That bore it, on the Plains of Liberty     [15]
Had burst innocuously, say more, the swarm
That came elate and jocund, like a Band
15  Of Eastern Hunters, to enfold in ring
Narrowing itself by moments and reduce
To the last punctual spot of their despair
A race of victims, so they seem'd, *themselves*
Had shrunk from sight of their own task, and fled
20  In terror; desolation and dismay
Remain'd for them whose fancies had grown rank
With evil expectations, confidence
And perfect triumph to the better cause.     [30]
The State, as if to stamp the final seal

[MSS. for Bk. X: A B C D E (*two leaves of* A, *containing ll.* 1–43, *are missing*); *ll.* 689–710 Z.]
Book Tenth: Residence *etc.* B: Book Tenth C.
1 It was] Upon C. B *adds* [4, 5].
4 Such day as heighten'd the regret it sooth'd,
  Mine eyes look'd back upon the gliding Loire
  Ere from his banks I parted: and through scenes C.
5–7 and tilth *etc.*]       and woods
  Bright with autumnal hues, pursued my course
  Towards the fierce Metropolis C.
14–20 That came like Hunters of the East, elate
      And jocund, to enfold within a ring,
      Contracted momently before the point
      Of the life-threatening spear, a timid herd

# BOOK TENTH

## RESIDENCE IN FRANCE—Continued

It was a beautiful and silent day
That overspread the countenance of earth,
Then fading with unusual quietness,—
A day as beautiful as e'er was given
To soothe regret, though deepening what it soothed,     5
When by the gliding Loire I paused, and cast
Upon his rich domains, vineyard and tilth,
Green meadow-ground, and many-coloured woods,
Again, and yet again, a farewell look;
Then from the quiet of that scene passed on,     10
Bound to the fierce Metropolis. From his throne
The King had fallen, and that invading host—
Presumptuous cloud, on whose black front was written
The tender mercies of the dismal wind
That bore it—on the plains of Liberty     15
Had burst innocuous. Say in bolder words,
They—who had come elate as eastern hunters
Banded beneath the Great Mogul, when he
Erewhile went forth from Agra or Lahore,
Rajahs and Omrahs in his train, intent     20
To drive their prey enclosed within a ring
Wide as a province, but, the signal given,
Before the point of the life-threatening spear
Narrowing itself by moments—they, rash men,
Had seen the anticipated quarry turned     25
Into avengers, from whose wrath they fled
In terror. Disappointment and dismay
Remained for all whose fancies had run wild
With evil expectations; confidence
And perfect triumph for the better cause.     30

The State, as if to stamp the final seal

> (So could they deem!) of victims in despair
> Shrunk back, and reckless of the issue fled
> In terror: disappointment or dismay C.
> 1-23 D *stuck over*: D² *as* 1850.

25 On her security, and to the world
   Shew what she was, a high and fearless soul, [33]
   Or rather in a spirit of thanks to those
   Who had stirr'd up her slackening faculties
   To a new transition, had assumed with joy
30 The body and the venerable name [40]
   Of a Republic: lamentable crimes
   'Tis true had gone before this hour, the work
   Of massacre, in which the senseless sword
   Was pray'd to as a judge; but these were past,
35 Earth free from them for ever, as was thought, [45]
   Ephemeral monsters, to be seen but once;
   Things that could only shew themselves and die.

    This was the time in which enflam'd with hope,
   To Paris I returned. Again I rang'd
40 More eagerly than I had done before
   Through the wide City, and in progress pass'd [50]
   The Prison where the unhappy Monarch lay,
   Associate with his Children and his Wife
   In bondage; and the Palace lately storm'd
45 With roar of cannon, and a numerous Host.
   I crossed (a black and empty area then) [55]
   The Square of the Carousel, few weeks back
   Heap'd up with dead and dying, upon these
   And other sights looking as doth a man
50 Upon a volume whose contents he knows
   Are memorable, but from him lock'd up, [60]
   Being written in a tongue he cannot read,
   So that he questions the mute leaves with pain
   And half upbraids their silence. But that night
55 When on my bed I lay, I was most mov'd

27–29 Or under rash resentment and in pride
    Of spiteful gratitude to the baffled League
    Who had stirr'd up her slackening faculties
    To a new transition, having crush'd the king
    Spared not the empty throne, and had assum'd  C.
[35] Or under rash resentment; or to taunt  D: D² *as* E.
30 and the] and most  B².
32 Had gone before, unspeakable misdeeds  C.   the] dire  B².
38 This was the time when chear'd by such belief  C.
40 With ardour inexperienced heretofore  B³ C.   done] rang'd  B².
41–45 C *as* 1850, *but* numerous *for* furious.
46–49 Explor'd with shuddering curiosity
    The Square of the Carousel by the wrath

On her security, and to the world
Show what she was, a high and fearless soul,
Exulting in defiance, or heart-stung
By sharp resentment, or belike to taunt                    35
With spiteful gratitude the baffled League,
That had stirred up her slackening faculties
To a new transition, when the King was crushed,
Spared not the empty throne, and in proud haste
Assumed the body and venerable name                        40
Of a Republic. Lamentable crimes,
'Tis true, had gone before this hour, dire work
Of massacre, in which the senseless sword
Was prayed to as a judge; but these were past,
Earth free from them for ever, as was thought,—            45
Ephemeral monsters, to be seen but once!
Things that could only show themselves and die.


Cheered with this hope, to Paris I returned,
And ranged, with ardour heretofore unfelt,
The spacious city, and in progress passed                  50
The prison where the unhappy Monarch lay,
Associate with his children and his wife
In bondage; and the palace, lately stormed
With roar of cannon by a furious host.
I crossed the square (an empty area then!)                 55
Of the Carrousel, where so late had lain
The dead, upon the dying heaped, and gazed
On this and other spots, as doth a man
Upon a volume whose contents he knows
Are memorable, but from him locked up,                     60
Being written in a tongue he cannot read,
So that he questions the mute leaves with pain,
And half upbraids their silence. But that night

Of the same day besprinkled or upheap'd
With dead and dying, but the heedless shower
And untaught breezes of a few short weeks
Had purified, though not from fancied stain
The blank and vacant area. Through the crowd
Bustling and busied with its own concerns
I march'd, and oft did these and kindred spots
Hold me enchain'd: gazing as doth a Man  C.
54–55 The first that came to fling its awful shades
Over this new Sojourn, I was most moved  C.

And felt most deeply in what world I was;
My room was high and lonely, near the roof
Of a large Mansion or Hotel, a spot
That would have pleased me in more quiet times,
60 Nor was it wholly without pleasure then.
With unextinguish'd taper I kept watch,                         [70]
Reading at intervals; the fear gone by
Press'd on me almost like a fear to come;
I thought of those September Massacres,
65 Divided from me by a little month,
And felt and touch'd them, a substantial dread;                [75]
The rest was conjured up from tragic fictions,
And mournful Calendars of true history,
Remembrances and dim admonishments.
70 'The horse is taught his manage, and the wind
Of heaven wheels round and treads in his own steps,
Year follows year, the tide returns again,
Day follows day, all things have second birth;
The earthquake is not satisfied at once.'
75 And in such way I wrought upon myself,                       [85]
Until I seem'd to hear a voice that cried,
To the whole City, 'Sleep no more.' To this
Add comments of a calmer mind, from which
I could not gather full security,
80 But at the best it seem'd a place of fear
Unfit for the repose which night requires,                     [92]
Defenceless as a wood where tigers roam.

56  was] breathed  B² C.
65  a little] one vanish'd  C.
66  dread;] dream!  C.        69  dim] stern  C.
70–82  i  The Horse is taught his manage, and the Stars
             Of wildest power wheel round in their own track
             So do the Currents of the salt Abyss
             Eddying with all their monstrous retinue,
        v  For the exhausted Hurricane the air
             Calm though it be prepares a successor
             Which at no distant interval shall reign
             With equal power of devastation arm'd,—
             The waxing Moon mimics the moon dismiss'd
        x  From her uneasy task—year follows year,
             The absent tide is bent on quick return
             Day follows day, all things have second birth
             The earthquake is not satisfied at once.

I felt most deeply in what world I was,
What ground I trod on, and what air I breathed.                    65
High was my room and lonely, near the roof
Of a large mansion or hotel, a lodge
That would have pleased me in more quiet times;
Nor was it wholly without pleasure then.
With unextinguished taper I kept watch,                           70
Reading at intervals; the fear gone by
Pressed on me almost like a fear to come.
I thought of those September massacres,
Divided from me by one little month,
Saw them and touched: the rest was conjured up                   75
From tragic fictions or true history,
Remembrances and dim admonishments.
The horse is taught his manage, and no star
Of wildest course but treads back his own steps;
For the spent hurricane the air provides                         80
As fierce a successor; the tide retreats
But to return out of its hiding-place
In the great deep; all things have second birth;
The earthquake is not satisfied at once;
And in this way I wrought upon myself,                           85
Until I seemed to hear a voice that cried,
To the whole city, 'Sleep no more.' The trance
Fled with the voice to which it had given birth;
But vainly comments of a calmer mind
Promised soft peace and sweet forgetfulness.                     90
The place, all hushed and silent as it was,
Appeared unfit for the repose of night,
Defenceless as a wood where tigers roam.


And thus did Fancy work upon herself
xv Until I seem'd to hear a voice that cried
To the whole City 'Sleep no more'. Relief
Succeeded, comments of a calmer mind,
That fail'd to bring entire security
Nor could those precincts not be deem'd unfit
xx For the repose which Night requires, defenceless
As a fear-haunted wood where Tygers roam. C.
A² *has ll.* ix–xiii *of* C, *followed by* v, vi, viii, xiv–xxi, *but in* v *reads* departed
*for* exhausted, *in* vi *provides for* prepares, *and in* xix And still, at best, those
precincts seem'd unfit. D *reads* 70, 71, *as* 1850, *then* ix–xi *of* C, *followed by*
For the spent hurricane the air provides A successor. All things *etc.*: D²
*as* 1850.

Betimes next morning to the Palace Walk
Of Orleans I repair'd and entering there
85  Was greeted, among divers other notes,
By voices of the Hawkers in the crowd
Bawling, *Denunciation of the crimes*        [100]
*Of Maximilian Robespierre*; the speech
Which in their hands they carried was the same
90  Which had been recently pronounced, the day
When Robespierre, well knowing for what mark
Some words of indirect reproof had been      [105]
Intended, rose in hardihood, and dared
The Man who had an ill surmise of him
95  To bring his charge in openness, whereat
When a dead pause ensued, and no one stirr'd,
In silence of all present, from his seat       [110]
Louvet walked singly through the avenue
And took his station in the Tribune, saying,
100  'I, Robespierre, accuse thee!' 'Tis well known
What was the issue of that charge, and how
Louvet was left alone without support
Of his irresolute Friends; but these are things  [120]
Of which I speak, only as they were storm
105  Or sunshine to my individual mind,
No further. Let me then relate that now
In some sort seeing with my proper eyes
That Liberty, and Life, and Death would soon  [125]

83–86  Day dawn'd and early to the Palace walk
      Of Orleans I repair'd. Though still the streets,
      Though unfrequented yet such public haunt,
      The spirit of those long arcades was rouz'd
      And mid a peal of ill-assorted sounds
      That greeted me on entering—I could hear
      Shrill voices rais'd by Hawkers, mid the throng C.
*So* A², *but*               yet the streets
      Were still, the spirit of that place was rouzed *etc.*
            the spirit of those long arcades
      Was rouzed, and mid a peal of ill match'd sounds A³.
86  voices of the] voices shrill of B².
[95–96]  Of Orleans I repaired, the streets were still;
      Not so the spirit of those long Arcades D: D² *as* 1850.
88–89  their hands Obtruded on the view a printed Speech
          The same which *etc.* A² C.
91  well knowing] not ignorant C.
100–2                 Well is known
      The inglorious issue of that strife; and how

With early morning towards the Palace-walk
Of Orleans eagerly I turned; as yet                    95
The streets were still; not so those long Arcades;
There, 'mid a peal of ill-matched sounds and cries,
That greeted me on entering, I could hear
Shrill voices from the hawkers in the throng,
Bawling, 'Denunciation of the Crimes                   100
Of Maximilian Robespierre;' the hand,
Prompt as the voice, held forth a printed speech,
The same that had been recently pronounced,
When Robespierre, not ignorant for what mark
Some words of indirect reproof had been                105
Intended, rose in hardihood, and dared
The man who had an ill surmise of him
To bring his charge in openness; whereat,
When a dead pause ensued, and no one stirred,
In silence of all present, from his seat               110
Louvet walked single through the avenue,
And took his station in the Tribune, saying,
'I, Robespierre, accuse thee!' Well is known
The inglorious issue of that charge, and how
He, who had launched the startling thunderbolt,        115
The one bold man, whose voice the attack had sounded,
Was left without a follower to discharge
His perilous duty, and retire lamenting
That Heaven's best aid is wasted upon men
Who to themselves are false.                           120
                         But these are things
Of which I speak, only as they were storm
Or sunshine to my individual mind,
No further. Let me then relate that now—
In some sort seeing with my proper eyes
That Liberty, and Life, and Death would soon           125

The one bold Man whose voice had thus been raised
Even while the Tyrant's cheek confessed his fear
Was left to plead alone without support A² B².
102-3 He who had launched this startling thunderbolt
The one bold Man whose voice the charge had sounded
Who led the way with sparkling eye that flash'd
Bright news of golden victory within reach,
Was left without a Follower etc. as 1850 [117–20] A³ C. *So* D, *but*
[116] attack *for* charge *and* [117] lament *for* discharge, *with omission
of* [118]: D² *as* 1850.

To the remotest corners of the land
110 Lie in the arbitrement of those who ruled
The capital City, what was struggled for,
And by what Combatants victory must be won,
The indecision on their part whose aim                    [130]
Seem'd best, and the straightforward path of those
115 Who in attack or in defence alike
Were strong through their impiety, greatly I
Was agitated; yea I could almost
Have pray'd that throughout earth upon all souls         [135]
By patient exercise of reason made
120 Worthy of liberty, upon every soul
Matured to live in plainness and in truth
The gift of tongues might fall, and men arrive
From the four quarters of the winds to do               [140]
For France what without help she could not do,
125 A work of honour; think not that to this
I added, work of safety; from such thought
And the least fear about the end of things
I was as far as Angels are from guilt.                   [145]

Yet did I grieve, nor only griev'd, but thought
130 Of opposition and of remedies,
An insignificant Stranger, and obscure,
Mean as I was, and little graced with power
Of eloquence even in my native speech,                   [150]
And all unfit for tumult or intrigue,
135 Yet would I willingly have taken up
A service at this time for cause so great,
However dangerous. Inly I revolv'd
How much the destiny of man had still                    [155]
Hung upon single persons, that there was,
140 Transcendent to all local patrimony,
One Nature as there is one Sun in heaven,
That objects, even as they are great, thereby
Do come within the reach of humblest eyes,               [160]
That Man was only weak through his mistrust
145 And want of hope, where evidence divine
Proclaim'd to him that hope should be most sure,
That, with desires heroic and firm sense,

[133] inmost D² E: very C D.          120–1, 126–7 A³ C *as* 1850.
135–7 A³ C *as* 1850, *but* [152] mind *for* heart.

To the remotest corners of the land
Lie in the arbitrement of those who ruled
The capital City; what was struggled for,
And by what combatants victory must be won;
The indecision on their part whose aim                    130
Seemed best, and the straightforward path of those
Who in attack or in defence were strong
Through their impiety—my inmost soul
Was agitated; yea, I could almost
Have prayed that throughout earth upon all men,          135
By patient exercise of reason made
Worthy of liberty, all spirits filled
With zeal expanding in Truth's holy light,
The gift of tongues might fall, and power arrive
From the four quarters of the winds to do                140
For France, what without help she could not do,
A work of honour; think not that to this
I added, work of safety: from all doubt
Or trepidation for the end of things
Far was I, far as angels are from guilt.                 145

     Yet did I grieve, nor only grieved, but thought
Of opposition and of remedies:
An insignificant stranger and obscure,
And one, moreover, little graced with power
Of eloquence even in my native speech,                   150
And all unfit for tumult or intrigue,
Yet would I at this time with willing heart
Have undertaken for a cause so great
Service however dangerous.  I revolved,
How much the destiny of Man had still                    155
Hung upon single persons; that there was,
Transcendent to all local patrimony,
One nature, as there is one sun in heaven;
That objects, even as they are great, thereby
Do come within the reach of humblest eyes;               160
That man is only weak through his mistrust
And want of hope where evidence divine
Proclaims to him that hope should be most sure;
Nor did the inexperience of my youth
Preclude conviction, that a spirit strong                165

144 is B D: was A C D².

A Spirit thoroughly faithful to itself,
Unquenchable, unsleeping, undismay'd,
150 Was as an instinct among Men, a stream
That gather'd up each petty straggling rill
And vein of water, glad to be roll'd on
In safe obedience, that a mind whose rest
Was where it ought to be, in self-restraint,
155 In circumspection and simplicity,                          [175]
Fell rarely in entire discomfiture
Below its aim, or met with from without
A treachery that defeated it or foil'd.

On the other side, I called to mind those truths          [191]
160 Which are the commonplaces of the Schools,
A theme for boys, too trite even to be felt,
Yet, with a revelation's liveliness,
In all their comprehensive bearings known               [195]
And visible to Philosophers of old,
165 Men who, to business of the world untrain'd,
Liv'd in the Shade, and to Harmodius known
And his Compeer Aristogiton, known
To Brutus, that tyrannic Power is weak,                  [200]
Hath neither gratitude, nor faith, nor love,
170 Nor the support of good or evil men
To trust in, that the Godhead which is ours
Can never utterly be charm'd or still'd,
That nothing hath a natural right to last                [205]

146–59 *After* 146 B² *reads*: Young, lonely, inexperienced, I perceived
                    That mid the loud distractions of the world
    *followed by* [183–90] *and* 147–57, *and for* 158
                    Treachery that blinds it overthrows or foils.
    C *reads* Why should we gasp as if the element
                    Of noble purposes were all inapt
                    For mortal respirations,—unto us
                    What land is to the natives of the deep ?
                    Not such is his condition who hath learnt
                    That mid the loud *etc. as* 1850 [182–90].
    *followed by*    Nor did the inexperience of my Youth
                    Preclude the knowledge that a Spirit wise
                    Heroic, thoroughly faithful to itself
                    Is for Society's *etc. as* 1850 [168–77], *and for* [178]
                    A treachery that defeats its power or foils.
D *as* 𝔄, *but omitting* 149 :  D² *as* 1850, *but for* [166] Trained in the School of
high-born aspirations: D³ *as* 1850.
  148 thoroughly *all MSS.*: throughly 1850.

In hope, and trained to noble aspirations,
A spirit throughly faithful to itself,
Is for Society's unreasoning herd
A domineering instinct, serves at once
For way and guide, a fluent receptacle                170
That gathers up each petty straggling rill
And vein of water, glad to be rolled on
In safe obedience; that a mind, whose rest
Is where it ought to be, in self-restraint,
In circumspection and simplicity,                     175
Falls rarely in entire discomfiture
Below its aim, or meets with, from without,
A treachery that foils it or defeats;
And, lastly, if the means on human will,
Frail human will, dependent should betray             180
Him who too boldly trusted them, I felt
That 'mid the loud distractions of the world
A sovereign voice subsists within the soul,
Arbiter undisturbed of right and wrong,
Of life and death, in majesty severe                  185
Enjoining, as may best promote the aims
Of truth and justice, either sacrifice,
From whatsoever region of our cares
Or our infirm affections Nature pleads,
Earnest and blind, against the stern decree.          190

On the other side, I called to mind those truths
That are the common-places of the schools—
(A theme for boys, too hackneyed for their sires,)
Yet, with a revelation's liveliness,
In all their comprehensive bearings known             195
And visible to philosophers of old,
Men who, to business of the world untrained,
Lived in the shade; and to Harmodius known
And his compeer Aristogiton, known
To Brutus—that tyrannic power is weak,                200
Hath neither gratitude, nor faith, nor love,
Nor the support of good or evil men
To trust in; that the godhead which is ours
Can never utterly be charmed or stilled;
That nothing hath a natural right to last             205

161 felt] priz'd A² C.

But equity and reason, that all else
175 Meets foes irreconcilable, and at best
Doth live but by variety of disease.

Well might my wishes be intense, my thoughts
Strong and perturb'd, not doubting at that time, [210]
Creed which ten shameful years have not annull'd,
180 But that the virtue of one paramount mind
Would have abash'd those impious crests, have quell'd
Outrage and bloody power, and in despite
Of what the People were through ignorance
And immaturity, and, in the teeth [216]
185 Of desperate opposition from without,
Have clear'd a passage for just government,
And left a solid birthright to the State,
Redeem'd according to example given [220]
By ancient Lawgivers.
In this frame of mind,
190 Reluctantly to England I return'd,
Compell'd by nothing less than absolute want
Of funds for my support, else, well assured
That I both was and must be of small worth,
No better than an alien in the Land,
195 I doubtless should have made a common cause
With some who perish'd, haply perish'd, too, [230]
A poor mistaken and bewilder'd offering,
Should to the breast of Nature have gone back
With all my resolutions, all my hopes,
200 A Poet only to myself, to Men
Useless, and even, beloved Friend! a soul [235]
To thee unknown.
When to my native Land
(After a whole year's absence) I return'd

176 A C D: D² as 1850. 179 A *deletes*; *not in* C.
183–4 𝔄 C D: D² as 1850.
190–2 Dragg'd by the chain of stern necessity
So seem'd it then, I now would rather say
Forc'd by the gracious Providence of Heaven
To England I return'd, else though assured A² C D: D² as 1850.
193 worth 𝔄: weight A².
194 𝔄 C D: D² as 1850.
202–20 A² C D as 1850, *but*
The seasons had performed
Their circuit since I heard the murmuring waves [236–8], my *for*
our [241]

But equity and reason; that all else
Meets foes irreconcilable, and at best
Lives only by variety of disease.

Well might my wishes be intense, my thoughts
Strong and perturbed, not doubting at that time          210
But that the virtue of one paramount mind
Would have abashed those impious crests—have quelled
Outrage and bloody power, and, in despite
Of what the People long had been and were
Through ignorance and false teaching, sadder proof          215
Of immaturity, and in the teeth
Of desperate opposition from without—
Have cleared a passage for just government,
And left a solid birthright to the State,
Redeemed, according to example given          220
By ancient lawgivers.
                              In this frame of mind,
Dragged by a chain of harsh necessity,
So seemed it,—now I thankfully acknowledge,
Forced by the gracious providence of Heaven,—
To England I returned, else (though assured          225
That I both was and must be of small weight,
No better than a landsman on the deck
Of a ship struggling with a hideous storm)
Doubtless, I should have then made common cause
With some who perished; haply perished too,          230
A poor mistaken and bewildered offering,—
Should to the breast of Nature have gone back,
With all my resolutions, all my hopes,
A Poet only to myself, to men
Useless, and even, beloved Friend! a soul          235
To thee unknown!
                              Twice had the trees let fall
Their leaves, as often Winter had put on
His hoary crown, since I had seen the surge
Beat against Albion's shore, since ear of mine
Had caught the accents of my native speech          240
Upon our native country's sacred ground.
A patriot of the world, how could I glide

How could I glide, a Patriot of the world, [242], *and*
Well pleased I found *for* It pleased . . . found [244–5]. D² *as* 1850.

I found the air yet busy with the stir                    [246]
205 Of a contention which had been rais'd up
Against the Traffickers in Negro blood,
An effort, which though baffled, nevertheless            [250]
Had call'd back old forgotten principles
Dismiss'd from service, had diffus'd some truths
210 And more of virtuous feeling through the heart
Of the English People. And no few of those
So numerous (little less in verity
Than a whole Nation crying with one voice)
Who had been cross'd in this their just intent
215 And righteous hope, thereby were well prepared
To let that journey sleep awhile, and join
Whatever other Caravan appear'd
To travel forward towards Liberty
With more success. For me that strife had ne'er
220 Fasten'd on my affections, nor did now                [255]
Its unsuccessful issue much excite
My sorrow, having laid this faith to heart,
That, if France prosper'd, good Men would not long
Pay fruitless worship to humanity,
225 And this most rotten branch of human shame,            [260]
Object, as seem'd, of a superfluous pains
Would fall together with its parent tree.


Such was my then belief, that there was one,
And only one solicitude for all;
230 And now the strength of Britain was put forth
In league with the confederated Host,                    [265]
Not in my single self alone I found,
But in the minds of all ingenuous Youth,
Change and subversion from this hour. No shock
235 Given to my moral nature had I known
Down to that very moment; neither lapse                  [270]
Nor turn of sentiment that might be nam'd
A revolution, save at this one time,
All else was progress on the self-same path
240 On which with a diversity of pace
I had been travelling; this a stride at once             [275]
Into another region. True it is,
'Twas not conceal'd with what ungracious eyes
Our native Rulers from the very first

Into communion with her sylvan shades,
Erewhile my tuneful haunt ? It pleased me more
To abide in the great City, where I found                          245
The general air still busy with the stir
Of that first memorable onset made
By a strong levy of humanity
Upon the traffickers in Negro blood ;
Effort which, though defeated, had recalled                        250
To notice old forgotten principles,
And through the nation spread a novel heat
Of virtuous feeling. For myself, I own
That this particular strife had wanted power
To rivet my affections ; nor did now                               255
Its unsuccessful issue much excite
My sorrow ; for I brought with me the faith
That, if France prospered, good men would not long
Pay fruitless worship to humanity,
And this most rotten branch of human shame,                        260
Object, so seemed it, of superfluous pains,
Would fall together with its parent tree.
What, then, were my emotions, when in arms
Britain put forth her free-born strength in league,
Oh, pity and shame! with those confederate Powers!                 265
Not in my single self alone I found,
But in the minds of all ingenuous youth,
Change and subversion from that hour. No shock
Given to my moral nature had I known
Down to that very moment ; neither lapse                           270
Nor turn of sentiment that might be named
A revolution, save at this one time ;
All else was progress on the self-same path
On which, with a diversity of pace,
I had been travelling : this a stride at once                      275

217–18 Their persons and unite their means in aid
   Of any other combatants that seemed
   To uphold the cause of general liberty A².
218 Advancing towards the land of liberty B².
222 being inwardly convinced A² C.  226 𝕬 C D: D² as 1850.
228–30. What then were my emotions when the strength
   The armed strength of Britain was put forth. A² C : D² as 1850
242–56 A² C as 1850 [276–80].
244–5 Our native Rulers from the first had look'd
   Upon the daring effort made by France A².

245 Had look'd upon regenerated France
    Nor had I doubted that this day would come.
    But in such contemplation I had thought
    Of general interests only, beyond this
    Had [never] once foretasted the event.
250 Now had I other business for I felt
    The ravage of this most unnatural strife
    In my own heart; there lay it like a weight
    At enmity with all the tenderest springs
    Of my enjoyments. I, who with the breeze
255 Had play'd, a green leaf on the blessed tree
    Of my beloved country; nor had wish'd                    [280]
    For happier fortune than to wither there,
    Now from my pleasant station was cut off,
    And toss'd about in whirlwinds. I rejoiced,
260 Yea, afterwards, truth most painful to record!
    Exulted in the triumph of my soul                        [285]
    When Englishmen by thousands were o'erthrown,
    Left without glory on the Field, or driven,
    Brave hearts, to shameful flight. It was a grief,
265 Grief call it not, 'twas anything but that,
    A conflict of sensations without name,                   [290]
    Of which he only who may love the sight
    Of a Village Steeple as I do can judge
    When in the Congregation, bending all
270 To their great Father, prayers were offer'd up,
    Or praises for our Country's Victories,                  [295]
    And 'mid the simple worshippers, perchance,
    I only, like an uninvited Guest
    Whom no one own'd sate silent, shall I add,
275 Fed on the day of vengeance yet to come?

        Oh! much have they to account for, who could tear [300]
    By violence at one decisive rent
    From the best Youth in England, their dear pride,
    Their joy, in England; this, too, at a time
280 In which worst losses easily might wear
    The best of names, when patriotic love                   [305]
    Did of itself in modesty give way
    Like the Precursor when the Deity
    Is come, whose Harbinger he is, a time
285 In which apostacy from ancient faith

Into another region.  As a light
And pliant harebell, swinging in the breeze
On some grey rock—its birth-place—so had I
Wantoned, fast rooted on the ancient tower
Of my beloved country, wishing not                               280
A happier fortune than to wither there:
Now was I from that pleasant station torn
And tossed about in whirlwind.  I rejoiced,
Yea, afterwards—truth most painful to record!—
Exulted, in the triumph of my soul,                              285
When Englishmen by thousands were o'erthrown,
Left without glory on the field, or driven,
Brave hearts! to shameful flight. It was a grief,—
Grief call it not, 'twas anything but that,—
A conflict of sensations without name,                           290
Of which *he* only, who may love the sight
Of a village steeple, as I do, can judge,
When, in the congregation bending all
To their great Father, prayers were offered up,
Or praises for our country's victories;                          295
And, 'mid the simple worshippers, perchance
I only, like an uninvited guest
Whom no one owned, sate silent, shall I add,
Fed on the day of vengeance yet to come.

Oh! much have they to account for, who could tear,   300
By violence, at one decisive rent,
From the best youth in England their dear pride,
Their joy, in England; this, too, at a time
In which worst losses easily might wean
The best of names, when patriotic love                           305
Did of itself in modesty give way,
Like the Precursor when the Deity
Is come Whose harbinger he was; a time
In which apostasy from ancient faith

249 never *added in pencil to* A *and* B.
250-1 Now, by experience rendered sensible
        I felt the ravage of the unnatural strife  A².
259 whirlwinds 𝔄 D: whirlwind  C D².
274 sate mute, I will not add  D²: D *as* 𝔄.
275 vengeance 𝔄 C D²: judgment  D.
280 wear *all MSS.*:  wean 1850.

Seem'd but conversion to a higher creed,                    [310]
Withal a season dangerous and wild,
A time in which Experience would have pluck'd
Flowers out of any hedge to make thereof
290  A Chaplet, in contempt of his grey locks.

Ere yet the Fleet of Britain had gone forth            [315]
On this unworthy service, whereunto
The unhappy counsel of a few weak Men
Had doom'd it, I beheld the Vessels lie,
295  A brood of gallant Creatures, on the Deep
I saw them in their rest, a sojourner
Through a whole month of calm and glassy days,        [320]
In that delightful Island which protects
Their place of convocation; there I heard
300  Each evening, walking by the still sea-shore,
A monitory sound that never fail'd,
The sunset Canon. While the Orb went down             [325]
In the tranquillity of Nature, came
That voice, ill requiem! seldom heard by me
305  Without a spirit overcast, a deep
Imagination, thought of woes to come,
And sorrow for mankind, and pain of heart.            [330]

In France, the Men who for their desperate ends
Had pluck'd up mercy by the roots were glad
310  Of this new enemy. Tyrants, strong before
In devilish pleas were ten times stronger now,
And thus beset with Foes on every side                [335]
The goaded Land wax'd mad; the crimes of few
Spread into madness of the many, blasts
315  From hell came sanctified like airs from heaven;
The sternness of the Just, the faith of those
Who doubted not that Providence had times             [340]
Of anger and of vengeance,—theirs who throned
The human understanding paramount
320  And made of that their God, the hopes of those
Who were content to barter short-lived pangs
For a paradise of ages, the blind rage                [345]

288–94 A³ C *as* 1850.        299–304 D *stuck over*: D² *as* 1850.
302 Canon 𝔄: Cannon C.
305–6 with dark Imagination of impending woes A³ C.

Seemed but conversion to a higher creed;                    310
Withal a season dangerous and wild,
A time when sage Experience would have snatched
Flowers out of any hedge-row to compose
A chaplet in contempt of his grey locks.


    When the proud fleet that bears the red-cross flag     315
In that unworthy service was prepared
To mingle, I beheld the vessels lie,
A brood of gallant creatures, on the deep;
I saw them in their rest, a sojourner
Through a whole month of calm and glassy days           320
In that delightful island which protects
Their place of convocation—there I heard,
Each evening, pacing by the still sea-shore,
A monitory sound that never failed,—
The sunset cannon. While the orb went down            325
In the tranquillity of nature, came
That voice, ill requiem! seldom heard by me
Without a spirit overcast by dark
Imaginations, sense of woes to come,
Sorrow for human kind, and pain of heart.              330


    In France, the men, who, for their desperate ends,
Had plucked up mercy by the roots, were glad
Of this new enemy. Tyrants, strong before
In wicked pleas, were strong as demons now;
And thus, on every side beset with foes,              335
The goaded land waxed mad; the crimes of few
Spread into madness of the many; blasts
From hell came sanctified like airs from heaven.
The sternness of the just, the faith of those
Who doubted not that Providence had times             340
Of vengeful retribution, theirs who throned
The human Understanding paramount
And made of that their God, the hopes of men
Who were content to barter short-lived pangs
For a paradise of ages, the blind rage                345

---

307 A² C *as* 1850.        311 ℨ C D: D² *as* 1850.
318 A² C *as* 1850.

Of insolent tempers, the light vanity
Of intermeddlers, steady purposes
325 Of the suspicious, slips of the indiscreet,
And all the accidents of life were press'd
Into one service, busy with one work;                    [350]
The Senate was heart-stricken, not a voice
Uplifted, none to oppose or mitigate;                    [355]
330 Domestic carnage now filled all the year
With Feast-days; the old Man from the chimney-nook,
The Maiden from the bosom of her Love,
The Mother from the Cradle of her Babe,
The Warrior from the Field, all perish'd, all,           [360]
335 Friends, enemies, of all parties, ages, ranks,
Head after head, and never heads enough
For those that bade them fall: they found their joy,
They made it, ever thirsty as a Child,
If light desires of innocent little Ones                 [365]
340 May with such heinous appetites be match'd,
Having a toy, a wind-mill, though the air
Do of itself blow fresh, and make the vane               [370]
Spin in his eyesight, he is not content
But with the plaything at arm's length he sets
345 His front against the blast, and runs amain,
To make it whirl the faster.
                              In the depth
Of those enormities, even thinking minds                 [375]
Forgot at seasons whence they had their being,
Forgot that such a sound was ever heard
350 As Liberty upon earth; yet all beneath
Her innocent authority was wrought,
Nor could have been, without her blessed name.           [380]
The illustrious Wife of Roland, in the hour
Of her composure, felt that agony
355 And gave it vent in her last words. O Friend!

328–9 A² C *as* 1850 [351–5].
336–46 Head after head shower'd dismally to earth
        Unglutted, unappeased; life after life
        Poured out for hourly increase of the thirst
        That sway'd the ruthless havock  Amid the depth A² C: D *stuck
        over*: D² *as* 1850.
338–41                        As a child
        Pleas'd on some blustering day to exercise
        A Toy that mimics with revolving arms
        The motions of a Windmill A³ (*deleted*).

Of insolent tempers, the light vanity
Of intermeddlers, steady purposes
Of the suspicious, slips of the indiscreet,
And all the accidents of life were pressed
Into one service, busy with one work.                    350
The Senate stood aghast, her prudence quenched,
Her wisdom stifled, and her justice scared,
Her frenzy only active to extol
Past outrages, and shape the way for new,
Which no one dared to oppose or mitigate.                 355

   Domestic carnage now filled the whole year
With feast-days; old men from the chimney-nook,
The maiden from the bosom of her love,
The mother from the cradle of her babe,
The warrior from the field—all perished, all—            360
Friends, enemies, of all parties, ages, ranks,
Head after head, and never heads enough
For those that bade them fall. They found their joy,
They made it proudly, eager as a child,
(If like desires of innocent little ones                  365
May with such heinous appetites be compared),
Pleased in some open field to exercise
A toy that mimics with revolving wings
The motion of a wind-mill; though the air
Do of itself blow fresh, and make the vanes               370
Spin in his eyesight, *that* contents him not,
But, with the plaything at arm's length, he sets
His front against the blast, and runs amain,
That it may whirl the faster.
                 Amid the depth
Of those enormities, even thinking minds                  375
Forgot, at seasons, whence they had their being;
Forgot that such a sound was ever heard
As Liberty upon earth: yet all beneath
Her innocent authority was wrought,
Nor could have been, without her blessed name.            380
The illustrious wife of Roland, in the hour
Of her composure, felt that agony,
And gave it vent in her last words. O Friend!

346–7 In the depth Of] Amid the depth Of A² C D²: Appalled, astounded
By D: By E (*v.* note).

It was a lamentable time for man
Whether a hope had e'er been his or not,                          [385]
A woeful time for them whose hopes did still
Outlast the shock; most woeful for those few,
360 They had the deepest feeling of the grief,
Who still were flattered, and had trust in man.
Meanwhile, the Invaders fared as they deserv'd;          [390]
The Herculean Commonwealth had put forth her arms
And throttled with an infant Godhead's might
365 The snakes about her cradle; that was well
And as it should be, yet no cure for those
Whose souls were sick with pain of what would be          [395]
Hereafter brought in charge against mankind;
Most melancholy at that time, O Friend!
370 Were my day-thoughts, my dreams were miserable;
Through months, through years, long after the last beat
Of those atrocities (I speak bare truth,                          [400]
As if to thee alone in private talk)
I scarcely had one night of quiet sleep
375 Such ghastly visions had I of despair
And tyranny, and implements of death,
And long orations which in dreams I pleaded          [411]
Before unjust Tribunals, with a voice
Labouring, a brain confounded, and a sense
380 Of treachery and desertion in the place
The holiest that I knew of, my own soul.                          [415]


When I began at first, in early youth
To yield myself to Nature, when that strong
And holy passion overcame me first,
385 Neither the day nor night, evening or morn
Were free from the oppression; but, Great God!          [420]
Who send'st thyself into this breathing world
Through Nature and through every kind of life,
And mak'st Man what he is, Creature divine,

---

358-61 A² C *as* 1850.
372-5                              atrocities the night to me
              Came seldom charged with unmolested sleep
              Such ghastly *etc.* A² C D: D³ *as* 1850: *for* D² *vide notes.*
[407] fond] forced D E.          382 A² C *as* 1850.
385-6 A C D: D² as 1850.
387-9 A² C D *as* 1850 [421-4], *but* care *for* call.

It was a lamentable time for man,
Whether a hope had e'er been his or not;                385
A woful time for them whose hopes survived
The shock; most woful for those few who still
Were flattered, and had trust in human kind:
They had the deepest feeling of the grief.
Meanwhile the Invaders fared as they deserved:          390
The Herculean Commonwealth had put forth her arms,
And throttled with an infant godhead's might
The snakes about her cradle; that was well,
And as it should be; yet no cure for them
Whose souls were sick with pain of what would be        395
Hereafter brought in charge against mankind.
Most melancholy at that time, O Friend!
Were my day-thoughts,—my nights were miserable;
Through months, through years, long after the last beat
Of those atrocities, the hour of sleep                  400
To me came rarely charged with natural gifts,
Such ghastly visions had I of despair
And tyranny, and implements of death;
And innocent victims sinking under fear,
And momentary hope, and worn-out prayer,                405
Each in his separate cell, or penned in crowds
For sacrifice, and struggling with fond mirth
And levity in dungeons, where the dust
Was laid with tears. Then suddenly the scene
Changed, and the unbroken dream entangled me            410
In long orations, which I strove to plead
Before unjust tribunals,—with a voice
Labouring, a brain confounded, and a sense,
Death-like, of treacherous desertion, felt
In the last place of refuge—my own soul.                415

When I began in youth's delightful prime
To yield myself to Nature, when that strong
And holy passion overcame me first,
Nor day nor night, evening or morn, was free
From its oppression. But, O Power Supreme!               420
Without Whose call this world would cease to breathe,
Who from the fountain of Thy grace dost fill
The veins that branch through every frame of life,
Making man what he is, creature divine,

390  In single or in social eminence                    [425]
     Above all these rais'd infinite ascents
     When reason, which enables him to be,
     Is not sequester'd, what a change is here!
     How different ritual for this after worship
395  What countenance to promote this second love      [430]
     That first was service but to things which lie
     At rest, within the bosom of thy will:
     Therefore to serve was high beatitude;
     The tumult was a gladness, and the fear
400  Ennobling, venerable; sleep secure,                [435]
     And waking thoughts more rich than happiest dreams.

     But as the ancient Prophets were enflam'd
     Nor wanted consolations of their own               [440]
     And majesty of mind, when they denounced
405  On Towns and Cities, wallowing in the abyss
     Of their offences, punishment to come;
     Or saw like other men with bodily eyes
     Before them in some desolated place                [445]
     The consummation of the wrath of Heaven,
410  So did some portions of that spirit fall
     On me, to uphold me through those evil times,
     And in their rage and dog-day heat I found
     Something to glory in, as just and fit,
     And in the order of sublimest laws;
415  And even if that were not, amid the awe
     Of unintelligible chastisement,                    [455]
     I felt a kind of sympathy with power,
     Motions rais'd up within me, nevertheless,
     Which had relationship to highest things.
420  Wild blasts of music thus did find their way       [461]
     Into the midst of terrible events,
     So that worst tempests might be listen'd to:
     Then was the truth received into my heart,

391  all these] the rest  A² C.
397-9  𝔄 C D:  D² as 1850.
405-16  stuck over in D:  D² as E, vide notes.
408  desolated  𝔄 C: desolate  D² E.
409  wrath of Heaven] threaten'd wrath  A² C.
411-12  On me uplifted from the vantage ground
            Of lamentation to a state of being
            That through the times exceeding fierceness saw  A² C.

In single or in social eminence,                                    425
Above the rest raised infinite ascents
When reason that enables him to be
Is not sequestered—what a change is here!
How different ritual for this after-worship,
What countenance to promote this second love!                       430
The first was service paid to things which lie
Guarded within the bosom of Thy will.
Therefore to serve was high beatitude;
Tumult was therefore gladness, and the fear
Ennobling, venerable; sleep secure,                                 435
And waking thoughts more rich than happiest dreams.

But as the ancient Prophets, borne aloft
In vision, yet constrained by natural laws
With them to take a troubled human heart,
Wanted not consolations, nor a creed                                440
Of reconcilement, then when they denounced,
On towns and cities, wallowing in the abyss
Of their offences, punishment to come;
Or saw, like other men, with bodily eyes,
Before them, in some desolated place,                               445
The wrath consummate and the threat fulfilled;
So, with devout humility be it said,
So, did a portion of that spirit fall
On me uplifted from the vantage-ground
Of pity and sorrow to a state of being                             450
That through the time's exceeding fierceness saw
Glimpses of retribution, terrible,
And in the order of sublime behests:
But, even if that were not, amid the awe
Of unintelligible chastisement,                                     455
Not only acquiescences of faith
Survived, but daring sympathies with power,
Motions not treacherous or profane, else why
Within the folds of no ungentle breast
Their dread vibration to this hour prolonged?                       460
Wild blasts of music thus could find their way
Into the midst of turbulent events;
So that worst tempests might be listened to.
Then was the truth received into my heart,

   417–19 A² C *as* 1850 [456–9].
   421 terrible 𝕬 C D: desperate D²: turbulent D³.

That under heaviest sorrow earth can bring,                [465]
425 Griefs bitterest of ourselves or of our kind,
If from the affliction somewhere do not grow
Honour which could not else have been, a faith,
An elevation, and a sanctity,
If new strength be not given, or old restored
430 The blame is ours not Nature's. When a taunt        [470]
Was taken up by Scoffers in their pride,
Saying, 'behold the harvest which we reap
From popular Government and Equality,'
I saw that it was neither these, nor aught
435 Of wild belief engrafted on their names            [475]
By false philosophy, that caus'd the woe,
But that it was a reservoir of guilt
And ignorance, fill'd up from age to age,
That could no longer hold its loathsome charge,
440 But burst and spread in deluge through the Land.   [480]

And as the desart hath green spots, the sea
Small islands in the midst of stormy waves,
So that disastrous period did not want
Such sprinklings of all human excellence,
445 As were a joy to hear of. Yet (nor less            [486]
For those bright spots, those fair examples given
Of fortitude, and energy, and love,
And human nature faithful to itself
Under worst trials) was I impell'd to think           [490]
450 Of the glad time when first I traversed France,
A youthful pilgrim, above all remember'd
That day when through an Arch that spann'd the street,
A rainbow made of garish ornaments,
Triumphal pomp for Liberty confirm'd,
455 We walk'd, a pair of weary Travellers,
Along the Town of Arras, place from which
Issued that Robespierre, who afterwards

425 A *deletes*; *not in* C.
434-8 𝔄 C D: D² *as* 1850.
442 in the midst of] planted amid A² C D: D² *as* 1850.
445-9 As were a . . . think A² C D *as* 1850, *but* graciously dispersed
Of human *for* in no age surpassed . . . human, *and* itself *for* herself [488].
D² *as* 1850.
451-3 𝔄 C D: D² *as* 1850.
455-7 We walk'd, a pair of gazing Travellers,

That, under heaviest sorrow earth can bring,          465
If from the affliction somewhere do not grow
Honour which could not else have been, a faith,
An elevation and a sanctity,
If new strength be not given nor old restored,
The blame is ours, not Nature's. When a taunt          470
Was taken up by scoffers in their pride,
Saying, 'Behold the harvest that we reap
From popular government and equality,'
I clearly saw that neither these nor aught
Of wild belief engrafted on their names          475
By false philosophy had caused the woe,
But a terrific reservoir of guilt
And ignorance filled up from age to age,
That could no longer hold its loathsome charge,
But burst and spread in deluge through the land.          480

   And as the desert hath green spots, the sea
Small islands scattered amid stormy waves,
So *that* disastrous period did not want
Bright sprinklings of all human excellence,
To which the silver wands of saints in Heaven          485
Might point with rapturous joy. Yet not the less,
For those examples in no age surpassed
Of fortitude and energy and love,
And human nature faithful to herself
Under worst trials, was I driven to think          490
Of the glad times when first I traversed France
A youthful pilgrim; above all reviewed
That eventide, when under windows bright
With happy faces and with garlands hung,
And through a rainbow-arch that spanned the street,          495
Triumphal pomp for liberty confirmed,
I paced, a dear companion at my side,
The town of Arras, whence with promise high
Issued, on delegation to sustain
Humanity and right, *that* Robespierre,          500
He who thereafter, and in how short time!

     Entering beneath a festive evening sky
     With weary steps the Town of Arras, whence
     Issued, on delegation to sustain
     The interests and rights of human kind,
     That Robespierre, who in succeeding days  A² C D: D² *as* 1850.

Wielded the sceptre of the atheist crew.                        [502]
When the calamity spread far and wide,
460  And this same City, which had even appear'd
To outrun the rest in exultation, groan'd                       [505]
Under the vengeance of her cruel Son,
As Lear reproach'd the winds, I could almost
Have quarrel'd with that blameless spectacle
465  For being yet an image in my mind
To mock me under such a strange reverse.                        [510]

O Friend! few happier moments have been mine
Through my whole life than that when first I heard
That this foul Tribe of Moloch was o'erthrown,
470  And their chief Regent levell'd with the dust.
The day was one which haply may deserve
A separate chronicle. Having gone abroad
From a small Village where I tarried then,
To the same far-secluded privacy
475  I was returning. Over the smooth Sands
Of Leven's ample Æstuary lay                                    [515]
My journey, and beneath a genial sun;
With distant prospect among gleams of sky
And clouds, and intermingled mountain tops,
480  In one inseparable glory clad,
Creatures of one ethereal substance, met                        [520]
In Consistory, like a diadem
Or crown of burning Seraphs, as they sit
In the Empyrean. Underneath this show
485  Lay, as I knew, the nest of pastoral vales
Among whose happy fields I had grown up                         [525]
From childhood. On the fulgent spectacle
Which neither changed, nor stirr'd, nor pass'd away,
I gazed, and with a fancy more alive
490  On this account, that I had chanced to find
That morning, ranging thro' the churchyard graves
Of Cartmell's rural Town, the place in which
An honor'd Teacher of my youth was laid.                         [534]

468-70 Than that which told me that this horrid Crew
        Of Moloch with their Regent, lay in dust. A².
  470 Prostrated with their Moloch in the dust *followed by* 471 D: D² *as*
1850.
  485-97 D *stuck over.*
  488-93 That neither passed away nor stirr'd nor changed

Wielded the sceptre of the Atheist crew.
When the calamity spread far and wide—
And this same city, that did then appear
To outrun the rest in exultation, groaned                        505
Under the vengeance of her cruel son,
As Lear reproached the winds—I could almost
Have quarrelled with that blameless spectacle
For lingering yet an image in my mind
To mock me under such a strange reverse.                         510

  O Friend! few happier moments have been mine
Than that which told the downfall of this Tribe
So dreaded, so abhorred. The day deserves
A separate record. Over the smooth sands
Of Leven's ample estuary lay                                     515
My journey, and beneath a genial sun,
With distant prospect among gleams of sky
And clouds, and intermingling mountain tops,
In one inseparable glory clad,
Creatures of one ethereal substance met                         520
In consistory, like a diadem
Or crown of burning seraphs as they sit
In the empyrean. Underneath that pomp
Celestial, lay unseen the pastoral vales
Among whose happy fields I had grown up                         525
From childhood. On the fulgent spectacle,
That neither passed away nor changed, I gazed
Enrapt; but brightest things are wont to draw
Sad opposites out of the inner heart,
As even their pensive influence drew from mine.                 530
How could it otherwise? for not in vain
That very morning had I turned aside
To seek the ground where, 'mid a throng of graves,
An honoured teacher of my youth was laid,

I gazed with fancy charmed and soothed but soon
Depressed for all bright things are apt to draw
Sad opposites out of the inner heart
As now they did—how could they else from mine
For I that morning not in vain had sought
Ground where a Teacher of my Youth was laid  D²: D³ *as* 1850.
490 For this, that I had sought and not in vain. A² C.
492–4 in which ... Schoolboys he]      where lay
     Interr'd, an honour'd Teacher of my Youth
     He in my Schoolboy time  A² C.

While we were Schoolboys he had died among us,
495 And was borne hither, as I knew, to rest
With his own Family. A plain Stone, inscribed
With name, date, office, pointed out the spot,
To which a slip of verses was subjoin'd,
(By his desire, as afterwards I learn'd)
500 A fragment from the Elegy of Gray.                    [536]
A week, or little less, before his death
He had said to me, 'my head will soon lie low;'
And when I saw the turf that cover'd him,                    [540]
After the lapse of full eight years, those words,
505 With sound of voice, and countenance of the Man,
Came back upon me; so that some few tears
Fell from me in my own despite. And now,
Thus travelling smoothly, o'er the level Sands,                    [545]
I thought with pleasure of the Verses, graven
510 Upon his Tombstone, saying to myself
He loved the Poets, and if now alive,
Would have loved me, as one not destitute
Of promise, nor belying the kind hope                    [550]
Which he had form'd, when I at his command,
515 Began to spin, at first, my toilsome Songs.

Without me and within, as I advanced,
All that I saw, or felt, or communed with
Was gentleness and peace. Upon a small
And rocky Island near, a fragment stood                    [555]
520 (Itself like a sea rock) of what had been
A Romish Chapel, where in ancient times
Masses were said at the hour which suited those
Who crossed the Sands with ebb of morning tide.                    [561]
Not far from this still Ruin all the Plain
525 Was spotted with a variegated crowd
Of Coaches, Wains, and Travellers, horse and foot,
Wading, beneath the conduct of their Guide                    [565]
In loose procession through the shallow Stream
Of inland water; the great Sea meanwhile
530 Was at safe distance, far retired. I paused,

500 𝔄 C D:  D² *as* 1850.
501-2 Not long before the day when Nature closed
            His sufferings in the quietness of death
            I heard him say 'my *etc.* A² C.

And on the stone were graven by his desire        535
Lines from the churchyard elegy of Gray.
This faithful guide, speaking from his death-bed,
Added no farewell to his parting counsel,
But said to me, 'My head will soon lie low;'
And when I saw the turf that covered him,        540
After the lapse of full eight years, those words,
With sound of voice and countenance of the Man,
Came back upon me, so that some few tears
Fell from me in my own despite. But now
I thought, still traversing that widespread plain,        545
With tender pleasure of the verses graven
Upon his tombstone, whispering to myself:
He loved the Poets, and, if now alive,
Would have loved me, as one not destitute
Of promise, nor belying the kind hope        550
That he had formed, when I, at his command,
Began to spin, with toil, my earliest songs.

As I advanced, all that I saw or felt
Was gentleness and peace. Upon a small
And rocky island near, a fragment stood        555
(Itself like a sea rock) the low remains
(With shells encrusted, dark with briny weeds)
Of a dilapidated structure, once
A Romish chapel, where the vested priest
Said matins at the hour that suited those        560
Who crossed the sands with ebb of morning tide.
Not far from that still ruin all the plain
Lay spotted with a variegated crowd
Of vehicles and travellers, horse and foot,
Wading beneath the conduct of their guide        565
In loose procession through the shallow stream
Of inland waters; the great sea meanwhile
Heaved at safe distance, far retired. I paused,

507-9 Fell in my own despite. And now I thought
        With tender pleasure, *etc.* D: D² *as* 1850.
510 saying 𝔄 C D: whispering D².        515 A² C *as* 1850.
520-6 A² C *as* 1850, *but* masses *for* matins.
[561] morning D²: even D.
529-30 A² C *as* 1850: *after* distance A² *has*, deleted, with her ravenous
Host Of foaming billows.
530-8 D *stuck over*: D² *as* 1850.

      Unwilling to proceed, the scene appear'd
      So gay and chearful, when a Traveller
      Chancing to pass, I carelessly inquired
      If any news were stirring; he replied
535  In the familiar language of the day           [572]
      That, *Robespierre was dead.* Nor was a doubt,
      On further question, left within my mind
      But that the tidings were substantial truth;
      That he and his supporters all were fallen.      [575]

540     Great was my glee of spirit, great my joy
      In vengeance, and eternal justice, thus
      Made manifest. 'Come now ye golden times,'
      Said I, forth-breathing on those open Sands
      A Hymn of triumph, 'as the morning comes     [580]
545  Out of the bosom of the night, come Ye:
      Thus far our trust is verified; behold!
      They who with clumsy desperation brought
      Rivers of Blood, and preach'd that nothing else
      Could cleanse the Augean Stable, by the might    [585]
550  Of their own helper have been swept away;
      Their madness is declared and visible,
      Elsewhere will safety now be sought, and Earth
      March firmly towards righteousness and peace.'
      Then schemes I framed more calmly, when and how  [590]
555  The madding Factions might be tranquillised,
      And, though through hardships manifold and long,
      The mighty renovation would proceed;
      Thus, interrupted by uneasy bursts
      Of exultation, I pursued my way      [595]
560  Along that very Shore which I had skimm'd
      In former times, when, spurring from the Vale
      Of Nightshade, and St. Mary's mouldering Fane,
      And the Stone Abbot, after circuit made
      In wantonness of heart, a joyous Crew     [600]
565  Of School-boys, hastening to their distant home,
      Along the margin of the moonlight Sea,
      We beat with thundering hoofs the level Sand.

531–4 Unwilling *etc.*] Loth to advance the scene appeared so gay,
                    So bright and chearful, but a Horseman soon
                    Approached of whom I carelessly inquired
                    If aught of news *etc.* A² C.
536–9 That Robespierre was dead.—Who?—when and how?
      Questions that thrust each other (out) of sight

Longing for skill to paint a scene so bright
And cheerful, but the foremost of the band                    570
As he approached, no salutation given
In the familiar language of the day,
Cried, 'Robespierre is dead!'—nor was a doubt,
After strict question, left within my mind
That he and his supporters all were fallen.                   575

    Great was my transport, deep my gratitude
To everlasting Justice, by this fiat
Made manifest. 'Come now, ye golden times,'
Said I forth-pouring on those open sands
A hymn of triumph: 'as the morning comes                      580
From out the bosom of the night, come ye:
Thus far our trust is verified; behold!
They who with clumsy desperation brought
A river of Blood, and preached that nothing else
Could cleanse the Augean stable, by the might                 585
Of their own helper have been swept away;
Their madness stands declared and visible;
Elsewhere will safety now be sought, and earth
March firmly towards righteousness and peace.'—
Then schemes I framed more calmly, when and how               590
The madding factions might be tranquillised,
And how through hardships manifold and long
The glorious renovation would proceed.
Thus interrupted by uneasy bursts
Of exultation, I pursued my way                               595
Along that very shore which I had skimmed
In former days, when—spurring from the Vale
Of Nightshade, and St. Mary's mouldering fane,
And the stone abbot, after circuit made
In wantonness of heart, a joyous band                         600
Of school-boys hastening to their distant home
Along the margin of the moonlight sea—
We beat with thundering hoofs the level sand.

      But no misgiving, not a doubt survived
      That he *etc.* (*found on an odd sheet*)
             Nor did a doubt
      On further question in my mind remain
      That he *etc.* $A^2$ C.
540 great my joy] deep my joy $A^2$ C.      551 is $\mathfrak{A}$ C D: stands $D^2$.
556 though] how $A^2$ C.
557 mighty] glorious $A^2$ C.      561 times $\mathfrak{A}$ C D: days $D^2$.

FROM this time forth, in France, as is well known,
Authority put on a milder face,
570 Yet everything was wanting that might give
Courage to those who look'd for good by light
Of rational experience, good I mean                          [5]
At hand, and in the spirit of past aims.
The same belief I, nevertheless, retain'd;
575 The language of the Senate and the acts
And public measures of the Government,
Though both of heartless omen, had not power                 [10]
To daunt me; in the People was my trust
And in the virtues which mine eyes had seen,
580 And to the ultimate repose of things
I look'd with unabated confidence;
I knew that wound external could not take
Life from the young Republic, that new foes
Would only follow in the path of shame                       [15]
585 Their brethren, and her triumphs be in the end
Great, universal, irresistible.
This faith, which was an object in my mind
Of passionate intuition, had effect
Not small in dazzling me; for thus, thro' zeal,
590 Such victory I confounded in my thoughts
With one far higher and more difficult,
Triumphs of unambitious peace at home                        [20]
And noiseless fortitude. Beholding still
Resistance strong as heretofore, I thought
595 That what was in degree the same, was likewise
The same in quality, that, as the worse
Of the two spirits then at strife remain'd                   [25]
Untired, the better surely would preserve
The heart that first had rouzed him, never dreamt

568–9 From that time forth Authority in France,
          As is well known, put on a milder face,  D:  D² *as* 1850.
571 those 𝔄 C D:  them  D².
572–3 A² C *as* 1850.

# BOOK ELEVENTH

### FRANCE—Concluded

FROM that time forth, Authority in France
Put on a milder face; Terror had ceased,
Yet every thing was wanting that might give
Courage to them who looked for good by light
Of rational Experience, for the shoots                    5
And hopeful blossoms of a second spring:
Yet, in me, confidence was unimpaired;
The Senate's language, and the public acts
And measures of the Government, though both
Weak, and of heartless omen, had not power               10
To daunt me; in the People was my trust:
And, in the virtues which mine eyes had seen,
I knew that wound external could not take
Life from the young Republic; that new foes
Would only follow, in the path of shame,                 15
Their brethren, and her triumphs be in the end
Great, universal, irresistible.
This intuition led me to confound
One victory with another, higher far,—
Triumphs of unambitious peace at home,                   20
And noiseless fortitude. Beholding still
Resistance strong as heretofore, I thought
That what was in degree the same was likewise
The same in quality,—that, as the worse
Of the two spirits then at strife remained               25
Untired, the better, surely, would preserve
The heart that first had roused him. Youth maintains,

574 How could I then retain the same belief? A² C. Yet unabated was
*my* confidence D E: E² *as* 1850.
    579 *not in* D: *restored to* D².     580–1 A *deletes*; *not in* C.
    587–93 This faith—this passionate intuition—led
            My inexperienced judgment to confound
            Such with a victory more arduous far,
            That unambitious peace alone could win
            And noiseless fortitude A² C.
    599–605 never dreamt . . . call'd to. A *deletes and also* I knew 605.
*Not in* C.

600  That transmigration could be undergone
     A fall of being suffer'd, and of hope
     By creature that appear'd to have received
     Entire conviction what a great ascent
     Had been accomplish'd, what high faculties
605  It had been call'd to. Youth maintains, I knew,
     In all conditions of society,
     Communion more direct and intimate
     With Nature, and the inner strength she has,                    [30]
     And hence, oft-times, no less, with Reason too,
610  Than Age or Manhood, even. To Nature then,
     Power had reverted: habit, custom, law,
     Had left an interregnum's open space
     For her to stir about in, uncontrol'd.
     The warmest judgments and the most untaught
615  Found in events which every day brought forth
     Enough to sanction them, and far, far more
     To shake the authority of canons drawn
     From ordinary practice. I could see
     How Babel-like the employment was of those                     [35]
620  Who, by the recent deluge stupefied,
     With their whole souls went culling from the day
     Its petty promises to build a tower
     For their own safety; laugh'd at gravest heads,
     Who, watching in their hate of France for signs               [40]
625  Of her disasters, if the stream of rumour
     Brought with it one green branch, conceited thence
     That not a single tree was left alive
     In all her forests. How could I believe
     That wisdom could in any shape come near                       [45]
630  Men clinging to delusions so insane?
     And thus, experience proving that no few
     Of my opinions had been just, I took
     Like credit to myself where less was due,
     And thought that other notions were as sound,                  [50]
635  Yea, could not but be right, because I saw
     That foolish men opposed them.
                                    To a strain
     More animated I might here give way,
     And tell, since juvenile errors are my theme,
     What in those days through Britain was perform'd               [55]
640  To turn *all* judgments out of their right course;

In all conditions of society,
Communion more direct and intimate
With Nature,—hence, ofttimes, with reason too—            30
Than age or manhood, even. To Nature, then,
Power had reverted: habit, custom, law,
Had left an interregnum's open space
For *her* to move about in, uncontrolled.
Hence could I see how Babel-like their task,              35
Who, by the recent deluge stupified,
With their whole souls went culling from the day
Its petty promises, to build a tower
For their own safety; laughed with my compeers
At gravest heads, by enmity to France                     40
Distempered, till they found, in every blast
Forced from the street-disturbing newsman's horn,
For her great cause record or prophecy
Of utter ruin. How might we believe
That wisdom could, in any shape, come near               45
Men clinging to delusions so insane?
And thus, experience proving that no few
Of our opinions had been just, we took
Like credit to ourselves where less was due,
And thought that other notions were as sound,            50
Yea, could not but be right, because we saw
That foolish men opposed them.
                              To a strain
More animated I might here give way,
And tell, since juvenile errors are my theme,
What in those days, through Britain, was performed        55
To turn *all* judgments out of their right course;

605–10                    Youth maintains
        A more direct communion, this I felt, *etc. as* 1850 [30–31]  A² C.
608     With Nature and that unapparent strength
        Which, if required, is given her to display  A³ (*deleted*).
614–18 A *deletes and reads* Hence with my ardent Comrades I could see.
*So* C.
624–8   Who by their keen hostility to France
        Distempered, found in every boastful blast *etc. as* 1850 [42–44]
        A² C.
632, 633, 635 my ... I ... myself ... I  𝔄 C: our ... we ... ourselves ...
we  A².

But this is passion over-near ourselves,
Reality too close and too intense,
And mingled up with something, in my mind,
Of scorn and condemnation personal,                    [60]
645 That would profane the sanctity of Verse.
Our Shepherds (this say merely) at that time
Thirsted to make the guardian Crook of Law
A tool of Murder; they who ruled the State,            [65]
Though with such awful proof before their eyes
650 That he who would sow death, reaps death, or worse,
And can reap nothing better, child-like long'd
To imitate, not wise enough to avoid,                  [69]
Giants in their impiety alone,
But, in their weapons and their warfare base
655 As vermin working out of reach, they leagu'd
Their strength perfidiously, to undermine
Justice, and make an end of Liberty.

But from these bitter truths I must return
To my own History. It hath been told                   [75]
660 That I was led to take an eager part
In arguments of civil polity
Abruptly, and indeed before my time:
I had approach'd, like other Youth, the Shield
Of human nature from the golden side                   [80]
665 And would have fought, even to the death, to attest
The quality of the metal which I saw.
What there is best in individual Man,
Of wise in passion, and sublime in power,
What there is strong and pure in household love,
670 Benevolent in small societies,                          [85]
And great in large ones also, when call'd forth
By great occasions, these were things of which
I something knew, yet even these themselves,
Felt deeply, were not thoroughly understood
675 By Reason; nay, far from it, they were yet,
As cause was given me afterwards to learn,
Not proof against the injuries of the day,             [90]
Lodged only at the Sanctuary's door,
Not safe within its bosom. Thus prepared,

643 mingled up] intermixed A² C.
644 Our Shepherds acted in those days like men A² D: D² *as* 1850.

But this is passion over-near ourselves,
Reality too close and too intense,
And intermixed with something, in my mind,
Of scorn and condemnation personal,                          60
That would profane the sanctity of verse.
Our Shepherds, this say merely, at that time
Acted, or seemed at least to act, like men
Thirsting to make the guardian crook of law
A tool of murder; they who ruled the State,                  65
Though with such awful proof before their eyes
That he, who would sow death, reaps death, or worse,
And can reap nothing better, child-like longed
To imitate, not wise enough to avoid;
Or left (by mere timidity betrayed)                          70
The plain straight road, for one no better chosen
Than if their wish had been to undermine
Justice, and make an end of Liberty.


But from these bitter truths I must return
To my own history. It hath been told                         75
That I was led to take an eager part
In arguments of civil polity,
Abruptly, and indeed before my time:
I had approached, like other youths, the shield
Of human nature from the golden side,                        80
And would have fought, even to the death, to attest
The quality of the metal which I saw.
What there is best in individual man,
Of wise in passion, and sublime in power,
Benevolent in small societies,                               85
And great in large ones, I had oft revolved,
Felt deeply, but not thoroughly understood
By reason: nay, far from it; they were yet,
As cause was given me afterwards to learn,
Not proof against the injuries of the day;                   90
Lodged only at the sanctuary's door,
Not safe within its bosom. Thus prepared,

---

669 A *deletes*; *not in* C.
672-4 By great occasions, these momentous objects
      Had exercised my mind, yet had they not
      Though deeply felt, been thoroughly understood  A² C.

680  And with such general insight into evil,
     And of the bounds which sever it from good,
     As books and common intercourse with life                [95]·
     Must needs have given; to the noviciate mind,
     When the world travels in a beaten road,
685  Guide faithful as is needed, I began
     To think with fervour upon management
     Of Nations, what it is and ought to be,                   [100]
     And how their worth depended on their Laws
     And on the Constitution of the State.


690      O pleasant exercise of hope and joy!                  [105]
     For great were the auxiliars which then stood
     Upon our side, we who were strong in love;
     Bliss was it in that dawn to be alive,
     But to be young was very heaven: O times,
695  In which the meagre, stale, forbidding ways               [110]
     Of custom, law, and statute took at once
     The attraction of a Country in Romance;
     When Reason seem'd the most to assert her rights
     When most intent on making of herself
700  A prime Enchanter to assist the work,                     [115]
     Which then was going forwards in her name.
     Not favour'd spots alone, but the whole earth
     The beauty wore of promise, that which sets,
     To take an image which was felt, no doubt,
705  Among the bowers of paradise itself,                      [120]
     The budding rose above the rose full blown.
     What temper at the prospect did not wake
     To happiness unthought of? The inert
     Were rouz'd, and lively natures rapt away:
710  They who had fed their childhood upon dreams,             [125]
     The Play-fellows of Fancy, who had made
     All powers of swiftness, subtlety, and strength
     Their ministers, used to stir in lordly wise
     Among the grandest objects of the sense,
715  And deal with whatsoever they found there                [130]
     As if they had within some lurking right

683 noviciate 𝔄 C D E: inexperienced E².
     685–8 𝔄 C D E, *but* D E depends upon *for* depended on: E² *as* 1850
[99–104].
     691 great] mighty A² B² C *and The Friend.*

And with such general insight into evil,
And of the bounds which sever it from good,
As books and common intercourse with life                    95
Must needs have given—to the inexperienced mind,
When the world travels in a beaten road,
Guide faithful as is needed—I began
To meditate with ardour on the rule
And management of nations; what it is                         100
And ought to be; and strove to learn how far
Their power or weakness, wealth or poverty,
Their happiness or misery, depends
Upon their laws, and fashion of the State.

  O pleasant exercise of hope and joy!                     105
For mighty were the auxiliars which then stood
Upon our side, us who were strong in love!
Bliss was it in that dawn to be alive,
But to be young was very Heaven! O times,
In which the meagre, stale, forbidding ways                   110
Of custom, law, and statute, took at once
The attraction of a country in romance!
When Reason seemed the most to assert her rights
When most intent on making of herself
A prime enchantress—to assist the work,                      115
Which then was going forward in her name!
Not favoured spots alone, but the whole Earth,
The beauty wore of promise—that which sets
(As at some moments might not be unfelt
Among the bowers of Paradise itself)                          120
The budding rose above the rose full blown.
What temper at the prospect did not wake
To happiness unthought of? The inert
Were roused, and lively natures rapt away!
They who had fed their childhood upon dreams,                 125
The play-fellows of fancy, who had made
All powers of swiftness, subtilty, and strength
Their ministers,—who in lordly wise had stirred
Among the grandest objects of the sense,
And dealt with whatsoever they found there                    130
As if they had within some lurking right

691–2 To them thrice pleasant who were strong in love Z: Z² *as* 𝕬.
692 we *all MSS.*: us 1850.        701 going 𝕬 Z²: carrying Z.
704 𝕬 C D: D² *as* 1850.

To wield it; they too, who, of gentle mood,
Had watch'd all gentle motions, and to these
Had fitted their own thoughts, schemers more mild,
720 And in the region of their peaceful selves,                    [135]
Did now find helpers to their hearts' desire,
And stuff at hand, plastic as they could wish,
Were call'd upon to exercise their skill,
Not in Utopia, subterraneous Fields,                             [140]
725 Or some secreted Island, Heaven knows where,
But in the very world which is the world
Of all of us, the place in which, in the end,
We find our happiness, or not at all.

Why should I not confess that earth was then              [145]
730 To me what an inheritance new-fallen
Seems, when the first time visited, to one
Who thither comes to find in it his home?
He walks about and looks upon the place
With cordial transport, moulds it, and remoulds,         [150]
735 And is half pleased with things that are amiss,
'Twill be such joy to see them disappear.

An active partisan, I thus convoked
From every object pleasant circumstance
To suit my ends; I moved among mankind                   [155]
740 With genial feelings still predominant;
When erring, erring on the better part,
And in the kinder spirit; placable,
Indulgent oft-times to the worst desires
As on one side not uninform'd that men
745 See as it hath been taught them, and that time
Gives rights to error; on the other hand              [161]
That throwing off oppression must be work
As well of licence as of liberty;
And above all, for this was more than all,
750 Not caring if the wind did now and then               [165]
Blow keen upon an eminence that gave

[136] A² C.          721 now] both A² C *and The Friend.*
724 subterraneous 𝔄 C D: subterranean D².
727 in which] where A² C *and The Friend.*
728 find 𝔄 *and The Friend*: reap A²: [        ] C.
733 place] spot A² C.
743 Indulgent often times to ill desires A² C.

To wield it;—they, too, who of gentle mood
Had watched all gentle motions, and to these
Had fitted their own thoughts, schemers more mild,
And in the region of their peaceful selves;—                135
Now was it that *both* found, the meek and lofty
Did both find helpers to their hearts' desire,
And stuff at hand, plastic as they could wish,—
Were called upon to exercise their skill,
Not in Utopia,—subterranean fields,—                       140
Or some secreted island, Heaven knows where!
But in the very world, which is the world
Of all of us,—the place where, in the end,
We find our happiness, or not at all!

   Why should I not confess that Earth was then            145
To me, what an inheritance, new-fallen,
Seems, when the first time visited, to one
Who thither comes to find in it his home?
He walks about and looks upon the spot
With cordial transport, moulds it and remoulds,            150
And is half pleased with things that are amiss,
'Twill be such joy to see them disappear.

   An active partisan, I thus convoked
From every object pleasant circumstance
To suit my ends; I moved among mankind                     155
With genial feelings still predominant;
When erring, erring on the better part,
And in the kinder spirit; placable,
Indulgent, as not uninformed that men
See as they have been taught—Antiquity                     160
Gives right to error; and aware, no less,
That throwing off oppression must be work
As well of License as of Liberty;
And above all—for this was more than all—
Not caring if the wind did now and then                    165
Blow keen upon an eminence that gave

[160] taught—Antiquity 1850: taught, and that Antiquity  D E.
                        taught, that privilege
           Which blinds the judgement like a mist
           Can like a mist imbibe soft light and feed
           Under its shade sweet flowers—Antiquity  A².

Prospect so large into futurity,
In brief, a child of nature, as at first,
Diffusing only those affections wider
755 That from the cradle had grown up with me,                    [170]
And losing, in no other way than light
Is lost in light, the weak in the more strong.

In the main outline, such, it might be said,
Was my condition, till with open war
760 Britain opposed the Liberties of France;                      [175]
This threw me first out of the pale of love;
Sour'd and corrupted upwards to the source
My sentiments, was not, as hitherto,
A swallowing up of lesser things in great;
765 But change of them into their opposites,                      [180]
And thus a way was opened for mistakes
And false conclusions of the intellect,
As gross in their degree and in their kind
Far, far more dangerous. What had been a pride
770 Was now a shame; my likings and my loves
Ran in new channels, leaving old ones dry,                        [185]
And hence a blow which, in maturer age,
Would but have touch'd the judgment struck more deep
Into sensations near the heart: meantime,
775 As from the first, wild theories were afloat,
Unto the subtleties of which, at least,                          [190]
I had but lent a careless ear, assured
Of this, that time would soon set all things right,
Prove that the multitude had been oppressed,
780 And would be so no more.
                                        But when events
Brought less encouragement, and unto these                       [195]
The immediate proof of principles no more
Could be entrusted, while the events themselves,
Worn out in greatness, and in novelty,
785 Less occupied the mind, and sentiments
Could through my understanding's natural growth               [200]
No longer justify themselves through faith
Of inward consciousness, and hope that laid
Its hand upon its object, evidence
790 Safer, of universal application, such

752 *after* futurity, A² B² *read* happy, *del.*
765 opposites 𝔄 C D: contraries D².

Prospect so large into futurity;
In brief, a child of Nature, as at first,
Diffusing only those affections wider
That from the cradle had grown up with me,                    170
And losing, in no other way than light
Is lost in light, the weak in the more strong.

    In the main outline, such it might be said
Was my condition, till with open war
Britain opposed the liberties of France.                      175
This threw me first out of the pale of love;
Soured and corrupted, upwards to the source,
My sentiments; was not, as hitherto,
A swallowing up of lesser things in great,
But change of them into their contraries;                     180
And thus a way was opened for mistakes
And false conclusions, in degree as gross,
In kind more dangerous. What had been a pride,
Was now a shame; my likings and my loves
Ran in new channels, leaving old ones dry;                    185
And hence a blow that, in maturer age,
Would but have touched the judgment, struck more deep
Into sensations near the heart: meantime,
As from the first, wild theories were afloat,
To whose pretensions, sedulously urged,                       190
I had but lent a careless ear, assured
That time was ready to set all things right,
And that the multitude, so long oppressed,
Would be oppressed no more.
                    But when events
Brought less encouragement, and unto these                    195
The immediate proof of principles no more
Could be entrusted, while the events themselves,
Worn out in greatness, stripped of novelty,
Less occupied the mind, and sentiments
Could through my understanding's natural growth               200
No longer keep their ground, by faith maintained
Of inward consciousness, and hope that laid
Her hand upon her object—evidence
Safer, of universal application, such

767–9, 776, 778–80 A² C *as* 1850.
784 and in 𝔄 C D E: stripped of E².      787 𝔄 C D E: E² *as* 1850.

As could not be impeach'd, was sought elsewhere.          [205]

And now, become Oppressors in their turn,
Frenchmen had changed a war of self-defence
For one of conquest, losing sight of all
795 Which they had struggled for; and mounted up,
Openly, in the view of earth and heaven,                  [210]
The scale of Liberty. I read her doom,
Vex'd inly somewhat, it is true, and sore;
But not dismay'd, nor taking to the shame
800 Of a false Prophet; but, rouz'd up I stuck              [214]
More firmly to old tenets, and to prove
Their temper, strained them more, and thus in heat
Of contest did opinions every day
Grow into consequence, till round my mind                 [220]
805 They clung, as if they were the life of it.

This was the time when all things tending fast
To depravation, the Philosophy
That promised to abstract the hopes of man                [225]
Out of his feelings, to be fix'd thenceforth
810 For ever in a purer element
Found ready welcome. Tempting region that
For Zeal to enter and refresh herself,
Where passions had the privilege to work,                 [230]
And never hear the sound of their own names;
815 But, speaking more in charity, the dream
Was flattering to the young ingenuous mind
Pleas'd with extremes, and not the least with that
Which makes the human Reason's naked self
The object of its fervour. What delight!                   [235]
820 How glorious! in self-knowledge and self-rule,
To look through all the frailties of the world,
And, with a resolute mastery shaking off
The accidents of nature, time, and place,
That make up the weak being of the past,
825 Build social freedom on its only basis,

795 and mounted up *all MSS.*: now mounted up 1850.
798 A² C *as* 1850.
800 but, rouz'd up I stuck] While Resentment rose
        In generous support of wounded pride
          And mortified presumption, I adhered  A² C.
803 Of altercation, every day opinions  A².

As could not be impeached, was sought elsewhere.          205

But now, become oppressors in their turn,
Frenchmen had changed a war of self-defence
For one of conquest, losing sight of all
Which they had struggled for: now mounted up,
Openly in the eye of earth and heaven,                    210
The scale of liberty. I read her doom,
With anger vexed, with disappointment sore,
But not dismayed, nor taking to the shame
Of a false prophet. While resentment rose
Striving to hide, what nought could heal, the wounds      215
Of mortified presumption, I adhered
More firmly to old tenets, and, to prove
Their temper, strained them more; and thus, in heat
Of contest, did opinions every day
Grow into consequence, till round my mind                 220
They clung, as if they were its life, nay more,
The very being of the immortal soul.

This was the time, when, all things tending fast
To depravation, speculative schemes—
That promised to abstract the hopes of Man                225
Out of his feelings, to be fixed thenceforth
For ever in a purer element—
Found ready welcome. Tempting region *that*
For Zeal to enter and refresh herself,
Where passions had the privilege to work,                 230
And never hear the sound of their own names.
But, speaking more in charity, the dream
Flattered the young, pleased with extremes, nor least
With that which makes our Reason's naked self
The object of its fervour. What delight!                  235
How glorious! in self-knowledge and self-rule,
To look through all the frailties of the world,
And, with a resolute mastery shaking off
Infirmities of nature, time, and place,

805    They clung as if they had no other life
        Than that which they had kindled and sustained. A² C: A³ D E
*as* 1850, *but* the life of it *for* its life, nay more; E² *as* 1850.
   807  the Philosophy 𝔄 C D E: E² *as* 1850.
   816–18  𝔄 C D: D² *as* 1850.

The freedom of the individual mind, [240]
Which, to the blind restraint of general laws
Superior, magisterially adopts
One guide, the light of circumstances, flash'd
830 Upon an independent intellect. [244]

For howsoe'er unsettled, never once
Had I thought ill of human kind, or been
Indifferent to its welfare, but, enflam'd
With thirst of a secure intelligence
835 And sick of other passion, I pursued [250]
A higher nature, wish'd that Man should start
Out of the worm-like state in which he is,
And spread abroad the wings of Liberty,
Lord of himself, in undisturb'd delight—
840 A noble aspiration, yet I feel [255]
The aspiration, but with other thoughts
And happier; for I was perplex'd and sought
To accomplish the transition by such means
As did not lie in nature, sacrificed
845 The exactness of a comprehensive mind
To scrupulous and microscopic views
That furnish'd out materials for a work
Of false imagination, placed beyond
The limits of experience and of truth.

850 Enough, no doubt, the advocates themselves [259]
Of ancient institutions had perform'd
To bring disgrace upon their very names,
Disgrace of which custom and written law
And sundry moral sentiments as props
855 And emanations of those institutes [265]
Too justly bore a part. A veil had been
Uplifted; why deceive ourselves? 'Twas so,
'Twas even so, and sorrow for the Man
Who either had not eyes wherewith to see,
860 Or seeing hath forgotten. Let this pass, [270]

831 never once 𝔄 C²: never—never A² C. 832 been] stood A² C D.
831–4 D as A² C: For not indifferent was I to mankind
  Howe'er unsettled, but enflamed with thirst
  Of an impregnable intelligence D².
831–49 E omits, E² restores, as A² C, but for 836 What seemed a brighter
nature, wished that man; 837 as 1850 [252] and for 841–50 The aspiration,

Build social upon personal Liberty,                                      240
Which, to the blind restraints of general laws
Superior, magisterially adopts
One guide, the light of circumstances, flashed
Upon an independent intellect.
Thus expectation rose again; thus hope,                                  245
From her first ground expelled, grew proud once more.
Oft, as my thoughts were turned to human kind,
I scorned indifference; but, inflamed with thirst
Of a secure intelligence, and sick
Of other longing, I pursued what seemed                                  250
A more exalted nature; wished that Man
Should start out of his earthly, worm-like state,
And spread abroad the wings of Liberty,
Lord of himself, in undisturbed delight—
A noble aspiration! *yet* I feel                                         255
(Sustained by worthier as by wiser thoughts)
The aspiration, nor shall ever cease
To feel it;—but return we to our course.

Enough, 'tis true—could such a plea excuse
Those aberrations—had the clamorous friends                             260
Of ancient Institutions said and done
To bring disgrace upon their very names;
Disgrace, of which, custom and written law,
And sundry moral sentiments as props
Or emanations of those institutes,                                       265
Too justly bore a part. A veil had been
Uplifted; why deceive ourselves? in sooth,
'Twas even so; and sorrow for the man
Who either had not eyes wherewith to see,
Or, seeing, had forgotten! A strong shock                                270

but with happier thoughts, Happier as wiser.—Turn we back:—'tis true,
More than enough the advocates themselves: E³ *as* 1850.
   836 start] rise  A² C D.
   837 in which he is] in which he creeps  Á² C: with new-fledged wings  D.
   842-8 D *deletes.*     849 Experience and unlimited by truth  D (*v. note*).
   850-2 Meanwhile the intemperate Advocates who spake
            For ancient institutions urged their way
            Into extremes that cover'd with disgrace
            The very name of things they wish'd to guard  A² C.
   [259] Enough if hostile bigotry could excuse  D.
       More than enough could such a plea excuse  E: E² *as* 1850.
   [260] clamorous friends  E²: advocates  D² E.
   857-63 𝔄 C D E: E² *as* 1850.

Suffice it that a shock had then been given
To old opinions; and the minds of all men
Had felt it; that my mind was both let loose,
Let loose and goaded. After what hath been
865 Already said of patriotic love,                    [274]
And hinted at in other sentiments
We need not linger long upon this theme.
This only may be said, that from the first
Having two natures in me, joy the one
870 The other melancholy, and withal
A happy man, and therefore bold to look
On painful things, slow, somewhat, too, and stern
In temperament, I took the knife in hand
And stopping not at parts less sensitive,
875 Endeavoured with my best of skill to probe
The living body of society                    [281]
Even to the heart; I push'd without remorse
My speculations forward; yea, set foot
On Nature's holiest places. Time may come
880 When some dramatic Story may afford
Shapes livelier to convey to thee, my Friend,
What then I learn'd, or think I learn'd, of truth,    [286]
And the errors into which I was betray'd
By present objects, and by reasoning false
885 From the beginning, inasmuch as drawn
Out of a heart which had been turn'd aside            [290]
From nature by external accidents,
And which was thus confounded more and more,
Misguiding and misguided. Thus I fared,
890 Dragging all passions, notions, shapes of faith,
Like culprits to the bar, suspiciously                [295]
Calling the mind to establish in plain day
Her titles and her honours, now believing,
Now disbelieving, endlessly perplex'd
895 With impulse, motive, right and wrong, the ground
Of moral obligation, what the rule                    [300]

866–7 A *deletes*; *not in* C.
868 This only will I add  A² C D E:  E² *as* 1850.
868–81 Ⅵ C D E:  E² *as* 1850 [275–85].
872–81 E *has rejected alternative*:
        On painful objects sternly I assayed
        To anatomize the frame of social life
        Probed to the quick. Without reserve I toiled

Was given to old opinions; all men's minds
Had felt its power, and mine was both let loose,
Let loose and goaded. After what hath been
Already said of patriotic love,
Suffice it here to add, that, somewhat stern          275
In temperament, withal a happy man,
And therefore bold to look on painful things,
Free likewise of the world, and thence more bold,
I summoned my best skill, and toiled, intent
To anatomise the frame of social life,                280
Yea, the whole body of society
Searched to its heart. Share with me, Friend! the wish
That some dramatic tale, endued with shapes
Livelier, and flinging out less guarded words
Than suit the work we fashion, might set forth        285
What then I learned, or think I learned, of truth,
And the errors into which I fell, betrayed
By present objects, and by reasonings false
From their beginnings, inasmuch as drawn
Out of a heart that had been turned aside             290
From Nature's way by outward accidents,
And which was thus confounded, more and more
Misguided, and misguiding. So I fared,
Dragging all precepts, judgments, maxims, creeds,
Like culprits to the bar; calling the mind,           295
Suspiciously, to establish in plain day
Her titles and her honours; now believing,
Now disbelieving; endlessly perplexed
With impulse, motive, right and wrong, the ground
Of obligation, what the rule and whence               300

> To fathom mysteries and crafts endeavoured
> To reach Authority's abiding place
> Whether it seemed a Sanctuary of good
> Or den of evil. Wish with me O friend
> That some dramatic Tale with livelier Shapes
> Replete and flinging out more passionate words
> Than suit our present labour might set forth

875 best of] nicest  A² C D E.          877 I push'd] pushing  A² C D E.
878–9 yea . . . places A *deletes*. *Not in* C D E.
883 was 𝔄 C D E: fell E².
887 𝔄 C D E: E² *as* 1850.
890 𝔄 C D E: feelings, notions, forms of faith E²: judgments, notions,
maxims, creeds E³: E⁴ *as* 1850.
891–2, 896–7 𝔄 C D E: E² *as* 1850.

And what the sanction, till, demanding *proof*,
And seeking it in everything, I lost
All feeling of conviction, and, in fine,
900 Sick, wearied out with contrarieties,
    Yielded up moral questions in despair,      [305]
    And for my future studies, as the sole
    Employment of the enquiring faculty,
    Turn'd towards mathematics, and their clear
905 And solid evidence—Ah! then it was
    That Thou, most precious Friend! about this time
    First known to me, didst lend a living help
    To regulate my Soul, and then it was
    That the belovèd Woman in whose sight      [335]
910 Those days were pass'd, now speaking in a voice
    Of sudden admonition, like a brook
    That does but cross a lonely road, and now
    Seen, heard and felt, and caught at every turn,
    Companion never lost through many a league,      [340]
915 Maintain'd for me a saving intercourse

902-8 A² *as* [306–33], *but for* [318–20] *reads*
    And still to acknowledged law rebellious would,
    As selfish passion prompted, act amiss.
*in* [321] confounded *for* bewildered, *and for* [328–33]
    But for my future studies as the sole
    Employment of the reasoning faculty
    To abstract Science turned, and its severe
    And solid evidence. Ah! then it was *So* C D: D² E *as* 1850, *but*
*omitting* [331–2] *and reading in* [333] Find no admission. Yet then it was
    [331] matters various, properties] matters various attributes E²: matters
various properties E³.
    913 Seen, heard and felt 𝔄 C D E: E² *as* 1850.

The sanction; till, demanding formal *proof*,
And seeking it in every thing, I lost
All feeling of conviction, and, in fine,
Sick, wearied out with contrarieties,
Yielded up moral questions in despair.　　　　305

　　This was the crisis of that strong disease,
This the soul's last and lowest ebb; I drooped,
Deeming our blessed reason of least use
Where wanted most: 'The lordly attributes
Of will and choice,' I bitterly exclaimed,　　　　310
'What are they but a mockery of a Being
Who hath in no concerns of his a test
Of good and evil; knows not what to fear
Or hope for, what to covet or to shun;
And who, if those could be discerned, would yet　　　　315
Be little profited, would see, and ask
Where is the obligation to enforce?
And, to acknowledged law rebellious, still,
As selfish passion urged, would act amiss;
The dupe of folly, or the slave of crime.'　　　　320

　　Depressed, bewildered thus, I did not walk
With scoffers, seeking light and gay revenge
From indiscriminate laughter, nor sate down
In reconcilement with an utter waste
Of intellect; such sloth I could not brook,　　　　325
(Too well I loved, in that my spring of life,
Pains-taking thoughts, and truth, their dear reward)
But turned to abstract science, and there sought
Work for the reasoning faculty enthroned
Where the disturbances of space and time—　　　　330
Whether in matters various, properties
Inherent, or from human will and power
Derived—find no admission. Then it was—
Thanks to the bounteous Giver of all good!—
That the beloved Sister in whose sight　　　　335
Those days were passed, now speaking in a voice
Of sudden admonition—like a brook
That did but *cross* a lonely road, and now
Is seen, heard, felt, and caught at every turn,
Companion never lost through many a league—　　　　340
Maintained for me a saving intercourse

With my true self; for, though impair'd and chang'd
Much, as it seem'd, I was no further chang'd
Than as a clouded, not a waning moon:                    [344]
She, in the midst of all, preserv'd me still
920 A Poet, made me seek beneath that name
My office upon earth, and nowhere else,
And lastly, Nature's Self, by human love                 [350]
Assisted, through the weary labyrinth
Conducted me again to open day,
925 Revived the feelings of my earlier life,
Gave me that strength and knowledge full of peace,
Enlarged, and never more to be disturb'd,
Which through the steps of our degeneracy,
All degradation of this age, hath still
930 Upheld me, and upholds me at this day
In the catastrophe (for so they dream,
And nothing less), when finally, to close
And rivet up the gains of France, a Pope
Is summon'd in to crown an Emperor;                      [360]
935 This last opprobrium, when we see the dog
Returning to his vomit, when the sun
That rose in splendour, was alive, and moved             [365]
In exultation among living clouds
Hath put his function and his glory off,
940 And, turned into a gewgaw, a machine,
Sets like an opera phantom.                              [370]
                              Thus, O Friend!
Through times of honour, and through times of shame,
Have I descended, tracing faithfully
The workings of a youthful mind, beneath

916-17 impair'd and chang'd Much as it seem'd 𝔄.
      impair'd in lustre And changed as seem'd A².
917 E *deletes and changes* Than (918) *to* Both *and* not *to* and (*v.* note).
[345] *added in* E.        921 A² C *as* 1850.
922 And lastly] And fear'd I not to encroach upon a theme
      Reserv'd to close my Song, I would declare
      That lastly *etc.* A² C.
922-6 *stuck over in* D: D² *as* 1850 [349-52].
[352-3] through opening day To E²: to open day And  D E.
928 degeneracy] degenerate course  A² C.
933 rivet up] rivet down  A² C D E: seal up all  1850.
938-44 *stuck over in* D.
939      Has put his soul-exalting glory off
         Disclaimed all functions by the Gods bestowed  D² E.
         Has put his glory off with reckless haste

With my true self; for, though bedimmed and changed
Much, as it seemed, I was no further changed
Than as a clouded and a waning moon:
She whispered still that brightness would return,          345
She, in the midst of all, preserved me still
A Poet, made me seek beneath that name,
And that alone, my office upon earth;
And, lastly, as hereafter will be shown,
If willing audience fail not, Nature's self,              350
By all varieties of human love
Assisted, led me back through opening day
To those sweet counsels between head and heart
Whence grew that genuine knowledge, fraught with peace,
Which, through the later sinkings of this cause,          355
Hath still upheld me, and upholds me now
In the catastrophe (for so they dream,
And nothing less), when, finally to close
And seal up all the gains of France, a Pope
Is summoned in, to crown an Emperor—                      360
This last opprobrium, when we see a people,
That once looked up in faith, as if to Heaven
For manna, take a lesson from the dog
Returning to his vomit; when the sun
That rose in splendour, was alive, and moved             365
In exultation with a living pomp
Of clouds—his glory's natural retinue—
Hath dropped all functions by the gods bestowed,
And, turned into a gewgaw, a machine,
Sets like an Opera phantom.                               370
                          Thus, O Friend!
Through times of honour and through times of shame
Descending, have I faithfully retraced
The perturbations of a youthful mind

      Disclaimed all functions *etc.* E²: E³ *as* 1850.
939–40 Puts off his function, and, his glory gone,
      Sets *etc.* A² B².
941–2                          Thus through times
      Of honour and through times of bitter shame  D².
  *So* E, *but omitting* bitter. E² *as* 1850.
943 𝔄 C D E: E² *as* 1850.
944–5 The perturbations of a youthful mind
      Swayed by the breath of great events, its joy
      Sublime and ardent, its capacious griefs,
      Its scorn and anger, after hopes, no less  A² C.

945 The breath of great events, its hopes no less
     Than universal, and its boundless love;
     A Story destined for thy ear, who now,                    [375]
     Among the basest and the lowest fallen
     Of all the race of men, dost make abode
950 Where Etna looketh down on Syracuse,
     The city of Timoleon! Living God!
     How are the Mighty prostrated! they first,                [380]
     They first of all that breathe should have awaked
     When the great voice was heard from out the tombs
955 Of ancient Heroes. If for France I have griev'd
     Who, in the judgment of no few, hath been
     A trifler only, in her proudest day,                      [385]
     Have been distress'd to think of what she once
     Promised, now is, a far more sober cause
960 Thine eyes must see of sorrow, in a Land
     Strew'd with the wreck of loftiest years, a Land          [388]
     Glorious indeed, substantially renown'd
     Of simple virtue once, and manly praise,
     Now without one memorial hope, not even
965 A hope to be deferr'd; for that would serve
     To chear the heart in such entire decay.

     But indignation works where hope is not,
     And thou, O Friend! wilt be refresh'd. There is
     One great Society alone on earth,
970 The noble Living and the noble Dead:                       [395]
     Thy consolation shall be there, and Time
     And Nature shall before thee spread in store
     Imperishable thoughts, the Place itself
     Be conscious of thy presence, and the dull
975 Sirocco air of its degeneracy
     Turn as thou mov'st into a healthful breeze
     To cherish and invigorate thy frame.

     Thine be those motions strong and sanative,
     A ladder for thy Spirit to reascend
980 To health and joy and pure contentedness;

948 𝔄 C D E: E² *as* 1850.
949 Of nations and of men dost make abode A² C D E. (E *deletes*.)
950 𝔄 C D E: E² *as* 1850.
951 Living God] Righteous Heaven A² C.
955-6 A² C D² *as* 1850.

Under a long-lived storm of great events—
A story destined for thy ear, who now,                               375
Among the fallen of nations, dost abide
Where Etna, over hill and valley, casts
His shadow stretching towards Syracuse,
The city of Timoleon! Righteous Heaven!
How are the mighty prostrated! They first,                          380
They first of all that breathe should have awaked
When the great voice was heard from out the tombs
Of ancient heroes. If I suffered grief
For ill-requited France, by many deemed
A trifler only in her proudest day;                                 385
Have been distressed to think of what she once
Promised, now is; a far more sober cause
Thine eyes must see of sorrow in a land,
To the reanimating influence lost
Of memory, to virtue lost and hope,                                390
Though with the wreck of loftier years bestrewn.


    But indignation works where hope is not,
And thou, O Friend! wilt be refreshed. There is
One great society alone on earth:
The noble Living and the noble Dead.                                395


    Thine be such converse strong and sanative,
A ladder for thy spirit to reascend
To health and joy and pure contentedness;

961–6                          a Land
        Of simple virtue once, and solid praise
        Now without one memorial energy
        To kindle hope, in absolute decay  D.
        Strewn with the wreck of (*glorious*) happier years, yet lost
        To memory, to glory lost, and hope  D².
        Strewn with *etc. as* D².
        To the reanimating influence sweet
        Of memory, to virtue lost and hope.  D³ E.
        Though with the wreck of loftier years bestrewn—
        To the *etc.* E² (*but* lost *for* sweet). *No MS. authority for order of
            lines in* 1850.
962–6  Mid these memorials of past glory left
        Without a hope, in absolute decay.  A² C.
971–2  𝔄 C D:  D *deletes.*
973–7  Imperishable beauty heard and felt
        Where'er thou mov'st along the faded place  A² C D:  D *deletes.*
978  those motions] such converse  A² C.

To me the grief confined that Thou art gone
From this last spot of earth where Freedom now          [400]
Stands single in her only sanctuary,
A lonely wanderer, art gone, by pain
985 Compell'd and sickness, at this latter day,
This heavy time of change for all mankind;
I feel for Thee, must utter what I feel:          [405]
The sympathies, erewhile, in part discharg'd,
Gather afresh, and will have vent again:
990 My own delights do scarcely seem to me
My own delights; the lordly Alps themselves,
Those rosy Peaks, from which the Morning looks          [410]
Abroad on many Nations, are not now
Since thy migration and departure, Friend,
995 The gladsome image in my memory
Which they were used to be; to kindred scenes,
On errand, at a time how different!
Thou tak'st thy way, carrying a heart more ripe          [415]
For all divine enjoyment, with the soul
1000 Which Nature gives to Poets, now by thought
Matur'd, and in the summer of its strength.
Oh! wrap him in your Shades, ye Giant Woods,
On Etna's side, and thou, O flowery Vale
Of Enna! is there not some nook of thine,          [420]
1005 From the first playtime of the infant earth
Kept sacred to restorative delight?

Child of the mountains, among Shepherds rear'd,
Even from my earliest school-day time, I lov'd
To dream of Sicily; and now a strong
1010 And vital promise wafted from that Land
Comes o'er my heart; there's not a single name
Of note belonging to that honor'd isle,

986 heavy time of change 𝔄 C D E: sorrowful reverse E².
993 are not now 𝔄 D² E: yield not now A² C D: are no more E².
994 𝔄 C D: D deletes.          995 𝔄 C D E: E² as 1850.
996 used to be] wont to yield A² C D: D² as 1850.
997 𝔄 C D E: E² as 1850.          998-9 𝔄 C D: D² as 1850.
1003 Vale] Field A² C.
1002-3 O lure him to recline within your shades
          Ye trees whose circumambient zone engirds
          Vast Etna's midway region! Sunny lawns
          Of fragrant Hybla offer to his lip
          Your choicest sweets, and thou O flowery Field  A² (deleted) B².

To me the grief confined, that thou art gone
From this last spot of earth, where Freedom now            400
Stands single in her only sanctuary;
A lonely wanderer art gone, by pain
Compelled and sickness, at this latter day,
This sorrowful reverse for all mankind.
I feel for thee, must utter what I feel:                   405
The sympathies erewhile in part discharged,
Gather afresh, and will have vent again:
My own delights do scarcely seem to me
My own delights; the lordly Alps themselves,
Those rosy peaks, from which the Morning looks             410
Abroad on many nations, are no more
For me that image of pure gladsomeness
Which they were wont to be. Through kindred scenes,
For purpose, at a time, how different!
Thou tak'st thy way, carrying the heart and soul.          415
That Nature gives to Poets, now by thought
Matured, and in the summer of their strength.
Oh! wrap him in your shades, ye giant woods,
On Etna's side; and thou, O flowery field
Of Enna! is there not some nook of thine,                  420
From the first play-time of the infant world
Kept sacred to restorative delight,
When from afar invoked by anxious love?

    Child of the mountains, among shepherds reared,
Ere yet familiar with the classic page,                    425
I learnt to dream of Sicily; and lo,
The gloom, that, but a moment past, was deepened
At thy command, at her command gives way;
A pleasant promise, wafted from her shores,
Comes o'er my heart: in fancy I behold                     430
Her seas yet smiling, her once happy vales;
Nor can my tongue give utterance to a name
Of note belonging to that honoured isle,

1009–11 To think, to dream of Sicily, and now
    A pleasant . . . happy vales *as* [429–31]
    Nor doth the book of Time display a name A² C.
  *After* [426] E *has rejected line*:
    Sensations changing as thoughts shift their ground,
[427–8] *added* E³: The apprehension and sad thoughts that rose
        At her command, at her command dispersed E².
1010 vital B: gladsome A: pleasant A² C.

Philosopher or Bard, Empedocles,
Or Archimedes, deep and tranquil Soul! [435]
1015 That is not like a comfort to my grief:
And, O Theocritus, so far have some
Prevail'd among the Powers of heaven and earth,
By force of graces which were their's, that they
Have had, as thou reportest, miracles [440]
1020 Wrought for them in old time: yea, not unmov'd,
When thinking of my own beloved Friend,
I hear thee tell how bees with honey fed
Divine Comates, by his tyrant lord
Within a chest imprison'd impiously [445]
1025 How with their honey from the fields they came
And fed him there, alive, from month to month,
Because the Goatherd, blessed Man! had lips
Wet with the Muse's Nectar.
　　　　　　　　　　Thus I soothe
The pensive moments by this calm fire side, [450]
1030 And find a thousand fancied images
That chear the thoughts of those I love, and mine.
Our prayers have been accepted; Thou wilt stand

1014 calm abstracted Soul A² C.
1015 That shines not for my comfort, like the lamp
　　　　Of some tall Pharos on a perilous coast
　　　　That with no questionable purpose sends
　　　　Its lustre streaming o'er the gloomy deep. A² C.
1018 𝔄 C D: D² as 1850.
1022 I hear thee tell how clustering bees sustain'd A² C.
1023 tyrant 𝔄 C D E: impious E². 　　1024–5 A² C D E: E² as 1850.
1024 impiously 𝔄 C D E: how they came E².
1025 𝔄 C D E; *but* burden *for* honey D E, *and* meads *for* fields A² C D:
E² as 1850.
1026 alive 𝔄 D²: preserv'd A² C D. From month to month 𝔄 C D E:
month after month E².
1030 fancied] bounteous A² C.
1031–9 [452–70] 　　　　　　　　　　and mine,
　　　　Teaching our souls to flow, though by a rough
　　　　And bitter world surrounded, as, unting'd
　　　　With aught injurious to her native freshness,
　　　　Flowed Arethusa under briny waves
　　　　Of the Sicilian Sea. Delicious Fount!
　　　　Our prayers have been accepted, at thy side
　　　　Lingers (or if thou be indeed no more
　　　　Then near some other Spring which by thy name
　　　　He gratulateth, willingly deceiv'd)
　　　　Lingers my Friend, a gladsome Votary

Philosopher or Bard, Empedocles,
Or Archimedes, pure abstracted soul!                      435
That doth not yield a solace to my grief:
And, O Theocritus, so far have some
Prevailed among the powers of heaven and earth,
By their endowments, good or great, that they
Have had, as thou reportest, miracles                    440
Wrought for them in old time; yea, not unmoved,
When thinking on my own beloved friend,
I hear thee tell how bees with honey fed
Divine Comates, by his impious lord
Within a chest imprisoned; how they came                 445
Laden from blooming grove or flowery field,
And fed him there, alive, month after month,
Because the goatherd, blessed man! had lips
Wet with the Muses' nectar.
                            Thus I soothe
The pensive moments by this calm fire-side,              450
And find a thousand bounteous images
To cheer the thoughts of those I love, and mine.
Our prayers have been accepted; thou wilt stand


    And not a Captive pining for his home
    In querulous lassitude. To Etna's top
    Foot-quickening Health shall guide him, there to stand
    No Exile, but a joyful Visitant
    A Conqueror wresting from the dwindled earth
    And from the invaded heavens, capacious thoughts
    Far-stretching views, magnificent designs
    Worthy of Poets, who attuned their Harps
    In woods and echoing caves, for discipline
    Of Heroes, and in reverence to the Gods
    Mid temples serv'd by sapient Priests and serv'd
    By Virgins crown'd with roses which their hands,
    At daybreak, gather'd from the dewy fields. A² C.
               *End of book* A².
D *as* 1850, *but for* [454–6] No exile but a joyful Visitant
    On Etna's top a conqueror, from the earth
    Under thee stretched, and from the invaded heavens
    Winning high thoughts, magnificent designs
*and for* [461–5]            roses that their hands
    At daybreak gathered from the dewy fields.
    Then from that height descending on the brink
    Of pastoral Arethusa shalt thou stand
D² E *for* [461–5] *have* Of Virgins crowned with flowers; or on the brink
            Thou wilt recline of pastoral Arethuse
*and for* [469] Wilt linger, a rejoicing Votary. E² *as* 1850.

Not as an Exile but a Visitant
On Etna's top; by pastoral Arethuse          [465]
1035 Or, if that Fountain be in truth no more,
Then near some other Spring, which by the name
Thou gratulatest, willingly deceived,
Shalt linger as a gladsome Votary,
And not a Captive, pining for his home.          [470]

[459] Of youthful heroes and delight of gods  D².

On Etna's summit, above earth and sea,
Triumphant, winning from the invaded heavens　　　455
Thoughts without bound, magnificent designs,
Worthy of poets who attuned their harps
In wood or echoing cave, for discipline
Of heroes; or, in reverence to the gods,
'Mid temples, served by sapient priests, and choirs　　　460
Of virgins crowned with roses. Not in vain
Those temples, where they in their ruins yet
Survive for inspiration, shall attract
Thy solitary steps: and on the brink
Thou wilt recline of pastoral Arethuse;　　　465
Or, if that fountain be in truth no more,
Then, near some other spring, which, by the name
Thou gratulatest, willingly deceived,
I see thee linger a glad votary,
And not a captive pining for his home.　　　470

# BOOK ELEVENTH

## IMAGINATION, HOW IMPAIRED AND RESTORED

LONG time hath Man's unhappiness and guilt
Detain'd us; with what dismal sights beset
For the outward view, and inwardly oppress'd
With sorrow, disappointment, vexing thoughts,
5 Confusion of opinion, zeal decay'd,                          [5]
And lastly, utter loss of hope itself,
And things to hope for. Not with these began
Our Song, and not with these our Song must end:
Ye motions of delight, that through the fields
10 Stir gently, breezes and soft airs that breathe             [10]
The breath of Paradise, and find your way
To the recesses of the soul! Ye Brooks
Muttering along the stones, a busy noise
By day, a quiet one in silent night,                           [20]
15 And you, ye Groves, whose ministry it is
To interpose the covert of your shades,                        [25]
Even as a sleep, betwixt the heart of man
And the uneasy world, 'twixt man himself,
Not seldom, and his own unquiet heart,

[MSS. for Bk. XII, A B C D E Z: *for ll.* 42–44, 138–51, 176–84, 199–257, 316–45 W: *for* 258–389 V; *for* 9–14 Y.]
Book Eleventh, Imagination, how impaired *etc.* B D E: 11 A: Book Eleventh C. And Taste *added to* E².
1–2 did human ignorance and guilt Detain B².
1–8 A² C *as* 1850.
9–11 Ye motions of delight, that haunt the sides
    Of the green hills in company with airs
    And Zephyrs whose least whisper finds an inlet A² C.
9–13 Ye gentle breezes lead me forth again
    Soft airs and gladdening sunbeams lead me on
    To the green haunts of chearfulness and peace
    And health and liberty, to pathways roads
    And fields with rural works to open earth
    And the calm bliss of an unbounded sky
    The woods the villages the pleasant farms
    Smoke rising up from tufted trees and brooks
    Muttering among the stones Y; *but* woods the *corr. from* scattered.
10–12 Stir gently vernal airs that find an inlet
    To the recesses of the Soul B².
[9–20] Ye sunbeams, glancing over the green hills,
    Ye spirits of air, that league your strength to rouze

# BOOK TWELFTH

## IMAGINATION AND TASTE, HOW IMPAIRED AND RESTORED

LONG time have human ignorance and guilt
Detained us, on what spectacles of woe
Compelled to look, and inwardly oppressed
With sorrow, disappointment, vexing thoughts,
Confusion of the judgment, zeal decayed,                    5
And, lastly, utter loss of hope itself
And things to hope for! Not with these began
Our song, and not with these our song must end.—
Ye motions of delight, that haunt the sides
Of the green hills; ye breezes and soft airs,              10
Whose subtle intercourse with breathing flowers,
Feelingly watched, might teach Man's haughty race
How without injury to take, to give
Without offence; ye who, as if to show
The wondrous influence of power gently used,               15
Bend the complying heads of lordly pines,
And, with a touch, shift the stupendous clouds
Through the whole compass of the sky; ye brooks,
Muttering along the stones, a busy noise
By day, a quiet sound in silent night;                     20
Ye waves, that out of the great deep steal forth
In a calm hour to kiss the pebbly shore,
Not mute, and then retire, fearing no storm;
And you, ye groves, whose ministry it is
To interpose the covert of your shades,                    25
Even as a sleep, between the heart of man
And outward troubles, between man himself,
Not seldom, and his own uneasy heart:

The sea whose surface in your gentle mood
Ye deign to ripple into elfin waves
Innumerable, ye whose intercourse
With breathing flowers might teach Man's haughty race
*etc. to* clouds [17] *as* 1850
Yet condescend to ripple Lake or Pool
In elfin waves innumerable, ye Brooks *etc.* D: D² *as* 1850, *but*
**one** *for* sound [20].
19 unquiet 𝔄 C D: (un)peaceful D²: uneasy D³.

20 Oh! that I had a music and a voice,
   Harmonious as your own, that I might tell          [30]
   What ye have done for me. The morning shines,
   Nor heedeth Man's perverseness; Spring returns,
   I saw the Spring return, when I was dead
25 To deeper hope, yet had I joy for her,
   And welcomed her benevolence, rejoiced
   In common with the Children of her Love,
   Plants, insects, beasts in field, and birds in bower.          [35]
   So neither were complacency nor peace
30 Nor tender yearnings wanting for my good
   Through those distracted times; in Nature still          [40]
   Glorying, I found a counterpoise in her,
   Which, when the spirit of evil was at height
   Maintain'd for me a secret happiness;
35 Her I resorted to, and lov'd so much
   I seem'd to love as much as heretofore;
   And yet this passion, fervent as it was,
   Had suffer'd change; how could there fail to be
   Some change, if merely hence, that years of life
40 Were going on, and with them loss or gain
   Inevitable, sure alternative.

     This History, my Friend, hath chiefly told
   Of intellectual power, from stage to stage          [45]
   Advancing, hand in hand with love and joy,
45 And of imagination teaching truth
   Until that natural graciousness of mind          [50]
   Gave way to over-pressure of the times
   And their disastrous issues. What avail'd,
   When Spells forbade the Voyager to land,
50 The fragrance which did ever and anon
   Give notice of the Shore, from arbours breathed          [55]
   Of blessed sentiment and fearless love?
   What did such sweet remembrances avail,
   Perfidious then, as seem'd, what serv'd they then?
55 My business was upon the barren sea,

24 A² C *as* 1850.          25, 26, 28, 35, 36 A *deletes*; *not in* C.
28 With plants the green herb and the bleating Lamb Z.
28–30 D *stuck over*: D² *as* 1850.
29–30 So neither stillness beauty or repose
     Order or peace were wanting *etc.* Z: Z² *as* 𝕬.
33 was at 𝕬 C D: reached its D².

Oh! that I had a music and a voice
Harmonious as your own, that I might tell                    30
What ye have done for me. The morning shines,
Nor heedeth Man's perverseness; Spring returns,—
I saw the Spring return, and could rejoice,
In common with the children of her love,
Piping on boughs, or sporting on fresh fields,              35
Or boldly seeking pleasure nearer heaven
On wings that navigate cerulean skies.
So neither were complacency, nor peace,
Nor tender yearnings, wanting for my good
Through these distracted times; in Nature still             40
Glorying, I found a counterpoise in her,
Which, when the spirit of evil reached its height,
Maintained for me a secret happiness.

This narrative, my Friend! hath chiefly told
Of intellectual power, fostering love,                      45
Dispensing truth, and, over men and things,
Where reason yet might hesitate, diffusing
Prophetic sympathies of genial faith:
So was I favoured—such my happy lot—
Until that natural graciousness of mind                     50
Gave way to overpressure from the times
And their disastrous issues. What availed,
When spells forbade the voyager to land,
That fragrant notice of a pleasant shore
Wafted, at intervals, from many a bower                     55
Of blissful gratitude and fearless love?

37-41 And yet this passion, fervent as it was,
    Had yielded to some change, for years of life
    Were going on, and with them loss or gain
    Inevitable, sure alternative  A² B² C.
    *So* D, *but* Yet had this *for* And yet this *and* Submitted *for* Had yielded.
D² *deletes*.
    42-44 My present labour hath till lately been
        A history of Love from stage to stage
        Advancing hand in hand with power and joy.  W.
    42-45 𝔄 C D E;  *but in* 42 D E *have* narrative *for* history *and in* 44 *for*
love and joy D² E *have* hope and joy: E² *as* 1850 [44-49].
    47 of the times 𝔄 C D:  D² *as* 1850.
    48  And their disastrous issues, whence ensued
        A lower tone of feeling in respect
        To human life and sad perplexities
        In moral knowledge. Ah, what then availed  Z *deleted*.
    50-52 𝔄 C D:  D² *as* 1850.        53-56 A *deletes*; *not in* C.

My errand was to sail to other coasts.
Shall I avow that I had hope to see,
I mean that future times would surely see
The Man to come parted as by a gulph,
From him who had been, that I could no more          [60]
Trust the elevation which had made me one
With the great Family that here and there
Is scatter'd through the abyss of ages past,
Sage, Patriot, Lover, Hero; for it seem'd
That their best virtues were not free from taint     [65]
Of something false and weak, which could not stand
The open eye of Reason. Then I said,
Go to the Poets; they will speak to thee
More perfectly of purer creatures, yet
If Reason be nobility in man,                        [70]
Can aught be more ignoble than the man
Whom they describe, would fasten if they may
Upon our love by sympathies of truth.

      Thus strangely did I war against myself;       [76]
A Bigot to a new Idolatry
Did like a Monk who hath forsworn the world
Zealously labour to cut off my heart
From all the sources of her former strength;         [80]
And, as by simple waving of a wand
The wizard instantaneously dissolves
Palace or grove, even so did I unsoul
As readily by syllogistic words
Some charm of Logic, ever within reach,
Those mysteries of passion which have made,          [85]
And shall continue evermore to make,
(In spite of all that Reason hath perform'd
And shall perform to exalt and to refine)
One brotherhood of all the human race
Through all the habitations of past years
And those to come, and hence an emptiness
Fell on the Historian's Page, and even on that
Of Poets, pregnant with more absolute truth.
The works of both wither'd in my esteem,
Their sentence was, I thought, pronounc'd; their rights
Seem'd mortal, and their empire pass'd away.

56 errand Z²: business Z.

60, 65, 70, 75, 80, 85, 90, 95 are the line numbers in the left margin.

Dare I avow that wish was mine to see,
And hope that future times *would* surely see,
The man to come, parted, as by a gulph,
From him who had been; that I could no more　　60
Trust the elevation which had made me one
With the great family that still survives
To illuminate the abyss of ages past,
Sage, warrior, patriot, hero; for it seemed
That their best virtues were not free from taint　　65
Of something false and weak, that could not stand
The open eye of Reason. Then I said,
'Go to the Poets; they will speak to thee
More perfectly of purer creatures;—yet
If reason be nobility in man,　　70
Can aught be more ignoble than the man
Whom they delight in, blinded as he is
By prejudice, the miserable slave
Of low ambition or distempered love ?'

In such strange passion, if I may once more　　75
Review the past, I warred against myself—
A bigot to a new idolatry—
Like a cowled monk who hath forsworn the world,
Zealously laboured to cut off my heart
From all the sources of her former strength;　　80
And as, by simple waving of a wand,
The wizard instantaneously dissolves
Palace or grove, even so could I unsoul
As readily by syllogistic words
Those mysteries of being which have made,　　85
And shall continue evermore to make,
Of the whole human race one brotherhood.

62–63 𝔄 C D: D² *as* 1850.　　64 A² C *as* 1850.
73 Upon us by affinities of truth Z: Z² *as* 𝔄.
74, 76, 77 𝔄 C D: D² *as* 1850.
75–128 *added to* Z; *in their place* Z *had originally*:
　　Nor here alone for even the lovely earth
　　To which I owed so much of noble thought
　　With its sweet groves and rivers, pomp of clouds
　　And all the visible universe was scann'd
　　In something of a kindred spirit, had fallen
　　　　*etc. as* 𝔄 117–20, *but with* benignant (119) *for* more noble.
83 charm 𝔄 Z²: spell Z.　　84 passion 𝔄 C D E: being E²
88 𝔄 C D: D² *as* 1850.

What then remained in such eclipse ? what light
To guide or chear ? The laws of things which lie
Beyond the reach of human will or power;
The life of nature, by the God of love
100 Inspired, celestial presence ever pure;
These left, the Soul of Youth must needs be rich,
Whatever else be lost, and these were mine,
Not a deaf echo, merely, of the thought
Bewilder'd recollections, solitary,
105 But living sounds. Yet in despite of this,
This feeling, which howe'er impair'd or damp'd,
Yet having been once born can never die.
'Tis true that Earth with all her appanage
Of elements and organs, storm and sunshine,
110 With its pure forms and colours, pomp of clouds
Rivers and mountains, objects among which
It might be thought that no dislike or blame,
No sense of weakness or infirmity
Or aught amiss could possibly have come,
115 Yea, even the visible universe was scann'd
With something of a kindred spirit, fell
Beneath the domination of a taste                                    [90]
Less elevated, which did in my mind
With its more noble influence interfere,
120 Its animation and its deeper sway.

There comes (if need be now to speak of this
After such long detail of our mistakes)
There comes a time when Reason, not the grand
And simple Reason, but that humbler power
125 Which carries on its no inglorious work
By logic and minute analysis
Is of all Idols that which pleases most
The growing mind. A Trifler would he be
Who on the obvious benefits should dwell
130 That rise out of this process; but to speak
Of all the narrow estimates of things
Which hence originate were a worthy theme
For philosophic Verse; suffice it here
To hint that danger cannot but attend
135 Upon a Function rather proud to be
The enemy of falsehood, than the friend

What wonder, then, if, to a mind so far
Perverted, even the visible Universe
Fell under the dominion of a taste                    90
Less spiritual, with microscopic view
Was scanned, as I had scanned the moral world ?

96–102 What then remained . . . lost: 𝔄 C D: D *goes on* Ah! then it
was [XI. 333–52] *with some changes, and deletes both passages, substituting*
1850 [88–92].
98/99 The one sensation evermore *del.* Z.
102–6 Whatever . . . feeling] A *deletes* and these were mine . . . despite of
this *and reads* Whatever else be lost. But in despite Of feelings, *so* C.
106–7 This feeling which once born can never die Z: Z² *as* 𝔄.
110 its 𝔄: her A² C.
114 come] risen A² C.
115 even the Z² 𝔄: the whole Z.
120 its deeper] profounder A² C.
125 Which . . . its] Who . . . her A² C.          129–37 *not in* Z.
130–1 speak Of all the] unfold The many A² B² C.
132 theme] toil B².
[92/93] *Between these lines* E *has* By glimmering lights perplexed
(*deleted*).

     Of truth, to sit in judgment than to feel.

       Oh! soul of Nature, excellent and fair,
     That didst rejoice with me, with whom I too
140   Rejoiced, through early youth before the winds      [95]
     And powerful waters, and in lights and shades
     That march'd and countermarch'd about the hills
     In glorious apparition, now all eye
     And now all ear; but ever with the heart      [100]
145   Employ'd, and the majestic intellect;
     Oh! Soul of Nature! that dost overflow
     With passion and with life, what feeble men
     Walk on this earth! how feeble have I been      [105]
     When thou wert in thy strength! Nor this through stroke
150   Of human suffering, such as justifies
     Remissness and inaptitude of mind,
     But through presumption, even in pleasure pleas'd
     Unworthily, disliking here, and there,      [110]
     Liking, by rules of mimic art transferr'd
155   To things above all art. But more, for this,
     Although a strong infection of the age,
     Was never much my habit, giving way
     To a comparison of scene with scene      [115]
     Bent overmuch on superficial things,
160   Pampering myself with meagre novelties
     Of colour or proportion, to the moods
     Of time or season, to the moral power
     The affections, and the spirit of the place,      [120]
     Less sensible. Nor only did the love
165   Of sitting thus in judgment interrupt
     My deeper feelings, but another cause
     More subtle and less easily explain'd
     That almost seems inherent in the Creature,      [125]
     Sensuous and intellectual as he is,
170   A twofold Frame of body and of mind;
     The state to which I now allude was one
     In which the eye was master of the heart,
     When that which is in every stage of life
     The most despotic of our senses gain'd

141 powerful 𝔄 C D: roaring D².
143 In glorious apparition, powers on whom
     I daily waited—now all eye A³ D: D² *as* 1850.

O Soul of Nature! excellent and fair!
That didst rejoice with me, with whom I, too,
Rejoiced through early youth, before the winds          95
And roaring waters, and in lights and shades
That marched and countermarched about the hills
In glorious apparition, Powers on whom
I daily waited, now all eye and now
All ear; but never long without the heart              100
Employed, and man's unfolding intellect:
O Soul of Nature! that, by laws divine
Sustained and governed, still dost overflow
With an impassioned life, what feeble ones
Walk on this earth! how feeble have I been            105
When thou wert in thy strength! Nor this through stroke
Of human suffering, such as justifies
Remissness and inaptitude of mind,
But through presumption; even in pleasure pleased
Unworthily, disliking here, and there                 110
Liking; by rules of mimic art transferred
To things above all art; but more,—for this,
Although a strong infection of the age,
Was never much my habit—giving way
To a comparison of scene with scene,                  115
Bent overmuch on superficial things,
Pampering myself with meagre novelties
Of colour and proportion; to the moods
Of time and season, to the moral power,
The affections and the spirit of the place,           120
Insensible. Nor only did the love
Of sitting thus in judgment interrupt
My deeper feelings, but another cause,
More subtle and less easily explained,
That almost seems inherent in the creature,           125
A twofold frame of body and of mind.
I speak in recollection of a time
When the bodily eye, in every stage of life
The most despotic of our senses, gained

144 D *as* 𝔄: D² *as* 1850.        145–7 𝔄 C D: D² *as* 1850.
162–3 Of time or ... Place  B D E  (*but* time and D E): Of Nature and the
spirit of the place  A² C (*original reading of* A *erased*).
164 Less sensible] Insensible  A² C.
167 subtle A: subtile  B.
171 A³ C *as* 1850.

175 Such strength in me as often held my mind     [130]
In absolute dominion. Gladly here,
Entering upon abstruser argument,
Would I endeavour to unfold the means
Which Nature studiously employs to thwart
180 This tyranny, summons all the senses each     [135]
To counteract the other and themselves,
And makes them all, and the objects with which all
Are conversant, subservient in their turn
To the great ends of Liberty and Power.
185 But this is matter for another Song;
Here only let me add that my delights,     [140]
Such as they were, were sought insatiably,
Though 'twas a transport of the outward sense,
Not of the mind, vivid but not profound:
190 Yet was I often greedy in the chace,
And roam'd from hill to hill, from rock to rock,
Still craving combinations of new forms,
New pleasure, wider empire for the sight,     [145]
Proud of its own endowments, and rejoiced
195 To lay the inner faculties asleep.
    Amid the turns and counter-turns, the strife
And various trials of our complex being,
As we grow up, such thraldom of that sense     [150]
Seems hard to shun; and yet I knew a Maid,
200 Who, young as I was then, conversed with things
In higher style, from Appetites like these
She, gentle Visitant, as well she might,
Was wholly free, far less did critic rules
Or barren intermeddling subtleties     [155]
205 Perplex her mind; but, wise as Women are
When genial circumstance hath favor'd them,
She welcom'd what was given, and craved no more.
Whatever scene was present to her eyes,
That was the best, to that she was attuned     [160]

176 Gladly here] Then gladly too  W.
178 Would 𝔄 C D E: Could E².     unfold Z²: explain Z.
178–80 Attempt to place in view the diverse means
    Which Nature studiously {puts forth / employs} to uphold
    This agency against the barren [          ?]
    Of use and habit, call the senses each  W. (Would we *added
      above* Attempt).

Such strength in *me* as often held my mind                 130
In absolute dominion. Gladly here,
Entering upon abstruser argument,
Could I endeavour to unfold the means
Which Nature studiously employs to thwart
This tyranny, summons all the senses each                   135
To counteract the other, and themselves,
And makes them all, and the objects with which all
Are conversant, subservient in their turn
To the great ends of Liberty and Power.
But leave we this: enough that my delights                  140
(Such as they were) were sought insatiably.
Vivid the transport, vivid though not profound;
I roamed from hill to hill, from rock to rock,
Still craving combinations of new forms,
New pleasure, wider empire for the sight,                   145
Proud of her own endowments, and rejoiced
To lay the inner faculties asleep.
Amid the turns and counterturns, the strife
And various trials of our complex being,
As we grow up, such thraldom of that sense                  150
Seems hard to shun. And yet I knew a maid,
A young enthusiast, who escaped these bonds;
Her eye was not the mistress of her heart;
Far less did rules prescribed by passive taste,
Or barren intermeddling subtleties,                         155
Perplex her mind; but, wise as women are
When genial circumstance hath favoured them,
She welcomed what was given, and craved no more;
Whate'er the scene presented to her view,
That was the best, to that she was attuned                  160

185-6 Let this be matter for another song
      Here only will I add that my delights  D E: E² *as* 1850.
188-9 It was a transport vivid though not profound  D.
      Vivid the transport, though not profound  D² E: E² *as* 1850.
190-1 𝔄 C D E: E² *as* 1850.        194 endowments A B²: enjoyments B.
196 B *begins new paragraph here.*
197 complex being  Y² 𝔄: faculties Z.
200-3 Who, though her years ran parallel with mine
      Did then converse with objects of the sense
      In loftier style; from appetites like these
      She gentle Visitant was wholly free
      Far less did rules prescribed by passive taste  A² C: D *illegible*:
D² *as* 1850.
203-5 her no critic rules . . . Ever perplex'd  Z: Z² *as* 𝔄.
      her rules of critic art . . . Never perplex'd  W.

210 Through her humility and lowliness,
     And through a perfect happiness of soul
     Whose variegated feelings were in this
     Sisters, that they were each some new delight:      [164]
     For she was Nature's inmate. Her the birds
215 And every flower she met with, could they but
     Have known her, would have lov'd. Methought such charm
     Of sweetness did her presence breathe around
     That all the trees, and all the silent hills
     And every thing she look'd on, should have had
220 An intimation how she bore herself      [170]
     Towards them and to all creatures. God delights
     In such a being; for her common thoughts
     Are piety, her life is blessedness.

     Even like this Maid before I was call'd forth
225 From the retirement of my native hills      [175]
     I lov'd whate'er I saw; nor lightly lov'd,
     But fervently, did never dream of aught
     More grand, more fair, more exquisitely fram'd
     Than those few nooks to which my happy feet
230 Were limited. I had not at that time      [180]
     Liv'd long enough, nor in the least survived
     The first diviner influence of this world,
     As it appears to unaccustom'd eyes;
     I worshipp'd then among the depths of things
235 As my soul bade me; could I then take part      [185]
     In aught but admiration, or be pleased
     With any thing but humbleness and love;
     I felt, and nothing else; I did not judge,
     I never thought of judging, with the gift
240 Of all this glory fill'd and satisfi'd.      [190]
     And afterwards, when through the gorgeous Alps
     Roaming, I carried with me the same heart:

     210 Through her benignity and lowliness D E: By her benign and
simple way of life E²: E³ *as* 1850.
     213 Sisters that each bestowed some new delight E²: E *as* 1850.
     214 inmate] Pupil A² B² C.
     216 charm] depth Z.      223 blessedness 𝔄 C: gratitude A² B² D E
     227-8 But deeply never dreamt of aught more fair
         More grand more choice more exquisitely framed W Z. A 227
*originally as* Z, *but scratched out.* 228 More fair, more grand B.
     230-40 Were limited. And why? upon myself
         I was dependent then else should I soon

By her benign simplicity of life,
And through a perfect happiness of soul,
Whose variegated feelings were in this
Sisters, that they were each some new delight.
Birds in the bower, and lambs in the green field,        165
Could they have known her, would have loved; methought
Her very presence such a sweetness breathed,
That flowers, and trees, and even the silent hills,
And every thing she looked on, should have had
An intimation how she bore herself        170
Towards them and to all creatures. God delights
In such a being; for her common thoughts
Are piety, her life is gratitude.

Even like this maid, before I was called forth
From the retirement of my native hills,        175
I loved whate'er I saw: nor lightly loved,
But most intensely; never dreamt of aught
More grand, more fair, more exquisitely framed
Than those few nooks to which my happy feet
Were limited. I had not at that time        180
Lived long enough, nor in the least survived
The first diviner influence of this world,
As it appears to unaccustomed eyes.
Worshipping then among the depth of things,
As piety ordained; could I submit        185
To measured admiration, or to aught
That should preclude humility and love?
I felt, observed, and pondered; did not judge,
Yea, never thought of judging; with the gift
Of all this glory filled and satisfied.        190
And afterwards, when through the gorgeous Alps
Roaming, I carried with me the same heart:

Have languish'd and familiar with the shape
And outside fabric of that little world
Have undelighted looked on all delight. W. *So Z, but for second
and third lines Z has*
Was my dependence then else must I needs
Have languish'd and accustom'd to *etc. Z deletes whole passage.*
235–8 As piety ordained; could I submit
To stinted admiration or be pleased
With aught that banished humbleness and love;
I felt observed and pondered, did not judge. A² D: B² C *as* A,
*but* felt observed and felt (238): D² *as* 1850.
242 I roamed W.

In truth, this degradation, howsoe'er
Induced, effect in whatsoe'er degree
245 Of custom, that prepares such wantonness          [195]
As makes the greatest things give way to least,
Or any other cause which hath been named;
Or lastly, aggravated by the times,
Which with their passionate sounds might often make
250 The milder minstrelsies of rural scenes          [200]
Inaudible, was transient; I had felt
Too forcibly, too early in my life,
Visitings of imaginative power
For this to last: I shook the habit off
255 Entirely and for ever, and again          [205]
In Nature's presence stood, as I stand now,
A sensitive, and a creative Soul.

There are in our existence spots of time,
Which with distinct pre-eminence retain
260 A vivifying Virtue, whence, depress'd          [210]
By false opinion and contentious thought,
Or aught of heavier or more deadly weight,
In trivial occupations, and the round
Of ordinary intercourse, our minds
265 Are nourished and invisibly repair'd,          [215]
A virtue by which pleasure is enhanced
That penetrates, enables us to mount
When high, more high, and lifts us up when fallen.
This efficacious spirit chiefly lurks
270 Among those passages of life in which          [220]
We have had deepest feeling that the mind

243–51   In truth this relaxation in the power
Of natural objects o'er my weaker mind
Though doubtless aggravated by the times
In various manners, for their passionate sounds
Without my knowledge oftentimes might make
The milder minstrelsies of rural scenes
Inaudible  Z.

243–57   In truth this malady of which I speak
Though aided by the times whose deeper sound
Without my knowledge sometimes might perchance
Make rural Nature's milder minstrelsies
Inaudible did never take in me
Deep (*root*) hold or larger action.  I had received
Impressions far too early and too strong
For this to last: I threw the habit off

In truth, the degradation—howsoe'er
Induced, effect, in whatsoe'er degree,
Of custom that prepares a partial scale          195
In which the little oft outweighs the great;
Or any other cause that hath been named;
Or lastly, aggravated by the times
And their impassioned sounds, which well might make
The milder minstrelsies of rural scenes          200
Inaudible—was transient; I had known
Too forcibly, too early in my life,
Visitings of imaginative power
For this to last: I shook the habit off
Entirely and for ever, and again          205
In Nature's presence stood, as now I stand,
A sensitive being, a *creative* soul.

There are in our existence spots of time,
That with distinct pre-eminence retain
A renovating virtue, whence, depressed          210
By false opinion and contentious thought,
Or aught of heavier or more deadly weight,
In trivial occupations, and the round
Of ordinary intercourse, our minds
Are nourished and invisibly repaired;          215
A virtue, by which pleasure is enhanced,
That penetrates, enables us to mount,
When high, more high, and lifts us up when fallen.
This efficacious spirit chiefly lurks
Among those passages of life that give          220
Profoundest knowledge to what point, and how,

　　　　Entirely and for ever, and again
　　　　In Nature's presence stood as I do now
　　　　A meditative and creative Soul W.
245-6 𝔄 C D: D² *as* 1850.　　247 Or  D E: Of 𝔄 C (*sic*).
249 𝔄 C D E: E² *as* 1850.　　251 felt] known A² B² C.
252 forcibly] deeply and Z.
257 𝔄 C D:  D² *as* 1850.　　258 V *begins again here.*
260 vivifying A Z²: fructifying V Z: renovating A² B C D E.
261-2 *not in* V; *added later to* Z.
264/265 (Especially the imaginative power) V.
266–73 *not in* V; *added later to* Z.　　269 efficacious Z² 𝔄: animating Z.
270-3　　　　　　　　　　life that give
　　　　Profoundest feeling to what point the mind
　　　　Is lord and master, and external sense
　　　　Obedient servant to her will. Such moments D:  D² *as* 1850.

Is lord and master, and that outward sense
Is but the obedient servant of her will.
Such moments, worthy of all gratitude,
275 Are scatter'd everywhere, taking their date
From our first childhood: in our childhood even [225]
Perhaps are most conspicuous. Life with me,
As far as memory can look back, is full
Of this beneficent influence. At a time
280 When scarcely (I was then not six years old)
My hand could hold a bridle, with proud hopes
I mounted, and we rode towards the hills:
We were a pair of Horsemen; honest James
Was with me, my encourager and guide. [230]
285 We had not travell'd long, ere some mischance
Disjoin'd me from my Comrade, and, through fear
Dismounting, down the rough and stony Moor
I led my Horse, and stumbling on, at length
Came to a bottom, where in former times [235]
290 A Murderer had been hung in iron chains.
The Gibbet-mast was moulder'd down, the bones
And iron case were gone; but on the turf,
Hard by, soon after that fell deed was wrought
Some unknown hand had carved the Murderer's name. [240]
295 The monumental writing was engraven
In times long past, and still, from year to year,
By superstition of the neighbourhood,
The grass is clear'd away; and to this hour
The letters are all fresh and visible. [245]
300 Faltering, and ignorant where I was, at length
I chanced to espy those characters inscribed
On the green sod: forthwith I left the spot
And, reascending the bare Common, saw
A naked Pool that lay beneath the hills,

274–81 Such moments chiefly seem to have their date
In our first childhood. I remember well,
'Tis of an early season that I speak,
The twilight of rememberable life,
While I was yet an urchin, one who scarce
Could hold a bridle, with ambitious hopes V.
277–80 Perhaps are most conspicuous. Vividly
How vividly in one particular scene
Now present to my memory did I feel
This fructifying influence at a time
When scarcely *etc.* Z: Z² *as* 1850.

The mind is lord and master—outward sense
The obedient servant of her will. Such moments
Are scattered everywhere, taking their date
From our first childhood. I remember well,                         225
That once, while yet my inexperienced hand
Could scarcely hold a bridle, with proud hopes
I mounted, and we journeyed towards the hills:
An ancient servant of my father's house
Was with me, my encourager and guide:                             230
We had not travelled long, ere some mischance
Disjoined me from my comrade; and, through fear
Dismounting, down the rough and stony moor
I led my horse, and, stumbling on, at length
Came to a bottom, where in former times                           235
A murderer had been hung in iron chains.
The gibbet-mast had mouldered down, the bones
And iron case were gone; but on the turf,
Hard by, soon after that fell deed was wrought,
Some unknown hand had carved the murderer's name.   240
The monumental letters were inscribed
In times long past; but still, from year to year,
By superstition of the neighbourhood,
The grass is cleared away, and to this hour
The characters are fresh and visible:                             245
A casual glance had shown them, and I fled,
Faltering and faint, and ignorant of the road:
Then, reascending the bare common, saw
A naked pool that lay beneath the hills,

276-80 [225-6] From earliest seasons. I remember well
       That once while yet a child      When (I was then but six years
         whose timid hand  A² C.        old) my hand  D: D² *as* 1850.
281 A² C D *as* [227].
282 rode 𝔄 C D E: journeyed E².
283 A² C *as* [229].
290-303 A man, the murderer of his wife, was hung
         In irons, moulder'd was the gibbet mast,
         The bones were gone, the iron and the wood,
         Only a long green ridge of turf remained
         Whose shape was like a grave. I left the spot
         And reascending the bare slope, I saw  V: Z *as* 𝔄.
[241] inscribed  D² E: engraven  D.
299 Remain the letters fresh and visible.  D: D³ *as* 1850.
     The far-famed characters are visible.  D².
301-2 Chancing to espy these far famed characters carved
       Fresh in the turf I hurried from the spot  D: D² *as* 1850.

305 The Beacon on the summit, and more near, [250]
    A Girl who bore a Pitcher on her head
    And seem'd with difficult steps to force her way
    Against the blowing wind. It was, in truth,
    An ordinary sight; but I should need
310 Colours and words that are unknown to man [255]
    To paint the visionary dreariness
    Which, while I look'd all round for my lost Guide,
    Did at that time invest the naked Pool,
    The Beacon on the lonely Eminence,
315 The Woman, and her garments vex'd and toss'd [260]
    By the strong wind. When, in a blessed season
    With those two dear Ones, to my heart so dear,
    When in the blessed time of early love,
    Long afterwards, I roam'd about
320 In daily presence of this very scene,
    Upon the naked pool and dreary crags,
    And on the melancholy Beacon, fell [265]
    The spirit of pleasure and youth's golden gleam;
    And think ye not with radiance more divine
325 From these remembrances, and from the power
    They left behind? So feeling comes in aid
    Of feeling, and diversity of strength [270]
    Attends us, if but once we have been strong.
    Oh! mystery of Man, from what a depth
330 Proceed thy honours! I am lost, but see
    In simple childhood something of the base
    On which thy greatness stands, but this I feel, [275]
    That from thyself it is that thou must give,
    Else never canst receive. The days gone by
335 Come back upon me from the dawn almost
    Of life: the hiding-places of my power
    Seem open; I approach, and then they close; [280]
    I see by glimpses now; when age comes on,
    May scarcely see at all, and I would give,
340 While yet we may, as far as words can give,

313 The Moor invested and the naked Pool D: D² *as* 1850.
315 Woman 𝔄 C D: Female D².
316-19             When in the blessed hours
      Of early love, alone or with the Maid
      To whom were breathed my first fond vows I roamed A² C.
316-45 When in a . . . conclude] *not in* V.
323 *followed in* D *by deleted line* Fell with a radiance brighter for the shade

The beacon on the summit, and, more near,   250
A girl, who bore a pitcher on her head,
And seemed with difficult steps to force her way
Against the blowing wind. It was, in truth,
An ordinary sight; but I should need
Colours and words that are unknown to man,   255
To paint the visionary dreariness
Which, while I looked all round for my lost guide,
Invested moorland waste, and naked pool,
The beacon crowning the lone eminence,
The female and her garments vexed and tossed   260
By the strong wind. When, in the blessed hours
Of early love, the loved one at my side,
I roamed, in daily presence of this scene,
Upon the naked pool and dreary crags,
And on the melancholy beacon fell   265
A spirit of pleasure and youth's golden gleam;
And think ye not with radiance more sublime
For these remembrances, and for the power
They had left behind ? So feeling comes in aid
Of feeling, and diversity of strength   270
Attends us, if but once we have been strong.
Oh! mystery of man, from what a depth
Proceed thy honours. I am lost, but see
In simple childhood something of the base
On which thy greatness stands; but this I feel,   275
That from thyself it comes, that thou must give,
Else never canst receive. The days gone by
Return upon me almost from the dawn
Of life: the hiding-places of man's power
Open; I would approach them, but they close.   280
I see by glimpses now; when age comes on,
May scarcely see at all; and I would give,
While yet we may, as far as words can give,

328 Attends on him who hath but once been strong W: W² *as* 𝕬.
329 Oh mystery of Man 𝕬 C D E: Mysterious soul of Man A² *deleted.*
333 is Z² 𝕬 C: comes Z D E.   335 𝕬 C D: D² *as* 1850.
338–45 *In place of these lines* W *reads*:
        Yet have I singled out not satisfied
        With general feelings, here and there have cull'd
        Some incidents that may explain whence came
        My restoration, and with yet one (more) of these
        I will conclude. One Christmas time
340 give] do Z.

A substance and a life to what I feel:
I would enshrine the spirit of the past                    [285]
For future restoration. Yet another
Of these, to me, affecting incidents
345  With which we will conclude.
                              One Christmas-time,
The day before the Holidays began,
Feverish, and tired, and restless, I went forth
Into the fields, impatient for the sight                    [290]
Of those two Horses which should bear us home;
350  My Brothers and myself. There was a crag,
An Eminence, which from the meeting-point
Of two highways ascending, overlook'd
At least a long half-mile of those two roads,
By each of which the expected Steeds might come,
355  The choice uncertain. Thither I repair'd            [296]
Up to the highest summit; 'twas a day
Stormy, and rough, and wild, and on the grass
I sate, half-shelter'd by a naked wall;
Upon my right hand was a single sheep,                  [300]
360  A whistling hawthorn on my left, and there,
With those Companions at my side, I watch'd,
Straining my eyes intensely, as the mist
Gave intermitting prospect of the wood
And plain beneath. Ere I to School return'd           [305]
365  That dreary time, ere I had been ten days
A dweller in my Father's House, he died,
And I and my two Brothers, Orphans then,
Followed his Body to the Grave. The event
With all the sorrow which it brought appear'd        [310]
370  A chastisement; and when I call'd to mind
That day so lately pass'd, when from the crag
I look'd in such anxiety of hope,
With trite reflections of morality,
Yet in the deepest passion, I bow'd low                 [315]

343–5              restoration. Then vouchsafe
        Philosopher and friend a willing Ear
        While I record a second incident
        With thankful memory. One  A² C.
V (*going on from l.* 316) *reads* Nor less I recollect
        (Long after, though my childhood had not ceased)
        Another scene which left a kindred power
        Implanted in my mind. One Christmas time
346 𝔄 C D:  D² *as* 1850.

Substance and life to what I feel, enshrining,
Such is my hope, the spirit of the Past　　　　　　285
For future restoration.—Yet another
Of these memorials:—
　　　　　　　　　One Christmas-time,
On the glad eve of its dear holidays,
Feverish, and tired, and restless, I went forth
Into the fields, impatient for the sight　　　　　　290
Of those led palfreys that should bear us home;
My brothers and myself. There rose a crag,
That, from the meeting-point of two highways
Ascending, overlooked them both, far stretched;
Thither, uncertain on which road to fix　　　　　　295
My expectation, thither I repaired,
Scout-like, and gained the summit; 'twas a day
Tempestuous, dark, and wild, and on the grass
I sate half-sheltered by a naked wall;
Upon my right hand couched a single sheep,　　　　300
Upon my left a blasted hawthorn stood;
With those companions at my side, I watched,
Straining my eyes intensely, as the mist
Gave intermitting prospect of the copse
And plain beneath. Ere we to school returned,—　　305
That dreary time,—ere we had been ten days
Sojourners in my father's house, he died,
And I and my three brothers, orphans then,
Followed his body to the grave. The event,
With all the sorrow that it brought, appeared　　　310
A chastisement; and when I called to mind
That day so lately past, when from the crag
I looked in such anxiety of hope;
With trite reflections of morality,
Yet in the deepest passion, I bowed low　　　　　315

349 two Horses 𝔄: three horses V Z: rough palfreys 𝔄² B² C D: led
palfreys D² E.　　　351-2 D² *as* 1850.　　　351-5 𝔄 C D.
353-5 Thither (for which of these two roads might first
　　　Show to my eager sight the expected steeds
　　　Was all uncertain) Scoutlike I repaired D² E: E² *as* 1850.
357 Stormy and rough and wild V 𝔄: bleak *for* rough B²; A² C *as* 1850.
359 was V Z 𝔄: couched A² C.　　　360 A² C *as* 1850.
361 With those] Those two V.
362 Straining my eyes intensely] With eyes intensely straining V.
364-6 I . . . I . . . A dweller V 𝔄: we . . . we . . . Sojourners A² C.
367 two V Z 𝔄 C: three D E.

375 To God, who thus corrected my desires;
And afterwards, the wind and sleety rain
And all the business of the elements,
The single sheep, and the one blasted tree,
And the bleak music of that old stone wall, [320]
380 The noise of wood and water, and the mist
Which on the line of each of those two Roads
Advanced in such indisputable shapes,
All these were spectacles and sounds to which
I often would repair and thence would drink, [325]
385 As at a fountain; and I do not doubt
That in this later time, when storm and rain
Beat on my roof at midnight, or by day
When I am in the woods, unknown to me
The workings of my spirit thence are brought. [331–2]

390 Thou wilt not languish here, O Friend, for whom
I travel in these dim uncertain ways
Thou wilt assist me as a Pilgrim gone
In quest of highest truth. Behold me then
Once more in Nature's presence, thus restored
395 Or otherwise, and strengthened once again
(With memory left of what had been escaped)
To habits of devoutest sympathy.

385 As at a favorite fountain, and belike  D E:  E² *as* 1850.
386–9 𝔄 C D.
[329–*end*] When in a grove I walk whose lofty trees
Laden with all their summer foliage, rock
High over head those workings of the mind
Of source and tendency to me unknown,
Some inward agitations thence are brought
Efforts and struggles tempered and restrained
By melancholy awe or pleasing fear.  D².

To God, Who thus corrected my desires;
And, afterwards, the wind and sleety rain,
And all the business of the elements,
The single sheep, and the one blasted tree,
And the bleak music from that old stone wall,　　320
The noise of wood and water, and the mist
That on the line of each of those two roads
Advanced in such indisputable shapes;
All these were kindred spectacles and sounds
To which I oft repaired, and thence would drink,　　325
As at a fountain; and on winter nights,
Down to this very time, when storm and rain
Beat on my roof, or, haply, at noon-day,
While in a grove I walk, whose lofty trees,
Laden with summer's thickest foliage, rock　　330
In a strong wind, some working of the spirit,
Some inward agitations thence are brought,
Whate'er their office, whether to beguile
Thoughts over busy in the course they took,
Or animate an hour of vacant ease.　　335

> When in a grove I walk whose lofty trees
> Laden with summer's thickest foliage, rock
> In a strong wind, some workings of the spirit
> Some inward agitations thence proceed
> To blend with all that impulse from without
> Inspires of effort tempered and restrained
> By melancholy awe or pleasing fear　D³ E:　E² *as* 1850.

390–7 A B *delete*: *not in* C.
393 highest] precious A².
395–7 Or otherwise behold me at her shrine
　　　Heal'd and accomplish'd, sensible of what
　　　Had been escap'd, and strengthen'd once again.
　　　To habits *etc.* Z.

# BOOK TWELFTH

## SAME SUBJECT—Continued

FROM nature doth emotion come, and moods
Of calmness equally are nature's gift,
This is her glory; these two attributes
Are sister horns that constitute her strength;  [4]
5 This twofold influence is the sun and shower
Of all her bounties, both in origin
And end alike benignant. Hence it is,
That Genius which exists by interchange  [5]
Of peace and excitation, finds in her
10 His best and purest Friend, from her receives
That energy by which he seeks the truth,
Is rouzed, aspires, grasps, struggles, wishes, craves,
From her that happy stillness of the mind
Which fits him to receive it, when unsought.  [10]

15    Such benefit may souls of humblest frame
Partake of, each in their degree; 'tis mine
To speak of what myself have known and felt
Sweet task! for words find easy way, inspired
By gratitude and confidence in truth.  [15]
20 Long time in search of knowledge desperate,
I was benighted heart and mind; but now
On all sides day began to reappear,
And it was proved indeed that not in vain
I had been taught to reverence a Power  [20]
25 That is the very quality and shape
And image of right reason, that matures
Her processes by steadfast laws, gives birth
To no impatient or fallacious hopes,

[MSS. for Bk. XII: A B D E Z: *ll.* 1–186 C; *ll.* 111–276 Y; *ll.* 185–204 J.]
  Book Twelfth: Same Subject continued B: 12 A: Book Twelfth C.
Subject concluded D E.
  1–2 From nature comes emotion; moods of peace And calmness A².
  3–5 This is her glory; for this twofold sway
      The very sunshine as it were and shower Z: Z² as 𝕬.
  7 is 𝕬 C: comes B².
  8 which exists 𝕬 C: born to thrive A².
  12 B: A *omits* wishes, craves, *and deletes defective line*: not in C.

# BOOK THIRTEENTH

## IMAGINATION AND TASTE, HOW IMPAIRED AND RESTORED—Concluded

FROM Nature doth emotion come, and moods
Of calmness equally are Nature's gift:
This is her glory; these two attributes
Are sister horns that constitute her strength.
Hence Genius, born to thrive by interchange     5
Of peace and excitation, finds in her
His best and purest friend; from her receives
That energy by which he seeks the truth,
From her that happy stillness of the mind
Which fits him to receive it when unsought.     10

   Such benefit the humblest intellects
Partake of, each in their degree; 'tis mine
To speak, what I myself have known and felt;
Smooth task! for words find easy way, inspired
By gratitude, and confidence in truth.     15
Long time in search of knowledge did I range
The field of human life, in heart and mind
Benighted; but, the dawn beginning now
To re-appear, 'twas proved that not in vain
I had been taught to reverence a Power     20
That is the visible quality and shape
And image of right reason; that matures
Her processes by steadfast laws; gives birth
To no impatient or fallacious hopes,

20–23 When in the search of knowledge desperate
    I was benighted both in heart and mind
    Soon as the day began to reappear
    Then was it prov'd indeed that not in vain Z: Z² Y *as* 𝔄.
    Desperate in search of knowledge long I roamed
    The path of life, benighted, heart and mind,
    But, day beginning now to reappear
    On every side, 'twas proved that not in vain A².
    Long time in search of knowledge desperate
    Roam'd I the plain of life in heart and mind
    Benighted but the dawn beginning now *etc. as* 1850 A³ C D: D² *as*
      1850.
25 very 𝔄 C D: visible D² E.

No heat of passion, or excessive zeal,                    [25]
30 No vain conceits, provokes to no quick turns
Of self-applauding intellect, but lifts
The Being into magnanimity;
Holds up before the mind, intoxicate
With present objects and the busy dance          [30]
35 Of things that pass away, a temperate shew
Of objects that endure, and by this course
Disposes her, when over-fondly set
On leaving her incumbrances behind
To seek in Man, and in the frame of life,          [35]
40 Social and individual, what there is
Desireable, affecting, good or fair
Of kindred permanence, the gifts divine
And universal, the pervading grace
That hath been, is, and shall be. Above all          [39]
45 Did Nature bring again that wiser mood
More deeply re-establish'd in my soul,
Which, seeing little worthy or sublime
In what we blazon with the pompous names
Of power and action, early tutor'd me
50 To look with feelings of fraternal love          [45]
Upon those unassuming things, that hold
A silent station in this beauteous world.


Thus moderated, thus composed, I found
Once more in Man an object of delight
55 Of pure imagination, and of love;          [50]
And, as the horizon of my mind enlarged,
Again I took the intellectual eye
For my instructor, studious more to see
Great Truths, than touch and handle little ones.
60 Knowledge was given accordingly; my trust          [55]
Was firmer in the feelings which had stood
The test of such a trial; clearer far
My sense of what was excellent and right;
The promise of the present time retired
65 Into its true proportion; sanguine schemes,          [60]
Ambitious virtues pleased me less, I sought

31–32 𝔄 C D: D² *as* 1850.          42–46 A² C *as* 1850.
48–49 In that Ambition which the Historian's pen
Delights to blazon . . . action D: D² *as* 1850 [42–44].

No heat of passion or excessive zeal,                        25
No vain conceits; provokes to no quick turns
Of self-applauding intellect; but trains
To meekness, and exalts by humble faith;
Holds up before the mind intoxicate
With present objects, and the busy dance            30
Of things that pass away, a temperate show
Of objects that endure; and by this course
Disposes her, when over-fondly set
On throwing off incumbrances, to seek
In man, and in the frame of social life,                 35
Whate'er there is desirable and good
Of kindred permanence, unchanged in form
And function, or, through strict vicissitude
Of life and death, revolving. Above all
Were re-established now those watchful thoughts      40
Which, seeing little worthy or sublime
In what the Historian's pen so much delights
To blazon—power and energy detached
From moral purpose—early tutored me
To look with feelings of fraternal love                  45
Upon the unassuming things that hold
A silent station in this beauteous world.

    Thus moderated, thus composed, I found
Once more in Man an object of delight,
Of pure imagination, and of love;                        50
And, as the horizon of my mind enlarged,
Again I took the intellectual eye
For my instructor, studious more to see
Great truths, than touch and handle little ones.
Knowledge was given accordingly; my trust       55
Became more firm in feelings that had stood
The test of such a trial; clearer far
My sense of excellence—of right and wrong:
The promise of the present time retired
Into its true proportion; sanguine schemes,         60
Ambitious projects, pleased me less; I sought

61 A² C *as* 1850.        62 clearer far  Z²: far more deep  Z.
63 𝔄 C D E:  D² E² *as* 1850.
65–66 schemes . . . sought  Z²: thoughts, . . . look'd  Z.
66 virtues  𝔄 C D E: projects  D² E².

For good in the familiar face of life
And built thereon my hopes of good to come.

With settling judgments now of what would last
70 And what would disappear, prepared to find          [65]
Ambition, folly, madness in the men
Who thrust themselves upon this passive world
As Rulers of the world, to see in these,
Even when the public welfare is their aim,
75 Plans without thought, or bottom'd on false thought     [70]
And false philosophy: having brought to test
Of solid life and true result the Books
Of modern Statists, and thereby perceiv'd
The utter hollowness of what we name
80 The wealth of Nations, where alone that wealth
Is lodged, and how encreased, and having gain'd
A more judicious knowledge of what makes          [80]
The dignity of individual Man,
Of Man, no composition of the thought,
85 Abstraction, shadow, image, but the man
Of whom we read, the man whom we behold
With our own eyes; I could not but inquire,
Not with less interest than heretofore,          [85]
But greater, though in spirit more subdued,
90 Why is this glorious Creature to be found
One only in ten thousand ? What one is,
Why may not many be ? What bars are thrown
By Nature in the way of such a hope ?          [90]
Our animal wants and the necessities
95 Which they impose, are these the obstacles ?
If not, then others vanish into air.
Such meditations bred an anxious wish
To ascertain how much of real worth          [95]
And genuine knowledge, and true power of mind
100 Did at this day exist in those who liv'd
By bodily labour, labour far exceeding

67 𝕬 C D: D² *as* 1850.
71 Ambition 𝕬 C D E: Presumption D² E².
75–80 D *stuck over*: D² *as* 1850.
76–78 And false philosophy; having brought the Books
     Of Modern Statists to their proper test—
      Life, human Life,—and clearly thence perceived A² C.
77–78 *added to* Z.
82 More feelingly to know wherein consists Z: Z² *as* 𝕬.

For present good in life's familiar face,
And built thereon my hopes of good to come.

With settling judgments now of what would last
And what would disappear; prepared to find                    65
Presumption, folly, madness, in the men
Who thrust themselves upon the passive world
As Rulers of the world; to see in these,
Even when the public welfare is their aim,
Plans without thought, or built on theories                    70
Vague and unsound; and having brought the books
Of modern statists to their proper test,
Life, human life, with all its sacred claims
Of sex and age, and heaven-descended rights,
Mortal, or those beyond the reach of death;                    75
And having thus discerned how dire a thing
Is worshipped in that idol proudly named
'The Wealth of Nations,' *where* alone that wealth
Is lodged, and how increased; and having gained
A more judicious knowledge of the worth                        80
And dignity of individual man,
No composition of the brain, but man
Of whom we read, the man whom we behold
With our own eyes—I could not but inquire—
Not with less interest than heretofore,                        85
But greater, though in spirit more subdued—
Why is this glorious creature to be found
One only in ten thousand? What one is,
Why may not millions be? What bars are thrown
By Nature in the way of such a hope?                           90
Our animal appetites and daily wants,
Are these obstructions insurmountable?
If not, then others vanish into air.
'Inspect the basis of the social pile:
Inquire,' said I, 'how much of mental power                    95
And genuine virtue they possess who live
By bodily toil, labour exceeding far

84 thought 𝔄 C D: brain D².      88–89 *added to* Z.
92 many 𝔄 C D: millions D².      94 𝔄² C *as* 1850.
94–96 *added to* Z.
95–101 A² *as* 1850, *after false start*:
        Look, said I, first at Men of low degree
        Enquire what genuine knowledge—
101 𝔄 C D: D² *as* 1850.      101 exceeding] beyond Z.

Their due proportion, under all the weight
Of that injustice which upon ourselves
By composition of society
105 Ourselves entail. To frame such estimate                    [100]
I chiefly look'd (what need to look beyond ?).
Among the natural abodes of men,
Fields with their rural works, recall'd to mind
My earliest notices, with these compared
110 The observations of my later youth,                    [105]
Continued downwards to that very day.

For time had never been in which the throes
And mighty hopes of Nations, and the stir
And tumult of the world to me could yield,
115 How far soe'er transported and possess'd,
Full measure of content; but still I craved                    [110]
An intermixture of distinct regards
And truths of individual sympathy
Nearer ourselves. Such often might be glean'd
120 From that great City, else it must have been
A heart-depressing wilderness indeed,                    [115]
Full soon to me a wearisome abode;
But much was wanting; therefore did I turn
To you, ye Pathways, and ye lonely Roads
125 Sought you enrich'd with everything I prized,
With human kindness and with Nature's joy.

Oh! next to one dear state of bliss, vouchsafed                    [120]
Alas! to few in this untoward world,
The bliss of walking daily in Life's prime
130 Through field or forest with the Maid we love,
While yet our hearts are young, while yet we breathe
Nothing but happiness, living in some place,                    [125]
Deep Vale, or anywhere, the home of both,
From which it would be misery to stir;
135 Oh! next to such enjoyment of our youth,

110 of my] made in  A² C.
111 *followed in* Z *by* (Though) Not with less interest than heretofore
                    But greater, though more temperate, more subdued.
111–14 And to that day continued. For the time
          Had never been in which the throes of nations
          And tumult of the world to me could yield  A² C D:  D² *as* 1850.
113–14 Of nations and their conflicts and the stir
          And turmoil of the world to me could yield  Y.

Their due proportion, under all the weight
Of that injustice which upon ourselves
Ourselves entail.' Such estimate to frame                    100
I chiefly looked (what need to look beyond?)
Among the natural abodes of men,
Fields with their rural works; recalled to mind
My earliest notices; with these compared
The observations made in later youth,                        105
And to that day continued.—For, the time
Had never been when throes of mighty Nations
And the world's tumult unto me could yield,
How far soe'er transported and possessed,
Full measure of content; but still I craved                  110
An intermingling of distinct regards
And truths of individual sympathy
Nearer ourselves. Such often might be gleaned
From the great City, else it must have proved
To me a heart-depressing wilderness;                         115
But much was wanting: therefore did I turn
To you, ye pathways, and ye lonely roads;
Sought you enriched with everything I prized,
With human kindnesses and simple joys.

Oh! next to one dear state of bliss, vouchsafed              120
Alas! to few in this untoward world,
The bliss of walking daily in life's prime
Through field or forest with the maid we love,
While yet our hearts are young, while yet we breathe
Nothing but happiness, in some lone nook,                    125
Deep vale, or any where, the home of both,
From which it would be misery to stir:
Oh! next to such enjoyment of our youth,

120–1 A² C *as* 1850.
122 A *deletes*; *not in* C.
126 𝔄 C D: D² *as* 1850.
131–2                    while we inhale
        At every respiration happiness;
        Or feed on cares that but inhance delight,
        Living together in some lonely spot  A² C.
                        while yet we breathe
        Nothing but happiness; or feed on cares
        That ruffle and stir up, but cannot stain,
        Living together in some lonely spot  D: D² *as* 1850.
134 misery 𝔄 C D² E²: punishment D E.

In my esteem, next to such dear delight
Was that of wandering on from day to day                    [130]
Where I could meditate in peace, and find
The knowledge which I love, and teach the sound
140 Of Poet's music to strange fields and groves,            [135]
Converse with men, where if we meet a face
We almost meet a friend, on naked Moors
With long, long ways before, by Cottage Bench              [140]
Or Well-spring where the weary Traveller rests.

145     I love a public road: few sights there are
That please me more; such object hath had power
O'er my imagination since the dawn                         [145]
Of childhood, when its disappearing line,
Seen daily afar off, on one bare steep
150 Beyond the limits which my feet had trod
Was like a guide into eternity,                            [151]
At least to things unknown and without bound.
Even something of the grandeur which invests
The Mariner who sails the roaring sea
155 Through storm and darkness early in my mind
Surrounded, too, the Wanderers of the Earth,              [155]
Grandeur as much, and loveliness far more;
Awed have I been by strolling Bedlamites,

136 *added to* Z.
139 The knowledge which I loved, or teach the sound  A² C.
[132–3] The knowledge which I loved, or like a bird  D: D² *as* 1850.
[136] *added to* D, *and* [137] *added to* A  (*after* 140).
142 naked 𝔄 C D E² Z²: lonely  Y Z.      Moors 𝔄 C D: heaths  D².
145–7 Who doth not love to follow with his eye
        An easy pathway's undulating flow
        Through Park or flowery Meadow, or to track
        The statelier course of some frequented road
        Climbing round hills or stretched along the plain
        Such object though familiar hath had power
        On my imagination . . . A².
    Who does not love to follow with his eye
    A winding Stream, even so a public road
    Familiar object as it is with me
    Hath exercised a salutary power
    Over imagination . . . A³.
    Few sights more please me than a public road
    'Tis my delight; such object hath had power
    O'er my imagination . . . B².
145–6 The wild meanderings of a liquid brook
        Who doth not love, what eye the stately course
        Of a large river tracks but with delight?

In my esteem, next to such dear delight,
Was that of wandering on from day to day                     130
Where I could meditate in peace, and cull
Knowledge that step by step might lead me on
To wisdom; or, as lightsome as a bird
Wafted upon the wind from distant lands,
Sing notes of greeting to strange fields or groves,          135
Which lacked not voice to welcome me in turn:
And, when that pleasant toil had ceased to please,
Converse with men, where if we meet a face
We almost meet a friend, on naked heaths
With long long ways before, by cottage bench,                140
Or well-spring where the weary traveller rests.

Who doth not love to follow with his eye
The windings of a public way ? the sight,
Familiar object as it is, hath wrought
On my imagination since the morn                             145
Of childhood, when a disappearing line,
One daily present to my eyes, that crossed
The naked summit of a far-off hill
Beyond the limits that my feet had trod,
Was like an invitation into space                            150
Boundless, or guide into eternity.
Yes, something of the grandeur which invests
The mariner who sails the roaring sea
Through storm and darkness, early in my mind
Surrounded, too, the wanderers of the earth;                 155
Grandeur as much, and loveliness far more.
Awed have I been by strolling Bedlamites;

With kindred pleasure doth my sight pursue
The humbler windings of a public road
Through shady grove or cultivated field
Or desert waste, such object hath had power  B³.
[143–5] The easy pathways undulating flow
      Familiar object as it is, hath fed
      Imagination ever since the morn  D:
      The windings of a public way ? the sight
      Hath wrought on my imagination since the morn  D² E.
149 steep] slope  Y.
152 At least . . . bound] And regions of illimitable space  A²: The region
*etc.*  C: An invitation into boundless space!  D:  D² *as* 1850.
153 invests  A Z²: surrounds  Z.
156 Surrounded  A Z²: Invested  Z.
158 strolling] wandering  Y.

From many other uncouth Vagrants pass'd
160 In fear, have walk'd with quicker step; but why
Take note of this? When I began to inquire,        [160]
To watch and question those I met, and held
Familiar talk with them, the lonely roads
Were schools to me in which I daily read
165 With most delight the passions of mankind,        [164]
There saw into the depth of human souls,
Souls that appear to have no depth at all
To vulgar eyes. And now convinced at heart
How little that to which alone we give
170 The name of education hath to do        [171]
With real feeling and just sense, how vain
A correspondence with the talking world
Proves to the most, and call'd to make good search
If man's estate, by doom of Nature yoked        [175]
175 With toil, is therefore yoked with ignorance,
If virtue be indeed so hard to rear,
And intellectual strength so rare a boon
I prized such walks still more; for there I found
Hope to my hope, and to my pleasure peace,        [180]
180 And steadiness; and healing and repose
To every angry passion. There I heard,
From mouths of lowly men and of obscure
A tale of honour; sounds in unison
With loftiest promises of good and fair.        [185]

185     There are who think that strong affections, love
Known by whatever name, is falsely deem'd
A gift, to use a term which they would use,
Of vulgar Nature, that its growth requires
Retirement, leisure, language purified        [190]
190 By manners thoughtful and elaborate,
That whoso feels such passion in excess
Must live within the very light and air
Of elegances that are made by man.

162 watch] search Y.
162–3 held Familiar talk with] speak Without reserve to A² C.
166 *Added to* D.          168 vulgar 𝔄 C D: careless D².
169 𝔄 C D: D² *as* 1850.
181–2 *Between these lines* Y *has* (*deleted*):
      And in the tongue of tru[est] eloquence
182–3 A² *as* 1850.

From many other uncouth vagrants (passed
In fear) have walked with quicker step; but why
Take note of this? When I began to enquire,                    160
To watch and question those I met, and speak
Without reserve to them, the lonely roads
Were open schools in which I daily read
With most delight the passions of mankind,
Whether by words, looks, sighs, or tears, revealed;            165
There saw into the depth of human souls,
Souls that appear to have no depth at all
To careless eyes. And—now convinced at heart
How little those formalities, to which
With overweening trust alone we give                           170
The name of Education, have to do
With real feeling and just sense; how vain
A correspondence with the talking world
Proves to the most; and called to make good search
If man's estate, by doom of Nature yoked                       175
With toil, be therefore yoked with ignorance;
If virtue be indeed so hard to rear,
And intellectual strength so rare a boon—
I prized such walks still more, for there I found
Hope to my hope, and to my pleasure peace                      180
And steadiness, and healing and repose
To every angry passion. There I heard,
From mouths of men obscure and lowly, truths
Replete with honour; sounds in unison
With loftiest promises of good and fair.                       185

There are who think that strong affection, love
Known by whatever name, is falsely deemed
A gift, to use a term which they would use,
Of vulgar nature; that its growth requires
Retirement, leisure, language purified                         190
By manners studied and elaborate;
That whoso feels such passion in its strength
Must live within the very light and air
Of courteous usages refined by art.

187 C *ends abruptly here.*      187–8 A gift of Nature that *etc.*  J.
188 vulgar 𝔄 D²: common B² D.    190 thoughtful 𝔄 J D: studied D².
191 excess] its strength J B².      192 within] even in  J.
193 𝔄 D: D² *as* 1850 [194].

True is it, where oppression worse than death                    [195]
195 Salutes the Being at his birth, where grace
Of culture hath been utterly unknown,
And labour in excess and poverty
From day to day pre-occupy the ground
Of the affections, and to Nature's self                          [200]
200 Oppose a deeper nature, there indeed,
Love cannot be; nor does it easily thrive
In cities, where the human heart is sick,
And the eye feeds it not, and cannot feed:                       [205]
Thus far, no further, is that inference good.
205    Yes, in those wanderings deeply did I feel
How we mislead each other, above all
How Books mislead us, looking for their fame
To judgments of the wealthy Few, who see
By artificial lights, how they debase                            [210]
210 The Many for the pleasure of those Few
Effeminately level down the truth
To certain general notions for the sake
Of being understood at once, or else
Through want of better knowledge in the men                      [215]
215 Who frame them, flattering thus our self-conceit
With pictures that ambitiously set forth
The differences, the outside marks by which
Society has parted man from man,
Neglectful of the universal heart.                               [220]

220    Here calling up to mind what then I saw
A youthful Traveller, and see daily now
Before me in my rural neighbourhood,
Here might I pause, and bend in reverence
To Nature, and the power of human minds,                         [225]
225 To men as they are men within themselves.
How oft high service is perform'd within,
When all the external man is rude in shew,

194–7 These deem that bonds of natural amity
        Do seldom lay strong hold upon the hearts
        Of men in low estates, true inference
        Where want and the excess of Poverty  J.
194–8 Where culture hath been utterly unknown,
        And labour in excess and Poverty
        Have from the first preoccupied the ground  Z: Z² *as* A.
        Where labour in excess and poverty, *etc. as* Z, Y.

True is it, where oppression worse than death          195
Salutes the being at his birth, where grace
Of culture hath been utterly unknown,
And poverty and labour in excess
From day to day pre-occupy the ground
Of the affections, and to Nature's self          200
Oppose a deeper nature; there, indeed,
Love cannot be; nor does it thrive with ease
Among the close and overcrowded haunts
Of cities, where the human heart is sick,
And the eye feeds it not, and cannot feed.          205
—Yes, in those wanderings deeply did I feel
How we mislead each other; above all,
How books mislead us, seeking their reward
From judgments of the wealthy Few, who see
By artificial lights; how they debase          210
The Many for the pleasure of those Few;
Effeminately level down the truth
To certain general notions, for the sake
Of being understood at once, or else
Through want of better knowledge in the heads          215
That framed them; flattering self-conceit with words,
That, while they most ambitiously set forth
Extrinsic differences, the outward marks
Whereby society has parted man
From man, neglect the universal heart.          220


Here, calling up to mind what then I saw,
A youthful traveller, and see daily now
In the familiar circuit of my home,
Here might I pause, and bend in reverence
To Nature, and the power of human minds,          225
To men as they are men within themselves.
How oft high service is performed within,
When all the external man is rude in show,—

200–1 there indeed] true it is Y.    nature, true no less  J, *omitting* 201.
201–2 A² B² *as* 1850 [202–4].        203 the eye Z²: knowledge Z.
207–8 looking for their fame To 𝕬 D: seeking their reward From D².
215–19 B² D *as* 1850 (*but* [216] pictures *for* words *and* [219] By which *for*
Whereby). D² *as* 1850.
222 𝕬 D: D² *as* 1850: *not in* Y, *added to* Z.
226 service is perform'd] reverence is paid D: D² *as* 𝕬 *and* 1850.

Not like a temple rich with pomp and gold
But a mere mountain-Chapel such as shields                    [230]
230  Its simple worshippers from sun and shower.
Of these, said I, shall be my Song; of these,
If future years mature me for the task,
Will I record the praises, making Verse
Deal boldly with substantial things, in truth                    [235]
235  And sanctity of passion, speak of these
That justice may be done, obeisance paid
Where it is due: thus haply shall I teach,
Inspire, through unadulterated ears
Pour rapture, tenderness, and hope, my theme                    [240]
240  No other than the very heart of man
As found among the best of those who live
Not unexalted by religious hope,
Nor uninformed by books, good books though few,
In Nature's presence: thence may I select                    [245]
245  Sorrow that is not sorrow, but delight,
And miserable love that is not pain
To hear of, for the glory that redounds
Therefrom to human kind and what we are.
Be mine to follow with no timid step                    [250]
250  Where knowledge leads me; it shall be my pride
That I have dared to tread this holy ground,
Speaking no dream but things oracular,
Matter not lightly to be heard by those
Who to the letter of the outward promise                    [255]
255  Do read the invisible soul, by men adroit
In speech and for communion with the world
Accomplish'd, minds whose faculties are then
Most active when they are most eloquent
And elevated most when most admired.                    [260]
260  Men may be found of other mold than these,
Who are their own upholders, to themselves
Encouragement, and energy and will,
Expressing liveliest thoughts in lively words
As native passion dictates. Others, too,                    [265]
265  There are among the walks of homely life
Still higher, men for contemplation framed,

229 such as shields] that protects B².
233 record ℑ Y² Z²: rehearse Y Z.
238 ears ℑ Y² Z²: hearts Y Z.

Not like a temple rich with pomp and gold,
But a mere mountain chapel, that protects                    230
Its simple worshippers from sun and shower.
Of these, said I, shall be my song; of these,
If future years mature me for the task,
Will I record the praises, making verse
Deal boldly with substantial things; in truth               235
And sanctity of passion, speak of these,
That justice may be done, obeisance paid
Where it is due: thus haply shall I teach,
Inspire, through unadulterated ears
Pour rapture, tenderness, and hope,—my theme                240
No other than the very heart of man,
As found among the best of those who live,
Not unexalted by religious faith,
Nor uninformed by books, good books, though few,
In Nature's presence: thence may I select                   245
Sorrow, that is not sorrow, but delight;
And miserable love, that is not pain
To hear of, for the glory that redounds
Therefrom to human kind, and what we are.
Be mine to follow with no timid step                        250
Where knowledge leads me: it shall be my pride
That I have dared to tread this holy ground,
Speaking no dream, but things oracular;
Matter not lightly to be heard by those
Who to the letter of the outward promise                    255
Do read the invisible soul; by men adroit
In speech, and for communion with the world
Accomplished; minds whose faculties are then
Most active when they are most eloquent,
And elevated most when most admired.                        260
Men may be found of other mould than these,
Who are their own upholders, to themselves
Encouragement, and energy, and will,
Expressing liveliest thoughts in lively words
As native passion dictates. Others, too,                    265
There are among the walks of homely life
Still higher, men for contemplation framed,

239-44                              my theme
    The joys and pains of man, of men who live
    In Nature's presence, among these may find  Y.
242 hope] faith A² B².        260 other mold  Y² A: better make  Y.

Shy, and unpractis'd in the strife of phrase,
Meek men, whose very souls perhaps would sink
Beneath them, summon'd to such intercourse:     [270]
270 Theirs is the language of the heavens, the power,
The thought, the image, and the silent joy;
Words are but under-agents in their souls;
When they are grasping with their greatest strength
They do not breathe among them: this I speak     [275]
275 In gratitude to God, who feeds our hearts
For his own service, knoweth, loveth us
When we are unregarded by the world.

Also about this time did I receive
Convictions still more strong than heretofore     [280]
280 Not only that the inner frame is good,
And graciously composed, but that no less
Nature through all conditions hath a power
To consecrate, if we have eyes to see,     [285]
The outside of her creatures, and to breathe
285 Grandeur upon the very humblest face
Of human life. I felt that the array
Of outward circumstance and visible form
Is to the pleasure of the human mind
What passion makes it, that meanwhile the forms     [290]
290 Of Nature have a passion in themselves
That intermingles with those works of man
To which she summons him, although the works
Be mean, have nothing lofty of their own;
And that the genius of the Poet hence     [295]
295 May boldly take his way among mankind
Wherever Nature leads, that he hath stood
By Nature's side among the men of old,
And so shall stand for ever. Dearest Friend,
Forgive me if I say that I, who long
300 Had harbour'd reverentially a thought
That Poets, even as Prophets, each with each     [301]
Connected in a mighty scheme of truth,
Have each for his peculiar dower, a sense
By which he is enabled to perceive

274 do not Z²: scarcely Z.     277 the world] mankind Y.
279 More deep impressions even than heretofore Z: Impressions still
more deep than heretofore Z².
282 A D: D² *as* 1850.     287–9 B² *as* 1850.

Shy, and unpractised in the strife of phrase;
Meek men, whose very souls perhaps would sink
Beneath them, summoned to such intercourse:            270
Theirs is the language of the heavens, the power,
The thought, the image, and the silent joy:
Words are but under-agents in their souls;
When they are grasping with their greatest strength,
They do not breathe among them: this I speak          275
In gratitude to God, Who feeds our hearts
For His own service; knoweth, loveth us,
When we are unregarded by the world.

Also, about this time did I receive
Convictions still more strong than heretofore,         280
Not only that the inner frame is good,
And graciously composed, but that, no less,
Nature for all conditions wants not power
To consecrate. if we have eyes to see,
The outside of her creatures, and to breathe           285
Grandeur upon the very humblest face
Of human life. I felt that the array
Of act and circumstance, and visible form,
Is mainly to the pleasure of the mind
What passion makes them; that meanwhile the forms      290
Of Nature have a passion in themselves,
That intermingles with those works of man
To which she summons him; although the works
Be mean, have nothing lofty of their own;
And that the Genius of the Poet hence                  295
May boldly take his way among mankind
Wherever Nature leads; that he hath stood
By Nature's side among the men of old,
And so shall stand for ever. Dearest Friend!
If thou partake the animating faith                    300
That Poets, even as Prophets, each with each
Connected in a mighty scheme of truth,
Have each his own peculiar faculty,
Heaven's gift, a sense that fits him to perceive

291–2 That intermingle with the works of man
        Engrafted on her objects, tho' the works  Z:  Z² *as* 𝕬.
299–300 𝕬 D: A reverential thought had long been mine  D²: D³ *as* 1850.
303–4 𝕬 D: A² B² Whereby *for* By which;  D² *as* 1850.
303–14 D *stuck over*: D² *as* 1850.

305 Something unseen before; forgive me, Friend,                    [305]
    If I, the meanest of this Band, had hope
    That unto me had also been vouchsafed
    An influx, that in some sort I possess'd
    A privilege, and that a work of mine,
310 Proceeding from the depth of untaught things,                  [310]
    Enduring and creative, might become
    A power like one of Nature's. To such mood,
    Once above all, a Traveller at that time
    Upon the Plain of Sarum was I raised;
315 There on the pastoral Downs without a track                    [315]
    To guide me, or along the bare white roads
    Lengthening in solitude their dreary line,
    While through those vestiges of ancient times
    I ranged, and by the solitude o'ercome,
320 I had a reverie and saw the past,
    Saw multitudes of men, and here and there,                     [321]
    A single Briton in his wolf-skin vest
    With shield and stone-axe, stride across the Wold;
    The voice of spears was heard, the rattling spear
325 Shaken by arms of mighty bone, in strength                     [325]
    Long moulder'd of barbaric majesty.
    I called upon the darkness; and it took,
    A midnight darkness seem'd to come and take
    All objects from my sight; and lo! again
330 The desart visible by dismal flames!                           [330]
    It is the sacrificial Altar, fed
    With living men, how deep the groans, the voice
    Of those in the gigantic wicker thrills
    Throughout the region far and near, pervades
335 The monumental hillocks; and the pomp
    Is for both worlds, the living and the dead.                   [335]
    At other moments, for through that wide waste
    Three summer days I roam'd, when 'twas my chance
    To have before me on the downy Plain
340 Lines, circles, mounts, a mystery of shapes
    Such as in many quarters yet survive,
    With intricate profusion figuring o'er
    The untill'd ground, the work, as some divine,

310 the depth] a source B². 315–16 𝔄 D: D² *as* 1850.
319–20 I wandered, from the solitude proceeded
        A reverie, and I beheld the past B² D: D² *as* 1850.

Objects unseen before, thou wilt not blame                     305
The humblest of this band who dares to hope
That unto him hath also been vouchsafed
An insight that in some sort he possesses,
A privilege whereby a work of his,
Proceeding from a source of untaught things               310
Creative and enduring, may become
A power like one of Nature's. To a hope
Not less ambitious once among the wilds
Of Sarum's Plain, my youthful spirit was raised;
There, as I ranged at will the pastoral downs             315
Trackless and smooth, or paced the bare white roads
Lengthening in solitude their dreary line,
Time with his retinue of ages fled
Backwards, nor checked his flight until I saw
Our dim ancestral Past in vision clear;                   320
Saw multitudes of men, and, here and there,
A single Briton clothed in wolf-skin vest,
With shield and stone-axe, stride across the wold;
The voice of spears was heard, the rattling spear
Shaken by arms of mighty bone, in strength,               325
Long mouldered, of barbaric majesty.
I called on Darkness—but before the word
Was uttered, midnight darkness seemed to take
All objects from my sight; and lo! again
The Desert visible by dismal flames;                      330
It is the sacrificial altar, fed
With living men—how deep the groans! the voice
Of those that crowd the giant wicker thrills
The monumental hillocks, and the pomp
Is for both worlds, the living and the dead.              335
At other moments (for through that wide waste
Three summer days I roamed) where'er the Plain
Was figured o'er with circles, lines, or mounds,
That yet survive, a work, as some divine,

327–8 I called on darkness and it came to take
330–1 The desart visible by flames that mount
          Up from the sacrificial altar, fed B² D: D² *as* 1850.
333 in the gigantic] that throng the giant A²; that crowd the giant B².
334 A *deletes*          338 rang'd Z: roam'd Z².
343 the work] rude work A². A work of mystery as some divine D: D²
*as* 1850.

            Of infant science, imitative forms
345  By which the Druids covertly express'd
            Their knowledge of the heavens, and imaged forth        [341]
            The constellations, I was gently charm'd,
            Albeit with an antiquarian's dream,
            And saw the bearded Teachers, with white wands          [345]
350  Uplifted, pointing to the starry sky
            Alternately, and Plain below, while breath
            Of music seem'd to guide them, and the Waste
            Was chear'd with stillness and a pleasant sound.


            This for the past, and things that may be view'd        [350]
355  Or fancied, in the obscurities of time.
            Nor is it, Friend, unknown to thee, at least
            Thyself delighted, who for my delight
            Hast said, perusing some imperfect verse
            Which in that lonesome journey was composed,
360  That also then I must have exercised                           [355]
            Upon the vulgar forms of present things
            And actual world of our familiar days,
            A higher power, have caught from them a tone,
            An image, and a character, by books
365  Not hitherto reflected. Call we this                           [360]
            But a persuasion taken up by Thee
            In friendship; yet the mind is to herself
            Witness and judge, and I remember well

344 B *deletes.*          345 express'd] preserved A².
345-7 B² *as* 1850.          348-9 𝔄 D: D² *as* 1850.
351-3                                  while notes
            Of music seemed to guide them, strains that chear'd
            The widely list'ning Waste with still delight
            Intense, from voice or viewless harp diffused A²: D *as* 𝔄: D²
                *as* 1850.
[352] monumental D E²: antiquarian E.      356-63 𝔄 D: D² *as* 1850.
357 Thyself pleased highly—for my pleasure, Thou A².
362 actual Z²: living Z.          363 higher] loftier A².
366-9 But a persuasion taken up by thee
            In friendship—no—that could not be—for then
            We two were strangers—and I must not speak
            Thus wrongfully of strains which were to thee ⎫
            An instantaneous opening from afar              ⎬ *deleted.*
            In splendid oneness (?) to thy youthful mind ⎭
            Thus wrongfully of verse to which I owe
            So much, so much of thy profounder Love
            I must have courage to proclaim thy joy

Shaped by the Druids, so to represent                340
Their knowledge of the heavens, and image forth
The constellations; gently was I charmed
Into a waking dream, a reverie
That, with believing eyes, where'er I turned,
Beheld long-bearded teachers, with white wands     345
Uplifted, pointing to the starry sky,
Alternately, and plain below, while breath
Of music swayed their motions, and the waste
Rejoiced with them and me in those sweet sounds.

   This for the past, and things that may be viewed   350
Or fancied in the obscurity of years
From monumental hints: and thou, O Friend!
Pleased with some unpremeditated strains
That served those wanderings to beguile, hast said
That then and there my mind had exercised           355
Upon the vulgar forms of present things,
The actual world of our familiar days,
Yet higher power; had caught from them a tone,
An image, and a character, by books
Not hitherto reflected. Call we this                360
A partial judgment—and yet why? for *then*
We were as strangers; and I may not speak
Thus wrongfully of verse, however rude,
Which on thy young imagination, trained
In the great City, broke like light from far.       365
Moreover, each man's Mind is to herself
Witness and judge; and I remember well

    And for a moment tread with steps serene
    The elevation of thy gratitude.
    Moreover my own mind is to herself
    Witness and judge A² (*deleted*).
    But a persuasion taken up by thee
    In friendship—yet not so, for at that time
    We were as strangers  A² B² Z
    and I may not speak
    Thus wrongfully of verse, however rude,
    Which to thy youthful Fancy did appear
    An instantaneous opening from afar
    Of verse to whose preparatory gifts
    I owe so much of thy profounder love
    Moreover my own mind is to herself *etc.*  A³.  *So* D, *but omitting*
Of verse . . . profounder love: D² *as* 1850.

That in life's every-day appearances
370 I seem'd about this period to have sight
Of a new world, a world, too, that was fit [370]
To be transmitted and made visible
To other eyes, as having for its base
That whence our dignity originates,
375 That which both gives it being and maintains
A balance, an ennobling interchange [375]
Of action from within and from without,
The excellence, pure spirit, and best power
Both of the object seen, and eye that sees.

369–70 Z² 𝔄: B² *as* 1850: That at this time I seem'd to have the sight Z.
372–5 𝔄 D: D² *as* 1850.
374 Z² 𝔄: That in which human dignity consists Z.
378 spirit 𝔄 D: function D².

That in life's every-day appearances
I seemed about this time to gain clear sight
Of a new world—a world, too, that was fit                    370
To be transmitted, and to other eyes
Made visible; as ruled by those fixed laws
Whence spiritual dignity originates,
Which do both give it being and maintain
A balance, an ennobling interchange                          375
Of action from without and from within;
The excellence, pure function, and best power
Both of the object seen, and eye that sees.

# BOOK THIRTEENTH

## CONCLUSION

In one of these excursions, travelling then
Through Wales on foot, and with a youthful Friend,
I left Bethkelet's huts at couching-time,
And westward took my way to see the sun                          [5]
5   Rise from the top of Snowdon. Having reach'd
The Cottage at the Mountain's foot, we there
Rouz'd up the Shepherd, who by ancient right
Of office is the Stranger's usual Guide;
And after short refreshment sallied forth.                       [10]

10     It was a Summer's night, a close warm night,
Wan, dull and glaring, with a dripping mist
Low-hung and thick that cover'd all the sky,
Half threatening storm and rain; but on we went
Uncheck'd, being full of heart and having faith
15  In our tried Pilot. Little could we see
Hemm'd round on every side with fog and damp,
And, after ordinary Travellers' chat                             [16]
With our Conductor, silently we sank
Each into commerce with his private thoughts:
20  Thus did we breast the ascent, and by myself
Was nothing either seen or heard the while                       [20]
Which took me from my musings, save that once
The Shepherd's Cur did to his own great joy

[MSS. for Bk. XIII: A B D E: *for ll.* 1–135, 154–65 W; *for ll.* 184–203 J;
*for ll.* 334–67, 374–85 Y.]
   Book Thirteenth Conclusion B: *no heading in* A.
   1 Once (but I must premise that several years
      Are overleap'd to reach this incident W (*deleted*).
   1–3 Once when a Youth and with a youthful friend
         Travelling along the region of North Wales
         We left *etc.* W.
   1–3 In one of those Excursions (may they neer
         Fade from my thoughts nor be with less delight
         Remember'd!) travelling with a youthful Friend
         Along the northern Tract of Wales, I left
         Bethkelert's peaceful Huts at Couching-time. A² B² D, *but* B² D mind
*for* thoughts: D² *as* 1850.
   3 Bethkelet  A: *corrected by W. W. in another draft to* Bethkeler.

# BOOK FOURTEENTH

## CONCLUSION

IN one of those excursions (may they ne'er
Fade from remembrance!) through the Northern tracts
Of Cambria ranging with a youthful friend,
I left Bethgelert's huts at couching-time,
And westward took my way, to see the sun   5
Rise from the top of Snowdon. To the door
Of a rude cottage at the mountain's base
We came, and roused the shepherd who attends
The adventurous stranger's steps, a trusty guide;
Then, cheered by short refreshment, sallied forth.  10

It was a close, warm, breezeless summer night,
Wan, dull, and glaring, with a dripping fog
Low-hung and thick that covered all the sky;
But, undiscouraged, we began to climb
The mountain-side. The mist soon girt us round,  15
And, after ordinary travellers' talk
With our conductor, pensively we sank
Each into commerce with his private thoughts:
Thus did we breast the ascent, and by myself
Was nothing either seen or heard that checked  20
Those musings or diverted, save that once
The shepherd's lurcher, who, among the crags,

5–8     To the door
Of a rude cottage near the mountain's     at
 base
Arrived, we rouzed the Shepherd who We came and rouz'd B² D:  D² *as*
 by right A².        1850.
           Having reached
   The cottage at the mountain's foot, we rouz'd
   The shepherd up who is the Stranger's guide  W.
 9 And after short repose we *etc.*  W.
 13–18 B² *as* 1850.
 13–14 But we were undismay'd such faith was ours  A².
 14 being full of heart] being young and blithe  W.
 17 chat 𝕬: talk  A² B².
 18 silently] pensively  B².
 21–22 𝕬 D:  D² *as* 1850.
 23–24 The shepherd's Mongrel to his own great joy
   Unearthed a Hedgehog in the crags and teased  D:  D² *as* 1850.

Unearth a Hedgehog in the mountain crags
25 Round which he made a barking turbulent.
This small adventure, for even such it seem'd [25]
In that wild place and at the dead of night,
Being over and forgotten, on we wound
In silence as before. With forehead bent
30 Earthward, as if in opposition set
Against an enemy, I panted up [30]
With eager pace, and no less eager thoughts.
Thus might we wear perhaps an hour away,
Ascending at loose distance each from each,
35 And I, as chanced, the foremost of the Band; 
When at my feet the ground appear'd to brighten, [35]
And with a step or two seem'd brighter still;
Nor had I time to ask the cause of this,
For instantly a Light upon the turf
40 Fell like a flash: I looked about, and lo!
The Moon stood naked in the Heavens, at height [40]
Immense above my head, and on the shore
I found myself of a huge sea of mist,
Which, meek and silent, rested at my feet:
45 A hundred hills their dusky backs upheaved
All over this still Ocean, and beyond,
Far, far beyond, the vapours shot themselves, [45]
In headlands, tongues, and promontory shapes,
Into the Sea, the real Sea, that seem'd
50 To dwindle, and give up its majesty,
Usurp'd upon as far as sight could reach.
Meanwhile, the Moon look'd down upon this shew

29-30 With forehead bent Earthward] With face towards The hill W.
32 pace] steps W.     33 perhaps an] a midnight A² B².
34 Ascending] Straggling W.
36-40 When at my feet the ground in gentle sort
        Brighten'd, at least I fancied that it looked
        More bright in that half dream which wrapp'd me up
        Nor had I time to ask if it were so
        For instantly a light before my eyes
        Fell like a flash etc. W.
37 seem'd brighter still A D²: became more bright B² D.
38 A² B² as 1850.     41 stood] hung B² D.
40     Fell like a flash; a startling gleam, yet mild
        The shock, and gentle: I look'd up, and lo! A².
43-44 Of a huge sea, in clear and open air
        I found myself, a billowy sea of mist A².
        I stood, and saw a billowy sea of mist D: D² as 1850.

Had to his joy unearthed a hedgehog, teased
His coiled-up prey with barkings turbulent.
This small adventure, for even such it seemed                         25
In that wild place and at the dead of night,
Being over and forgotten, on we wound
In silence as before. With forehead bent
Earthward, as if in opposition set
Against an enemy, I panted up                                        30
With eager pace, and no less eager thoughts.
Thus might we wear a midnight hour away,
Ascending at loose distance each from each,
And I, as chanced, the foremost of the band;
When at my feet the ground appeared to brighten,                     35
And with a step or two seemed brighter still;
Nor was time given to ask or learn the cause,
For instantly a light upon the turf
Fell like a flash, and lo! as I looked up,
The Moon hung naked in a firmament                                   40
Of azure without cloud, and at my feet
Rested a silent sea of hoary mist.
A hundred hills their dusky backs upheaved
All over this still ocean; and beyond,
Far, far beyond, the solid vapours stretched,                        45
In headlands, tongues, and promontory shapes,
Into the main Atlantic, that appeared
To dwindle, and give up his majesty,
Usurped upon far as the sight could reach.
Not so the ethereal vault; encroachment none                         50
Was there, nor loss; only the inferior stars
Had disappeared, or shed a fainter light

46/47 *Between these lines* A B *add* Throughout the wide dominion of the
West; *but* A *deletes.*
47 vapours shot themselves] solid vapours stretched A² B².
49 Into the Atlantic [ ] A²: B² *as* 1850.
51-56 Not so the ethereal vault—encroachment none
         Was there, save only that the inferior stars
         Had disappear'd before the full orb'd Moon
         That from her sover[eign] . . .
         In plenitude of solitary state:
         And while we stood, the hoary mists our feet
         Touching, we saw, at distance from the shore
         Not twice the measure of an arrow's flight
         A dark blue chasm *etc.* A³.
[51-77] *stuck over in* D: D² [51-60] *as* 1850.
52 Meanwhile, the] The radiant A².

In single glory, and we stood, the mist
Touching our very feet; and from the shore
55 At distance not the third part of a mile
Was a blue chasm; a fracture in the vapour,
A deep and gloomy breathing-place through which
Mounted the roar of waters, torrents, streams
Innumerable, roaring with one voice.                      [60]
60 The universal spectacle throughout
Was shaped for admiration and delight,
Grand in itself alone, but in that breach
Through which the homeless voice of waters rose,
That dark deep thoroughfare had Nature lodg'd
65 The Soul, the Imagination of the whole.

A meditation rose in me that night
Upon the lonely Mountain when the scene
Had pass'd away, and it appear'd to me
The perfect image of a mighty Mind,                      [70]
70 Of one that feeds upon infinity,

53 single W²: lonesome W.
55 Not distant more perchance than half a mile  W:  W³ *as* 𝔄.
56 a blue A W: all a  A². vapour] mist W: amid the vapoury [?]  W².
59 Innumerable] Inseparable  W.
60–65 The universal . . . whole]
        The universal spectacle was shaped
        For admiration; for delight was framed
        In all that it displayed but in that breach *etc.*  A².
        The universal spectacle was shaped
        For admiration, with magnificence
        Impregnated, but in that stedfast breach *etc. as*  𝔄 E:
[61–62] Heard over earth and felt (for so it seemed
        At that still hour) up to the starry heavens.  E²:  E³ *as* 1850.
62 in itself alone] in its single self  W.
[63–71] When into air had quietly dissolved
        That vision, given to Spirits of the night
        And three chance human wanderers, when the marvel
        Was seen no more, it offered to my thoughts
        The type or image of a mighty mind
        That feeds upon infinity, that broods  D² E:  E² *as* 1850.
66–89 Even yet thou wilt vouchsafe an ear my Friend
        As to this prelude thou I know hast done
        And something too of a submissive mind
    ·  As in thy mildness Thou I know hast done
        While with a winding but no devious song
        Through [        ] processes I make my way
        By links of tender thought. My present aim
        Is to contemplate for a needful while
        Following a track which would in season [        ]

In the clear presence of the full-orbed Moon,
Who, from her sovereign elevation, gazed
Upon the billowy ocean, as it lay                                    55
All meek and silent, save that through a rift—
Not distant from the shore whereon we stood,
A fixed, abysmal, gloomy, breathing-place—
Mounted the roar of waters, torrents, streams
Innumerable, roaring with one voice!                                 60
Heard over earth and sea, and, in that hour,
For so it seemed, felt by the starry heavens.

　　When into air had partially dissolved
That vision, given to spirits of the night
And three chance human wanderers, in calm thought                   65
Reflected, it appeared to me the type
Of a majestic intellect, its acts
And its possessions, what it has and craves,
What in itself it is, and would become.
There I beheld the emblem of a mind                                  70
That feeds upon infinity, that broods

　　　(Passage which will conduct in season due
　　　Back to the tale which we have left behind)
　　　The diverse manner in which Nature works
　　　Oft times, upon the outward face of things,
　　　As if with an imaginative power
　　　I mean so moulds, exalts, indues, combines,
　　　Impregnates, separates, adds, takes away
　　　And makes one object sway another so
　　　By unhabitual influence or abrupt
　　　That even the grossest minds must see and hear
　　　And cannot chuse but feel. The power which these
　　　Acknowledge, ⎫
　　　Are touch'd by, ⎭ being so mov'd, which Nature thus
　　　Thrusts ⎫
　　　Puts 　 ⎭ forth upon the senses (not to speak
　　　Of finer operations) is in kind
　　　A Brother of the very faculty  W.
68–69　it appeared to me The perfect *etc.*] to my thoughts it showed
　　　　　　　　Embodied in material portraiture
　　　　　　　　The perfect *etc.*  A² B².
68–72　　　　　and to my thoughts it gave
　　　A shadowy image of a mighty Mind
　　　That while it copes with visible shapes hears also
　　　Through vents and openings in the ideal world
　　　The astounding chorus of infinity
　　　Exalted by an underconsciousness
　　　Of depth not faithless, the sustaining thought
　　　Of God in human Being, *Another draft by W. W. in* A.

That is exalted by an under-presence,
The sense of God, or whatsoe'er is dim
Or vast in its own being, above all
One function of such mind had Nature there
75 Exhibited by putting forth, and that
With circumstance most awful and sublime,                 [80]
That domination which she oftentimes
Exerts upon the outward face of things,
So moulds them, and endues, abstracts, combines,
80 Or by abrupt and unhabitual influence
Doth make one object so impress itself
Upon all others, and pervade them so
That even the grossest minds must see and hear           [85]
And cannot chuse but feel. The Power which these
85 Acknowledge when thus moved, which Nature thus
Thrusts forth upon the senses, is the express
Resemblance, in the fulness of its strength
Made visible, a genuine Counterpart
And Brother of the glorious faculty
90 Which higher minds bear with them as their own.         [90]
That is the very spirit in which they deal
With all the objects of the universe;
They from their native selves can send abroad
Like transformation, for themselves create
95 A like existence, and, whene'er it is                    [95]
Created for them, catch it by an instinct;
Them the enduring and the transient both                 [100]

71 Exalted by an underconsciousness A² B².
73 in its own being, above all] in the sustaining power profound
        Of its own human being. Above all  A² B².
75-76 and that With] with pomp Of  A² B².
[74] A mind instinct with faculties sustained  D²: D³ as 1850.
[76] conducting to  D³ E: exalted by  D².
79-83 Moulds them; abstracts, combines; and so endows
        With interchangeable supremacy
        Making one object so diffuse its influence
        Among all others and pervade and fill
        Their several frames with such commanding virtue
        That even etc.  A².
86-88 Exhibits to the senses, is the express
        Resemblance, say a genuine counterpart  D: D² as 1850.
91-92 not in W.        92 ℔ D: D² as 1850.
93 ff. These from their native selves can deal about
        Like transformation, to one life impart
        The functions of another, shift, create,

Over the dark abyss, intent to hear
Its voices issuing forth to silent light
In one continuous stream; a mind sustained
By recognitions of transcendent power,                    75
In sense conducting to ideal form,
In soul of more than mortal privilege.
One function, above all, of such a mind
Had Nature shadowed there, by putting forth,
'Mid circumstances awful and sublime,                     80
That mutual domination which she loves
To exert upon the face of outward things,
So moulded, joined, abstracted, so endowed
With interchangeable supremacy,
That men, least sensitive, see, hear, perceive,           85
And cannot choose but feel. The power, which all
Acknowledge when thus moved, which Nature thus
To bodily sense exhibits, is the express
Resemblance of that glorious faculty
That higher minds bear with them as their own.            90
This is the very spirit in which they deal
With the whole compass of the universe:
They from their native selves can send abroad
Kindred mutations; for themselves create
A like existence; and, whene'er it dawns                  95
Created for them, catch it, or are caught
By its inevitable mastery,
Like angels stopped upon the wing by sound
Of harmony from Heaven's remotest spheres.
Them the enduring and the transient both                  100

Trafficking with immeasurable thoughts. W (*for continuation of*
**W** *v. notes*).

93 They from the seats of passion or calm thought Within their native
selves *etc.* B².

96-97                              catch it by an instinct,
        Say rather by an intellectual sense
        Or attribute, inevitably fine;
        Enraptur'd, awed, suspended or inspired
        As Angels on the wing when Music speaks
        In the remotest quarters of the heavens,
        So they perceive, and so they think, though then
        Mortal, and Tenants of this nether sphere
        Where change and grief and wretchedness prevail
        Them the enduring *etc.* A² B².
                              catch it by the aid
        Of attributes inevitably fine
        Them the enduring *etc.* A³.

Serve to exalt; they build up greatest things
From least suggestions, ever on the watch,
100 Willing to work and to be wrought upon,
They need not extraordinary calls
To rouze them, in a world of life they live,                    [105]
By sensible impressions not enthrall'd,
But quicken'd, rouz'd, and made thereby more fit
105 To hold communion with the invisible world.
Such minds are truly from the Deity,
For they are Powers; and hence the highest bliss
That can be known is theirs, the consciousness
Of whom they are habitually infused                    [115]
110 Through every image, and through every thought,
And all impressions; hence religion, faith
And endless occupation for the soul
Whether discursive or intuitive;                    [120]
Hence sovereignty within and peace at will
115 Emotion which best foresight need not fear
Most worthy then of trust when most intense.
Hence chearfulness in every act of life
Hence truth in moral judgements and delight
That fails not in the external universe.

120      Oh! who is he that hath his whole life long                    [130]
Preserved, enlarged this freedom in himself?
For this alone is genuine Liberty.
Witness, ye Solitudes! where I received

104 fit 𝔄: apt A²; But by their quickening virtue made more apt D.
105 𝔄 D E: E² *as* 1850 [108–11].
[108-10] To hold apt converse [To hold communion D] with the invisible
        world
          And with the generations of mankind
          Spread o'er past time, time present and to come E²: E³ *as* 1850.
[109–11] *not in* D: *added to* E, *with, as earlier drafts of* [110],
          (1) Both of past time, time present and to come,
          (2) From present time to past, from both to future,
108 That can be known] That Man can know A²: That Man may know
B²: Earth *for* Man D: D² *as* 1850.
111 impressions] perceptions A².
[115–27] D *stuck over*: D² *as* [116–29], *but in* [128] this pure source D³ E:
Power divine D: God's free gift D².
123–8 Among the living or the mighty dead
          Where is the favoured Being who hath held
          Such course uncheck'd, unerring and untired
          In one perpetual progress bright and pure?
     v A humbler destiny have we retraced
          And told of lapse and devious wandering, yet
          Encompassed round by mountain solitudes

Serve to exalt; they build up greatest things
From least suggestions; ever on the watch,
Willing to work and to be wrought upon,
They need not extraordinary calls
To rouse them; in a world of life they live,     105
By sensible impressions not enthralled,
But by their quickening impulse made more prompt
To hold fit converse with the spiritual world,
And with the generations of mankind
Spread over time, past, present, and to come,     110
Age after age, till Time shall be no more.
Such minds are truly from the Deity,
For they are Powers; and hence the highest bliss
That flesh can know is theirs—the consciousness
Of Whom they are, habitually infused     115
Through every image and through every thought,
And all affections by communion raised
From earth to heaven, from human to divine;
Hence endless occupation for the Soul,
Whether discursive or intuitive;     120
Hence cheerfulness for acts of daily life,
Emotions which best foresight need not fear,
Most worthy then of trust when most intense.
Hence, amid ills that vex and wrongs that crush
Our hearts—if here the words of Holy Writ     125
May with fit reverence be applied—that peace
Which passeth understanding, that repose
In moral judgments which from this pure source
Must come, or will by man be sought in vain.

Oh! who is he that hath his whole life long     130
Preserved, enlarged, this freedom in himself?
For this alone is genuine liberty:

> Within whose holy Temple I received . . . powers (*as* A 124–7)
> Before their presence with a grateful heart
> x Do I declare in accents which by truth
> And harmony exalted shall not fear
> To blend their murmur with these solemn streams
> That whatsoever falls my better mind *etc.* A². *So* B², *but* Spirit (ii)
*for* Being *and* (vii) by these *for* round by.
> *So* A³, *but for* vi–vii:
> Of lapse and devious wandering have we told
> Yet bear ye witness mountain solitudes *etc.*, *and in* x While I
affirm *etc.*; D *as* B², *but omitting* And yet . . . grateful heart, *and reading in*
xii To blend while from my grateful heart they flow: D² *as* 1850.

My earliest visitations, careless then                    [141]
125 Of what was given me, and where now I roam,
A meditative, oft a suffering Man,                         [143]
And yet, I trust, with undiminish'd powers,
Witness, whatever falls my better mind,
Revolving with the accidents of life,
130 May have sustain'd, that, howsoe'er misled,
I never, in the quest of right and wrong,              [150]
Did tamper with myself from private aims;
Nor was in any of my hopes the dupe
Of selfish passions; nor did wilfully
135 Yield ever to mean cares and low pursuits;
But rather did with jealousy shrink back               [155]
From every combination that might aid
The tendency, too potent in itself,
Of habit to enslave the mind, I mean
140 Oppress it by the laws of vulgar sense,
And substitute a universe of death,                     [160]
The falsest of all worlds, in place of that
Which is divine and true. To fear and love, ·
To love as first and chief, for there fear ends,
145 Be this ascribed; to early intercourse,
In presence of sublime and lovely Forms,            [165]
With the adverse principles of pain and joy,
Evil as one is rashly named by those
Who know not what they say. From love, for here
150 Do we begin and end, all grandeur comes,
All truth and beauty, from pervading love,
That gone, we are as dust. Behold the fields          [170]
In balmy spring-time, full of rising flowers
And happy creatures; see that Pair, the Lamb
155 And the Lamb's Mother, and their tender ways

---

[157–61] D *stuck over.* D² *as* 1850.
139 Of use and custom to enslave the mind A².
142–3 The falsest of all worlds for the divine
       And actual universe. To *etc.* A².
146 and lovely] or beauteous A².          149 say] speak A².
154 happy] sportive A²: joyous A³: gladsome A⁴: blissful B².

Where is the favoured being who hath held
That course unchecked, unerring, and untired,
In one perpetual progress smooth and bright ?—  135
A humbler destiny have we retraced,
And told of lapse and hesitating choice,
And backward wanderings along thorny ways:
Yet—compassed round by mountain solitudes,
Within whose solemn temple I received  140
My earliest visitations, careless then
Of what was given me ; and which now I range,
A meditative, oft a suffering man—
Do I declare—in accents which, from truth
Deriving cheerful confidence, shall blend  145
Their modulation with these vocal streams—
That, whatsoever falls my better mind,
Revolving with the accidents of life,
May have sustained, that, howsoe'er misled,
Never did I, in quest of right and wrong,  150
Tamper with conscience from a private aim ;
Nor was in any public hope the dupe
Of selfish passions ; nor did ever yield
Wilfully to mean cares or low pursuits,
But shrunk with apprehensive jealousy  155
From every combination which might aid
The tendency, too potent in itself,
Of use and custom to bow down the soul
Under a growing weight of vulgar sense,
And substitute a universe of death  160
For that which moves with light and life informed,
Actual, divine, and true. To fear and love,
To love as prime and chief, for there fear ends,
Be this ascribed ; to early intercourse,
In presence of sublime or beautiful forms,  165
With the adverse principles of pain and joy—
Evil as one is rashly named by men
Who know not what they speak. By love subsists
All lasting grandeur, by pervading love ;
That gone, we are as dust.—Behold the fields  170
In balmy spring-time full of rising flowers
And joyous creatures ; see that pair, the lamb
And the lamb's mother, and their tender ways

Shall touch thee to the heart; in some green bower
Rest, and be not alone, but have thou there
The One who is thy choice of all the world,                    [178]
There linger, lull'd and lost, and rapt away,
160  Be happy to thy fill; thou call'st this love
And so it is, but there is higher love                    [175]
Than this, a love that comes into the heart
With awe and a diffusive sentiment;
Thy love is human merely; this proceeds
165  More from the brooding Soul, and is divine.

This love more intellectual cannot be
Without Imagination, which, in truth,
Is but another name for absolute strength                    [190]
And clearest insight, amplitude of mind,
170  And reason in her most exalted mood.
This faculty hath been the moving soul
Of our long labour: we have traced the stream
From darkness, and the very place of birth
In its blind cavern, whence is faintly heard                    [195]
175  The sound of waters; follow'd it to light
And open day, accompanied its course
Among the ways of Nature, afterwards
Lost sight of it, bewilder'd and engulph'd,
Then given it greeting, as it rose once more                    [200]
180  With strength, reflecting in its solemn breast

156–60 In some green bower . . . fill  B: *not in* W *or* A (*orig. text*):
156–66              In some green bower
        Rest *etc.* . . . world
        There linger, soothed and lost and rapt away,
        Lulled by her voice, enchanted by her eyes,
        Be happy to thy fill. Thou callest this love
        Rightly bestow'st that name on both delights
        The mild and passionate; but higher love
        Exists a love that breathes not without awe
        Thy love is human *etc.* . . . divine. A².
        To both delights the mild and passionate
        Though different in kind and in degree
        Do thy affections give the name of love
        And rightly so, but there is higher love
        Thy love is human *etc.* A³.
    *Then, added later,*
        Passion from all disturbing influence pure
        Foretaste of beatific sentiment
        Bestowed in mercy on a world condemned
        To mutability [to] pain and grief

Shall touch thee to the heart; thou callest this love,
And not inaptly so, for love it is,                                    175
Far as it carries thee. In some green bower
Rest, and be not alone, but have thou there
The One who is thy choice of all the world:
There linger, listening, gazing, with delight
Impassioned, but delight how pitiable!                                 180
Unless this love by a still higher love
Be hallowed, love that breathes not without awe;
Love that adores, but on the knees of prayer,
By heaven inspired; that frees from chains the soul,
Lifted, in union with the purest, best,                                185
Of earth-born passions, on the wings of praise
Bearing a tribute to the Almighty's Throne.

This spiritual Love acts not nor can exist
Without Imagination, which, in truth,
Is but another name for absolute power                                 190
And clearest insight, amplitude of mind,
And Reason in her most exalted mood.
This faculty hath been the feeding source
Of our long labour: we have traced the stream
From the blind cavern whence is faintly heard                          195
Its natal murmur; followed it to light
And open day; accompanied its course
Among the ways of Nature, for a time
Lost sight of it bewildered and engulphed:
Then given it greeting as it rose once more                            200
In strength, reflecting from its placid breast

Terrestrial Nature's sure inheritance.
Such love *etc. as* 𝔄 166.
[181] still higher E²: far higher E.
[185–7] Lifted above the fairest, purest, best
    Of mortal passions, on the wings of praise,
    Its tribute bearing *etc.* D;
    Bearing in union with the purest best
    Of earthborn passions on the wings of praise
    A mutual tribute *etc.* E². (*No MS. authority for* 1850.)
165/6 Passion from all disturbing influence pure
    Foretaste of beatific sentiment
    Bestowed in mercy on a world condemned
    To mutability [and] pain and grief
    Terrestrial nature's sure inheritance A².
166 love more intellectual] intellectual feeling B².
173–80 B² *as* 1850.

The works of man and face of human life,
And lastly, from its progress have we drawn
The feeling of life endless, the great thought
By which we live, Infinity and God.      [205]
185 Imagination having been our theme,
So also hath that intellectual love,
For they are each in each, and cannot stand
Dividually.—Here must thou be, O Man!
Strength to thyself; no Helper hast thou here;      [210]
190 Here keepest thou thy individual state:
No other can divide with thee this work,
No secondary hand can intervene
To fashion this ability; 'tis thine,
The prime and vital principle is thine      [215]
195 In the recesses of thy nature, far
From any reach of outward fellowship,
Else 'tis not thine at all. But joy to him,
Oh! joy to him who here hath sown, hath laid
Here the foundations of his future years!      [220]
200 For all that friendship, all that love can do,
All that a darling countenance can look
Or dear voice utter to complete the man,
Perfect him, made imperfect in himself,
All shall be his: and he whose soul hath risen      [225]
205 Up to the height of feeling intellect
Shall want no humbler tenderness, his heart
Be tender as a nursing Mother's heart;
Of female softness shall his life be full,
Of little loves and delicate desires,      [230]
210 Mild interests and gentlest sympathies.

Child of my Parents! Sister of my Soul!
Elsewhere have strains of gratitude been breath'd
To thee for all the early tenderness
Which I from thee imbibed. And true it is      [235]
215 That later seasons owed to thee no less;
For, spite of thy sweet influence and the touch
Of other kindred hands that open'd out

183-4 𝔄 D (*but* A² B² D one *for* great): D² *as* 1850.
189 𝔄 D: Power to D²: Strength and resource and succour to thyself A².
190 thy individual 𝔄 D: in singleness thy D².
209 little loves] humble cares A² B².      212-13 B² *as* 1850.

The works of man and face of human life;
And lastly, from its progress have we drawn
Faith in life endless, the sustaining thought
Of human Being, Eternity, and God.　　　　205

　　Imagination having been our theme,
So also hath that intellectual Love,
For they are each in each, and cannot stand
Dividually.—Here must thou be, O Man!
Power to thyself; no Helper hast thou here;　　　210
Here keepest thou in singleness thy state:
No other can divide with thee this work:
No secondary hand can intervene
To fashion this ability; 'tis thine,
The prime and vital principle is thine　　　215
In the recesses of thy nature, far
From any reach of outward fellowship,
Else is not thine at all. But joy to him,
Oh, joy to him who here hath sown, hath laid
Here, the foundation of his future years!　　　220
For all that friendship, all that love can do,
All that a darling countenance can look
Or dear voice utter, to complete the man,
Perfect him, made imperfect in himself,
All shall be his: and he whose soul hath risen　　　225
Up to the height of feeling intellect
Shall want no humbler tenderness; his heart
Be tender as a nursing mother's heart;
Of female softness shall his life be full,
Of humble cares and delicate desires,　　　230
Mild interests and gentlest sympathies.

　　Child of my parents! Sister of my soul!
Thanks in sincerest verse have been elsewhere
Poured out for all the early tenderness
Which I from thee imbibed: and 'tis most true　　　235
That later seasons owed to thee no less;
For, spite of thy sweet influence and the touch
Of kindred hands that opened out the springs

214 true it is] 'tis most true B².
217-18 D *as* 1850, *but* in infancy or childhood *for* in childhood, and in spite.

The springs of tender thought in infancy,
And spite of all which singly I had watch'd                              [240]
220 Of elegance, and each minuter charm
In nature and in life, still to the last
Even to the very going out of youth,
The period which our Story now hath reach'd,
I too exclusively esteem'd that love,
225 And sought that beauty, which, as Milton sings,                     [245]
Hath terror in it. Thou didst soften down
This over-sternness; but for thee, sweet Friend,
My soul, too reckless of mild grace, had been
Far longer what by Nature it was framed,
230 Longer retain'd its countenance severe,                             [250]
A rock with torrents roaring, with the clouds
Familiar, and a favorite of the Stars:
But thou didst plant its crevices with flowers,
Hang it with shrubs that twinkle in the breeze,
235 And teach the little birds to build their nests                     [255]
And warble in its chambers. At a time
When Nature, destined to remain so long
Foremost in my affections, had fallen back
Into a second place, well pleas'd to be
240 A Handmaid to a nobler than herself,                                [260]
When every day brought with it some new sense
Of exquisite regard for common things,
And all the earth was budding with these gifts
Of more refined humanity, thy breath,
245 Dear Sister, was a kind of gentler spring                           [265]
That went before my steps.
                                    With such a theme,                  [275]
Coleridge! with this my argument, of thee

219–23 𝔄 D: D² *as* 1850.
228 too reckless 𝔄 D: not studious A². been] stood A² B².
229–30 Confiding in its own original frame
            And held too long its countenance severe. A².    Retained too long
*etc.* A³ B² D: *but* self *for* frame B² D: D² *as* 1850.
[266–74] *Not in* 𝔄:
                                    Thereafter came
            One who in friendship had been early pair'd
            No more an apparition to ador[n]
            A moment, but an Inmate of the heart
            In feminine humility arrayed
            And yet a Spirit still, by words and looks
            And nameless influences, high and low,

Of genial thought in childhood, and in spite
Of all that unassisted I had marked                          240
In life or nature of those charms minute
That win their way into the heart by stealth
(Still to the very going-out of youth),
I too exclusively esteemed *that* love,
And sought *that* beauty, which, as Milton sings,            245
Hath terror in it. Thou didst soften down
This over-sternness; but for thee, dear Friend!
My soul, too reckless of mild grace, had stood
In her original self too confident,
Retained too long a countenance severe;                      250
A rock with torrents roaring, with the clouds
Familiar, and a favourite of the stars:
But thou didst plant its crevices with flowers,
Hang it with shrubs that twinkle in the breeze,
And teach the little birds to build their nests             255
And warble in its chambers. At a time
When Nature, destined to remain so long
Foremost in my affections, had fallen back
Into a second place, pleased to become
A handmaid to a nobler than herself,                         260
When every day brought with it some new sense
Of exquisite regard for common things,
And all the earth was budding with these gifts
Of more refined humanity, thy breath,
Dear Sister! was a kind of gentler spring                    265
That went before my steps. Thereafter came
One whom with thee friendship had early paired;
She came, no more a phantom to adorn
A moment, but an inmate of the heart,
And yet a spirit, there for me enshrined                     270
To penetrate the lofty and the low;
Even as one essence of pervading light
Shines, in the brightest of ten thousand stars,
And, the meek worm that feeds her lonely lamp
Couched in the dewy grass.
                          With such a theme,                 275
Coleridge! with this my argument, of thee

     Pervading as one quality of light
     Shines in the brightest of a thousand stars
     And the meek worm that feeds its single lamp
     Among the dewy grass A²: D *stuck over*: D² *as* 1850.

Shall I be silent ? O most loving Soul!
Placed on this earth to love and understand,
250 And from thy presence shed the light of love,
Shall I be mute ere thou be spoken of ?                    [280]
Thy gentle Spirit to my heart of hearts
Did also find its way; and thus the life
Of all things and the mighty unity
255 In all which we behold, and feel, and are,
Admitted more habitually a mild                    [288]
Interposition, closelier gathering thoughts
Of man and his concerns, such as become                    [290]
A human Creature, be he who he may!
260 Poet, or destined for a humbler name;
And so the deep enthusiastic joy,
The rapture of the Hallelujah sent
From all that breathes and is, was chasten'd, stemm'd
And balanced by a Reason which indeed                    [296]
265 Is reason; duty and pathetic truth;
And God and Man divided, as they ought,
Between them the great system of the world
Where Man is sphered, and which God animates.

And now, O Friend! this history is brought
270 To its appointed close: the discipline
And consummation of the Poet's mind
In everything that stood most prominent                    [305]
Have faithfully been pictured; we have reach'd
The time (which was our object from the first)
275 When we may, not presumptuously, I hope,
Suppose my powers so far confirmed, and such
My knowledge, as to make me capable                    [310]
Of building up a work that should endure.
Yet much hath been omitted, as need was;
280 Of Books how much! and even of the other wealth
That is collected among woods and fields,

248 most loving 𝔄 D: capacious D².
252 gentle Spirit] genial spirit A² B² D: kindred influence D².
253–69 D *stuck over*: D² *as* 1850 [282–95], *but* [284] helped *for* learned *and*
[285–6] unity The mighty unity *for* mystery, The incumbent mystery,
[296–302] *torn off.*
259 A² B² *as* 1850.
266–8 And in the presence of his God Man stood
     Bound by a chain of order to the part

Shall I be silent ? O capacious Soul!
Placed on this earth to love and understand,
And from thy presence shed the light of love,
Shall I be mute, ere thou be spoken of ?                    280
Thy kindred influence to my heart of hearts
Did also find its way. Thus fear relaxed
Her overweening grasp; thus thoughts and things
In the self-haunting spirit learned to take
More rational proportions; mystery,                         285
The incumbent mystery of sense and soul,
Of life and death, time and eternity,
Admitted more habitually a mild
Interposition—a serene delight
In closelier gathering cares, such as become               290
A human creature, howsoe'er endowed,
Poet, or destined for a humbler name;
And so the deep enthusiastic joy,
The rapture of the hallelujah sent
From all that breathes and is, was chastened, stemmed   295
And balanced by pathetic truth, by trust
In hopeful reason, leaning on the stay
Of Providence; and in reverence for duty,
Here, if need be, struggling with storms, and there
Strewing in peace life's humblest ground with herbs,     300
At every season green, sweet at all hours.


    And now, O Friend! this history is brought
To its appointed close: the discipline
And consummation of a Poet's mind,
In everything that stood most prominent,                    305
Have faithfully been pictured; we have reached
The time (our guiding object from the first)
When we may, not presumptuously, I hope,
Suppose my powers so far confirmed, and such
My knowledge, as to make me capable                         310
Of building up a Work that shall endure.
Yet much hath been omitted, as need was;
Of books how much! and even of the other wealth
That is collected among woods and fields,

Assigned him in the system where all flesh
Is sphered and which God animates and rules. B².

Far more: for Nature's secondary grace,          [315]
That outward illustration which is hers,
Hath hitherto been barely touch'd upon,
285 The charm more superficial, and yet sweet
Which from her works finds way, contemplated
As they hold forth a genuine counterpart
And softening mirror of the moral world.

Yes, having track'd the main essential Power,
290 Imagination, up her way sublime,
In turn might Fancy also be pursued
Through all her transmigrations, till she too
Was purified, had learn'd to ply her craft
By judgment steadied. Then might we return
295 And in the Rivers and the Groves behold
Another face, might hear them from all sides
Calling upon the more instructed mind
To link their images with subtle skill
Sometimes, and by elaborate research
300 With forms and definite appearances
Of human life, presenting them sometimes
To the involuntary sympathy
Of our internal being, satisfied
And soothed with a conception of delight
305 Where meditation cannot come, which thought
Could never heighten. Above all how much
Still nearer to ourselves we overlook
In human nature and that marvellous world
As studied first in my own heart, and then          [324]
310 In life among the passions of mankind
And qualities commix'd and modified
By the infinite varieties and shades
Of individual character. Herein
It was for me (this justice bids me say)
315 No useless preparation to have been
The pupil of a public School, and forced
In hardy independence, to stand up
Among conflicting passions, and the shock
Of various tempers, to endure and note          [335]
320 What was not understood though known to be;
Among the mysteries of love and hate,
Honour and shame, looking to right and left,
Uncheck'd by innocence too delicate

Far more: for Nature's secondary grace                 315
Hath hitherto been barely touched upon,
The charm more superficial that attends
Her works, as they present to Fancy's choice
Apt illustrations of the moral world,
Caught at a glance, or traced with curious pains.      320

Finally, and above all, O Friend! (I speak
With due regret) how much is overlooked
In human nature and her subtle ways,
As studied first in our own hearts, and then
In life among the passions of mankind,                 325
Varying their composition and their hue,
Where'er we move, under the diverse shapes
That individual character presents
To an attentive eye. For progress meet,
Along this intricate and difficult path,               330
Whate'er was wanting, something had I gained,
As one of many schoolfellows compelled,
In hardy independence, to stand up
Amid conflicting interests, and the shock
Of various tempers; to endure and note                 335
What was not understood, though known to be;
Among the mysteries of love and hate,
Honour and shame, looking to right and left,
Unchecked by innocence too delicate,

283 𝕬 *deletes.*
285-7 and yet sweet *etc.*]         that awaits
        Upon her works contemplated or caught
        As they hold forth *etc.* A².
285-8                              that attends
        Her works contemplated as they hold forth
        A softening mirror *etc.* B² D: D² *as* 1850.
289-308 𝕬 D: D² *as* 1850 [321-3].
298 subtle A: subtile B.
311-15 Varying their composition and their hue
          Under the infinite diversities
Of individual character. For this        That individual character presents
Whate'er of fitness nature had          To observation; for this exercise
denied
Or art had failed to cultivate, I        I had not lack'd preparatory aids B².
lack'd not                                    *So* D (. . . eye): D² *as* 1850.
An early preparation, having been A².
  316 and forced] compelled A² B²              318 passions 𝕬 D: interests D².

And moral notions too intolerant,                              [340]
325  Sympathies too contracted. Hence, when call'd
     To take a station among Men, the step
     Was easier, the transition more secure,
     More profitable also; for the mind
     Learns from such timely exercise to keep            [345]
330  In wholesome separation the two natures,
     The one that feels, the other that observes.

     Let one word more of personal circumstance,
     Not needless, as it seems, be added here.
     Since I withdrew unwillingly from France,           [349]
335  The Story hath demanded less regard
     To time and place; and where I lived, and how
     Hath been no longer scrupulously mark'd.
     Three years, until a permanent abode
     Receiv'd me with that Sister of my heart
340  Who ought by rights the dearest to have been
     Conspicuous through this biographic Verse,
     Star seldom utterly conceal'd from view,
     I led an undomestic Wanderer's life.
     In London chiefly was my home, and thence
345  Excursively, as personal friendships, chance
     Or inclination led, or slender means
     Gave leave, I roam'd about from place to place
     Tarrying in pleasant nooks, wherever found
     Through England or through Wales. A Youth (he bore
350  The name of Calvert; it shall live, if words        [355]
     Of mine can give it life,) without respect
     To prejudice or custom, having hope
     That I had some endowments by which good
     Might be promoted, in his last decay
355  From his own Family withdrawing part
     Of no redundant Patrimony, did
     By a Bequest sufficient for my needs
     Enable me to pause for choice, and walk             [360]
     At large and unrestrain'd, nor damp'd too soon
360  By mortal cares. Himself no Poet, yet
     Far less a common Spirit of the world,
     He deem'd that my pursuits and labors lay
     Apart from all that leads to wealth, or even        [365]

332-4  circumstance . . . France]      concern
            Be added here: Since I withdrew from France  A².
            When with reluctance I withdrew from France  Y.

And moral notions too intolerant,                          340
Sympathies too contracted. Hence, when called
To take a station among men, the step
Was easier, the transition more secure,
More profitable also; for, the mind
Learns from such timely exercise to keep              345
In wholesome separation the two natures,
The one that feels, the other that observes.

   Yet one word more of personal concern—
Since I withdrew unwillingly from France,
I led an undomestic wanderer's life,                       350
In London chiefly harboured, whence I roamed,
Tarrying at will in many a pleasant spot
Of rural England's cultivated vales
Or Cambrian solitudes. A youth—(he bore
The name of Calvert—it shall live, if words           355
Of mine can give it life,) in firm belief
That by endowments not from me withheld
Good might be furthered—in his last decay
By a bequest sufficient for my needs
Enabled me to pause for choice, and walk            360
At large and unrestrained, nor damped too soon
By mortal cares. Himself no Poet, yet
Far less a common follower of the world,
He deemed that my pursuits and labours lay
Apart from all that leads to wealth, or even         365

340 been] shone A².
344-9 In London chiefly harboured, whence I roamed
    Excursively, in many a pleasant spot
    Tarrying mid chearful England's populous haunts
    Or Cambrian solitudes A². *So* B², *but* merry *for* chearful.
346-7 Or chance directed, or my slender means
    Gave leave in pleasant nooks wherever found  Y: Y² *as* A.
351 without respect] in firm belief (*deleting next line*)  B² D: D² *as* 1850.
355-6 Withdrawing, and from kindred whom he loved,
    A part of no redundant Patrimony  B² D E *with* Enabled 358.
    (*No MS. authority for omission in* 1850.)
361 Spirit A D: Follower D².     362 pursuits] delights Y.
363 Apart from all that fosters wealth or leads A².
    Distinct *for* Apart  B² D².
363-5 Among the lonely places of the earth
    Far out of reach of all that leads to wealth
    Or even to necessary maintenance
    Without some (*injury*) danger to the finer sense
    And since in this he did not falsely take
    The measure of my soul  Y (*but last two lines deleted*).

Perhaps to necessary maintenance,
365 Without some hazard to the finer sense;
He clear'd a passage for me, and the stream
Flow'd in the bent of Nature.
                                    Having now
Told what best merits mention, further pains          [370]
Our present labour seems not to require,
370 And I have other tasks. Call back to mind
The mood in which this Poem was begun,
O Friend! the termination of my course
Is nearer now, much nearer; yet even then             [375]
In that distraction and intense desire
375 I said unto the life which I had lived,
Where art thou? Hear I not a voice from thee
Which 'tis reproach to hear? Anon I rose
As if on wings, and saw beneath me stretch'd          [380]
Vast prospect of the world which I had been
380 And was; and hence this Song, which like a lark
I have protracted, in the unwearied Heavens
Singing, and often with more plaintive voice
Attemper'd to the sorrows of the earth;               [385]
Yet centring all in love, and in the end
385 All gratulant if rightly understood.


Whether to me shall be allotted life,
And with life power to accomplish aught of worth
Sufficient to excuse me in men's sight
For having given this Record of myself,               [391]
390 Is all uncertain; but, beloved Friend,
When, looking back, thou seest in clearer view
Than any sweetest sight of yesterday
That summer when on Quantock's grassy Hills           [395]
Far ranging, and among the sylvan Coombs,
395 Thou in delicious words, with happy heart,
Didst speak the Vision of that Ancient Man,
The bright-eyed Mariner, and rueful woes              [400]

[366] A² D² *as* 1850.
372 𝔄 D E²: The termination of my earthly course  D² E.
374 In such distraction such intense desire  Y.
383 𝔄 D: D² *as* 1850.
388 𝔄 D: D² E² *as* 1850: That may suffice to excuse me in men's sight E.
392 sweetest] liveliest  A² B².

A necessary maintenance insures,
Without some hazard to the finer sense;
He cleared a passage for me, and the stream
Flowed in the bent of Nature.
                    Having now
Told what best merits mention, further pains     370
Our present purpose seems not to require,
And I have other tasks. Recall to mind
The mood in which this labour was begun,
O Friend! The termination of my course
Is nearer now, much nearer; yet even then,     375
In that distraction and intense desire,
I said unto the life which I had lived,
Where art thou? Hear I not a voice from thee
Which 'tis reproach to hear? Anon I rose
As if on wings, and saw beneath me stretched     380
Vast prospect of the world which I had been
And was; and hence this Song, which like a lark
I have protracted, in the unwearied heavens
Singing, and often with more plaintive voice
To earth attempered and her deep-drawn sighs,     385
Yet centring all in love, and in the end
All gratulant, if rightly understood.

    Whether to me shall be allotted life,
And, with life, power to accomplish aught of worth,
That will be deemed no insufficient plea     390
For having given the story of myself,
Is all uncertain: but, beloved Friend!
When, looking back, thou seest, in clearer view
Than any liveliest sight of yesterday,
That summer, under whose indulgent skies,     395
Upon smooth Quantock's airy ridge we roved
Unchecked, or loitered 'mid her sylvan coombs,
Thou in bewitching words, with happy heart,
Didst chaunt the vision of that Ancient Man,
The bright-eyed Mariner, and rueful woes     400

393–6 𝔄 D: D² *as* 1850. That one blest summer whose indulgent sky
    Supplied a progeny of golden days
    To lead us forth, on Quantock's grassy ridge
    Far ranging, or amid her sylvan coombs
    Embower'd beside the crystal springs, where thou
    Didst in delicious words with happy heart
    Rehearse the Vision *etc.* A². A³ D² *as* 1850.

Didst utter of the Lady Christabel;
And I, associate with such labour, walk'd
400 Murmuring of him who, joyous hap! was found,
After the perils of his moonlight ride                    [405]
Near the loud Waterfall; or her who sate
In misery near the miserable Thorn;
When thou dost to that summer turn thy thoughts,
405 And hast before thee all which then we were,
To thee, in memory of that happiness                    [410]
It will be known, by thee at least, my Friend,
Felt, that the history of a Poet's mind
Is labour not unworthy of regard:
410 To thee the work shall justify itself.

The last and later portions of this Gift                    [415]
Which I for Thee design, have been prepared
In times which have from those wherein we first
Together wanton'd in wild Poesy,
415 Differ'd thus far, that they have been, my Friend,
Times of much sorrow, of a private grief
Keen and enduring, which the frame of mind                    [420]
That in this meditative History
Hath been described, more deeply makes me feel;
420 Yet likewise hath enabled me to bear
More firmly; and a comfort now, a hope,
One of the dearest which this life can give,
Is mine; that Thou art near, and wilt be soon                    [425]
Restored to us in renovated health;
425 When, after the first mingling of our tears,
'Mong other consolations we may find
Some pleasure from this Offering of my love.

Oh! yet a few short years of useful life,                    [430]
And all will be complete, thy race be run,
430 Thy monument of glory will be raised.
Then, though, too weak to tread the ways of truth,
This Age fall back to old idolatry,
Though men return to servitude as fast                    [435]
As the tide ebbs, to ignominy and shame

399 walk'd] A² B² as 1850 [402–3].
412–13 Destined for thee, have been prepared in times
          From those, alas, far differing when we first A².

Didst utter of the Lady Christabel;
And I, associate with such labour, steeped
In soft forgetfulness the livelong hours,
Murmuring of him who, joyous hap, was found,
After the perils of his moonlight ride,　　　405
Near the loud waterfall; or her who sate
In misery near the miserable Thorn;
When thou dost to that summer turn thy thoughts,
And hast before thee all which then we were,
To thee, in memory of that happiness,　　　410
It will be known, by thee at least, my Friend!
Felt, that the history of a Poet's mind
Is labour not unworthy of regard:
To thee the work shall justify itself.

The last and later portions of this gift　　　415
Have been prepared, not with the buoyant spirits
That were our daily portion when we first
Together wantoned in wild Poesy,
But, under pressure of a private grief,
Keen and enduring, which the mind and heart,　　　420
That in this meditative history
Have been laid open, needs must make me feel
More deeply, yet enable me to bear
More firmly; and a comfort now hath risen
From hope that thou art near, and wilt be soon　　　425
Restored to us in renovated health;
When, after the first mingling of our tears,
'Mong other consolations, we may draw
Some pleasure from this offering of my love.

Oh! yet a few short years of useful life,　　　430
And all will be complete, thy race be run,
Thy monument of glory will be raised;
Then, though (too weak to tread the ways of truth)
This age fall back to old idolatry,
Though men return to servitude as fast　　　435
As the tide ebbs, to ignominy and shame

Have been prepared under enduring grief
　　In times from those far differing, when we first  D:  D² *as* 1850.
421-3 now, a hope . . . Is mine] now is mine, . . . A hope  A².
422 A *and* B *delete*. *Not in* D.　　　426 find 𝔄 D: draw D².

435  By Nations sink together, we shall still
     Find solace in the knowledge which we have,
     Bless'd with true happiness if we may be
     United helpers forward of a day                    [440]
     Of firmer trust, joint-labourers in a work
440  (Should Providence such grace to us vouchsafe)
     Of their redemption, surely yet to come.
     Prophets of Nature, we to them will speak
     A lasting inspiration, sanctified                  [445]
     By reason and by truth; what we have loved,
445  Others will love; and we may teach them how;
     Instruct them how the mind of man becomes
     A thousand times more beautiful than the earth
     On which he dwells, above this Frame of things     [450]
     (Which, 'mid all revolutions in the hopes
450  And fears of men, doth still remain unchanged)
     In beauty exalted, as it is itself
     Of substance and of fabric more divine.

          436  we have] is ours  A² B².
          438  of a day] to a day  A² B² D:  D² *as* 1850.
          441  redemption  𝔄 D:  deliverance  D².

By nations sink together, we shall still
Find solace—knowing what we have learnt to know,
Rich in true happiness if allowed to be
Faithful alike in forwarding a day      440
Of firmer trust, joint labourers in the work
(Should Providence such grace to us vouchsafe)
Of their deliverance, surely yet to come.
Prophets of Nature, we to them will speak
A lasting inspiration, sanctified      445
By reason, blest by faith: what we have loved,
Others will love, and we will teach them how;
Instruct them how the mind of man becomes
A thousand times more beautiful than the earth
On which he dwells, above this frame of things      450
(Which, 'mid all revolution in the hopes
And fears of men, doth still remain unchanged)
In beauty exalted, as it is itself
Of quality and fabric more divine.

444 and by truth] blest by truth B² D: blest by faith D².
452 substance and of 𝔄 D: quality and D².

# NOTES

*The Prelude* was published by Moxon on July 20, 1850, and the statement of accounts, sent to Wordsworth's executors on July 3, 1851, proves that by that date the whole edition of 2,000 copies was exhausted. They received in payment the sum of £414. 15*s.* 8*d.*, two-thirds of the profits. A second edition appeared in 1851.

The following 'Advertisement' was prefixed to the Poem in 1850:

THE following Poem was commenced in the beginning of the year 1799, and completed in the summer of 1805.

The design and occasion of the work are described by the Author in his Preface to the EXCURSION, first published in 1814, where he thus speaks:—

'Several years ago, when the Author retired to his native mountains with the hope of being enabled to construct a literary work that might live, it was a reasonable thing that he should take a review of his own mind, and examine how far Nature and Education had qualified him for such an employment.

'As subsidiary to this preparation, he undertook to record, in verse, the origin and progress of his own powers, as far as he was acquainted with them.

'That work, addressed to a dear friend, most distinguished for his knowledge and genius, and to whom the author's intellect is deeply indebted, has been long finished; and the result of the investigation which gave rise to it, was a determination to compose a philosophical Poem, containing views of Man, Nature, and Society, and to be entitled the RECLUSE; as having for its principal subject the sensations and opinions of a poet living in retirement.

'The preparatory poem is biographical, and conducts the history of the Author's mind to the point when he was emboldened to hope that his faculties were sufficiently matured for entering upon the arduous labour which he had proposed to himself; and the two works have the same kind of relation to each other, if he may so express himself, as the Ante-chapel has to the body of a Gothic Church. Continuing this allusion, he may be permitted to add, that his minor pieces, which have been long before the public, when they shall be properly arranged, will be found by the attentive reader to have such connection with the main work as may give them claim to be likened to the little cells, oratories, and sepulchral recesses, ordinarily included in those edifices.'

Such was the Author's language in the year 1814.

It will thence be seen, that the present Poem was intended to be introductory to the RECLUSE, and that the RECLUSE, if completed, would have consisted of Three Parts. Of these, the Second Part alone, viz. the EXCURSION, was finished, and given to the world by the Author.

The First Book of the First Part of the RECLUSE still [1850] remains in manuscript; but the Third Part was only planned. The materials of which it would have been formed have, however, been incorporated, for the most part, in the Author's other Publications, written subsequently to the EXCURSION.

The Friend, to whom the present Poem is addressed, was the late SAMUEL TAYLOR COLERIDGE, who was resident in Malta, for the restoration of his health, when the greater part of it was composed.

Mr. Coleridge read a considerable portion of the Poem while he was abroad; and his feelings, on hearing it recited by the Author (after his return to his own country) are recorded in his Verses, addressed to Mr. Wordsworth, which will be found in the 'Sibylline Leaves', p. 197, ed. 1817, or 'Poetical Works, by S. T. Coleridge', vol. i, p. 206.

RYDAL MOUNT,
*July* 13*th*, 1850.

As will be gathered from the Introduction (pp. xxxiii, xxxiv), this 'Advertisement' is not quite accurate. The 'review of the poet's mind' was conceived, and portions of it written, in 1798, when Wordsworth was in Germany, i.e. *before* he had 'retired to his native mountains'. Moreover the idea of writing it arose out of his determination to compose *The Recluse*, and not, as here suggested, *vice versa*.

At the end of MS. D is the note (in M. W.'s hand): 'The composition of this poem was finished early in 1805—it having been begun about 1798.' To this E adds, 'The Life is brought up to the time of the Composition of the first Edition of the Lyrical Ballads' (in Dora W.'s hand).

# BOOK I

**1–271 [1–269].** The 'preamble', 1–54 [1–45], referred to in VII. 4 *infra*, together with the succeeding lines, 155–271 [46–269], constitute a passage difficult to date confidently: it does not appear in any MS. before MS. M written in March–April 1804. All the earlier MSS. open with a half-line:

'Was it for this' (l. 271).

If we assume that by the 'glad preamble' Wordsworth means the opening ll. 1–54 of Book I then we should accept his statement that these lines were composed extempore (ll. 55–59) on the very autumn day when he walked down to Racedown from Bristol in September 1795 (*v. infra* note to l. 74). His anticipations of settling at the chosen cottage fit Racedown but not Grasmere. His words about quitting the sea, and dwelling on shore

If not *a Settler on the soil*, at least
To drink wild water, and to pluck green herbs, (36–37)

imply that he is seeking a temporary residence. The house at Racedown lent them by the Pinneys was exactly that. When they took Dove Cottage they meant to settle permanently. If the lines (1–54) were composed extempore they were perhaps not written down at the time: some fragmentary reminiscences of them appear in MS. JJ written at Goslar 1798–9, *q.v.* p. 633 *infra*. Cf. in particular I. 20 and 43–47 with MS. JJ, Z verso.

The succeeding passage, ll. 55–271, was perhaps written in this form in October 1803, but it probably represents a fusing into one account of his memories, dating from Racedown and Alfoxden days, of abortive attempts to get started upon his great poem.

**1.** *Oh there is blessing in this gentle breeze*: It is worth noting how often Wordsworth's imagination conceives of the coming of creative energy to the soul as a 'breeze'. Cf. I. 41–45 (and *app. crit.*), II. 245, the lines quoted in note to I. 577–93, VII. 2, and *Excursion*, IV. 600, 'The breeze of nature stirring in his soul'.

**7.** [*vast city*:] clearly reminiscent of Milton's invocation of London in *Areopagitica*: 'Behold this vast city . . .'. 'Yon city' in the MS. version (1805) must be London, where Wordsworth had resided from February to August 1795. The freedom came from the legacy of £900 left him by Raisley Calvert (*v.* XIII. 349–67). Calvert died in January that year (his funeral was on Jan. 12), but doubtless the law's delays were partly responsible for the months that elapsed before Wordsworth settled with his sister at Racedown.

**15.** *The earth is all before me*: the first of the many Miltonic echoes in the poem. Cf. *Paradise Lost*, xii. 646: 'The world was all before them, where to choose' (*v.* Introduction, p. xlii).

**23–24.** *That burthen . . ., weary day*: Cf. *Lines composed a few miles above Tintern Abbey*, 37–41, written July 13, 1798:

that blessed mood,
In which the burthen of the mystery,
In which the heavy and the weary weight
Of all this unintelligible world,
Is lightened.

The phrase 'undisturb'd delight' (28) recalls *A Nightpiece*, composed January 25, 1798, 'Not undisturbed by the delight it feels.' The phrase reappears in X. 839, 'Lord of himself in undisturb'd delight.'

**55–56.** *not used to make A present joy the matter of my Song*: 'I have said that Poetry is the spontaneous overflow of powerful feelings: it takes its origin from emotion recollected in tranquillity: the emotion is contemplated till by a species of reaction the tranquillity gradually disappears, and an emotion, similar to that which was before the subject of contemplation, is gradually produced, and does itself

actually exist in the mind. In this mood successful composition generally begins,' *etc*. Preface to *Lyrical Ballads*, 1800. Wordsworth, as
Garrod points out, calls special attention here to the fact that ll. 1–54
differed in this respect from his other poetry.

**58–59.** *Even in the very words which I have here Recorded*: a statement modified in D and E, owing to the changes introduced in the
previous lines. In the 'preamble' as written in 1795 there was nothing
about 'punctual service high' or 'Matins and vespers'.

**74.** *'Twas Autumn*: Wordsworth and Dorothy arrived at Racedown on September 26, 1795. The autumnal scene which he describes
does not fit the date and occasion of his departure from Goslar in
February 1799, nor that of his journey to take up his abode in Grasmere, December 1799. We must not look for factual exactitude in
Wordsworth's poetic autobiography, where a running together of
memories of two or more significant occasions is often to be found.
In this preamble (ll. 1–54) and in the post-preamble (ll. 55–271)
Wordsworth seems to combine memories of his journey to Racedown
and sojourn there 1795–7 with equally significant memories of his
arrival at Dove Cottage in December 1799 and subsequent period of
habitation. The walk itself seems to correspond with the walk from
Bristol to Racedown (50 miles).

**82.** *one sweet Vale*: This suggests Grasmere rather than Racedown:
Racedown Lodge stands on the side of a hill 400 feet above the sea.

**104 [96].** *Eolian visitations*: thoughts that come and go with the
breeze, as the Aeolian harp sounds when the wind passes over it. Cf.
Coleridge, *The Eolian Harp*, 39–43:

> Full many a thought uncall'd and undetain'd,
> And many idle flitting phantasies,
> Traverse my indolent and passive brain,
> As wild and various as the random gales
> That swell and flutter on this subject Lute!

**[102–3].** *the mellowing sun, that shed Mild influence*: an echo of
Milton, *Paradise Lost*, vii. 375, where the Pleiades dance before the Sun
'Shedding sweet influence'.

**117.** *The admiration and the love*: to Wordsworth the true sustenance of the spiritual Life. Cf. the passage from notebook Y quoted on
p. 571.

**122 [113].** *the happiness entire*: This is hardly a true picture of
Wordsworth's frame of mind in the early days at Racedown, though
it could apply more justly to the end of his stay there, when under the
influence of Dorothy's companionship and Coleridge's friendship he
recovered his natural balance. But here again he is probably fusing
into one account his memory of days at Racedown, Alfoxden, and
Dove Cottage.

**143–4 [133–4].** *present gifts Of humbler industry*: The *Alfoxden*
notebook (*v*. Introduction, p. **xxv**) proves that in the early months of

1798 he was engaged on the character of the Wanderer (*Excursion* I), *The Cumberland Beggar*, and 'The Discharged Soldier' (*Prelude* IV). A little later he wrote the simpler poems to be included in the *Lyrical Ballads*, and *Peter Bell*.

**151–2 [140–1].** *as the Mother Dove, Sits brooding*: Cf. *Paradise Lost*, i. 21: Dove-like satst brooding on the vast Abyss.

**153–4 [142–3].** *goadings on That drive her as in trouble through the groves*: Cf. the portrait which Wordsworth has drawn of himself in *Stanzas written in my pocket copy of Thomson's Castle of Indolence*, 1–36, especially the lines

> Oft could we see him driving full in view . . .
> And his own mind did like a tempest strong
> Come to him thus, and drove the weary wight along.

**179–80 [168–9].**        *some British theme, some old*
>        *Romantic tale, by Milton left unsung;*

It is significant that Wordsworth's first ambition is to emulate Milton. In the Milton MS. at Trinity, Cambridge, is a list of subjects for a projected epic, in which the history of Britain before the Conquest is divided into thirty-three heads. Cf. also the *Epitaphium Damonis*, in which Milton tells of his project for writing a poem on the subject of King Arthur.

**182–3 [171–2].**    *Within the groves of Chivalry, I pipe*
>        *Among the Shepherds, with reposing Knights*

cf. Spenser, *Faerie Queene*, Book VI. Notice the manner in which Wordsworth develops this passage later, giving it a definite moral turn, of which, when he wrote in 1798, he was quite innocent.

**[185].** *faithful loves*: Spenser, *Faerie Queene*, I. i. 1. 'Fierce warres and faithful loves shall moralize my song.'

**186–95.** *Mithridates . . . Odin . . . Sertorius*: To these themes Wordsworth was attracted by his reading of Plutarch and Gibbon. 'There were only two provinces of literature', says De Quincey (*Works*, ii. 288, ed. Masson), 'in which Wordsworth could be looked upon as decently well read—Poetry and Ancient History. Nor do I believe that he would much have lamented, on his own account, if all books had perished, excepting the entire body of English Poetry, and, perhaps, Plutarch's Lives. . . . His business with Plutarch was not for purposes of research: he was satisfied with his fine moral effects.' This statement, like many of De Quincey's, is fantastically exaggerated, for Wordsworth was more widely read than is often supposed (*v.* notes *passim*, and pp. xl–xliii), but at least it points to two of his three favourite classes of reading. Of Mithridates (131–63 B.C.) he read in Plutarch's *Lives* of *Sulla* and *Pompey*. After his defeat by Pompey in 66 B.C. Mithridates marched into Colchis and thence to the Cimmerian Bosphorus, where he planned to pass round the north and west coasts of the Euxine, through the tribes of Sarmatians and Getae, and invade Italy from the north. The connexion of Odin with Mithridates was suggested, as Worsfold points out, by Gibbon (*Decline and Fall of the Roman Empire*, chap. x). 'It is supposed that Odin was the chief of a tribe of barbarians which dwelt on the banks of the lake Maeotis, till the fall of Mithridates and the arms of Pompey menaced the north with servitude; that Odin, yielding with indignant fury to a power which he was unable to resist, conducted his tribe from the frontiers of the Asiatic Sarmatia into Sweden, with the great design of forming, in that inaccessible retreat of freedom, a religion and a people which, in some remote age, might be subservient to his immortal revenge; when his invincible Goths, armed with martial fanaticism, should issue in numerous swarms from the neighbourhood of the Polar circle, to chastise the oppressors of mankind.' Gibbon appends to this passage a note which, doubtless, suggested the theme to Wordsworth. 'This wonderful expedition of Odin, which, by deducing the enmity of the Goths and Romans from so memorable a cause, might supply the noble groundwork of an Epic poem, cannot safely be received as authentic history.' The identification of Mithridates with Odin is probably Wordsworth's own contribution to the legend: *v.* Addenda, p. 632.

*Sertorius*: the famous Roman general who for eight years resisted the tyranny of the Senatorial party and kept the armies of Metellus and Pompey at bay till, in 72 B.C., he was assassinated. Mithridates sent him ships and men to support him against their common enemy. Plutarch relates that on one occasion Sertorius went to north Africa and on his return 'passed the strait of *Gibralter*, and turning on his right hand landed upon the coast of *Spaine*, lying towards the great Westerne sea, a little above the mouth of the river of *Baetis*. There certaine sailers met with him that were newly arrived from the Iles of the *ocean Atlanticum*, which the ancients called, the fortunate ilands. . . . They have raine there very seldome, howbeit a gentle wind commonly that bloweth in a little silver deaw, which moisteneth the earth so finely, that it maketh it fertile and lusty. . . . The weather is faire and pleasant continually and never hurteth the body . . . insomuch as the very barbarous people themselves do faithfully believe that there are the *Elysian* fields, the aboad of blessed creatures, which Homer hath so much spoken of. *Sertorius* hearing report of these Ilands (upon a certain desire now to live quietly out of tyranny and warres) had straight a marvellous mind to go dwell there' (Plutarch's *Lives: Sertorius*, tr. by North). Wordsworth seems to have read Plutarch in the French translation of Thevet (1676) of which a copy was in his library. The legend is that the followers of Sertorius, after his death, in order to escape the tyranny of Rome, fled to the Canary Islands, called by the ancients the Fortunate Isles, which were in this way peopled. It was their heroic descendants, then, who fought so valiantly and tenaciously to keep out the invading Spaniards from Teneriffe in 1493; their final subjugation was due not to the valour of the Spaniards, but to a terrible pestilence which decimated them in 1494.

Their race died out completely. The story is told by Alonso de Espinosa in *The Guanches of Teneriffe*, first published in Spanish in 1594.

**205.** *that one Frenchman*: 'Dominique de Gourges, a French gentleman who went in 1568 to Florida to avenge the massacre of the French ·by the Spaniards there' (note in 1850). In 1562 Jean Ribault, a Huguenot, with a band of French emigrants, landed in Florida and claimed the country for France; in 1565 Pedro Menendez de Aviles followed him there, with the resolve to uproot the French colony, and hanged all the settlers he could lay hands on—'not as Frenchmen, but as Lutherans'. The French court received the news with indifference, but Dominique de Gourges, a friend of Ribault, organized an expedition of vengeance, and reached Florida in 1567, 'where he most justly valiantly and sharply revenged the bloody and inhumane massacre committed by the Spaniards upon his countrymen in the yere 1565'. He hanged all his prisoners, saying 'I do not this as unto Spaniards, but as unto Traitors, Robbers, and Murtherers'. De Gourges returned to France in June 1568, but was ill received at court. He died in 1582. Wordsworth owed his knowledge of the incident to Hakluyt's *Voyages*, *etc*., from which the above quotations are taken.

**211.** *Gustavus*: Gustavus I (1496–1560) freed his country from the tyranny of Denmark. Dalecarlia, a mining district in the west midlands of Sweden, is known as 'the cradle of Swedish civil and religious liberty'. Here Gustavus arranged and matured his schemes for the liberation of his country, and the district is full of mementoes of his life there, when he had often to assume the guise of a peasant or miner to escape capture by the Danes.

**213.** *Wallace*: Knight and Worsfold refer to D. W.'s *Journal* for August 21, 1803: 'Passed two of Wallace's caves. There is scarcely a noted glen in Scotland that has not a cave for Wallace, or some other hero.' In a MS. version of *Excursion* I Wordsworth tells us that the exploits of Wallace were among the tales that Drummond, the original of the Wanderer, used to relate to him as a boy.

**233–4.** *immortal verse Thoughtfully fitted to the Orphean lyre*: Cf. Milton, *L'Allegro*, 137, and *Paradise Lost*, iii. 17. So Coleridge, in his poem, *To a Gentleman, composed on the night after his recitation of a poem on the growth of an individual mind*, speaks of *The Prelude* as

> An Orphic song indeed,
> A song divine of high and passionate thoughts
> To their own music chaunted!

**248 [246].** *Doth lock my functions up*: cf. Pope, *Imit. of 1st Epistle of 1st Book of Horace*, 39, 40:

> So slow the unprofitable moments roll
> That lock up all the functions of my soul.

**277.** *Derwent*: the river that flows through Derwentwater and

Bassenthwaite, and joins the Cocker under the walls of Cockermouth Castle.

**278.** *my 'sweet Birthplace'*: a quotation from Coleridge's *Frost at Midnight*, l. 28. And in his *Sonnet to the River Otter*, Coleridge has told how

so deep imprest
Sink the sweet scenes of childhood, that mine eyes
I never shut amid the sunny ray,
But straight with all their tints thy waters rise.

Wordsworth by this quotation subtly associates the reminiscences of his own childhood with those of the friend for whom he writes.

**286–7.** *the Towers Of Cockermouth*: 'At the end of the garden of my father's house at Cockermouth was a high terrace that commanded a fine view of the river Derwent and Cockermouth Castle. This was our favourite playground' (I. F. note to *The Sparrow's Nest*). In Sonnet vii of *Poems . . . of 1833* (*Oxf. W.*, p. 464) Wordsworth tells us that it was in the 'green courts' of the castle that as a boy he chased the butterfly. Cf. *To a Butterfly*. 'Stay near me—do not take thy flight!' *etc.*

**308.** *that beloved Vale*: Esthwaite, at the north-west end of which is Hawkshead, where Wordsworth spent his schooldays. The family account-books prove conclusively that, with his elder brother Richard, he entered the school at Whitsuntide 1779. Whitsuntide falls in the middle of the summer term, but apparently it was not an unusual time for boys to enter. Thus Mr. Gordon Wordsworth finds the following corroborative note in Sir Daniel Fleming's accounts for June 4, 1683, 'Given to George, Michael, Richard and Roger when they went to Hawkeshead School 4*s*.' In the autumn following, therefore, Wordsworth had seen *ten* summers, and not *nine*, as stated in A 311. Still more inaccurate is the V text, which states that when he went to school he had not seen eight summers (*v.* p. 161, *app. crit.*).

**315.** *the smooth Hollows*: probably, as Knight suggests, on 'the round-headed grassy hills that lead up and on to the moor between Hawkshead and Coniston'.

**[327].** *Moved we as plunderers*: For 'Moved', the reading in both D and E is 'Roved'. The mistake in 1850 is due to the fact that the copyist of E wrote her 'M's and 'R's almost alike. But the 'R' in D is unmistakable. The scene of these adventures was probably Raven's Crag in Yewdale.

**351–72.** For the last six lines of V's version of this passage V has the deleted reading:

With me though rarely in my boyish days
They communed for as I have said there are
Teachers of different character who use *etc.*

Another version after 'miseries' (356) gives the line 'The medley of aversions and desires' and after 'believe' (362) 'That some are trained by milder discipline.'

It is interesting to notice that when Wordsworth began to write *The Prelude* he still delighted to conceive of Nature not merely as the expression of one divine spirit, but as in its several parts animated by individual spirits who had, like human beings, an independent life and power of action. This was obviously his firm belief in the primitive paganism of his boyhood (*v.* ll. 329–50, 405–27); and long after he had given up definite belief in it, he cherished it as more than mere poetic fancy. The passages which illustrate this are chiefly found in the readings of MS. V: (cf. *app. crit.* to I. 351, 490, and *Nutting* with its concluding words 'there is a Spirit in the woods'), but it finds expression in the reading of A² for I. 29–32, and is at least suggested in the A text of II. 139. But though the 'Spirits of air' reappear in the D text of [XII. 9–12], he would doubtless have regarded them, at that time, as merely 'a pretty piece of Paganism'.

**376.** *'Twas by the shores of Patterdale*: The scene of this famous boating episode has always been supposed to be Esthwaite, and critics have vainly sought to identify the 'rocky Cave' and 'the craggy steep' upon its level banks, and to name the 'huge cliff' that rose above it, when it was viewed at some distance from the shore. Ullswater, now shown to be the lake referred to, is far more suited to the adventure. Stybarrow crag, about 1¼ miles from the inn at Patterdale, well answers to the description of the 'craggy steep', and where the crag touches the water there are several little inlets, in which a boat might well be moored, answering to the description of 'rocky caves'. The 'huge peak' which appears due west behind Stybarrow Crag on rowing out from shore is called Black Crag (2,000 ft.). Mr. Gordon Wordsworth, however, holds the view that the boat was taken from the spot, now occupied by the Patterdale Hall boat-house, where the road from Patterdale first touches the lake. The 'huge peak' would then be St. Sunday's Crag. The objection to his view is that the shore is flat at this spot, and there is nothing that by any poetic licence could be regarded as a 'rocky cave'.

**387–8.** *Even like a Man, etc.*: an echo of *Paradise Lost*, xii. 1–2, As one who in his journey bates at Noon, Though bent on speed.

**399 [371].** *for behind*: As Mr. Nowell Smith conjectured, 'far' in the 1850 text should be 'for'. 'Far' is only found in E, where it is clearly a copyist's error.

**425–7 [398–400].** In *The Times Literary Supplement* for April 4, 1922, Mr. Garrod suggested that these lines should be punctuated thus:

But huge and mighty forms that do not live,

Like living men moved slowly through the mind *etc.*

It will be noted that A B and C have no commas after 'forms', 'live', or 'men'. This would support Mr. Garrod's interpretation, for the natural pause at the end of the line would connect the word 'live' with what preceded rather than with what followed it. V has the commas: but as they are in a blacker ink and were clearly added later, they do not necessarily represent Wordsworth's intention when he wrote the lines. The meaning, however, would seem to be rightly rendered without the comma.

**428–89 [401–63].** *Wisdom and Spirit, etc.*: 'These lines have already been published in the Author's Poetical Works, vol. i, p. 172, ed. 1849—p. 62 of the edition in one volume' (note in 1850). They were first published in *The Friend*, December 28, 1809, and were included in the 1815 ed. of *Poems*. In 1849 Wordsworth dates them 1799. The passage first appeared as part of *The Prelude* in MS. M. Lines 452–73 were sent to S. T. C. by D. W. in December or January 1798–9 introduced thus: 'It is from a description of William's boyish pleasures.' Soon after receiving this letter, S. T. C. wrote to his wife (Jan. 14, 1799): 'When very many are skating together the sounds and the noises give an impulse to the icy Trees, and the woods all round the lake *tinkle*.' (Cf. Wordsworth's l. 469.) Much of Coleridge's letter was afterwards adapted for an Essay in *The Friend*, December 1809.

**485–6 [459–60].** *as if the earth had rolled*
*With visible motion her diurnal round*:
Cf. the second stanza of '*A slumber did my spirit seal*' which, like this passage, was written at Goslar in 1799:

No motion has she now, no force;
She neither hears nor sees;
Rolled round in earth's diurnal course,
With rocks, and stones, and trees.

**490–2** *app. crit.* In V this passage was first introduced after l. 441 and later transferred to its place after l. 489. On a blank half-sheet is a line not used: 'Ye thoughts that travel round the world like winds'.

**520–4.** *The kite high up . . . storm.* Another draft of these lines is found in Wordsworth's hand at the end of MS. V, intended for insertion at 532:

Yet had ye
Your own dear pastimes and your own delights
The kite sent up among the driven clouds
And breasting the strong wind then [   ?   ]

**543 [516].** *Lu*: spelt thus in all MSS.: Loo 1850. *Lu* is the 18th-century spelling of this popular game.

**549 [522].** *plebeian cards*: Wordsworth, who had committed much of Pope to memory (*Memoirs*, ii. 470), could hardly fail, when he wrote this passage, to recall the famous game of cards in *The Rape of the Lock*. As Knight notes, he borrows the phrase from that poem (iii. 54):
Gained but one trump, and one plebeian card.

**563–4 [536–7].** *the frost . . . with keen and silent tooth*: Cf. *As You Like It*, ii. vii. 177.

**566–70 [539–43].** *the splitting ice, etc.*: Notice the change introduced into the text of this passage, due to a desire for greater scientific accuracy. Wordsworth's own experience of the noise occasioned by the splitting ice may have been reinforced by recollection of Coleridge's vivid description in the *Ancient Mariner*:

> It cracked and growled and roared and howled,
> Like noises in a swound.

**571 [544].** *Nor, sedulous as I have been to trace How Nature*: an echo of *Paradise Lost*, ix. 27, 'Not sedulous by Nature to indite.'

**577–93.** Knight (iii. 150) quotes a parallel passage of 33 lines beginning 'I tread the mazes of this argument and paint', and ending 'Of waters coloured by the clouds of Heaven', which he found written in a copy of the *Poems* belonging to the poet's son. This passage is substantially the same as that on pp. U and U verso of MS. JJ; *q.v. infra*, pp. 636–7.

**586–8.**          *when the changeful earth,*
> *And twice five seasons on my mind had stamp'd*
> *The faces of the moving year,*

Cf. ll. 502–4 *supra*. Wordsworth's feeling for the seasons is often expressed in language which recalls the poet Thomson. Cf.

> Nature! great parent! whose unceasing hand
> Rolls round the seasons of the changeful year
> > (*The Seasons*, Winter, 106).

**631 [603].** *discipline of fear*: for the part taken by fear in the natural education of the child cf. also the passage in MS. Y (*v.* p. 572).

**[613].** The confusion in the text of E, which led to an unmetrical line, was due to a misreading of D, in which 'I began' written below l. [612] is taken to belong to l. [613]. Intermediary between the readings recorded as D and D² is the reading 'not exempt, I fear, From some infirmity' *etc.*

**643 [615].** *birth of spring*: There is no MS. authority for 'breath of spring' (ed. 1850), which is therefore a printer's error.

**644 [616].** *Planting my snowdrops among winter snows*: The text of 1850 here follows D and not E, the copy sent to press. The explanation of this may be that owing to the error in E [613] the printer made a hash of the passage, and the editor, referring back to D, copied into the proof (either from mistake or choice) the reading of D in this line rather than that of D².

Botanically the metaphor is inaccurate, for it implies, at least, that snowdrops are normally 'planted' in the spring, and its meaning is obscure. Garrod (p. 196) interprets it as referring to the time of year (winter) at which Wordsworth began the composition of *The Prelude*. But the poet seems to mean not 'I began my story early in the year' —a remark which would be pointless in this context, and would give to the word 'early' as applied to the second part of the sentence a meaning different from that which it bore in the first—but rather 'I started my story far back in the earliest period of my Life, dealing

with incidents of my babyhood of which, I admit, I have no distinct
memories.' In the words 'ere the birth of spring planting' *etc.*, he aims
at expressing his misgivings at his attempt to go back to days 'disowned by memory'. In his last revision Wordsworth noticed the
weakness of the metaphor, for he deleted it, and substituted in its
place:

> fancying flowers where none
> Not even the sweetest do or can survive
> For him at least whose dawning day they cheered.

There is no doubt that he wished this reading to stand in the final text,
but unfortunately his editor did not accept the correction.

# BOOK II

**1.** *app. crit.* In MS. 18*a* under the heading 'Part II' appears an
abortive beginning of this book (*v. app. crit. supra*, p. 42).

**1-54.** This passage first appears in MS. RV, and then in U. In
MS. V two pages carrying the passage have been torn out. It must
have been composed after Wordsworth's return to Hawkshead, 'after
long absence', on November 2, 1799, with John Wordsworth and
Coleridge. He refers to the changes in Hawkshead in his letter to his
sister, November 7, 1799.

**39.** *A smart Assembly-room*: This is the Town Hall built in 1790
partly on the site of an older Market House on the south side of the
Hawkshead Market Square (*v. Hawkshead: its history, archaeology,
industries etc.*, by Henry Swainson Cowper, 1899).

**44-45.** *that old Dame From whom the stone was named*: The reading
of A² in l. 38 gives her name, which appears to be Rowe.

**57.** *To beat along the plain of Windermere*: Knight compares *Excursion*, IX. 485-88:

> When, on thy bosom, spacious Windermere!
> A Youth, I practised this delightful art:
> Tossed on the waves alone, or 'mid a crew
> Of joyous comrades . . .

**59-65.** *an Island etc.*: In the fourth ed. of Wordsworth's *Guide to
the Lakes* is the following note on the Islands of Windermere. 'This
Lake has seventeen islands. Among those that lie near the largest,
formerly called "Great Holm", may be noticed "Lady Holm", so
called from the Virgin who had formerly a Chapel or Oratory there. On
the road from Kendal to the Great-Boat, might lately, and perhaps
may still be seen, the ruins of the Holy Cross; a place where the pilgrims
to this beautifully situated shrine must have been in the habit of offering up their devotions. Two other of these islands are named from the
Lily of the Valley, which grows there in profusion.'

**83.** *A little weekly stipend* . . .: The weekly stipend paid by Ann Tyson, began at three pence and rose to sixpence as the boys grew older. Sums varying from 5*s*. 3*d*. to one guinea were paid to the boys at the close of some vacations. The half-yearly holidays came at Midsummer and Christmas, lasting approximately from June 20 to August 4, and from December 20 to January 20. *v*. 'The Boyhood of Wordsworth', by G. G. Wordsworth, *Cornhill Magazine*, April 1920.

**[90–91].** *or by a river side Or shady fountains*: Hutchinson, and others following him, have read here 'by a river's side Or shady fountain's'. But 'river's side' is a cacophony of which Wordsworth was never guilty (cf. I. [173], V. 349, VI. 452, *Peter Bell*, 446, in all of which Wordsworth writes 'river side'), and 'fountains' is not an error for 'fountain's' but for 'fountain', which in D is followed by a large comma, mistaken by E for an 's'. Hence the reading of 1850.

**[98].** *courteous*: So E, but 'courteous' is a copyist's error for 'cautious', the more appropriate epithet taken by D from l. 108 of A.

**[101–2].** *some famed temple where of yore The Druids worshipped*: Knight annotates: 'probably Conishead Priory on the Cartmel Sands'. But, as Mr. Norman Nicholson points out, this Priory has no connexion with the Druids, and he suggests that the reference must be to the Stone Circle at Swinside above the lower Duddon—always known as the Druids' Circle. Wordsworth refers to this Stone Circle in *An Evening Walk*, 1793, l. 171, and again in *The River Duddon*: Sonnet 17—his note to which gives its exact locality: 'The Druidical Circle is about half a mile to the left of the road ascending Stoneside from the Vale of Duddon: the country people call it "Sunken Church".'

**110 [103].** *that large Abbey*: Furness Abbey. Its distance from Hawkshead is twenty-one miles.

**139.** *that still Spirit of the evening air*: Note the textual alteration of this line, and cf. note to I. 351–72.

**144 [137].** *We beat with thundering hoofs the level sand*: The passage in Book X. 567 where this incident is recalled proves that the sands referred to were those of 'Leven's ample estuary', that lie between Cartmel and Ulverston.

**147.** *an Inn*: The White Lion at Bowness. Part of the bowling-green is still extant. It was this bowling-green that the Jacobite and Whig, described in *Excursion*, VI. 405–521, 'filled with harmless strife' (*ibid*. 466).

**152 [145].** *or ere*: 'and ere' (1850) is a mistake made by the copyist of E.

**155 [148].** *its one bright fire*: 'own' (1850) is a copyist's error for 'one'.

**174 [168].** *The Minstrel of our troop*: 'Robert Greenwood, afterwards Senior Fellow of Trinity College, Cambridge' (*Memoirs*, i. 41).

**181–3.** In draft B(2) of this passage 'nor less pleased . . . fair' is a correction of

> with pleased heart
> To stand beneath the vacant sky, whose fair . . .

In B(3) 'loved to watch Their shifting colours' is a correction of 'with delight To watch their colours', 'hours' a correction of 'days' and 'And the dread labours of the Earth' a correction of 'Earth's first remote disturbances'. 'Rested', 'was', 'stay'd', and 'linger'd' were altered later to 'Resteth', 'is', 'stays', and 'lingers'.

On the flysheets at the beginning of B there is another, probably the latest, draft of the passage. It omits ll. 2–5 of B(3) and then runs on, as B(3), to 'Insensibly', but omitting 'My native region's own peculiar boast', and for 'thoughts within the mind itself' reading 'thought within the human mind'. After 'Insensibly' it goes on

> Behold a fleecy Host
> Voluminous, hurrying with the lofty wind
> In squadrons hurrying out of sight while That

*etc.*, as B(3), down to 'permanence serene', after which it reads

> Nor was I unaccustomed with delight
> As keen to stand *etc.* as B(3).

The idea expressed in the lines 'To records listening . . . permanence serene' seems to have been suggested to Wordsworth by reading Thomas Burnet's *The Theory of the Earth containing an account of the Original of the Earth and of all the general changes which it hath already undergone or is to undergo till the consummation of things*. Latin ed. 1681, trs. 1684–9. The edition of 1697 was in Wordsworth's library. In chap. 6 Burnet likens the antediluvian earth to an egg with a thick crust filled with water. The flood, he says, was caused by the action of the sun upon the water, which had no room to expand. After the flood the earth settled down into its present form, the broken shell forming dry land and the water the seas. 'The earth is a hollow sphere with water in it which the heat of the Fire rarefies and burns into vapours and wind. The Sun here is as the Fire, and the exterior Earth is as the Shell, and the Abysse as the water within it. Now when the heat of the Sun had pierced through the Shell and reached the Waters, it began to rarefy them and raise them into vapours, which rarefication made them require more space. . . . And finding themselves pressed in by the exterior earth they pressed with violence against that Arch to make it yield and give way to their dilatation and eruption. If the mouth be stoppt that gives the vent, the water rarefied will burst the vessel with its force. . . . Thus the whole fabric brake.' Wordsworth quotes Burnet in a note to *Excursion* III, and Coleridge refers to him in the *Biographia Literaria*. His book was much read and discussed in the eighteenth century; and he seems to have influenced the geological conceptions of the poet Thomson (*v. Spring*, 309–16, *Liberty*, iv. 461 ff.).

**219 [214].** *succedaneum*: The only other employment of this word in verse with which I am familiar is in Cowper's humorous *Lines to the Rev. William Bull*:

> Oh for a succedaneum then
> To accelerate a creeping pen!

In Cowper's line the word is more suited to its context than it is here.

**220–4 [216–19].** *that false secondary power*: cf. note on 434–5 *infra*.

**232 [228].** *Hard task*: So Raphael speaks of his difficulty in relating the 'invisible exploits of warring Spirits' as 'sad task and hard'. *Paradise Lost*, v. 564.

**246.** *Even* [*in the first trial of its powers*]: This line must have been illegible in the MS. from which A and B were taken. It is supplied from RV, V and M.

**263–4.** *The gravitation and the filial bond etc.*: In an article on Wordsworth's reading of Addison (*R.E.S.* April 1927) Mr. T. E. Casson compares this passage with *Spectator*, No. 571: 'Every particle of matter is actuated by this Almighty Being which passes through it. The heavens and the earth, the stars and planets, move and gravitate by virtue of this great principle within them.' Cf. also *Spectator*, No. 120.

**285–6 [270–1].** *infant sensibility, Great birthright of our Being*: Cf. the passage found in Y, following Book VIII. 159 (notes, p. 571), where Wordsworth shows how infant sensibility develops through the instincts of admiration and love.

**314 [295].** '*best society*': *Paradise Lost*, ix. 249.

> For solitude somtimes is best societie ...

**316 [297].** *By silent inobtrusive sympathies*: another of those few cases (*v.* I. 613–16) where 1850 has followed, not E, but an earlier text.

It is probable that the reading of D² E, 'By inward concords, silent, inobtrusive' seemed to the editor metrically irregular, and that in his distress he referred to an earlier MS.

**321–41.** Two drafts of this passage are found in the *Alfoxden* notebook, among other fragments of passages in *The Excursion*, Book I. It was evidently written in the first place to form part of the description of the Wanderer. The second of them opens:

> he wandered there
> In storm and tempest and beneath the beam
> Of quiet moons he wandered there—and there
> Would feel *etc.* as in A text, but in l. 326 'there would he' for 'and I would', in l. 330 'he' for 'I', in 337 'at' for 'to'. The first draft has ll. 324–9 in contracted form, followed by

> There would he stand
> In the still covert of some [lonesome ?] rock
> Would gaze upon the moon until its light
> Fell like a strain of music on his soul
> And seem'd to sink into his very heart.

This passage is thus among the first parts of *The Prelude* to be written.

**338-9 [319-20].** *With growing faculties she doth aspire,*
*With faculties still growing*:
an imitation of one of the most characteristic features of Milton's poetic style, a studied repetition of words or phrases, the repetition both emphasizing the idea and giving a peculiar musical effect.

**349 [330].** *hours of School*: 'The daily work in Hawkshead School began—by Archbishop Sandys' ordinance—at 6 a.m. in summer, and 7 a.m. in winter' (Knight).

**352 [333].** *a Friend*: the late Rev. John Fleming, of Rayrigg, Windermere (note in 1850). Knight suggests that the friend was the Rev. Charles Farish, author of *The Minstrels of Windermere* and *Black Agnes*, but he gives no authority for his suggestion.

**[341-2].** *or the vernal thrush*
*Was audible; and sate among the woods*:
There is no MS. authority for the reading of 1850. The editor may have disliked the word 'reveillé', and reconstructed the line after reference to earlier texts.

**362 [343].** *some jutting eminence*: Knight has attempted to identify the eminence, but by the word 'some' Wordsworth implies that the same eminence was not chosen every morning. Hence the attempt to identify it is futile.

**368-71 [349-52].** *I forgot That I had bodily eyes etc.*: Cf. the I. F. note to the *Ode: Intimations etc.* 'I was often unable to think of external things as having external existence, and I communed with all that I saw as something not apart from, but inherent in, my own immaterial nature. Many times while going to school have I grasped at a wall or tree to recall myself from this abyss of idealism to the reality. At that time I was afraid of such processes. In later periods of life I have deplored, as we all have reason to do, a subjugation of an opposite character, and have rejoiced over the remembrances, as is expressed in the lines "Obstinate questionings *etc.*" To that dream-like vividness and splendour which invests objects of sight in childhood, every one, I believe, if he would look back, could bear testimony.' Cf. also *Lines composed . . . above Tintern Abbey*, describing the 'serene and blessed mood' in which

> the breath of this corporeal frame,
> And even the motion of our human blood
> Almost suspended, we are laid asleep
> In body, and become a living soul.

and ll. 432-4 *infra*, and VI. 529-42.

**380-1 [361-2]** *That by the regular action of the world*
*My soul was unsubdu'd*:
Wordsworth speaks in several places of the danger to the growing soul when the novelty and wonder of the world begins to wear off, and things are taken for granted: Cf. *Ode*, 130-2,

> Full soon thy Soul shall have her earthly freight,
> And custom lie upon thee with a weight,
> Heavy as frost, and deep almost as life!

and MS. passage in Y (pp. 571–4).

**430.** *I saw one life, and felt that it was joy*: Notice that the definitely Christian explanation of this 'joy' [412–14] is among the latest of the additions to the poem—in MS. E.

**434/435.** MS. RV has a passage here which was not transcribed in MSS. U and V and was never used in the published text of *The Prelude*:

> By such communion I was early taught
> That what we see of forms and images
> Which float along our minds and what we feel
> Of active, or recognizable thought
> 5 Prospectiveness, intelligence or will
> Not only is not worthy to be deemed
> Our being, to be prized as what we are
> But is the very littleness of life
> Such consciousnesses seemed but accidents
> 10 Relapses from the one interior life
> Which is in all things, from that unity
> In which all beings live with God, are lost
> In god and nature, in one mighty whole
> As undistinguishable as the cloudless east
> 15 At noon is from the cloudless west when all
> The hemisphere is one cerulean blue

A version of this passage is found, written in Wordsworth's neat hand, on a page of MS. 2 of *Peter Bell* with the following variants: or intellect *for* intelligence (5); consciousness I deem *for* consciousnesses seemed (9); *and for* (11–14):

> That lives in all things, sacred from (far beyond) the touch
> Of that false secondary power by which
> In weakness we create distinctions, then
> Believe that (*all*) our puny boundaries are things
> Which we perceive and not which we have made
> —In which all beings live with god, themselves
> Are god, existing in one mighty whole

The reference here to the 'false secondary power' does not occur in the parallel passage in RV, which, however, introduces it at l. 220 in this same book. It seems likely, therefore, that the RV version is later than the *Peter Bell* version (date 1799–1800).

In 'the forms and images which float along our minds' and 'what we feel of active *etc.*' Wordsworth is contrasting, like Coleridge in *Biographia Literaria*, chap. v, the passive and active processes of the mind. The 'passive' are those based on the law of association ('the passive fancy and mechanical memory', *Biog. Lit.* i. 73, ed.

Shawcross, and for the phrase 'float along the mind' cf. Coleridge's note, written 1804 (*v. Anima Poetae*, p. 65), on 'the streamy nature of the associative faculty'). The 'active' processes would correspond to Coleridge's 'understanding'.

Wordsworth dismisses both as nugatory in comparison with a state of being deeper and more vital than thought. This state, which he knew in his own experience, he often tries to describe, but it baffles description. Its essential features are (1) the overwhelming consciousness of God (2) the sense that God in Nature is one with God in the soul, so that the soul seems to *be* God or *be* Nature (3) (a natural consequence of (2)) the sense of creative power in the soul. Cf. V. 16, III. 172, 192, 540, and passage found in MS. Y, ll. 137–9 (*v.* p. 575). Hence sprang the 'fear and awe' which fell upon him when he looked into the Mind of Man (*Prospectus to Excursion*, 38–40).

**448–56 [432–40].** *if in these times of fear etc.*: Legouis was the first to point out that this passage was suggested to Wordsworth by a letter he received from Coleridge in the summer of 1799 (quoted *Memoirs*, i. 159): 'I wish you would write a poem, in blank verse, addressed to those, who, in consequence of the complete failure of the French Revolution, have thrown up all hopes of the amelioration of mankind, and are sinking into an almost epicurean selfishness, disguising the same under the soft titles of domestic attachment and contempt for visionary *philosophes*. It would do great good, and might form a part of *The Recluse*.' At this time Wordsworth intended to make it so, for in the five books which formed the original scheme of *The Prelude* his relations with the French Revolution were not touched upon (*v.* Introduction, p. 1).

**461–2.** *app. crit. Ye mists* [*winds* C² D E] *and sounding cataracts 'tis yours*: This line is in all the MSS. from B² onwards: not in A.

**466–7 [451–2].** *Thou . . . wert rear'd In the great City*: Wordsworth here recalls the lines written by Coleridge himself in his *Frost at Midnight*:

I was reared
In the great city, pent 'mid cloisters dim.

# BOOK III

**44.** *The Evangelist St. John*: Wordsworth entered St. John's College on October 30, 1787.

**[17].** *And at the* Hoop *alighted, famous Inn*: 'This line', says Matthew Arnold (*Lectures on translating Homer*), 'shews excellently how a poet may sink with his subject by resolving not to sink with it.' Arnold prefaces the quotation with the statement: 'When Wordsworth having to narrate a very plain matter tries not to sink with it, tries, in short, to be what is falsely called poetical, he does sink, although he sinks by being pompous, not by being low.' This is doubtless a sound general criticism, especially applicable to Wordsworth's later style, but is surely inapplicable here. It is obvious that in recounting a part of his experience as an undergraduate he is in playful mood, as befits the theme, and he treats it in something of the mock-heroic manner. Cf. e.g. ll. 33–43. But from this he can rise as occasion demands.

**[62–63].**     *The marble index of a mind for ever*
          *Voyaging through strange seas of Thought, alone*:
These lines, only introduced into the poem as a correction of D, show that Wordsworth's poetic inspiration was not so shortlived as is sometimes supposed. Legouis has suggested (p. 79) that they owe something to Thomson's *To the Memory of Sir Isaac Newton*:

          The noiseless tide of time, all bearing down
          To vast eternity's unbounded sea,
          Where the green islands of the happy shine,
          He stemmed alone.

**81 ff.** *But wherefore be cast down? etc.*: It is significant that the almost defiant justification of his life at Cambridge, found in the A text and developed in the lines added to A (*v. app. crit.*), is toned down to apology in D E. The parenthesis in 1850 text [83–87], however admirable its sentiment, is wholly irrelevant to his feelings in 1787. In the A text he is interpreting his actual feelings as an undergraduate: in 1850 he reflects upon them from the outlook of an elder brother of the Master of Trinity, just as, after l. [110], he interpolates a gloss on 'earth and heaven' quite foreign to the spirit of the A text.

**85–88.** *To apprehend all passions etc.*: Cf. II. 267–80; 377 ff.

**102–8.** *this first absence etc.*: One of Wordsworth's chief debts to Cambridge was that here first he realized that great source of his poetic inspiration—the 'spiritual presences of absent things'.

**[104–7].** *In youth . . . night of death*: In place of these four lines the text of 1857 simply reads 'In youth, or to be changed in after years'. This text is followed without comment by Dowden and Hutchinson, but there can be no authority for it, and if there were one, it would have been as valid in 1850 as in 1857. It is probable that the change was made by Bishop Wordsworth on its being pointed out to him that the original reading of 1850 was grammatically obscure.

**113 [117].** *spread my thoughts*: Cf. II. 253.

**115 [119].** *incumbences*: cf. IX. 68 *app. crit.* where B reads *incumbences*, A *incumbencies*. Both forms were possible in Wordsworth's day, *incumbences* the older and less usual.

**121 [127].** *A track pursuing not untrod before*: Note that in the A text a fresh paragraph begins here, and the comma after 'subdued' (123) connects ll. 121–3 with what follows, whereas the fullstop in 1850 connects them with what precedes.

**136–7 [140–1].**   *To the sky's motion; in a kindred sense*
*Of passion was obedient etc.*:
The punctuation of A is correct and that of 1850 obviously wrong.
In D the semicolon after 'motion' and in D² after 'influence' was
strengthened to a colon. But E put commas after both 'influence'
and 'passion', and the semicolon after 'passion' was a further mistake
made by 1850.

**178–81 [180–2].** Cf. *Ode: Intimations of Immortality*. This passage
would probably have been written in February 1804 (*v.* Introduction,
p. xlix *supra*) about the time when Wordsworth finished the *Ode*
(*v. P.W.* iv. 465).

**182.** *This is, in truth, heroic argument*: Wordsworth, like Milton,
insists on the heroic nature of his theme. Cf. *Paradise Lost*, ix. 13–29
                              . . . argument
         Not less but more Heroic than the wrauth
         Of stern Achilles . . .
         Not sedulous by Nature to indite
         Warrs, hitherto the onely Argument
         Heroic deemd.
Cf. also Wordsworth's *Prospectus to the Excursion*, 25–41. Both there
and in this passage he infers that as Milton deemed his subject more
'heroic' (i.e. worthy of epic treatment) than Homer's or Virgil's, so
his theme, 'the might of Souls', is more heroic than Milton's.

**[191].** *But is not each a memory to himself*: The sense obviously
requires a note of interrogation, which Knight supplies in his text.

**201.** *Uphold . . . my fainting steps*: an echo of Milton: *Samson
Agonistes*, 666, 'And fainting spirits uphold'. The change of 'Uphold'
to 'Support', introduced in A, was due to the presence of 'told' in the
next line.

**207.** *Observance less devout*: The reading of M here, with its suggestion of the disturbing influence of a sceptical friend, is interesting, but
the friend cannot be identified.

**218–19.** *than sodden clay On a sea River's bed at ebb of tide*: a simile
vividly recalling the sands of Leven and Duddon, known to Wordsworth from boyhood.

**259.** *the opening act*: rightly altered in D to 'second act'. The first
act of his new life had been more significant in his spiritual development, for then it was that he first became conscious of what he owed
to the country he had left behind. Cf. *supra*, ll. 102–8 and note.

**261–2.** *print . . . steps*: Cf. Milton, *Arcades*, 85, 'Where no print of
step hath been'.

**269.** *nobler* [noble]. 'nobler' is the correct reading, 'noble' is a copyist's error in E.

**276–81.** The punctuation of A is obviously correct (*v. app. crit.* for
its gradual deterioration). For the phrasing cf. Milton, *L'Allegro*,
67–68:

And every Shepherd tells his tale
Under the Hawthorn in the dale.

'Trumpington, nat fer fro Canterbrigge' was the scene of Chaucer's
*Reve's Tale*.

**277, 281, 297.** *Chaucer . . . Spenser . . . Milton*: Spenser was at
Pembroke Hall, Milton at Christ's. 'When I began to give myself up
to the profession of a poet for life, I was impressed with a conviction,
that there were four English poets whom I must have continually
before me as examples—Chaucer, Shakespeare, Spenser, and Milton.
These I must study, and equal *if I could*; and I need not think of the
rest.' *Memoirs*, ii. 470.

**284–5.** *who, in his later day, Stood almost single, uttering odious
truth*: So Milton, depicting under the figure of Abdiel his own position
at the Restoration, insists on the same point:

Nor number, nor example with him wrought
To swerve from truth, or change his constant mind
Though single.         (*P.L.* v. 901–3)
            well hast thou fought
The better fight, who single hast maintaind
Against revolted multitudes the Cause
Of Truth         (*P.L.* vi. 29–32).

**286.** *Darkness before, and danger's voice behind*: Cf. *Paradise Lost*,
vii. 27, 'In darkness, and with dangers compast round . . .'

**295–7.** *My Class-fellow at school*: Edward Joseph Birkett, the only
schoolfellow from Hawkshead who was at Christ's at this time: he
was admitted April 19, 1786. *v.* John Peile, *Biographical Register of
Christ's College*, ii. 322.

**305.** *Within my private thoughts*: It is significant that Wordsworth
does not impart to his companions, who would be in no mood to
understand it, what was passing in his mind. The reading of A in the
next line, too, is suggestive, and his various modifications of the A text
(*v. app. crit.*) a little amusing.

**326–8.** In  *Ye will forgive the weakness of that hour
In some of its unworthy vanities,
Brother of many more*

the punctuation of neither A nor 1850 is correct. There should be a
comma after 'hour', but not after 'vanities'.

**340–1.** *A floating island . . . of spungy texture*: Cf. *Guide to Lakes*
(present editor's reprint p. 38). 'There occasionally appears above the
surface of Derwent-water, and always in the same place, a considerable tract of spongy ground covered with aquatic plants, which is
called the Floating, but with more propriety might be named the
Buoyant, Island; and on one of the pools near the Lake of Esthwaite,
may sometimes be seen a mossy Islet, with trees upon it, shifting
about before the wind, a *lusus naturae* frequent on the great rivers of
America, and not unknown in other parts of the world.' Cf. also

D. W.'s poem 'Harmonious Powers with Nature work' *etc. P.W.* iv. 162.

**400–1 [394–5].** *and to endure. The passing Day*: The punctuation of A, which had been conjectured by Professor Garrod as an emendation of 1850, is clearly correct. All MSS. before E have the full stop after 'endure'. E had originally no stop after either 'endure' or 'day', and a later hand added the comma after 'day', which 1850 strengthened into a semicolon.

**410–27 [404–21].** It is interesting to notice that this attack upon compulsory attendance at College Chapel was toned down in later texts; in M (*v. app. crit.*) it was far stronger than in A. It speaks eloquently for Wordsworth's independence of mind that in his most conventional days it was not altogether deleted. Christopher Wordsworth, the poet's brother, made himself unpopular as Master of Trinity College by his rigid enforcement of the rules for attendance at Chapel. *v.* D. A. Winstanley, *Early Victorian Cambridge*, 388–93.

**442–54.** *a Virgin grove etc*: Professor Lane Cooper has called attention to the fact that this passage is a striking example of Wordsworth's debt to that literature of travel and adventure, which, next to poetry and ancient history, was his favourite reading:

'I ascended this beautiful river on whose fruitful banks the generous and true sons of liberty securely dwell, fifty miles above the white settlements . . . My progress was rendered delightful by the sylvan elegance of the groves, cheerful meadows, and high distant forests, which in grand order presented themselves to view. The winding banks of the rivers, and the high projecting promontories, unfolded fresh scenes of grandeur and sublimity. The deep forests and distant hills re-echoed the cheering social lowings of domestic herds. The air was filled with the loud and shrill hooping of the wary sharp-sighted crane. Behold, on yon decayed, defoliated cypress tree, the solitary wood pelican, dejectedly perched upon its utmost elevated spire; he there, like an ancient venerable sage, sets himself up as a mark of derision, for the safety of his kindred tribes.' Bartram, *Travels through North and South Carolina, etc.*, 1794, pp. 47–48.

**486–7 [476–7].** '*an obolus, a penny give To a poor scholar*': The allusion is to Belisarius, the general of the Byzantine Empire, who according to the popular story (dismissed by Gibbon as an idle fable), after he had been disgraced and his eyes put out, begged in the streets of Constantinople, saying 'Date obolum Belisario'. Wordsworth owed his knowledge of the story to Coleridge; for in a letter to him, dated March 29, 1804, he writes, 'I ought to have asked your permission for the scholars and their obolus *etc.*' Perhaps the '*etc.*' is meant to include the references to Bucer and Melanchthon also, which are more in Coleridge's line of reading than Wordsworth's. Bucer (1491–1551), a German Greek scholar brought over to England on Cranmer's invitation, taught theology at Cambridge, and died there. Erasmus came to England in 1497 and taught for some time at Oxford. Melanchthon (1497–1560), Professor of Greek at Wittenberg, friend and associate of Martin Luther.

**511–16 [500–5].** *Far more I griev'd etc.*: On these lines Mrs. Davy's report of a conversation with Wordsworth, June 5, 1846 (quoted Grosart, iii. 456), provides an interesting commentary. 'Some talk concerning school led Mr. Wordsworth into a discourse, which, in relation to himself, I thought very interesting, on the dangers of emulation, as used in the way of help to school progress. Mr. Wordsworth thinks that envy is too likely to go along with this, and therefore would hold it to be unsafe. "In my own case," he said, "I never felt emulation with another man but once, and that was accompanied by envy. This once was in the study of Italian, which I entered on at College along with ——. I never engaged in the proper studies of the university, so that in these I had no temptation to envy anyone; but I remember with pain that I *had* envious feelings when my fellow student in Italian got before me. I was his superior in many departments of mind, but he was the better Italian scholar, and I envied him. The annoyance this gave me made me feel that emulation was dangerous for *me*, and it made me very thankful that as a boy I never experienced it. I felt very early the force of the words 'Be ye perfect even as your Father in heaven is perfect,' and as a teacher, or friend, or counsellor of youth, I would hold forth no other motive to exertion than this. . . . There must always be a danger of incurring the passion of vanity by emulation. Oh! one other time," he added, smiling, "one other time in my life I felt envy. It was when my brother was nearly certain of success in a foot race with me. I tripped up his heels. This *must* have been envy."'

So in his College days Wordsworth annoyed his uncle by declining to compete for the prize offered for elegiac stanzas on the late master of his College. Cf. ll. 533–6 *infra*.

**535.** *dissolute pleasure*: Cf. Wordsworth's statement in a letter to De Quincey, written March 6, 1804, just after completing this book of *The Prelude*, that when he was at Cambridge 'the manners of the young men were very frantic and dissolute'.

**546–9.** *Even as a shepherd on a promontory*: Mr. Oswald Doughty compares Thomson, *The Castle of Indolence*, I. xxx.

**592–4.**      *Of colours, lurking, gleaming up and down*
         *Through that state arras woven with silk and gold;*
         *This wily interchange of snaky hues*:
A reminiscence of Spenser, *Faerie Queene*, III. xi. 28:
         For round about, the wals yclothed were
         With goodly arras of great majesty,
         Woven with gold and silke so close and nere
         That the rich metall lurked privily,
         As faining to be hid from envious eye;

Yet here, and there, and every where, unwares
It shewd itselfe and shone unwillingly;
Like a discolourd Snake, whose hidden snares
Through the greene gras his long bright burnisht backe declares.

**616.** *goings-on*: a favourite word of both Coleridge and Wordsworth. Cf. VI. 350, a fragment of *Michael* (*v. P.W.* ii. 482) 'the goings-on Of earth and sky', and *Gipsies* (1807), 1. 23, 'The silent Heavens have goings on', of which W. W. wrote to Barron Field in October 1828, '"Goings-on" is precisely the word wanted; but it makes a weak and apparently prosaic line, so near the end of a poem.' So also in Preface 1802 Wordsworth speaks of the Poet as 'a man pleased with his own passions and volitions . . . delighting to contemplate similar volitions and passions as manifested in the goings-on of the Universe' *etc.* Cf. Coleridge: *Frost at Midnight*, 11–12,

Sea, and hill, and wood,
With all the numberless goings-on of life;

and *The Friend*, where he translates Bruno's 'ex visibilium aeterno immenso et innumerabili effectu' as 'the perpetual immense and innumerable goings-on of the visible world'. The word is not found in the final text of any poem of Wordsworth's.

**636–7 [604–5].** *Guile; Murmuring Submission*: The punctuation of 1850 is obviously an improvement, but it is not likely that Wordsworth is responsible for it, for it only occurs in E, which is throughout careless in its punctuation.

# BOOK IV

**1–15 [1–26].** These lines describe the walk from Kendal, which Wordsworth reached by coach, over to the Ferry on Windermere, and after crossing the lake, up through Sawrey, past Esthwaite, to Hawkshead. The inapt allusion to 'the Charon of the flood' [14] does not occur before the D text.

**11 [19].** *that sweet valley*: Hawkshead (note in 1850).

**17 [28].** *my old Dame*; Hawkshead Grammar School was a day-school: boys whose homes were at a distance were housed with cottagers in Hawkshead or its near neighbourhood. The Wordsworth boys lodged with Ann Tyson and her husband, first in a cottage in Hawkshead, and afterwards, when the Tysons moved to Colthouse, in a cottage known as Green-end, half a mile east of the town: *v.* Moorman, pp. 84–85; and William Bennett's record of a conversation with Wordsworth in 1846: 'We spoke of his education: nine years, nine to eighteen, had been spent at Hawkshead then a celebrated school, during a great part of which time he lodged at Colthouse.' Dove Cottage MS.: *v. Cumbria*, December 1957. The family account-books record a payment for each boy of £10 per half-year.

**26 [37].** *more than eighty*: Ann Tyson died on May 25, 1796, aged 83.

**35–37 [46–48].** *the court, the garden were not left*
*Long unsaluted, and the spreading Pine*
*And broad stone Table*:

Dr. Cradock (quoted by Knight) calls attention to the reminiscence of *Peter Bell*, 155–6:

To the stone table in my garden
Loved haunt of many a summer hour.

**40 [51].** *The froward Brook*: So all MSS. before E. 'Famous' for 'froward' is a copyist's error in E, which thus found its way into 1850. The brook, now as then, is 'boxed in' as it runs through the garden.

**73.** *In my accustomed Bed*: The following lines, found in a volume containing *Peter Bell* MS. 2 and some fragments of verse belonging to 1798–1800, were obviously jotted down with a view to introduction into *The Prelude*, but were either forgotten or rejected. But they have their interest, as throwing additional light upon Wordsworth as a child:

when in my bed I lay
Alone in darkness, I have seen the gloom
Peopled with shapes arrayed in hues more bright
Than flowers or gems, or than the evening sky;
Processions, multitudes in wake or fair
Assembled, puppet shews with tru[m]pet, fife,
Wild beasts, and standards waving in the [field ?].
These mounting ever in a sloping line
Were foll(ow)ed by the tumult of the shew
Or horses [                    ]
These vanishing, appeared another scene—
Hounds, and the uproar of the ch[ase ?], or steeds
That galloped like the wind through standing corn.
Then headless trunks and faces horrible,
Then came a thron[g] of forms all [           ]
Unutterably, horribly arranged
In parallel lines, in feature and in look
All different, yet marvellously akin;
Then files of soldiery with dazzling arms
Still mounting, mounting upwards, each to each
Of all these spectres every band and cl[ass ?]
Succeeding with fa[n]tastic difference
And instant, unimaginable change.
[                    ] phantoms [                    ]

*(punctuation supplied by editor)*.

**104–8.** *Some fair enchanting image etc.* Cf. his schoolboy poem on *The Dog—an Idyllium*, *P.W.* i. 264, ll. 18–24, where the image and the incident were first recorded.

**110–11 [119–20].** *like a river murmuring And talking to itself*: 'Though the accompaniment of a musical instrument be dispensed with, the true Poet does not therefore abandon his privilege distinct from that of the mere Proseman:

He murmurs near the running brooks
A music sweeter than their own.'    (*Preface to Poems*, 1815.)

**140–1.** *my soul Put off her veil*: Cf. Exod. xxxiv. 33–35; 2 Cor. iii. 13–16.

**148 [157].** *weariness*: 'weakness' (MƷ) is clearly a copyist's error, which at first escaped detection, but can never have been written by Wordsworth. I have therefore substituted 'weariness' in the text. Similarly 'rapt' in 153, which is copied 'wrapped' as late as the D text.

**[198].** *Far otherwise) amid this rural solitude*: In altering this line from its original form Wordsworth has made it hypermetric. Cf. *infra* [289], VI. [261].

**199 [208].** *To deck some slighted Playmate's homely cheek*: a curious echo of Milton: *Lycidas*, 65: 'To tend the homely slighted Shepherds trade.'

**[289].** *And damp those yearnings which had once been mine*: As pointed out in the *app. crit.*, E reads 'daily yearnings', which makes the line hypermetric. Hence the editor of 1850 cut out 'daily'. On the same principle he ought to have cut out 'rural' in [198], but he did not.

**296.** *Th' authentic sight of reason*: Cf. *The Friend* (ed. 1818, i. 268) where Coleridge defines reason as 'the mind's eye', 'an organ bearing the same relation to spiritual objects . . . as the eye bears to material and contingent phenomena.'

**335 [328].** *Grain-tinctured, drench'd in empyrean light*: a Miltonic line. 'Grain-tinctured' is a reminiscence of Milton's 'skie-tinctur'd grain' (*P.L.* v. 285). On its meaning cf. a long and interesting note in Masson's edition (III. 465–7). The word 'grain', now used as equivalent to 'texture' or 'fibre' as of wood or stone (cf. the phrase 'hard in grain'), originally implied colour (cf. *Il Penseroso*, 33, 'All in a robe of darkest grain'); and not merely colour, but a particular colour, i.e. a clear red (*granum*, a seed or kernel, applied to the seed-like bodies of insects of the Coccus genus, from which dark red dye was procured). The literary associations of the word, which would influence Wordsworth in his use of it, are with scarlet or crimson. Cf. Chaucer, *Sir Thopas*, 'His rode is lyk scarlet in grayn', and Spenser, *Epithalamion*, 226–8:

How the red roses flush up in her cheekes,
And the pure snow with goodly vermill stayne,
Like crimsin dyde in grayne.

Thus in the word 'grain-tinctured' Wordsworth describes the mountains as drenched in the crimson of the sky at dawn.

The phrase 'melody of birds' (338) is also found in Milton (*P.L.* viii. 528).

Many conjectures have been made as to the possible route of this memorable walk, for Wordsworth has given no clue as to the situation of the house from which he was coming. If he had spent the evening at a farm in Yewdale, High Arnside, or in the region of Skelwith and Elterwater, he would strike across the high ground which lies between the Oxenfell and Barn Gates roads from Coniston to Ambleside. The mountain panorama here is magnificent, but the views of the sea, which can be obtained in one or two places, are so slight and distant that they hardly can be said to form a real feature of the view. Moreover the distance from Hawkshead of any house in these directions would be considerably greater than the two miles mentioned in the A text.

If he was coming from High Wray, or the west bank of Windermere, he might cross Claife Heights, and at the top of Latterbarrow Crag obtain a really magnificent view of the sea in front, but rather to the left of him; but the mountains could hardly be described as 'near'.

Robertson (*Wordsworthshire*, pp. 142–3) suggests that the poet was walking from a farm at Grizedale, about three miles SSW. from Hawkshead. On the height known as Sans Keldin, to the right of the road thence, a fine view of the sea can be obtained. The objections to this suggestion are that it would be distinctly off the route to ascend Sans Keldin, that the mountains are rather too distant, and that the sea would be behind him and not in front. A final possibility is that he was coming from the head of Coniston Lake or from Atkinson Ground. The direct route would be through meadow and copse near the lake and up on to Hawkshead Moor. His direction would be ENE. and the track would naturally take him over a high point known as Ligging Shaw. As he reached this point he would have a view of the sea in front, somewhat to his right. The sea is rather more distant than in the last-mentioned route, but the mountains are nearer, and the total length of the walk would be little over two miles. I incline to agree with Mr. Gordon Wordsworth that this last route answers best to the description.

**345.** After this line MS. W goes on:

> Thus deep enjoyments did not fail me then
> Even deeper sometimes, as they found a mind
> Engross'd with other matters and estr[anged]
> Instructing it to value, and to know
> What it possess'd though slighted and unused.
> For surely at that time a falling off
> Had taken place, no [        ?        ]

On the next two pages W has rough jottings, in several places quite illegible, of a passage which bears obvious relation to XIII. 101–5, *q.v.* and note, pp. 620–1 ; but when written, it may have been intended for Book V, for *The Prelude* was at that time to be complete in five books.

**346 [339].** *Strange rendezvous my mind was at that time,* : There is no manuscript authority for the punctuation of 1850, which makes non-sense of the passage. Wordsworth would hardly describe this greatest moment of his life, in which he received his poetic baptism, as 'a strange rendez-vous'. The meaning of the A text is clear enough. The mistake arose through E's omission of the comma after 'time', whence 1850, finding the line unpunctuated, interpolated the note of exclamation.

**363–6.** *A favourite pleasure etc.*: cf. XII. 145 ff.: 'I love a public road' *etc.*

**[354–65].** Wordsworth added this passage, doubtless, to explain the strange effect produced upon him by his meeting with the soldier. But it was unnecessary, and the rather elaborate style in which it is written contrasts awkwardly with the bare, telling simplicity of the narration that follows. The addition of ll. [370–8], on the other hand, is valuable: (1) because they enable us to locate the incident as having taken place on the road from Windermere to Hawkshead through Sawrey (the brook being Sawrey brook and the long ascent the rise between the two Sawreys); and (2) because they furnish another illustration of the fact that many of the most impressive moments of the life of Wordsworth arose when they were least expected, in striking contrast with the triviality of the experiences which immediately preceded them. Just as his poetic dedication had come to him on his way back from a dance, so this impressive episode is all the more impressive from his having just

> left a flower-decked room
> (Whose in-door pastime, lighted up, survived
> To a late hour), and spirits overwrought
> Were making night do penance for a day
> Spent in a round of strenuous idleness.

It is interesting to note that the phrase 'strenuous idleness' (cf. Milton's 'strenuous liberty', *S.A.* 271) occurs also in the poem 'This Lawn, a carpet all alive', written in 1829. It is only introduced into *The Prelude* in D², Book IV of D being written on paper with the watermark 1828, and the correction of the whole D text finished by 1839.

**400–504.** Wordsworth's meeting with the discharged soldier, which must have occurred in his first Long Vacation at Hawkshead (he was then 18 years old), clearly haunted his imagination, and some of the details are even more vividly presented in fragments in the *Alfoxden* notebook (early 1798), and in the *Christabel* notebook and MS. 18*a* (1798–1800) than in the version of 1805.

The *Alfoxden* notebook preserves the following fragments:

(a)                        He frets me sore I do not know
    What 'tis that ails him but I think the dog
    Howls to the murmur of the village stream
(b) And every second moment rang a peal
    Felt in my very heart. I could have thought
    His wrath was bent on me—there was no noise
    Nor any foot abroad—I do not know
    What ail'd him but it seemed as if the dog
    Howl'd to the murmur of the village stream
(c) At this I turn'd and through the open trees
IV. 450 Look'd down into the village. All were gone
    To rest nor hearth nor taper-light appear'd
    But every silent window to the moon
    Shone with a yellow glitter. No one there
    Said I is waking we must measure back
    The way which we have come—behind yon wood
    A labourer dwells an honest man and kind
    He will not murmur should we break his rest
    And he shall give you food, if food you need
    And lodging for the night—so back we turned
    And to the cottage bent our steps. He appeared
    To travel without pain and I beheld
    With ill-suppressed astonishment his thin
    And [       ] moving at my side
    With gentle steps and as our walk advanc'd
    I ask'd him why he tarried thus alone
(d) I asked him why he [     ] he answered
IV. 494 My trust is in the God of heaven
    And in the eye of him that passes me

With (a) and (b) cf. ll. 432–4 as given in *Christabel* MS. and 18a *infra*.
The *Christabel* MS. and MS. 18a (slightly later) give a fully worked-
out version of the episode corresponding with *Prelude* 404–504, but
retaining some of the vivid details of the fragmentary passages in
the *Alfoxden* MS. The howling dog, suggested surely by the manu-
facturer's dog whose 'strange, uncouth howl' D. W. noticed at
Alfoxden: 'It howls at the murmur of the village stream' [*Alfoxden
Journal*, Jan. 27, 1798], was banished from the version of 1805.

The following lines are of interest:

406–9 And lank and upright. There was in his form
    A meagre stiffness. You might almost think
    That his bones wounded him. His legs were long
    So long and shapeless that I looked at them
    Forgetful of the body they sustained
              *Christabel* MS., and MS. 18a *del.*
415 Though faded yet entire. His face was turn'd
    Towards the road yet not as if he sought

For any living spirit ⌊thing 18*a*]: he appeared
Forlorn and desolate, a man cut off
From all his kind, and more than half detached
From his own nature. He was alone
      *Christabel* MS., and MS. 18*a del.*

419–20 . . . to solitude. I think
If but a glove had dangled in his hand
It would have made him more akin to man
Long time I scann'd him with a mingled sense
      *Christabel* MS., and MS. 18*a del.*

424–5 Kept the same fearful steadiness. His shadow
Lay at his feet    *Christabel* MS., and MS. 18*a del.*

432 A groan scarce audible, but all the while
The chained mastiff in his wooden house
Was vexed and from among the village trees
Howled in the stillness. Not without reproach
Had I prolonged my watch and now confirmed
And my heart's specious cowardice subdued
      *Christabel* MS. and MS. 18*a del.*

478–9 I asked him wherefore he had tarried there
At such late hour nor had demanded rest
At any inn or cottage: he replied
'Twas not from [carelessness ?] when I had stopped
My weakness made me loth to move, in truth
I felt myself at ease and much reliev'd
But that the village mastiff fretted me
And every second moment rang a peal
Felt in my very heart. I could have thought
His wrath was bent on me—there was no noise
Nor any foot abroad. I do not know
What ail'd him but it seem'd as if the dog
Howl'd to the murmur of the village stream.
      *Christabel* MS.

491–2 But at the door of cottage or of inn
Demand the succour which his state required
And told him feeble as he was 'twere fit
He asked relief or alms. At this reproof
      *Christabel* MS. and 18*a.*

502 And so we parted   *Christabel* MS. *ends here.*
MS. 18*a adds the last words in a different hand.*

The story of the meeting with the discharged soldier must have been
one of the first parts of *The Prelude* to be written, early in 1798
(clearly it was intended for *The Recluse*). Readers will notice in the
style and phrasing a distinct similarity with parts of *The Cumberland
Beggar* and *Old Man Travelling*, written at the same period (*v.* espe-

cially ll. 442–9, 474–8). It belongs to the time when Wordsworth was influenced by Godwin in his views of war.

**468.** *ghastly*: E reads 'ghostly' which is a copyist's error. The 'o's and 'a's in D are often indistinguishable, and here E reads as an 'o' what was meant for an 'a'.


# BOOK V

**1–10.** MS. E begins this book with the word 'Hitherto' (10). In D the previous lines are written out at the end of the book after the 'Overflow' (*v. infra*, note to l. 345), other versions of the passage having been deleted. The copyist of E, taking them to be a part of the 'Overflow', failed to insert them in their proper place, and they were probably supplied to the printer on a loose sheet now lost.

**16.** *A soul divine which we participate*: The later reading of this line removes from it all trace of Wordsworth's early Pantheism. Cf. note to II. 434–5.

**25.** *Might almost 'weep to have' what he may lose*: a quotation from Shakespeare, *Sonnet* lxiv:

> This thought is as a death, which cannot choose
> But weep to have that which it fears to lose.

This sonnet is among those which Wordsworth singled out 'for their various merits of thought and language' (*Essay, supplementary to Preface*, 1815).

**55–139.** In his articles on Wordsworth in *Tait's Magazine* for January, February, and April 1839 (*v. Collected Works*, ed. Masson, ii. 268), De Quincey writes: 'In a great philosophical poem of Wordsworth's, which is still in manuscript, there is, at the opening of one of the books, a dream, which reaches the very *ne plus ultra* of sublimity, in my opinion, expressly framed to illustrate the eternity, and the independence of all social modes or fashions of existence, conceded to those two hemispheres, as it were, that compose the total world of human power—mathematics on the one hand, poetry on the other.' He proceeds to give, with quotations, 'though not refreshed by a sight of the poem for more than twenty years,' an interesting critical account of this passage—a striking proof of the impression it had made upon him. This remarkable dream-experience as recounted by Wordsworth has been noted with admiration by many critics, and it has been generally assumed that the dream was dreamt, or at least invented, by Wordsworth himself. But an excellent critical handling of it by Jane Worthington Smyser (*P.M.L.A.* March 1956, vol. lxxi. 1) puts the dream in a new light. In all MSS. prior to the corrected D (i.e. 1839) Wordsworth gives this dream to a friend (a Philosophic Friend A² C) and not to himself. In the final text where the dream is attributed to himself, the 'studious friend' is retained (ll. 50–56), but pointlessly. Mrs. Smyser establishes the dream as, in its central motif and in the symbols which carry it (the two books), the very dream, one of three, dreamt by Descartes on November 10, 1619 (v. Baillet's *Life of Descartes*, 1691). In this third dream Descartes records that he dreamt he beheld on his table a dictionary, and found that it contained all the Sciences gathered together. Almost at once he saw another book entitled *Corpus Poetarum*. An unknown man appeared, conversed with him and disappeared. Descartes was enraptured with the two books, which he thought must contain all scientific knowledge, and all the imaginative wisdom of poetry. (Wordsworth with poetic licence calls the first book a Stone, and the second a Shell.) If this dream came from Descartes, then who was the studious or philosophic friend who told it to Wordsworth ? Most probably Coleridge, who had a special interest in dreams and also in Descartes. Wordsworth transformed the dream and made it the expression of his own mind by linking it with a deep and awful moral, and by giving it a romantic setting suggested by his own early reading of Cervantes and of Eastern tales.

**106.** *undisturbed by space or time*: cf. VI. 155 and [XI. 330–3].

**164.** *immortal Verse*: from Milton, *L'Allegro*, 137, and *Comus*, 516.

**166–72 [166–73].** Mr. Nowell Smith has already called attention to the punctuation of 1850, which makes nonsense of the passage : in A the meaning is quite clear. The development of the text shows how the error arose. A² C put a note of exclamation after 'thoughts' (168) and kept the comma after 'Infancy' (169). D², in adding [169] naturally removed the stop at the end of the previous line, and has no stop after 'Infancy' [170] or 'even' [171], but a comma after 'unthanked' [169] and 'childhood' [171]. No doubt a full stop was intended after 'unpraised', but, as often at the end of a line, it was omitted. E puts in a comma after 'unpraised', and the erroneous semicolon after 'infancy' [170] was added later.

**178–9.** *some tale That did bewitch me then*: The reading of Wordsworth's boyhood may be conjectured from his reference to Fortunatus, Jack the Giant-killer, Robin Hood, and Sabra and St. George in ll. 364–9, to the Arabian Nights (484), to Fairy Land and the Forests of Romance (477), and from the following statement in his Autobiographical Memoranda (*Memoirs*, i. 10): 'Of my earliest days at school I have little to say, but that they were very happy ones, chiefly because I was left at liberty, then and in the vacations, to read whatever books I liked. For example, I read all Fielding's works, Don Quixote, Gil Blas, and any part of Swift that I liked ; Gulliver's Travels and the Tale of a Tub, being both much to my taste.' From *Memoirs* (i. 34) we learn 'that the poet's father set him very early to learn portions of the works of the best English poets by heart, so that at an early age he could repeat large portions of Shakespeare, Milton, and Spenser.'

**201.** *Whether by native prose or numerous verse*: *Paradise Lost*, v. 150.

**205–6.**   *And that, more varied and elaborate,*
        *Those trumpet-tones of harmony*:

i.e. Milton; cf. 'Scorn not the sonnet', ll. 11–14, and fragment of Poem, *P.W.* v. 362.

**209.** *For Cottagers and Spinners at the wheel*: Cf. the words of the Duke in *Twelfth Night* of the 'old and plain song' which

        The spinsters and the sitters in the sun
        Do use to chant.

**219–22.** *speak of them as Powers ... only less ... Than Nature's self*: Cf. XII. 309–12, where Wordsworth expresses the hope

            that a work of mine,
        Proceeding from the depth of untaught things,
        Enduring and creative, might become
        A power like one of Nature's.

It was by this power, which Wordsworth always insisted was the distinctive mark of great literature, that he wished his own work to be judged. Crabb Robinson (ed. E. J. Morley, p. 53) records a conversation in which a friend of his 'estimated Wordsworth's poems chiefly for the purity of their morals. Wordsworth, on the other hand, valued them only according to the power of mind they presupposed in the writer, or excited in the hearer.' Cf. *Essay suppl. to Pref.* 1815 (*Oxf. W.*, p. 952). The clearest statement of Wordsworth's position is found in De Quincey's Essay on Pope: 'There is', says De Quincey, 'first the literature of *knowledge*; and secondly the literature of *power*. The function of the first is to *teach*; of the second is to *move*. The first speaks to the *mere* discursive understanding; the second speaks ultimately to the higher understanding or reason, but always *through* affections of pleasure and sympathy. . . . There is a rarer thing than truth, namely *power* or deep sympathy with truth. . . . What you owe to Milton is not any knowledge; what you owe is *power*, i.e. exercise and expansion to your own latent capacity of sympathy with the infinite, where every pulse and each separate influx is a step upwards.' And elsewhere he writes: 'The true antithesis to knowledge is not pleasure but *power*. All that is literature seeks to communicate power; all that is not literature, to communicate knowledge.' To this, De Quincey adds, in a note, 'For which distinction, as for most of the sound criticism on poetry, or any subject connected with it that I have ever met with, I must acknowledge my obligations to many years' conversation with Mr. Wordsworth' (*De Q. Works*, ed. Masson, xi. 55; x. 48).

In the earlier scheme of *The Prelude*, which was to consist of five books only, the last book was to be devoted in part to illustrating this 'power' as gained from Nature and Books, and to showing by examples the kinship of the emotion aroused by both of them (*v.* pp. 623–8 *infra*).

**[222].** *Or His pure Word by miracle revealed*: a characteristic addition which only occurred to Wordsworth, in its first form, after C had been copied, i.e. about 1820.

**226 ff.** *I was reared Safe from an evil*: Much has been written on the influence of Rousseau on Wordsworth's theories of education, but though he had certainly read *Émile*, and as a young man was surrounded by warm advocates of Rousseau, he based his views on his own experience, and only seems to refer to Rousseau when he differs from him. Like Rousseau he held that Nature was fundamentally good and her creatures pure until they had been perverted by society; that education, therefore, must be directed to the development rather than the repression of natural instinct, and that much harm was done by premature appeals to the reason; but whilst Rousseau, not trusting Nature to do her work unaided, advocates the close guidance of the child in the path of Nature, Wordsworth is content to stand aside, and leave Nature and the child to themselves. The praise he accords his mother in this respect (ll. 270–85) is an implicit criticism of Rousseau's 'tutor', with his artificial manipulation of Nature's lessons. In contrast, too, to Rousseau's attack on books, and especially on tales of wonder and magic, as the bane of childhood, Wordsworth insists on their value as the firmest ally of Nature in educating the child, stimulating his imagination, saving him from vanity and self-consciousness (354–69), keeping alive his sense of wonder when it tends to lose its hold upon him (*v.* pp. 573–4, ll. 80–98), and softening the effects of Nature's sterner lessons (ll. 473–81 *infra*). Moreover, Wordsworth raises no protest against the school tasks which fell to his own lot at an age long before Rousseau would admit any formal instruction, and instead of advocating a childhood free from contamination with his fellows, pays special tribute to his debt to the rough and tumble of public school life (XIII. 314–31).

His chief protests, however, are not against Rousseau, but against those who, stimulated by the enthusiasm for education kindled by Rousseau, but without his genius, devoted their lives to 'child study', substituted for the old-time classics of the nursery, such as *Robin Hood* and the *Arabian Nights, etc.*, edifying tales designed to inculcate scientific information or moral truth, and invented systems which, under a show of developing the latent powers of the child, fettered that development at every turn, and produced not the child of Nature, but the self-conscious prig. It is interesting to note D. W.'s account of the training that she and her brother gave to little Basil Montagu, of whom they had charge in 1796–7. 'You ask to be informed of our system respecting Basil; it is a very simple one: so simple that in this age of systems you will hardly be likely to follow it. We teach him nothing at present but what he learns from the evidence of his senses. He has an insatiable curiosity, which we are always careful to satisfy to the best of our ability. It is directed to everything he sees, the sky, the fields, trees, shrubs, corn, the making of tools, carts, etc. He knows his letters, but we have not attempted any further step in the path of *book-learning*' (*E.L.* 164). The last decades of the eighteenth century and the first years of the nineteenth saw an alarming growth of theories about education. Locke in his *Some thoughts concerning education* (1693) had started with the conception of the mind at birth as a *tabula rasa* on which the experience of the senses can be inscribed: his system of education was therefore based on the training of the senses. Rousseau's *Émile*, published in 1762, and translated into English in the same year, made a profound impression. Like Locke he condemned current systems for over-emphasis on book-learning. In 1798 the Edgeworths, stimulated by Locke and Rousseau, produced their *Practical Education*, published in late summer and read by Coleridge in September when he was abroad with Wordsworth and Dorothy: they must have agreed with him in condemning the Edgeworths' distrust of the imagination—'a good servant, but a bad master'. Wordsworth to the end of his life insisted on the necessary part to be played by imagination. 'We must not only have Knowledge but the means of wielding it, and that is done infinitely more thro' the imaginative faculty assisting both in the collection and application of facts than is generally believed' (Letter on reforms in education, *L.Y.* 1269).

The absurd results of the Edgeworths' carefully planned schemes for the education of children are unintentionally exposed in Thomas Day's *Sandford and Merton*, originally written as a story for a book of the Edgeworths for their children. Cf. notes *infra* to ll. 304 and 331. Wordsworth's views on education are based on a sound sense of fact. No system isolating the boy under the vigilant care of a tutor could appeal to him:[1] what he asked for was companionship in regular schooling and in sports and games, together with plenty of freedom for solitary wandering. He said with pride in his old age that 'no man in England had been more regularly educated: nine years from nine to nineteen had been spent at Hawkshead, then a celebrated school' (Notes of William Bennet, 1846. Dove Cottage MS.). But this regular drilling with his fellows in school was accompanied by the experience of 'one who spent half of his boyhood in running wild among the Mountains' (*L.Y.* 1269). Cf. notes on ll. 345 and 370–7 *infra*.

**235.** *bye-spots*: a word not found in the *Oxford English Dictionary*, but recorded in Wright's *Dialect Dictionary* as peculiar to Cumberland ( = lonely spots). It is interesting to find Wordsworth using, and then deleting, a dialect word.

---

[1] The classical example of an intensive system of education carried out by a highly intelligent tutor is found in James Mill's attempt to educate his gifted son; the result, revealed in John Stuart Mill's *Autobiography*, was a near breakdown, from which he completely recovered, significantly enough, through the chance reading of a volume of Wordsworth's poetry.

**236–7.** These two lines were added to A soon after it was copied. The one line which originally stood in their place has been carefully scratched out as well as the last word of the previous line, and the two new lines inscribed in a smaller writing. The earlier reading was probably that of M. The B text was only begun when eight books of A were already copied; hence it shows no sign here of a correction.

**256–7.** *Early died My honour'd Mother*: i.e. in March 1778, at Penrith, her former home.

**268.** *shaping novelties from those to come*: The reading 'from', which persists through M, A, B, and C, was probably a scribal error for 'for', due to the 'from' in the line above.

**290–1.** *My drift hath scarcely, I fear, been obvious*: It is strange that though the poem underwent such continued revision, Wordsworth did not improve this prosaic and unnecessary statement.

**303 [305].** *The wandering Beggars propagate his name*: Legouis points out (p. 62) that here Wordsworth is in agreement with Rousseau, who protested in *Émile* (Book II) against Locke's opinion that the child should be incited to liberality.

**304.** *Dumb creatures find him tender as a Nun*: Thomas Day's little hero, Harry Sandford (in *Sandford and Merton*), is brave, generous to beggars, kind to animals, even cockchafers, calm in the presence of an angry bull. Even the cattle were glad when he came back after an absence.

**315–18 [307–9].** *fear itself . . . Touches him not*: To Wordsworth 'the discipline of fear' was among the most educative of Nature's agencies. Cf. I. 329–441 and passage found in Y (*v.* note to VIII. 159–72).

**316.** *Natural or Supernatural alike*: omitted in MS. M. *v.* letter of W. W. to S. T. C. March 29, 1804, *E.L.* 380.

**331.** *Ships he can guide across the pathless sea*: Harry Sandford finds his way home by the Pole-Star when he is lost.

**335.** *Can string you names of districts, cities, towns*: The five-year-old son of a friend of Locke's brought up on Locke's principles, could trace upon the globes 'all the noted parts, countries and cities of the world'.

**337.** Upon a gossamer thread, *boundless th'embrace Of his intelligence,* he sifts etc.: words in italics omitted in MS. M as noted by W. W. in the letter referred to above at l. 316, and never restored to the text. Two other lines, V. 437–8, mentioned by W. W. in the same letter as omitted from his copy, appear however in MS. M.

There must have been a third copy with these lines omitted, perhaps that which was lost but recovered in January 1806 (*v. M.Y.* 2 and 3).

**345.** D has here the following passage, afterwards struck out:

> Now let us ask: for this preposterous growth
> Who shall be blamed ? The Trainers; let the tree
> Be pitied rather, wonder not unlike

> [For this preposterous growth the Trainer blame
> Pity the tree a wonder not unlike]   D²
> To one of China's vegetable dwarfs
> Where Nature stands subjected to such freaks
> Of human care unceasingly perverse,
> *Here* to advance the growth and *there* retard,
> That the proportions of the full-grown oak
> Its roots, trunk, boughs, its foliage all appear
> In living miniature expressed, produced
> The Oak beneath whose umbrage freely spread
> Within its native fields, whole herds repose!

The revision of D and E reduced the passage to 47 lines, but evidently this reduction went against the grain, for he preserved fourteen of the rejected lines in the MSS. of D and E, in each case at the end of the Book, heading them 'Overflow'. They run as follows:

> What need of more? in him we strive to paint
> The Child is lost, but see for recompense
> The noon-tide shadow of a man complete
> Say rather a fond marvel, not unlike
> To one of China's vegetable dwarfs
> Whose trunk, whose branches ye(a) whose very leaves
> Are here perversely checked and there advanced
> Till the proportions of the forest oak
> Are in one miniature produced, the Oak
> Beneath whose full grown majesty of shade
> Stretched o'er its native plain whole herds repose
> For this unnatural growth the trainer blame
> Pity the tree, poor human vanity
> Were that extinguished nothing would be left.

**370–7.** An early draft of this passage which satirizes modern scientific systems of education is found in MS. 18*a*.

> There are who tell us that in recent times
> We have been great discoverers, that by dint
> Of nice experience we have lately given
> To education principles as fixed
> And plain as those of a mechanic trade
> Fair books and pure have been composed that act
> Upon the infant mind as does the Sun
> Upon a flower, in the corrected scheme
> Of modern days all error is block'd out
> So jealously that wisdom thrives apace
> And in our very boyhood we become
> Familiar friends with cause and consequence.
> Great feats have been performed, a smooth high-way
> So they assert has lately overbridged
> The random chaos of futurity.

> Hence all our steps are firm and we are made
> Strong in the power of knowledge. Ample cause
> Why we now living in this happy age
> Should bless ourselves.
>             For briefly 'tis maintained
> We now have rules and theories so precise
> That by the inspection of unwearied eyes
> We can secure infallible results.
> But if the shepherd to his flock should point
> The herb which each should feed on were it not
> Service redundant and ridiculous ?
> And they the tutors of our youth our guides
> And Masters, Wardens of our faculties . . . .

This was probably written in 1797–8. Wordsworth's revulsion against high-flown systems of education for children is seen in perspective against the background of the scheme for the education of a genius, which Thomas Wedgwood was at this time pressing upon Godwin, and in which he was attempting to engage the interest of Wordsworth and Coleridge, *v.* 'Coleridge, Wordsworth and the Wedgwood Fund', by David V. Erdman, *Bulletin of the New York Library*, September and October 1956.

**384–6.** *in the unreasoning . . . better eye than theirs*: These lines but with *ours* for *theirs* were first published as a quotation in the *Postscript to the Poems* of 1835, where Wordsworth gives them a significance and a moral of which he was quite innocent when he wrote them in 1804.

**389–422 [364–97].** *There was a boy etc.*: written in Germany, October–December 1798 (*v.* MS. JJ, p. 639 *infra*), and sent to Coleridge, who acknowledged it in a letter dated December 10, 1798: 'The blank lines gave me as much direct pleasure as was possible in the general bustle of pleasure with which I received and read your letter. I observed, I remember, that the "fingers woven" etc. only puzzled me ; and though I liked the twelve or fourteen first lines very well, yet I like the remainder much better. Well, now I have read them again, they are very beautiful, and leave an affecting impression. That

>             Uncertain heaven received
> Into the bosom of the steady lake,

I should have recognized anywhere ; and had I met these lines running wild in the deserts of Arabia, I should have instantly screamed out "Wordsworth!"' Dykes Campbell has suggested that l. 396, which is not found in an early MS., was added later 'in deference to S. T. C.'s expression of puzzlement'.

The lines were first published in the *Lyrical Ballads*, 1800, and afterwards included in the *Poems in Two Volumes* (1815). At different times slight changes were introduced into the text. Thus, ed. 1800 reads 'a wild scene' for 'concourse wild' (403), omits ll. 414–15, and at l. 422, reads:

Mute—for he died when he was ten years old.
Ed. 1827 reads in ll. 416–17:
    Pre-eminent in beauty is that Vale
    Where he was born and bred. The churchyard hangs
and ed. 1836 reads in ll. 404–5:
            and when there came a pause
    Of silence such as baffled his best skill.

In 1815 'There was a boy' stands first among the *Poems of the Imagination* and is referred to in the Preface in the following passage (omitted in 1845):

'I dismiss this subject with observing—that in the series of Poems placed under the head of Imagination, I have begun with one of the earliest processes of Nature in the development of this faculty. Guided by one of my own primary consciousnesses, I have represented a commutation and transfer of internal feelings, co-operating with external accidents to plant, for immortality, images of sound and sight, in the celestial soil of the Imagination. The Boy, there introduced, is listening, with something of a feverish and restless anxiety, for the recurrence of the riotous sounds which he had previously excited; and, at the moment when the intenseness of his mind is beginning to remit, he is surprized into a perception of the solemn and tranquillizing images which the Poem describes.'

**397–8 [372–3].** *he, as through an instrument, Blew mimic hootings*: 'This practice of making an instrument of their own fingers is known to most boys, though some are more skilful at it than others. William Raincock of Rayrigg, a fine spirited lad, took the lead of all my schoolfellows in this art' (I. F. note). Robertson (*Wordsworthshire*, pp. 67–68) after consultation of the village burial records, identified the 'boy' of the poem with either George Graham Gibson, died June 26, 1779, or John Vickars, died July 28, 1782. It could hardly be the former as Wordsworth only came to school after Whitsuntide 1779.

**450–81 [426–59].** *Well do I call to mind etc.*: possibly written in Germany in the winter of 1798–9 (*v.* Introduction, p. xlv). On the date when Wordsworth went to school *v.* I. 308 note.

**465–6 [441–2].** *a fish up-leaping, snapp'd The breathless stillness*: cf. *Fidelity* (written 1805):
    There sometimes doth a leaping fish
    Send through the tarn a lonely cheer . . .

**513 [488].** *a sudden bound of smart reproach*: It is characteristic of Wordsworth and the hold that Nature had upon him, that he reproaches himself on what some boys would regard as a matter of congratulation.

**532–3 [508–9].** *Our simple childhood sits upon a throne*
             *That hath more power than all the elements*:
Cf. *Personal Talk*, 23–25:
    Children are blest, and powerful; their world lies

More justly balanced; partly at their feet,
And part far from them:

**552 [528].** *Who make our wish our power, our thought a deed*: The punctuation of A is obviously right and that of 1850 wrong. D reads our wish our power, our thought, our deed. E omits all stops, and 1850 has no authority but that of the printer or editor.

**554 [530].** *And Seasons serve; all Faculties; to whom*: Again A's punctuation is correct, and its significance is still further emphasized by D, which reads 'all Faculties;—'. But E again omits all stops, and 1850, while restoring the semicolon after 'serve', omits the equally important one after 'Faculties'.

**556.** *Northern lights*: Cf. note to *The Complaint etc.* (*P.W.* ii, p. 40).

**560.** *A tract of the same isthmus*: Mr. Doughty compares Pope, *Essay on Man*, ii. 3, 'Plac'd on this isthmus of a middle state'.

**575–6 [552–3].** *Thirteen years Or haply less*: More probably correct than the reading of 1850. 'Less than twice five years' would mean on his entrance to Hawkshead school.

**581–601 [558–77].** De Quincey adds an interesting detail in summarizing this passage in his article on Wordsworth ('Lake Reminiscences: William Wordsworth II') in *Tait's Magazine*, February 1839: 'At another period of the year, when the golden summer allowed the students a long season of early play before the studies of the day began, he describes himself as roaming, hand-in-hand, with one companion along the banks of Esthwaite Water, chanting, with one voice, *the verses of Goldsmith and Gray*—verses which, at the time of recording the fact, he had come to look upon as either in parts false in the principles of their composition, or, at any rate, as wofully below the tone of high poetic passion; but which, at that time of life, when the profounder feelings were as yet only germinating, filled them with an enthusiasm which he describes as brighter than the dreams of fever or of wine.' In this article De Quincey implies that he is citing from memory a MS. of *The Prelude* which he had seen more than twenty years back: his quotations (all except one) correspond in fact with MS. A (*v.* John Edwin Wells, 'De Quincey and *The Prelude* in 1839', *Philological Quarterly*, Jan. 1941).

**583–4 [561].**                              *with that dear Friend*
                     *The same whom I have mention'd heretofore*:
The reading of 1850 'with a dear friend' has left room for speculation as to who the friend was. Text A makes this clear (*v.* II. 352 and note).

**[595–6].**                                    *Visionary power*
                     *Attends the motions of the viewless winds*:
Cf. II. 326–9. 'Viewless winds' is a reminiscence of the great speech of Claudio in *Measure for Measure*, III. 1:

> To be imprisoned in the viewless winds,
> And blown with restless violence about
> The pendant world.

**630–7.** There is no MS. authority for the omission of these lines in 1850. They are found unerased in both D and E. The lines might justly be omitted on poetic grounds, but they are valuable biographically, as probably written a few days after Wordsworth had given up the idea of completing the poem in five books, i.e. after March 6, 1804, when the opening of XIV was headed 'Fifth Book'. The reading of M points to a section of *The Prelude* on the influence of bad books, which unfortunately was never written.

# BOOK VI

*Among the notes on this Book will be found, marked 'S. T. C.', the annotations made by Coleridge in MS. B (v. Introduction, p.* xix).

**[11].** *Clothed in the sunshine of the withering fern*: a magnificent line of which there is no trace in A. It is interesting to follow its evolution from the reading of A² C, through D, to D².

**25 [22].** *Two winters may be pass'd*: the winters of 1788–9 and 1789–90.

**26–28 [23–24].** *many books . . . devour'd, Tasted or skimm'd, or studiously perus'd*: Cf. Bacon, *Essays*, 'Of Studies': 'Some books are to be tasted, others to be swallowed, and some few to be chewed and digested'. Because Wordsworth himself lays stress on the less studious side of his life at Cambridge, and speaking of himself as 'an Idler among academic Bowers' (VIII. 649) and of reading with 'no settled plan', accepts in later years that apologetic attitude to his undergraduate days common enough to mature graduates, the extent of his reading has often been absurdly minimized and its whole character misconceived. As a matter of fact he read more widely and with better result than many students who win unqualified approval from their tutors. As to mathematics he himself explains (*Memoirs*, i. 14) that he did so much at school that 'I had a full twelve months' start of the freshmen of my year, and accordingly got into rather an idle way'. 'William', wrote Dorothy, June 26, 1791, 'lost the chance indeed the certainty of a fellowship, by not combating his inclinations, He gave way to his natural dislike of studies so dry as many parts of the Mathematics, consequently could not succeed at Cambridge. He reads Italian, Spanish, French, Greek, Latin, and English, but never opens a mathematical book. . . . He has a great attachment to poetry, . . . which is not the most likely thing to produce his advancement in the world; his pleasures are chiefly of the imagination, he is never so happy as when in a beautiful country. Do not think in what I have said that he reads not at all, for he does read a great deal, and not only poetry, and those languages he is acquainted with, but history *etc. etc.*' It is true that he writes himself to Mathews (Nov. 1791) that he knows 'little of Latin and scarce anything of Greek. A pretty confession for a young gentleman whose whole life ought to have been devoted to study', but though he was not in any technical sense a scholar he 'read classic authors according to my fancy' and he knew enough, at least, of the classics to be able to appreciate Virgil, Horace, and Theocritus (cf. VIII. 312–24, X. 1016–28). For a close study of Wordsworth's reading at Cambridge *v*. B. Schneider.

**43 [31].** *more*: The reading of 1850, 'now', has no MS. authority and is obviously a misprint.

**55 [42].** *The Poet's soul was with me at that time*: It was in his first long vacation that he was dedicated a poet. Cf. IV. 340–5.

**61 [48].** *Four years and thirty, told this very week*: i.e. the first week in April 1804. Thursday, April 7, 1804, was the anniversary of his birthday.

**63–64 [51–52].** Another example of a fine late correction, only reaching perfection after E had been copied, i.e. about 1839.

**66 [54].** *lightly*: so all MSS. and 1850: 'slightly', the reading of Hutchinson, Nowell Smith, and Moore Smith, has no authority.

**77–79.** *I lov'd, and I enjoy'd etc.*: Cf. the description of the poet in *A Poet's Epitaph*, ll. 53–56.

**[65].** *achieve*: a misprint in 1850. MSS. D and E both read 'admire' though in E it might carelessly be misread 'achieve'. Hence the error. To 'achieve' was just what, at this time, Wordsworth did *not* do.

**90 [76].** *A single Tree*: In August 1810 D. W., then on a visit to Cambridge, wrote to Lady Beaumont: 'We walked in groves all the morning and visited the Colleges. I sought out a favourite ash-tree which my brother speaks of in his poem on his own life—a tree covered with ivy.' It was, perhaps, of this tree that Wordsworth was thinking in the *Ode : Intimations etc.*, 51- 53:

> But there's a tree, of many, one,
> A single field that I have looked upon,
> Both of them speak of something that is gone.

**124–34 [106–14].** An interesting passage which should be read in connexion with the Appendix 'on what is usually called Poetic Diction' (1802), and with XII. 253–74. It is evident that Wordsworth's later views on the subject of poetic style were a strong reaction from the taste of his undergraduate days. For if, as he says in ll. 117–18, the books which he 'then lov'd the most' are dearest to him now, as he writes *The Prelude* in 1804 (i.e. Spenser, Shakespeare, and Milton), his outward taste (l. 116) was for the most artificial and elaborate of the eighteenth-century poets, for it was they whom he strove to imitate and overgo in *An Evening Walk* (written at Cambridge). On the style of his early poems, *v*. the acute criticism in Legouis trs., pp. 127–57. Wordsworth was doubtless attracted to this style of writing, as he himself suggests in the Appendix, by its 'influence in impressing a notion of the peculiarity and exaltation of the Poet's character, and in flattering the Reader's self-love by bringing him nearer to a sympathy with that character'. As a child, poetry had appealed to him, as to most children, from a love of fine language and rhythm for their own sakes (V. 567–81).

On the 'delusion to young scholars incident', cf. the remarks of Coleridge, *Biographia Literaria*, chap. i.

**135–87.** For Wordsworth's interest in mathematics *v.* note to ll. 26–28, V. 64–139, and X. 902 ff.

**192.** *A melancholy from humours of the blood*: It is worth noting that in the A text Wordsworth definitely connects this melancholy with his physical health (cf. X. 870 and note). Both here and in Book X the text is altered.

**194.** *piping winds*: Cf. *Il Penseroso*, 126, 'While rocking winds are piping loud.'

**195 [175].** *Autumn than Spring*: His sister Dorothy shared this youthful taste. Cf. her letter to Jane Pollard, August 1793: 'I grant that the sensations autumn excites are not so chearful as those excited by the birth of Nature's beauties in the spring months, yet they are more congenial to my taste, the melancholy pleasure of walking in a grove or wood, while the yellow leaves are showering around me, is grateful to my mind beyond even the exhilarating charms of the budding trees.' ·

**200–2 [180–2].** *the Bard who sang etc.*: James Thomson in *The Castle of Indolence*, I. xv:

> Here nought but candour reigns, indulgent ease,
> Good-natured lounging, sauntering up and down.

**[188–9].** *the fault, This I repeat, was mine*: Note the self-reproach of these late-added lines, and contrast them with the A text III. 81–120.

**208 [190].** *In summer*: i.e. the long vacation of 1789. The 'works of art', i.e. of architecture, were not sought in Dovedale or his 'own native region', but in Yorkshire, e.g. Bolton and Fountains Abbeys.

**[193].** *spiry rocks*: a phrase found in Dyer's *Fleece*, I. 658: used by W. W. in a note to *Descriptive Sketches* (*v.* note to l. 70). Cf. also p. 198, l. 33 *supra*.

**212–13 [197–8].** *that seem'd another morn Risen on mid noon*: the words used by Adam to describe the 'presence' of Raphael—*Paradise Lost*, v. 310–11.

**214 [199].** *she*: The 'her' of 1850 is a correction not found in any of the MSS.

**214–17 [199–202].** *Of that sole Sister . . .*
> *Now, after separation desolate Restor'd to me*:

Wordsworth's reunion with his sister after a long break can be dated July–August 1787 when he was with her in Penrith (*v.* D. W.'s letters, *E.L.* 2–8). But he is probably running together events which took place in three summers, 1787, 1788, and 1789. He very likely visited Brougham Castle and the Beacon with her and with Mary Hutchinson during his stays in Penrith in 1787 and 1788, and he may have taken

walks in that district with Mary Hutchinson when she was still in
Penrith in 1789. Dorothy had left Penrith for Forncett in November
1788: she visited William at Cambridge early in that month. Since the
death of their mother and Dorothy's departure for Halifax in 1778
they had been together little, so that in 1794 Dorothy wrote: 'such
have been the circumstances of my life that I may be said to have
enjoyed his company only for a *very few* months'. But from childhood it had been their dream to live together, and after their reunion
at Racedown in September 1795 they were never parted for more
than a few weeks at a time until Wordsworth's death. Those passages
in which Wordsworth refers to his companionship with Dorothy and
what he owed to it, are among the most deeply moving in all his
poetry. Cf. X. 908–30, XIII. 211–46, *Lines composed a few miles
above Tintern Abbey*, 114–59, *The Sparrow's Nest, To a Butterfly*,
'On Nature's invitation do I come' (*Recluse*, 71–97, *P.W.* v. 316),
and *Poems on the Naming of Places*, III. 14–16, in which Dorothy is
spoken of as

> She who dwells with me, whom I have loved
> With such communion that no place on earth
> Can ever be a solitude to me.

**215–18.** *Thy Treasure also . . . A gift then first bestow'd.* For the play
on the meaning of Dorothy's name cf. Coleridge's phrase 'our Sister
Gift-of-God' in his letter to W. W. July 23, 1803.

**220 [205].** *that monastic castle*: Brougham Castle, a mile and a half
east of Penrith, at the junction of the rivers Lowther and Emont.

**223 [208].** *Sidney*: The evidence that Sir Philip Sidney ever visited
Brougham Castle is hardly trustworthy, and it will be noticed that the
text of 1850 is less confident on the point than the A text. Mr. W. G.
Collingwood points out to me that Wordsworth probably got the idea
from Clarke, *Survey of the Lakes* (2nd ed. 1789), p. 10, where, speaking
of 'the great Countess of Pembroke', Clarke says, 'Sir Philip Sidney,
whose intelligence was very great, resided with her at Brougham
Castle during the time he wrote part of his *Arcadia*'. 'He didn't',
adds Mr. Collingwood, 'for Sidney died in 1586 and the Countess was
only born about 1594, and came to live at Brougham Castle as lady
of the place in 1649. She might have had visits from her cousin
Sir Philip Musgrave, and that might have started the legend. But
her father George, third Earl of Cumberland (1570–1605), lived at
Brougham Castle and Sidney might have visited him. There was a
tradition that he came to Coniston Hall', and this, though unauthen-
ticated, strengthens the evidence of his connexion with this district.
Wordsworth was attracted to the story, and doubtless introduced it
here, because, like so much of his own best work, the *Arcadia* was 'by
fraternal love inspired'.

As Hutchinson has pointed out (ed. of *Poems* of 1807, i, p. xii) there
are many traces in the poems written in the first few years following

Wordsworth's settling at Grasmere, of a careful study of the Eliza-
bethans; and the poems themselves contain two quotations from
Sidney and one from Lord Brooke's *Life of Sidney*.

**231–2.** *Lay listening to the wild flowers and the grass,*
    *As they gave out their whispers to the wind*:
two lines which in their delicate simplicity are far more beautiful than
the three which were substituted for them later.

**233 [224].** *Another Maid there was*: Mary Hutchinson. Cf. XI.
316–18 (A²) [XIV. 266–75] and notes.

**242 [233].** *the Border Beacon*: a little north-east of Penrith, the
scene of the episode described XI. 280–323. The two visits are definitely
associated by the repetition, at XI. 323, of l. 245 'A spirit of pleasure
and youth's golden gleam'.

**[261].** *For whom it registers the birth, and marks the growth*: The
development of the text explains how this line comes to be hypermetric. It was doubtless an oversight which Wordsworth would have
corrected.

**276 [266].** *a liveried School-Boy*: i.e. at Christ's Hospital, situated
till a few years ago in the heart of the City. The boys wore a distinctive costume of long dark blue coat reaching below the knee,
yellow stockings, and no hat (cf. II. 466–7 and note). Coleridge
entered the 'Blue-coat School' in 1782, and almost certainly did not
see his Devonshire birthplace again till 1789—hence Christ's Hospital
is here spoken of as his 'Home and School'. He went to Cambridge
in October 1791, Wordsworth having left in the previous January
(ll. 286–8).

**281.** *to shut thine eyes etc.*: an allusion to Coleridge's 'Sonnet to the
River Otter' (publ. 1797):    so deep imprest

    Sink the sweet scenes of childhood, that mine eyes
    I never shut amid the sunny ray
    But straight with all their tints thy waters rise.

**291–2 [281–2].** *What a stormy course Then follow'd*: Coleridge's college career began well, and in his first year he gained the Browne Gold
Medal for a Sapphic Ode, and was chosen by Porson as one of four to
compete for the Craven Scholarship. But his politics became too revolutionary to please the authorities, he was in debt and crossed in love;
and in December 1793 he enlisted in the King's Regiment of Light
Dragoons under the name of Silas Tomkyn Comberbach. He returned
to Cambridge the following April, but left in December without taking
a degree. In the intervening summer he had visited Oxford, met
Southey and with him evolved his schemes for Pantisocracy, and for
emigration to the banks of the Susquehanna. A precarious life in
London and at Bristol followed, spent in journalism and in lecturing,
but always in financial straits. It was probably in September 1795,
at Bristol, that he met Wordsworth for the first time.

**308–16 [297–305].** *Thy subtle speculations, toils abstruse etc.*: Cf. the

words of Lamb in his essay *Christ's Hospital Five and Thirty Years Ago*:
'How have I seen the casual passer through the cloisters stand still,
entranced with admiration (while he weighed the disproportion between the *speech* and the *garb* of the young Mirandula), to hear thee
unfold, in thy deep and sweet intonations, the mysteries of Jam-
blichus, or Plotinus (for even in those years thou waxedst not pale at
such philosophic draughts), or reciting Homer in his Greek, or Pindar,
while the walls of the old Grey Friars re-echoed to the accents of the
*inspired charity boy*!'

**339 [323].** *A Fellow Student*: Robert Jones, to whom Wordsworth
dedicated *Descriptive Sketches*, a poem written in 1792 to commemorate the tour. Wordsworth visited him at his home at Plas-yn-llan,
Denbighshire, in the summer of 1791, expected to be joined by him at
Blois in May 1792, and was with him again in August 1793 (*E.L.* 105).
He was a guest at Dove Cottage in September 1800. He remained
throughout life one of the poet's most intimate and valued friends.
Jones took orders, and had a curacy in Wales, and in later life he had
a living in Oxfordshire (cf. *Sonnet*, 'A genial hearth, a hospitable
board' and I. F. note, *P.W.* iii. 393), but continued spending much of
his time in Wales, where Wordsworth visited him in 1824, noting that his
'plumpness, ruddy cheeks and smiling countenance' seemed to those
who met him 'little suited to a hermit living in the Vale of Meditation'. This picture of him, and that by Dorothy when he came to
Rydal Mount in 1832, 'fat and roundabout and rosy, and puffing and
panting while he climbs the little hill from the road to our house',
suggest some of the charm that drew him to his austerer friend.

**342 [326] ff.** *An open slight etc.*: 'to *me* were obscure, and *now*
appear rather *awkwardly* expressed. I should wish to trace the classical
use of the word "concern". These are the passages, which it is so
difficult and fretsome to correct; because, if once amiss, no after
genial moment can be pressed into the dull service of emending them.
Yet I venture to propose, thinking dilatation better than awkwardness,

> A disregard
> Of College objects was our scheme, say rather,
> A mere slight of the studies and the cares
> Expected from us, we too being then
> Just at the close of our novitiate:
> Nor was it formed by me without some fears,
> And some uneasy forethought of the pain,
> The Censures, and ill-omening of those,
> To whom my worldly Interests were dear—'     (S. T. C.)

Notice that in MS. B, in which the above note is written, Wordsworth has accepted several of Coleridge's suggestions (*v. app. crit.* B²),
and that he retains some of them in the last version.

**350.** *goings-on*: *v.* note to III. 616.

**353 [340].** *France standing on the top of golden hours*: a reminiscence of Shakespeare, *Sonnet* xviii: 'Now stand you on the top of happy hours.' The substitution of 'golden' for 'happy' makes the passage no less Shakespearian, for 'golden' is one of Shakespeare's favourite epithets. Cf. 'golden time' in *Sonnet* iii. Wordsworth uses the phrase 'golden days' in l. 655.

**355–7 [344–6].**        *it was our lot*
            *To land at Calais on the very Eve*
            *Of that great federal Day*:

i.e. July 13, 1790. 'I set off for the Continent, in companionship with Robert Jones. . . . We went staff in hand, without knapsacks, and carrying each his needments tied up in a pocket handkerchief, with about twenty pounds apiece in our pockets. We crossed from Dover and landed at Calais on the eve of the day when the king was to swear fidelity to the new constitution: an event which was solemnized with due pomp at Calais. On the afternoon of that day we started, and slept at Ardres' (*Memoirs*, i. 14–15). For details of their itinerary, *v.* Harper, i. 90–95, Knight, *Poems*, i. 332–3, and Wordsworth's letter to Dorothy, September 6, 1790 (*E.L.* 30–37).

This tour was the subject of *Descriptive Sketches*, which Wordsworth wrote during his second stay in France (1791–2). But the melancholy of *Descriptive Sketches* is far less true to his actual feeling during the tour than this record of it written in 1804, nearly ten years later, for *The Prelude*. Of this the evidence is his letter to Dorothy above referred to, in which he writes: 'I am in excellent health and spirits, and have had no reason to complain of the contrary during our whole tour. My spirits have been kept in a perpetual hurry of delight.' Indeed, the only source of any uneasiness 'during this delightful tour' was the fear that Dorothy might be feeling some anxiety as to his safety. The poet's tender melancholy, and fond conceit of sadness (377–8), was never at this time potent enough to be depressing.

**359–60 [348–9].** *How bright a face is worn when joy of one*
            *Is joy of tens of millions*:

'We crossed . . . at the time when the whole nation was mad with joy in consequence of the revolution. It was a most interesting period to be in France; and we had many delightful scenes, where the interest of the picture was owing solely to this cause' (letter quoted above). Cf. also *Sonnet*, 'Jones! as from Calais' *etc.*

**378.** *to the noise*: so 𝔄 C. If the reading is correct 'to' must mean 'to the accompaniment of'. But perhaps 'to' is a mistake of the copyist not noted before D, where 'with the sound' is substituted for 'to the noise'.

**382 [372].** *dances in the open air*: The late addition of ll. [373–4] records a protest at which Wordsworth felt no concern either in 1790 or 1804.

**386 [378].** *we cut*: 'May "we cut" be used neutrally in pure language? if so, the "right of the best", if not "we flew" or "we rush'd"' (S. T. C.). Note that in deference to Coleridge's criticism Wordsworth added [379], which makes 'cut' transitive.

**396–7.** *Spousals newly solemniz'd At their chief City*: Cf. note to IX. 41–51.

**417 [410].** *The rapid River flowing without noise*: On one of the blank front pages of MS. B (Vol. I) is the following note in Wordsworth's hand, evidently a description of what he and Jones experienced in their walk along the Rhône: 'The[re] we cared little for the roaring of the wind, and the River was most magnificent winding away before us; its voice seemed stifled beneath the very weight of the water; and except when the wind encountered some trees by its edge it moved along to all appearance without noise: but on these occasions you could not help fearing that the noise was caused by the Water, then there was the silent Moon above our heads, now driving among the clouds and now resting herself in the steady blue sky.'

**422 [418].** *Convent of Chartreuse*: Wordsworth reached the Chartreuse on August 4. Cf. note to VIII. 410.

**[420–88].** In an unpublished poem entitled *A Tuft of Primroses*, and dated by internal evidence 1808 (i.e. soon after Wordsworth's return from Coleorton), occurs another draft of this passage, related closely to B iii (p. 200) and probably intermediary between B iii and A². 

It seems likely, therefore, that the whole account of Wordsworth's impressions at the Chartreuse had its inception at Coleorton, and arose out of a conversation with Coleridge after reading this book to him on his visit there (Dec. 1806–Feb. 1807). The version runs as follows:

> 'And is thy doom
> Pronounc'd' (I said, a stripling at that time
> Who with a Fellow-pilgrim had been driv'n
> Through madding France before a joyous gale
> And to the solemn haven of Chartreuse
> Repair'd for timely rest) 'and are we twain
> The last, perchance the very last, of men
> Who shall be welcom'd here, whose limbs shall find
> Repose within these modest cells, whose hearts
> Receive a comfort from these awful spires ?
> Alas! for what I see, the flash of arms,
> O Sorrow and yon military glare;
> And hark, those Voices! let us hide in gloom
> Profoundest of St. Bruno's wood, these sighs
> These whispers that pursue or meet me, whence
> [          ] are they but a common [          ]
> From the two Sister streams of Life and Death,
> Or are they by the parting Genius sent
> Unheard till now and to be heard no more?'

> Yes, I was moved and to this hour am moved;
> What Man would bring to nothing, if he might,
> A natural power or element ? and who,
> If the ability were his, would dare
> To kill a species of insensate life,
> Or to the bird of meanest wing would say,
> Thou, and thy kind, must perish. Even so
> So consecrated, almost, might be deem[ed]
> That power, that organ, that transcendent frame
> Of social being. 'Stay your impious hand,'

The version goes on as A² 24–32, but omitting 'this transcendent ...
Being', and then

> I heard, or seemed to hear, and thus the voice
> Proceeded: 'Honour *etc.*

as A² 48 ... 75 ('consoled'), but reading 'life' for 'pride' (49), 'All hail ye' for 'Hail to the' (50), and in place of 63–69, 'Of faith ... inhabitants':

> Of Heaven-descended truth and humbler claim
> Of these majestic floods, my noblest boast,
> These shining cliffs pure as their home the sky.

The text of A², except in ll. 1, 4, 7, 23, 39, 56, 75, is unpunctuated. In l. 3 'region's' is a correction of 'monstrous'.

[425–6]. *riotous men commissioned to expel The blameless inmates*: In this, as Legouis has pointed out, Wordsworth was mistaken. The armed occupation of the Chartreuse did not take place till May 1792 —the soldiers were at this time paying no more than a domiciliary visit, followed perhaps by confiscation. In *Descriptive Sketches*, 53 ff., with which this passage should be compared, he expresses himself in stronger language.

[439]. *sister streams of Life and Death*: Cf. *Descriptive Sketches*, 73, 'mystic streams of Life and Death', and Wordsworth's note 'Names of rivers at the Chartreuse'. The two streams are the *Guiers vif* and the *Guiers mort*, torrents which unite to form the river Guiers in the valley below the Grande Chartreuse.

[448–50]. *Past and Future . . . knowledge*: These lines were first printed in the *Essay, Supplementary to Preface*, 1815.

[480]. *Vallombre*: 'Name of one of the vallies of the Chartreuse'. Wordsworth's note in *Descriptive Sketches*.

[484–5]. *The cross of Jesus stand erect, as if*
        *Hands of angelic powers had fixed it there*:
Cf. *Descriptive Sketches*, 70–71:

> The cross with hideous laughter Demons mock
> By angels planted on the aereal rock.

And Wordsworth's note 'Alluding to crosses seen on the tops of the spiry rocks of the Chartreuse which have every appearance of being inaccessible'.

**[509–10].** *compassed round With danger*: Milton, *Paradise Lost*, vii. 27.

**446.** *My heart leap'd up when first I did look down*: 'leap'd *up*', 'look'd down', | 'leap'd high', or rather 'O! my heart leap'd when first' *etc.* (S. T. C.). In deference to S. T. C., A² C reads 'How leap'd my heart' *etc.* The lyric 'My heart leaps up' *etc.* was written in 1802.

**448 [518–19].** *A green recess, an aboriginal vale*: D. W. tells in her *Tour of the Continent* 1820 of their finding themselves, after ascending from Martigny, on the brow of the precipice above 'a shady deep recess, the very image of pastoral life, stilness and seclusion. William came up to me, and, if my feelings had been moved before, how much more interesting did the spot become when he told me it was the same dell, that *aboriginal vale*, that *green recess* so often mentioned by him— the first of the kind that he had passed through in Switzerland.' D. W.'s *Journals*, ii. 280.

**467 [539].** *Descending from the mountain to make sport*: 'This line I would omit; as it clearly carries on the metaphor of the Lion, and yet is contradictory to the idea of a *"tamed" Lion.* *"to make sport"* *etc.* is here at once the proof of his having been "tamed" and the object of his "descending from the mountains", which appear incompatible' (S. T. C.). Wordsworth altered the text in A² C in deference to Coleridge, but in D reverted to the previous reading, save that he changed 'tamed' to 'well-tamed'.

**489 [558].** *something of stern mood*: Cf. X. 872, XIII. 217–32.

**525–7 [592–5].** An early version of these lines is quoted in an article on Miss E. Trevenen's Album in *The West Country Magazine*, No. 3, vol. 2, Autumn, 1947:

> Imagination lifting up herself
> In sudden apparition like a cloud
> Whose fleecy substance mounts upon the wind
> Into the vacant sky, or like the form
> Ghostly and wan of some unfather'd mist ...

**525–48 [592–616].** *Imagination!* *etc.*: No passage illustrates better than this at once Wordsworth's relation with the sensationist, empirical philosophy of the eighteenth century and the manner in which he transcends and spiritualizes it. All intellectual and spiritual growth comes from the reaction of the senses, chiefly of eye and ear, to the external world, which is 'exquisitely fitted to the mind', but the highest vision is superinduced upon this in a state of ecstasy, in which the light of sense goes out and the soul feels its kinship with that which is beyond sense. Cf. *Lines composed . . . above Tintern Abbey*, 35–49. And this great spiritual experience comes generally not immediately after the sense-experience which has inspired it, but perhaps years later, when the original emotion, recollected in tranquillity, is rekindled.

Wordsworth made many efforts to give a satisfactory philosophic account of the imagination. It was easier to him to say what it was not than what it was. It was a higher quality than fancy; it had nothing to do with the processes of the analytic reason, but rather seemed to have some relation with the affections and the moral nature. But his inability to understand or to define it did not affect his faith in its reality. It was to him 'the vision and the faculty divine', for it was a vital part of his mystical experience, by reason of which, to put it baldly, the poet *is* a poet: cf. note to XIII. 1–119, *infra*.

**526.** *the eye and progress of my Song*: this use of the so-called 'doublet' is suggested by Shakespeare. Cf. *King John*, II. i. 208: 'Before the eye and prospect of your town.' Wordsworth uses it again at VII. 724: 'The measure and the prospect of the soul.'

**537 [603].** *There harbours whether we be young or old.*: there is no manuscript authority for the punctuation of the 1850 text: 'harbours; ... old,' which is due to E's unfortunate habit of omitting the full stop at the end of a line.

**544–5.** *aught . . . thoughts*: 'aught: thoughts: was a hitch to my ear:       ? seeks for no trophies, struggles for no spoils
              That may attest' *etc.*       (S. T. C.)
Wordsworth accepts the correction.

**548 [616].** *Which hides it like the overflowing Nile*: 'Was it by mere caprice or a beginning of an impulse to alter, from having looked over the latter half of this Book for the purpose of correcting, which I employed myself on for the deadening of a too strong feeling, which the personal Passages, so exquisitely beautiful, had excited—that I wished this faultless line to stand "Spread o'er it, like the fertilizing Nile"? For fear it should be so, I will leave off. Ὕστερον ἄδιον ᾀσῶ' (S. T. C.). Notice that in D, E, Wordsworth adopts the idea of the 'fertilizing Nile'. It is significant that this book, written just after Coleridge had left for Malta, and most full of tender affection for him, is the one to which Coleridge turns in his mood of depression.

**553–72 [621–40].** *brook and road etc.*: 'See *Poetical Works*, ii. 99. p. 143 of the Edition in One Volume' (note in 1850), i.e. ii. 99 of the 1849 edition of the *Poems*, and p. 143 of the 1845 edition. The lines were first published in 1845, with ll. 554 and 556 as A, and l. 559 as 1850. In both editions the passage is dated 1799.

**566 [634].** *The unfetter'd clouds, and region of the Heavens*: a curiously Shakespearian line. Shakespeare in several places uses 'region', with the meaning of 'sky' or 'upper air'. Cf. 'the region clouds' (*Sonnet* xxiii); 'Her eyes in heaven Would through the airy region stream so bright', *Romeo and Juliet*, II. ii. 21.

**573–80 [641–8].** *That night our lodging was an Alpine House*: D. W. in her *Journal* for September 10, 1820 (*v. Journals*, ii. 258–9) records that William recognized this Alpine House as 'the very same where he and his Companion had passed an awful night'.

**579 [647].** *innocent Sleep*: *Macbeth*, II. ii. 36.

**587 [655].** *Locarno's Lake*: i.e. Maggiore. On the whole description given here Wordsworth's letter to Dorothy, September 1790, affords an interesting commentary: 'After passing two days in the environs of Chamouny, we returned to Martigny, and pursued our route up the Valais, along the Rhone, to Brig. At Brig we quitted the Valais, and passed the Alps at the Simplon, in order to visit part of Italy. The impressions of three hours of our walk among the Alps will never be effaced. From Duomo d'Ossola, a town of Italy which lay in our route, we proceeded to the Lake of Locarno, to visit the Borromean Islands there, and thence to Como. A more charming path was scarcely ever travelled over ... The banks of many of the Italian and Swiss lakes are so steep and rocky, as not to admit of roads; that of Como is partly of this character. A small foot-path is all the communication by land between one village and another, on the side along which we passed, for upwards of thirty miles. We entered upon this path about noon, and owing to the steepness of the banks, were soon unmolested by the sun, which illuminated the woods, rocks, and villages of the opposite shore. The lake is narrow, and the shadows of the mountains were early thrown across it. It was beautiful to watch them travelling up the side of the hills for several hours, to remark one half of a village covered with shade, and the other bright with the strongest sunshine. . . .

'The shores of the lake consist of steeps, covered with large sweeping woods of chestnut, spotted with villages; some clinging from the summits of the advancing rocks, and others hiding themselves within their recesses. Nor was the surface of the lake less interesting than its shores; part of it glowing with the richest green and gold, the reflection of the illuminated woods and part shaded with a soft blue tint. ... It was impossible not to contrast that repose, that complacency of spirit, produced by these lovely scenes, with the sensations I had experienced two or three days before, in passing the Alps. At the lake of Como, my mind ran through a thousand dreams of happiness, which might be enjoyed upon its banks, if heightened by conversation and the exercise of the social affections. Among the more awful scenes of the Alps, I had not a thought of man, or a single created being; my whole soul was turned to him who produced the terrible majesty before me.'

**590–2 [660–2].** *And Como, thou, a treasure by the earth*
*Kept to itself, a darling bosom'd up*
*In Abyssinian privacy* . . .
Cf. *Descriptive Sketches*, 81: 'Como bosom'd deep in chestnut groves'. The pathway is particularly noted in l. 90 and in Wordsworth's note.

**600–5 [670–5].** *While yet a Youth, undisciplin'd in Verse*: Wordsworth cannot help contrasting the easy descriptive verse of *Descriptive Sketches* (published in 1793) with the verse he is now writing in

1805 under a nobler impulse and with a fuller knowledge of his art: *v.* Introduction *supra*, p. xliii.

**667 [737].** *a mean pensioner*: The 'mere' in 1850 is possibly due to an undetected error of the copyist of D.

**691 [764].** *We cross'd the Brabant Armies on the fret*: The 'Etats belgiques unis' had been declared in January 1790, and had aroused great enthusiasm in Paris, where, for example, Camille Desmoulins wrote proudly of 'les révolutions de France et de Brabant'. But this new Republic was soon rent by dissension, and after the death of Joseph II his successor Leopold saw an opportunity for enforcing his authority. Through his ambassador in London he pointed out that 'the general interest of the whole of Europe demands a restitution of the old constitution', and he gained the sympathy of England, Prussia, and Holland. Early in October he collected his forces to march on Belgium, but under the guarantee of the three powers he promised the Belgians to maintain the charters of the provinces; and proclaiming an amnesty, invited the submission of his rebellious subjects before the end of the following month. The Three Powers advised the Belgians to accept, but they refused, though their internal quarrels made them powerless to offer any effective resistance. 'The Brabant armies on the fret', witnessed by Wordsworth in this October, must have been the republican troops preparing to oppose Leopold.

# BOOK VII

**3.** *issuing from the City's Walls*: 'The city of Goslar in Lower Saxony' (note in 1850). But this is clearly wrong (*v.* pp. 510 and 512).

**12–13.** *a little space Before last primrose-time*: This is more accurate than the later reading.

**16 [14].** *At thy departure to a foreign Land*: Coleridge did not actually leave for Malta till April 9, but by the end of the previous November he had already decided to go abroad, and early in January he paid his farewell visit to Dove Cottage; after which Wordsworth, 'to beguile his heavy thoughts' at his friend's departure, and doubtless urged on by Coleridge's entreaties, had restarted on *The Prelude*.

**35–36 [29–30].** *ye and I will be Brethren*: In 1808 the *Simpliciad* laughed at Wordsworth for his habit of expressing fraternity and equality with the humbler creatures; and, in particular, in the couplet:

> With brother lark or brother Robin fly
> And flutter with half-brother butterfly,

had held up to scorn the lines in *The Redbreast and the Butterfly* (1802, publ. 1807):

> 'All men who know thee call thee Brother' (the robin)
> 'A brother he seems of thine own' (the butterfly).

This last line Wordsworth omitted in 1815, and doubtless he altered 'Brethren' here to 'Associates' in recollection of the same criticism. Indeed, he seems to have become nervous about using the word brother, for he removes it from the text of VI. 478 and XIII. 89, in both cases with a loss of strength to the line. But in III. 328, where it might well have been altered, for its use confuses the sense, he retains it.

**50 [44].** *my favourite Grove*: known in the Wordsworth family as 'Brother John's Grove', situated below White Moss Common, in Ladywood. Cf. *Poems on the naming of Places*, VI. 'Wheri to the attractions of the busy world', *etc.*

**57 [52].** *Return'd from that excursion, etc.*: i.e. his foreign tour with Robert Jones, described in the previous Book. He returned to Cambridge early in November 1790, spent a six-weeks Christmas vacation at Forncett, Norfolk, in the company of Dorothy, and was at Cambridge again to take his degree on January 21, 1791.

**68–72.** With what he says here as to his character, cf. III. 531–6.

**73–74.** *when I first beheld That mighty place*: There is no other record of this early visit to London except the allusion to it in VIII. 688–709. It may have been at Christmas 1789 (*v.* M. Moorman, *William Wordsworth. The Early Years*, pp. 124–5).

**81–88 [77–84].** *There was a time etc.*: a passage written in the Miltonic style and with reminiscence, partly of *Paradise Lost*, partly of Purchas, *His Pilgrimes.* Cf. *Paradise Lost*, i. 717–19:

> Not *Babilon*
> Nor great *Alcairo* such magnificence
> Equald in all thir glories

**[118].** *not knowing each the other's name*: There is no manuscript authority for reading 'not'; 'nor' is found in both D and E.

**123 [121].** *Vauxhall and Ranelagh*: Fashionable resorts of pleasure in the eighteenth century; *v.* Walpole's *Letters*, passim, and Fanny Burney's *Evelina*: Letters xlvi and xii, and *Cecilia*, chap. xii. Cf. also Austin Dobson, *Eighteenth Century Vignettes*.

**131.** *the Giants of Guildhall*: Gog and Magog. Cf. Horace Walpole's *Letter to Montague*, September 24, 1761, where he likens Lord Errol to 'one of the Giants in Guildhall, new gilt'.

**132.** *Bedlam*: The famous hospital for lunatics, situated in Moorfields, and one of the sights of eighteenth-century London. It was pulled down in 1814.

**137.** *in season due*: a Miltonic phrase. Cf. *Lycidas*, 7.

**176–80 [160–4].** The punctuation of 1850 is obviously incorrect, and to elucidate the passage it has been suggested that ll. 178 and 179 are in the wrong order. But Mr. Nowell Smith has already anticipated the true solution, which is found in the punctuation of the A text.

**186.** *sequester'd nook*: Cf. *Comus*, 500.

**200.** *May then entangle us awhile*: The incompleteness of this line is explained by the X text, where the words 'at length' are deleted, and nothing substituted for them. The mistake was not rectified till the revision of D.

**209 [193].** *Here files of ballads dangle from dead walls*: 'The railing adjacent to the gate (i.e. Cumberland Gate, now the Marble Arch) was at that period (about 1812) permitted to be strung with rows of printed old-fashioned ballads, such as *Cruel Barbara Allen, etc.*' Mrs. Cowden Clarke, *My Long Life*, quoted by Nowell Smith.

**228 [212].** *distinguishable shapes*: *Paradise Lost*, ii. 667–8, 'that shape had none Distinguishable'.

**267 [250].** *shading colours*: The 'shading' colours (altered to 'blended' in D) is probably an unconscious echo of *Paradise Lost*, iii. 509: 'By *Model*, or by *shading* Pencil drawn.'

**275 [255].** *Of Tivoli etc.*: In copying the A text Dorothy wrote thus:

> Of Tivoli
> And high upon the steep that mouldering Fane
> The Temple of the Sybil.

Obviously she had the X text before her, but with the words 'and dim Frescati's (*sic*) bowers' deleted from them (deleted because Wordsworth realized that as the lines stood they would give the impression that 'Frascati's bowers' were on the same steep as the Temple of the Sybil). Wordsworth filled in the blank left by Dorothy with the words 'and high upon that steep', deleting Dorothy's next line. He failed, however, to insert the change in B, where it was made later.

**280 [260].** *'And'*, the reading of 1850, is obviously incorrect. In D the word 'Add' is so indistinctly written that E took it for 'And'; hence the error in 1850.

**288 [267].** *Half-rural Sadler's Wells*: situated at Islington, then a suburb of London. In the seventeenth and early eighteenth century it consisted of a Tea Garden with a Music House attached, and was a popular resort of entertainment, for rope dancers and tumblers could be seen there. When, in 1765, a Theatre was erected on the site of the Music House, it retained its 'popular' character, and in 1783 Horace Walpole refers to it as 'a place of low buffoonery': *v.* Addenda, p. 632.

**306 [284].** A quotation from Milton, *Samson Agonistes*, 87–89:

> silent as the Moon,
> When she deserts the night,
> Hid in her vacant interlunar cave.

**[288].** *'forms and pressures of the time'*: *Hamlet*, iii. ii. 28.

**321 [297].** *the Maid of Buttermere*: John Hatfield, a vulgar adventurer, came to Keswick in 1802, and giving himself out to be Alexander Augustus Hope, M.P. for Linlithgowshire, and brother to the Earl of Hopetoun, imposed upon all the tradesmen of the district. He married Mary, daughter of the innkeeper of the Fish, Buttermere, at Lorton Church on October 2, but before the end of the month his frauds were detected, and he fled the country, leaving behind him papers which proved that he had another wife living, and several children. He was caught soon afterwards, and tried for forgery at the Carlisle Assizes on the prosecution of the Post Office, for franking letters under the name of Hope. He was hanged at Carlisle on September 3, 1803. Wordsworth and Coleridge were much interested in the incident, and Coleridge contributed three papers upon it to the *Morning Post* of October 11, October 22, and November 5, 1802, under the titles of *Romantic Marriage* and *The Fraudulent Marriage*. (They were afterwards collected in *Essays on His Own Times*, 1850.) A further paper on the subject, not from Coleridge's hand, appeared in the *Morning Post* of November 6. The case caused a considerable stir in the country and was made the subject of a successful melodrama. The play was produced at Sadler's Wells (*v.* note to 288) on April 25, 1803, and was described by its author, Charles Dibdin the younger, the manager of the theatre, as an operatic piece in rhyme. It was entitled *Edward and Susan or the Beauty of Buttermere*. It ran till the end of May and was revived towards the end of June. Mary Lamb wrote to D. W. in the following July: 'We went last week with Southey and Rickman and his sister to Sadler's Wells, the lowest and most London-like of our amusements. The entertainments were Goody Two Shoes, Jack the Giant Killer, and *Mary of Buttermere*! Poor Mary was very happily married at the end of the piece, to a sailor, her former sweetheart. We had a prodigious fine view of her father's house in the vale of Buttermere—mountains very like large haycocks, and a lake like nothing at all. If you had been with us, would you have laughed the whole time like Charles and Miss Rickman, or gone to sleep as Southey and Rickman did ?' (*Letter*, July 9, 1803). De Quincey, in his article on Coleridge in *Tait's Magazine* of October 1834, gave a detailed account of the whole story (*Works*, ii. 177–84, ed. Masson), and in 1841 a novel *James Hatfield and the Beauty of Buttermere, a Story of Modern Times*, was published by Henry Colburn. This book was in the library of Rydal Mount, bearing witness to Wordsworth's continued interest in the story.

**322.** '*a bold bad man*': a quotation from Spenser, *Faerie Queene*, I. i. 37.

**327-9 [303-5].** Wordsworth and Coleridge were at Buttermere on or about November 11, 1799, in the course of their tour of the Lake Country: *v. Coleridge Letters*, Griggs, i. 543-4.

**341-2.**      *For we were nursed, as almost might be said,*
         *On the same mountains; Children at one time*:
a reminiscence of Milton, *Lycidas*, 23, 'For we were nurst upon the selfsame hill.' Mary of Buttermere was born in 1772, and was thus only two years younger than Wordsworth: the Cocker (345) flows from Buttermere through Crummock Water to Cockermouth.

**412 [382].** *little more than three short years*: i.e. on his first journey to Cambridge, in October 1787.

**[406].** *By Siddons trod*: It is curious that in the early version of this book there is no allusion to Mrs. Siddons or the more serious theatre.

**460 [428].** *Prate somewhat loudly of the whereabout*: *Macbeth*, II. i. 58.

**471 [439].** *a Kitten when at play, etc.*: *The Kitten and the Falling Leaves* was written in the same year (1804) as this passage.

**486–7.** *when on our beds we lie etc.*: Cf. IV. 72–78.

**506 [476].** *the suburbs of the mind*: Shakespeare: *Julius Caesar*, II. i. 285–6: 'Dwell I but in the suburbs Of your good pleasure?'

**526–8 [496–8].** *Familiarly a household term, like those,*
       *The Bedfords, Glocesters, Salisburys of old,*
       *Which the fifth Harry talks of*:
Cf. *Henry V*, IV. iii. 51–55: Then shall our names
       Familiar in his mouth as household words
       Harry the King, Bedford and Exeter,
       Warwick and Talbot, Salisbury and Gloucester,
       Be in their flowing cups freshly remember'd.
In 1850 'Salisburys' was printed 'Salsburys', but noted in a *corrigendum*.

**538.** *He winds away his never-ending horn*: an echo of Milton: *Lycidas*, 28: 'What time the Gray-fly winds her sultry horn.'

**[512–43]** and *app. crit.* This passage, which does not occur in C, and was therefore not written before 1820, records an impression of Burke which certainly would not have been true of Wordsworth's earlier attitude to politics. It is interesting also to notice, as a sign of the growing conservatism of Wordsworth's later years, that the allusion to Fox was removed from the text somewhere between 1828 and 1832. Haydon in his *Autobiography* notes (*Journal*, May 23, 1815): 'Wordsworth speaking of Burke, Fox and Pitt, said: You always went from Burke with your mind filled; from Fox with your feelings excited: and from Pitt with wonder at his having had the power to make the worse appear the better reason.'

**[544–50].** These reflections on the higher triumphs of the pulpit and the impression made by 'the awful truths delivered', are a characteristic late addition to the text.

**546–65 [551–72].** *There have I seen a comely Bachelor, etc.*: Cf. the attack on the 'theatrical clerical coxcomb' made by Cowper in *The Task*, ii. 414–62.

**559 [564].** *The Death of Abel*: Gessner's *Tod Abels* was written in 1758 and translated into English soon afterwards. It ran through many editions. Its great popularity was due to its 'süssliche und weinerliche Ton' which appealed to the sentimentality of the time. Young's *Night Thoughts* (1742–5) appealed to the more morbid and gloomy aspects of the same sentimental tendency. For Wordsworth's views on Macpherson's *Ossian*, v. *Essay supplementary to Preface* (1815) and *Lines written in a blank leaf of Macpherson's Ossian* (1824).

**649–51.** *the Fair Holden where Martyrs suffer'd*: St. Bartholomew's Fair, formerly held on St. Bartholomew's Day, August 24, was in 1753, following alteration in the Calendar, proclaimed on September 3, and was thereafter held on the four days succeeding that date. Lamb conducted W. W. and D. W. to 'Bartlemy Fair' in September 1802 (*v.* his letter to S. T. C. Sept. 8).

**698 ff.**: In J, and therefore written before May 1802 and thought of in relation with *Michael*, are the following lines, obviously related to this passage:

> Shall he who gives his days to low pursuits
> Amid the indistinguishable world
> Of cities mid the same eternal flow
> Of the same objects melted and reduced
> To one identity, by differences
> That have no law no meaning and no end
> Shall he feel yearning to those lifeless forms
> And shall we think that Nature is less kind
> To them who all day long through a long life
> Have walk'd within her sight—it cannot be

Knight quotes the lines (inaccurately) in *Poems*, iii. 269, and states that they 'were dictated to' D. W. or 'copied by her'. But they are in Wordsworth's own hand (*v.* note on J, p. xxviii).

**713 [737].** *This, of all acquisitions first, awaits*: The punctuation of A, not that of 1850, is obviously correct.

**716–29 [740–62].** *Attention comes etc.*: In the *Alfoxden* notebook (*v.* Introduction, p. xxv), in a draft of the character of the Wanderer, occur lines which are obviously the first suggestion of this passage:

> There is a holy indolence
> Compared to which our best activity
> Is oftimes deadly bane.
> They rest upon their oars
> Float down the mighty stream of tendency
> In the calm mood of holy indolen(ce)
> A most wise passiveness in which the heart
> Lies open and is well content to feel
> As nature feels and to receive her shapes
> As she has made them
> The mountain's outlines and its steady forms
> Gave simple grandeur to his mind, nor less
> The changeful language of its countenance
> Gave movement to his thoughts and multitude
> With order and relation.

A little farther on in the *Alfoxden* notebook are the lines:

> Of untamed nature he had skill to draw
> A better and less transitory power
> An influence [*more permanent*] less transient

To his mind
The mountain's outline and its steady form
Gave simple grandeur and its presence shaped
The measure and the prospect of his soul
To majesty, such virtue had these forms
[*Perennial*] Of mountains and the aged hills nor less
*etc.* as above, but 'their' for 'its'.

**724.** *The measure and the prospect of the soul*: cf. VI. 526 note.


# BOOK VIII

**1–61.** It is evident from Y that these lines describing Helvellyn fair were an afterthought, and that in their place Wordsworth originally wrote that passage which he afterwards adapted for the opening of *Excursion* II. For Y has a page on which, after an illegible line, ending, as *Excursion* II, 1, with 'far'd', we have ll. 2–5 as *Excursion* II. 2–5; l. 6 'And now a' (*rest illegible*), ll. 7–8 *as Excursion* II. 10–11, followed by:

Withal from Robbers and from dangers safe
By melody and by the charm of verse
And with his harp still pendent at his side
Familiarly and [*sic.* as ?] now our Labourer(s) wear
Their Satchels when they plod to distant fields.
Yet such a Man so favour'd could not draw
By his glad faculties more earnest bliss
From that [*his vagrant*] eventful and way-faring life
Than I unknown uncountenanc'd and obscure
Accoutred with a knapsack and a staff.

This is followed by an almost illegible passage which can be identified with *Prelude* VIII. 74–86, whence the manuscript runs on as A.

In a letter dated 1805 Wordsworth sent ll. 1–61 to Sir George Beaumont, in a form which tallies substantially with that of the A text.

**10 [11].** *It is a summer festival, a Fair*: Cf. D. W.'s *Journal* for September 2, 1800. 'The fair day. . . . There seemed very few people and very few stalls, yet I believe there were many cakes and much beer sold. . . . It was a lovely moonlight night. We talked much about a house on Helvellyn. The moonlight shone only upon the village. It did not eclipse the village lights, and the sound of dancing and merriment came along the still air.'

**[42].** *half pleased with half ashamed*: an example of the bad punctuation of 1850.

**[48–52].** 'These lines are from a descriptive poem—"Malvern Hills"—by one of Mr. Wordsworth's oldest friends, Mr. Joseph Cottle' (note in 1850). 'The *Malvern Hills*', wrote Wordsworth to Cottle in 1829, 'was always a favourite of mine. Some passages, and especially

one, closing "To him who slept at noon and wakes at eve"—I thought
super-excellent.' It is interesting to note that ll. [45–52], which are
clearly a tribute to the poet's wife, find their way into the text as a
correction of E, i.e. in 1839.

Joseph Cottle (1770–1853) was a bookseller in Bristol from 1791 to
1799; he first met Southey and Coleridge in 1794, and Wordsworth
probably in the following year. He was the joint publisher, with
Messrs. Robinson of London, of Coleridge's *Poems on various subjects*,
1796, for which he had paid thirty guineas in advance, and of the
*Poems. Second Edition, To which are added Poems by Charles Lamb
and Charles Lloyd*, 1797. He also printed and bore the expense of
Coleridge's *Watchman*. In 1798 he published *The Lyrical Ballads*, as
well as his own poem, *Malvern Hills*. His *Early Recollections chiefly
relating to the late Samuel Taylor Coleridge during his long residence in
Bristol* appeared in 1837 (2nd ed. 1847): it is a book full of inaccuracies,
ill-conceived and in the worst taste, and Garnett (*D.N.B.*) speaks of
Cottle with justice as a 'typical example of the moral and religious
Philistine'; but there is no question that he was a good friend to
Coleridge in his early days at Bristol; and Wordsworth always retained a warm affection for him.

**64–73.** What is evidently a first draft of these lines, but expressed
generally and not as a personal experience, is found in Y, where, after
eleven lines illegible from the effects of damp, we read:

must read the inner heart.
[Few pleasures ?] are more dear than this, above all
If he already shall have learned to love
His fellow beings to such habits trained
By nature in the woods and fields [     ]
Did there first find a teacher to enlarge
His thoughts and carry his affection forth
Beyond the bosom of his family.

**86.** After this line Y has 'Like those that have been recently described'. It is hard to see what Wordsworth had in mind unless he is
thinking of the lines in W (*v.* p. 623 *infra*) describing the storm on
Coniston. These were already written, and he may have thought of
introducing them before this passage.

**116–19:** cf. [471–5].

**119–45 [74–99].** This passage, in which Wordsworth describes the
beauty of 'the Paradise where I was reared', is strongly reminiscent in
style, construction, and phrasing of *Paradise Lost*, iv. 208–47, and other
lines in which Milton calls to memory various scenes famed in history
or fiction, only to dismiss them as unworthy of comparison with Eden:

in this pleasant soile
His farr more pleasant Garden God ordaind.

Cf. also especially 'boon Nature' (128) with 'Nature boon' (*P.L.* iv.
242), and 129 ff. with

> sweet interchange
> Of Hill and Vallie, Rivers, Woods, and Plaines,
> Now Land, now Sea, and Shores with Forrest crownd,
> Rocks, Dens, and Caves (*P.L.* ix. 115–18).

For the comparison with Gehol's matchless Gardens Wordsworth draws on Lord Macartney's description, quoted by John Barrow (*Travels in China*, 1804, pp. 127–33): 'The Emperor was pleased to give directions to his first minister to shew us his park or garden at Gehol. It is called in Chinese Van-shoo-yuen, or the Paradise of ten thousand trees. We rode about three miles through a very beautiful park kept in the highest order . . . the grounds gently undulated and chequered with various groups of well-contrasted trees in the offskip. . . . An extensive lake appeared before us, the extremities of which seemed to lose themselves in distance and obscurity. The shores of the lake have all the varieties of shape which the fancy of a painter can delineate. Nor are islands wanting, but they are situated only where they should be, each in its own proper place and having its proper character: one marked by a pagoda or other building; one quite destitute of ornaments; some smooth and level, some steep and uneven, and others frowning with wood or smiling with culture. . . . In the course of our journey we stopped at forty or fifty different places or pavilions. . . . The western garden . . . forms a strong contrast with the other, and exhibits all the sublimer beauties of nature in as high a degree as the part which we saw before possesses the attractions of softness and amenity. It is one of the finest forest scenes in the world; wild, woody, mountainous and rocky. . . In many places immense woods . . . grow on almost perpendicular steeps. There at proper distances you find palaces, banquetting houses, and monasteries, adapted to the situation and peculiar uses of the place; sometimes with a rivulet on one hand, gently stealing through the glade, at others with a cataract tumbling from above raging with foam, and rebounding with a thousand echoes from below, or silently engulfed in a gloomy pool or yawning chasm. . . . On a mound so elevated as perfectly to command the whole surrounding country I saw everything before me as on an illuminated map—palaces, pagodas, towns, villages, plains, vallies watered by innumerable streams, hills waving with woods, meadows covered with cattle of the most beautiful marks and colours.' The 'Domes of Pleasure' (130–1) recall Coleridge's *Kubla Khan.*

**159–72.** Instead of these lines Y has the following passage, illegible in places, partly through rapid and careless writing, partly through the effects of damp. It was never corrected or incorporated into the text of *The Prelude*, and exhibits the loose and uneven texture of a rough draft. But its drift is perfectly clear, and it is deeply interesting, as a variation, with unique autobiographical detail, upon the main theme of *The Prelude*, the growth of the poet's soul under the interacting influences of Nature and Man.

The preceding lines (1–158) pay tribute to the happy union of man with Nature in Wordsworth's native country-side; ll. 159–72 tell briefly how the human associations of Nature fasten imperceptibly upon the child's mind; and the alternative passage found in Y sets this thought in an extended perspective. Wordsworth goes back again to the beginning, making as it were a parenthetical introduction, from a new point of view, to the argument of Book VIII—*Love of Nature leading to Love of Man*. Of this tendency to retrace his steps, to 'turn and return with intricate delay', he was himself thoroughly aware. (Cf. the opening to Book IX, where he compares the 'motions retrograde' of his course with that of a river that 'turns ... far back, Towards the very regions which he cross'd In his first outset'.)

The new point of view is stated in the opening lines 'We live by admiration and by love' *etc.* In the *Letter to the Editor of the Friend* (1809) Wordsworth lays stress on love and admiration as motive forces in the education of youth. In the lines before us these feelings are shown to be the source and feeding streams of our spiritual life; and the soul's growth is traced from infancy to manhood. Love and admiration for Nature prepare the way for love and admiration of Man. The babe, first at the instance of its elders, and then of its own accord, feels wonder and delight at the simplest objects in Nature (6–16); the child proceeds to admire things of 'Nature's rarer workmanship' (21–36); and then his mind is awakened to 'thoughtful wonder' by the inexplicable appearances that meet him everywhere in the works of Nature and Man (37–51). Fear mingles sometimes with his wonder (51–54). But by degrees his mind is lulled into acquiescence in the divine miracle, and in the 'name of God', the oft-repeated answer to his questions, he finds a satisfying solution (55–62). His perpetual challenge to other existences unlike his own gives place to a passive acceptance of their differing and independent life (63–79). The instinct of wonder, now unsatisfied by an outer world which he has come to take for granted, finds new food in the world of fable and romance (80–98), and of travellers' tales (99–109). But romance has its dangers; it tends to pervert the child's simple wonder and joy in Nature into a taste for the strange and the bizarre (110–19). Minds untutored by Nature advance no farther: in after-life they will always need gross stimulants to awaken thought and feeling (120–4). But the more favoured child, creature of sense though he is, apparently careless of the world about him, intent on his own pursuits, and regarding himself as the centre of things—though to the casual observer a mere vulgar animal—is yet haunted by the memory of what has impressed his earlier years (124–37). He undergoes a change which is like a 'second birth'. Nature has early entered into his soul: now her power begins to quicken his mind into a new and more active communion with the universe. He realizes the boundless field for thought offered to him by Nature, and he enters with a fuller understanding into that experience, familiar to him from childhood, in which sense merges with spirit. 'Bodily eye and spiritual need' seem now to have become 'one great faculty' (137–58). His earliest memories redound upon him. The pure vigour of his wonder and love are revived, accompanied by a new reliance on the strength and independence of his developing mind (158–94). At this stage Nature becomes all-absorbing, and he shrinks from man with his sordid and transitory occupations (194–213). But this 'slight' of Man is only superficial: his deeper sympathies have intertwined from the first the forms of Nature with the human affections. 'Habits of ear and eye' with their inevitable human associations are really preparing him for a fuller communion with his fellows. The distinction between Man and Nature he finds to be unreal, for they are indissolubly bound together; without Man Nature has no significance, even to its Maker (214–40). The passage is as follows:

Two feelings have we also from the first,
[    ?    ] of grandeur and of tenderness;
We live by admiration and by love
And ev'n as these are well and wisely fixed
5     In dignity of being we ascend.
There doth our life begin; how long it is,
To pass things nearer by, ere the delight
Abate or with less eagerness return
Which flashes from the eyes of babes in arms
10   When they have caught, held up for that intent,
A prospect of the Moon, or that with which
When, born[e] about on [       ] days, they greet
Unheeded objects of their own accord;
Discoveries of their own—a little rill
15   Of water sparkling down a rocky slope
By the way side, a beast, a bird, a flower.
When these few works of earliest [      ?      ],
Gifts and enchanting toys by [     ?     ]
Thus [                    ?                    ]
20   Become familiar, agitate us less,
Than doth an after transport, to the first

---

3–5 Cf. *Excursion*, IV. 763–5. *This passage is unpunctuated except in* ll. 16, 42, 43, 51, 62, 63, 65, 71, 85, 87, 89, 98, 100, 103, 105, 109, 137, 139, 144, 152, 173, 194, 199, 203.

6 *This line is deleted; in its place are written four lines, only partly legible*:
[        ] sympathies of tender love are slow
[        ] motions scarcely visible
[        ] admiration that is near
[        ] and spreading fast how long it is
9–11 Cf. Coleridge, *The Nightingale*, 96–105.
13–14          All uninvited of their own accord
                Some unregarded sight (*deleted*).

Succeeding lawfully, nor less intense,
Attend the Child when he can stir about;
Brac'd, startled into notice, lifted up
25       As if on plumes, with sudden gift of [flight ?],
By things of Nature's rarer workmanship,
Her scatter'd accidents of sight and sound—
The peacock's fan with all its [     ] eyes
Unfurled, the rainbow, or the Cuckoo's shout,
30       An echo, or the glow-worm's faery lamp,
Or some amazement and surprize of sense,
When it hath pass'd away, returns again
In later days,—-the fluid element
That yields [not ?] when we touch it, lake or pool.
35       [    ?    ] transparent as the liquid deep
And safe with all its dangers underfoot.
Then everyday appearances, which now
The spirit of thoughtful wonder first pervades,
Crowd in and give the mind its needful food;
40       Nature's unfathomable works, or Man's
Mysterious as her own,—a ship that sails
The seas, the lifeless arch of stones in air
Suspended, the cerulean firmament
And what it is; the River that flows on
45       Perpetually, whence comes it, whither tends,
Going and never gone; the fish that moves
And lives as in an element of death;
Or aught of more refin'd astonishment,
Such as the Skylark breeds, singing aloft
50       As if the Bird were [*roosted in*] native to the heavens,
There planted like a Star: with these combine
Objects of fear, yet not without their own
Enjoyment,—lightning and the thunder's roar,
Snow, rain and hail, and storm implacable.
55       In turn these also slacken in their hold,
And the world's native produce, as it meets
The sense with less habitual stretch of mind,
Is ponder'd as a miracle, and words
By frequent repetition take the place
60       Of theories, repeated till faith grows

---

29–30 The echo, rainbow, cuckoo, and glowworm all haunt Wordsworth's poetry as they haunted his mind from childhood.

42 *the lifeless arch*: cf. *Miscellaneous Sonnets*, III. xlviii. 9–10.

50–51 Cf. *A Morning Exercise*, 26–30.

55 A correction of two lines of which is legible 'Brings somewhat' (*deleted*) 'Becoming somewhat like a [?] The faith in turn less passionate'.

Through acquiescence, and the name of God
Stands fix'd a keystone of the mighty arch.
Meantime, while we have been advancing thus
Through hesitations that do evermore

65 Revive; and when the impersonating power,
The faculty that gives sense, motion, will,
[ ? ] is at length
Beaten of [ ? ] betwixt the depth
Of our existence, and admits, though loth,

70 Divided sway, things, qualities that are
And not as we are; when the Child hath long
Ceased to enquire of his own thoughts whence Day
Whence Night, and whither they betake themselves,
Or, told of something pleasant to be done

75 When summer comes, no more within himself
Marvels what summer is; and when in fine
That great Magician, the unresting year,
Hath play'd his changes off, till less and less
They excite in us a passionate regard;

80 Then attestations new of growing life,
Distinct impressions and unbounded thought,
To appease the absolute necessities
That struggle in us, opportunely come
From the universe of fable and [romance ?]—

85 Trees that bear gems for fruit, rocks spouting milk,
And diamond palaces, and birds that sing
With human voices, formidable hills,
Or magnets which, leagues off, can witch away
Iron, disjointing in a moment's space

90 The unhappy ship that comes within their reach,
Enchanted armour, talismanic rings,
Dwarfs, Giants, Genii, creatures that can shape
Themselves and be or not be at their will;
Others, the slaves and instruments of these,

95 That neither are beast, bird, insect or worm,
But shapes of all, and powers intemperately
Upon each other heap'd, or parcell'd out

---

78–79 Y$^2$: Hath in our presence play'd his changes off
Till they excite less passionate regard Y.

84 *fable and romance*: cf. V. 365–89; 477–82. It is interesting to notice how fully Wordsworth draws his illustrations of the 'universe of fable' from the *Arabian Nights*. 'Trees that bear gems for fruit' and 'diamond palaces' are found in 'Aladdin', the bird with the human voice in 'The Story of the Three Sisters', the unhappy disjointed ship in 'The History of the Third Calender'. I have not traced the story in which 'rocks spout milk'.

86 Y$^2$: And palaces of diamond, birds that sing Y.

In boundless interchange. Nor less esteem
Bear at this season the more sober tales
100  Of travellers through foreign climes, that shew
A face as if it were another earth,
As if another Nature flourishd [*govern'd*] there ;—
Bananas, palm-trees, citrons, orange groves
And jasmine bowers, or desart wastes of sand
105  Helpless and hopeless, or in desart woods
The enormous Snake that is a tree in size,
The burning Mountain, the huge Cataract,
Or lands that see the Sun through half a year
And lie as long in night, beneath the stars.

110  Meantime the Spirits are in dance if aught
At home of glaring spectacle or new
Be interwoven with the common sights
Which Earth presents, and contrasts strong and harsh
And fanciful devices, temples, grots,
115  Statue and terrace sward and trim cascade,—
In short whatever object savours least
Of mind's right understanding and [      ],
Is least in nature, seems to please us most,
Affects us with most vehement delight.

120  Untutor'd minds stop here, and after life
Leads them no farther ; vivid images
To them and strong sensations must be given :
They cannot make these [      ?      ] without harm
In the eye of nature.
                            Fast outstripping these
125  The child, by constitution of his frame,
And circumstances favored from the first,
Grows in the common [      ], an animal
Like others, only [            ]
Within him burns ; he irradiates all without,
130  Vulgar impostor seems and unrefin'd,
Careless of Nature's presence, and unaw'd
[                                                    ]
And his own person, senses, faculties,
Centre and soul of all :—yet haunted oft
135  By what has been his life at every turn,
Unfolding a proud length of [      ].

---

99–100 *tales Of travellers*: cf. p. xli, 625–8.
118–19 Cf. VIII. 510–62.
129 Within him burns Y²: Burning within Y.

Why need we track the process ? Then will come
Another soul, spring, centre of his being,
And that is Nature. As his powers advance,
140 He is not like a man who sees in the heavens
A blue vault merely and a glittering cloud,
One old familiar likeness over all,
A superficial pageant, known too well
To be regarded ; he looks nearer, calls
145 The stars out of their shy retreats, and part(s)
The milky stream into its separate forms,
Loses and finds again, when baffled most
Not least delighted ; finally he takes
The optic tube of thought that patient men
150 Have furnished with the toil [        ],
Without the glass of Galileo sees
What Galileo saw ; and as it were
Resolving into one great faculty
Of being bodily eye and spiritual need,
155 The converse which he holds is limitless ;
Nor only with the firmament of thought,
But nearer home he looks with the same eye
Through the entire abyss of things. And now
The first and earliest motions of his life,
160 I mean of his rememberable time,
Redound upon him with a stronger flood ;
In speculation he is like a Child,
With this advantage, that he now can rest
Upon himself ; authority is none
165 To cheat him of his boldness, or hoodwink
His intuitions, or to lay asleep
The unquiet stir of his perplexities ;
And in this season of his second birth,

137-9 Cf. l. 513 *infra*, where Imagination is described as 'an Element of
the nature's inner self'. Cf. also II. 341-8.

141 cloud] written 'crowd'.

145 Cf. *Recluse* (*Home at Grasmere*), I. i. 122-3 :

> Clustered like stars some few, but single most,
> And lurking dimly in their shy retreats

Cf. also Wordsworth's *Letter to the Editor of the Friend* (1809) : 'Hitherto the
youth has been content to look at his own mind, after the manner in which
he ranges along the stars in the firmament with naked unaided sight : let
him now apply the telescope of art, to call the invisible stars out of their
hiding-places ; and let him endeavour to look through his whole being, with
the organ of reason, summoned to penetrate, as far as it has power, in discovery of the impelling forces and the governing laws.'

149 *optic tube* : *Paradise Lost*, iii. 590. The reference to Galileo is, o
course, a Miltonic reminiscence (*P.L.* i. 288).

[      ] submission and a slavish world
170    [      ] making a redemption of his mind,
He feels that, be his mind however great
In aspiration, the universe in which
He lives is equal to his mind, that each
Is worthy of the other; if the one
175    Be insatiate, the other is inexhaustible.
Whatever dignity there be [     ]
Within himself, from which he gathers hope,
There doth he feel its counterpart the same
In kind before him outwardly express'd,
180    With difference that makes the likeness clear,
Sublimities, grave beauty, excellence,
Not taken upon trust, but self-display'd
Before his proper senses; 'tis not here
Record of what hath been, is now no more,
185    Nor secondary work of mimic skill,
Transcripts that do but mock their archetypes;
But primary and independent life,
No glimmering residue of splendour past,
Things in decline or faded. [     ]
190    What hidden greater far than what is seen,
No false subordination, fickleness,
Or thwarted virtue, but inveterate power
Directed to best ends, and all things good
Pure and consistent. If upon mankind
195    He looks, and on the human maladies
Before his eyes, what finds he there to this
Fram'd answerably? what but sordid men,
And transient occupations, and desires
Ignoble and deprav'd? Therefore he cleaves
200    Exclusively to Nature as in her
Finding his image, what he has, what lacks,
His rest and his perfection. From mankind,
Like earlier monk or priest, as if by birth
He is sequester'd; to her altar's laws
205    Bound by an irrefutable decree;
No fellow labourer of the brotherhood,
Single he is in state, monarch and king;

--------

185–9 Y:      And imitations are not here that mock
                Their archetypes no single residue
                Of a departed glory [     ] a world
                Living and to live   Y.

The lines in the text above are found on another page, but are obviously
meant to come in here, though it is not clear how many of the lines in Y they
are meant to replace.

        Or like an Indian, when, in solitude
        And individual glory, he looks out
210     From some high eminence upon a tr(act)
        Boundless of unappropriated earth;
        So doth he measure the vast universe,
        His own by right of spiritual sovereignty.

        Yet who can tell while he this [   ?   ] path
215     Hath been ascending, in apparent slight
        Of man and all the mild humanities
        That overspread the surface of the heart,
        What subtle virtues from the first have been
        In midst of this, and in despite of [   ?   ]
220     At every moment finding out their way
        Insensibly to nourish in the heart
        Its tender sympathies, to keep alive
        Those yearnings, and to strengthen them and shape,
        Which from the mother's breast were first receiv'd?
225     The commonest images of nature—all,
        No doubt, are with this office charg'd,—a path,
        A taper burning through the gloom of night,
        Smoke breathing up by day from cottage trees,
        A beauteous sunbeam in a sunny shed,
230     A garden with its walks and banks of flowers,
        A churchyard, and the bell that tolls to church,
        The roaring ocean and waste wilderness,

---

208–13 Cf. *Excursion*, III. 928–40, *with Wordsworth's note on the passage*:

      But contemplations, worthier, nobler far
      Than her destructive energies, attend
      His Independence, when along the side
      Of Mississippi, or that Northern Stream
      Which spreads into successive seas, he walks;
      Pleased to perceive his own unshackled life,
      And his innate capacities of soul,
      There imaged: or, when having gained the top
      Of some commanding Eminence, which yet
      Intruder ne'er beheld, he thence surveys
      Regions of wood and wide Savannah, vast
      Expanse of unappropriated earth,
      With mind that sheds a light on what he sees.

227 *A taper etc.*: Cf. Wordsworth's *Letter to the Editor of the Friend* (quoted *supra*), where he describes the feelings of the schoolboy as he watches the 'sullen light which had survived the extinguished flame' of his candle: 'This is nature teaching seriously and sweetly through the affections, melting the heart, and, through that instinct of tenderness, developing the understanding.'

231 'tolls' written 'tholls', as though Wordsworth had started to write 'chimes' and written 't' over the 'c', omitting to delete the 'h'.

          Familiar things and awful, the minute
          And grand, are destined here to meet, are all
235       Subservient to this end, near or remote;
          One serv[ice ?] have in which they all [partake ?];—
          Namely, to make those gracious charities
          Habits of eye and ear and every sense,—
          Endearing union, without which the Earth
240       Is valueless, even in its Maker's eye.

**191–203 [144–56].** *Nor such as Spenser fabled etc.*: cf. *Shepheard's Calender*: *May*, 9–14, 19–24, 27–34.

          Yougthes folke now flocken in euery where,
          To gather may buskets and smelling brere:
          And home they hasten the postes to dight,
          And all the Kirke pillours eare day light,
          With Hawthorne buds, and swete Eglantine,
          And girlonds of roses and Sopps in wine.

          .     .     .     .     .     .     .

          Sicker this morrowe, ne lenger agoe,
          I saw a shole of shepheardes outgoe,
          With singing, and shouting, and iolly chere:
          Before them yode a lusty Tabrere,
          That to the many a Horne pype playd,
          Whereto they dauncen eche one with his mayd, . . .
          Tho to the greene Wood they speeden hem all,
          To fetchen home May with their musicall:
          And home they bringen in a royall throne,
          Crowned as king: and his Queene attone
          Was Lady Flora, on whom did attend
          A fayre flocke of Faeries, and a fresh bend
          Of Louely Nymphes. (O that I were there,
          To helpen the Ladyes their Maybush beare) . . .

Cf. also *Epithalamion*, 207–8:

          And all the postes adorne as doth behove,
          And all the pillours deck with girlands trim.

**221.** *my Household Dame*: i.e. Ann Tyson. Cf. IV. 17, 55, 208–21.

**222–311.** This story, not in D or E, is shown by J to have been originally written as an incident in the life of Michael and Luke, and therefore must be the work of October–December 1800, when Wordsworth was occupied with *Michael*. It was first printed, with some errors, in Knight's edition of the *Poems* (VIII. 224–30).

---

236 The second word is clearly 'servant', probably a scribal error due to the presence of the word 'subservient' in the previous line. The last word of the line seems to begin 'part', but there is no 'k' in the latter half. Wordsworth may have hesitated between 'partake' and 'pertain', intending if he decided on 'pertain' to alter 'in which' to 'to which'.

**236–7.** *that cloud-loving Hill, Seat Sandal, etc.*: Wordsworth used these lines more than thirty years later in *Musings near Aquapendente*, April 1837:

> Transported over that cloud-wooing hill,
> Seat Sandal, a fond suitor of the clouds . . .

**241.** *Russet Cove* (printed by Knight 'Sheepcot' Cove). There is no Russet Cove in the neighbourhood of Helvellyn. Mr. Gordon Wordsworth points out to me that the spot referred to is Ruthwaite (pronounced 'Ruthet') Cove, about a mile north of Grisedale Tarn and north-east of Dollywaggon Pike. Wordsworth's mistake is pardonable if we remember that he had settled at Grasmere less than a year before he wrote the line.

**312–24 [173–85].** A passage which bears witness to a knowledge and love of Latin poetry with which Wordsworth is not always credited. Galaesus is a river in Calabria, flowing into the bay of Tarentum, celebrated by Virgil and Horace for the sheep that fed upon its banks; cf. *Georgics*, iv. 126, and Horace, *Odes*, II. vi. 10 (Wordsworth had written an adaptation of this Ode in his schooldays under the title *Septimi Gades*, *P.W.* i. 296):

> Unde si Parcae prohibent iniquae
> Dulce pellitis ovibus Galaesi
> Flumen . . . petam.

Clitumnus was a river in Calabria whose waters were so pure that it whitened the coats of the herds that fed upon its banks and made them fit for sacrifice: cf. *Georgics*, ii. 146–8:

> Hinc albi, Clitumne, greges et maxima taurus
> Victima, saepe tuo perfusi flumine sacro,
> Romanos ad templa deum duxere triumphos;

Lucretilis (now Monte Gennaro), a hill overlooking Horace's Sabine farm. Cf. *Odes*, I. xvii:

> Velox amoenum saepe Lucretilem
> Mutat Lycaeo Faunus et igneam
> Defendit aestatem capellis
> Usque meis pluviosque ventos.

Horace identifies Faunus with Pan, the pipe-player, cf. ll. 10–12 (utcumque dulci . . . fistula . . . Levia personuere saxa). 'Horace', said Wordsworth in his later life, 'is my great favourite: I love him dearly.'

**339.** *His flute . . . resounding*: cf. *Sonnet*: 'The fairest brightest' etc. 3–4:

> O Friend! thy flute has breathed a harmony
> Softly resounded through this rocky glade.

**349 [211].** *Goslar, once Imperial!*: 'In this town the German emperors of the Franconian line were accustomed to keep their court, and it retains vestiges of its ancient splendour. . . . I walked daily on the ramparts, or in a sort of public ground or garden' (I. F. note to *Lines written in Germany*).

**353 [215].** *Hercynian forest*: The 'Hercynia silva' in the time of Julius Caesar stretched over a vast mountainous tract of South and East Germany. The name Hartz is derived from it.

**[241-4].** Cf. IX. 302-4.

**401 [266].** *In size a giant, stalking through the fog*: cf. Thomson, *Autumn*, 726-30, where the poet describes how, when 'sits the general fog Unbounded o'er the world', 'o'er the waste the shepherd stalks gigantic'.

**410 [275].** *Chartreuse*: cf. VI. 422 [482-8], and D. W.'s letter to Crabb Robinson, December 21, 1822, 'My Br. is very sorry that you should have missed the Chartreuse. I do not think that any one spot which he visited during his youthful Travels with Robert Jones made so great an impression on his mind: and in my young days he used to talk so much of it to me.'

**420 [285], 422 [287].** *Corin, Phillis*: typical names from the classical and Elizabethan pastoral; cf. *As You Like It*, and *L'Allegro*.

**428 [293], 449 [314].** Two hypermetric lines. The MSS. suggest no explanation in either case.

**442 [307].** *whencesoever*: The reading of 1850 'wheresoever' is clearly a mistake in copying; first found in D, and from D copied into E.

**483 [349].** The change from 'three' (A) to 'two' (D) 'and twenty' puts the date right. Wordsworth was born in April 1770. The time when 'two and twenty summers had been told' must, therefore, be after the summer of 1791 and before the summer of 1792. Garrod (p. 58) holds that two and twenty summers necessarily points to the autumn of 1791, and adds 'it means that the interest in Man was not first acquired in France, as is commonly supposed, and under the influence of Beaupuy, but that it was this interest, which, acquired in England, took him to France for the second time in 1792'. Against this view it can be argued:

(i) When Wordsworth went to France for the second time (it was in November 1791, not as Garrod states in 1792) his chief reason, as he says in the A text, was to learn the language.

(ii) His own account in *The Prelude* makes it clear that Nature was still first with him in the London period (VIII. 860-9) and that the winter of 1791-2 witnessed a shifting of his love from Nature to Man. Even in Paris, though he 'visited each spot of recent fame' (IX. 41-42), he 'affected more emotion than he felt' (*ibid.* 71): it was only after he reached the Loire that

my heart was all
Given to the People, and my love was theirs (ibid. 124-5).

If my interpretation is correct, this shifting of interest from Nature to Man would coincide with his plunge into humanitarian politics and the dawning of his love for Annette (Dec.-Jan. 1791-2).

**491 [357].** Cf. *Paradise Lost*, iv. 264-6:

The Birds thir quire apply; aires, vernal aires,

> Breathing the smell of field and grove, attune
> The trembling leaves.

The 'minute obeisances of tenderness' (493–4) Wordsworth owed to the influence of Dorothy at Racedown (*v.* XIII. 226–36).

**497.** After this line Y has a deleted passage, parts of which were afterwards utilized in *Excursion*, IV. 404–12 and IX. 437–48. But the vivid touch of personal detail, with which this version closes, gives it an autobiographical and poetic value absent from the lines as they appear in the *Excursion*:

> Whether the whistling kite wheel'd in the storm
> Maze intricate, above me or below,
> As if in mockery or in proud display
> Of his own gifts compar'd with feeble Man;
> Or facing some huge breast of rock I heard,
> As I have sometimes done, a solemn bleat
> Sent forth as if it were the mountain's voice,
> As if the visible [mountain made the cry]

(*Here follow three illegible deleted lines.*)

> And hark again!
> No other, and the region all about
> Is silent, empty of all shape of life;
> It is a lamb left somewhere to itself,
> The plaintive spirit of the solitude.
> In those same careless rambles of my youth,
> Once coming to a bridge that overlook'd
> A mountain torrent, where it was becalm'd
> By a flat meadow, at a glance I saw
> A twofold image; on the grassy bank
> A snow-white ram, and in the peaceful flood
> Another and the same; most beautiful
> The breathing creature; nor less beautiful,
> Beneath him, was his shadowy counterpart;
> Each had his [glowing] mountains, each his sky,
> [And each seem'd centre of his own] fair world.
> A stray temptation seiz'd me to dissolve
> The vision,—but I could not, and the stone,
> Snatch'd up for that intent, dropp'd from my hand.
> Why need I mention Tillers of the Soil? *etc.*

The words enclosed in brackets, which are illegible in the MS., have been supplied from the corresponding lines in the *Excursion*. In the MS. the passage is entirely without punctuation.

**498–510.** These lines were perhaps omitted in later texts because they interrupt the train of thought, but they are well worthy of preservation. They give a vivid picture of the occupations of the men and women among whom the poet grew up, and who were unconsciously leading him from love of nature to love of man. And the picture of Echo and her sister Silence, added to A, has a touch of suggestive beauty that recalls *Comus*.

**559 [406] ff.** *There was a Copse etc.*: The house in which Wordsworth lodged at Colthouse which seems to be rightly identified as Greenend Cottage (*v.* M. Moorman, pp. 84–85) has a view of Spring Wood on the slope of Claife Height opposite.

**584–5 [421–3].** *wilful fancy . . . imagination*: for the relation of fancy to imagination, and the distinction between them, cf. XIII. 282–306, and Preface to 1815 ed. of *Poems*.

**605–7 [433–4].** Cf. II. 466–7 and note.

**[458–75].** This passage is founded on one of the experiences of boyhood which Wordsworth originally intended to incorporate in Book II. In MSS. V and U they follow II. 144, as follows:

> There was a row of ancient trees, since fallen
> That on the margin of a jutting land
> Stood near the lake of Coniston and made
> With its long boughs above the water stretch'd
> A gloom through which a boat might sail along
> As in a cloister. An old Hall was near
> Grotesque and beautiful, its gavel end
> And huge round chimneys to the top o'ergrown
> With fields of ivy. Thither we repair'd,
> Twas even a custom with us, to the shore
> And to that cool piazza. They who dwelt
> In the neglected mansion-house supplied
> Fresh butter, tea-kettle, and earthen-ware,
> And chafing dish with smoking coals, and so
> Beneath the trees we sate in our small boat
> And in the covert eat our delicate meal
> Upon the calm smooth lake. It was a joy
> Worthy the heart of one who is full grown
> To rest beneath those horizontal boughs
> And mark the radiance of the setting sun
> Himself unseen, reposing on the top
> Of the high eastern hills. And there I said,
> That beauteous sight before me, there I said,
> (Then first beginning in my thoughts to mark
> That sense of dim similitude which links
> Our moral feelings with external forms)
> That in whatever region I should close
> My mortal life I would remember you
> Fair scenes! that dying I would think on you
> My soul would send a longing look to you:
> Even as that setting sun while all the vale
> Could nowhere catch one faint memorial gleam
> Yet with the last remains of his last light

Still linger'd and a farewell lustre threw
On the dear mountain tops where first he rose.

'Twas then my fourteenth summer and these words
Were utter'd in a casual access
Of sentiment, a momentary trance
That far outran the habit of my mind.

Thurston-mere is an old name for Coniston Lake.

**[471–5]**. See *P.W.* i. 1 (note in 1850), i.e. *Extract from the conclusion of a poem, composed in anticipation of leaving school*:

Dear native regions, I foretell,
From what I feel at this farewell,
That, wheresoe'er my steps may tend,
And whensoe'er my course shall end,
If in that hour a single tie
Survive of local sympathy,
My soul will cast the backward view,
The longing look alone on you.

Thus, while the Sun sinks down to rest
Far in the regions of the west,
Though to the vale no parting beam
Be given, not one memorial gleam,
A lingering light he fondly throws
On the dear hills where first he rose.

On these lines the I. F. note runs: 'The beautiful image with which this poem concludes suggested itself to me while I was resting in a boat along with my companions under the shade of a magnificent row of sycamores, which then extended their branches from the shore of the promontory upon which stands the ancient and at that time the more picturesque Hall of Coniston, the Seat of the Le Flemings from very early times. The Poem of which it is the conclusion was of many hundred lines, and contained thoughts and images most of which have been dispersed through my other writings.'

It is characteristic of Wordsworth that this experience of his fourteenth year, when he could not have thought of leaving school, was turned into poetry two years later, and again, when he came to write *The Prelude*, in 1799.

**634 [487]**. *As of all visible natures crown*: Notice the theological limitation to man's glory added to the 1850 text.

**646 [500]**. *eclips'd*: eclipse (D, E, 1850) is probably an uncorrected copyist's error.

**680–1 [533–4]**. An unconscious echo of Milton, *Lycidas*, 104–6:

His *mantle* hairy and his bonnet sedge,
*Inwrought* with figures dim, and on the edge
Like to that sanguine flower . . .

**689–93 [540–3]**. Cf. VII. 73.

**711 [560]** ff. Another passage in the Miltonic style ('sees, or thinks He sees' is reminiscent of *Paradise Lost*, i. 783–4, 'sees, Or dreams he sees').

**713 [562]**. *Antiparos*: a small island among the Cyclades.

**714 [564]**. *Yordas*: near Ingleton, Yorkshire, and visited by Wordsworth with his brother John in May 1800 (*v. E.L.* 151).

**735.** *pressure*: used in Shakespearian sense; cf. VII. [288].

**742–51 [590–6]**. Originally written to form part of Book VII (*v.* Introduction, p. lii).

**763 [610]**. *punctual*: i.e. confined to one spot, a Miltonic use of the word. Cf. *Paradise Lost*, viii. 23: 'this punctual spot'.

**771.** *Greece . . . and Rome*: For Wordsworth's interest in ancient history cf. I. 190 (note).

**775.** *Stript of their harmonising soul*: 'their' refers, of course, to 'events' (772). When 772–3 were omitted from the text 'their' should have been altered to 'its'. As it stands in the 1850 text 'their' is ungrammatical.

**823 [664]**. From Milton, *Paradise Lost*, xi. 204 (note in 1850). But the quotation is of more than one line:

> why in the East
> Darkness ere Dayes mid-course, and Morning light
> More orient in yon Western Cloud that draws
> Ore the blew Firmament a radiant white,
> And slow descends, with something heav'nly fraught.

**[680]**. '*busy hum*': cf. Milton, *L'Allegro*, 117–18:

> Towred Cities please us then,
> And the busie humm of men.

# BOOK IX

**13–17.** The reading of A, and still more that of A² C, suggests that at the back of Wordsworth's mind was the opening of *Paradise Lost*, ix, where Milton turns from the delineation of sinless Paradise to describe

> foul distrust, and breach
> Disloyal on the part of Man, revolt,
> And disobedience; On the part of Heav'n
> Now alienated, distance and distaste,
> Anger and just rebuke, and judgement giv'n.

**24.** *Looking as from a distance*: possibly omitted from D E because it repeats the statement made in VI. 695–6 of his feeling towards the Revolution in the previous year. But the A text of this passage (23–30) gives as a whole a more discerning account of what London had contributed to the growth of his mind than the versions in D and E.

**31 [28]**. *A year thus spent*: 'Scarcely a year' E. The time was really much shorter. Wordsworth went to London in February 1791, and from a letter of his sister's, dated May 23, we learn that he was then already in Wales; and though he was probably in London again in October, on November 23 he was at Brighton, *en route* for France.

**34–39.** A[2] reads:

> To lure the valiant Saunterer from his Track)
> I quitted, and betook myself once more
> To that attractive Land which I had crossed
> Erewhile in eager pilgrimage—but now
> Relinquishing the well-tried Staff and Scrip
> I went prepared to take up my abode
> And be a Dweller in a pleasant town
> Washed by the Waters of the stately Loire.

**36–37.** The reading of A disposes of the view advanced by some critics that Wordsworth was chiefly drawn to France by a newly awakened interest in man, and hence a sympathy with the Revolution. Cf. also ll. 74–79, 85–107, and note on VIII. 483.

**39 [41].** *A City on the Borders of the Loire*: i.e. Orleans, which Wordsworth reached on December 6, 1791; at some date in the early months of the next year, 1792, he removed to Blois. As Professor Harper has pointed out, Wordsworth does not distinguish in *The Prelude* between his experiences at Orleans and at Blois. He dated a letter to his brother Richard on December 19 from Orleans, and on May 17 following wrote that he was 'overwhelmed by a sense of shame' for leaving so long unanswered a letter from Matthews which had reached him just as he 'was busy in preparing to quit Orleans', since when, 'day after day and week after week have stolen insensibly over my head with inconceivable rapidity'. At the lowest computation this would take us back to March, and Harper adduces good evidence (*Life*, i. 155) that he was already at Blois in February. The 'knot of military Officers' (126) were certainly stationed there, for Blois, and not Orleans, was at the time a garrison city. Wordsworth was still at Blois when the king was *suspendu* on August 10 (*Memoirs*, i. 15), and on September 3, when he dates a letter from there, but at Orleans in the next day or two during the September massacres, and also in the following month (*v. Descriptive Sketches*, 1793 ed., 760–3). At the end of October he was again in Paris, where he remained till the end of the year, or possibly till early in January 1793.

**41–51 [43–53].** *visited In haste each spot of old and recent fame etc.*: All those 'spots' mentioned here by Wordsworth were 'of recent fame'. The *field of Mars* (43), in the west of Paris, was the scene of the Federation fête held on July 14, 1790, to commemorate the fall of the Bastille. The Federated States were invited to send delegates, and great preparations were made for the festivities. A huge *arc de triomphe* was erected, and in the middle was placed the *autel de la Patrie*. Fifteen thousand workmen were not enough to complete the work, so that the whole population was invited to volunteer. At the altar a solemn oath was administered to the deputies and to the newly formed National Guards, and here Louis XVI swore fidelity to the new constitution. But in the July following (1791), after the king's flight, a petition asking for the deposition of the monarch was exposed on the altar, to receive signatures. The National Guard under Lafayette was called out to check riotous meetings, and blood flowed even up to the steps of the altar.

**44 [46].** *The Suburbs of St. Antony*: The Faubourg St. Antoine, in the east of the city, and abutting on the Bastille, was the workmen's quarter, where much of the revolutionary violence was fomented.

**45 [47].** *Mont Martyr*: i.e. Montmartre, in the north of Paris, where revolutionary meetings were held, possibly in two convents evacuated by the order of the Government in the preceding year.

**45–46 [47–48].** *the Dome Of Geneviève*: i.e. the Panthéon, in the south of Paris, was a church built to the classic designs of the architect Soufflot on the site of the old Abbey of Ste Geneviève. It was in course of erection at the outbreak of the Revolution. On the death of Mirabeau (April 1791) the Assembly wished for a place of burial, like Westminster Abbey, in which to deposit the remains of those who had deserved well of their country. Soufflot's building seemed well suited for the purpose, and *dans un transport civique* it was baptized, and 'henceforth received a soul and a meaning' (Quinet). It was still called Ste Geneviève, however, as the separation of Church and State had not yet taken place, and at Mirabeau's funeral the clergy officiated. Voltaire's remains were brought there in July of the same year, and when, a few days later, a petition was submitted that the body of Rousseau should be placed there also, the name Panthéon was suggested.

**47 [49].** *The National Synod*: The National Assembly at this time met in the *salle de Manège* or Riding Hall at the east corner of the Rue de Rivoli. The Hall was demolished in 1810.

*the Jacobins*: The Jacobin Club met in the library of the convent of the Dominicans, near the Rue Saint Honoré. The Dominicans were known as Jacobins because their earliest convent in Paris (A.D. 1218) was a hospice bearing the title of St. Jacques, and the name was transferred to the revolutionaries who met there.

**50–51 [52–53].** *The Arcades . . . in the Palace huge Of Orleans*: i.e. in the Palais Royal. On three sides of the courtyard arcades of shops had been built (51–52), and this was the chief centre in Paris both for business and for idle lounging (53–54). 'The beauty of the buildings and magnificence of the shops did not impress us', writes a visitor in 1787, 'so much as the crowds of people who flocked there at mid-day. It is the rendez-vous of strangers, of the idle Parisians, and charming women' (J. Letaconnoux, *La Vie parisienne au xviii^{me} siècle*, p. 55). Cf. also X. 83–84.

**56 [58].** *hubbub wild*: cf. *Paradise Lost*, ii. 951–2:

At length an universal hubbub wilde
Of stunning sounds and voices all confus'd . . .

**68.** *incumbences*: i.e. spiritual broodings or visitations. Cf. III. 115 and note.

**77.** *the Magdalene of le Brun*: Charles le Brun (1616–90), court painter to Louis XIV, painted this picture for the Carmelite convent in the Rue d'Enfer. 'It was regarded as one of the "sights" of the day. Religious music was played for the benefit of those who came to view it' (Legouis trans., p. 194). It is now in the Louvre. Wordsworth never acquired any sound taste in pictorial art, and was able later to express a genuine admiration for the canvases of his friends Haydon and Sir George Beaumont.

**96 [97].** *the master Pamphlets of the day*: Among the many pamphlets issued at this time Aulard (*Hist. pol. rev.*) mentions those of the royalist Peltier, the *constituant* Drouet (*Voilà ce qu'il faut faire*), and the extremists Marat and Robespierre (on universal suffrage); also the anonymous *Grande visite de Mademoiselle République*, and *Deux Brutus au peuple français*. At the sale of W. W.'s library in 1859 'Lot 405' was 'Pamphlets and Ephemera—French; a bundle'.

**107–10.**　　*At that time, . . . Lock'd up in quiet*:
On September 30, 1791, the Constituent Assembly had dispersed and on the following day the Legislative Assembly heard from the throne the statement that 'le terme de la Révolution est arrivé. Que la nation reprenne son heureux caractère.' This internal peace was not disturbed till after November 29, when the strong measures taken against those priests who were not loyal to the new constitution began to embitter good Catholics. Abroad, the *émigrés* (*v.* note to l. 185 *infra*) had as yet achieved no dangerous success with foreign powers, and the king and queen rather feared their zeal than favoured their intrigues. Wordsworth's description of the state of things on his arrival in France is therefore quite accurate.

**124 [123].** *Patriot*: Wordsworth could not be a 'patriot' of France in the ordinary acceptance of the term. But Camille Desmoulins in his *Révolutions de France et de Brabant* had given the word the special political meaning of 'republican'. Both here and in ll. 295, 553, W. W. uses it in this technical sense.

**126 [125].** *A knot of military Officers*: Wordsworth's first associates were all anti-revolutionary in their sympathies. Cf. the letter to his brother Richard, December 19: 'I had imagined . . . there were some people of wealth and circumstance favourers of the Revolution, but here is no one to be found.' He had not yet met Beaupuy.

**178 [176].** *Carra, Gorsas*: journalist deputies of Girondist sympathy, who sat in the National Convention. Gorsas was the first Girondist to be guillotined (Oct. 7, 1793). In 1840 Wordsworth told Carlyle that he was present at the execution. If this was so, and Carlyle is hardly likely to have misunderstood Wordsworth on a matter which would interest him so deeply, Wordsworth must have paid a flying visit to France at that time.

**185 [183].** *To augment the band of Emigrants*: The first *émigrés* were the extreme reactionaries who, exasperated by the king's early concessions to the National Assembly, left France with the avowed object of returning to reconquer the country for the *ancien régime*. On the general attack upon the châteaux throughout France they were joined, for reasons of personal safety, by many more of the nobility and gentry ; and, after the flight of the king to Varennes (June 1791), by the majority of the army officers. They made their headquarters at Coblenz, and formed later the nucleus of the Royalist armies ranged against France.

**293 [288].** *Among that band of Officers was one*: Michel Armand Beaupuy (wrongly spelt in l. 425 Beaupuis), born at Mussidan, Périgord, in 1755, and thus fifteen years older than Wordsworth. He was of noble family, and descended on the female side from Montaigne ; but his sympathy, and that of his mother and four brothers, was entirely with the revolutionary cause, and he was, moreover, a student, and widely read in the philosophy of the eighteenth century. For a full account of his life and character *vide* Legouis, *Early Life of Wordsworth*, and Bussière and Legouis, *Le Général Michel Beaupuy*. It is clear from M. Legouis's researches that Beaupuy was well worthy of Wordsworth's enthusiastic but discerning praise of him, and that his influence on the poet's mind was only equalled by that exercised later by Coleridge. Before his intimacy with Beaupuy Wordsworth's interest in the Revolution was largely sentimental (cf. ll. 63–79, 200–16): it now became practical, and reasoned, if a little doctrinaire. Harper is surely right in his suggestion that when Wordsworth drew his portrait of *The Happy Warrior* (less than two years after this sketch of Beaupuy was written) his French friend was at the back of his mind.

**340 [333].** *Than afterwards*: i.e. in 1793–5, the period with which he deals in Book X [X–XI].

**369–70 [362–3].** *As just etc.*: the meaning here is not clear and the construction awkward. Wordsworth probably means 'making the life of society as a whole as pure and as well-regulated, as is the life of the individual wise and good man'. Cf. the remark made by Dicey (*Statesmanship of Wordsworth*, p. 32): 'Beaupuy and Wordsworth were in 1792 democrats who hoped to obtain every kind of socialistic reform by means which would have met with the approval of zealous individualists.'

**414–23 [408–17].** *Such conversation ... Did Dion hold with Plato etc.*: Wordsworth owed his knowledge of this story to Plutarch (*v.* note to I. 186–95), and the poem which he wrote later (1816) upon Dion is full of reminiscences of Plutarch's *Life of Dion*. Dion was the brother-in-

law of Dionysius the elder, tyrant of Syracuse. On Plato's first visit to
Sicily Dion became his disciple, and after the accession of Dionysius
the younger (367 B.C.), a weak and dissolute tyrant, he induced Plato
to return in the hope of influencing his nephew. But his plans for the
young man's reformation, though for a time successful, were under-
mined by flatterers and proved abortive ; he was himself banished and
retired to Athens, where once more he associated with Plato and other
philosophers. Plato paid a third visit to Syracuse in the hope of effect-
ing the recall of Dion, but Dionysius refused, confiscated Dion's property, and married his wife, Arete, to another husband. 'These things
went to *Dions* heart, so that shortly after he shewed himselfe an open
enemie unto *Dionysius*, but specially when he heard how he handled
his wife . . . *Dion* from thenceforth disposed himself altogether unto
war, against *Platoes* counsel and advise ; . . . Howbeit, on the other
side, *Speusippus* and his other friends did provoke him unto it, and
perswade him to deliver *Sicile* from the slaverie and bondage of the
tyrant, the which held up her hands unto him, and would receive him
with great love and goodwill. . . . The philosophers do set forward
*Dions* warres ; many citizens dealing in the affaires of the commonwealth, did aide him, and divers of them also that only gave their
minds to the studie of Philosophie : and among them *Eudemus Cyprian*
. . . *Timonides Leucadian*, went with him. . . The place where they appointed to meete was the *Ile* of *Zacynth* where they leavied all their
souldiers. . . . So *Dions* souldiers were embarked into two great ships
of burden' (Plutarch, *Dion*: North's trans.). Dion succeeded in de-
posing Dionysius (357 B.C.) but was himself assassinated in 353 B.C.

　　**430 [424].** *He perish'd fighting*: In this statement Wordsworth was
mistaken. Beaupuy was dangerously wounded in the Vendée, but recovered, and served the republican cause with distinction and unswerving loyalty till 1796, when he fell at the battle of the Elz, on
November 19 (*v.* Legouis, p. 214).

　　**441 [435].** *High woods and over-arch'd etc.*: Cf. *Paradise Lost*, ix.
1106–7 :

a Pillard shade
High overarcht, and echoing Walks between

　　**453 [451].** *Angelica*: the heroine of Ariosto's *Orlando Furioso* (*v.*
Canto I. 13) :

La donna il palafreno addietro volta,
e per la selva a tutta briglia il caccia ;
nè per la rara più che per la folta,
la più sicura e miglior via procaccia ;
ma pallida, tremando, e di sè tolta,
lascia cura al destrier che la via faccia.

　　**455 [453].** *Erminia*: the heroine of Tasso's *Gerusalemme Liberata*
(*v.* Canto VII. 1) :

In tanto Erminia in fra l'ombrose piante

d'antica selva dal cavallo è scorta:
nè più governa il fren la man tremante,
e mezza quasi par tra viva a morta.
Per tante strade si raggira e tante
il corridor che in sua balía la porta,
ch' al fin da gli occhi altrui pur si delegua;
ed è soverchio omai ch' altri la segua.

Wordsworth studied Italian at Cambridge under Isola, who had formerly been Gray's teacher.

**461 [459].** *Satyrs in some viewless glade etc.*: Cf. Spenser, *Faerie Queene*, I. vi. 13, where Una is rescued from Sansloy by the satyrs who
> lead her forth, about her dauncing round,
> Shouting, and singing all a shepheards ryme,
> And with greene braunches strowing all the ground,
> Do worship her as Queene, with olive girlond cround.

Cf. also the picture of Hellenore among the Satyrs (*F.Q.* III. x. 43–44):
> Now when among the thickest woodes they were,
> They heard a noyse of many bagpipes shrill,
> And shrieking Hububs them approaching nere,
> Which all the forrest did with horror fill;
>
> .    .    .    .    .    .    .    .    .
>
> The jolly Satyres full of fresh delight,
> Came dauncing forth, and with them nimbly ledd
> Faire Hellenore, with girlonds all bespredd.

The hermits (447) are possibly suggested by Archimago (*F.Q.* I. i. 34).

**475 [473].** *I could not but bewail a wrong so harsh, etc.*: Cf. his feelings at the Chartreuse, described in VI. [420–87].

**482–92.** *Romorentin . . . Edifice of Blois . . . Chambord*: *Romorantin* (*not* Romorentin), a small château, twenty-five miles from Blois, beloved by Louise de Savoie, the mother of Francis I. Francis spent much time there as a boy with his sister. It was here that Louise saw the comet in the sky which was supposed to presage the first military success of her son at Marignano. *The imperial Edifice of Blois* was reconstructed by Louis XII; here the Emperor Charles V visited Francis in 1539. *Chambord* is on the plain of Sologne, nine miles south-east of Blois, and one of the finest examples of Renaissance architecture. Originally an old *maison de chasse*, Francis began its transformation in 1519, and on his return from captivity in Madrid the building and decoration were his delight, and he lived there at least three years (1526–30). The episode referred to by Wordsworth must belong to this time. In 1526 his mother, hoping to dissociate him from Françoise de Chateaubriant, produced from her suite a young maid of honour, Anne de Pisseleu d'Heilly, who forthwith became his mistress, and was 'in constant company with the king in his daily examination of the progress at Chambord'. Of the three châteaux within a radius of ten miles from Chambord, and on the heights, Chaverney was not built till 1640, and

Chaumont, which is on a hill and commands a long view of the Loire, was occupied after 1561 by Diane; and she did not come on the scene till 1537, when Francis's interest in Chambord had waned. The third, Beauregard, was a hunting lodge built by Francis, 4½ miles from Blois, and on one of the roads to Chambord. This seems therefore the most likely to have been the 'rural Castle' (483) whose name Wordsworth had forgotten, and Anne the lady to whom the king signalled. There seems no trustworthy source for the suggestion (taken by Nowell Smith from Hachette's *Guide*) that Thoury was the castle and the Comtesse of Thoury the lady—still less for Knight's statement that the lady was Claude, daughter of Louis XII.

**537.** *mandate without law*: i.e. *lettre de cachet*, or letter expressing the personal will of the sovereign or his government, not a legal decision, and sent *cachetée* to the officer charged with the execution of the order contained in it.

**540 [539].** *not*: So all MSS., but the sense clearly requires 'but'.

**[547].** *repeat a tale*: the tale of *Vaudracour and Julia* (note in 1850). *Vaudracour and Julia* was first published in 1820.

**553–4.** *related by my patriot Friend And others*:
In the 1850 version Wordsworth speaks of the tale simply as 'told by my patriot friend'. In the I. F. note to *Vaudracour and Julia* he stated that it was 'faithfully narrated, though with the omission of many pathetic circumstances, from the mouth of a French lady, who had been an eye and ear witness of all that was done and said. Many long years after, I was told that Dupligne was then a monk in the Convent of La Trappe.' This incompatibility has more than once been commented on, and M. Legouis has suggested that its object was 'to avert suspicion rather than to give information to the public' (*William Wordsworth and Annette Vallon*, 1922). But it is difficult to see why the mouth of a French lady would awaken less suspicion than the mouth of his patriot friend. The reading of A perhaps explains the discrepancy. If, as Wordsworth said in 1820 (and his statements of fact can be trusted), 'the facts are true; no invention as to these has been exercised, as none was needed', the events would naturally be much talked of at the time of their occurrence; and it is not unlikely that Wordsworth would hear the story not only from Beaupuy, but from others; among them, with much detail in which Beaupuy would not be interested, from the French lady referred to in the I. F. note. The statement, also made in 1820, that 'the following tale was written as an episode in a work from which its length may perhaps exclude it', does not imply that its length was the only reason of its exclusion. Doubtless he omitted it in part to avert suspicion, just as he included it, in spite of its length, when he wrote *The Prelude*, that he might not leave without allusion an important episode of his own life in France—i.e. his love for Annette. He has been accused of a reticence amounting to insincerity in tracing 'the growth of the poet's mind' without any reference to an

event which must have borne some part in that growth. The explanation is twofold. (1) Quite apart from his own feelings in the matter, it was impossible for him to relate the facts without causing pain to those who had every claim upon his consideration—not only his own wife and family, but also Annette and Caroline : on the other hand, he could hardly pass over the matter without some allusion to it. Consequently he adopts the compromise of telling the story in veiled language through the tale of Vaudracour and Julia. The fates of these two lovers were sufficiently like and sufficiently unlike those of Wordsworth and Annette to tell Coleridge (for whom, it must be remembered, *The Prelude* was specially written) the state of his own feelings at the time. Few students of Wordsworth, realizing how much his genius was dependent for all its greatest manifestations upon actual personal experience, will doubt that in the great passages of *Vaudracour and Julia*, which stand out all the more clearly from the inferiority of the poem as a whole,—the account of the ecstasy of young love (580–93), the exciting passion of stolen interviews (625–32) (ed. 1820, 94–101), and the distracted state of mind of the separated lovers (744–9)—Wordsworth is drawing on his own experience. Certainly Coleridge would so understand it. (2) This passion for Annette, overwhelming as it was at the time, could not have left him the same man as he was before. Yet in retrospect it seemed to him to have been transient rather than permanent in its effects upon him, and perhaps to have arrested rather than developed the natural growth of his poetic mind. It had, for example, none of that formative and continually stimulating effect upon his imagination which he recognized in the experiences of his childhood. Consequently, however vital a part of his biography as a man, it seemed less vital in the history of his mind. That it had more influence upon his mind and art than he believed it to have is probable ; it can hardly be doubted, for example, that he owed to it that sympathetic penetration into the heart of the deserted woman, and the relations of mother and child, which is a marked feature of his poetry from 1795 to 1805. But it is one thing to differ from Wordsworth as to the importance of the episode in the development of his mind, and another to accuse him of wilfully misrepresenting that development.

It is evident from the amount of revision that *Vaudracour and Julia* underwent before its publication in 1820 that Wordsworth was deeply affected by it, equally evident that as a whole it is among the weakest of his attempts in narrative verse. Its most radical fault lies in that part which was probably true to fact, but farthest removed from his own experience, i.e. the character of the hero, with whose meek resignation it is as impossible to sympathize as with the patience of a Griselda. But whereas Chaucer has the dramatic and narrative power to awaken, for the time at least, enough poetic faith to make us accept his story, Wordsworth completely fails in presenting a character so unlike his own; and the matter-of-fact detail which he supplies, often so effective and moving in his narratives, only makes *Vaudracour and Julia* more ludicrous, till in ll. 906–7 it reaches a climax of absurdity difficult to parallel in our literature: *v.* Addenda, p. 632.

**575 [24–29].** The image added to A² of two birds parted and reunited in the storm he had already used in *The Recluse*, I, writing in 1800, of his winter walk with Dorothy to take up their abode at Grasmere:

> Like two birds, companions in mid-air
> Parted and reunited by the blast.

**583.** *Arabian fiction*: For Wordsworth's fondness for the *Arabian Nights* cf. V. 484–99 and MS. Y (p. 573).

**595–6.** *whether through effect Of some delirious hour*: the obvious psychological explanation, which is ill replaced by the shocked morality of the 1820 version.

**911.** Altered, doubtless, in later texts to escape odious comparison with *Othello*, v. ii. 303, 'From this time forth I never will speak word.'

**933–4.** This is an unwitting departure from fact, but it was only years after that Wordsworth learnt that Dupligne (i.e. Vaudracour) was a monk at La Trappe (*v.* I. F. note, quoted p. 591).

# BOOK X

**9–37.** *The King had fallen etc.*: On July 25, 1792, the Duke of Brunswick signed a manifesto inspired by Marie-Antoinette, to the effect that if the least violence or outrage were done upon the king the allies would avenge it by a military execution in Paris. Two days later the Princes issued a declaration that not only Paris should suffer the extremity of martial law, but every town to which the king might be removed. These manifestoes, intended to terrorize Paris, only strengthened the hands of the more violent section; as a counterstroke, the Revolutionists led by Danton decided to depose the king and hold him as a hostage. On the night of August 9 the Tuileries was stormed by the mob and on the following day the king was deposed and confined in prison 'for his own security'. On August 19 the allied forces entered France and took Longwy (Aug. 24) and Verdun (Sept. 1). In retaliation the committee of the Commune, of whom Marat, Danton, and Robespierre were chief, organized the September massacres (Sept. 2, 3, and 4), in which over 3,000 Royalist suspects were taken from prison and slaughtered. After the poor resistance of the Republican troops at Longwy and Verdun, the allied forces anticipated no difficulty in reaching Paris; but the French troops under Dumouriez made an unexpected stand at Valmy on September 20, and early in the following months the allies had completely evacuated French territory. The Republic was decreed on the day of the victory of Valmy and was proclaimed on September 22. In the new assembly, which had just been elected, Paris was represented by Jacobin extremists, but the September massacres had not appealed to the country as a whole, and there was a large majority of moderates who were prepared to follow the Girondists—if the Girondists would lead. Hence Wordsworth's optimism in ll. 34–37.

The changes which Wordsworth introduced into the text of this passage are noteworthy, as showing his increased horror of the Revolution in his later life. The statement that 'in a spirit of thanks' to the victors of Valmy she 'assumed with joy' the name of a Republic is replaced by the assertion that it was an act of defiance and resentment, and prompted by the desire 'to taunt the baffled League'. Similarly he tones down the expression of his own enthusiasm at the time from 'enflamed with hope' to 'cheered with this hope'.

**17.** *punctual spot*: a Miltonic phrase, *Paradise Lost*, viii. 23 (cf. *The Prelude*, VIII. 763). It is worth noting that, whilst this phrase goes out in later versions, the simile of the 'eastern hunters' is elaborated in the Miltonic manner, with a definite debt to *Paradise Lost*, xi. 391, '*Agra* and *Lahor* of great *Mogul*', and i. 776, 'the signal giv'n' (of the narrowing of the giants into pigmies).

**19–20 [26–27].** *fled In terror*: a somewhat exaggerated description of the retreat of the allied army from France.

**29.** *assumed with joy*: 'Wordsworth was probably present on September 21 at the civic feast given at Orleans to celebrate the suppression of monarchy, during which deputy Manuel made a speech before the assembly. As a symbol of the fall of royalty, fire was set to a big wood-pile: "Le feu est solennellement mis à l'énorme bûcher, composé de fagots élevés en une haute pyramide couronnée d'un bouquet d'artifice qui bientôt tombe en mille flammèches étincelantes, et les citoyens se livrent à la joie qu'ils ressentent de l'établissement de la République française: dans leur enthousiasme, avec les élans qui n'appartiennent qu'à des hommes vraiement dignes de la liberté, les cris de 'Vive la République! Vive la nation française!' éclatent de toutes parts."' Legouis, *William Wordsworth and Annette Vallon*, p. 24 (quoted from *Histoire de la ville d'Orléans* by Bimbenet).

**42 [51].** *The Prison where the unhappy Monarch lay*: the 'Temple', in north-east Paris, built in the second half of the twelfth century for the Order of Templars. When they were suppressed in the fourteenth century, it became the seat of the Grand Priory of France. The tower of the 'Temple' was a thick-walled building, square, and flanked with turrets at the four corners. It was demolished in 1811.

**44 [53].** *the Palace lately storm'd*: the Tuileries, situated between the Louvre and the Champs-Élysées.

**47 [56].** *The Square of the Carrousel*: a vast square in front of the Tuileries and only separated from it by an iron paling. It was so called because in 1662 Louis XIV gave here a magnificent tournay or 'carrousel'. On August 10, 1792, a mob composed chiefly of the

Marseillese and of workmen from the Faubourg St-Antoine attacked the Tuileries; they were fired on by the Swiss guards, and many of them fell in the Place du Carrousel before entry was gained into the Palace.

**50–69.** A loose sheet containing these lines is extant. It represents a text intermediary between A and C, for it has throughout the readings of C, and 'dread' (66) is so written that it might easily be mistaken for 'dream', with the last stroke of the 'm' curled up.

**70 [77].** *The horse is taught his manage*: Cf. *As You Like It*, I. i. 13: 'His horses are bred better: . . . they are taught their manage.'

**76–77 [86–87].** *A voice that cried, . . . 'Sleep no more'*: *Macbeth*, II. ii. 35.

**83.** *Betimes next morning*: From this passage it is natural to suppose that Wordsworth arrived in Paris on the very day, October 29, on which Louvet made his accusation, which would be hawked about the streets on the next morning. Louvet accused Robespierre of having 'perverted the Jacobin Club and exercised a despotism of opinion. These bloody men', he said, and he mentioned Marat also by name, 'wished to satiate their cruel eyes with the spectacle of 28,000 bodies sacrificed to their fury. I accuse you of having dispersed and persecuted the Legislative Assembly, of having exhibited yourself as an object of idolatry, of having aimed at supreme power; and in this accusation your own conduct will speak more strongly than words' (Report in *Morning Chronicle*, Nov. 3–6). Robespierre was given a week in which to prepare his answer to Louvet, and in the meantime popular feeling ran strong against him, and 'there was a marvellous clamour for the heads of Robespierre, Marat and Danton', who were burnt in effigy on November 4. But in his speech on Monday, November 5, he succeeded in turning the tide back in his favour. He denied any hand in the September massacres. 'They were', he said, 'the act of men raised to defend their country after the Verdun disaster. If people will lament, let them lament the patriots massacred by despotism. I am always suspicious of that sensibility which is exclusively excited by the fate of the enemies of the State' (*St. James's Chronicle*, Nov. 8–10). It is easy to imagine Wordsworth's feelings as he saw 'with my own proper eyes' that Robespierre now 'ruled the capital City' (111), and that 'Liberty and Life and Death' in the whole land would soon lie in his 'arbitrement' (110).

**100–3.** The readings of A² A³, given in the *app. crit.*, are preserved on reverse side of page containing ll. 69–92.

**107–17 [124–34].** The Girondists were idealists whose speeches were full of references to ancient Greece and Rome; but they had no definite policy, and used all their efforts in a vain attempt to discredit the Jacobins. Hence, though they could command a majority they could make no use of it, and the power remained in the hands of the extremist minority. Cf. Coleridge, *Conciones ad Populum* (1795): 'The

Girondists . . . were men of enlarged views and great literary attainments; but they seem to have been deficient in that vigour and daring activity, which circumstances made necessary. Men of genius are rarely either prompt in action or consistent in general conduct: their early habits have been those of contemplative indolence; and the day-dreams with which they have been accustomed to amuse their solitude, adapt them for splendid speculation, not temperate and practical counsels. Brissot, the leader of the Gironde party, is entitled to the character of a virtuous man and an eloquent speaker; and his excellences equally with his faults rendered him unfit for the helm in the stormy hour of Revolution. Robespierre, who displaced him, possessed a glowing ardour that still remembered the *end*, and a cool ferocity that never either overlooked or scrupled the means.'

**119–20 [136–7].** *patient exercise of reason made Worthy of liberty*: an echo of Milton, *Samson Agonistes*, 1287 ff.:

> But patience is more oft the exercise
> Of saints, the trial of thir fortitude,
> Making them each his own Deliverer
> And Victor over all
> That tyrannie or fortune can inflict.

**166–7 [198–9].** *Harmodius . . . And his compeer Aristogiton*: two noble Athenians who raised a conspiracy against the tyranny of the Pisistratae, 514 B.C. They lost their lives, but gained from the later generations of Athenians the character of patriots and deliverers.

**179.** *Creed which ten shameful years have not annull'd*: Such was Wordsworth's faith in 1804; but evidently he had lost it before 1820, for the line does not appear in C.

**180 [211].** *one paramount mind*: v. note to ll. 107–17.

**191–2.** *Compell'd by nothing less than absolute want*
*Of funds for my support*:
Both Harper (i. 178) and Garrod (p. 57) have raised doubts whether the 'chain of harsh necessity' [222] was really an empty purse. But the reading of A proves that interpretation to be correct.

**196 [230].** *some who perished*: Brissot and his Girondist followers vainly fought against the growing Jacobin strength, but in the following June they were put under arrest in their own houses, imprisoned in July, and guillotined in October 1793.

**202 [236].** *To thee unknown*: Wordsworth did not meet Coleridge till nearly three years later, i.e. in the autumn of 1795.

**203.** *After a whole year's absence*: Wordsworth was in France from November 1791 to December 1792. The reading of A is, therefore, more accurate than the more decorative version of 1850. On his return he went to London, where he stayed till the summer.

**206 [249].** *Against the Traffickers in Negro blood*: The Society for the suppression of the Slave Trade was founded by Clarkson and

Wilberforce in 1787. In the following year Wilberforce brought a bill for abolition before Parliament, but without success; in 1792 a bill passed the Commons but was thrown out by the Lords. The Act was finally passed in March 1807. Cf. Wordsworth's *Sonnet*, 'Clarkson! it was an obstinate hill to climb.'

**230–1 [264–5].** *Britain . . . In league with the confederated Host*: France declared war on England and Holland, February 1, 1793; England declared war in return, February 11.

**234–42 [267–76].** An important passage. It is too often forgotten that it was not the Revolution, but the definite siding of England *against* the Revolution, that caused the first great moral shock to Wordsworth. The Revolution had seemed to him

> nothing out of nature's certain course
> A gift that rather was come late than soon.   IX. 252–3.

(Cf. Garrod, pp. 59–61.) And the shock was not less because, as he tells us in the A text, he had anticipated it from the hostility of English politicians. But he had never realized what the effect would be upon his own nature.

**262 [286].** *When Englishmen by thousands were o'erthrown*: The English troops had some slight success at first, and the Duke of York besieged Dunkirk, but in September he was defeated in the Battle of Hondshoote, and obliged to retreat.

**269–70 [293–4].** *bending all To their great Father*: a reminiscence of *The Ancient Mariner*, 607: 'While each to his great Father bends.'

**280 [304].** *wear*: Despite Worsfold's eloquent defence of the reading 'wean', it has no MS. authority. But the 'r' in E might easily be mistaken for an 'n'; hence the error in 1850.

**293.** *The unhappy counsel of a few weak Men*: Note the omission in later texts of this attack upon the English government.

**298 [321].** *In that delightful Island*: 'During the latter part of the summer of 1793, having passed a month in the Isle of Wight, in view of the fleet which was then preparing for sea off Portsmouth at the commencement of the war, I left the place with melancholy forebodings. The American war was still fresh in memory. The struggle which was beginning, and which many thought would be brought to a speedy close by the irresistible arms of Great Britain being added to those of the allies, I was assured in my own mind would be of long continuance, and productive of distress and misery beyond all calculation. This conviction was pressed upon me by having been a witness, during a long residence in revolutionary France, of the spirit which prevailed in that country.' *Advertisement* to *Guilt and Sorrow*, 1842. Wordsworth's companion in the Isle of Wight was William Calvert, brother of Raisley Calvert.

**310–11 [333–4].** *Tyrants, strong before In devilish pleas*: Cf. Milton, *Paradise Lost*, iv. 393–4:

So spake the Fiend, and with necessitie,
The Tyrants plea, excus'd his devilish deeds.

**314–15 [337–8].** *blasts From hell came sanctified like airs from heaven*:
Cf. *Hamlet*, I. iv. 41:

Bring with thee airs from heaven or blasts from hell.

**318–19 [341–2].** *who throned The human understanding paramount*:
For this Chaumette, 'the glowing patriarch of irreligious belief', was
chiefly responsible. On November 10, 1793, 'Chaumette opened the
Cathedral of Notre Dame to the religion of Reason. The Convention
stood aloof, in cold disdain. But an actress, who played the leading
part, and was variously described as the Goddess of Reason or the
Goddess of Liberty, and who possibly did not know herself which she
was, came down from her throne in the church, proceeded to the
Assembly, and was admitted to a seat beside the President, who gave
her what was known as a friendly accolade, amid loud applause. After
that invasion, the hesitating deputies yielded, and about half of them
attended the goddess back to her place under the Gothic towers.
Chaumette decidedly triumphed. He had already forbidden religious
service outside the buildings. He had now turned out the clergy whom
the state had appointed, and had filled their place with a Parisian
actress.' Acton, *Lectures on the French Revolution*, p. 178.

**330–81 [356–415].** *Domestic carnage etc.*: The Reign of Terror may
be dated from September 25, when Robespierre obtained a unanimous
vote of confidence against the Dantonists. The 'Reign' was inaugur-
ated by the execution of the Girondist leaders in October and November, and lasted till the fall of Robespierre on July 26, 1794.

**339 [365].** *light*: obviously the correct reading, for which 'like' is a
copyist's error. If the 'desires of innocent little ones' were 'like', there
would be no reason to apologize for the comparison; it is only apo-
logized for because they *were* 'light', whereas those of the Jacobins
were 'heinous'.

**346–7 [374–5].** *the faster. In the depth Of those*: The reading of D here
is covered by the overlapping of the paper on which D² is written.
The words 'Amid the depth', moreover, are cut through in D², so
that less than half of them is left. Hence E, in copying from D², was at
a loss, and seeing neither 'Appalled, astounded' in D which was
covered up, nor 'Amid the depth' in D² which was cut through, left
l. 346 blank after 'faster', and began l. 347 with 'By'. The editor of
1850 must have consulted C or D.

**353 [381].** *The illustrious Wife of Roland*: Madame Roland, a leading
Girondist, was guillotined on November 8, 1793. Her last words, as
she looked on the statue of Liberty, were 'O Liberté, que de crimes l'on
commet en ton nom!'

**372–81 [400–15].** For this passage D² reads:

Of those atrocities, the hours of rest
For me came seldom charged with natural sleep,

> Such ghastly visions clung to me of strife
> And persecution—strugglings of false mirth
> And levity in dungeons where the dust
> Was laid with tears, such hauntings of distress
> And anguish fugitive in woods, in caves
> Concealed, of scaffolds, implements of death
> And long orations which in dreams I pleaded
> Before unjust Tribunals, with a voice
> Labouring, a brain confounded, and a sense
> Of blank desertion, trecherous cowardise
> In the last place of refuge, my own soul.

[407]. *fond*: a printer's error for 'forced', the reading of both D and E. But in E it might be misread 'fond'.

[421]. *call*: E's error for 'care'; but in D the top of both the 'r' and the 'e' is joined on to the bottom of letters in the previous line, so that the word could easily be mistaken for 'call'. Hence the error in E and 1850. Note the theological turn given to this passage in revision, in place of the natural religion of the original reading; also the manner in which the confidence of the next paragraph is toned down, and the weak change of 'As were a joy to hear of' to

> To which the silver wands of saints in heaven
> Might point with rapturous joy [485–6].

**456 [498].** *the Town of Arras*: Wordsworth passed through Arras on July 16, 1790, on his tour with Robert Jones, en route from Calais to Switzerland. For his impressions of the state of France at that time *v.* VI. 352–425 and *Sonnet*, 'Jones! as from Calais southward you and I', 1–8. Robespierre was born at Arras in 1758, and came to Paris as a deputy where he sat in the first legislative Assembly. It was by his motion that all those who sat in the first Assembly were excluded from the second. He became the chief speaker in the Jacobin clubs, and a leading spirit in dictating their policy. He was elected President of the Committee of Public Safety in 1793. But though Chaumette carried on his anti-religious policy in the days of Robespierre's supremacy, Robespierre was never, as Wordsworth seems to imply, an atheist, but like his master Rousseau, a worshipper of the Supreme Being. 'He denounced Chaumette's irreligious masquerades, and declared that the Convention never intended to proscribe the Catholic worship.' In March 1792 he had proposed a resolution that the belief in Providence and a future life is a necessary condition of Jacobinism, and in November argued that 'the essential principles of politics might be found in the sublime teaching of Christ . . . and on May 7, 1794, brought forward his famous motion that the Convention acknowledge the existence of a Supreme Being' (Acton, *op. cit.*, pp. 285–6). On June 8 he headed the Procession at the Feast of the Supreme Being.

**458 [502].** *atheist crew*: a Miltonic phrase. Cf. *Paradise Lost*, vi. 370.

**463 [507].** *As Lear reproach'd the winds*: *King Lear*, III. ii. 1–24, iv. 22–32.

**469.** *this foul Tribe of Moloch*: This description of Robespierre and his crew has an added significance when we realize that Wordsworth had in mind *Paradise Lost*, i. 392–5:

> *Moloch*, horrid King besmeard with blood
> Of human sacrifice, and parents tears,
> Though for the noise of Drums and Timbrels loud
> Thir childerns cries unheard.

**471 [513].** *The day*: Robespierre was guillotined July 28, 1794. Hence Knight states that Wordsworth 'must have made this journey across the Ulverston sands in the first week of August'. But it was certainly not before the third week. On Saturday August 16 the first (inaccurate) account of Robespierre's fall appeared in *The Times*, announcing that he had been murdered in the Convention with poniards. On the 18th there was a definite statement of his execution and a full report of the events which occurred on July 27; on the 19th, reports from Paris of what had taken place down to August 1, when all was quiet again, and a definite statement that on the 28th, at night, Robespierre had been guillotined.

**473.** *From a small Village*: probably Rampside, a village in Low Furness, Lancashire, opposite Peel Castle, where Wordsworth spent four weeks this summer, 1794, with his cousin Mrs. Barker. Cf. *Elegiac stanzas suggested by a picture of Peele Castle*, 1805:

> I was thy neighbour once, thou rugged Pile!
> Four summer weeks I dwelt in sight of thee.

Hutchinson (*Oxf. W.*, p. xxvi) has thought that Wordsworth's visit to Rampside was in the long vacation of 1788, or in 1794: but 1794 is much more likely. There is no other 'village of far-secluded privacy' at which Wordsworth is known to have stayed at this time, to which he could have returned from this walk over Leven Sands: moreover the description of the fulgent spectacle

> Which neither changed, nor stirr'd, nor pass'd away (488)

recalls significantly the language in which he describes his impression of Peel Castle as seen from Rampside.

**480–7 [519–26].** *In one inseparable glory clad, etc.*: These lines ring with Miltonic echoes. 'Ethereal substance', *Paradise Lost*, vi. 330, 'in Consistory', *Paradise Regained*, i. 42, 'burning seraphs', *At a Solemn Music*, l. 10 ('Where the bright Seraphim in burning row'), 'the Empyrean', *passim*. 'Fulgent' (487) is also a Miltonic word.

**493 [534].** *An honor'd Teacher of my youth*: In the churchyard of Cartmel Priory the following epitaph can still be read: 'In memory of the Rev. William Taylor, A.M., son of John Taylor of Outerthwaite who was for some years a Fellow of Emmanuel College Cambridge; Master of the Free School at Hawkshead. He departed this life June the 12th, 1786, aged 32 years 2 months and 13 days.

> His merits, stranger, seek not to disclose,
> Or draw his Frailties from their dread abode;
> There they alike in trembling Hope repose
> The bosom of his Father and his God.'

It was thus 'full eight years' in 1794 from the time when Wordsworth, then a schoolboy, took leave of Taylor on his death-bed. Cf. *Address to the scholars of the village school of* ——, *Matthew, The two April Mornings,* and *The Fountain,* all of which, as Wordsworth says, are 'composite' pictures, but owed much to his memory of Taylor, though the schoolmaster delineated in these poems is an old man.

**515 [552].** *my earliest songs*: 'The first verses that I wrote were a task imposed by my master, the subject, "The Summer Vacation"; and of my own accord I added others upon "Return to School". There was nothing remarkable in either poem; but I was called upon, among other scholars, to write verses upon the completion of the second centenary from the foundation of the school, in 1585, by Archbishop Sandys. The verses were much admired, far more than they deserved, for they were but a tame imitation of Pope's versification, and a little in his style. This exercise, however, put it into my head to compose verses from the impulse of my own mind, and I wrote, while yet a schoolboy, a long poem running upon my own adventures, and the scenery of the country in which I was brought up. The only part of it which has been preserved is the conclusion of it.' *Memoirs,* i. 10–13 (*q.v.* for the lines imitative of Pope; for the others, *v.* p. 583 *supra*).

**519 [555].** *rocky Island*: known as Chapel Island from the remains of a small oratory, still extant in Wordsworth's time, built by the monks of Furness.

**560–7 [596–603].** Cf. II. 108–44, and notes.

**575–583 [XI. 8–14].** The faulty punctuation of this passage in 1850, which has been noticed and corrected by several editors, is explained by a study of the development of the text. C, in omitting 580–1, forgot to change the comma after 'confidence' into a semicolon, and E omitted even the comma after 'seen'. So that 1850 had to reconstruct the punctuation for itself. In this, as often, it was not successful.

**599–605.** *never dreamt . . . call'd to*: a passage deleted from A, and not appearing in later texts, probably because of its awkwardness of expression. The meaning is 'I never dreamt that men inspired by the spirit of the early Revolutionists, instead of realizing the significance of their achievement and the greatness of their mission, could suffer a change of heart and a fall from their ideal'.

**612 [XI. 33].** *an interregnum's . . . space*: i.e. after the fall of Robespierre.

**626.** *conceited*: an obsolete form of the verb 'conceive' used also by Wordsworth in his adaptation of *Troilus and Cressida* (1801), 104–5,

> All which he of himself conceited wholly
> Out of his weakness and his melancholy.

The whole sentence 'if the stream . . . forests' was altered, doubtless, because of its perversion of an incident in the story of the deluge. The appearance of the green branch would naturally suggest to the plain man, and not only 'to gravest heads', that the tree from which it came was *not* dead, but alive.

**646–57 [XI. 62–73].** *Our Shepherds etc.*: Cf. Coleridge, *The Friend: Essay on Party Spirit*: 'In order to oppose Jacobinism they imitated it in its worst features: in personal slander, in illegal violence, and even in the thirst for blood.' Early in 1793 the Habeas Corpus Act was suspended, and the law-courts filled with government prosecutions of those who argued for political reform, or seemed in any way to favour a policy sympathetic with France. Muir, Palmer, and others were tried for treason and sent to Botany Bay; and in the next year (i.e. soon after the fall of Robespierre—which Wordsworth has just recounted) the government made an effort to get Hardy, the founder of the Corresponding Society, and the organizer of political movement among the working classes, condemned to death as a traitor. He was defended by Erskine, and London, though anti-Jacobin as a whole, rejoiced at his acquittal. It is to the government attack on Hardy (acquitted Nov. 5), Horne Tooke, and Thelwall that Wordsworth specially alludes here. With this passage should be compared his remarks in his *Letter to the Bishop of Llandaff, Apology for the French Revolution,* 1793: 'At this moment have we not daily the strongest proofs of the success with which, in what you call the best of monarchical governments, the popular mind may be debauched ? Left to the quiet exercise of their own judgments, do you think the people would have thought it necessary to set fire to the house of the philosophic Priestley, and to hunt down his life like that of a traitor or a parricide ?'

The A version of this passage brings a much stronger indictment against the character and motives of the government than do the later texts, in which its action is not denounced as impiety and underhand perfidy, with the express design of undermining liberty, but is attributed, probably with more justice, merely to weakness and timidity.

**658–757 [XI. 74–172].** Wordsworth now reverts from describing the conduct of the English government in 1793–4, to recount his own relation to public events from the time of his arrival in France (Nov. 1791) till his return to England. He is therefore traversing again the ground covered by Books IX and X. 1–227.

**690–728 [XI. 105–44].** First published in *The Friend*, October 26, 1809, then in the 1815 and subsequent editions of the *Poems*. The text of *The Friend* shows already those changes towards the final version which are found in A² C. In 1815 other changes appear in ll. 700, 713, 715, 721. This does not prove that C as a whole was copied before 1815; for this passage might well have been revised with a view to its immediate publication, and the corrections not inserted in a full copy of *The Prelude* till later. Coleridge was at Grasmere when he wrote

*The Friend,* and some of the changes may have been his suggestion.

**704–5.** In B, l. 704 is deleted, and in its place is written:

The budding rose (as could not but be felt
Among the bowers of paradise itself)
The budding rose *etc.*

This is deleted and the original reading replaced in pencil.

**758–80 [XI. 173–94].** Another statement of Wordsworth's feelings after the declaration of war in February 1793, and thus a restatement of ll. 228–307.

**775 [XI. 189].** *wild theories were afloat*: In February 1793 William Godwin's *Enquiry concerning Political Justice* was published, and there can be no doubt that in this passage Wordsworth is referring to its early influence upon him. For a full and connected statement of Godwin's theories, *vide* Legouis (*op. cit.*), Leslie Stephen, *English Thought in the Eighteenth Century,* and Brailsford, *Shelley, Godwin, and their Circle*; it is enough for the present purpose to recall that he was a necessitarian; that he denied the doctrine of innate ideas and insisted that sense-impressions and experience can be the only source of knowledge; that he exalted reason at the expense of the passions, and had boundless faith in the perfectibility of man when his passions had become subordinate to his reason; that he exalted the individual at the expense of the collective reason and hence rejected Rousseau's 'general will', and denied the right of government or society to coerce the individual either in action or opinion. Lastly that his writing was inspired with a genuine passion for justice and a noble humanitarianism. When Wordsworth says, in the A text, that he 'lent but a careless ear' to the 'subtleties' of Godwinism, he must be understood to mean that at first he accepted such of Godwin's creed as did not militate against his faith in the Revolution, but that he did not realize as yet its fuller implications. Thus at this time, if we may judge from *Guilt and Sorrow,* conceived on Salisbury Plain in August 1793, and finished before the end of 1794, he only accepted Godwin's necessitarianism (the crimes of the murderer being due to his circumstances), and hence his attack on criminal law and especially on capital punishment, his sympathy with the outcasts of society, who are what society has made them, his protest against wealth and property, and his hatred of war, and exposure of the calamities of war as they affect individuals.

During the next year (1794) the influence of the Revolution waned before his growing tendency to accept the fuller implications of Godwin's individualism. The fall of Robespierre at the end of July reawakened his faith in the immediate future; but when Frenchmen 'changed a war of self defence to one of conquest' he became for the time a wholehearted Godwinian. The question arises, when was that time, and how long did his subjection to Godwinism last?

Some critics have given the date 1798 to Wordsworth's recognition of the French as 'oppressors'. In this they are misled by the statement found in the second paragraph of the pamphlet on the *Convention of Cintra* (1809) to the effect that 'only after the subjugation of Switzerland and not till then' had 'the body of the people who had sympathized with the Revolution begun to regard the war against France as both just and necessary'. The subjugation of Switzerland was, indeed, the event which arrested the popular imagination, but it was significant of a change in French policy which had been noted by Wordsworth, and had brought about his second moral crisis, some years before. To accept 1798 as the date of Wordsworth's renunciation of France would be to falsify the whole chronology of *Prelude* X [XI], and that view is, indeed, falsified by all we know of Wordsworth's life and poetry in the Alfoxden days. He was doubtless deeply stirred by the subjugation of Switzerland, but politics were clearly not his prime interest at that time, and his moral crisis was over.

The date most usually accepted (Knight, Worsfold, Moore Smith) is 1796, when Napoleon undertook his first campaign in Italy; and Garrod has placed it slightly earlier, i.e. after the Directory (Oct. 25, 1795). But even this is too late to fit in with my interpretation of his changing states of mind as recorded in *The Prelude*, and it seems to me more likely that Wordsworth is referring to the close of 1794 and early months of 1795. The change in the policy of the French was in reality dictated by necessity rather than by the definite renunciation of an ideal. After the fall of Robespierre the Thermidorians, with a treasury drained dry, had to choose between disbanding their starving army (with the imminent danger that it would refuse to be disbanded and that its generals would come to Paris and effect another Revolution) and sending it beyond the frontiers to feed upon other nations. They chose what was obviously to them the lesser of two evils; but to Wordsworth, to whom the Revolution was the ideal of universal freedom and brotherhood, this was the renunciation of their faith. In the reports of the progress of the French armies which appeared in the English papers of this period Wordsworth found plenty of evidence of French aggression. In September and October 1794 France had successes in Spain and Italy, and still more in Holland, where they demanded 10 millions of Antwerp and took hostages to ensure its receipt; in Germany they were fighting for possession of all the country west of the Rhine, and this they had obtained by January 16 following. The conquests of France, it is reported in *The Times* of February 18, 'though they increase the glory of the Republic, are considered in Paris only as means of spreading ruin in foreign countries'. 'For eight months', said Hauffman in the National Convention of February 24, 'our armies have subsisted on the produce of the conquered countries.' 'Let the public wealth of Holland', said Crétier two days later, 'be carried into France. It may be injustice, but any other policy is folly.'

There was plenty in all this to convince Wordsworth that the French 'had become oppressors in their turn'. In the last months of 1794 he was at Penrith at the bedside of his friend Raisley Calvert. In January Calvert died, leaving him the legacy which freed him from all immediate financial anxiety. Forthwith he hurried to London to be able to watch the progress of events at closer quarters, and here he stayed till he went to Bristol early in September, and then with Dorothy proceeded to Racedown, Dorsetshire. His change from faith in the practical issue of the Revolution to abstract Godwinism, I incline to date some time in the spring of that year, 1795,[1] when he gives up his faith in the 'general will' and becomes for the time a pure individualist. But in my view his complete subservience to Godwin satisfied him for a much shorter period than is usually supposed, and indeed was passed by the time that, in September, he went to Racedown. At that time 'he had yielded up moral questions in despair'—a state from which he was rescued partly by Dorothy and partly by Coleridge 'about that time first known to me' (X. 906. N.B.—W. W. and S. T. C. met in September 1795). The period of moral despair is often confused with that of complete Godwinism. But Godwin, with his sublime optimism, was very far from giving up any question in despair. Despair came to Wordsworth from that scepticism and disillusionment which was the inevitable result of his discovery that Godwinism did not satisfy his nature. His cure from this state was slow and gradual, and cannot be said to have been completed till the summer of 1797. During that period, while he had given up Godwinism, or at least found it unsatisfying to his whole nature, he could yet find no faith with which to replace it. Hence I take the view supported by Hale White and Legouis, but denied by Garrod, that *The Borderers*, written in 1795–6, though unquestionably Godwinian in plot, is written rather as an exposure than an exposition of Godwinism. This is clear also from the essay which Wordsworth wrote as preface to *The Borderers*.[2] The essay was obviously written early (according to the I.F. note, while he was actually writing the play); for it is prefixed to a much corrected and obviously early draft. 'The general moral', says Wordsworth in that essay, 'is obvious—to show the dangerous use which may be made of reason when a man has committed a great crime', i.e. he seeks to show that reason when it sins against the emotions is a dangerous guide. Garrod asserts that both Oswald and Marmaduke fail because they do not trust their intellects enough, i.e. are not good Godwinians. But Wordsworth's meaning surely is that they failed because they declined to listen to the call of the emotions which, on Godwinian principles, they rejected as unreasonable. Certainly Coleridge would not have admired *The Borderers* so immoderately if he had regarded it as Godwinian; for though he went through a period of modified Godwin-

---

[1] Godwin's Diaries record five meetings with Wordsworth between February and August, 1795. M. Moorman, p. 262.

[2] Published in *Oxford Lectures on Poetry*, by E. de Selincourt, 1934.

ism himself, and addressed a *Sonnet* to Godwin in the *Morning Post* of
January 10, 1795, he was exposing the fallacies of Godwin before the
end of the year.

**820–30**. *How glorious . . . independent intellect*: Cf. the words put
into the mouth of the Godwinian Oswald, addressing his dupe Marmaduke after Herbert has been left to starve on the moor:

> You have obeyed the only law that sense
> Submits to recognize; the immediate law,
> From the clear light of circumstances, flashed
> Upon an independent Intellect. (*Borderers*, 1493–6.)

Legouis points out that ll. 822–30 are an exact poetical version of a
saying of Godwin: 'The true dignity of human reason is, as much as
we are able to go beyond them [i.e. general rules], to have our faculties
in act upon every occasion that occurs, and to conduct ourselves accordingly', *Enquiry concerning Political Justice* (2nd ed. i. 347). Cf. also
*ibid*. i. 398, 'He who regards all things past present and to come as links
of an indissoluble chain, will, as often as he recollects this comprehensive view, be superior to the tumult of passion; and will reflect
upon the moral concerns of mankind with the same clearness of perception, the same unalterable firmness of judgement, and the same
tranquillity as we are accustomed to do upon the truths of geometry.'
The fact that Wordsworth soon found himself obliged to turn from
the moral concerns of mankind and give them up in despair in
favour of geometry shows that he was no longer a whole-hearted
Godwinian.

**838–9 [XI. 253–4]**. *And spread abroad the wings of Liberty etc.*:
A reminiscence of Spenser's *Muiopotmos, or, The tale of the Butterflie*,
209–11:

> What more felicitie can fall to creature,
> Then to enjoy delight with libertie,
> And to be lord of all the workes of Nature!

In *The Beggars* (composed 1802) Wordsworth draws upon this same
stanza of *Muiopotmos* for the phrase 'a weed of glorious feature'.

**849**. D retains this line, though it should have been deleted with
842–8.

**850–6 [XI. 259–66]**. *Enough no doubt . . . part*: Cf. 646–57 and
note.

**869–70**.     *Having two natures in me, joy the one*
                *The other melancholy*:

It is interesting to notice that in the A text Wordsworth refers to an
element in his character which was doubtless in part responsible for
the hold which Godwin had upon him—his addiction to melancholy.
'Now it is a question', writes Mark Rutherford ('Godwin and Wordsworth', in *More Pages from a Journal*, p. 209), 'whether Wordsworth's
temporary subjugation by *Political Justice* was due to pure intellectual conviction. I think not. Coleridge noticed that Wordsworth

Be little profitted, would see, and ask
Where is the obligation to enforce?
And to acknowledged law rebellious, still
As selfish passion urged, would act amiss,
The dupe of folly, or the slave of crime.

                     bewildered
          Depressed, ~~confounded~~ thus I did not walk
With scoffers, seeking light and gay revenge
From indiscriminate laughter, nor sate down
In reconcilement with an utter waste
Of Intellect; such sloth I could not brook
(Too well I loved in that my spring of life
pains taking thoughts and truth their dear reward)
But turned to abstract science, and there sought
Work for the reasoning faculty enthroned

Where the disturbances of space and time
the matter various attributes properties
or admissions. — Then it was,
Depressed, find Thanks to the bounteous Giver of all Good!
That the beloved woman in whose sight
Those days were passed, now speaking in a voice
Of sudden admonition like a brook
That does but cross a lonely road, and now
Seen, heard, and felt, and caught at every turn,
Companion never lost thro' many a league,
                         I went

suffered much from hypochondria. He complains that during the Scotch tour in 1803 "Wordsworth's hypochondriacal feelings keep him silent and self-centred ". He again says to Richard Sharp, in 1804, that Wordsworth "has occasional fits of hypochondriacal uncomfortableness, from which, more or less, he has never been wholly free from his very childhood ", and that he "has a hypochondriacal graft in his nature ". Wordsworth himself speaks of times when

> fears and fancies thick upon me came;
> Dim sadness—and blind thoughts, I knew not nor could name.

. . . During 1793, 1794 and part of 1795 this tendency to hypochondria must have been greatly encouraged. His hopes in the Revolution had begun to fail, but the declaration of war against France made him wretched. He wandered about from place to place, unable to conjecture what his future would be. "I have been doing nothing," he tells Matthews, "and still continue to do nothing. What is to become of me I know not." . . . Hypochondriacal misery is apt to take an intellectual shape. The most hopeless metaphysics or theology which we happen to encounter fastens on us, and we mistake for an unbiased conviction the form which the disease assumes. The *Political Justice* found in Wordsworth the aptest soil for germination; it rooted and grew rapidly. [It] was falsified in him by Racedown, by better health, by the society of his beloved sister, and finally by the friendship with Coleridge. . . . Certain beliefs, at any rate with men of Wordsworth's stamp, are sickness, and with the restoration of vitality and the influx of joy they disappear.'

[XI. 287]. *fell, betrayed*: This is probably what Wordsworth meant, 'felt betrayed' (E²) being a copyist's error.

[XI. 331–2].　*Whether in matters various, properties*
　　　　　　　　*Inherent, or from*:
The passage should read, as a glance at the facsimile page of MS. E will show, 'matter's various properties'. There is no manuscript authority for the comma after 'various'. The passage had evidently puzzled Carter, for he has written in the margin of E, 'Qy, is this sense ?' It did not occur to him, as it did to Mr. Garrod, who emended the passage correctly without reference to the MS., that 'matters' should be 'matter's'. One should add that the possessive apostrophe is omitted from several other places in E.

**905–6.** *then it was That Thou, most precious Friend*: omitted, doubtless, from later texts because the influence of Coleridge succeeded and did not precede that of Dorothy.

**909 [XI. 335].** *the belovèd Woman*: *vide* note to VI. 214–18.

**918 [XI. 344].** *Than as a clouded, not a waning moon*: The 'and' in E, in place of 'not', is an error. When [345] was added, [343] was omitted, and 'Than' [344] changed to 'Both'; when [343] was restored, the 'not' of [344] should also have been restored.

**933 [XI. 359].** *rivet up*: There is no MS. authority for 'seal up all', the reading of 1850.

**933–4 [XI. 359–60].** *a Pope Is summoned in to crown an Emperor*: on December 2, 1804, a ceremony to which Pope Pius VII had been summoned. But when the Pope was about to crown him, Napoleon took the crown from the altar, and put it on his own head himself.

**950–1 [XI. 378–9].** *Syracuse, The city of Timoleon*: Coleridge was in Sicily from early in August to the beginning of November 1804 (*v.* Introduction, p. 1).

Some time after the murder of Dion in 353 B.C. (cf. IX. 414 ff., note) Dionysius the younger again obtained possession of Syracuse, but in 343 B.C. was driven out by Timoleon, who came from Corinth at the request of the Greek cities in Sicily, to repel the Carthaginians from the island. Timoleon took Syracuse and 'at the sute of the citizens, made counsel hals, and places of justice to be built there: and did by this means stablish a free state and popular government, and did suppress all tyrannical power'. He then defeated a large force of the Carthaginians and drove them from the island, establishing democracies in the different cities. He died in 337 B.C. 'Thus did Timoleon roote out all tyrants out of *Sicilie* and made an end of all warres there. And whereas he found the whole Ile, wild, savage, and hated of the naturall countrymen and inhabitants of the same for the extreme calamities and miseries they suffered, he brought it to be so civill, and so much desired of all straungers, that they came far and neare to dwell there, where the naturall inhabitants of the country selfe before, were glad to fly and forsake it. For *Agrigentum* and *Gela*, two great cities, did witnesse this . . . whom *Timoleon* did not only assure of peace and safety to live there, but willingly did helpe them besides, with all other things necessarie, to his uttermost meane and ability, for which they loved and honoured him as their father and founder. And this his good love and favour was common also to all other people of *Sicilie* whatsoever.' Plutarch, *Life of Timoleon*, trans. by North.

**969–70 [XI. 394–5].** *One great Society alone on earth,*
*The noble Living and the noble Dead*:
Cf. *Convention of Cintra* (1809) (Grosart, i. 170). 'There is a spiritual community binding together the living and the dead; the good, the brave and the wise, of all ages. We would not be rejected from that community: and therefore do we hope.'

**986.** *This heavy time of change*: *Lycidas*, 37: 'But O the heavy change now thou art gone.' The phrase was clearly put into Wordsworth's mind by his previous use of 'thou art gone' in l. 981 *supra*.

**998.** *carrying a heart more ripe*: i.e. more ripe than Wordsworth's was when he visited the Alps in 1790.

**1003–4 [XI. 419–20].** *O flowery Vale Of Enna!*: Cf. *Paradise Lost*, iv. 268–71:

Not that faire field

> Of Enna, where Proserpin, gathring flours
> Herself a fairer Floure, by gloomie Dis
> Was gatherd.

**1013 [XI. 434].** *Empedocles*: the philosopher of Agrigentum (*fl. c.* 444 B.C.), who according to tradition threw himself into the burning crater of Etna that he might be deemed a god. Cf. Matthew Arnold, *Empedocles on Etna.*

**1014 [XI. 435].** *Archimedes*: of Syracuse, born 287 B.C., the most famous of ancient mathematicians. He constructed engines of war for Hiero, when defending Syracuse against Marcellus, and is said to have been killed by the Roman soldiers in 212 B.C., when intent on a mathematical problem.

**1023 [XI. 444].** *Divine Comates*: Theocritus, *Idyll*, vii. 78 (note in 1850). 'And he shall sing how, once upon a time, the great chest prisoned the living goatherd by his lord's infatuate and evil will, and how the blunt-faced bees, as they came up from the meadow to the fragrant cedar chest, fed him with food of tender flowers, because the muse still dropped sweet nectar on his lips. O blessed Comates, surely these things befell thee, and thou wast enclosed within the chest, and feeding on the honeycomb through the springtime didst serve out thy bondage.' *Idyll*, vii. 78–83, trans. by Lang.

**1039 [XI. 470].** *a Captive, pining for his home*: The reading of A² C, which adds to these words 'in querulous lassitude', a vivid description of Coleridge's habitual frame of mind, was quite rightly never incorporated in the text.

On a sheet at the end of Book X in A is a passage which, if not intended for incorporation in the poem, was evidently a reflection upon Coleridge's visit to Sicily:

> Time who makes war on temples till they fall
> Towers till they waste away, tho' Nature love
> Their mouldering ruins, cannot treat with words
> Like an omnipotent—Tho' Babylon
> Be dust, and Agrigentum wrapt in weeds
> Homer survives for everlasting praise
> Plato for converse on the soil which now
> Thy footsteps tread, the soil which once he trod.

# BOOK XI [XII]

Z, the earliest authority for most of this book, proves that originally the book began at l. 42 ('This History, my Friend, *etc.*), for ll. 1–42 are stitched on the front. It is headed 'Book 12th', which suggests that Books X and XI were originally divided as in 1850, and not run into one Book as in A. Z, however, runs together Books XI and XII [XII and XIII] so that the number of Books would still be thirteen, and not fourteen.

**15–22.** *And you, ye Groves . . . done for me*: In this passage, and in
II. 214–21, and also in XII. 47–52, Wordsworth is returning to an
idea which he was attempting to work out in 1798 in various blank-
verse passages connected loosely with his theme in *Nutting*, and later
to be published in part under that title in *Lyrical Ballads*, 1800. The
surviving manuscripts are: *Christabel* notebook, MS. 18*a*, MS. JJ
(*v.* P verso, Transcript, p. 641 *infra*), and D. W.'s letter to S. T. C.
December–January 1798–9. The central idea is the spiritual sympathy
between man and Nature. Incidents are drawn in to illustrate the
violation of that sympathy (1) by the wild maiden (*v. P.W.* ii. 504–5:
Ah what a crash! . . .) (2) by the boy Nutter, who is Wordsworth
himself. The passage which is here recalled stands in MS. 18*a* as
follows:

Ye gentle Stewards of a Poet's time!
Ye Powers! without whose aid the idle man
Would waste full half of the long summers day,
Ye who by virtue of this dome of leaves
And its cool umbrage, [*these cool pathways*] make the forenoon walk,
When July suns are blazing, to his verse
Propitious, as a range o'er moonlight cliffs
Above the breathing sea—And ye no less
Ye too who with most necessary care
Amid the concentration of your groves
Restore the springs of his exhausted frame,
And ye whose general ministry it is
To interpose the coverts of these shades
Even as a sleep, betwixt the heart of man
And the uneasy world, 'twixt man himself,
Not seldom, and his own unquiet heart
Oh! that I had a music and a voice
Harmonious as your own, to tell the world
What ye have done for me

Wordsworth said of the poem *Nutting*: 'Written in Germany: intended
as a part of a poem on my own life [i.e. *The Prelude*] but struck out as
not being wanted there' (I.F. note).

**24–25.** *when I was dead To deeper hope etc.*: The time referred to is
clearly the spring of 1796 at Racedown, when Wordsworth, dissatisfied with Godwinism, yet having found no theory of life to take its
place, had 'given up moral questions in despair'. These lines, fuller in
A than in 1850, explain how it was that though he was 'dead to
deeper hope' he could yet at times be cheerful, as both his own letters
and Dorothy's written in the early Racedown days prove him to have
been. They are thus a complete answer to Harper's scepticism as to
his mental depression at this time (*v.* Harper, i. 289–90).

**59–60.**        *The man to come parted as by a gulph,*
                    *From him who had been*:

Cf. Godwin, *Political Justice*, 1st ed. ii. 494: 'Nothing can be more un-reasonable than to argue from men as we now find them, to men as they may hereafter be made.' The whole passage down to l. 137 sums up the influence upon Wordsworth of his Godwinian hopes that the world would start afresh on the basis of pure Reason. 'A bigot to a new idolatry', he does not seem to realize that the 'mysteries of passion' (84), so strongly rooted in his own nature, are the true bond of brotherhood to the human race. Hence he gives up first history and then poetry; and even Nature becomes less deeply valuable to him (99–120).

**64.** *Patriot, Lover*: significantly changed later to 'warrior, patriot'. When Wordsworth first wrote the lines he would not allow the warrior, as distinct from the patriot, to be one of 'the great family'.

**121–37.** An interesting passage on the dangers of the analytic or scientific reason, though Wordsworth at the same time recognizes its value as a stage in mental development. Its result is presumption (152), superficiality (159), and a lack of penetrative imagination. Cf. *The Tables Turned*, 26–28.

**171–99 [XII. 127–51].** The attitude to Nature described in these lines is that which he first experienced on his visit to Tintern in 1793. On his return to England Man had absorbed his whole interest, but after the war with France had brought about his first moral crisis (i.e. in Spring 1793) he made a fresh return to Nature—

> more like a man
> Flying from something that he dreads than one
> Who sought the thing he loved.
> . . . The sounding cataract
> Haunted me like a passion: the tall rock,
> The mountain, and the deep and gloomy wood,
> Their colours and their forms, were then to me
> An appetite; a feeling and a love,
> That had no need of a remoter charm,
> By thought supplied, nor any interest
> Unborrowed from the eye.

It is a new thing, and typical of his psychological state at this time, that he should come to Nature fleeing from something that he dreads, i.e. in reaction from his moral sufferings. He now finds distraction in purely sensuous pleasure, from which moral feeling and all his deeper 'inner faculties' are excluded. This attitude to Nature seems to have been dominant with him until, gradually, his cure was effected.

**191.** *from rock to rock*: Cf. *To the Daisy*:

> In youth from rock to rock I went,
> From hill to hill in discontent
> Of pleasure high and turbulent.

**199.** *I knew a Maid*: I differ here from Professor de Selincourt, who identifies this maid with Dorothy. Everything points to Mary

Hutchinson: 'her years ran parallel with mine' (200, *app. crit.*)—she
was born in August 1770, only four months after Wordsworth, whereas
Dorothy, born in December 1771, was a year and eight months younger.
And the description of her placid character fits Mary and not Dorothy.

  **204 [XII. 155].** *barren intermeddling subtleties*: cf. *The Tables
Turned*, 26–28:      Our meddling intellect
                     Misshapes the beauteous forms of things:—
                     We murder to dissect.

  **214–21.** *For she was Nature's inmate* (v. note on 15–22 *supra*).
A further passage from MS. 18*a* is drawn upon here: it is a careful copy
by the poet himself, but almost without punctuation. I have added
stops, and printed in italics lines which are struck out in the MS.

                     I would not strike a flower
          As many a man will strike his horse; at least,
          If, from the wantonness in which we play
          With things we love, or from a freak of power,
5         Or from involuntary act of hand
          Or foot unruly with excess of life,
          It chanc'd that I ungently used a tuft
          Of meadow-lillies, or had snapp'd the stem
          Of foxglove bending o'er his native rill,
10        I should be loth to pass along my way
          With unreprov'd indifference,—I would stop
          Self-question'd, asking wherefore that was done.
          And ye who, judging rashly, deem that such
          Are idle sympathies, the toys of one
15        More curious than need is, say, have ye not
          Your gardens with their individual flowers
          Which ye would spring to rescue from the hand
          Of any rude destroyer *with the same
          Instinctive eagerness as if a child,*
20        *Your own, were sleeping near a lion's mouth?*
          Ye have my wishes for a recompense
          The best which your devotion can bestow;
          But some there are, and such as I have known
          Far happier, chiefly one beloved maid;
25        For she is Nature's inmate, and her heart
          Is everywhere; even the unnoticed heath
          That o'er the mountains spreads its prodigal bells
          Lives in her love; friends also more than one
          Are hers who feed among the woods and hills
30        A kindred joy. And blessed are your days
          That such delights are yours. For though we prize,
          And by a [          ] law, the things
          Our hands have form'd, and though, as I believe,
          The love of order is a sentiment

35   Inherent in the mind, yet does it seem
     That each access of strength this passion gains
     From human labours, by a course direct
     Or sinuous, is productive evermore
     Of littleness and pride.
                              Then is he wise
40   Who with unweari'd diligence repairs
     To Nature as to an unerring rule
     And measure of ennobling principles
     Eternal and unchang'd,—correcting thus
     Deformities that steal by easy steps
45   Into our heart, and raising up his thoughts
     From that abasement into which perforce
     The mind must sink that hangs on its own works
     With an exclusive dotage. And the man
     Who has been taught this lesson will so feel
50   Its wholesome influence, with such silent growth
     Of tenderness and gratitude will bless
     His teacher, that even meanest objects, else
     Despis'd or loath'd or dreaded, as a part
     Of this great whole, insensibly will cleave
55   To his affections, that at length, by power
     Of such communion, he will cease to look
     Upon the earth as on some charter'd ground,
     A spot where children unreproved may act
     Their wanton pranks, but it will be to him
60   A temple—made for reverence and love.
     And thus by salutary awe controul'd,
     *Even like a man still present with a judge*
     *Unwarp'd, unbiass'd,* while he regulates
     His notions of the beautiful and grand,
65   In him will admiration be no weak
     Fantastic quality that doth betray
     Its owner, but a firm support, a source
     Perennial of new faculties and powers;
     His pleasures will be pure, his frame of heart
70   Sound, and a strengthening judgement will sustain
     Affections ever strengthening. For can he
     Who thus respects a mute insensate form,
     Whose feelings do not need the gross appeal
     Of tears and of articulate sounds, can he
75   Be wanting in his duties to mankind
     Or slight the pleadings of a human heart?
     *Hence too will he another habit gain*
     *Of precious tendency; for tutor'd thus*
     *He needs must carry into moral things*

80     *A like forbearance: never will he touch*
        *The ark in rashness, tempering thought with fear*
        *And love with contemplation.* Need I add
        That while he fosters such regard for things
        In which he finds no traces of himself,
85     By this pure intercourse those bastard loves,
        Those low and fickle yearnings of the heart,
        The wayward brood of vanity, must die
        Within him, and benevolence be spread
        Like the Sun's light upon the open sea ?

**235.** *As my soul bade me*: Notice Wordsworth's earlier insistence on natural emotion prompted by experience of the senses—'I felt, and nothing else' (238) rather than, as later, on external sanction—'as piety ordained' [185], supported by reflection—'I felt, observed, and pondered' [188]. The change in the text really obscures his meaning.

**262–3 [XII. 212–13].** *Or aught of heavier and more deadly weight*
             *In trivial occupations etc.*:
cf. *Sonnet*, 'I am not one who much or oft delight', and the lines which, in MS. W, follow XIII. 165 (*infra*, p. 629, note).

**279–316.** Mr. Gordon Wordsworth has identified the scene of this episode as the Cowdrake Quarry on the Edenhall side of the Penrith Beacon. Here Thomas Parker was murdered on November 18, 1766 by Thomas Nicholson who was executed near the scene of the murder on August 31, 1767. J. Walker in his *History of Penrith* says that the letters cut upon the turf were TPM which he interprets as *Thomas Parker Murdered*. This seems unlikely. We should expect Thomas Nicholson's initials. Mr. C. Roy Huddleston tells me that in Daniel Scott's copy of Walker's *History* Scott has written *No* against Walker's interpretation of the initials. Professor MacGillivray makes the clever suggestion that the initials may originally have been T. N. with the sign of the gallows between the two letters thus: T Γ N—the gallows sign coming in course of time to look like capital P, and N degenerating into M. I have not solved the puzzle.

**283.** *honest James*: his father's servant, not to be confounded with that James, one of his grandfather's servants, whose insolence was so galling to the Wordsworth children (*v.* Dorothy's letter to Jane Pollard, quoted in Harper, i. 76–77).

**323 [XII. 266].** *The spirit of pleasure and youth's golden gleam*: This line is repeated from VI. 245, where he recounts this same visit to the Border Beacon, near Penrith. (For the difficulty in dating this visit *v.* note to VI. 214–17.) Hence the 'two dear Ones to my heart so dear', words which he omits from 1850. The reading of A² C, 'with the Maid To whom were breathed my first fond vows', is important, as it suggests that Mary Hutchinson was in fact the poet's first love, forgotten for the time in his passion for Annette. If so, she was, possibly, the inspiration of the 'Lucy' poems also.

**326–43 [XII. 269–86].** A statement of the central point of Words-worth's creed, that poetry is 'emotion recollected in tranquillity', drawing its inspiration and its material from the great moments of the past, especially from the scenes of childhood and early youth, when feeling is strongest. Hence, perhaps, the falling off in the inspiration of his later poetic life, which he might be said to prophesy in ll. 338–9. Lines 333–4 owe something to Coleridge, *Ode to Dejection*, 47–48:

> O Lady! we receive but what we give,
>   And in our life alone does Nature live.

It will be noted that ll. 316–45 were not in MS. V (1799), but were added when this episode was transferred from Book I to its present place in the poem. For the idea expressed in the whole passage cf. *The Waggoner*, iv. 197–217, but especially the reference (210–12) to

> a shy spirit in my heart,
>   That comes and goes—will sometimes leap
>   From hiding-places ten years deep.

**345 [XII. 287].** *One Christmas-time*: December 1783, at which time there would be three boys at school, William and his brothers Richard and John. Christopher did not go to Hawkshead till two years later. Wordsworth seems to have been in some doubt as to the number of horses sent, but two is probably correct. The scene of the look-out crag has been a matter of much discussion; and three out of four of Knight's conjectures are based on the false assumption that the horses were coming from Penrith, whereas they were coming from Cocker-mouth. Hence their route would run either over the Wrynose Pass, or via Grasmere and Keswick—in neither case through Ambleside, as Knight imagines. Knight's fourth suggestion—by Randy Pike—is just possible, but far more likely is Mr. Gordon Wordsworth's—a short half-mile north of Borwick Lodge, on the ridge that overlooks the road to Skelwith and the now little-used track to Oxenfell.

**367. [XII. 308].** *two Brothers*: altered to 'three' in D text. The text of 1805 is correct: *v.* D. W.'s letter to C. Clarkson, *M.Y.* 165: 'my three eldest Brothers [viz. Richard, William, and John] followed him (my father) to the Grave: Christopher was at Penrith, and I was in Yorkshire'.

**382 [XII. 323].** *Advanced in such indisputable shapes*: an echo of Hamlet: 'Thou camst in such a questionable shape', i.e. a shape that can be questioned.

## BOOK XII (XIII)

**31–32 [XIII. 27–28].** *but lifts the Being into magnanimity*: Notice the significant change in the text, not introduced before 1832.

**47–52 [XIII. 41–47].** *seeing little worthy or sublime . . . beauteous world*: another passage found in MS. 18*a*, *vide* note to XI. 15–22. These lines immediately precede the passage quoted there beginning:

Ye gentle Stewards of a Poet's time,

and are thus introduced:

> Well! blessed be the Powers
> That teach philosophy and good desires
> In this their still Lyceum, hand of mine
> Wrought not this ruin—I am guiltless here—
> For seeing little worthy or sublime

*etc.* as A text, but with 'I was early taught' for 'early tutor'd me' (49).

**66–68.**                    *I sought*
> *For good in the familiar face of life*
> *And built thereon my hopes of good to come*:

a contrast, deliberately stated, with his faith when as a Godwinian he had hope to see,

> I mean that future times would surely see,
> The man to come parted as by a gulph,
> From him who had been.   (XI. 57–60.)

The 'individual man', in whom he is now interested, is 'no composition of the thought, Abstraction, image, shadow' (i.e. the ideal man of Godwin's *Political Justice*). The lines that follow (97–219) describe the frame of mind in which, in revulsion from Godwinism, Wordsworth set himself to compose the more homely of the *Lyrical Ballads*. The attribution of 'genuine knowledge' to the rustic in l. 99 (altered later to the less debatable 'genuine virtue') was a definite defiance of Godwin. 'Godwin', says Legouis (trs., p. 307) 'had taught him to believe that virtue was dependent on the intelligence, which can itself be exercised only on knowledge already acquired. He had said that "in order to choose the greatest possible good" one "must be deeply acquainted with the nature of man, its general features and varieties" (*Pol. Just.*, 1st ed., pp. 232–3). He had asserted that "virtue cannot exist in an eminent degree, unaccompanied by an extensive survey of causes and their consequences" (*ibid.*, p. 232). He had sneered at Tertullian for saying "that the most ignorant peasant under the Christian dispensation possessed more real knowledge than the wisest of ancient philosophers", and had shown the absurdity of pretending that "an honest ploughman could be as virtuous as Cato" (*ibid.*, p. 254).'

**149–50 [XIII. 146–9].** *one bare steep Beyond the limits which my feet had trod*: i.e. the road to the village of Isel over the Hay or Watch Hill, which can be seen from the garden and the back of the house at Cockermouth where Wordsworth passed the first years of his life.

**185–204.** A passage found with slight variations in J and therefore written before 1802, probably in 1800. Wordsworth's strong sympathy with the poor and with the working man, while it made him aware of the capacity for deep feeling in 'men who do not wear fine clothes' (*v.* his letter to Charles James Fox, Jan. 14, 1801), did not blind him to the corroding effect of 'labour in excess and poverty'. Cf. passage in *Alfoxden* notebook, *P.W.* v. 344–5, Appendix B, IX.

**223–77.** This passage was first printed as the conclusion of the Appendix to *Poems* 1835 (*Of Legislation for the Poor, the Working Classes, and the Clergy*).

**231–98.** The whole of this passage should be compared with the lines written in 1798 and afterwards printed as the *Prospectus* to *The Excursion*; and also with the *Preface* to the *Lyrical Ballads*, 1802, especially with that part in which Wordsworth defends his choice of subject. 'Low and rustic life was generally chosen, because, in that condition, the essential passions of the heart find a better soil in which they can attain their maturity, are less under restraint, and speak a plainer and more emphatic language; because in that condition of life our elementary feelings coexist in a state of greater simplicity, and, consequently, may be more accurately contemplated, and more forcibly communicated; because the manners of rural life germinate from those elementary feelings, and, from the necessary character of rural occupations, are more easily comprehended, and are more durable; and, lastly, because in that condition the passions of men are incorporated with the beautiful and permanent forms of nature.' Cf. also the passage which follows, on the language of men of humble and rustic life, with ll. 253–64.

**313–14.** *a Traveller at that time Upon the Plain of Sarum*: After a month with William Calvert in the Isle of Wight in July–August 1793, the friends travelled across Salisbury Plain in a whiskey, but their journey was interrupted by an accident, and Wordsworth continued his rambles from Salisbury for two or three days over the Plain on foot.[1] In his 'Advertisement' to *Guilt and Sorrow*, published in 1842, Wordsworth writes: 'After leaving the Isle of Wight I spent two days in wandering on foot over Salisbury Plain.' The 'three days' mentioned in *Prel.* XII. 338 is more likely to be right.

**357–65.** *who for my delight Hast said . . . reflected*: 'I was in my twenty-fourth year, when I had the happiness of knowing Mr. Wordsworth personally, and while memory lasts, I shall hardly forget the sudden effect produced on my mind, by his recitation of a manuscript poem, which still remains unpublished,[2] but of which the stanza, and tone of style, were the same as those of the *Female Vagrant*, as originally printed in the first volume of the *Lyrical Ballads*. There was here no mark of strained thought, or forced diction, no crowd or turbulence of imagery; and as the poet hath himself well described in

---

[1] *v.* D. W. to J. Pollard, *E.L.*, p. 105.

[2] *Guilt and Sorrow* was published complete, but doubtless much altered, in 1842. What was read to Coleridge in 1796 must have been an early MS. of *Guilt and Sorrow*: *v. P.W.* i. 330–1.

his lines "on revisiting the Wye", manly reflection, and human associations had given both variety, and an additional interest to natural objects, which in the passion and appetite of the first love they had seemed to him neither to need or permit. . . . It was not however the freedom from false taste, whether as to common defects, or to those more properly his own, which made so unusual an impression on my feelings immediately, and subsequently on my judgment. It was the union of deep feeling with profound thought; the fine balance of truth in observing, with the imaginative faculty in modifying the objects observed: and above all the original gift of spreading the tone, the atmosphere, and with it the depth and height of the ideal world around forms, incidents and situations, of which, for the common view, custom had bedimmed all the lustre, had dried up the sparkle and the dew drops.' Coleridge, *Biographia Literaria*, chap. 4. Professor Garrod and Mr. Nowell Smith have independently suggested that in this passage Wordsworth 'in effect quotes and versifies from the *Biographia Literaria*' (published 1817). But the reading of A (1805–6) proves that the borrowing, if any, was the other way. More probably, both Wordsworth in this passage and Coleridge, *op. cit.*, are recalling an actual conversation which remained an ineffaceable memory with both.

**365–7.** *Call we this . . . friendship*: it is noticeable that in the A text Wordsworth makes no mention of himself and Coleridge being 'as strangers' when *Guilt and Sorrow* was read; nor indeed were they. It is clear that in later versions Wordsworth is confusing and combining the impression made on Coleridge by *Guilt and Sorrow* with that of *Descriptive Sketches* some time earlier. Cf. *Biog. Lit.*, chap. 4, 'During the last year of my residence at Cambridge. I became acquainted with Mr. Wordsworth's first publication entitled *Descriptive Sketches*, and seldom, if ever, was the emergence of an original poetic genius above the literary horizon more evidently announced.'

**369–79.** This passage in its original form expresses a vital element in Wordsworth's thought, and puts into intellectual terms a part of his own deepest experience. The growth of his mind was bound up with a process of continual action and interaction between his own inner life and the world without:

> my mind hath look'd
> Upon the speaking face of earth and heaven
> As her prime Teacher, intercourse with man
> Establish'd by the sovereign Intellect,
> Who through that bodily Image hath diffus'd
> A soul divine which we participate,
> A deathless spirit.   (V. 11–17.)

Here he differed from Coleridge, who held that

> we receive but what we give
> And in our life alone doth Nature live.

To Wordsworth, as to Coleridge, the poetic mind was creative, but unlike Coleridge, he held that it was stimulated and worked upon by the creative power of Nature, since Nature was possessed by that same divine being, which ran through all things, of whose presence he was conscious in his 'own interior life'. Hence the poet is a *sensitive* being, a *creative* soul (XI. 257). The first version of this passage simply asserts that the source of our inner life, 'that whence our dignity originates', is an active power which maintains a continual interaction between the mind and the objects of its vision, and is itself 'the excellence, pure spirit, and best power' of both. The later version substitutes for this 'power' a system of 'fixed laws', and makes the 'spirit' into a 'function', thus covering up the true significance of the passage in its relation with his earlier Pantheism.

# BOOK XIII (XIV)

**1–119.** The memory of his ascent of Snowdon by night in the days of his youth and the reflections that arose from it were clearly what Wordsworth had in mind in the first months of 1804 as the climax of his poem. At this time, as the letters of March 6 to Coleridge and De Quincey, read in conjunction with the letter to Wrangham (early February), show, he hoped to finish the poem in five books. MS. W, a small notebook used at the beginning of 1804, gives most of Book IV, passages from Book XI, and V, and then under the heading *5th Book* passes on at once to the Snowdon ascent, followed by lines corresponding to XIII. 66–165, and other passages not finally used in *The Prelude* (*v.* p. 623 *infra*). Writing to Coleridge on March 6, he says he has finished another book of his poem (clearly Book IV): 'And now I am positively arrived at the subject I spoke of in my last.' [His 'last' letter has not survived.] This subject must clearly be the nature and function of the creative mind. Significantly, when in the end he extended the scope of his poem to thirteen (finally fourteen) books, he still used the Snowdon ascent, with its unforgettable revelation to him of the transcendent power of the imagination, as the taking-off place for the culminating argument of his last book: it held the core of his inner experience and therefore it had to be the climax of the story of his poetic education. In his reflections that arose from the scene on Snowdon (*Prelude*, XIII. 66–210) Wordsworth follows two lines of thought: first, the function of the human imagination; and secondly, beyond and beneath this, the essential character and activity, no less spiritual than intellectual, of the 'higher mind' itself.

There is evidence in MS. W that whilst he was working on Book IV in February and March 1804 he was probing into the nature of the 'higher mind' and attempting to define it, for in the early pages of this MS. we find some abortive 'try-out' passages (written apparently at different times but within the same period—early 1804—on pages that had been left blank) in which he is trying to penetrate to the very core of the mental character and experience of the man who is fitted to be a poet. The passages, tentative and incomplete, are in the form of rough notes.

(a)                For he is one who must be such in truth
                     Whatever be the object of his thought
Cf. II. 344–5  familiar with the essences of things[1]
                     Active and prompt to see, and to enjoy
                     Because he sees. A brooding spirit
XIII. 100      Willing to work and to be wrought upon
                     and haply in his [        ] heart
                     Enters the better awful presences

                     ·     ·     ·     ·     ·

                     And chiefly must the sense have stirr'd in him
                     Of two great presences

The poet must seek 'the essences of things'[1]: he does so primarily through his senses. Sight was for Wordsworth the leading sense, standing as a symbol for the rest. Of the Pedlar in *The Excursion* he writes:

                     But in the mountains did he *feel* his faith
                     . . . and there his spirit shaped
                     Her prospects: nor did he believe—he *saw*.

The next 'try-out' passage reveals what he means by the *two great presences*.

(b)                But also such an one must have been used
XIII. 70–73  To feed his soul upon infinity
                     To deal with whatsoe'er be dim or vast
                     In his own nature [*blending*] in a form
                     Of unity through truth-inspiring thoughts
                     By one sensation, either be it that
                     Of his own mind the power by which he thinks
XIII. 183–4  Or lastly the great feeling of the world,
                     God and the immortality of life
                     Beneath all being evermore to be

The thought here passes from the soul's apprehension of infinity (somewhat gropingly reached after) into the compelling sense of unity in which it becomes absorbed, and finally into the affirmation of the truth he now reaches of *the two great presences*—which indeed are one:

                     God and the immortality of life
                     Beneath all being evermore to be

This is the simplest statement which Wordsworth ever made of the

---

[1] Mr. William L. Payne notes from Thomas Rymer's *Preface to Rapin*: 'He [the poet] must by a particular chymistry extract the essence of things, without soiling his wit with the gross and trumpery.'

central experience of the mystic—not to be expressed, as all true mystics testify, except in the words *being* and *to be*. He is here trying to define the *way-in* to this ultimate experience, and he needs all three words: sensation, thought, and feeling.

In speaking of the 'great feeling of the world' he seems to suggest that the feeling he had in his communion with Nature (the way-in was through his senses) of what he was to call 'the one Presence, and the Life Of the great whole' (III. 130) passes into thought—for feeling and thought were always in his mind vitally connected. The idea is concisely expressed in the 1805 version of Book XIII. 183–4:

> The feeling of life endless, the great thought [one thought MS. B]
> By which we live, Infinity and God

The final version of these last lines in the text of 1850 [XIV. 204–5] draws the idea under the covering shield of the Christian conception:

> Faith in life endless, the sustaining thought
> Of human Being, Eternity and God.

(c) Another passage bears relation to *Prelude* (1805) XIII, ll. 66–106, and shows Wordsworth trying to define the moral qualities essential to the poet. The passage is in the rough, unfinished and partly illegible:

> For he is one whose habits must have needs
> Been such as shall have fitted him no less
> For moral greatness: made him [*rich in truth*] clear in
> Whatever be the object of his thoughts　　　　[soul
> A man not easily perplexed but . . .
> A man of unobstructed sight and trained
> To take the measure and the scale
> Of moral greatness:
> A spirit unencumber'd unperplex'd
> Whatever be the [object ?] of his thought
>
> .　　.　　.　　.　　.
>
> To catch the [　　　] qualities of things
> By instinct to enjoy because he sees
> And see by reason that he can enjoy
> Prompt, watchful [direct ?] comprehensive sure

XIII. 103–5　　By objects of the senses not enslaved
> But strengthened rouzed and made by them more fit
> To hold communion with the invisible world.

XIII. 97　　The enduring and the transitory both
> Contribute to exalt him while he bends
> To general laws he [　　　　　]
> That [　　　　] within him might have . . .
> The first

XIII. 79　　By which he adds or separates takes away
> Or multiplies, doth to one form impart
> The functions of another

And to [invention ?] . . .

A profitable servant of the Truth

The scribbled passages in this MS. reveal Wordsworth's searching attempt to define the experience and the qualities essential to the poet: lively sensuous experience comes first; imaginative use of that experience comes next; spiritual insight of the deepest and purest kind is the centre (for Wordsworth this is clearly the experience of the mystic); but the rational and moral basis of the poet's thought is also insisted upon: he must 'bend to general laws'—he must be a 'profitable servant of the Truth'.

**2.** *with a youthful friend*: Robert Jones (*v.* VI. 339 and note). This excursion was in the summer of 1791: *v. Memoirs*, I. 71, and Havens, 607.

**5–8.** A has two other readings (omitted from the *apparatus criticus*):

(i)                    Having reached

A Cottage seated near the Mountain's base

In a green Hollow, at the silent door

We knocked and to fulfill our purpose, rouzed

From sleep the shepherd who by antient right

(ii)                   Soon was reached

A ragged Cottage at the Mountain's base

Where knocking at the silent door, we rouzed

From sleep the shepherd, who by antient right

[XIV. 63–76]. A leaf tacked on to the end of A contains what appears to be the first draft of the reading of D² E. After 'When into air . . . mind' [70] as D² E, it goes on:

Through her own world, for depth for height, for width

And for the fellowship of silent light

With speaking darkness—opening her embrace

A mind that feeds upon infinity

[*Ever sustained by an underconsciousness*]

Sustained by more than perishable power

In sense subservient to ideal Form.

[XIV. 71 -72]. *that broods Over the dark abyss*: Milton, *Paradise Lost*, i. 21.

**71.** *under-presence*: Note the significance of Wordsworth's use of nouns compounded with the prefix 'under'. Here, 'under-presence' and 'under-consciousness' (A², B²—neither of them in the *Oxford English Dictionary*); 'Under-Powers' (I. 163; *O.E.D.* gives no other ex.), 'under-soul' (III. 540; *O.E.D.*, no ex. before 1868), 'under-countenance' (VI. 236; not in *O.E.D.*), 'under-thirst' (VI. 489 [558]; not in *O.E.D.*). He needed these words to express his profound consciousness of that mysterious life which lies deep down below our ordinary, everyday experience, and whence we draw our power—that one interior life

In which all beings live with God, themselves

Are God, existing in the mighty whole (note to II. 434/5).

The relation of this conception to the subconscious or subliminal self of the modern psychologist is obvious.

**81–83.** The reading of A² is a correction of:

> Doth make one object with a subtle reach
> And comprehensive sway impress its virtue
> Upon all others till the whole reflect
> Upon all others and their several frames
> Pervade, to such an eminent degree
> That even the grossest minds *etc.*

**95.** After 'Trafficking with immeasurable thoughts' W goes on:

> Oft tracing this analogy betwixt
> The mind of man and nature, doth the scene
> Which from the side of Snowden I beheld
> Rise up before me, followed too in turn
> 5   By sundry others, whence I will select
> A portion, living pictures to embody
> This pleasing argument.
>                 It was a day
> Upon the edge of Autumn, fierce with storm;
> The wind blew through the hills of Coniston
> 10   Compress'd as in a tunnel, from the lake
> Bodies of foam took flight, and the whole vale
> Was wrought into commotion high and low—
> Mist flying up and down, bewilder'd showers,
> Ten thousand thousand waves, mountains and crags,
> 15   And darkness, and the sun's tumultuous light.
> Green leaves were rent in handfuls from the trees,
> The mountains all seem'd silent, din so near
> Pealed in the traveller's ear, the clouds [   ?]
> The horse and rider stagger'd in the blast,
> 20   And he who look'd upon the stormy lake
> Had fear for boat or vessel where none was.
> Meanwhile, by what strange chance I cannot tell,
> What combination of the wind and clouds,
> A large unmutilate[d] rainbow stood

---

1–7 To this one scene which I from Snowdon's breast
Beheld might more be added to set forth
The manner in which oftener Nature works
Herself upon the outward face of things
As if with an imaginative power (*alternative lines on another page of* W).

7–30 No punctuation in W, except after 'tunnel' (10), 'darkness' (15), and 'adamant' (30).

13 W²: A roaring wind mist and bewilder'd showers W.

17 The mountains all W²: All distant things W.

18 W²: Block'd up the listener's ear W.

25   Immoveable in heav'n, kept standing there
     With a colossal stride bridging the vale,
     The substance thin as dreams, lovelier than day,—
     Amid the deafening uproar stood unmov'd,
     Sustain'd itself through many minutes space;
30   As if it were pinn'd down by adamant.
       One evening, walking in the public way,
     A Peasant of the valley where I dwelt
     Being my chance Companion, he stopp'd short
     And pointed to an object full in view
35   At a small distance. 'Twas a horse, that stood
     Alone upon a little breast of ground
     With a clear silver moonlight sky behind.
     With one leg from the ground the creature stood
     Insensible and still,—breath, motion gone,
40   Hairs, colour, all but shape and substance gone,
     Mane, ears, and tail, as lifeless as the trunk
     That had no stir of breath; we paused awhile
     In pleasure of the sight, and left him there
     With all his functions silently sealed up,
45   Like an amphibious work of Nature's hand,
     A Borderer dwelling betwixt life and death,
     A living Statue or a statued Life.
       To these appearances which Nature thrusts
     Upon our notice, her own naked work
50   Self-wrought, unaided by the human mind,
     Add others more imperious; those I mean
     Which on our sight she forces, calling man
     To give new grandeur to her ministry,
     Man suffering or enjoying. Meanest minds
55   Want not these monuments, though overlook'd
     Or little prized; and books are full of them,—
     Such power,—to pass at once from daily life
     And our inevitable sympathy
     With passions mingled up before our eyes,—

---

26 W²: With stride colossal bridging the whole vale W.

35–47 No punctuation in W except commas after 'still' (39) and 'breath' (42).      38 leg] written 'left'.

40 Hairs: For this rather unusual plural cf. *Sonnet*, 'Brook! whose society' *etc.* l. 10.

48–104 No punctuation in W except after 'enjoying' (54) 'priz'd', 'them' (56) 'course' (64) 'more' (79) 'eye' (81) 'Africa' (82) 'us' (89) 'on' (95) 'calm', 'at length' (101) 'bow' (103) 'purpose' (108) and 'length' (111).

51 more imperious W²: still more obvious W.      52 calling W²: taking W.
53 W²: Takes man into the bosom of her works W.
55–56 though . . . priz'd W²: if they would look Back on the past W.

60        Such presence is acknowledg'd, when we trace
           The history of Columbus, think of him
           And of his followers when, in unknown seas
           Far travell'd, first they saw the needle take
           Another course, and faltering in its office
65        Turn from the Pole. Such object doth present,
           To those who read the story at their ease,
           Sir Humphrey Gilbert, that bold voyager,
           When after one disastrous wreck he took
           His station in the pinnace, for the sake
70        Of Honour and his Crew's encouragement;
           And they who followed in the second ship,
           The larger Brigantine which he had left,
           Beheld him while amid the storm he sate
           Upon the open deck of his small bark
75        In calmness, with a book upon his knee—

---

60–64       Such power was with Columbus and his Crew
             When first far travell'd into unknown seas
             They saw the needle faltering in its office W,
*followed by short and partly illegible version of* 65–79. W² *as text.* The story of Columbus would be familiar to Wordsworth from many Collections of travels. He certainly knew *The Life and Actions of C. Columbus* by his son Ferdinand Columbus, where he read 'He also perceived, that at night the compass vary'd a whole point to the NW., and at break of day it came right with the Star. These things confounded the Pilots, till he told them the cause of it was the compass the star took about the Pole, which was some satisfaction to them, for this variation made them apprehend some danger in such an unknown distance from Home and such strange Regions.'

65–79 Wordsworth owes this story to the *Report of the Voyage ... 1583 ... by Sir Humphrey Gilbert . . . written by Edward Haie* and preserved in Hakluyt's *Principall Navigations etc.* The pertinent passages are as follows: The vehement persuasion and intreatie of his friends could nothing availe, to divert him from a wilfull resolution of going through in his Frigat . . . But when he was intreated by the Captain Master and other his well willers of the Hinde, not to venture in the Frigat, this was his answer: I will not forsake my little company going homeward, with whom I have passed so many storms and perils . . . So we committed him to God's protection and set him aboord his Pinnesse, we being more than 300 leagues onward of our way home. . . .

Munday the ninth of September, in the afternoone the Frigat was neere cast away, oppressed by waves, yet at that time recovered: and giving foorth signes of joy, the General sitting abaft with a booke in his hand, cried out unto us in the Hind (so oft as we did approch within hearing) We are as neere to heaven by sea as by land. Reiterating the same speech, well beseeming a souldier, resolute in Jesus Christ, as I can testifie he was. The same Monday night, about twelve of the clocke, or not long after, the Frigat being ahead of us in the Golden Hinde, suddenly her lights were out, wherof as it were in a moment, we lost the sight, and withall our watch cryed, the Generall was cast away, which was too true. For in that moment, the Frigat was devoured and swallowed up in the Sea.

To use the language of the Chronicle,
'A Soldier of Christ Jesus undismay'd,'—
The ship and he a moment afterwards
Engulph'd and seen no more. Like spectacle
80      Doth that Land Traveller, living yet, appear
To the mind's eye, when, from the Moors escap'd,
Alone, and in the heart of Africa,
And having sunk to earth, worn out with pain
And weariness that took at length away
85      The sense of Life, he found when he awaked
His horse in quiet standing at his side,
His arm within the bridle, and the Sun
Setting upon the desert. Kindred power

---

79–88 *Land Traveller living yet*: Mungo Park (1771–1805), who made the
first of his famous journeys to the river Niger in West Africa in 1795, and
published his account of it in 1799. 'A little before sunset, having reached
the top of a gentle rising, I climbed a high tree, from the topmost branches
of which I cast a melancholy look over the barren wilderness. . . . Descending from the tree, I found my horse devouring the stubble and brushwood
with great avidity; and as I was now too faint to attempt walking, and my
horse too much fatigued to carry me, I thought it but an act of humanity,
and perhaps the last I should ever have it in my power to perform, to take
off his bridle and let him shift for himself; in doing which I was suddenly
affected with sickness and giddiness, and falling upon the sand felt as if the
hour of death was fast approaching.
    '*Here then (thought I), after a short ineffectual struggle, terminate all my
hopes of being useful in my day and generation; here must the short span of my
life come to an end.*'
    I cast (as I believed) a last look on the surrounding scene, and whilst
I reflected on the awful change that was about to take place, this world with
all its enjoyments seemed to vanish from my recollection. Nature however
at length resumed its functions, and on recovering my senses I found myself
stretched upon the sand with the bridle still in my hand, and the sun just
sinking behind the trees. I now summoned all my resolution, and determined to make another effort to prolong my existence.' *Travels in the
Interior of Africa* by Mungo Park, ed. 1878, p. 163.
    88–114 On May 15, 1688, Dampier left Nicobar for Achin in a Nicobar
canoe, accompanied by three Englishmen, four (not three) Malayans, and
one Portuguese half-caste. The following extracts from Dampier's account
of the voyage show Wordsworth's fidelity, often verbal, to the source upon
which he was drawing:
    'We then had also a very ill Presage, by a great Circle about the Sun (five
or six times the Diameter of it) which seldom appears, but Storms of Wind
and much Rain ensue. . . . We commonly take great notice of these . . .
observing if there be any breach in the Circle, and in what quarter the
breach is; for from thence we commonly find the greatest stress of Wind
will come. . . . The evening of this day was very dismal. . . . The Sea was
already roaring in a white Foam about us: a dark Night coming on, and no
Land in sight to shelter us, and our little Ark in danger to be swallowed by

```
        Is with us, in the suffering of that time
90      When, flying in his Nicobar Canoe
        With three Malayan Helpers, Dampier saw
        Well in those portents of the broken wheel
        Girding the sun, and afterwards the sea
        Roaring and whitening at the night's approach,
95      And danger coming on, not in a shape
        Which in the heat and mettle of the blood
        He oft had welcom'd, but deliberate
        With dread and leisurely solemnity.
        Bitter repentance for his roving life
100     Seized then upon the ventrous mariner,
        Made calm, at length, by prayer and trust in God.
        Meanwhile the bark went forward like an arrow
        Shot from a bow, the wind for many hours
        Her Steersman. But a slackening of the storm
105     Encouraged them at length to cast a look
```

every Wave: and what was worst of all, none of us thought ourselves prepared for another World. . . . I had been in many imminent Dangers before now, . . . but the worst of them all was but a Playgame in comparison with this. Other Dangers came not upon me with such a leisurely and dreadful Solemnity. A sudden Skirmish or Engagement, or so, was nothing when one's blood was up. . . . I must confess that my courage failed me here: and I made very sad reflections on my former Life, and looked back with Horrour and Detestation on Actions which I before detested, but now I trembled at the remembrance of. I had long before this repented me of that roving Course of Life, but never with such concern as now. I did also call to mind the many miraculous acts of God's Providence towards me in the whole Course of my Life, of which kind I believe few men have met with the like. For all these I returned Thanks in a peculiar manner, and this once more asked God's Assistance and composed my mind as well as I could in the Hopes of it. . . .

At 10 oclock it began to thunder, lighten and rain. . . . The Wind at first blew harder than before, but within half an hour it abated and became more moderate: and the Sea also assuaged of its Fury; and then by a lighted Match, of which we kept a Piece burning on purpose, we looked at our Compass, to see how we steered, and found our Course to be still East. . . .

At 2 oclock we had another Gust of Wind with much Thunder, Lightning, and Rain: which lasted until Day and obliged us to put before the Wind again steering thus for several Hours. It was very dark, and the hard Rain soaked us so thoroughly that we had not one dry Thread about us. . . . In this wet starveling Plight we spent the tedious Night. Never did poor Mariners on a Lee Shore more earnestly long for the dawning Light than we did now. At length the Day appeared, but with such dark black Clouds near the Horizon, that the first Glimpse of the Dawn appeared 30 or 40 Degrees high, which was dreadful enough: for it is a common Saying among Seamen, and true, as I have experienced, that a *high Dawn* will have *high Winds*, and *a low Dawn small winds*.'

102–3 W[2]:       shot forward like an arrow
                For many hours abandoned to the wind    W.

Upon the compass by a lighted match
Made visible, which they in their distress
Kept burning for the purpose. Thus they fared
Sitting all night upon the lap of death
110     In wet and starveling plight, wishing for dawn,—
A dawn that came at length, with gloomy clouds
Covering the horizon; the first [glassy hue ?]
Far from the horizon's edge, high up in heaven,
High Dawn prognosticating winds as high.

**98–99.** *they build up greatest things From least suggestions*: These words recall the first of Wordsworth's printed attempts to define the imagination, 'the faculty which produces impressive effects out of simple elements' (note to 'The Thorn', *Lyr. Ball.*, 1800).

**101–2.** *They need not extraordinary calls*
*To rouze them*:
cf. *Preface*, 1802: 'the human mind is capable of being excited without the application of gross and violent stimulants; and he must have a very faint perception of its beauty and dignity who does not know . . . that one being is elevated above another in proportion as he possesses this capability.' In the passage found in MS. Y (*v.* pp. 574–5) Wordsworth makes this same distinction between those who need 'vivid images and strong sensations' to rouse them, and those who find all they need in the life that lies at their door.

Cf. also note to IV. 345.

**113 [XIV. 120].** *Whether discursive or intuitive*: Cf. Milton, *Paradise Lost*, v. 486–8:

Fansie and understanding, whence the Soule
Reason receives, and reason is her being,
Discursive or Intuitive.

**141 [XIV. 160].** *a universe of death*: a Miltonic phrase. Cf. *Paradise Lost*, ii. 622–4:

A Universe of death, which God by curse
Created evil, for evil onely good,
Where all life dies, death lives.

**151.** *All truth and beauty, from pervading love*: In later versions than A and B Wordsworth omits the statement that love is the source of all truth and beauty.

**161–5 [XIV. 181–7].** *there is higher love etc.*: The change in the text here, with the introduction of a definitely Christian interpretation of the character of that 'higher love', is noteworthy, as is the change in the next line of 'intellectual' into 'spiritual'. Wordsworth would not, in 1804–5, have denied that the love was spiritual, but he prefers to emphasize his belief that it is essentially a part of the natural equipment

---

112 Covering W²: Blackening W. The words 'glassy hue' are almost illegible, and I may have misread them.

of man as man, and does not depend, as in the later text, upon a definitely Christian faith and attitude to religion. The religion of the original version of *The Prelude* is the religion of the *Lines composed a few miles above Tintern Abbey*, and not the religion of the *Ecclesiastical Sonnets*. Cf. Aubrey de Vere, *Recollections of Wordsworth* (Grosart, iii. 491): 'It has been observed that the Religion of Wordsworth's poetry, at least of his earlier poetry, is not as distinctly "Revealed Religion" as might have been expected from this poet's well-known adherence to what he has called emphatically "The Lord and mighty paramount of Truths". He once remarked to me himself on this circumstance, and explained it by stating that when in youth his imagination was shaping for itself the channel in which it was to flow, his religious convictions were less definite and less strong than they had become on more mature thought, and that when his poetic mind and manner had once been formed, he feared that he might, in attempting to modify them, have become constrained.'

It will be noted that the 1850 text of [185–7] has no MS. authority, but is a compromise between E and E². Apparently the editor did not understand, or approve of, the word 'mutual' as applied to the 'tribute'.

**165/166.** Between these lines, after one line which is quite illegible, MS. W goes on:

<blockquote>
The unremitting warfare from the first<br>
Waged with this faculty;—its various foes<br>
Which for the most continue to increase<br>
With growing life and burthens which it brings<br>
5    Of petty duties and degrading cares—<br>
Labour and penury, disease and grief,<br>
Which to one object chain the impoverished mind<br>
Enfeebled, and devouring vexing strife<br>
At home, and want of pleasure and repose,<br>
10   And all that eats away the genial spirits,<br>
May be fit matter for another song.<br>
Nor less the misery brought into the world<br>
By the perversion of this power misplaced<br>
And misemployed, [          ]      ·<br>
15   Blinding [     ] ambition obvious<br>
And all the superstitions of this life<br>
A mournful catalogue. Then gladly too[1]
</blockquote>

Here W goes on to XI. 176, *q.v.*

**183 [XIV. 204].** *The feeling of life endless, the great thought*: Notice

---

[1] W has only two stops in this passage, a comma after 'disease' (6), where it is not needed, and a full stop after 'catalogue' (17). In l. 7 'object' is written 'objects'.

the very significant change of this line, coming in as late as D², to 'Faith in life endless, the sustaining thought'. Cf. note to ll. 1–119 *supra*.

[XIV. 230]. *Of humble cares and delicate desires*: Cf. *The Sparrow's Nest* (a poem paying a tribute to Dorothy), l. 18: 'And humble cares and delicate fears.'

212 [XIV. 233]. *Elsewhere*: Cf. note to VI. 214–17.

219–24 [XIV. 239–44]. The punctuation of 1850, as Mr. Nowell Smith pointed out, is obviously incorrect. The MSS. explain how it arose. D enclosed ll. 222–3 in brackets, and D² in changing the words found in A and D to those of 1850, after replacing 'Even' by 'Still' forgot to remove the bracket before it. Then, noticing a bracket after the deleted line (The period . . . reach'd) moved it up to follow 'youth'.

225–6 [XIV. 245–6]. *that beauty, which, as Milton sings, Hath terror in it*: cf. *Paradise Lost*, ix. 489–91:

> Shee fair, divinely fair, fit Love for Gods,
> Not terrible, though terrour be in Love
> And beautie

[XIV. 266–75]. It is significant that in the early text these lines are not found. Nor should they be. For in *The Prelude*, written to recount the growth of his mind up to the year 1798, when he conceived his powers and his knowledge equal to the task 'of building up a work that should endure' (ll. 274–8), Mary Hutchinson has properly no important place. His escape from the slough of despond was due, as far as it was due to external influence, to Dorothy and to Coleridge. When Wordsworth completed the original *Prelude* he realized this, and wishing to pay a tribute to his wife wrote a separate poem for the purpose, i.e. 'She was a phantom of delight' (1804). Later, when he decided to place her by the side of Dorothy and Coleridge in this passage, he drew largely upon that lyric. It is worth noting that the first version, written into A, with its 'apparition to adorn ("adore" is probably a slip of the pen) a moment' and in 270 'And yet a spirit still', is even closer to the lyric than is the final version.

[XIV. 272–5]. As Mr. Nowell Smith pointed out, the punctuation of these lines in the 1850 text makes nonsense of them. The MSS. have no commas after either 'Shines' or 'And'. The error was corrected in the edition of 1857.

246–68 [XIV. 275–301]. *Coleridge, with this my argument, of thee Shall I be silent?*:
It is curious that whilst this passage pays a beautiful tribute to Wordsworth's love for his friend, so little acknowledgement is made of his incalculable intellectual debt to him. Yet it was through Coleridge that he came first to understand himself and his poetic aims, and he readily admits elsewhere how much he owed to Coleridge's inspired conversation. Thus he writes to Sir George Beaumont (Aug. 1, 1806) of *The Recluse*: 'Should Coleridge return, so that I might have some conversation with him on the subject, I should go on swimmingly.'

exquisite regard for common things,
And all the earth was budding with these gifts
Of more refined humanity, thy breath
Dear Sister was a kind of gentler spring
That went before my steps. Thereafter came
                           with thee
One, whom friendship had ~~both thee been~~ early paired

She came, no more a Phantom to adorn
A moment, but an Inmate of the heart,
And yet a Spirit there for me enshrined
To penetrate the lofty & the low;
Even as one essence of pervading light
Shines in the brightest of ten-thousand stars,
And the meek worm that feeds her lonely lamp
Couched in the dewy grass.
                                   With such a theme
~~That feed to the lonely lamp~~
~~And the meek worm that~~
~~Shrouded~~
~~.~~               With such a theme,
              my
Coleridge! with this argument of these
Shall I be silent? O ~~capacious~~ soul!

And years later he said of Coleridge: 'He was most wonderful in the power he possessed of throwing out in profusion grand central truths from which might be evolved the most comprehensive systems.' In later texts Wordsworth did something to correct this deficiency, but even so it is hardly a complete expression of his debt.

**350 [XIV. 355].** *The name of Calvert*: Raisley Calvert, brother of William Calvert with whom Wordsworth stayed in the Isle of Wight in the summer of 1793. The Calverts were sons of the steward of the Duke of Norfolk, who owned a large estate at Greystoke, four miles from Penrith (Harper, i. 248). Raisley was consumptive and Wordsworth proposed in October 1794 to accompany him to Lisbon on a voyage of health, and when this plan fell through, attended him through his last illness. He died in January 1795 and left Wordsworth £900. This legacy, by freeing him from financial anxiety, enabled him definitely to devote his life to poetry: *vide* also *Sonnet: To the Memory of Raisley Calvert*.

**393.** *Quantock's grassy Hills*: Wordsworth was at Alfoxden from July 1797 to June 1798; Coleridge was living three miles off at Nether Stowey; the Quantock hills rise behind both places. Both *The Ancient Mariner* and *Christabel* was written in the late autumn of 1797 (*The Ancient Mariner* in Nov.); the 'summer' therefore which Wordsworth here recalls was the warm spring and early summer of 1798. *The Thorn* and *The Idiot Boy* were both written in 1798 (*The Thorn* on March 19).

**416 [XIV. 419].** *a private grief*: the loss of his brother John. Cf. *Elegiac Verses, In Memory of my Brother, John Wordsworth, Commander of the E. I. Company's Ship, The Earl of Abergavenny, in which he perished by calamitous shipwreck, February 6th, 1805. Elegiac Stanzas, suggested by a Picture of Peele Castle etc.* were inspired by this same loss, and in drawing his portrait of *The Happy Warrior* Wordsworth had in mind, he tells us (I.F. note to the poem), many elements in his brother's character. There is every evidence in the letters and elsewhere that Wordsworth was passionately devoted to his brother, and the shock of his loss seems to have made a turning-point in the poet's thought. The beginning of the change from the naturalism and sensationalism of his early poetry to a more definitely orthodox attitude dates from this time.

**444.** *By reason and by truth*: notice the significant alteration of the early text to 'By reason, blest by faith'.

# ADDENDA TO NOTES

**I. 186–95** (p. 514). Cf. also Southey's Poem 'The Race of Odin' in *Poems* by R. Lovell and R. Southey, 1795.

**VII. 288 [267]** (p. 563). Professor Chester L. Shaver has drawn my attention to an account of the rope-dancing at Sadler's Wells quoted in *Theatre Note-book*, vi (October 1951—July–September 1952). The season began in 1795 on 6 April, and tight-rope dancing was evidently one of the most popular items in the programme.

**IX. 553–4** (p. 593). F. M. Todd, in *Politics and the Poet*, 1958, has drawn attention to a close parallel to the story of Vaudracour and Julia in Miss Helen Williams's *Letters written in France in the summer of 1790, containing Memoirs of Mons. and Madame F*. These memoirs refer to a Monsieur and Madame du Fossé, friends of Miss Williams, who tells the story of their sufferings—a story corresponding in its main lines to that of Vaudracour and Julia, 'as an example of the deep-rooted nature of the tyranny of the "ancien régime".' Professor Shaver (*T.L.S.* 21 February 1958) has tracked the probable source of the name Vaudracour to a certain Lieutenant de Vaudrecourt who was one of the officers of Beaupuy's battalion at Tours in May 1791 and presumably at Blois from the following August. Wordsworth liked to adopt the name of a real person for his characters (witness Martha Ray, heroine of *The Thorn*) and Vaudracour was an appropriately aristocratic and sonorous name.

# APPENDIX
## MANUSCRIPT JJ[1]

*Last page Z recto*

I. 271                         Was it for this
        That one, the fairest of all rivers loved
        To blend his murmurs with my nurse's song
        And from his alder shades and rocky falls
275 And from his fords and shallows sent a voice
        To intertwine my dreams, for this didst thou
        O Derwent travelling over the green plains
        [Giving ceaseless music to the]
        Near my sweet birthplace [to the night and day]
                         didst thou beauteous stream
        Give ceaseless music to the night & day
280 Which with its steady cadence tempering
        Our human waywardness compose(d) my thought
        To more than infant softness giving me
        Amid the fretful [tenements of man] dwellings of mankind
        A knowledge, a dim earnest of the calm
285 Which Nature breathes among her woodland [haunts ?[2]]
        Was it for this [for these perhaps] & now I speak of things
        [That have been & that are, no gentle (dreams ?)]
        Complacent fashioned fondly to adorn
        The time [years] of unrememberable being
        Was it for this that I a four years child[3]

*Y verso*

        [Beneath thy scars & in] A naked boy among thy silent
          pools
        Made one long bathing of a summers day
295 Basked in the sun or plunged into thy stream
        Alternate all a summers day, or coursd
        Over the sandy [plains] fields & dashed the flowers
        Of yellow grundsel or when the hill tops
        The woods & all the [distant] glorious mountains
300 Were bronzed with a deep radiance stood alone
304 A naked savage in the thunder shower

333 [For this] Nor less in spring time when on southern banks
        The shining sun had from [his] its knot of leaves
        Decoyed the primrose flower and when the vales
        And woods were warm was I a rover then

---

[1] I have placed in brackets but without italics words which are obviously written as alternative readings but often not deleted.

[2] *haunts* supplied by *Christabel* MS.

[3] *v.* MS. V. 286–94, note, pp. 18–19 *supra*.

In the high places, on the [lonely] lonesome peaks
Among the mountains & the winds. Though mean
340 And though inglorious were my views the end
Was not ignoble. Oh when I have hung
Above the ravens nest, have hung alone
By half inch fissures in the slippery rock
But ill sustained and almost as it seemed
345 Suspended by the [wind] blast which blew amain
[Against] Shouldering the naked cragg ah then

*X verso*

With what strange utterance did the [loud dry] wind
349 Blow through my ears
                     the colours of the sky
                        the sky was [then no sky ?]
350 Of earth & with what motion move[d] the cloud[s]
As on the perilous [brink] cliff

---

While on the perilous [edge] [ridge] cliff I hung alone
With what strange utterance did the loud dry wind
Blow through my ears the sky seemd not a sky
350 Of earth, and with what motion moved the clouds

Ah not in vain ye beings of the hills[1]
And ye that walk the woods and open heaths
432 By moon or starlight thus from my first dawn
Of childhood did ye love to interweave
The passions
435 Not with the mean & vullgar works of man
But with high objects with eternal things
With life & nature, purifying thus
The elements of feeling & of thought

*Y recto*

And sanctifying by such discipline
440 Both pain & fear untill we recognize
A grandeur in the beatings of the heart.
490–2 Ah! not [in vain] for this ye spirits of the springs[2]
*app. crit.*
And ye that are $\begin{cases} \text{familiars of the clouds} \\ \text{have your voices in the clouds} \end{cases}$
Through pleasant da(ys ?)
Through snow & sunshine & through rain & storm
Did ye with such assiduous love pursue
Your favourite & your joy did ye delight
[Thus by the agency of boyish sports
To fix upon the streams the woods the hills
To fix upon all forms the character

---

[1] *v.* MS. V. 428–33, note, p. 26 *supra.*
[2] *v.* MS. V. 490–2, note, p. 28 *supra.*

498 Of danger & desire & so to [make ?]
   The surface of the universal earth
   With meanings of delight of hope and fear
   [Nor belike a]
493 A vullgar hope was yours when [ye employed]
   Such ministry not vainly for ye [know?]]][1]

*W recto*

   The mountains & the fluctuating hills

490–2 Ye powers of earth
*app. crit.* Ah not in vain ye spirits of the springs
   And ye that have your voices in the clouds
   And ye that are familiars of the lakes
   And standing pools,[2] ah not for trivial ends
   Through snow & sunshine & through [rain and storm]
                              the sparkling plains
   Of moonlight frost and through the stormy [day ?]
   Did ye with such assiduous love pursue

*W verso*

   Your favorite and your joy.
492                      I may not think
   A vulgar hope was yours when ye employed
   Such ministry when ye through many a year
   Thus by the agency of boyish sports
   [Impressd upon the streams the woods the hills
496 Upon the caves the trees the woods the hills]
   Impressd upon all forms the character
   Of danger or desire and thus did make
   The surface of the universal earth
500 With meanings of delight of hope & fear
   Work like a sea.—

---

311 For this[3] when on the witherd mountain slope[4]
   The frost and breath of frosty wind had snapped
   The last autumnal crocus did I love
   To range [wander] through half the night among the cliffs
315 And the smooth hollows where the woodcocks ran
   Along the moonlight turf. In thought and wish
   That time my shoulder all with springes hung
   I was a fell destroyer.

---

[1] This whole passage (9 lines) is struck out.
[2] Cf.   Ye elves of hills, brooks, standing lakes and groves
       And ye that on the sands with printless foot (*Tempest*, v. 1).
[3] *v.* MS. V. 305–11, note, p. 19 *supra*. Nor without kindred self-reproach ...
[4] A first draft of this passage (22 lines) is found on *V verso* and *W recto*
in pencil and largely illegible.

Gentle powers,
Who give us happiness, & call it peace

*X recto*

When [running] scudding on from snare to snare I plied
320 My anxious visitation hurrying on
Still hurrying hurrying onward, how my heart
panted: among the lonely eugh trees & the crags
That looked upon me how my bosom beat
325 With hope & fear [expectation]. And sometimes strong
desire
Resistless overcame me & the bird
That was the captive of another's toils
Became my prey, and [then] [when the deed] I heard
I heard among the solitary hills
330 Low breathings coming after me and sounds
Of undistinguishable motion steps
Almost as silent as the turf they trod

94[1]

*U recto*

Nor while, thou(gh) doubting yet not lost I tread
The mazes of this argument, and paint
I. 572 How Nature by collateral interest
And by extrinsic passion peopled first
My mind with beauteous objects may I well
Forget what might demand a loftier song
For oft th' eternal spirit, he that has
His life in unimaginable things
And he who painting what he is in all
The visible imagery of all the world
Is yet apparent chiefly as the soul
Of our first sympathies—Oh bounteous power
In childhood, in rememberable days
How often did thy love renew for me
Those naked feelings which when thou wouldst form
A living thing thou sendest like a breeze[2]
Into its infant being. Soul of things

*U verso*

How often did thy love renew for me
578 Those hallowed & pure motions of the sense
Which seem in their simplicity to own
An intellectual charm: that calm delight
Which if I err not surely must belong
To those first born affinities which fit
Our new existence to existing things

---

[1] W. W. has written this number clearly at the foot of the page.
[2] Cf. II. 244, MS. RV, p. 56: This passion is the awakening breeze of life.

And in our dawn of being constitute
585 The bond of union betwixt life & joy.
Yes, I remember when the changeful earth
And twice five seasons on my mind had stamped
The faces of the [changeful] moving year, even then,
A child I held unconscious intercourse
590 With the eternal beauty drinking in
A pure organic pleasure from the lines
Of curling mist or from the smooth expanse
Of waters coloured by the [cloudless moon] clouds of heaven

*V recto*

The sands of Westmorland the creeks & bays
595 Of Cumbria's rocky limits they can tell
How when the sea threw off his evening shade
And to the shepherds hut beneath the craggs
Did send sweet notice of the rising moon
How I have stood to images like these
601 A stranger linking with the spectacle
No body of associated forms . . .
And bearing with [me?] no peculiar sense
Of quietness or peace yet I have stood
605 Even while my eye has moved o'er three long leagues
Of shining water, gathering as it seemd
[                                    ]¹
608 New pleasure like a bee among the flowers—
Nor unsubservient even to noblest ends
Are these primordial feelings how serene
How calm those seem amid the swell
Of human passion even yet I feel
Their tranquillizing power

*Margin of*
*U verso*                              for often-times
577 In that tempestuous season I have felt
Even in that [ *blank left* ] & tempestuous time

*Margin of*
*U recto*      How while I ran wher'eer the (working ?) heat
Of passion drove me at that thoughtless time
365 A power unknown would open out the clouds
366 As with the touch of lightning seeking me
With gentle visitation [then unknown ?]

*T verso*
Nor in that thoughtless season [          ?          ]
575 That [purer] other pleasures have been mine
And joys of purer origin for oft

---

¹ Space left for a line.

[While ?] thus I wander'd doubting[1]

363 Yes there are genii which when they would form
[A favour'd spirit] open out the clouds
As with the touch of lightning seeking him
367 With gentle visitation. Others use
[Less homely ?] interference ministry
370 Of grosser kind & of their school was I
368 Though haply aiming at the selfsame end
And made me love them

*S verso*

I. 373 I went alone into a shepherd's boat
A skiff which to a willow tree was tied
With [ *blank left* ] it(s) usual home
383 The moon was up the lake was shining clear
Among the hoary mountains: from the shore
I push'd and struck the oars and struck again
In cadence and my little boat moved on
Just like a man who walks with stately step
Though bent on speed. A rocky steep uprose
395 Above the cavern of the willow-tree
[so as fitted ?]
And as beseemd a man who proudly rowed
With his best speed I fixd a steady view
Upon the top of that same shaggy ridge
The bound of the horizon for behind
400 Was nothing but the stars & the grey sky.
She was an elfin pinnace, twenty times
I dipp'd my oars into the silent lake
And (as) I rose upon the stroke my boat
Went heaving through the water like a swan

---

388                                    It was an act of stealth
And troubled pleasure not without the voice
390 Of mountain echoes did my boat move on
Leaving behind (her) still on either side
Small circles glittering idly in the moon
Untill they melted all into one track

*T recto*

Of sparkling light
When from behind that rocky steep till then
399 The bound of the horizon just between
The summit & the stars a huge high cliff
As if with voluntary power instinct

---

[1] Space has been left here, afterwards filled with four lines beginning
'with trembling hands I turn'd': *v.* p. 639, *T verso*.

      Upreared its head I struck and struck again
409 And growing still (in) stature the huge (cliff)
      With measured motion like a living thing
      Strode after (me)
410 Rose up between me & the stars & still
      With measured motion like a living thing
      Strode after me. Unusual was the power
      Of that strange spectacle for many days
421 There was a darkness in my thoughts no show
      Of usual objects images of trees
      Of sea or sky no colours of green fields
425 But huge and mighty forms that do not live
      Like living men [   *blank left*   ]
      By day and were the trouble of my dreams
419 Working with an undetermined sense
      Of unknown modes of being
                      and [as before ?] the solitary cliff
      Rose up between me & the
*T verso*
412          with trembling hands I turn'd
      And through the silent water stole my way
414 Back to the cavern of the willow
      And to my [     age.] in
*S recto*
V. 389 There was a boy ye knew him well, ye rocks
      And islands of Winander & ye green
      Peninsulas of Esthwaite many a time
                when the stars began
      To move along the edges of the hills
      Rising or setting would he stand alone
      Beneath the trees or by the glimmering lake
395 And through his fingers woven in one close knot
      Blow mimic hootings to the silent owls
      And bid them answer him. And they would shou
400 Across the watry vale and shout again
      Responsive to my call with tremulous sobs
      And long halloes & screams & echoes loud
      Redoubled & redoubled a wild scene
      Of mirth & jocund din. And when it chanced
405 That pauses of deep silence mocked my skill
      Then often,[1] in that silence, while I hung
      Listening a sudden[2] shock of mild surprize
      Would carry far into my heart the voice

---

[1] sometimes *written in pencil above.*
[2] gentle *written in pencil above.*

Of mountain torrents: or the visible scene
410 Would enter unawares into my mind
With all its solemn imagery its rocks
Its woods & that uncertain heaven received
Into the bosom of the steady lake

*R verso*

I. 405 When from behind that rocky steep, till then
2nd version The bound of the horizon a huge cliff
As if with voluntary power instinct
Uprear'd its head. I struck & struck again
409 And growing still in stature the huge cliff
Rose up between me and the stars & still
With measured motion like a living thing
Strode after me. With trembling hands I turn'd
And through the silent water stole my way
414 Back to the willow tree, the mooring place
Of my small [boat] pinnace

$\begin{Bmatrix} \text{A most unusual power} \\ \text{Unusual was the power} \end{Bmatrix}$

418 $\begin{Bmatrix} \text{Had} \\ \text{Of} \end{Bmatrix}$ that strange sight for many days my brain
Workd with a dim and undetermind sense
420 Of unknown modes of being in my thought
There was a darkness call it solitude [vacancy]
Or blank desertion no familiar shapes
Of hourly objects images of trees
Of sea or sky no colours of green fields
425 But huge & mighty forms that do not live
Like living men moved slowly through my mind
By day and were the trouble of my dreams

And straightway through [          ] I went
417 Though fearless with a grave & serious [mind ?]

*R recto*

351 The soul of man is fashioned & built up
D. W.'s   Just like a strain of music I believe
hand   That there are spirits which when they would form
A favor'd being open out the clouds
366 As at the touch of lightning
Seeking him with gentle visitation and with such
Though rarely in my wanderings I have held
Communion. Others too there are who use
Yet haply aiming at the selfsame end
370 Severer interventions, ministry
Of grosser kind, & of their school was I
311 And oft when on the withered mountain slope
The frost & breath

W. W.'s
hand

I have held

Communion with them in my boyish [days ?]

Though rarely

*P verso*

I would not strike a flower[1]

As many a man [would] will strike his horse ; at least

If from the wantonness in which we play

With things we love, or from a freak of [power] thought

Or from involuntary act of hand

Or foot unruly with excess of life

It eer should chance that I ungently used

A tuft of [     *left blank*     ] or snapp'd the stem

Of foxglove bending oer his native rill

I should be loth to pass along my road

With unreproved indifference. I would stop

Self questioned, asking wherefor that was done

XII. 47   For seeing little worthy or sublime

In what we blazon with the names [of power

And action] I was early taught to love.

Of power & action I was early taught

*Q recto*

To love those unassuming things that [occupy ?] hold

52   A silent station in this beauteous world

let [all things have] each thing have

[Their lot of life] Its little lot of life but more than all

The things that live in [ ?]

Then dearest maiden on whose lap I rest[2]

My head [      ] do not deem[3] that these

Are idle sympathies—

*Q verso*

Those beauteous colours of my [our] early years [time]

Which make the starting-place of being fair

And worthy of the goal to which they tend

I. 660   Those hours that cannot die [those] and lovely forms

And sweet sensations which throw back our life

And make our infancy a visible scene

663   On which the sun is shining

Those recollect(ed) hours that have the charm

Of visionary things—

[      ] islands in the unnavigable depth

Of our departed time

---

[1] *v.* overflow from *Nutting*, p. 612 *supra*.

[2] Cf. *Nutting*, ll. 54–56.

[3] *Possibly* dream, as in *Christabel* notebook.

*Z verso*

I. 43 [a gentle inspiration] a mild creative breeze[1]
      A vital breeze that passes gently on
      Oer things which it hath made and soon becomes
      A tempest a redundant energy
      That sweeps the waters and the [      ] this power
  47 Creating not but as it may
      disturbing things created
                         a storm not terrible but strong
      With lights and shades and with a rushing (power ?)
      With loveliness and power
I. 20                                      trances of thought
      And mountings of the mind compared to which
      The wind that drives along th' autumnal [leaf ?]
      Is meekness
                               what there is
      Of subtler feeling of remembered joy
      Of soul & spirit in departed sound
      That cannot be remembered[2]
                           a plain of leaves
      Whose matted surface spreads for many leagues
Cf. III. A level prospect such as shepherds view
  546 From some high promontory when the sea
      Flames, & the sun is setting.
               familiars of the lakes & standing [          ][3]
On the inside of the cover of the book
      How often in the silence of the woods

      The mountains & the fluctuating hills.

---

[1] Cf. *Prelude* I. 43–47.
[2] Cf. *Prelude* II. 324–34.
[3] *v. W recto ante.*

# INDEX

PRINTED IN GREAT BRITAIN
AT THE UNIVERSITY PRESS, OXFORD
BY VIVIAN RIDLER
PRINTER TO THE UNIVERSITY